T0201192

Cybersecurity Law

Cybersecurity Law

Jeff Kosseff

Registered Offices
John Wiley & Sons, Inc., 111 River Street, Hoboken, NJ 07030, USA

Editorial Office
111 River Street, Hoboken, NJ 07030, USA

For details of our global editorial offices, customer services, and more information about Wiley products visit us at www.wiley.com.

Wiley also publishes its books in a variety of electronic formats and by print-on-demand. Some content that appears in standard print versions of this book may not be available in other formats.

Library of Congress Cataloging-in-Publication Data:

Names: Kosseff, Jeff, 1978- author.
Title: Cybersecurity law / Jeff Kosseff.
Description: Hoboken, New Jersey : John Wiley & Sons, [2017] | Includes
  bibliographical references and index.
Identifiers: LCCN 2016038242| ISBN 9781119231509 (cloth) | ISBN 9781119232025
  (epub)
Subjects: LCSH: Computer security – Law and legislation – United States. | Data
  protection – Law and legislation – United States. | Hacking – United
  States – Prevention. | Cyberterrorism – Prevention. | Privacy, Right
  of – United States. | Computer networks – Security measures. | Computer
  security – Law and legislation.
Classification: LCC KF1263.C65 K67 2017 | DDC 343.7309/99 – dc23
LC record available at https://lccn.loc.gov/2016038242

Cover image: Westend61/Gettyimages
Cover design by Wiley

Set in 10/12pt Warnock by SPi Global, Chennai, India

Printed in the United States of America

V10013837_091019

This book is dedicated to my two biggest supporters, my wife, Crystal Zeh, and my daughter, Julia Kosseff.

Contents

About the Author

Jeff Kosseff is an Assistant Professor of Cybersecurity Law at the United States Naval Academy in Annapolis, Maryland. He practiced cybersecurity and privacy law at Covington & Burling LLP, and clerked for Judge Milan D. Smith, Jr. of the U.S. Court of Appeals for the Ninth Circuit and for Judge Leonie M. Brinkema of the U.S. District Court for the Eastern District of Virginia. Mr. Kosseff is a graduate of Georgetown University Law Center and the University of Michigan. Before becoming a lawyer, he was a journalist for *The Oregonian* and was a finalist for the Pulitzer Prize for national reporting.

Acknowledgment

The author would like to extend his gratitude and recognize the contribution of copyeditor Z. Dana Andrus for her excellence in editing this book.

About the Companion Website

This book is accompanied by a companion website:

www.wiley.com/go/kosseff/cybersecurity

The website includes:

- Class discussion questions for each chapter
- News updates
- New cybersecurity laws
- Cybersecurity legislative proposals
- Recent cybersecurity policy developments

Introduction

In recent years, cybersecurity has become not only a rapidly growing industry, but an increasingly vital consideration for nearly every company and government agency in the United States. A data breach can lead to high-stakes lawsuits, significant business disruptions, intellectual property theft, and national security vulnerabilities. Just ask any executive from Sony, Target, Home Depot, or the scores of other companies that experienced costly data breaches or the top officials at the U.S. Office of Personnel Management, which suffered a breach that exposed millions of federal workers' highly confidential security clearance applications. In short, it is abundantly clear that companies, governments, and individuals need to do more to improve cybersecurity.

Many articles and books have been written about the technical steps that are necessary to improve cybersecurity. However, there is much less material available about the legal rules that require – and, in some cases, restrict – specific cybersecurity measures. Legal obligations and restrictions should be considered at the outset of any cybersecurity strategy, just as a company would consider reputational harm and budgetary issues. Failure to comply with the law could lead to significant financial harms, negative publicity, and, in some cases, criminal charges.

Unfortunately, the United States does not have a single "cybersecurity law" that can easily apply to all circumstances. Rather, the United States has a patchwork of hundreds of state and federal statutes, regulations, binding guidelines, and court-created rules regarding data security, privacy, and other issues commonly considered to fall under the umbrella of "cybersecurity." On top of that, if U.S. companies have customers or employees in other countries, they must consider the privacy and data security laws and regulations of those nations.

This book aims to synthesize the cybersecurity laws that are most likely to affect U.S. corporate and government operations. The book is intended for a wide range of audiences that seek to learn more about cybersecurity law: undergraduate, graduate, and law school students; technology professionals; corporate executives; and lawyers. For lawyers who use this book as a reference treatise, this book contains detailed footnotes to the primary source materials, such as statutes and case citations. However, this book is not intended only for those with law degrees; it is written with the intent of being a guide for lawyers and nonlawyers alike. Similarly, in addition to being a desk reference, this book can be used as a primary or supplemental text in a cybersecurity law class.

The book focuses on the cybersecurity obligations of U.S. companies, but because cyberspace involves global private and public infrastructure, the book does not focus only on U.S. legal obligations of private companies. The book examines the efforts of the public sector and private sector to work together on cybersecurity, as well as the limits on government cyber operations under the U.S. Constitution and various statutes. Moreover, the book discusses some of the foreign cybersecurity laws that U.S. companies are most likely to encounter.

At the outset, it is important to define the term "cybersecurity law." Unlike more established legal fields, such as copyright, contracts, and torts, cybersecurity law is relatively new and not clearly defined. Indeed, some people think of cybersecurity law as consisting only of data security requirements for companies that are designed to reduce the likelihood of data breaches. Others think of cybersecurity law as anti-hacking laws. And to some, cybersecurity law is a subset of privacy law.

To all of those suggestions, I say "yes." Cybersecurity encompasses all of those subjects and more. The U.S. Department of Homeland Security's National Initiative for Cybersecurity Careers and Studies defines cybersecurity as "[t]he activity or process, ability or capability, or state whereby information and communications systems and the information contained therein are protected from and/or defended against damage, unauthorized use or modification, or exploitation." This definition is a good – and largely complete – starting point for the purposes of this book. The DHS definition captures the "CIA Triad" – confidentiality, integrity, and availability – that typically is associated with cybersecurity. Under this definition, we should be concerned with data security laws, data breach litigation, and anti-hacking laws. However, I have two additions to the DHS definition. First, it is impossible to fully evaluate cybersecurity without understanding the limits on the government's ability to conduct electronic surveillances. Accordingly, the Fourth Amendment to the U.S. Constitution and statutes that restrict government surveillance must be considered as part of an examination of cybersecurity law. Second, cybersecurity law is heavily intertwined with privacy law, which restricts the ability of companies and governments to collect, use, and disclose individuals' personal information.

To simplify, this book categorizes cybersecurity law as consisting of six broad areas of law:

- Private sector data security laws
- Anti-hacking laws
- Public–private cybersecurity efforts

- Government surveillance laws
- Cybersecurity requirements for government contractors
- Privacy law

Private Sector Data Security Laws (Chapters 1–4)

Among the most complex – and rapidly changing – areas of cybersecurity are the many requirements that apply to U.S. companies' handling of customers' and employees' personal data. A number of state and federal laws require companies to implement specific data security safeguards, and if a company faces a data breach, it may be required to notify customers, regulators, and credit bureaus. Breaches also could expose companies to costly regulatory actions and class action lawsuits.

Chapter 1 provides an overview of the state and federal laws that generally apply to data security and data breaches. Unlike other nations, the United States does not have a general law that imposes specific privacy and data security requirements on all companies. The closest analogue in the United States is Section 5 of the Federal Trade Commission Act, which prohibits unfair and deceptive trade practices. Chapter 1 examines dozens of complaints that the Federal Trade Commission has filed under this statute arising from allegedly inadequate data security. The chapter next examines the laws in nearly every state that require companies to notify regulators, customers, and credit bureaus of data breaches in certain circumstances. Finally, the chapter examines the dozen state laws that impose specific data security requirements for personal information.

Chapter 2 examines the various types of private class action lawsuits that companies could face after they experience data breaches. First, the chapter examines a concept known as Article III standing, which is among the most significant barriers to plaintiffs' lawsuits arising from data breaches. In short, Article III standing requires that plaintiffs demonstrate that they suffered an injury-in-fact that is fairly traceable to the defendant's conduct and redressable by a lawsuit. Courts are divided as to what types of injuries a data breach plaintiff must demonstrate to have Article III standing. The chapter then reviews common legal claims that arise from data breaches, including negligence, misrepresentation, breach of contract, invasion of privacy, unjust enrichment, and state consumer protection laws. The chapter also reviews the procedural requirements that data breach plaintiffs must satisfy to be permitted to sue on behalf of a larger class of plaintiffs. It examines whether commercial insurance coverage helps cover companies' liability in data breach lawsuits. Finally, the chapter examines how companies can reduce the likelihood that their internal cybersecurity communications and reports will be subject to discovery and used against them in litigation.

Chapter 3 examines the additional data security requirements that U.S. companies face if they handle particularly sensitive personal information. The

Gramm-Leach-Bliley Act requires financial institutions to adopt specific security safeguards for customers' nonpublic financial information. The Payment Card Industry Data Security Standard contractually imposes data security safeguards for companies that handle credit and debit card information. Doctors, health insurers, and other healthcare companies and their business associates face stringent data security requirements under the Health Insurance Portability and Accountability Act. Finally, the chapter examines the cybersecurity requirements for electric utilities and nuclear licensees.

Chapter 4 provides an overview of data security requirements that affect corporations. The Securities and Exchange Commission expects publicly traded companies to disclose material risks, and in recent years, it has urged companies to be transparent about their cybersecurity vulnerabilities and explain how those vulnerabilities might affect shareholders. This chapter examines the level of disclosure that the SEC expects in publicly traded companies' public filings, and provides examples of various levels of transparency and disclosure. The chapter also examines the possibility of shareholders suing executives and directors if the company experiences a costly data breach. Next, the chapter explores the cybersecurity expectations of the Committee on Foreign Investment in the United States, which must approve any foreign investments in U.S. companies. Finally, the chapter examines how the ongoing debate over corporate export controls could make it more difficult for U.S. companies to conduct cybersecurity research.

Anti-Hacking Laws (Chapter 5)

Anti-hacking laws – notably the federal Computer Fraud and Abuse Act (CFAA) – are intended to help promote cybersecurity. However, some critics argue that these laws are outdated and not only fail to help protect private and government computers but also penalize individuals for conducting entirely legitimate activities, such as cybersecurity research.

Chapter 5 reviews the seven offenses that are prohibited by the CFAA, such as hacking computers to obtain information and damaging computers. The CFAA applies to activities that are conducted "without authorization" or "exceed[ing] authorized access," and the chapter examines how different courts have applied these rather ambiguous terms. The chapter briefly reviews state hacking laws that are based on the CFAA. The chapter then examines Section 1201 of the Digital Millennium Copyright Act, which restricts the ability of individuals to circumvent access controls that protect copyrighted material, and therefore imposes significant limits on cybersecurity vulnerability research. Finally, the chapter examines the Economic Espionage Act, a criminal law that companies increasingly see as a tool to penalize individuals that steal trade secrets. In 2016, Congress amended the Economic Espionage Act to allow companies to file civil lawsuits against hackers and others who steal trade secrets.

Public–Private Security Efforts (Chapter 6)

Cybersecurity law often is associated with punitive measures, such as FTC investigations and data breach class action lawsuits. While those considerations surely are an important component of cybersecurity law, the federal government also has taken a number of proactive steps to work with companies to improve cybersecurity throughout the public and private sectors. Such collaboration is particularly necessary and common in cybersecurity because public and private cyber infrastructure often is interconnected.

Chapter 6 provides an overview of the organization of the federal government's cybersecurity efforts, with the Department of Homeland Security taking an increasingly large and central role in the government's collaboration with the private sector. The chapter examines private–public information sharing, which likely will expand due to the Cybersecurity Act of 2015. The chapter examines the National Institute of Standards and Technology's 2014 cybersecurity framework, which many companies voluntarily adopt as the basis of their own cybersecurity plans. Finally, the chapter briefly examines the U.S. military's involvement with private sector cybersecurity, and the limits imposed by the Posse Comitatus Act.

Government Surveillance Laws (Chapter 7)

Government surveillance laws often restrict the government's ability to increase the security of cyberspace. By "security," what is meant is more than merely preventing the transmission of malware and other harmful programs. Security also encompasses government efforts to fight cybercrime, such as child pornography, terrorist recruitment, and other harmful online activities. The government – and, in some cases, the private sector – often is restricted by constitutional provisions and statutes.

Chapter 7 begins with an examination of how the Fourth Amendment's prohibition on unreasonable searches and seizures applies to electronic surveillance. The chapter then examines the Electronic Communications Privacy Act, a comprehensive statute that limits the ability of the government to obtain stored communications, use wiretaps to obtain data in transit, and obtain metadata via pen registers. The chapter further examines the government's ability to issue National Security Letters to obtain certain information regarding electronic communications, and the obligations of communications companies to assist law enforcement under the Communications Assistance for Law Enforcement Act. The chapter concludes with an examination of law enforcement's attempts, using the All Writs Act, to compel technology companies to help them access encrypted communications.

Cybersecurity Requirements for Government Contractors (Chapter 8)

Many small and large companies rely on the federal government as a significant client for a wide range of products and services. Increasingly, the federal government is expecting these companies to implement specific standards for cybersecurity.

Chapter 8 examines the key cybersecurity requirements for U.S. government contractors. First, the chapter examines the Federal Information Security Management Act (FISMA), the primary statute that governs data security for the federal government and its contractors. The chapter next provides an overview of the information security controls that the National Institute of Standards and Technology has developed for government agencies and their contractors as part of FISMA. The chapter then examines specific cybersecurity requirements for government contractors that handle classified information, controlled unclassified information, and covered defense information.

Privacy Law (Chapter 9)

Any examination of cybersecurity law would be incomplete without an overview of privacy law. Privacy law restricts the ability of companies to use, share, collect, and retain personal information. While data security laws traditionally focus on the measures that companies take to prevent unauthorized access to information, privacy laws restrict the ability of companies to voluntarily use or disclose customers' personal information. Privacy law should be considered alongside data security and other cybersecurity laws because they form a company's overall approach to handling personal information. Moreover, a company's statements about its data security in its privacy policy can lead to significant liability under various privacy laws.

Chapter 9 begins with an overview of the FTC's approach to privacy regulation. As with data security, the FTC uses Section 5 of the Federal Trade Commission Act to bring complaints against companies that violate their consumers' privacy rights or fail to meet the guarantees of their privacy policies. The chapter then examines the privacy laws that restrict healthcare providers and insurers and financial institutions. The chapter describes the CAN-SPAM Act, which limits the ability of companies to send email marketing materials. It explores the Video Privacy Protection Act, which restricts the ability of companies to share online and offline video viewing information, and the Children's Online Privacy Protection Act, which limits the collection of information from children under 13 years old. Finally, the chapter examines state laws in California and Illinois that require website privacy policies, require the deletion of certain information provided by minors, and restrict the use of biometric information, including facial recognition.

Chapters 1 through 9 therefore focus primarily on the U.S. federal and state cybersecurity laws that bind U.S. companies. However, very few U.S. companies can operate without considering the cybersecurity requirements of other countries. If the companies have employees, customers, or business partners in other countries, they may also be bound by those countries' cybersecurity laws. And many countries – particularly those in the European Union – have enacted privacy and data security laws that are much more restrictive than those in the United States. For that reason, Chapter 10 examines the primary privacy and data security legal requirements of the five largest trading partners of the United States: the European Union, Canada, Mexico, China, and Japan.

As with all emerging areas of the law, cybersecurity law is rapidly evolving. At any time, legislatures, regulators, and courts may change some of the laws that are described in this book. Accordingly, this book is not intended to be a substitute for legal advice from qualified counsel.

Cybersecurity law is a complex, nascent, and rapidly changing field. As we continue to define and build this exciting new area of law, this book attempts to provide a reference for students, lawyers, information technology professionals, and others who are interested in helping companies and government agencies improve the security of their computers, systems, and networks.

1

Data Security Laws and Enforcement Actions

CHAPTER MENU
FTC Data Security 2
State Data Breach Notification Laws 36
State Data Security Laws 42
State Data Disposal Laws 49

The United States does not have a national law that prescribes specific data security standards for all industries. The only *federal* data security laws apply to companies that handle specific types of data, such as financial information or health records (discussed in Chapter 3). This comes as a surprise to many, and is frustrating to businesses that want to assure customers and regulators that they comply with all legal requirements, particularly for securing customers' personal information. Likewise, consumer advocates and privacy groups criticize the federal government for failing to enact data security requirements. In recent years, members of Congress and the White House have introduced legislation to set minimum data security standards, but, as of publication of this book, Congress has not enacted any such legislation.

Despite the lack of a statute that sets minimum data security requirements, the Federal Trade Commission aggressively polices data security. In recent years, the FTC has brought dozens of enforcement actions against companies that it believes have failed to take reasonable steps to secure the personal data of their customers. The FTC brings these actions under Section 5 of the FTC Act, a century-old law that was designed to protect consumers and competitors from unfair business practices. Although the law does not explicitly address cybersecurity, it is one of the primary tools that the government uses to bring enforcement actions against companies that failed to take adequate steps to protect consumer information.

This chapter provides an overview of data security requirements under Section 5 of the FTC Act, as well as under state data security laws and private tort claims.

Cybersecurity Law, First Edition. Jeff Kosseff.
© 2017 John Wiley & Sons, Inc. Published 2017 by John Wiley & Sons, Inc.
Companion Website: www.wiley.com/go/kosseff/cybersecurity

First, we examine what the FTC considers to constitute "unfair" trade practices that violate Section 5. Next, we pay special attention to challenges to the FTC's cybersecurity authority. These challenges have been raised by two companies, Wyndham Worldwide Resorts and LabMD, and we conclude that, for now, it is largely accepted that the FTC has some authority to bring Section 5 complaints against companies that fail to adequately secure customer data. We then review how the FTC has applied that reasoning to cybersecurity, both in guidance and the dozens of complaints that it has filed against companies that allegedly failed to adequately secure personal information.

After reviewing the FTC's data security guidance and enforcement actions, we review the laws of 47 states and the District of Columbia that require companies to notify individuals, regulators, and credit bureaus after certain types of personal information are disclosed in a data breach. These laws are fairly complex, and the notification requirements vary by state. Failure to comply with the requirements in each of these statutes could lead to significant regulatory penalties and, in some cases, private lawsuits.

This chapter also provides an overview of the dozen state laws that require companies to implement reasonable data security programs and policies, and the 31 state laws that require companies to securely dispose of personal information.

1.1 FTC Data Security

The FTC is the closest thing that the U.S. federal government has to a centralized data security regulator. Many other agencies – including the Department of Health and Human Services, Education Department, and Federal Communications Commission – have jurisdiction to regulate privacy and data security for particular sectors. However, only the FTC has the authority to regulate companies in a wide range of sectors, provided that they engage in interstate commerce.

1.1.1 Overview of Section 5 of the FTC Act

The FTC claims its data security authority under Section 5 of the Federal Trade Commission Act,[1] which declares illegal "unfair or deceptive acts or practices in or affecting commerce."[2] The statute does not explicitly mention data security. The FTC commonly claims authority for data security enforcement actions under the "unfairness" prong of Section 5.

---

1 For the full text of § 5, *see* app. A.
2 15 U.S.C. § 45(a)(1).

Throughout the 1960s and 1970s, the FTC was criticized for broadly imposing its own value judgments when determining whether a practice is unfair. The Commission considered:

> (1) whether the practice, without necessarily having been previously considered unlawful, offends public policy as it has been established by statutes, the common law, or otherwise – whether, in other words, it is within at least the penumbra of some common-law, statutory, or other established concept of unfairness; (2) whether it is immoral, unethical, oppressive, or unscrupulous; (3) whether it causes substantial injury to consumers (or competitors or other businessmen).[3]

This three-part test became known as the Cigarette Rule because the Commission articulated it as it was considering how to regulate cigarette advertising. Although the FTC did not frequently use this authority, the United States Supreme Court quoted it with approval in 1972, describing the three prongs as "the factors it considers in determining whether a practice that is neither in violation of the antitrust laws nor deceptive is nonetheless unfair."[4]

The FTC recognized the need to clarify the Cigarette Rule to focus more specifically on the injury to customers and benefits to society, rather than value judgments about whether the practice "offends public policy," is immoral, or unscrupulous. In 1980, the Commission issued the Unfairness Policy Statement, which the Commission wrote provides a "more detailed sense of both the definition and the limits of these criteria."[5] The statement articulates a new three-part test for unfairness claims: (1) "the injury must be substantial," (2) "the injury must not be outweighed by any offsetting consumer or competitive benefits that the sales practice also produces," and (3) "the injury must be one which consumers could not reasonably have avoided."[6]

In 1994, Congress amended the FTC Act to codify the 1980 Unfairness Policy Statement into law, Section 5(n) of the FTC Act. The statute states that "unfair" practices are those that cause or are likely to cause "substantial injury to consumers which is not reasonably avoidable by consumers themselves and not outweighed by countervailing benefits to consumers or to competition."[7] This has created a three-part test that the FTC (and courts) must conduct to assess a trade practice.

---

3 Unfair or Deceptive Advertising and Labeling of Cigarettes in Relation to the Health Hazards of Smoking, 16 C.F.R. 408, 29 Fed. Reg. 8344 (July 2, 1964).
4 FTC v. Sperry & Hutchinson Co., 405 U.S. 233 (1972).
5 FTC Policy Statement on Unfairness, Appended to International Harvester Co., 104 F.T.C. 949, 1070 (1984).
6 *Id.*
7 15 U.S.C. § 45(n).

First, has the trade practice caused or is likely to cause *substantial* injury to customers? In other words, a minor injury will not constitute an unfair trade practice. The FTC has stated that a substantial injury often "involves monetary harm, as when sellers coerce consumers into purchasing unwanted goods or services or when consumers buy defective goods or services on credit but are unable to assert against the creditor claims or defenses arising from the transaction."[8] Emotional harm, and nothing more, likely will not constitute unfairness, according to the Commission.[9] In the cybersecurity world, this means that a company is more likely to face an FTC action if the Commission finds that a data breach led to actual consumer harm, such as identity theft. Absent such actual harm, the FTC is less likely to bring an action for a data breach.

Second, do benefits to consumers outweigh the injury?[10] The FTC states that it "will not find that a practice unfairly injures consumers unless it is injurious in its net effects."[11] The Commission states that it considers "the various costs that a remedy would entail," including:

- direct costs to the parties;
- paperwork;
- restrictions on information flows;
- reduced innovation; and
- restrictions on capital formation.

This means that if a company suffers a data breach that leads to substantial consumer injury, a company may be able to avoid an FTC action if the company can demonstrate that it would have been very difficult for the company to avoid the data breach. Note that this is a very high bar; a company cannot merely argue that cybersecurity safeguards were too expensive. The company must be able to demonstrate that either the remedy would have been impossible or the costs would have been so high that customers would have suffered even more than they did because of the data breach.

Third, the Commission considers whether consumers, exercising reasonable care, could have avoided the injury in the first place.[12] This prong reflects the FTC's market-based approach to consumer protection. The Commission states that it relies on "consumer choice – the ability of individual consumers to make their own private purchasing decisions without regulatory intervention."[13] The Commission becomes more likely to find a practice to be unfair if the consumer

---

8 FTC Unfairness Policy Statement.
9 *Id.*
10 *Id.*
11 *Id.*
12 *Id.*
13 *Id.*

was unable to reasonably avoid the harm.[14] Applying this to cybersecurity, the FTC is unlikely to take action against a company for a breach or other attack if customers could have taken simple steps to avoid harm. For instance, if a customer's failure to install updates on an operating system led to a virus that deleted all of the customer's files from the hard drive, the customer is not very likely to succeed in a lawsuit against the maker of the operating system. In contrast, a consumer might successfully sue a company whose internal servers were hacked, leading to disclosure of the customer's personal financial information and, subsequently, identity theft. In that circumstance, it is difficult to imagine how the customer would have reasonably avoided the harm.

The FTC has not issued binding regulations that explain how these three principles apply to cybersecurity. That has led a number of businesses and industry groups to criticize the agency for failing to provide concrete standards. After all, they argue, a company will be more hesitant to invest significant time, money, and resources in cybersecurity measures if it is not even sure whether these investments would satisfy the FTC's expectations. The FTC and its defenders, however, argue that cybersecurity is not a one-size-fits-all solution, and a company's safeguards should depend on its unique needs. For instance, a hospital likely stores vast amounts of highly confidential medical data; thus, it might be expected to take greater security precautions than a company that does not typically process or store personal information. Likewise, if a company has experienced a cybersecurity incident, it would be on notice of such vulnerabilities and expected to take reasonable steps to prevent future incidents.

1.1.2 Wyndham: Does the FTC have Authority to Regulate Data Security under Section 5 of the FTC Act?

An August 2015 opinion from the U.S. Court of Appeals for the Third Circuit – arising from a cybersecurity complaint that the FTC filed against the Wyndham hotel chain – is the most important court decision to date involving the Commission's cybersecurity authority. In short, the opinion provides the most compelling authority for the Commission to use Section 5 to bring cases against companies that have failed to adequately secure personal information.

Up to this point, the FTC's regulation of privacy and data security had been a source of frustration for many companies. As discussed above, Congress has not passed a statute that provides the FTC with the general authority to regulate

---

14 *Id*. ("[I]t has long been recognized that certain types of sales techniques may prevent consumers from effectively making their own decisions, and that corrective action may then become necessary. Most of the Commission's unfairness matters are brought under these circumstances. They are brought, not to second-guess the wisdom of particular consumer decisions, but rather to halt some form of seller behavior that unreasonably creates or takes advantage of an obstacle to the free exercise of consumer decisionmaking.")

cybersecurity. Instead, the FTC claims that inadequate data security may constitute an unfair or deceptive trade practice under Section 5 of the FTC Act, which Congress initially passed more than a century ago.

Although many commentators have long challenged the FTC's cybersecurity authority, it typically has been widely accepted. In the vast majority of cases, if the FTC threatens to file a lawsuit against a company arising from allegedly inadequate cybersecurity, the company agrees to a consent order. Although the terms vary by company, the orders generally require companies to develop comprehensive information security programs, obtain periodic independent assessments of their information security, and provide the FTC with broad oversight and access into the company's programs for up to twenty years. Failure to adhere to the order can result in significant fines. Despite the potential for draconian penalties, companies generally do not risk the publicity and costs of challenging the FTC's findings in court, and instead agree to a consent order.

Wyndham Worldwide Corporation, a hotel chain, decided to become among the first companies to mount a serious challenge to the FTC's cybersecurity enforcement authority.[15] In 2008 and 2009, hackers stole hundreds of thousands of Wyndham customers' financial information and charged more than $10 million to consumer accounts.[16] After investigating the breaches, the FTC claimed that Wyndham failed to take numerous steps to safeguard customer information, leading to the compromises. Patent among the failures that the FTC cited were:

- storing credit card data in clear text;
- allowing simple passwords for the systems that store the sensitive data;
- failure to use firewalls and similarly standard cybersecurity technology;
- failure to adequately oversee the cybersecurity of hotels that connect to Wyndham's central servers;
- allowing vendors to have unnecessary access to Wyndham servers; and
- failure to take "reasonable measures" for security investigations or incident response.[17]

Altogether, the FTC alleged that these failures constituted unfair trade practices that violated Section 5 of the FTC Act. Rather than agree to a consent order, Wyndham allowed the FTC to file a lawsuit against the company in federal court. Wyndham moved to dismiss the lawsuit, arguing, among other things, that Section 5 does not provide the FTC with the authority to bring cybersecurity-related actions against companies.[18] The gravamen of Wyndham's argument was that Congress has addressed data security in industry-specific

---

15 FTC v. Wyndham Worldwide Corp., 799 F.3d 236 (3d Cir. 2015).
16 *Id*. at 240.
17 *Id*. at 240–41.
18 *Id*. at 242.

statutes for healthcare, banking, and credit reporting, and therefore, if Congress had intended to provide the FTC with the authority to regulate data security for all businesses, it would have explicitly granted the Commission such power. The district court disagreed and denied the motion to dismiss, holding that "the FTC's unfairness authority over data security can coexist with the existing data-security regulatory scheme."[19] Soon after the ruling, the district court granted Wyndham's request for the U.S. Court of Appeals for the Third Circuit to review its ruling. This was particularly significant because, until that point, no federal appellate court had ever ruled whether the FTC has the authority to bring cybersecurity-related actions.

After hearing oral argument, the Third Circuit in March 2015 issued a 47-page opinion in which it upheld the District Court and ruled that the "unfairness" prong of Section 5 provides the Commission with the authority to regulate data security. Although the Court's ruling is only binding in the Third Circuit – Delaware, New Jersey, Pennsylvania, and the U.S. Virgin Islands – it was widely seen as an affirmation of the FTC's jurisdiction over cybersecurity.

Relying on dictionary definitions, Wyndham argued that "unfair" conditions only exist if they are "not equitable" or are "marked by injustice, partiality, or deception."[20] The Third Circuit declined to rule whether such deception is necessary to demonstrate unfairness; it concluded that a company "does not act equitably when it publishes a privacy policy to attract customers who are concerned about data privacy, fails to make good on that promise by investing inadequate resources in cybersecurity, exposes its unsuspecting customers to substantial financial injury, and retains the profits of their business."[21]

Wyndham also argued that a business "does not treat its customers in an 'unfair' manner when the business *itself* is victimized by criminals."[22] The Third Circuit rejected this argument, concluding that the fact "that a company's conduct was not *the most* proximate cause of an injury does not immunize liability from foreseeable harms."[23] The Court noted that Wyndham did not argue that the breaches were unforeseeable, a stance that the Court believed "would be particularly implausible as to the second and third attacks."[24]

The Third Circuit also gave little weight to Wyndham's argument that allowing the lawsuit to proceed would effectively provide the FTC with unlimited authority under the unfairness prong. Wyndham argued that such a result would mean that the Commission could use Section 5 to "regulate the locks on hotel room doors, ... to require every store in the land to post an armed guard at the door, and to sue supermarkets that are sloppy about sweeping up banana

---

19 FTC v. Wyndham Worldwide Corp., 10 F.Supp. 3d 602, 613 (D. N.J. 2014).
20 FTC v. Wyndham Worldwide Corp., 799 F.3d 236, 245 (3d Cir. 2015).
21 *Id.*
22 *Id.* at 246.
23 *Id.*
24 *Id.*

peels."[25] The Court dismissed this argument as "alarmist," noting that "were Wyndham a supermarket, leaving so many banana peels all over the place that 619,000 customers fall hardly suggests it should be immune" from a Section 5 action.[26]

Like the District Court, the Third Circuit disagreed with Wyndham's argument that Congress's passage of data security laws for banking, credit reporting, and other specific sectors demonstrates that the FTC does not have general authority over cybersecurity. The FTC noted that many of these laws focus on the *collection* of data, and do not conflict with regulation of the data *security*.[27]

In addition to arguing that the FTC lacked the statutory authority to bring general data security enforcement actions, Wyndham also asserted that the FTC's action violates the Due Process Clause of the U.S. Constitution because it failed "to provide a person of ordinary intelligence fair notice of what is prohibited, or is so standardless that it authorizes or encourages seriously discriminatory enforcement."[28] As the Third Circuit accurately summarized, Wyndham's position is that "the FTC has not yet declared that cybersecurity practices can be unfair; there is no relevant FTC rule, adjudication or document that merits deference; and the FTC is asking the federal courts to interpret [Section 5 of the FTC Act] in the first instance to decide whether it prohibits the alleged conduct here."[29]

The Third Circuit concluded that Wyndham was only entitled to "fair notice that its conduct could fall within the meaning of the statute," and it was not entitled "to know with ascertainable certainty the FTC's interpretation of what cybersecurity practices are required" by Section 5 of the FTC Act.[30] The Third Circuit concluded that Wyndham had such notice, as the Commission, for years, had filed complaints arising from similar data security practices.[31]

Rather than asking all the judges on the Third Circuit to review the opinion *en banc*, or request the United States Supreme Court to hear the case, in December 2015 Wyndham settled the charges with the FTC. Wyndham agreed to implement a companywide data security program, undergo extensive payment card security audits, and take other precautions.[32] The order is in place for twenty years, as is standard for FTC data security settlements.

Although the *Wyndham* case has settled – and likely will not reappear unless the Commission alleges that Wyndham has violated its consent order – the case's

---

25 *Id.* at 246–47.

26 *Id.* at 247.

27 *Id.* at 248.

28 *Id.* at 249, quoting FCC v. Fox Television Stations, Inc., ___ U.S. ___, 132 S. Ct. 2307, 2317 (2012).

29 *Id.* at 253.

30 *Id.* at 255.

31 *Id.* at 257–58.

32 Press Release, Federal Trade Commission, Wyndham Settles FTC Charges It Unfairly Placed Consumers' Payment Card Information at Risk (Dec. 9, 2015).

impact cannot be understated. Even though the ruling is only binding in the Third Circuit, it is the only federal appellate court ruling to consider whether the FTC has general data security enforcement authority. The ruling was a significant boost to the FTC's position that Section 5 allows it to regulate cybersecurity.

The ruling also led critics to bolster their criticisms of the FTC. While there is little dispute that private sector cybersecurity needs government support *and* regulation, a number of critics question whether an agency tasked with antitrust and consumer protection is the best equipped to carry out that mission.[33] Unless the Supreme Court overrules the Third Circuit's ruling, it is likely that the FTC's role as the de facto regulator of private sector data security will become more entrenched.

1.1.3 LabMD: What Constitutes "Unfair" or "Deceptive" Data Security?

In the only other significant challenge to the FTC's cybersecurity enforcement authority, LabMD, a medical testing laboratory, convinced an FTC administrative law judge to rule that the Commission's lawyers had failed to demonstrate that the company's alleged inadequate data security safeguards had caused or was likely to cause substantial injury to the company's consumers. However, in July 2016, the full Federal Trade Commission reversed the judge's ruling, in a significant victory for data security regulators.

In the LabMD case, the FTC's Complaint focused on two data security incidents at the company. The first arose from a report by a third party that a LabMD insurance aging report containing personal information of more than 9000 patients had been made public on a peer-to-peer network in 2008.[34] In the second incident, in 2012, documents containing personal information including names and Social Security numbers were found in the possession of unauthorized individuals.[35]

The Commission alleged in its Complaint that these two security incidents were due to a number of failures to take adequate safeguards, including:

- developing an information security program;
- identifying risks;

---

33 *See, e.g.*, Paul Rosenweig, The FTC Takes Charge – FTC v. Wynham, Lawfare (Aug. 26, 2015). ("All of this means that the FTC now owns cybersecurity in the private sector. Which is an odd result. One would surely have thought that DHS (or DoD or DOJ or even the Department of Commerce) would have had a more salient role in defining standards for the private sector. But somehow, we've converted a consumer protection mandate into a cybersecurity obligation and assigned that role to an independent agency. Candidly, I don't think the FTC is up to the task – not in terms of staffing nor in terms of expertise – but we will soon see how that turns out.")
34 In the Matter of LabMD Inc., No. 9537 (FTC Administrative Law Judge Nov. 13, 2015) at 1–2.
35 *Id.* at 2.

- preventing LabMD employees from unnecessarily accessing personal information;
- training employees regarding information security;
- requiring common authentication security for remote access to LabMD's network;
- maintaining and updating LabMD operating systems; and
- employing "readily available" prevention and detection measures.[36]

The FTC Administrative Law Judge (ALJ) collected extensive evidence, and ultimately granted LabMD's motion to dismiss the complaint. The ALJ focused on Section 5(n)'s requirement that the trade practice cause or be likely to cause substantial injury to customers. The ALJ ruled that the section "is clear that finding of actual or likely substantial consumer injury, which is also not reasonably avoidable by consumers themselves and not outweighed by countervailing benefits to consumers or to competition, is a legal precondition to finding a respondent liable for unfair conduct."[37] The ALJ concluded that the preponderance of the evidence did not show that LabMD's "alleged unreasonable data security caused, or is likely to cause, substantial consumer injury."[38]

The FTC lawyers argued that even though there was not *actual* harm of identity theft, Section 5(n) also allows actions arising from "likely" harm. The ALJ, however, concluded that the failure to produce any evidence of consumer harm, "even after the passage of many years," undermines this argument.[39] After reviewing extensive Section 5 case law, the ALJ concluded that there is no known case in which "unfair conduct liability has been imposed without proof of actual harm, on the basis of predicted 'likely' harm alone."[40]

The ALJ's LabMD ruling is so important to data security because it stands for the proposition that the mere threat of identity theft after a data breach is not sufficient grounds for a Section 5 claim. This ruling, if it had become binding law, could have made it significantly harder for the FTC to bring cases under Section 5.

Accordingly, consumer and privacy advocates were relieved on July 29, 2016, when the full Federal Trade Commission reversed the ALJ's dismissal of charges against LabMD. The Commission's unanimous ruling was not entirely surprising, as the Commissioners had long defended the Commission's authority to regulate data security under Section 5. In its opinion, the Commission wrote that a demonstration of a "significant risk" of injury is sufficient to meet Section 5's "likely to cause" requirement.[41] Exposing sensitive personal information to millions of people via peer-to-peer networking, the Commission

---

36 *Id.*
37 *Id.* at 48.
38 *Id.* at 49.
39 *Id.* at 52.
40 *Id.* at 53.
41 In the Matter of LabMD Inc., No. 9537 (Commission Opinion and Order, July 29, 2016) at 21.

reasoned, creates a significant risk of injury and therefore satisfies this requirement.[42]

As of the publication of this book, LabMD was expected by some commentators to appeal the FTC's ruling to the U.S. Court of Appeals for the Eleventh Circuit but had not yet done so.

1.1.4 FTC June 2015 Guidance on Data Security

In the face of criticism that it did not clearly articulate the standards to which it holds companies for data security, in June 2015, the FTC released a highly publicized document, *Start with Security: A Guide for Business.*[43] The guide was not formally approved by the Commission as a regulation, and therefore it is not binding in court, as regulations would be. Instead, the booklet draws on the facts of data security-related enforcement actions that the FTC has brought against companies, and provides ten over-arching principles to help guide companies as they develop their cybersecurity programs.

Even though the guide does not carry the force of law, it is noteworthy because the FTC rarely provides any guidance whatsoever regarding data security. Accordingly, it is important to consider the ten principles that the FTC articulated in the guide, and an analysis of how these principles might apply to businesses:

1) ***Start with security.*** The Commission urges businesses to consider security in every aspect of their decision making. Businesses should not collect unnecessary information, and they should dispose of information after it has served its purpose. Companies also should avoid unnecessary use of personal information.

2) ***Control access to data sensibly.*** The Commission advises businesses to allow employees to access sensitive data, such as financial account numbers, only if those employees have a valid business reason to access that data. For example, a human resources manager may have a valid reason to have access to employees' payroll data. But an entry-level marketing employee probably does not have a valid reason to access the payroll records of all employees. The Commission also recommends that companies limit the number of employees who have administrative access to make changes to the entire system.

3) ***Require secure passwords and authentication.*** A common vulnerability that leads to data breaches and other incidents is the failure of organizations to require strong passwords. Indeed, a recent survey found that the five most common passwords in 2014 were 123456, password, 12345, 12345678, and

---

42 *Id.*
43 Federal Trade Commission, Start with Security: A Guide for Business (June 2015).

qwerty.[44] To compound problems, people often fail to change their passwords. Forty-seven percent of passwords in 2014 were at least five years old.[45] The FTC suggests that organizations require individuals to choose complex passwords. The Commission does not specify a minimum number of characters, but it suggests prohibiting passwords that are common dictionary words. The Commission also urges organizations to prevent employees from unnecessarily exposing passwords, such as by storing them in personal email accounts. Finally, the Commission notes that hackers often guess passwords through "brute force attacks" in which automatic programs guess combinations of characters until they hit the correct passwords. The Commission said that companies can reduce the threat of brute force attacks by limiting the number of attempted log-ins. Some risk-averse companies limit the number of failed log-in attempts to five or three. After that point, the account is locked, and the user must call an administrator to reactivate access.

4) ***Store sensitive personal information securely and protect it during transmission.***   The Commission appears to recognize that certain types of sensitive personal information, such as health records, require particularly strong security measures. Although the Commission does not provide a specific definition of "sensitive" information, it strongly encourages businesses to use strong cryptography – such as hashes and Transport Layer Security/Secure Sockets Layer – on any information that they deem to be sensitive. The Commission urges companies to use industry-standard security measures, and to avoid adopting encryption methods that have not been tested (though the Commission did not point to a specific industry standard). Sensitive data should be secured throughout its life cycle, both in transit and at rest on a company's server.

5) ***Segment your network and monitor who's trying to get in and out.***   The Commission suggests that companies segregate particularly sensitive data from other parts of the network. For instance, a retail company should segment the computers that store credit card information so that the card numbers are not accessible from every computer on the network. Furthermore, the Commission urges companies to monitor access logs to detect unusual activity.

6) ***Secure remote access to your network.***   Bring Your Own Device (BYOD) programs[46] and virtual private networks are increasingly popular options

---

44 Carly Okyle, *Password Statistics: The Bad, the Worse, and the Ugly*, Entrepreneur (June 3, 2015).

45 *Id.*

46 *See* Matt Straz, *Employees Feel the Love When Companies Embrace BYOD*, Entrepreneur (June 15, 2015). ("BYOD is when a business allows employees to use personal devices at work, ranging from smartphones to tablets to laptops, or devices sanctioned by the company and supported alongside devices that are business-owned.")

that enable employees to access corporate email and files on their own mobile devices. However, these devices present a number of serious cyber-security challenges. The Commission urges businesses to ensure that these devices and computers contain adequate security measures. For instance, if an employee accesses a company's VPN via a personal computer that is infected with malware, a hacker could track all of that employee's keystrokes – including usernames and passwords. Accordingly, companies would be wise to require employees to have antivirus programs and firewalls on their computers. Companies also should require that mobile devices used for BYOD be secured with sufficiently complex passwords. It is increasingly common, for example, for companies to require employees to use device passcodes that are longer than many smartphones' default minimum of four characters.[47] For VPN access, it is increasingly common – and wise – for companies to require two-factor authentication (e.g., a password and a token).

7) ***Apply sound security practices when developing new products.*** The Commission has made it crystal clear that it will not allow companies to avoid responsibility for cybersecurity incidents by blaming engineers or other technical employees. Indeed, the FTC expects those who design products and services to have the same understanding of security practices as lawyers and managers. The FTC requires employees at all levels of the organization – including engineers – to prioritize cybersecurity. The Commission expects companies to provide all engineers with secure coding training, and it has brought actions against companies whose engineers did not employ industry-standard coding practices. Furthermore, if a platform such as IOS has default security settings, the Commission expects that app or software developers will not circumvent that security. The Commission also urges companies to test apps and software to ensure that the security measures function properly, and to regularly test software and apps for vulnerabilities.

8) ***Make sure your service providers implement reasonable security measures.*** Just as companies cannot avoid responsibility for breaches by blaming employees, they cannot shift the responsibility to service providers. The FTC warns that companies must "keep a watchful eye" on their service providers. In the age of subcontractors and sub-subcontractors, of course, this can be quite a difficult task. However, it is necessary, at minimum, to require adequate security in contractors with service providers, and to monitor their compliance with these standards. The FTC states that companies could reduce the risks of security vulnerabilities caused by subcontracts by "asking questions and following up with the service provider during the development process."

---

47 *See 13 Best Practices for Developing Your Mobile Device Policy*, NetStandard (Aug. 6, 2013).

9) ***Put procedures in place to keep your security current and address vulnerabilities that may arise.*** The Commission urges companies to keep in mind that cybersecurity "Isn't a one-and-done deal." If a software provider provides a patch, the FTC expects that a company will promptly install that patch. If companies receive "credible security warnings," the Commission says, they must quickly remediate those problems. For instance, independent security researchers often alert companies to vulnerabilities that they have detected. The FTC has made clear that companies cannot turn a blind eye to such warnings. The Commission suggests that companies establish a dedicated email address for security reports.

10) ***Secure paper, physical media, and devices.*** Cybersecurity involves both data *and* physical security. The Commission has brought actions against companies that have failed to secure papers that contain sensitive information. Moreover, the Commission expects companies to physically secure computers and devices that contain sensitive information. Likewise, the Commission has brought enforcement actions against companies whose data has been compromised because employees have lost laptops. If employees store sensitive information on laptops, it is wise to encrypt the laptops. Finally, the FTC expects that companies securely dispose of all data – whether in electronic or paper form.

1.1.5   FTC *Protecting Personal Information* Guide

In November 2011, the FTC released *Protecting Personal Information: A Guide for Businesses*. The 15-page guide is less specific about particular technologies than *Start with Security*. Also unlike the subsequent guidance, *Protecting Personal Information* does not cite specific FTC actions or complaints for its guidance. Instead, *Protecting Personal Information* provides a five-step framework that companies should consider when developing their cybersecurity plans:

1) ***Take stock.*** Businesses should conduct routine and comprehensive inventories of the personal information on all of their computers, servers, and other storage facilities. Businesses should know who can access the data, the types of data that businesses maintain, and where the data is stored.

2) ***Scale down.*** The Commission urges businesses to only retain personal information that is necessary for business operations and customer services. Moreover, a number of statutory restrictions limit the types of information that can be stored and distributed. For instance, Social Security numbers may not be used as general customer identifiers, and businesses are required to redact all but the last five digits of a payment card number from a receipt.

3) ***Lock it.*** To the extent that businesses have a legitimate need to retain personal information, they must take proper physical, administrative, and

technical safeguards to protect that information from unauthorized access and disclosure. The Commission is particularly focused on the need to employ technical measures such as firewalls and encryption to safeguard personal information. The Commission also urges businesses to restrict employee access to mobile storage – such as laptops. The FTC encourages businesses to regularly train employees regarding proper security practices, and to conduct thorough inquiries of the data security of potential service providers.

4) ***Pitch it.*** The Commission encourages businesses to securely destroy personal information once it is no longer necessary. For paper documents, the FTC encourages effective shredding. For computers and other electronic storage, companies must use software that fully deletes the data before discarding the equipment.

5) ***Plan ahead.*** The Commission encourages companies to develop detailed incident response plans that delegate roles and duties immediately after a data breach. In particular, companies should consider how to prevent further harm, as well as their obligations to notify individuals, regulators, law enforcement, and others.

1.1.6   Lessons from FTC Cybersecurity Complaints

With rare exceptions such as the *Wyndham* cases, the vast majority of FTC cybersecurity investigations do not result in court opinions or judgments. That is because most of these cases quietly settle, with the company agreeing to remediation measures and oversight by the FTC for up to twenty years.

The FTC's *Start with Security* guidance, described above, is perhaps the Commission's clearest statement about some factors that it considers when determining whether a cybersecurity measure (or lack thereof) constitutes "unfair" or "deceptive" trade practice. However, the document is relatively short and does not even purport to cover every possible cybersecurity safeguard and vulnerability.

The complaints that the FTC has filed against companies provide the most useful guidance as to what types of cybersecurity safeguards (or lack thereof) are most likely to result in the FTC investigating a company and filing an enforcement action. (Indeed, the FTC's guidance is based on its positions in these cases.) Below is a more complete summary of the cybersecurity-related complaints that the FTC has filed in the past decade, with a focus on the incidents that the FTC alleges to constitute a violation of Section 5. Keep in mind that all of these complaints resulted in a settlement agreement before the FTC even had the opportunity to file a lawsuit in court, so there is a chance that a court would disagree with the FTC and conclude that the company had implemented adequate data security safeguards. By settling with the FTC, the companies did not admit any wrongdoing.

Although all of the complaints involve Section 5 allegations, I have categorized them into three general types of complaints: (1) security of highly sensitive personal information, (2) security of payment card information, and (3) security violations that contradict privacy policies. The FTC also has brought a number of complaints that allege inadequate cybersecurity practices by financial institutions, in violation of the Gramm–Leach–Bliley Act; those cases are discussed in Chapter 9.

The FTC also brings Section 5 cases against companies that it believes violated customer privacy. For instance, if a company promises to keep customer personal information confidential, and proceeds to sell that data to third parties, the FTC may bring a Section 5 complaint against that company. Because the focus of this section is *security*, I have not included purely privacy-focused Section 5 cases. However, I included cases that include both privacy- *and* security-related claims.

When possible, the docket numbers for the FTC cases are included below. To obtain the full case information, including FTC complaints, press releases, and consent decrees, visit www.ftc.gov and enter the docket number.

1.1.6.1 Failure to Secure Highly Sensitive Information

Unlike other jurisdictions, such as the European Union, the FTC does not have a formal definition of "sensitive" information. However, the FTC is more likely to bring a complaint against a company if it has failed to safeguard particularly sensitive forms of information. As the cases below demonstrate, the FTC considers data to be particularly "sensitive" if it reveals a health condition or other highly personal trait, or if its unauthorized disclosure is likely to lead to identity theft (e.g., a Social Security number or full credit card number).

The FTC general expects companies to adopt industry-standard practices for sensitive data. Among these practices are strong encryption, securing both electronic *and* physical access, routine audits, penetration testing, and other common safeguards.

1.1.6.1.1 Use Industry-Standard Encryption for Sensitive Data

In the Matter of Henry Schein Practice Solutions, Inc., Docket No. C-4575 (2016) Henry Schein Practice Solutions makes software that dentists use to enter and store patient medical records. The company used a database engine provided by an outside vendor. The engine protected the data with a proprietary algorithm that the vendor told Henry Schein was less secure than industry-standard encryption algorithms that are recommended by the Department of Health and Human Services and the National Institute of Standards and Technology. Nonetheless, Henry Schein promoted its software as offering "new encryption capabilities that can help keep patient records safe and secure." In 2013, the U.S. Computer Emergency Readiness Team issued an alert about the company's software as containing a "weak obfuscation algorithm," yet for several months after that alert, the company continued to market the claim that it "encrypts" patient data. The FTC brought a complaint against Henry Schein, alleging that despite its representations, the software "used technology that was less secure than industry-standard encryption."

Key Lesson Although NIST and the U.S. Computer Emergency Readiness Team do not regulate agencies, they are among the leading voices on encryption and data protection. Accordingly, if either of those agencies specifically criticizes a company's data security technology, there is a good chance that an FTC complaint will soon follow.

1.1.6.1.2 Routine Audits and Penetration Testing are Expected

In the Matter of Reed Elsevier Inc. and Seisint Inc., **No. C-4226 (2008)** Reed Elsevier operates LexisNexis, which provides companies with databases of information about individuals. Companies that used these verification services include landlords, debt collectors, and potential employers. Among the data in the company's databases were individuals' credit reports, driving records, and Social Security numbers. Recognizing the sensitivity of the information, the company imposed a number of safeguards, including authentication of customers who accessed the databases, formatting requirements for the credentials that customers use to authenticate, and restrictions on access to nonpublic personal information. These safeguards, however, were not strong enough to prevent a breach of these databases. Unauthorized users obtained a customer's user ID and password and accessed the sensitive information – including names, addresses, birth dates, and Social Security numbers – of more than 300,000 individuals. In some cases, the thieves used this information to open credit accounts in the individuals' names. The FTC filed a complaint against the company, alleging that the breach was caused, in part, by the company's failure to take the following precautions:

- Prohibiting customers from using common dictionary words as their passwords and user IDs;
- Allowing LexisNexis customer to share credentials with others;
- Failing to require users to change their passwords routinely (the FTC used every 90 days as an example);
- Failing to limit the number of unsuccessful attempts to log-in before suspending access;
- Allowing customers to log into Lexis-Nexis automatically by storing their credentials in cookies;
- Not requiring encryption of credentials or searches in transit;
- Failing to confirm a customer's identity before allowing the customer to create new credentials;
- Failing to assess the company website's vulnerability to certain common forms of attacks;

Key Lesson Companies cannot assume that data is secure merely because data is password protected. Companies must regularly assess the strength of their authentication procedures and ensure that bad actors cannot bypass the authentication safeguards.

1.1.6.1.3 *Health-Related Data Requires Especially Strong Safeguards*

In the Matter of Eli Lilly and Company, **No. 012 3214 (2002)**   Eli Lilly, which manufactures the psychiatric drug Prozac, offered an email service, "Medi-Messenger," which provided customers with personal reminders regarding their medications. For instance, if a customer was due for a thirty-day refill of Prozac, the Medi-Messenger site, via Prozac.com, would email a reminder to the customer. As one might imagine, the mere fact that an individual has been prescribed an antidepressant is viewed as highly sensitive information.

About three months after launching Medi-Messenger, Eli Lilly decided to terminate the service. The company informed customers via a blast email. However, the email addresses of all 669 Medi-Messenger customers were visible in the "To" line of the email (rather than in the "BCC" line). This resulted in every recipient of the email being able to see the email addresses of the 668 other Eli Lilly customers who had registered for the Prozac medication reminder service.

The FTC alleged that Eli Lilly violated Section 5 by failing to adequately train and oversee the employee who sent out this particularly sensitive email. The Commission also argued that Eli Lilly should have reviewed the email before sending and tested the email system to ensure that such a communication would not reveal the email addresses of the customers.

This complaint – one of the FTC earliest data security-related enforcement actions – is instructive on two fronts. First, it demonstrates that the FTC will hold a company accountable for the actions of one employee, no matter how inept or negligent. The employer ultimately is responsible for ensuring that *every* employee safeguards customer data. Second, the complaint illustrates that the FTC does not treat all types of data the same; it considers the sensitivity. The FTC's concern was not merely that email addresses were exposed; the truly egregious violation occurred because those email addresses were associated with the fact that the individuals had been prescribed psychiatric medications. Had the program instead been a weekly reminder for customers to go grocery shopping or pay their water bills, it is unclear whether the FTC would have shown a similar level of concern.

Key Lesson Companies that handle particularly sensitive information should carefully oversee the employees who handle that information, and provide regular, comprehensive cybersecurity training. Although health-care-related data also is subject to requirements under the Health Information Portability and Accountability Act (HIPAA), disclosure of particularly sensitive information also could give rise to a Section 5 complaint from the FTC.

In the Matter of CBR Systems, Inc., Docket No. C-4400 (2013)   CBR collects umbilical cord blood during the delivery of babies, and banks it for potential future medical use. When processing orders from potential clients, CBR collects personal information including the names, addresses, Social Security numbers, credit card numbers, blood types, medical histories, and adoption histories of families. Information about nearly 300,000 individuals was backed up on four unencrypted tapes, which a CBR employee placed in a backpack to transport between two CBR facilities in California. The employee left the backup tapes, along with a CBR laptop and hard drive, in a personal vehicle that was broken into overnight. The laptop and hard drive contained unencrypted information that could enable an unauthorized user to access other personal information on the company's network.

The FTC brought a complaint against CBR, alleging that it violated the FTC Act by allowing its employee to transport unencrypted personal information in a backpack, and failing to "employ sufficient measures to prevent, detect, and investigate unauthorized access to computer networks, such as by adequately monitoring web traffic, confirming distribution of anti-virus software, employing an automated intrusion detection system, retaining certain system logs, or systematically reviewing system logs for security threats."

Key Lesson   This case demonstrates that the FTC expects companies to take exceptional care when handling information such as medical histories and adoption records. The Commission also expects companies to ensure that they safeguard not only the personal information stored on their networks but also the credentials and other tools that could be used to access that information.

1.1.6.1.4   Data Security Protection Extends to Paper Documents
In the Matter of CVS Caremark Corporation, C-2459 (2009)   CVS, one of the largest pharmacy chains in the United States, improperly disposed of papers containing customers' personal information in pharmacies in fifteen cities. Among the records were pharmacy labels, credit card receipts, and prescription purchase refunds. Journalists reported that CVS had disposed of these records in public dumpsters. The FTC alleged that CVS failed to implement "reasonable and appropriate measures to protect personal information against unauthorized access," and violated its own privacy policy, which stated that "nothing is more central to our operations than maintaining the privacy of your health information."

Key Lesson   Discussions about "data security" typically involve information that is stored on computers. Indeed, although FTC data security enforcement typically focuses on computer data, the Commission also will bring actions against companies that fail to properly safeguard data in physical form, such as paper records and credit card receipts. Likewise, physically disposing of a computer could raise concerns with the FTC if the company has not taken proper steps to ensure that all personal information has been permanently removed from the computer before disposal.

PLS Financial Services, **Case 1:12-cv-08334 (E.D. Ill.)**   Similarly, the FTC filed a complaint in the federal court against PLS, which operated payday loan retailers in Illinois. The FTC accused the company of disposing of boxes of consumer records that included a great deal of sensitive information, including bank account numbers, wage data, applications for loans, and consumer reports. The FTC alleged that the company "failed to implement policies and procedures in key areas, including the physical security of sensitive consumer information; the proper collection, handling, and disposal of sensitive consumer information; and employee training regarding such matters."

Key Lesson   The Commission's complaint focused on the failure of PLS to develop *written* policies regarding both electronic *and* physical data security. Accordingly, it is in a company's best interests to develop such policies, and to train employees to follow them. Too often, data security policies focus on electronic data and do not account for the possibility that physical records can contain highly sensitive data.

In the Matter of Rite Aid Corporation, **Docket No. C-4308 (2010)**   Television stations reported that Rite Aid, a large nationwide operator of retail pharmacies, had disposed of pharmacy labels, employment applications, and other documents containing sensitive information, in unsecured dumpsters. The FTC alleged that this data "could be misused to commit identity theft or to steal prescription medicines." The FTC attributed this incident to Rite Aid's failure to:

- implement secure disposal policies and procedures that would ensure that sensitive information is no longer readable;
- train employees on proper disposal methods;
- evaluate its data disposal procedures; and
- establish a "reasonable process" to mitigate disposal-related risks.

Key Lesson   As with the CVS case, this case demonstrates that companies need not only care about the data that they store in their files and on servers but the data that they dispose of once it is no longer necessary for business purposes. Companies must not only discard the data, but they must ensure that it is no longer readable or capable of being reconstructed by a bad actor.

1.1.6.1.5   Business-to-Business Providers also are Accountable to the FTC For Security of Sensitive Data

In the Matter of Ceridian Corporation, **Docket No. C-4325 (2011)**   Ceridian provides online payroll processing services for small businesses that do not have internal payroll departments. To process employee payroll, the company must collect employees' personal information, including addresses, Social Security numbers, birth dates, and bank account numbers. The company's website promised employers that its "comprehensive security program is designed in accordance with ISO 27000 series standards, industry best practices and federal, state and local regulatory requirements." Despite these promises, hackers used an SQL injection attack – a common hacking tool – to access the personal information of more than 27,000 individuals whose employers used Ceridian. The FTC determined that Ceridian had failed to take a number of reasonable security steps. Among the alleged failures: storing the information in clear text, storing the information indefinitely, neglecting to test its applications and networks for SQL injection attacks, and failing to employ standard detection and prevention measures.

Key Lesson   Unlike retailers and other companies that collect personal information directly from consumers, Ceridian receives the information from a third party. Nonetheless, the FTC will hold service providers responsible for the security of personal information that they receive from business customers.

***In the Matter of Lookout Services,* C-4326 (2011)**   Just as Ceridian is an outsourced payroll provider, Lookout Services outsources the employee citizenship verification required under federal law. To perform this service, Lookout collected a great deal of sensitive information, including employee Social Security numbers and passport numbers. Lookout's advertisements to potential customers stated that this data is transmitted securely and its interface "will protect your data from interception, as well as keep the data secure from unauthorized access." Lookout's website stated that its servers "are continuously monitoring attempted network attacks on a 24 × 7 basis, using sophisticated software tools."

Despite these alleged precautions, Lookout allegedly failed to implement a number of common security safeguards, including complex passwords, required password changes, and monitoring for unauthorized access. Users also were able to circumvent Lookout's authentication procedures altogether by typing a Lookout URL directly into their web browser. Such "backdoor access" is an easily preventable vulnerability. A Lookout user took advantage of this weakness and obtained more than 37,000 individuals' sensitive personal information. Two months later, the user guessed common passwords, such as "test," to again access the sensitive information.

Key Lesson   Even if a company has implemented significant technical data security safeguards, its failure to implement adequate authentication policies may leave it vulnerable to scrutiny by the FTC. All companies – and particularly those that store and process particularly sensitive information – should ensure that their authentication procedures are industry standard, and that only properly authenticated users have access to the data.

In the Matter of Accretive Health, Inc., **Docket No. C-4432 (2014)**   Accretive Health provides hospitals with a variety of administrative services, including bill collection, registration services, and transcription. Its employees work on-site at hospitals. In 2011, a laptop containing highly sensitive personal information about more than 23,000 patients of an Accretive client was stolen from an Accretive employee's car. The FTC complaint against Accretive alleged that the company did not take adequate steps to prevent employees from transporting personal information in an unsecure manner, and that Accretive had a duty to limit employee access to personal data only if the employees had a business need to access the information.

Key Lesson   Even though the personal information belonged to customers of Accretive's clients – and not to Accretive's direct clients – the FTC nonetheless held Accretive fully responsible for the failure to safeguard the information.

1.1.6.1.6   Companies are Responsible for the Data Security Practices of Their Contractors

In the Matter of GMR Transcription Services, Inc., **Docket No. C-4482 (2014)**   GMR Transcription services transcribes audio recordings for a variety of clients, including doctors and medical institutions. GMR customers typically upload audio files via GMR's website. GMR typists transcribe the audio into a Word document, and provide the transcript to the customer either via email or GMR's computer network. The FTC alleges that Fedtrans, an India-based contractor for GMR, stored audio files and transcripts on an unsecure FTP application that was accessible to unauthenticated users. Indeed, the FTC was able to find thousands of GMR transcripts via a major search engine. These files contained particularly sensitive information, including names, medications, employment history, and medical records. The FTC complaint alleged that GMR caused this exposure by failing to require that its contractors adhere to standard data security safeguards, such as requiring Fedtrans and other service providers, in the service contracts, to implement "reasonable and appropriate security measures to protect personal information in audio and transcript files" that are stored on the contractors' networks. For instance, the FTC cited GMR's failure to require contractors to encrypt storage and transmission of audio and transcript files, and to require strong authentication measures before typists could access the data. The FTC also asserted that GMR failed to adequately oversee the contractor's data security practices through audits or requests for written security policies and procedures.

Key Lesson   Just as the FTC holds service providers responsible for how they handle the personal information of their clients' customers, the FTC also will hold companies accountable for the data security practices of their service providers. Accordingly, it is a best practice to contractually require service providers to adopt industry-standard data security measures, particularly for sensitive information. Moreover, the FTC believes that companies have a duty to regularly oversee the data security practices of their contractors, through audits and other routine reviews.

1.1.6.1.7   *Make Sure that Every Employee Receives Regular Data Security Training for Processing Sensitive Data*

In the Matter of Franklin's Budget Car Sales, Inc., also dba Franklin Toyota Scion, C-4371 (2012)   Personal information of about 95,000 customers of Franklin's Budget Car Sales, a car dealership, was made available on a peer-to-peer network that a Franklin's employee had installed on his work computer. Among the information allegedly disclosed were drivers' license numbers and Social Security numbers. Peer-to-peer networks are not only the source of a great deal of intellectual property infringement (through sharing videos and music) and illegal content (e.g., child pornography), they also carry viruses and other malware that exposes a computer – and the network to which it was connected – to data theft. After an investigation, the FTC criticized Franklins for failing to implement a number of safeguards, including employee data security training, network monitoring, and promulgation of information security policies.

Key Lesson   Employee behavior remains one of the most significant data security vulnerabilities for businesses. To avoid regulatory action after data breaches, employers must provide ongoing employee training, and reasonably monitor employees' use of information technology to ensure that the employees are not taking large risks, particularly if the employer's computers contain sensitive consumer information.

1.1.6.1.8   *Privacy Matters, Even in Data Security*

In the Matter of Compete, Inc., No. C-4384 (2013)   Compete, a marketing company, provided customers with a free web browser tool bar, which provided them with information about the sites that they were surfing. It also offered a "Consumer Input Panel," which provided customers with the opportunity to win prizes in exchange for their product reviews. Compete's privacy policy stated that if a customer opted in, the company would only collect anonymous data about their web-browsing habits. The FTC alleged that this was untrue, and that the company, in fact, collected information about customers' online shopping, credit card numbers, web searches, and Social Security numbers. Although at first glance, this appears to be a privacy issue, it also involved data security because the FTC alleged that Compete failed to adequately safeguard this data, including by sending full bank account information in clear text. The FTC alleged that Compete's failure to adequately safeguard data created "unnecessary risk to consumers' personal information."

Key Lesson   The FTC will take a particularly close look at a potential data security violation if the company had collected that data without obtaining the proper permission from consumers. Although such an act could be the basis for a separate privacy-based claim, it could increase the chances that any subsequent data breach will receive extra regulatory scrutiny.

1.1.6.1.9 *Limit the Sensitive Information Provided to Third Parties*

In the Matter of GeneLink, Inc., **Docket Nos. C-4456 and 4457 (2014)**   GeneLink provides cheek-swab kits to consumers, which collects their DNA information. After analyzing the DNA, GeneLink sells skincare products and nutritional supplements based on what the company determines to be their genetic needs. The FTC filed a lengthy complaint against GeneLink, largely focusing on the company's claims in its advertising and marketing. However, the complaint also included claims arising from inadequate data security. GeneLink's privacy policy stated that it provides some personal information to third-party subcontractors and agents, which "do not have the right to use the Personal Customer Information beyond what is necessary to assist or fulfill your order" and are "contractually obligated to maintain the confidentiality and security of the Personal Customer Information[.]" The FTC claimed that GeneLink took a number of "unnecessary risks" with customers' personal information, including providing all customer information to service providers, regardless of whether the providers needed that data.

Key Lesson   Even if a company reserves the right to provide third parties with access to personal information, the FTC may closely scrutinize whether the company is unnecessarily putting customers' personal information at risk of unauthorized disclosure.

1.1.6.2   Failure to Secure Payment Card Information

As with particularly "sensitive" information such as health records and Social Security information, the FTC pays close attention to any breaches or exposures that involve payment card information, such as full credit card numbers, expiration dates, and security codes. It is important to note that companies that process or store payment card information also must comply with the Payment Card Industry Data Security Standard (PCI DSS), an industry-run program discussed in Chapter 3 of this book. However, in addition to the PCI DSS obligations, companies risk enforcement actions from the FTC if they do not properly handle payment card data.

1.1.6.2.1   *Adhere to Security Claims about Payment Card Data*

In the Matter of Guess?, Inc., **Docket No. C-4091 (2003)**   This case, one of the FTC's earliest data security actions, arose when a hacker used an SQL injection attack on the clothing producer's ecommerce website to access customer credit card numbers. The Commission alleged that Guess? failed to adequately secure the data, by storing it in clear, unencrypted, and readable text. This was contrary to the company's privacy policy, which stated that Guess? uses SSL technology, which "encrypts files allowing only Guess? to decode your information." The FTC alleged that the company failed to "detect reasonably foreseeable vulnerabilities of their website and application" and "prevent visitors to the website from exploiting such vulnerabilities and gaining access to sensitive consumer data," and therefore the claims in its privacy policy were misleading.

Key Lesson Any claims about security of payment card information must be strictly followed. If a breach later occurs, the FTC will closely scrutinize whether a company lived up to its claims about data security.

In the Matter of Guidance Software, Inc., **Docket No. C-4187 (2007)** Guidance Software provides business customers with a variety of information technology software and services, often focused on data security and breaches. As would be expected from a company in the cybersecurity field, Guidance issued a privacy policy that promised users that their sensitive information is protected, and that "information is encrypted and is protected with the best encryption software in the industry – SSL." The privacy policy also claimed that the company also does "everything in our power to protect user-information off-line" and "is committed to keeping the data you provide us secure and will take reasonable precautions to protect your information from loss, misuse, or alteration." A hacker used an SQL injection attack to obtain thousands of customer credit card numbers, security codes, and expiration dates, along with other personal information. In its complaint, the FTC noted that although Guidance did, in fact, use SSL encryption during transit, it allegedly stored the payment card data in clear text. The FTC also claimed that Guidance failed to adopt standard security measures and safeguards, nor did it regularly monitor outside connections to its network. The Commission asserted that the company failed to "detect reasonably foreseeable web application vulnerabilities" and "prevent attackers from exploiting such vulnerabilities and obtaining unauthorized access to sensitive personal information."

Key Lesson Companies that actively promote their cybersecurity safeguards – such as companies that sell security software and services – should be especially careful about the promises and guarantees that they provide to the public regarding payment card data.

1.1.6.2.2 *Always Encrypt Payment Card Data*
In the Matter of Genica Corporation and Compgeeks.com and Geeks.com, **Docket No. C-4252 (2009)** Genica Corporation and its subsidiary, Compgeeks.com, operated a website, geeks.com, that sold computers and accessories. Its privacy policy stated that it uses "secure technology, privacy protection controls and restrictions on employee access in order to safeguard your personal information" and that it uses "state of the art technology (e.g., Secure Socket Layer, or SSL) encryption to keep customer personal information as secure as

possible." In fact, the website allegedly did not encrypt data, and instead stored payment card data and other personal customer information in clear text. During the first half of 2007, hackers repeatedly launched SQL injection attacks on the website and obtained hundreds of customers' payment card data.

Key Lesson   Companies that collect and store credit card information should always encrypt the data, particularly if they promise security in their privacy policies.

1.1.6.2.3   *Payment Card Data Should be Encrypted Both in Storage and at Rest*

In the Matter of Petco Animal Supplies, Inc. (2004)   Petco, a large pet supply retailer, operates Petco.com, which sells products directly to consumers. The website's privacy policy assured customers that entering their credit card numbers "is completely safe," and that Petco.com's server "encrypts all of your information; no one except you can access it." In 2003, a hacker used an SQL injection attack to obtain complete credit card information from Petco.com's database. After investigating, the FTC determined that although the credit card data was encrypted in transit between the consumer's computer and Petco.com's server, Petco.com stored the data in unencrypted, clear text. The Commission, in its complaint, alleged that Petco "did not implement reasonable and appropriate measures to protect personal information it obtained from consumers through www.PETCO.com against unauthorized access."

Key Lesson   Although encrypting payment card information while it is transit is a good first step, it is not sufficient to satisfy the FTC's standards. Payment card information also must be encrypted while it is stored on servers; otherwise, it could be vulnerable to relatively simple hacking.

In the Matter of Life is good Retail, Inc., **Docket No. C-4218 (2008)**   Life is good, an online apparel retailer, promised customers in its privacy policy that "[a]ll information is kept in a secure file and is used to tailor our communications with you." In 2006, a hacker used an SQL injection attack on the company's website to access thousands of payment card numbers, security codes, and expiration dates. The FTC attributed this breach to the company's storage of payment card information in clear text, and its storage of the payment card information for an indefinite period of time. The Commission also alleged that the company failed to implement standard safeguards for payment card information, such as monitoring mechanisms and defensive measures.

Key Lesson   Particularly if payment card data will be stored for a long period of time, the FTC likely will expect it to be encrypted while in storage.

1.1.6.2.4   *In-Store Purchases Pose Significant Cybersecurity Risks*

In the Matter of BJ's Wholesale Club, Inc., **Docket No. C-4148 (2005)**   At the time of the FTC Complaint, BJ's operated 150 warehouse wholesale stores in the United States. The retailer accepted credit cards, and used its computers to receive authorization from the issuing banks for the card purchases. BJ's usually transmitted the credit card data, obtained from the magnetic stripes on the cards, to a central BJ's data center, and then would send the information from there to the banks. BJ's also used wireless scanners, connected to its store computer networks, to collect information about its store inventory. In 2003 and 2004, BJ's customers' credit cards were used for numerous fraudulent purposes, causing thousands of customers to cancel and replace their credit and debit cards. The FTC alleged that BJ's inadequate security practices caused the fraudulent purposes. In particular, the FTC claimed that BJ's payment card security was inadequate because it failed to:

- encrypt payment card information both in transit and at rest;
- implement authorization safeguards that prohibit anonymous access to the data;
- restrict access to the in-store wireless networks;
- implement industry-standard intrusion detection programs; and
- delete the information after there is no business need (BJ's had been storing the data for 30 days, regardless of business need).

Key Lesson Retailers must take care to ensure that security of payment card data collected in stores is secure from unauthorized access. Particularly when a company operates hundreds of locations nationwide with thousands of employees, it may be difficult to control how each of those employees protects customer payment card data. However, it is clear that the FTC will hold companies accountable for in-store cybersecurity shortfalls.

In the Matter of DSW Inc., **Docket No. C-4157 (2006)** DSW, a footwear retailer that operated nearly 200 stores nationwide, suffered a data breach. In March 2005, DSW issued a press release announcing that credit card and purchase data was compromised. The next month, DSW announced in a second press release that checking account numbers, along with driver's license information, was compromised. In total, according to the FTC, the information for more than 1.4 million payment cards and 96,000 checking accounts was compromised, resulting in fraudulent charges on some of those accounts. The FTC asserted in its complaint that the breach was caused by DSW's failure "to provide reasonable and appropriate security for personal information collected at its stores." The data security shortfalls that the FTC identified include:

- storing payment card data in multiple files even though there was not a legitimate need to continue to retain the data;
- failing to secure its in-store wireless networks;
- failing to encrypt payment card information while it was in storage;
- allowing DSW in-store computers to connect to computers in other DSW stores and the corporate network, without adequate limits; and
- installing and implementing sufficient intrusion detection systems.

Key Lesson   The DSW case illustrates the difficulty that many companies face when communicating with the public after a data breach or other security incident. Ideally, DSW would have only issued one press release that described all categories of data that had been compromised. However, such announcements involve a difficult balancing act: although data breach announcements should be thorough and complete, companies face pressure to inform the public of a data breach as quickly as possible to stem further damage.

***In the Matter of The TJX Companies, Inc.*, Docket No. C-4227 (2008)**   In 2007, nationwide retailer The TJX Companies announced what at that time was believed to be the largest data breach in U.S. history. The company, which operates TJ Maxx and Marshalls retail chains, suffered a massive breach in which a hacker downloaded the payment card information of hundreds of thousands of customers between July 2005 and December 2006. The hacker accessed much of this data via Internet connections to TJX computers, where it was stored in clear text. Additionally, the hacker obtained some of the data while it was in transit between stores and TJX's central network. In total, TJX reports more than 45 million payment card numbers worldwide were stolen, though banks that later sued TJX argued that the number was closer to 100 million. In the year following the breach, TJX reported spending $250 million on the incident. The FTC filed a complaint against TJX, alleging that the breach was due to numerous cybersecurity shortcomings, including a failure to encrypt personal information while in transit and at rest, and a lack of "readily available security measures" for wireless access to its in-store networks. The Commission also noted that TJX failed to require strong passwords for authentication to its network, and did not use a firewall to isolate computers that stored payment card information.

Key Lesson   The TJX data breach was enormous for its time, and led to some of the largest private sector cybersecurity lawsuits from customers and issuing banks (discussed in more detail later in Chapter 2). However, companies should keep in mind that besides private contract and tort litigation, they still could face an additional investigation and enforcement action from the FTC. In other words, private litigation and FTC actions are not mutually exclusive.

1.1.6.2.5   *Minimize Duration of Storage of Payment Card Data*
***In the Matter of CardSystems Solutions, Inc.*, Docket No. C-4168 (2006)**   CardSystems Solutions provides credit card authentication services for retailers, and in 2005 processed at least $15 billion in purchases. In short, CardSystems acts as an intermediary between the retailer and the issuing bank, and communicates whether the purchase is approved or denied. A hacker used an SQL injection attack on CardSystems' website to obtain tens of millions of payment card numbers that the company had processed. The FTC alleges that this hack led to "several million dollars in fraudulent credit and debit card purchases that

had been made with counterfeit cards." The Commission, in its complaint, stated that CardSystems "created unnecessary risks to the information by storing it in a vulnerable format for up to 30 days." Additionally, the FTC alleged that CardSystems failed to assess whether its website was vulnerable to SQL injection attacks, failed to require employees to authenticate access with strong passwords, and neglected to implement a number of standard security and intrusion detection procedures and technologies.

Key Lesson   Companies should *immediately* dispose of payment card data once it is no longer necessary for business purposes. CardSystems' blanket policy for retaining all payment card data for 30 days was clearly below the FTC's standards, particularly because the information was not encrypted.

1.1.6.2.6   Monitor Systems and Networks for Unauthorized Software

In the Matter of Dave & Busters, Inc., Docket No. C-4291 (2010)   Dave & Busters, which operates more than 50 indoor entertainment centers nationwide, experienced a breach of about 130,000 customer payment card numbers. Hackers obtained this information by installing unauthorized software on the company's networks, allowing them to obtain the payment card data while it traveled from the stores to the company's credit card processing service provider. In its complaint against Dave & Busters, the FTC alleged that the company failed to adequately detect unauthorized access to its network and to monitor the third-party access to its network.

Key Lesson   As with many data breaches, the hackers in the Dave & Busters case relied on software that they installed on the network to export the payment card data. Companies should routinely audit their systems to ensure that unauthorized software has not been installed by a third party.

1.1.6.2.7   Apps Should Never Override Default App Store Security Settings

In the Matter of Fandango, LLC, Docket No. C-4481 (2014)   Fandango provides an app for smartphones that allows customers to search for movie listing information and purchase tickets with their credit cards. When a customer purchases a ticket, the customer's app transmits the customer's complete payment card information to Fandango's servers. Fandango's privacy policy informs customers that when they purchase tickets via the iPhone app, the "information is securely stored on your device and transferred with your approval during each transaction." Apple, which provides the iOS system for the iPhone, uses application programming interfaces (APIs) that enable secure SSL connections, which provide encrypted communications. SSL communications use SSL certificates for both authentication and encryption. This prevents hackers from acting as middlemen and intercepting payment card data, a significant risk when customers use Wi-Fi connections at coffee shops, libraries, and other public locations. The default setting for iOS requires apps to use SSL certificates.

Apple warned developers that if they disable this default SSL setting, they will eliminate "any benefit you might otherwise have gotten from using a secure connection. The resulting connection is no safer than sending the request via unencrypted HTTP because it provides no protection from spoofing by a fake server." The FTC alleges that Fandango overrode this default setting and did not use the iOS SSL certificates. Fandango also failed to do any security testing that would have revealed that it was not using SSL. The FTC claimed that due to this failure, "attackers could have, in connection with attacks that redirect and intercept network traffic, decrypted, monitored, or altered any of the information transmitted from or to the application, including the consumer's credit card number, security code, expiration date, billing code, email address, and password."

Key Lesson As companies increasingly accept payment card information via apps, they should ensure that they accept all of the default app store security settings, unless they have a valid reason to do otherwise.

1.1.6.3 Failure to Adhere to Security Claims

Although the FTC pays particular attention to data breaches that compromise the security of sensitive information and payment card data, it is important to keep in mind that compromises of less sensitive information also could be on the FTC's radar. This is particularly true if the company's privacy policy, advertising, or other publicly available statement claims to provide specific data security protections, and the company nonetheless falls short. In other words, the FTC expects companies to adhere to their claims about cybersecurity, and it will pursue companies that it believes have broken their promises.

Even if a company's privacy policy or marketing materials do not explicitly guarantee a specific data security safeguard, the FTC may read broad statements about security and privacy to implicitly guarantee certain precautions. For instance, if a company's marketing materials guarantee customers that "we take every step to ensure the security of your information," and the company does not deactivate employees' log-in credentials after they leave the company, the FTC could reasonably conclude that the company's promise of security was misleading.

1.1.6.3.1 Companies Must Address Commonly Known Security Vulnerabilities
In the Matter of MTS, Inc., d/b/a/ Tower Records/Books/Video and Tower Direct, LLC, Towerrecords.com, **Docket No. C-4110 (2004)** The companies operated TowerRecords.com, which sold music, videos, and other products via the Internet. The website's privacy policy claimed to "use state-of-the-art technology to safeguard your personal information." The policy also promised that the site "takes steps to ensure that your information is treated securely and in accordance with the relevant Terms of Service and this Privacy Policy." The FTC states that in 2002, when the website operator redesigned the site's

check-out functions, they created a vulnerability to enable any customer who entered an order number to view "the consumer's name, billing and shipping addresses, email address, phone number, whether the product purchased was a gift, and all Tower products purchased online." The FTC alleges that more than 5000 consumers' purchase information was accessed, and Internet chat rooms contained discussions about this security loophole. The FTC attributes this vulnerability to the companies' failure to "implement appropriate checks and controls on the process of writing and revising Web applications, adopt and implement policies and procedures regarding security tests for its Web applications, and provide appropriate training and oversight for their employees regarding Web application vulnerabilities and security testing." The FTC stated that such "broken account and session management" security risks had been "widely known" in the technology industry for years, and therefore, the companies misled consumers when they did not "implement measures reasonable and appropriate under the circumstances to maintain and protect the privacy and confidentiality of personal information obtained from or about consumers through the Tower Web site."

Key Lesson If a company makes a general promise to take reasonable steps to secure customer information, the FTC will expect that its data security measures will anticipate commonly known vulnerabilities. A company's failure to adopt such safeguards could attract FTC scrutiny, even if the company had not exposed payment card data or highly sensitive information.

1.1.6.3.2 *Ensure that Security Controls are Sufficient to Abide by Promises about Security and Privacy*

In the Matter of Twitter, Inc., **Docket No. 4316 (2011)** Social media company Twitter collects a great deal of nonpublic information about its users, including IP addresses, email addresses, and mobile phone numbers. The site also enables users to exchange nonpublic direct messages, and to make certain tweets nonpublic. In its privacy policy from 2007 to 2009, Twitter's privacy policy stated that it employs "administrative, physical, and electronic measures designed to protect your information from unauthorized access." The policy also stated that direct messages "are not public; only author and recipient can view direct messages" and that users can switch the status of their accounts to "protected" in order to "control who is able to follow them, and keep their updates away from the public eye." The FTC alleged that Twitter failed to enact controls that would enable them to live up to this promise. For instance, the FTC alleged that the company "granted almost all of its employees the ability to exercise administrative control of the Twitter system, including the ability to: reset a user's account password, view a user's nonpublic tweets and other nonpublic user information, and send tweets on behalf of a user. Such employees have accessed these administrative controls using administrative credentials, composed of a user name and administrative password." Moreover, the FTC alleged that Twitter failed to require complex administrative passwords, prohibit employees from storing administrative passwords in their personal email folders, disable accounts after a certain number of unsuccessful attempts, and require password changes after a specified period of days. In 2009, hackers used unsecured administrative accounts to access users' nonpublic information, reset their passwords, and send public tweets from these accounts. For instance, one hacker accessed Barack Obama's Twitter account and offered his followers the chance to win $500 in gasoline if they completed a survey. The FTC alleged that Twitter "did not use reasonable and appropriate security measures to prevent unauthorized access to nonpublic user information."

Key Lesson   A company must ensure that its administrative accounts have adequate controls to enable it to abide by all of the promises about data security that it makes in its privacy policy and other public statements. Employees should not have robust administrative accounts as default; instead, employees only should have the authorization that is necessary for them to perform their jobs.

In the Matter of Upromise, **Docket No. C-4351 (2012)**   Upromise is a membership-based service that teams with merchants and provides online deals to customers that sign up for its service. Among its services is the Upromise TurboSaver toolbar, which promotes Upromise merchant partners in customers' search results and personalizes offers to customers based on their web-browsing information. The tool collected web-browsing information, as well as the data that customers entered into web pages. The Upromise TurboSaver privacy policy stated that the toolbar would only "infrequently" collect personal information, that a Upromise filter "would remove any personally identifiable information" before the data is transmitted, and that Upromise would make "every commercially viable effort … to purge their databases of any personally identifiable information." The Upromise security statement separately promised that Upromise "automatically encrypts your sensitive information in transit from your computer to ours." The FTC alleges that Upromise never prevented the toolbar from collecting and transmitting personal information such as PIN numbers, credit card numbers, and expiration dates. For example, assume that a customer was entering bank account information on a bank website. Even if the bank's website employed the necessary SSL encryption technology, the Upromise toolbar allegedly would transmit that data via clear text, thus defeating any security protections that the bank's website had provided to this sensitive information. An external security researcher in 2010 announced that this information was collected by Upromise and conveyed via clear text. In its complaint against Upromise, the FTC alleged that the company "created unnecessary risks of unauthorized access to consumer information by the Targeting Tool transmitting sensitive information from secure web pages, such as financial account numbers and security codes, in clear readable text over the

Internet," and that the company "failed to use readily available, low-cost measures to assess and address the risk that the targeting tool would collect such sensitive consumer information it was not authorized to collect."

Key Lesson If a company promises to protect and encrypt information, the FTC will hold it accountable if it fails to do so. Moreover, the Upromise case is one of many in recent years in which the FTC has brought a complaint after an independent security researcher has discovered and announced a company's security vulnerability. A number of such researchers have obtained large followings on the Internet, and their findings can prompt immediate and severe regulatory action.

1.1.6.3.3 Omissions about Key Security Flaws also can be Misleading

In the Matter of Oracle Corporation, **Docket No. C-4571 (2016)** Oracle makes Java, the software that enables consumers to use a variety of online programs. Java has long been known for being the target of hackers, and Oracle routinely releases updates to patch vulnerabilities. Oracle typically delivered these updates to consumers via a pop-up prompt, and when the consumer installed the update, Oracle informed the consumer that "Java provides safe and secure access to the world of amazing Java content," and informed the customer that the computer would have the latest "security improvements." Unfortunately, even if the consumer installed the update, the older, vulnerable Java version remained on the consumer's computer. The FTC brought a complaint against Oracle, alleging that it should have informed customers that updating Java still left their computers vulnerable unless they removed the older Java versions. In the complaint, the FTC alleged that by "failing to inform consumers that the Java SE update process did not remove all prior iterations of the software, Oracle left some consumers vulnerable to a serious, well-known, and reasonably foreseeable security risk that attackers would target these computers through exploit kits, resulting in the theft of personal information[.]"

Key Lesson If a company is aware of a major security vulnerability that could expose consumer information, it should disclose that vulnerability – and ways to fix it.

1.1.6.3.4 Companies Must Abide by Promises for Security-Related Consent Choices

In the Matter of HTC America, Inc., **Docket No. C-4406 (2013)** HTC manufactures Windows- and Android-based smartphones. The FTC's complaint against HTC focused primarily on HTC's Android-based phones. Android, which is Google's operating system, has a "permission-based security model" that requires a customer to explicitly provide a third-party application with permission before that application can access that customer's sensitive information (e.g., geolocation information or payment card data). HTC's user manual for its Android devices stated that apps "may require access to your personal information (such as your location, contact data, and more) or access to certain functions or settings of your device" and that during installation, a screen "notifies you whether the app will require access to your personal information or access to certain functions or settings of your device. If you agree to the conditions, tap OK to begin downloading and installing your app." As the FTC concluded, this statement led consumers to believe that "through the Android permission-based security model, a user of an HTC Android-based mobile device would be notified when a third-party application required access to the user's personal information or to certain functions or settings of the user's device before the user completes installation of the third-party application." However, the FTC alleges that HTC devices contained numerous security vulnerabilities that prevented such notice and consent. For instance, HTC had circumvented the Android permission model through a number of "permission re-delegation" vulnerabilities, which occurs when one app that has permission to access sensitive information transfers that permission to another app, even if the consumer has not provided consent for that second app to obtain the information. Separately, the FTC alleged that HTC allowed customers to install apps that were not downloaded through the Android app store, creating another avenue for third-party apps to circumvent the notice-and-consent process that Android requires. Those shortcomings, along with other vulnerabilities in HTC devices, meant that "third-party applications could access a variety of sensitive information and sensitive device functionality on HTC Android-based mobile devices without notifying or obtaining consent from the user before installation," the FTC alleged in its complaint against HTC.

Key Lesson   As with the Fandango case, the FTC takes a very aggressive stance against companies that actively disable security settings that are provided as the default by app stores or operating systems. As online life increasingly moves from the traditional web to apps, the security policies of intermediaries such as app stores will play an increasingly important role in determining whether an app or device-maker's security practices are unfair under Section 5.

1.1.6.3.5 *Companies that Promise Security Must Ensure Adequate Authentication Procedures*

In the Matter of Trendnet, Inc., **Docket No. C-4426 (2014)**   Trendnet manufactures and sells a number of connected devices, including SecurView IP-connected cameras, which enable users to install cameras in their homes (e.g., in a baby's room) and view the video live on the Internet. SecurView's website allows its users to choose whether to require a log-in or password to access the live video (because in some cases, users may want a live video to be publicly accessible). For those who did not want the video to be available to the public, Trendnet assured them that the system was secure. Indeed, SecurView's packaging contained a sticker with a padlock and the word "security." However, from April 2010 to February 2012, 20 models of Trendnet's camera allegedly did not require log-in credentials, even if users had chosen to require them. In other words, any member of the public could access *any* of the camera feeds. Indeed, hackers posted links to live feeds of almost 700 Trendnet cameras, publicly displaying scenes such as babies asleep in cribs and children playing. The FTC took this breach particularly seriously, stating that it "increases the likelihood that consumers or their property will be targeted for theft or other criminal activity, increases the likelihood that consumers' personal activities and conversations or those of their families, including young children, will be observed and recorded by strangers over the Internet." The FTC asserted that consumers "had little, if any reason to know that their information was at risk, particularly those consumers who maintained login credentials for their cameras or who were merely unwitting third parties present in locations under surveillance by the cameras."

Key Lesson The Trendnet case was a particularly newsworthy complaint due to the sensitive nature of the information that was disclosed. However, from a legal standpoint, perhaps the biggest lesson from the case is that if a company markets a product or service as "secure" (and, in fact, includes "secure" in the name of its product), then the FTC is far more likely to scrutinize its practices if later there is a security vulnerability.

1.1.6.3.6 Adhere to Promises about Encryption
In the Matter of Credit Karma, Inc., **Docket No. C-4480 (2014)** Credit Karma provides a mobile app that allows customers to view their credit reports and scores. The company's app privacy policy stated that it uses SSL "to establish a secure connection between your computer and our servers, creating a private session." Apple, which manufactures the iPhone and provides the iOS operating system, provides application programming interfaces that, by default, use encrypted SSL communications. Apple warns developers that disabling this default setting "eliminates any benefit you might otherwise have gotten from using a secure connection. The resulting connection is no safer than sending the request via unencrypted HTTP because it provides no protection from spoofing by a fake server." Credit Karma allegedly overrode those default settings and therefore did not use SSL communications. Accordingly, the FTC alleged, "attackers could, in connection with attacks that redirect and intercept network traffic, decrypt, monitor, or alter any of the information transmitted from or to the application, including Social Security numbers, dates of birth, 'out of wallet' information, and credit report information." Moreover, the FTC alleged that hackers could "intercept a consumer's authentication credentials, allowing an attacker to log into the consumer's Credit Karma web account to access the consumer's credit score and a more complete version of the credit report." The FTC asserted that misuse of this information "can lead to identity theft, including existing and new account fraud, the compromise of personal information maintained on other online services, and related consumer harms."

Key Lesson   As with the Fandango and HTC cases, here the FTC had little tolerance for a company that circumvented a mobile operating system's default security settings. Such settings are quickly becoming the de facto standard of care for mobile app security.

1.2   State Data Breach Notification Laws

At the state level, perhaps the most pervasive cybersecurity-related laws are data breach notification laws. Forty-seven states and the District of Columbia have enacted such laws, which require companies and government agencies to notify consumers, regulators, and credit bureaus about data breaches under specified circumstances.

Companies must be aware of every breach notification law, even if it does not have any employees or property in that state. Each breach notification law applies to the unauthorized disclosure of that state's residents. For example, if a California company discloses the personal information of New York residents, the New York law will determine whether and how the company is required to notify consumers, regulators, and credit bureaus. As a practical matter, because companies often process data about customers and other individuals who are located across the United States, they are subject to all 48 breach notification laws in the United States.

Determining whether a company's breach notice obligations are triggered can be quite time-consuming because this determination requires a careful review of the facts of the data breach. Although many of the state laws have similar provisions – indeed, some contain identical phrases and requirements – there are important differences. Because of these deviations among breach notification laws, quite often, a company is required to report a data breach under the laws of some states but not under the laws of others.

If companies do not properly issue data breach notifications, they face significant fines and private litigation in many states. Yet, they must fulfill these legal obligations during a chaotic period after a data breach, when they often have incomplete information about the incident. Companies must balance their legal duties to disclose with the equally compelling need to ensure that their disclosures are accurate. If a company incorrectly describes a data breach, it could face an action from a state regulator or the FTC under Section 5, discussed in Section 1.1.1 of this chapter. Moreover, a company's initial breach disclosures could have a significant impact on the company's brand and public relations.

This Section provides an overview of the key elements of breach notification laws. The first subsection examines the circumstances under which state laws require companies to issue data breach notifications to customers. The second subsection outlines the required contents of the customer notifications. The third subsection examines companies' obligations to notify state regulators and credit bureaus. The fourth subsection examines the penalties and litigation that companies can face if they do not comply with the statutes.

This section discusses the most common rules under the state data breach notification statutes, and also notes many of the state laws that differ from these default rules. However, many of these state laws are unique and contain particular requirements that vary considerably, so companies should always consult the current version of the states' data breach notification law to understand the precise requirements in each state. For ease of reference, a summary of all 48 U.S. data breach notification laws, current as of 2016, is published in Appendix B.

Keep in mind that certain industries that process highly sensitive data – including healthcare companies and financial institutions – *also* face breach notification requirements under federal law, discussed in Chapter 3.

1.2.1 When Consumer Notifications are Required

After many data breaches, the state breach notification laws do not require companies to notify customers, regulators, or credit bureaus. In many cases, the information that was compromised is not covered by the state laws, and therefore notification is required. Moreover, every state except Tennessee does not require notification if the breached personal information was encrypted and the encryption key was not disclosed. There also are a number of exceptions that allow companies to avoid breach notifications even if unencrypted personal information was accessed without authorization, including provisions in most laws that allow companies to withhold notifications if they determine that the disclosure will not create a reasonable likelihood of harm to the customers.

Even if companies are not required to notify a state's residents of a data breach, many do so anyway. Many companies view breach notifications as a matter of good business and transparency. Moreover, if a company is required to notify residents in even one state, news of the breach may be quickly reported in the media. That would leave customers in other states wondering whether their information also was compromised, and questioning why the company did not notify them.

1.2.1.1 Definition of Personal Information

State data breach laws only apply to unauthorized acquisition of *personal information*, a term that is defined in each statute. If a data breach only exposes data that does not fall under the statute's definition of "personal information," then a company is not required to notify customers. In many cases, data that is not classified as "personal information" still may be quite sensitive and valuable to identity thieves or other criminals, but the notification rule does not apply.

In nearly every state with a data breach law, the definition of personal information includes, at minimum, an individual's first name or initial and last name, in combination with at least *one* of the following categories of information: (1) Social Security number; (2) driver's license or state identification number; or (3) account number, credit card number, or debit card number, along with any required password or access code.

In addition to those three elements, a number of other states include elements that, combined with an individual's name, trigger a data breach requirement (specific definitions for each state, as of mid-2016, are summarized in Appendix B):

Medical information: Arkansas, California, Florida, Missouri, North Dakota, Oregon, Texas
Health insurance information: California, Florida, North Dakota, Oregon
Online account information (including username and unencrypted password):   California, Florida
Biometric data (e.g., fingerprints):   Iowa, Nebraska, North Carolina, Oregon, Wisconsin
Taxpayer identification number: Maryland, North Carolina
Tribal identification number: Montana, Wyoming
Any federal or state identification number: Wyoming
Date of birth: North Dakota
Mother's maiden name: North Dakota
Employment identification number: North Dakota
Passport number: North Carolina, Oregon
Digital signature: North Carolina, North Dakota

A handful of states also require notification of the unauthorized access to information even if the individual's names are not disclosed. California and Florida require notification for the disclosure of a user name or email address, in combination with a password or security question and answer that would allow access to an online account. Maine and Oregon require notification of the breach of certain categories of information, without the individual's name, if the information could be used for identity theft. Texas requires notification for the disclosure of any information related to an individual's healthcare, even if it is not disclosed with the individual's name.

Many breach notification laws explicitly state that they do not cover information that is lawfully made public by the government or media.

1.2.1.2 Encrypted Data

All state data breach notification laws, except Tennessee's, do not require notification of the breach of personal information that is encrypted. Most of these laws do not provide technical specifics for encryption; however, Massachusetts requires encryption with at least a 128-bit processed. Additionally, many of the state encryption exceptions only apply if the encryption key was not accessed. In 2015, Tennessee amended its breach notification law and became the first and only state to require notification even if the personal information was encrypted. This change had a significant impact nationwide and caught many data security professionals by surprise. Until this change, companies that properly encrypted their data could avoid any notification obligation; now, encryption does not fully absolve companies of this obligation. However, Tennessee still has an exception to the notice requirement if the company determines that the breach did not create a risk of harm – discussed below. Companies would have a very strong argument that if all of the personal data was encrypted, a breach would not pose a risk of harm.

1.2.1.3 Risk of Harm

In thirty-eight of the states with breach notification laws, companies can avoid notification obligations if, after investigating the breach, they determine that the incident did not create a risk of harm for individuals whose personal information was exposed. The exact wording of this exception varies by state. For example, in Michigan, companies are not required to notify individuals if they determine that "the security breach has not or is not likely to cause substantial loss or injury to, or result in identity theft" with respect to Michigan residents. Oregon's exception is a bit narrower, applying if the company "reasonably determines that the consumers whose personal information was subject to the breach of security are unlikely to suffer harm." New York's exception only applies if the company determines that the breach did not compromise the security, confidentiality, or integrity of the personal information. Florida's risk-of-harm exception only applies if the company provides to the Florida Department of Legal Affairs its written determination that the disclosure will not result in harm, and retains that determination for five years.

Ten of the data breach notification statutes do not have risk-of-harm provisions, and therefore require notification regardless of whether the company concludes that the breach is likely to lead to harm to individuals. These "strict liability" jurisdictions are California, the District of Columbia, Georgia, Illinois, Massachusetts, Maine, Minnesota, Nevada, North Dakota, and Texas.

1.2.1.4 Safe Harbors and Exceptions to Notice Requirement

Most states have some additional, narrow exceptions to the breach notification rules. Commonly, if a company follows the breach notification procedures of its own information security policy, then it does not have to notify consumers pursuant to the specific requirements of the state law, as long as the timing of its notice is consistent with the state law. Additionally, many states allow regulated financial institutions and healthcare providers to notify consumers under applicable federal laws and regulations, rather than following the state breach notice provisions.

1.2.2 Notice to Individuals

The U.S. breach notification process is not one-size-fits-all. State laws differ as to the timing of the notices, the form in which they can be delivered, and the content of the notices. Failure to comply with these technical requirements can lead to liability, so companies are wise to double-check the current version of each state's breach notification law to ensure that they are providing proper notice.

1.2.2.1 Timing of Notice

Most breach notification laws require companies to notify customers as expediently as possible and without unreasonable delay, although the exact wording of that requirement varies by state (and is summarized by state in Appendix B). Although these states do not require notification within a specified number of days after discovering the breach, state regulators likely will not tolerate an unjustified delay of more than a month or two.

Eight states require notice within a specified period after discovery of the breach. The shortest time frame is in Florida, which requires individual notice within 30 days of discovery of a breach. Ohio, Rhode Island, Tennessee, Washington state, Wisconsin, and Vermont require notice within 45 days, and Connecticut requires notice within 90 days of discovery of a breach.

All breach notification laws allow companies to delay notification if the delay would harm an ongoing law enforcement investigation. Many of the laws also allow companies to delay notice to determine the scope of the breach, identify affected individuals, and restore the confidentiality, integrity, and availability of the company's computer systems and data.

1.2.2.2 Form of Notice

Companies also must ensure that they deliver the notice in a medium that is approved by each statute. The breach notification laws all allow written notice, mailed to the last known address on record for the individual. The laws also typically allow electronic notice delivered via email to the last known email address that the company has on record. Some states only allow electronic notice if email was the primary method of communication between the company and customer. The states also generally only allow electronic communication if the company obtained valid consent to delivery electronic notices pursuant to the federal E-SIGN Act. About half of the statutes also allow companies to deliver the notices via telephone, and a handful also allow notice to be delivered via fax machine.

Additionally, state breach notification laws allow companies to provide "substitute" notice if the company does not have sufficient contact information to deliver the other forms of notice, if the total cost of notification would exceed an amount specified in the statute, or if the company would be required to notify more than a certain number of people specified in the statute. Substitute notice generally consists of three elements: (1) email notice to any individuals for whom the business has an email address on file; (2) if the company has a website, conspicuous notice of the breach on the site; and (3) notice to major statewide media.

1.2.2.3 Content of Notice

Most state breach notification laws do not require a breach notice to contain specific information. A minority of states, however, require notices to individuals to contain certain statements or data. These requirements are listed in detail, by jurisdiction, in Appendix B. Among the most common requirements are:

- contact information for the company;
- a general description of the breach;
- the categories of personal information compromised in the breach;
- the date(s) of the breach;
- contact information for major credit bureaus, the state attorney general, and the Federal Trade Commission;
- advice to remain vigilant about identity theft by reviewing financial account records and credit reports; and
- information about identity theft protection services (California and Connecticut require companies to provide the services for 12 months).

Some states prohibit individual notices from containing certain types of information. For instance, Illinois prohibits companies from notifying individuals of the number of Illinois residents whose data was compromised. Massachusetts also prohibits companies from stating the number of state residents affected, and it also bars companies from describing the nature of the breach.

1.2.3 Notice to Regulators and Consumer Reporting Agencies

If a company notifies individuals about a data breach, it also may be required to notify state regulators or the three major credit bureaus.

Eighteen states (listed in Appendix B) require companies to notify state officials – typically the Attorney General – if individuals were notified. In six of those states, regulator notification is required only if the number of individuals notified exceeds a specified threshold (typically 500 or 1000 state residents). About half of these states require the regulator notice to contain specific content, such as a general description of the breach, the number of the state residents affected, and the steps that the company has taken to remediate harm. Some statutes require companies to provide regulators with samples of the notices that were sent to individuals. Some states, including California, New York, and North Carolina, provide companies with a form to complete.

Most – but not all – states also require notification of the major credit bureaus (Experian, EquiFax, and TransUnion). Typically, credit bureau notification is only required if more than 1000 residents of the states have been notified, though some have higher thresholds. The breach notice laws often require companies to inform the credit bureaus of the date that the notices were sent to individuals.

1.2.4 Penalties for Violating State Breach Notification Laws

Typically, state attorneys general may bring enforcement actions against companies that fail to comply with their states' data breach notification laws. Although the remedies vary by state, the officials typically can seek injunctions ordering disclosure of the breach and civil fines. In fourteen states[48] and the District of Columbia, individuals can bring private lawsuits seeking damages, often under state consumer protection statutes.

1.3 State Data Security Laws

Twelve states have enacted statutes that impose data security requirements on companies that own or process personal information from the states' residents. As with the data breach notification laws, the location of a company's headquarters is irrelevant to determining whether these laws apply to the company. Instead, a state's data security law will apply if a company owns or processes personal information of even one resident of that state. Because most midsized and large companies process the personal information of residents of all fifty states, companies must pay attention to the requirements of all state data security laws.

Of the twelve data security laws, eight are relatively flexible, requiring companies to implement reasonable security procedures, but not specifying precisely

---

48 The jurisdictions that allow private parties to sue for violations of data breach notification statutes are Alaska, California, Hawaii, Louisiana, Maryland, Massachusetts, Nevada, New Hampshire, North Carolina, Oregon, South Carolina, Tennessee, Virginia, Washington state, and the District of Columbia.

what constitutes "reasonable." Those states are Arkansas,[49] California,[50] Connecticut,[51] Florida,[52] Indiana,[53] Maryland,[54] Texas,[55] and Utah.[56]

A note about statutes, laws, regulations, and government guidelines described throughout this book: when possible, we use the language directly from the original text. However, for brevity and clarity, some of these descriptions are shortened or modestly edited. Moreover, Congress and state legislatures occasionally amend data security requirements. Accordingly, before citing any of these laws in an official document, consult the primary source, which is accessible via the citation in the footnotes.

1.3.1 Oregon

Oregon's data security law, which was significantly revised in 2015, also requires companies that own or possess Oregon consumers' personal

---

49 ARK. CODE. 4-110-104(b) ("A person or business that acquires, owns, or licenses personal information about an Arkansas resident shall implement and maintain reasonable security procedures and practices appropriate to the nature of the information to protect the personal information from unauthorized access, destruction, use, modification, or disclosure.").

50 CAL. CIV. CODE 1798.81.5 ("A business that owns, licenses, or maintains personal information about a California resident shall implement and maintain reasonable security procedures and practices appropriate to the nature of the information, to protect the personal information from unauthorized access, destruction, use, modification, or disclosure.").

51 CONN. PUB. ACTS No. 08-167(a) ("Any person in possession of personal information of another person shall safeguard the data, computer files and documents containing the information from misuse by third parties, and shall destroy, erase or make unreadable such data, computer files and documents prior to disposal.").

52 FLA. STAT. 501.171(2) ("Each covered entity, governmental entity, or third-party agent shall take reasonable measures to protect and secure data in electronic form containing personal information.").

53 IND. CODE 24-4.9-3-3.5 ("A data base owner shall implement and maintain reasonable procedures, including taking any appropriate corrective action, to protect and safeguard from unlawful use or disclosure any personal information of Indiana residents collected or maintained by the data base owner.").

54 MD. CODE COM. LAW 14-3503(a) ("To protect personal information from unauthorized access, use, modification, or disclosure, a business that owns or licenses personal information of an individual residing in the State shall implement and maintain reasonable security procedures and practices that are appropriate to the nature of the personal information owned or licensed and the nature and size of the business and its operations.").

55 TEX. BUS. & COM. CODE 48.102(a) ("A business shall implement and maintain reasonable procedures, including taking any appropriate corrective action, to protect and safeguard from unlawful use or disclosure any sensitive personal information collected or maintained by the business in the regular course of business.").

56 UTAH CODE 13-44-201(a) ("Any person who conducts business in the state and maintains personal information shall implement and maintain reasonable procedures to … prevent unlawful use or disclosure of personal information collected or maintained in the regular course of business[.]").

information to develop and implement reasonable safeguards.[57] However, the Oregon law provides more detail about how companies can satisfy the requirement.

Under the Oregon law, the company could satisfy the "reasonableness" requirement by developing an information security plan that contains the following safeguards:

- Administrative safeguards, such as:
  - designating a coordinator for the security program;
  - identifying "reasonably foreseeable" internal and external risks;
  - assessing if existing safeguards control those risks;
  - training and managing employees in security;
  - selecting service providers that can maintain safeguards, and requiring them, by contract, to maintain the safeguards; and
  - adjusting the security program when necessary.
- Technical safeguards, such as:
  - assessing risks in network and software design;
  - assessing risks in information processing, transmission, and storage;
  - detecting, preventing, and responding to attacks or system failures; and
  - testing and monitoring regularly the effectiveness of information security safeguards.
- Physical safeguards, such as:
  - assessing risks of information storage and disposal;
  - detecting, preventing, and responding to intrusions;
  - protecting against unauthorized access during or after collecting, transporting, destroying, or disposing of the personal information; and
  - disposing of personal information after it is no longer needed for business or legal purposes by adequately destroying it so it cannot be read or reconstructed.[58]

Alternatively, companies could satisfy the Oregon law by complying with the Gramm-Leach-Bliley Act (if the company is a financial institution),[59] the Health Insurance Portability and Accountability Act (if the company is subject to HIPAA),[60] or a state or federal law that provides greater protection to personal information than the procedures.[61]

---

57 O.R.S. 646A.622(1) ("A person that owns, maintains or otherwise possesses data that includes a consumer's personal information that the person uses in the course of the person's business, vocation, occupation or volunteer activities shall develop, implement and maintain reasonable safeguards to protect the security, confidentiality and integrity of the personal information, including safeguards that protect the personal information when the person disposes of the information.").

58 O.R.S. 646A.622(2)(d).

59 O.R.S. 646A.622(2)(b).

60 O.R.S. 646A.622(2)(c).

61 O.R.S. 646A.622(2)(a).

1.3.2 Rhode Island

Rhode Island's data security law, which, like Oregon's, was amended significantly in 2015, requires state agencies and firms to have "reasonable security procedures and practices."[62] The statute requires the program to be appropriate to:

- the size and scope of the organization;
- the nature of the information; and
- "the purpose for which the information was collected in order to protect the personal information from unauthorized access, use, modification, destruction, or disclosure and to preserve the confidentiality, integrity, and availability of such information."[63]

Rhode Island prohibits organizations from retaining personal information for a period longer than is reasonably required to provide requested services, to meet the purpose for which the personal information was collected, or in accordance with a written retention policy or as required by law.

Organizations that disclose Rhode Island residents' personal information to third parties (e.g., service providers) must require those third parties, by contract, to implement and maintain reasonable security procedures and practices.

1.3.3 Nevada

Nevada requires data collectors that maintain records containing Nevada residents' personal information to "implement and maintain reasonable security measures to protect those records from unauthorized access, acquisition, destruction, use, modification, or disclosure."[64] Companies that disclose Nevada residents' personal information to service providers must contractually require those companies to adopt reasonable security measures.

Nevada's data security law is unique in that it requires companies to use encryption before either (1) electronically transferring Nevada residents' personal information or (2) moving any data storage device containing Nevada residents' personal information beyond the logical or physical controls of the data collector, its data storage contractor, or, if the data storage device is used by or is a component of a multifunctional device, a person who assumes the obligation of the data collector to protect personal information.[65] The encryption requirements do not apply to telecommunications providers acting solely in the role of conveying communications of other persons.[66]

---

62 R.I. GEN. LAW 11-49.3-2(a).
63 *Id.*
64 N.R.S. 603A.210.
65 N.R.S. 603A.215.
66 N.R.S. 603A.215(4).

Nevada's statute does not provide specific technological requirements for encryption to satisfy this requirement. The statute states that the technology could be one that was adopted by a standards-setting body, such as the Federal Information Processing Standards issued by the National Institute of Standards and Technology.[67] The encryption also should use "[a]ppropriate management and safeguards of cryptographic keys to protect the integrity of the encryption" using guidelines that have been published by a standards-setting body, such as NIST.[68]

Nevada also requires data collectors that accept payment card information to comply with the Payment Card Industry Data Security Standard (PCI DSS), which is explained in Chapter 3 of this book. Although companies that accept payment card information typically must comply with PCI DSS due to contractual requirements with credit card companies, Nevada's law is unique in that it requires companies, by law, to comply.

1.3.4 Massachusetts

Massachusetts has enacted the most detailed and comprehensive general data security requirements in the United States. These requirements have quickly become de facto national standards for mid-sized and large businesses that have customers nationwide, as they most likely process some personal information of Massachusetts residents.

Massachusetts' data security law requires the state's Department of Consumer Affairs and Business Regulation to adopt data security regulations to safeguard Massachusetts residents' personal information. The statute requires the regulations to:

- "insure the security and confidentiality of customer information in a manner fully consistent with industry standards";
- "protect against anticipated threats or hazards to the security or integrity of such information"; and
- "protect against unauthorized access to or use of such information that may result in substantial harm or inconvenience to any consumer.[69]"

The Massachusetts Department of Consumer Affairs issued comprehensive data security regulations[70] to comply with this mandate. The regulations, modestly edited below for clarity and brevity, require every company and person who owns or licenses personal information about a Massachusetts resident to develop a comprehensive written information security program

---

67 N.R.S. 603A.215(5)(b).
68 *Id.*
69 Mass. Gen. Law 93H § 2(a).
70 201 C.M.R. 17.00 et seq.

that contains administrative, technical, and physical safeguards that are appropriate to:

- the size, scope, and type of business of the company;
- the amount of resources available to the company;
- the amount of stored data; and
- the need for security and confidentiality of both consumer and employee information.[71]

The Massachusetts regulations are unique in their specificity of the *required* components of a written information security plan. The regulations require all information security plans to include the following:

- At least one employee who is designated to maintain the security program.
- Identification and assessment of reasonably foreseeable internal and external risks to security, confidentiality, and integrity of records that contain personal information.
- Evaluating and improving the effectiveness of the current safeguards for limiting the risks, including but not limited to
  - ongoing employee training,
  - employee compliance with information security policies and procedures, and
  - means for detecting and preventing security system failures.
- Developing records storage, access, and transportation security policies.
- Disciplinary measures for information security violations.
- Preventing terminated employees from accessing personal information.
- Overseeing service providers that have access to consumers' personal information by
  - taking "reasonable steps" to select and retain providers that can maintain adequate security measures, and
  - contractually requiring service providers to maintain appropriate security measures.
- Reasonably restricting physical access to personal information.
- Regular monitoring to ensure proper operation of information security program.
- Reviewing scope of security measures at least annually or whenever there is a material change in business practices.
- Documenting responsive actions after a breach.[72]

---

71 201 C.M.R. 17.03(1).
72 201 C.M.R. 17.03(2).

The Massachusetts regulations also require information security programs to contain the following technical security measures when feasible:

- Secure user authentication protocols, including
  - control of identifiers,
  - a "reasonably secure" method of assigning passwords and other access mechanisms,
  - control of storage of passwords,
  - restricting access to active user accounts, and
  - blocking access to log-ins after multiple unsuccessful log-in attempts.
- Secure access control measures that
  - restrict access to personal information to those who need the information to perform their jobs, and
  - assign unique identifications plus passwords that are not default credentials and are reasonably designed to maintain integrity of access controls.
- Encryption of all personal information that travels across public networks or is transmitted wirelessly or stored on laptops or portable devices.
- Reasonable monitoring for unauthorized use.
- Up-to-date firewall protection and operating system patches.
- Reasonably up-to-date malware protection and anti-virus software.
- Employee computer security training.[73]

The Massachusetts regulations are, by far, the most detailed general data security requirements in the United States. Despite the length of the regulations, they are not significantly more onerous than the general expectations that regulators long have had for companies that handle personal information. For instance, it is unlikely that the FTC would agree to allow a company to store personal information on unencrypted laptops, nor would the California Attorney General suggest that companies allow multiple employees to access personal information with a single log-in credential. The Massachusetts regulations merely spell out what is generally considered in the industry to constitute "reasonable" data security. Even if a company does not own or process personal information of Massachusetts residents, it would be well advised to use the Massachusetts regulations as guidelines for its own data security programs.

---

73 201 C.M.R. 17.04.

1.4 State Data Disposal Laws

Thirty-one states require companies to take reasonable steps to dispose of records that contain personal information.[74] Although the wordings of the laws vary by state, they generally require steps such as shredding or otherwise rendering the personal information unreadable or undecipherable, and preventing the information from being reconstituted. Nonetheless, most statutes do not provide much detail on the "reasonable measures" necessary to satisfy the requirements of data disposal laws.

Massachusetts provides some additional detail about the minimum standards for disposal of personal information. Paper records should be either "redacted, burned, pulverized or shredded" so that the personal information cannot be read or reconstituted, and nonpapermedia (e.g., electronic media) should be "destroyed or erased so that personal information cannot practicably be read or reconstructed."[75]

Hawaii's law provides some detail about the oversight of vendors that destroy information. It states that a business can satisfy this requirement by exercising "due diligence" over records destruction contractors. Due diligence consists of:

- reviewing an independent audit of the disposal business' operations and compliance with the state data disposal law;
- obtaining information about the disposal business from several references or other reliable sources and requiring the disposal business be certified by a recognized trade association or similar third party with a reputation for high standards of quality review; or
- reviewing and evaluating the disposal business' information security policies or procedures, or taking other appropriate measures to determine the competency and integrity of the disposal business.[76]

---

74 ALASKA STAT. 45.48.500 (Alaska); ARIZ. REV. STAT. § 44-7601 (Arizona); ARK. CODE § 4-110-104 (Arkansas); CAL. CIV. CODE 1798.81 (California); COLO. REV. STAT. § 6-1-713 (Colorado); CONN. GEN. STAT. § 42-471 (Connecticut); DEL. CODE TIT. 6 § 5002C (Delaware); FLA. STAT. § 501.171(8) (Florida); GA. CODE § 10-15-2 (Georgia); HAW. REV. STAT 487R-2 (Hawaii); 815 ILCS 530/40 (Illinois); IND. CODE 24-4-14-8 (Indiana); KAN. STAT. § 50-7a03 (Kansas); KY. REV. STAT. § 365.725 (Kentucky); MASS. GEN. LAWS Ch. 93I, § 2 (Massachusetts); MD. STATE. GOV. CODE 10-1303 (Maryland); MCL § 445.72a (Michigan); MONT. CODE § 30-14-1703 (Montana); NEV. REV. STAT. § 603A.200 (Nevada); N.J. STAT. § 56:8-162 (New Jersey); N.Y. GEN. BUS. LAW § 399-H (New York); N.C. GEN. STAT. § 75-64 (North Carolina); ORE. REV. STAT. § 646A.622 (Oregon); R.I. GEN. LAWS § 6-52-2 (Rhode Island); S.C. CODE 30-2-190 (South Carolina); TENN. CODE § 39-14-150(g) (Tennessee); TEX. BUS. & COM. CODE § 72.004 (Texas); UTAH CODE § 13-44-201(2) (Utah); 9 VT. STAT. § 2445(b) (Vermont); WASH. REV. CODE § 19.215.020 (Washington state); WISC. STAT. § 134.97 (Wisconsin).
75 MASS. GEN. LAW Ch. 93I, § 2.
76 HAW. REV. STAT. 487R-2.

2

Cybersecurity Litigation

For good reason, businesses pay close attention to the FTC's statements about data security. After all, the FTC is, by far, the leading regulator when it comes to data security. However, businesses are just as concerned about the threat of class action litigation arising from data breaches and other cybersecurity incidents. Using centuries-old common law claims such as negligence, misrepresentation, and breach of contract – as well as private actions available under some state consumer protection statutes – plaintiffs' lawyers are increasingly seeking large damages from companies that they argue failed to adequately safeguard customer data. Indeed, after high-profile data breaches, it is common to see plaintiffs' lawyers battle to represent the class of individuals whose data was exposed (entitling the lawyers to a rather hefty fee if they prevail).

To understand the concepts in this chapter, it is helpful to briefly review the key procedural stages of civil lawsuits. Civil litigation in U.S. federal courts begins with the filing of a complaint, in which the plaintiffs provide a short and plain statement of the facts of their lawsuit, and describe why the defendant's actions violated either a common-law cause of action (e.g., negligence or breach of contract) or a statute (e.g., a state consumer protection law). The defendant then has a chance to file a motion to dismiss, in which the defendant argues that even if all of the facts in the complaint were true, the plaintiff does not state a viable legal claim. Even if a defendant has a strong argument, it may not succeed on a motion to dismiss because, at that stage, the judge must accept all facts as pleaded by the plaintiff, and the defendant does not have the opportunity to present its own evidence. If a judge does not grant a motion to dismiss, the case will proceed to discovery, in which both parties will have the

Cybersecurity Law, First Edition. Jeff Kosseff.
© 2017 John Wiley & Sons, Inc. Published 2017 by John Wiley & Sons, Inc.
Companion Website: www.wiley.com/go/kosseff/cybersecurity

opportunity to request relevant information from each other and third parties through document requests, interrogatories, and depositions. After discovery, either party may file for a motion for summary judgment, in which they present evidence gathered in discovery to the judge, and argue that, even when viewing the evidence in the light most favorable to the other party, no reasonable jury would find in favor of the opponent. Typically in breach cases, the defendant moves for summary judgment. If the judge does not grant summary judgment, the case proceeds to trial. Quite often, parties in data breach cases reach a settlement after a ruling on a motion to dismiss or summary judgment motion but before trial.

Although data breach lawsuits commonly are brought by consumers, businesses that suffer breaches face other potential plaintiffs. Often, banks that provide or process credit card payments will sue retailers for failing to adhere to payment card industry data security standards.

Fortunately, for companies, there are a number of legal obstacles to plaintiffs in class-action lawsuits that arise after data breaches. In short, plaintiffs often have a difficult time demonstrating that they actually have suffered damage that entitles them to compensation by the company that failed to safeguard their personal data. As we demonstrate below, customers who have suffered a concrete harm – such as identity theft – are more likely to prevail than those who only can demonstrate that their data merely was stolen.

2.1   Article III Standing

Before examining the specific types of lawsuits that companies could face for data breaches and inadequate data security, we first must consider whether the plaintiffs even have the constitutional right to sue. In many recent data breach cases, this has been among the primary barriers to private litigation.

Under Article III of the U.S. Constitution, federal courts only have jurisdiction over actual "cases" and "controversies." More than four decades ago, the United States Supreme Court stated that "[n]o principle is more fundamental to the judiciary's proper role in our system of government than the constitutional limitation of federal-court jurisdiction to actual cases or controversies."[1]

Among the most prominent requirements for demonstrating an Article III case or controversy is a concept known as "standing." As the Supreme Court has stated, the inquiry into whether a plaintiff has standing "focuses on whether the plaintiff is the proper party to bring this suit … although that inquiry often turns on the nature and source of the claim asserted."[2]

---

1 Simon v. Eastern Ky. Welfare Rights Organization, 426 U.S. 26, 37 (1976).
2 Raines v. Byrd, 521 U.S. 811, 818 (1997) (internal citations and quotation marks omitted).

What is Article III Standing?

Article III Standing is the constitutional right of a plaintiff to bring a lawsuit. Plaintiffs only have Article III standing if they have suffered an injury that is traceable to the defendant and repressible by a civil lawsuit.

Do Data Breach Victims Automatically have Article III Standing?

It depends on which judge you ask. Some judges have ruled that if your information has been breached, you have standing to sue the company that failed to protect your information because you are at greater risk of identity theft. Other judges have ruled that data breach victims only have standing if they have *actually* suffered identity theft.

For a plaintiff to demonstrate that he or she has standing, the plaintiff "must allege personal injury fairly traceable to the defendant's allegedly unlawful conduct and likely to be redressed by the requested relief."[3] In other words, the plaintiff has the burden of demonstrating three separate prongs in order to prove standing: (1) that she has suffered an injury-in-fact, (2) that the injury-in-fact is fairly traceable to the defendant's unlawful conduct, and (3) redressability.

Although courts allow plaintiffs to make general factual allegations to establish standing, their complaints still must "clearly and specifically set forth facts sufficient to satisfy" the standing requirement.[4]

2.1.1 Applicable Supreme Court Rulings on Standing

The primary barrier to establishing standing in data breach cases is the requirement that the plaintiff demonstrate that he or she suffered an actual injury. Also known as the "injury-in-fact" requirement, the plaintiff must demonstrate "an invasion of a legally protected interest which is "(a) concrete and particularized ... and (b) "actual or imminent, not conjectural or hypothetical."[5] Courts have held that mere "[a]llegations of possible future injury" are not sufficient to demonstrate the injury-in-fact that is necessary to establish Article III standing.[6] A threatened injury may constitute an injury in fact, but only if it is "certainly impending."[7]

Although the Supreme Court has ruled on the injury-in-fact standing requirement many times over the years, it has not issued any decisions in data

---

3 Allen v. Wright, 468 U.S. 737, 751 (1984).
4 Whitmore v. Arkansas, 495 U.S. 149, 155 (1990).
5 Lujan v. Defenders of Wildlife, 504 U.S. 555, 560–61 (1992) (internal quotation marks omitted).
6 Whitmore v. Arkansas, 495 U.S. 149, 158 (1990).
7 *Id.*

breach litigation regarding Article III standing. Therefore, we do not know with certainty whether the Supreme Court would conclude that the mere possibility of identity theft after a data breach is sufficient to establish an injury-in-fact for Article III standing. However, two recent privacy-related Supreme Court opinions shed some light on the factors that the Supreme Court likely would consider if it were to hear a data breach case.

In 2016, the Supreme Court issued its opinion in *Spokeo v. Robins*,[8] which many believed had the potential to completely change the landscape for standing in private litigation. However, the decision was fairly narrow and did not cause a major revolution in standing jurisprudence, perhaps because the Court was operating with only eight members, after the death of Justice Antonin Scalia. However, the *Spokeo* case is important because it provides some insight into the Supreme Court's overall thought process about standing in cases that do not clearly involve harm that has *already* occurred.

The case involved Spokeo, a website that provides detailed information about individuals, such as their home addresses, phone numbers, age, finances, and marital status. Spokeo is available to the general public. Plaintiff Thomas Robins alleged that an unidentified individual searched for Robins's name on Spokeo and obtained a profile that contained incorrect information about his family status, age, employment status, and education. He filed a class action lawsuit against Spokeo, alleging that the company violated the Fair Credit Reporting Act's requirements that consumer reporting agencies follow reasonable procedures to ensure the accuracy of their information and to limit the circumstances in which their reports are used for employment purposes. Spokeo moved to dismiss the lawsuit, arguing that Robins had not alleged an injury-in-fact, and the district court granted that motion. The U.S. Court of Appeals for the Ninth Circuit reversed the dismissal, concluding that Robins alleged that Spokeo violated his rights under the FCRA – not only the statutory rights of others, and that was sufficient to establish an injury-in-fact and standing.

The Supreme Court sent the case back to the Ninth Circuit for further analysis, concluding that the appellate court did not apply the proper test for standing. As discussed above, an injury-in-fact must be *both* (1) concrete and particularized, *and* (2) actual or imminent. The Supreme Court concluded that although the Ninth Circuit concluded that the alleged injury was particularized (i.e., that Robins claimed *his* statutory rights were violated), the Ninth Circuit failed to also consider whether the alleged injury was "concrete," which the Supreme Court said is a separate inquiry from particularization. For an injury to be "concrete," the Supreme Court ruled, it "must actually exist."

In a partial victory to plaintiffs' lawyers, the Supreme Court in *Spokeo* said that "concreteness" does not necessarily require an injury be tangible. For instance, the Court noted that violations of free speech or free exercise of

---

8 Spokeo, Inc. v. Robins, No. 13-1339, – U.S. – (2016).

religion may be sufficiently concrete to constitute injuries-in-fact. The Court also left open the door for the possibility of satisfying Article III's standing requirement with the allegation of the "risk-of-real-harm."[9]

However, the Court in *Spokeo* indicated that there are some limits to this ruling. The Court concluded that an allegation of a "bare procedural violation," without any further indication of harm, is not sufficiently concrete to constitute an injury-in-fact. [10]

Applying these principles to the dispute between Spokeo and Robins, the Supreme Court ordered the Ninth Circuit to analyze whether the violations of Robins's FCRA rights were sufficiently concrete. The Supreme Court indicated that such analysis could result in either dismissing the lawsuit or allowing it to proceed:

> On the one hand, Congress plainly sought to curb the dissemination of false information by adopting procedures designed to decrease that risk. On the other hand, Robins cannot satisfy the demands of Article III by alleging a bare procedural violation. A violation of one of the FCRA's procedural requirements may result in no harm. For example, even if a consumer reporting agency fails to provide the required notice to a user of the agency's consumer information, that information regardless may be entirely accurate. In addition, not all inaccuracies cause harm or present any material risk of harm. An example that comes readily to mind is an incorrect zip code. It is difficult to imagine how the dissemination of an incorrect zip code, without more, could work any concrete harm.[11]

Another recent Supreme Court opinion to address standing and the injury-in-fact issue was *Clapper v. Amnesty International USA*,[12] issued in 2013. In that case, a group of attorneys, media organizations, labor groups, and others that often communicate with individuals abroad filed a lawsuit against the federal government, challenging the Foreign Intelligence Surveillance Act, which allows surveillance of non-U.S. persons reasonably believed to be located abroad.[13] At issue in this case was both the requirement that the plaintiffs allege an injury-in-fact and that they allege the injury was fairly traceable to the surveillance program.

---

9 *Id.* ("Just as the common law permitted suit in such instances, the violation of a procedural right granted by statute can be sufficient in some circumstances to constitute injury in fact. In other words, a plaintiff in such a case need not allege any additional harm beyond the one Congress has identified.")
10 *Id.*
11 *Id.*
12 Clapper v. Amnesty International USA, 133 S. Ct. 1138 (2013).
13 *Id.* at 1142.

The plaintiffs did not argue that the government actually intercepted their communications; rather, they argued that (1) there is a "reasonable likelihood" that the government will obtain their communications at some point, and (2) this risk is so great that they will be forced to "take costly and burdensome measures to protect the confidentiality of their international communications[.]"[14]

The Supreme Court rejected the plaintiffs' first argument, concluding that the plaintiffs' "speculative chain of possibilities does not establish that injury based on potential future surveillance is certainly impending or is fairly traceable" to FISA.[15] The Court focused on the plaintiffs' failure to allege that the government had actually targeted any of them for surveillance. Instead, the Court wrote, the plaintiffs "merely speculate and make assumptions about whether their communications with their foreign contacts will be acquired[.]"[16]

Likewise, the Court rejected the plaintiffs' second argument, reasoning that "allowing respondents to bring this action based on costs they incurred in response to a speculative threat would be tantamount to accepting a repackaged version of respondents' first failed theory of standing."[17]

The Court concluded that standing simply does not exist because the plaintiffs "cannot demonstrate that the future injury they purportedly fear is certainly impending and because they cannot manufacture standing by incurring costs in anticipation of non-imminent harm."[18]

Taken together, *Spokeo* and *Clapper* demonstrate that the Supreme Court has set a very high bar for plaintiffs who bring a lawsuit based on the risk of a future, intangible injury. However, the Court has not entirely ruled out the possibility of allowing such lawsuits to proceed, provided that the potential risk of harm is particularized as to the plaintiffs bringing the lawsuit, and sufficiently concrete.

These standing rules matter immensely for lawsuits arising from data breaches, since in many of these cases the plaintiffs are alleging that the defendants' inadequate data security left them open to *future* harm. It would not be surprising if the Supreme Court eventually agrees to hear a standing challenge to a data breach lawsuit. Until then, the lower federal courts are free to develop their own rules as to whether a plaintiff has standing in a data breach case.

---

14 *Id.* at 1143.
15 *Id.* at 1150.
16 *Id.* at 1148–49 ("Simply put, respondents can only speculate as to how the Attorney General and the Director of National Intelligence will exercise their discretion in determining which communications to target.").
17 *Id.* at 1151.
18 *Id.* at 1155.

2.1.2 Lower Court Rulings on Standing in Data Breach Cases

The lower courts of appeals are not unified in their standing requirements for data breach lawsuits. Some courts will only allow a lawsuit to proceed if the defendant has demonstrated that a breach already has led to actual harm, such as identity theft. Other courts, however, have found standing when plaintiffs concretely allege that the breach could reasonably lead to future harm.

The decisions often are difficult to reconcile, and the practical effect is that data breach class actions are more likely to be dismissed for lack of standing in some federal courts than in others.

2.1.2.1 Injury-in-Fact

The Article III standing requirement – and, particularly, the injury-in-fact requirement – has proved to be a significant hurdle for data breach lawsuits. In the cases in which courts have found plaintiffs to have standing, the plaintiffs have made substantial and concrete demonstrations of injury. However, the result often depends on whether the courts have taken a broad or narrow view of the types of harms that constitute an injury-in-fact.

2.1.2.1.1 Broad View of Injury-in-Fact

Two opinions in which federal appellate courts have found plaintiffs to have Article III standing to sue over data breaches – *Krottner v. Starbucks Corp* from the Ninth Circuit and *Pisciotta v. Old National Bancorp* from the Seventh Circuit – present the most useful roadmap for demonstrating injury-in-fact. However, the results in these cases also depend on a court's willingness to consider the mere *risk* of harm as an injury-in-fact.

In *Krottner v. Starbucks Corp.*,[19] an unencrypted Starbucks laptop containing nearly 100,000 current and former Starbucks employees' names, addresses, and Social Security numbers was stolen. Three current and former employees filed a putative class action lawsuit against the company, in which they alleged claims of negligence and breach of implied contract. The first plaintiff claimed in the complaint that she spent a "substantial amount of time" monitoring her banking and retirement accounts because of the breach. The second plaintiff claimed that he "has spent and continues to spend substantial amounts of time checking his 401(k) and bank accounts" and "has generalized anxiety and stress regarding the situation." The third plaintiff stated that within a few months of the laptop theft, he was alerted by his bank of a third party's attempt to open a bank account with his Social Security number. The district court dismissed the case, finding that the plaintiffs failed to demonstrate the injury necessary to establish Article III standing.

The Ninth Circuit reversed the dismissal, finding that the plaintiffs' complaints sufficiently alleged injury because they "have alleged a credible threat of

---

19 628 F.3d 1139 (9th Cir. 2010).

real and immediate harm stemming from the theft of a laptop containing their unencrypted personal data." However, the Court noted that "more conjectural or hypothetical" allegations of harm may not have established Article III standing – "for example, if no laptop had been stolen, and Plaintiffs had sued based on the risk that it would be stolen at some point in the future."

The *Krottner* case quickly made it easier for data breach plaintiffs to establish standing in the Ninth Circuit. For instance, in 2014, the U.S. District Court for the Southern District of California found that plaintiffs had standing to bring a class action lawsuit against Sony Computer Entertainment America, LLC for a breach of the network that stores personal and financial information of Play Station Network customers.[20] The only injuries claimed by the named plaintiffs were the inability to access the Play Station Network while Sony was responding to the breach, and the cost of credit monitoring. Ten of the 11 named plaintiffs did not allege unauthorized charges on their financial accounts or other identity theft resulting from the breach.[21] One of the named plaintiffs alleged that he later received two unauthorized charges on his credit card, but the complaint did not state whether he was reimbursed for those charges.[22] Sony moved to dismiss the lawsuit, alleging that the plaintiffs did not sufficiently allege an injury-in-fact to establish Article III standing. Applying the Ninth Circuit's standard from *Krottner*, the Court held that the plaintiffs' claims that Sony collected and later wrongly disclosed it is "sufficient to establish Article III standing at this stage in the proceedings."[23] The Court held that even though the plaintiffs did not claim that a third party actually accessed their personal information, *Krottner* only requires a plausible allegation of "a 'credible threat' of impending harm based on disclosure of their Personal Information following the intrusion."[24] Notably, the Court held that even though the Supreme Court appeared to tighten its standing requirement in *Clapper* – decided after *Krottner* – the *Clapper* decision did not overrule the *Krottner* framework for analyzing standing in data breach cases.[25] One court, however, said that in the post-*Clapper* era, "courts have been even more emphatic in rejecting 'increased risk' as a theory of standing in data-breach cases."[26]

---

20 *In re* Sony Gaming Networks and Customer Data Security Data Breach Litigation, 996 F. Supp.2d 942 (S.D. Cal. 2014).
21 *Id.* at 956–57.
22 *Id.* at 957.
23 *Id.* at 962.
24 *Id.*
25 *Id.* at 961 ("Therefore, although the Supreme Court's word choice in *Clapper* differed from the Ninth Circuit's word choice in *Krottner*, stating that the harm must be 'certainly impending,' rather than 'real and immediate,' the Supreme Court's decision in *Clapper* did not set forth a new Article III framework, nor did the Supreme Court's decision overrule previous precedent requiring that the harm be 'real and immediate.'").
26 *In re* Science Applications International Corp. (SAIC) Backup Tape Data Theft Litigation, 45 F. Supp. 3d 14, 28 (D.D.C. 2014).

In *Pisciotta v. Old National Bancorp,*[27] two plaintiffs brought a putative class action lawsuit against a bank whose website allegedly was hacked, enabling a hacker to obtain a great deal of personal information about thousands of customers, including names, Social Security numbers, birth dates, financial account numbers, and mothers' maiden names. In their complaint, the two named plaintiffs – consumers whose data was disclosed – did not allege that they already had suffered a financial loss because of the breach. Instead, the complaint stated that the plaintiffs "have incurred expenses in order to prevent their confidential personal information from being used and will continue to incur expenses in the future."[28] They sought compensation "for all economic and emotional damages suffered as a result of the Defendants' acts which were negligent, in breach of implied contract or in breach of contract," and "[a]ny and all other legal and/or equitable relief to which Plaintiffs ... are entitled, including establishing an economic monitoring procedure to insure [sic] prompt notice to Plaintiffs ... of any attempt to use their confidential personal information stolen from the Defendants."[29] The district court granted the bank's motion to dismiss, concluding that the plaintiffs' complaint did not allege a cognizable injury-in-fact, and that "expenditure of money to monitor one's credit is not the result of any present injury but rather the anticipation of future injury that has not yet materialized."[30] On appeal, the Seventh Circuit upheld the dismissal of the case but, importantly, disagreed with the district court's ruling on Article III standing. The Court concluded that a data breach plaintiff can establish an injury-in-fact by alleging "a threat of future harm or by an act which harms the plaintiff only by increasing the risk of future harm that the plaintiff would have otherwise faced, absent the defendant's actions."[31] Courts nationwide have relied on the *Pisciotta* ruling to find that plaintiffs have standing in data breach cases.[32]

Indeed, since *Pisciotta,* the Seventh Circuit has found standing in two other large data breach class actions. In *Remijas v. Neiman Marcus Grp., LLC,*[33] the Seventh Circuit allowed a lawsuit to proceed against a department store chain that experienced a breach of a system that stored payment card data. Although

---

27 499 F.3d 629 (7th Cir. 2007).
28 *Id.* at 632.
29 *Id.*
30 *Id.* at 632–33.
31 *Id.* at 634.
32 *See, e.g.,* Ruiz v. Gap, Inc., 622 F. Supp. 2d 908, 912 (N.D. Cal. 2009) ("The Court finds that Ruiz has standing to bring this suit. Like the plaintiffs in *Pisciotta,* Ruiz submitted an online application that required him to enter his personal information, including his social security number."); Caudle v. Towers, Perrin, Forster & Crosby, Inc., 580 F. Supp. 2d 273 (S.D.N.Y. 2008) ("[T]his Court concludes that plaintiff has alleged an adequate injury-in-fact for standing purposes. [S]tanding simply means that the plaintiff is entitled to 'walk through the courthouse door' and raise his grievance before a federal court") (internal citations omitted).
33 794 F.3d 688 (7th Cir. 2015).

the plaintiffs did not allege that any identity theft or fraud had actually occurred, they claimed that the fear of future charges prompted them to take "immediate preventative measures."[34] The department store argued that the plaintiffs had not alleged an injury-in-fact and, instead, merely speculated without any actual evidence of impending harm. The Seventh Circuit rejected this claim, reasoning that the department store's customers "should not have to wait until hackers commit identity theft or credit-card fraud in order to give the class standing, because there is an 'objectively reasonable likelihood' that such an injury will occur."[35] The next year, the Seventh Circuit extended this pro-plaintiff holding when it refused to dismiss a data breach class action lawsuit brought against a restaurant chain.[36] The restaurant argued that there was no standing because, unlike the plaintiffs in *Remijas*, the restaurant's customers were only at risk of unauthorized credit card – not identity theft – and therefore they had not suffered an injury-in-fact. The Court found this distinction irrelevant.[37]

2.1.2.1.2 Narrow View of Injury-in-Fact

Other courts, however, have gone to great lengths to distinguish other data breach cases from *Krottner* and *Pisciotta* and hold that plaintiffs do not have Article III standing. For instance, in *Reilly v. Ceridian Corp.*,[38] plaintiffs filed a putative class action lawsuit against their employer's payroll processing company, Ceridian, after Ceridian experienced a data breach that exposed the personal and financial data of approximately 27,000 people.[39] There was no evidence in the record as to whether the hacker read or copied the breached information.[40] The district court granted Ceridian's motion to dismiss for lack of standing, and the U.S. Court of Appeals for the Third Circuit affirmed the dismissal, holding that "allegations of an increased risk of identity theft resulting from a security breach are therefore insufficient to secure standing."[41] The Third Circuit reasoned that hypothetical harm – and nothing more – does not establish an injury-in-fact: "we cannot now describe how Appellants will be injured in this case without beginning our explanation with the word 'if': *if* the hacker read, copied, and understood the hacked information, and *if* the hacker attempts to use the information, and *if* he does so successfully, only then will Appellants have suffered an injury."[42] Some federal district courts have adopted similar reasoning for data breach cases and held that the mere risk of identity

---

34 *Id.* at 692.
35 *Id.* at 693.
36 Lewert v. P.F. Chang's China Bistro, Inc., No. 14-3700 – F.3d – (7th Cir. 2016).
37 *Id.*
38 664 F.3d 38 (3d Cir. 2011).
39 *Id.* at 40.
40 *Id.*
41 *Id.* at 43.
42 *Id.*

theft after a breach – without any additional showing of imminent or actual harm – is insufficient to establish an injury-in-fact.[43]

The Third Circuit acknowledged that the courts in *Pisciotta* and *Krottner* found that data breach victims had standing to sue, but differentiated those cases because the harm was more "imminent" and "certainly impending" than the harm alleged by the plaintiffs suing Ceridian:

> In *Pisciotta*, there was evidence that "the [hacker's] intrusion was sophisticated, intentional and malicious." … In *Krottner*, someone attempted to open a bank account with a plaintiff's information following the physical theft of the laptop. … Here, there is no evidence that the intrusion was intentional or malicious. Appellants have alleged no misuse, and therefore, no injury. Indeed, no identifiable taking occurred; all that is known is that a firewall was penetrated. Appellants' string of hypothetical injuries do not meet the requirement of an "actual or imminent" injury.

Accordingly, at least according to the Third Circuit, a data breach plaintiff cannot have standing unless there has been *some* indication of potential harm,

---

43 *See, e.g., In re* Science Applications International Corp. (SAIC) Backup Tape Data Theft Litigation, 45 F. Supp. 3d 14, 28 (D.D.C. 2014) ("increased risk of harm alone does not constitute an injury in fact. Nor do measures taken to prevent a future, speculative harm."); Galaria v. Nationwide Mut. Ins. Co., 998 F.Supp.2d 646, 654-55 (S.D. Ohio 2014) ("an increased risk of identity theft, identity fraud, medical fraud or phishing is not itself an injury-in-fact because Named Plaintiffs did not allege — or offer facts to make plausible — an allegation that such harm is 'certainly impending'"); Whitaker v. Health Net of Cal., Inc., No. 11-910, 2012 WL 174961, at *2 (E.D. Cal. Jan. 20, 2012) ("[P]laintiffs do not explain how the loss here has actually harmed them … or that third parties have accessed their data. Any harm stemming from their loss thus is precisely the type of conjectural and hypothetical harm that is insufficient to allege standing."); Allison v. Aetna, Inc., No. 09-2560, 2010 WL 3719243, at *5 (E.D. Pa. Mar. 9, 2010) ("Plaintiff's alleged injury of an increased risk of identity theft is far too speculative."); Amburgy v. Express Scripts, Inc., 671 F.Supp.2d 1046, 1052 (E.D. Mo.2009) ("plaintiff does not claim that his personal information has in fact been stolen and/or his identity compromised"); Randolph v. ING Life Ins. and Annuity Co., 486 F. Supp. 2d 1 (D. D.C. 2007) ("Plaintiffs' allegation that they have incurred or will incur costs in an attempt to protect themselves against their alleged increased risk of identity theft fails to demonstrate an injury that is sufficiently 'concrete and particularized' and 'actual or imminent.'"); Key v. DSW, INC., 454 F. Supp. 2d 684, 690 (S.D. Ohio 2006) (dismissing data breach lawsuit for lack of standing because the plaintiff "has not alleged evidence that a third party intends to make unauthorized use of her financial information or of her identity" and that the "mere inquiry as to who would cause harm to Plaintiff, when it would occur, and how much illustrates the indefinite, and speculative nature of Plaintiffs alleged injury."); Giordano v. Wachovia Sec., Civ. No. 06-476JBS (D. N.J. July 31, 2006) ("the plaintiff's allegations here, if true, create only the possibility that the Plaintiff will be harmed at some future date by the loss of plaintiff's information or through identity theft."); Forbes v. Wells Fargo 420 F.Supp.2d 1018 (D. Minn. 2006) (plaintiffs' "expenditure in time and money was not the result of any present injury, but rather the anticipation of future injury that has not materialized.")

such as an attempt to open a credit account or a high level of sophistication of the hacker. The distinction seems a bit artificial, and suggests that it may be easier for data breach plaintiffs to establish standing in certain circuits – such as the Seventh and the Ninth – than other circuits – such as the Third.

The courts that have held that a data breach – and nothing more – is insufficient proof of injury-in-fact have reasoned that the mere possibility of identity theft or other harm is far too uncertain and depends on unknown variables. The U.S. District Court for the Eastern District of Missouri articulated this concern when it dismissed a lawsuit against a prescription drug benefit provider that suffered a security breach:

> For plaintiff to suffer the injury and harm he alleges here, many "if's" would have to come to pass. Assuming plaintiff's allegation of security breach to be true, plaintiff alleges that he would be injured "if" his personal information was compromised, and "if" such information was obtained by an unauthorized third party, and "if" his identity was stolen as a result, and "if" the use of his stolen identity caused him harm. These multiple "if's" squarely place plaintiff's claimed injury in the realm of the hypothetical. If a party were allowed to assert such remote and speculative claims to obtain federal court jurisdiction, the Supreme Court's standing doctrine would be meaningless.[44]

Moreover, if a plaintiff sues a company for inadequate data security but a breach has not yet occurred, it is unlikely that the court will conclude that an injury-in-fact exists. For instance, in *Katz v. Pershing*,[45] the plaintiff sued a financial services company because she believed that the company did not implement adequate data security safeguards, and that, as the court described it, "her nonpublic personal information has been left vulnerable to prying eyes[.]"[46] However, she did not allege that her information actually had been exposed to an unauthorized party. The First Circuit swiftly affirmed the dismissal of her lawsuit for lack of standing, concluding that "because she does not identify any incident in which her data has ever been accessed by an unauthorized person, she cannot satisfy Article III's requirement of actual or impending injury."[47]

2.1.2.2 Fairly Traceable

Even if a data breach plaintiff can demonstrate an injury-in-fact, the plaintiff also must credibly allege that the injury is "fairly traceable" to the defendant's failure to adopt adequate data security measures.

---

44 Amburgy v. Express Scripts, Inc., 671 F. Supp. 2d 1046, 1053 (E.D. Mo. 2009).
45 672 F.3d 64 (1st Cir. 2012).
46 *Id*. at 70.
47 *Id*. at 80.

For instance, in *Resnick v. AvMed, Inc.*,[48] laptops containing patients' personal information were stolen from AvMed, a healthcare company, exposing personal information such as Social Security numbers of more than one million customers. Customers who later were victims of identity theft – and had credit accounts opened in their names without their authorization – sued AvMed. The company filed a motion to dismiss claiming, and the district court dismissed the complaint, briefly stating that the complaint "fails to allege any cognizable injury."[49] On appeal, the U.S. Court of Appeals for the Eleventh Circuit disagreed, and found that plaintiffs established an injury-in-fact because they "allege that they have become victims of identity theft and have suffered monetary damages as a result."[50] The more difficult questions for the Court, however, was whether this injury was "fairly traceable" to the company's actions and whether the injury was redressable through the litigation. The Court concluded that a "fairly traceable" finding "requires less than a showing of 'proximate cause,'" and therefore the plaintiffs established this prong by alleging that they "became the victims of identity theft after the unencrypted laptops containing their sensitive information were stolen."[51]

2.1.2.3 Redressability

Finally, in order to demonstrate that standing exists, a plaintiff must sufficiently allege that the injury likely could be redressed by a ruling favorable to the plaintiff. As with the fairly traceable requirement, this prong is relatively easy for plaintiffs to satisfy.

In *AvMed*, the Court also found that the plaintiffs satisfied the final prong, redressability, because they "allege a monetary injury and an award of compensatory damages would redress that injury."[52] Accordingly, the Court concluded that the plaintiffs had standing to sue AvMed for harm arising from the data breach. Similarly, in 2014, a federal district judge in Minnesota held that plaintiffs had standing to sue Target after the retail chain's massive 2013 data breach because they alleged "unlawful charges, restricted or blocked access to bank accounts, inability to pay other bills, and late payment charges or new card fees."[53] The Court concluded that these are injuries-in-fact that are fairly traceable to Target's data security measures and redressable through the litigation.[54]

---

48 Resnick v. AvMed, Inc., 693 F.3d 1317 (11th Cir. 2012).
49 *Id.* at 1323.
50 *Id.*
51 *Id.* at 1324.
52 *Id.*
53 *In re* Target Corp. Data Sec. Breach Litigation, 66 F. Supp. 3d 1154, 1159 (D. Minn. 2014).
54 *Id.* at 1159–61.

Similarly, in the data breach lawsuit against P.F. Chang's,[55] the Seventh Circuit concluded that the plaintiffs had pleaded redressability because they "have some easily quantifiable financial injuries: they purchased credit monitoring services."[56]

In short, Article III standing often is the largest barrier for plaintiffs in data breach cases. Especially since the Supreme Court's decision in *Clapper*, courts are reluctant to allow a lawsuit to proceed merely because of the remote possibility that identity theft or another harm might occur at a later point. Many – but not all – courts will require a greater showing of harm, such as actual or imminent identity theft. However, as described above, the courts are somewhat split on this issue, and some courts are more likely to find that a plaintiff has standing than other courts.

2.2 Common Causes of Action Arising from Data Breaches

If a court concludes that a plaintiff has standing to sue over a data breach, the court then must consider the merits of the plaintiff's claims, and whether the plaintiff credibly alleges the violation of any legal duties.

Private litigation arises from two types of law: common law and statutes. First, common-law claims are created by state courts in decades or centuries of legal precedent. They include negligence, breach of contract, some warranty cases, and negligent misrepresentation. Second, statutes are passed by legislatures. State consumer protection laws – which prohibit unfair and deceptive trade practices – frequently are cited as the basis for class action lawsuits after data breaches.

2.2.1 Negligence

A common claim related to data breach-related lawsuits is negligence. This common-law claim is a frequent basis for lawsuits against companies. Customers frequently claim that retailers are negligent if the customers slip on freshly washed or waxed floors. Similarly, plaintiffs who are injured in car accidents may sue the driver for negligence. In recent years, customers have claimed that companies' inadequate data security measures also are negligent.

Because negligence is a common-law tort, precise rules have developed over centuries by court rulings. Accordingly, the exact requirements for negligence vary by state (the highest courts in each state – and not federal courts – ultimately are responsible for creating common-law torts). Typically, common-law negligence requires that a plaintiff demonstrate four

---

55 Lewert v. P.F. Chang's China Bistro, Inc., No. 14-3700 – F.3d – (7th Cir. 2016).
56 *Id.*

Frequent Claims in Data Breach Litigation

- *Negligence.* The defendant owed the plaintiff a legal duty, breached that duty, and caused injury to the plaintiff.
- *Negligent misrepresentation.* The defendant, in the course of business, failed to exercise reasonable care and supplied false information, causing the plaintiff to suffer pecuniary loss.
- *Breach of contract.* The defendant breached a bargained-for contract with the plaintiff.
- *Breach of implied warranty.* The defendant's product or services failed to satisfy basic expectations of fitness.
- *Invasion of privacy/publication of private facts.* The publication of private facts that are offensive and are not of public concern.
- *Unjust enrichment.* The defendant knowingly obtained a benefit from the plaintiff in a manner that was so unfair that it would be inequitable for the defendant to retain the benefit without paying fair value for it.
- *State consumer protection laws.* The defendant's conduct constituted unfair competition, unconscionable acts, and unfair or deceptive acts of trade or commerce.

elements: (1) the defendant owed a "legal duty" to the plaintiff (e.g., a duty to protect the plaintiff's personal information), (2) the defendant breached that duty (e.g., by failing to adequately safeguard the plaintiff's personal data), (3) the defendant's breach caused (4) a "cognizable injury" to the plaintiff.[57]

2.2.1.1 Legal Duty and Breach of Duty

The first two elements typically are not the subject of significant dispute in data breach litigation. Courts have generally assumed that businesses have a legal duty to safeguard the personal information of their customers and employees, and that a failure to meet that duty constitutes a breach. For instance, in the Sony data breach litigation, the district court held that finding a legal duty is supported not only by state law but by "common sense:"

> [B]ecause Plaintiffs allege that they provided their Personal Information to Sony as part of a commercial transaction, and that Sony failed to employ reasonable security measures to protect their Personal Information, including the utilization of industry-standard encryption, the Court finds Plaintiffs have sufficiently alleged a legal duty and a corresponding breach.[58]

---

57 *In re* Sony Gaming Networks and Customer Data Security Data Breach Litigation, 996 F. Supp.2d 942, 963 (S.D. Cal. 2014).
58 *Id.* at 966.

If the court is subject to mandatory security requirements, such as an industry standard set of protocols, courts may view those requirements as a legal duty for the purposes of a negligence lawsuit. For instance, the retailer Michaels experienced a breach of the PIN code entry system for its in-store debit and credit card processing systems. Michaels had not been in compliance with the payment card industry's PIN Security Requirements, which, among other things, required retailers to ensure that counterfeit devices were not collecting PIN numbers from retail terminals. The Court reasoned:

> Plaintiffs allege that Michaels failed to comply with various PIN pad security requirements, which were specifically designed to minimize the risk of exposing their financial information to third parties. Because the security measures could have prevented the criminal acts committed by the skimmers, Michaels' failure to implement such measures created a condition conducive to a foreseeable intervening criminal act.[59]

As the *Michaels* case demonstrates, companies must be aware of industry best practices and suggested security standards, as those are likely to create a standard of care that could trigger liability in negligence lawsuits.

Defendant companies occasionally argue that if their computer systems were hacked by a third party, the defendant did not breach a duty of care to the plaintiffs. The gravamen of this argument is that the harm was caused by a third party, and not the defendant. Courts generally reject such an argument in data breach cases. Target made this argument in its attempt to dismiss the class action that arose out of its 2013 data breach and was brought by financial institutions. The Court rejected Target's position, concluding that "[a]lthough the third-party hackers' activities caused harm, Target played a key role in allowing the harm to occur."[60] The Court considered the following factors in determining whether a duty exists: "(1) the foreseeability of harm to the plaintiff, (2) the connection between the defendant's conduct and the injury suffered, (3) the moral blame attached to the defendant's conduct, (4) the policy of preventing future harm, and (5) the burden to the defendant and community of imposing a duty to exercise care with resulting liability for breach," and ultimately concluding that imposing a legal duty on Target to protect customers' personal information "will aid Minnesota's policy of punishing companies that do not secure consumers' credit- and debit-card information."[61]

---

59 *In re* Michaels Stores Pin Pad Litigation, 830 F. Supp. 2d 518, 522 (N.D. Ill. 2011).

60 *In re* Target Corporation Customer Data Security Breach Litigation, 64 F.Supp.3d 1304, 1309 (D. Minn. 2014).

61 *Id.* at 1309–10.

2.2.1.2 Cognizable Injury

Perhaps the largest barrier to plaintiffs in negligence claims arising from data breaches is demonstrating that the breach of the legal duty caused a *cognizable injury*. That is due to a rule known as the Economic Loss Doctrine, which applies in many – but not all – state common law negligence claims. The Doctrine dates back to a 1927 opinion in which the United States Supreme Court concluded that "a tort to the person or property of one man does not make the tortfeasor liable to another merely because the injured person was under a contract with that other, unknown to the doer of the wrong."[62] As the Pennsylavania Supreme Court stated in 1985, this general rule leads to the conclusion that "negligent harm to economic advantage alone is too remote for recovery under a negligence theory."[63]

Over the past century, state courts have determined how – and if – to adopt this doctrine for common-law negligence claims. Keep in mind that the Economic Loss Doctrine can differ greatly by state, and therefore a data breach plaintiff who might have a viable claim in one state might be unsuccessful in a state that has a more defendant-friendly Economic Loss Doctrine. For instance, in the Target data breach consumer class action lawsuit, Target moved to dismiss negligence claims from consumers in 11 states, citing those states' Economic Loss Doctrines.[64] After an extensive analysis of the common law in each of those states, the Court concluded that the Economic Loss Doctrine requires dismissal of the negligence claims from five of the 11 states, while the claims in the remaining states should not be dismissed under those states' versions of the doctrine.[65] The court noted two primary differences among the various versions of the Economic Loss Doctrine. First, some states recognize an "independent duty" exception to the doctrine, meaning that "the rule does not apply where the duty alleged is an independent duty that does not arise from commercial expectations."[66] Second, some states recognize an exception to the doctrine if there is a "special relationship" between the plaintiff and defendant.[67]

The most stringent (and defendant-friendly) formulation of the doctrine "bars recovery unless the plaintiffs can establish that the injuries they suffered due to the defendants' negligence involved physical harm or property damage, and not solely economic loss."[68] For instance, a data breach of the payment card data at retailer BJ's Wholesale Club, Inc. resulted in unauthorized charges at a

---

62 Robins Dry Dock and Repair Co. v. Flint, 275 U.S. 303 (1927).

63 Aikens v. Baltimore and Ohio R. Co., 501 A.2d 277 (1985).

64 *In re* Target Corporation Customer Data Security Breach Litigation, 66 F. Supp. 3d 1154, 1171 (D. Minn. 2014).

65 *Id.* at 1176 ("The economic loss rule in Alaska, California, Illinois, Iowa, and Massachusetts appears to bar Plaintiffs' negligence claims under the laws of those states. Plaintiffs' negligence claims in the remaining states may go forward.").

66 *Id.* at 1171.

67 *Id.* at 1172.

68 Cumis Insurance Society, Inc. v. BJ's Wholesale Club, Inc., 455 Mass. 458, 469 (Mass. 2009).

number of credit unions. The credit unions, and the insurer that partially reimbursed the credit unions, sued BJ's for negligence arising from costs of replacing breached credit cards. The Massachusetts Supreme Judicial Court affirmed the dismissal of the negligence claims under the Economic Loss Doctrine, concluding that the credit cards were "canceled by the plaintiff credit unions for the purpose of avoiding future economic losses."[69] Other courts similarly have relied on the Economic Loss Doctrine to dismiss negligence claims filed by companies against businesses that have experienced data breaches that have led the plaintiffs to experience financial losses.[70]

The Economic Loss Doctrine also presents a barrier to customers who are suing businesses for failing to adequately safeguard their personal information. For instance, despite finding that Michaels had breached a legal duty to protect payment card PIN data, the Illinois federal judge dismissed the negligence claim filed by customers. The judge noted that "other courts dealing with data breach cases have also held that the economic loss doctrine bars the plaintiff's tort claim because the plaintiff has not suffered personal injury or property damage."[71] Similarly, in the Sony Play Station Network data breach litigation, the court relied on the Economic Loss Doctrine for its dismissal of negligence claims under California and Massachusetts laws.[72]

In some states, in contrast, the Economic Loss Doctrine is more limited. For instance, in Maine, the doctrine means that courts "do not permit tort recovery for a defective product's damage to itself."[73] A federal court in Maine, applying Maine common law, refused to dismiss a negligence claim arising from a breach of the defendant's computer system, concluding that "[t]his is not a case about a defective product that [the defendant] has sold to the customer."[74] In these states, it may be easier for a plaintiff to successfully bring a claim for negligence arising from a data breach.

As with establishing Article III standing, plaintiffs suing for data breaches or inadequate data security face their best chances at succeeding in negligence claims if they can demonstrate *actual* harm that has occurred as a result of the defendant's poor data security. However, it still is possible to recover even if

---

69 *Id.* at 470.

70 *See, e.g., In re* TJX Companies Retail Security Breach Litigation, 564 F.3d 489, 498 (1st Cir. 2009) (affirming dismissal of negligence claim by banks against retail chain that suffered a data breach because "purely economic losses are unrecoverable in tort and strict liability actions in the absence of personal injury or property damage."); Sovereign Bank v. BJ's Wholesale Club, Inc., 533 F. 3d 162 (3d Cir. 2008) (affirming dismissal of bank's negligence claim against retailer).

71 *In re* Michaels Stores Pin Pad Litigation, 830 F. Supp. 2d 518, 530-31 (N.D. Ill. 2011).

72 *In re* Sony Gaming Networks and Customer Data Security Data Breach Litigation, 996 F. Supp.2d 942, 967 (S.D. Cal. 2014).

73 *In re* Hannaford Bros. Co. Customer Data Security breach Litigation, 613 F.Supp.2d 108, 127 (D. Me. 2009), aff'd in part and rev'd in part on other grounds, Anderson v. Hannaford Bros. Co., 659 F. 3d 151 (1st Cir. 2011).

74 *Id.*

harm such as identity theft has not occurred, depending on the scope of the state's Economic Loss Doctrine and other legal rules surrounding negligence.

2.2.1.3 Causation

Even if a negligence plaintiff has demonstrated that the defendant breached a duty to safeguard the plaintiff's information, and that the plaintiff suffered cognizable injury, the plaintiff *still* must demonstrate that the breach of duty *caused* the injury. In other words, the defendant must link the inadequate data security to the identity theft or other harm. Causation is not disputed nearly as frequently as the other elements of negligence in data breach lawsuits; however, it potentially could present a barrier to an otherwise successful claim.

Nevertheless, courts are willing to make reasonable assumptions if the allegations in a lawsuit led to the likely conclusion that the breach caused harm to the plaintiffs. For example, in the *AvMed* case discussed above, the two plaintiffs were victims of identity theft approximately one year after an unencrypted laptop with their personal information was stolen.[75] Both plaintiffs stated that they take a number of steps to protect their personal information, and that they had not previously been the victims of identity theft.[76] The Court recognized that whether the breach caused the identity theft was a close call, particularly because the breach occurred approximately a year before the identity theft. The plaintiffs succeeded in convincing the Eleventh Circuit that they plausibly alleged causation because the information that was used in the identity theft was identical to the information on the stolen laptop.[77] Applying "common sense" to the allegations, the Court concluded that the plaintiffs' allegations of causation "move from the realm of the possible into the plausible," and it therefore denied AvMed's motion to dismiss.[78] However, the Court noted that if the Complaint had contained fewer factual allegations, the negligence claim likely would have been dismissed.[79]

Causation is easier to establish when the duration between the data breach and the identity theft is shorter. For instance, in *Stollenwerk v. Tri-West Health Care Alliance,*[80] the plaintiff suffered identity theft six weeks after computers containing his personal information were stolen from defendant Tri-West's headquarters. The Ninth Circuit concluded that the plaintiff had demonstrated causation because "(1) he gave Tri-West his personal information; (2) the identity fraud incidents began six weeks after the hard drives containing Tri-West's customers' personal information were stolen; and (3) he previously had not suffered any such incidents of identity theft."[81] However, the court cautioned

---

75 Resnick v. Avmed, Inc., 693 F.3d 1317, 1322 (11th Cir. 2012).
76 *Id*. at 1326.
77 *Id*.
78 *Id*.
79 *Id*.
80 Stollenwerk v. Tri-West Health Care Alliance, 254 Fed. Appx. 664 (9th Cir. 2007) (unpublished opinion).
81 *Id*. at 667.

that plaintiffs cannot prove causation merely because two incidents occurred within weeks of each other. Here, causation also was *logically* plausible because "[a]s a matter of twenty-first century common knowledge, just as certain exposures can lead to certain diseases, the theft of a computer hard drive certainly *can* result in an attempt by a thief to access the contents for purposes of identity fraud, and such an attempt *can* succeed."[82]

2.2.2 Negligent Misrepresentation or Omission

In a claim somewhat related to general negligence, some consumers and businesses bring data breach lawsuits against companies for misrepresenting their data security practices or omitting crucial details about their failure to adequately safeguard customer data.

In many states, negligent misrepresentation claims require the same elements as general negligence claims: legal duty, breach, causation, and injury. But some states allow negligent misrepresentation claims to proceed even if the plaintiffs only allege economic losses. This makes it easier, in those states, for plaintiffs to bring claims under the tort of negligent misrepresentation than general negligence.

For instance, a Nevada federal judge refused to dismiss negligent misrepresentation claims that customers brought against online retailer Zappos.com after a data breach. Quoting a Nevada Supreme Court case, the federal judge reasoned that liability "is proper in cases where there is significant risk that the law would not exert significant financial pressures to avoid such negligence," and that such cases include "negligent misstatements about financial matters."[83] The Court reasoned that because the customers did not have a "highly interconnected network of contracts" outlining the company's data security obligations, the customers did not have the ability to exert pressure to prevent such negligence, and therefore the tort of negligent misrepresentation should be available to them.[84]

Many state courts have adopted the definition of negligent misrepresentation from the Restatement (Second) of Torts, which states that negligent misrepresentation occurs under the following circumstances:

> One who, in the course of his business, profession or employment, or in any other transaction in which he has a pecuniary interest, supplies false information for the guidance of others in their business transactions, is subject to liability for pecuniary loss caused to them by their justifiable reliance upon the information, if he fails to exercise reasonable care or competence in obtaining or communicating the information.[85]

---

82 *Id.*

83 *In re* Zappos.com, Inc. Customer Data Security Breach Litigation, No. 3:12-cv-00325-RCJ-VPC, MDL No. 2357 (D. Nev. Sept. 9, 2013).

84 *Id.*

85 Restatement (Second) of Torts, Section 522 (1977).

In the banks' lawsuit against TJX, negligent misrepresentation was among the claims against the retailer. The banks claimed that because TJX accepted Visa and Mastercard credit cards, the retailer had implied that it would comply with credit card companies' data security rules. To determine whether this amounted to negligent misrepresentation, the U.S. Court of Appeals for the First Circuit applied Massachusetts common law, which has adopted the Restatement's test for negligent misrepresentation. The Court was highly skeptical about the banks' argument that merely accepting credit cards constitutes a representation about TJX's data security, stating that the "implication is implausible and converts the cause of action into liability for negligence – without the limitations otherwise applicable to negligence claims."[86] Although conduct "can be part of a representation," the Court reasoned, "the link between the conduct and the implication is typically tight."[87] However, because the Court only was considering a motion to dismiss – a stage at which all factual claims must be viewed in the light most favorable to the plaintiff – the Court allowed the negligent misrepresentation claim to survive "on life support."[88]

The financial institutions suing Target alleged that Target "failed to disclose material weaknesses in its data security systems and procedures," and therefore was liable for negligent misrepresentation by omission.[89] The district court concluded that the plaintiffs plausibly alleged that Target owed a duty to disclose because it "knew facts about its ability to repel hackers that Plaintiffs could not have known, and that Target's public representations regarding its data security practices were misleading."[90] The Court also found that the plaintiffs complied with Federal Rule of Civil Procedure 9(b), which requires plaintiffs alleging fraud or mistake to "state with particularity the circumstances constituting fraud or mistake." The Court concluded that the plaintiffs complied with this rule because they "have identified the omitted information, namely Target's failure to disclose that its data security systems were deficient and in particular that Target had purposely disengaged one feature of those systems that would have detected and potentially stopped the hackers at the inception of the hacking scheme."[91] However, the Court ultimately found that the financial institutions' Complaint fell short of properly alleging negligent misrepresentation because it did not plead that the institutions relied on Target's omissions. The Court rejected the plaintiff's claims that they were not required to plead reliance, and held that although securities fraud-by-omission claims do not require

---

86 *In re* TJX Companies Retail Security Breach Litigation, 564 F.3d 489, 494 (1st Cir. 2009).
87 *Id.*
88 *Id.* at 495.
89 *In re* Target Corporation Customer Data Security Breach Litigation, 64 F.Supp.3d 1304, 1310 (D. Minn. 2014).
90 *Id.* at 1311.
91 *Id.*

such an allegation, "courts have not extended this presumption of reliance outside of the securities fraud context."[92]

2.2.3 Breach of Contract

Consumers whose information has been compromised in a data breach often allege claims that the companies with which they entrusted their information breached a contract with the customer. As with torts, the precise elements of breach of contract may vary by state. For services, contract laws are set by courts under the common law, and for the sale of goods, contract laws are set by the state legislature's adoption of the Uniform Commercial Code. Typically, however, a plaintiff must demonstrate (1) a contract between the plaintiff and defendant, (2) the defendant's breach of a duty imposed by that contract, and (3) damage caused to the plaintiff as a result of that breach.[93]

If a company enters into a contract in which it guarantees a specific level of data security, then the company fails to provide that data security, and a breach exposes customers' information and leads to identity theft or other harm, the customer would have a fairly strong claim for breach of contract. The company would have breached an express duty in the contract, and that breach would have caused damage to the plaintiff. However, breach of contract claims in data breach cases often are not so clear-cut.

Data breach plaintiffs have attempted to bring breach of contract claims against companies for promises that they have made in their privacy policies or other public statements. Such claims will fail unless the plaintiff can prove that these statements are part of the bargained-for agreement between the plaintiff and defendant. For example, in 2016, a California district court dismissed a breach of contract claim in the class action lawsuit against Anthem, Inc., the health insurer that had experienced a large data breach. The plaintiffs alleged that Anthem had failed to adhere to a statement in its privacy notice, which stated "We keep your oral, written and electronic [PII] safe using physical, electronic, and procedural means."[94] The court dismissed this claim, concluding that the plaintiffs' Complaint fails to "allege that the privacy notices or public website statements were part of or were incorporated by reference" into the plaintiffs' contracts with Anthem.[95]

In some cases, the plaintiff alleges that a company – such as a service provider – breached an agreement with an intermediary by failing to safeguard information, and that in turn caused harm to the plaintiff. In that case, the plaintiff must convince a court that he was a third-party beneficiary to this agreement. Unless a contract explicitly names a third party as a beneficiary of

---

92 *Id.*
93 *See generally* Kaymark v. Bank of America, NA, 783 F.3d 168, 182 (3d Cir. 2015).
94 *In re* Anthem, Inc. Data Breach Litigation (N.D. Cal. 2016).
95 *Id.*

a contract, a court must determine whether a third party was an "intended beneficiary" of the contract's data security provisions.

A number of state courts have adopted the test for intended beneficiaries as articulated in Section 302 of the Restatement (Second) of Contracts:

Intended and Incidental Beneficiaries

1) Unless otherwise agreed between promisor and promisee, a beneficiary of a promise is an intended beneficiary if recognition of a right to performance in the beneficiary is appropriate to effectuate the intentions of the parties and either
   a) the performance of the promise will satisfy an obligation of the promisee to pay money to the beneficiary; or
   b) the circumstances indicate that the promisee intends to give the beneficiary the benefit of the promised performance.
2) An incidental beneficiary is a beneficiary who is not an intended beneficiary.[96]

In 2008, the U.S. Court of Appeals for the Third Circuit applied this definition of intended beneficiary in a case arising from the BJ's retailer data breach described above. A number of lawsuits arose out of that breach, including a lawsuit by Sovereign Bank, a credit card issuer, against BJ's and the retailer's bank, Fifth Third. Among the many claims by Sovereign was a breach of contract action, alleging that Fifth Third breached its agreement with Visa to ensure that BJ's adequately secured credit card information. Sovereign claimed that BJ's breached this agreement, and banks whose customers' data were breached – such as Sovereign – were intended third-party beneficiaries of the agreement between Fifth Third and Visa.[97] Fifth Third argued that the contract was not intended to benefit issuing banks such as Sovereign, but instead to "benefit the Visa system as a whole."[98] The district court dismissed this claim, but the Third Circuit reversed, finding that a Visa executive's testimony that the data security requirements are intended to benefit "the members that participate in it" was sufficient to allow a reasonable jury to conclude that Sovereign was an intended beneficiary, and therefore could sue Fifth Third for breach of contract.[99]

Some contracts, however, clearly preclude third-party beneficiary claims. For instance, Pershing LLC, which provides an electronic platform for financial services institutions, was sued by the customer of a financial institution that used Pershing's platform. The plaintiff filed a lawsuit against Pershing, alleging

---

96 Restatement (Second) of Contracts Sec. 302.
97 Sovereign Bank. v. B.J.'s Wholesale Club, Inc., 533 F.3d 162, 168 (3d Cir. 2008).
98 *Id.* at 169.
99 *Id.* at 172.

that the company failed to adequately secure her personal information by using safeguards such as encryption and proper end-user authentication.[100] Among her legal claims was that Pershing breached the data confidentiality provision of an agreement between Pershing and the plaintiff's financial institution. The U.S. Court of Appeals for the First Circuit swiftly rejected this claim, noting that the agreement stated that it "is not intended to confer any benefits on third-parties[.]'"[101] The Court held that when the intent to preclude third-party beneficiaries is "unambiguously disclaimed, a suitor cannot attain third-party beneficiary status."[102]

In many data breach cases, there is not an express contract between a consumer and company. For instance, if a customer walks into a store and purchases a product with her credit card, the customer typically does not first require the retailer to agree to adequately safeguard her credit card number and other personally identifiable information. However, in many states, it is possible to allege that a company's failure to safeguard data breaches an *implied* term of a contract.

For instance, in the *Hannaford* case, which consumers brought against a retailer after a breach of payment card information, the plaintiffs relied on Maine common law, which states that contracts can include "all such implied provisions as are indispensable to effectuate the intention of the parties and as arise from the language of the contract and circumstances under which it was made," provided that the provision is "absolutely necessary to effectuate the contract."[103] In the *Hannaford* case, the plaintiffs allege that when they provided their credit cards to the grocers' cashier at the cash register, they entered into an implied contract for the grocer to protect their credit card numbers. The grocer moved to dismiss this claim, stating that such an assumption is not absolutely necessary to engage in the payment transaction. The district court disagreed with the grocer and refused to dismiss the claim. The judge reasoned that a jury "could reasonably find that customers would not tender cards to merchants who undertook zero obligation to protect customers' electronic data."[104] However, the judge recognized that such an implied contract is limited, because "in today's known world of sophisticated hackers, data theft, software glitches, and computer viruses, a jury could not reasonably find an implied merchant commitment against every intrusion under any circumstances whatsoever (consider, for example, an armed robber confronting the

---

100 Katz v. Pershing, LLC, 672 F.3d 64, 69–70 (1st Cir. 2012).
101 *Id.* at 73.
102 *Id.*
103 *In re* Hannaford Bros. Co. Customer Data Security Breach Litigation, 613 F.Supp.2d 108, 118 (D. Me. 2009), aff'd in part and rev'd in part on other grounds, Anderson v. Hannaford Bros. Co., 659 F. 3d 151 (1st Cir. 2011).
104 *Id.* at 119.

merchant's computer systems personnel at gunpoint)."[105] In short, the court held that a jury could find an implied contract for the grocer to enact *reasonable* safeguards, similar to the negligence standard. However, the court does not believe that the implied contract creates an absolute prohibition on all data breaches because such a duty would be impossible in light of modern cyber threats. Nor did the judge agree with the plaintiff that there is an implied contract for the grocer to notify consumers of data breaches because such notification is not "absolutely necessary" for the contract.[106] The grocer appealed the district court's refusal to dismiss the claim entirely, and the U.S. Court of Appeals for the First Circuit affirmed the district court's conclusion, stating that a jury "could reasonably conclude, therefore, that an implicit agreement to safeguard the data is necessary to effectuate the contract."[107]

In contrast, the plaintiff in the case against Pershing, described above, claimed that in addition to being a third-party beneficiary to an express contract between Pershing and her service provider, she had an implied contract with Pershing, in which Pershing implicitly agreed to protect her personal information.[108] The First Circuit rejected this argument, holding that a contract did not exist between the plaintiff and Pershing because there was not any consideration (i.e., the plaintiff did not provide a "bargained-for benefit," nor did she suffer any "bargained-for detriment in exchange for the defendant's supported promises."[109]

In sum, there are three primary methods that a plaintiff could attempt to bring a breach of contract lawsuit arising from a data breach or poor data security. First, the plaintiff could sue for breaching an express contract between the plaintiff and a defendant in which the defendant agreed to provide a specified level of data security. This is the most likely route for success for the plaintiff, but in many recent data breach cases, such contracts did not exist. Second, the plaintiff could claim that she was the *intended* third-party beneficiary of a contract between the defendant and another party, in which the defendant agreed to provide a certain level of data security. As demonstrated above, it often is difficult to prove that the plaintiff was an intended third-party beneficiary of a contract. Third, the plaintiff can claim that even though there was not an express contract with the defendant, the parties had an *implied* contract in which the defendant agreed to provide a reasonable level of data security. Such claims are fact-specific and their success is difficult to predict with great certainty.

---

105 *Id.*
106 *Id.*
107 Anderson v. Hannaford Bros. Co., 659 F. 3d 151, 159 (1st Cir. 2011).
108 Katz v. Pershing, LLC, 672 F.3d 64, 69-74 (1st Cir. 2012).
109 *Id.*

2.2.4 Breach of Implied Warranty

Consumers also have claimed that companies breached implied warranties by failing to safeguard their data. Under this claim, plaintiffs typically argue that by selling the plaintiffs a product, the defendants provided an implied warranty that the good was fit for a particular purpose. The defendants breached that warranty, they argue, by failing to provide proper data security.

In the United States, there are two general sources of implied warranties: Article 2 of the Uniform Commercial Code, which applies to the sale of goods, and the common law (rulings by state court judges over many decades), which applies to the sale of services. Implied warranties under both the Uniform Commercial Code and the common law have arisen in data breach cases.

Most states have adopted the implied warranty provisions of Article 2 of the Uniform Commercial Code, which governs the sale of goods. Article 2 creates two implied warranties that are relevant to data breach cases: warranty of merchantability and warranty of fitness for a particular purpose.

Section 2-314 of the Uniform Commercial Code, which creates an implied warranty of merchantability, requires goods to be "merchantable," which the statute defines as:

a) pass without objection in the trade under the contract description; and

b) in the case of fungible goods, are of fair average quality within the description; and

c) are fit for the ordinary purposes for which such goods are used; and

d) run, within the variations permitted by the agreement, of even kind, quality and quantity within each unit and among all units involved; and

e) are adequately contained, packaged, and labeled as the agreement may require; and

f) conform to the promise or affirmations of fact made on the container or label if any.[110]

The implied warranty of merchantability only applies to merchants who sell "goods of that kind." In other words, a car dealer implicitly warrants the merchantabilities of cars that it sells, but if it sells an old desk that it had used in its office, it will not imply merchantability of the desk.

---

110 UNIFORM COMMERCIAL CODE 2-314.

Section 2-315 of the Uniform Commercial Code, which creates an implied warranty of fitness for a particular purpose, states:

> Where the seller at the time of contracting has reason to know any particular purpose for which the goods are required and that the buyer is relying on the seller's skill or judgment to select or furnish suitable goods, there is unless excluded or modified under the next section an implied warranty that the goods shall be fit for a particular purpose.[111]

Data breach plaintiffs have alleged that by failing to provide adequate security for personal information, the company breached both the implied warranties of merchantability and fitness.

The UCC allows merchants to "disclaim" implied warranties – and thus avoid the obligations imposed by these requirements. To do so, the UCC states, the disclaimer must be "by a writing and conspicuous."[112] To disclaim implied warranties, the UCC states that it is sufficient for the written disclaimer to use expressions such as "with all faults," "as is," or "There are no warranties which extend beyond the description on the face hereof."[113] Many states prohibit disclaimers from being buried in contracts; therefore, user agreements often contain the disclaimers in capital letters.

However, the UCC is only a *model* for states to use as a framework for adopting their own laws governing the sale of goods. Some states do not allow companies to disclaim the UCC's implied warranties. For instance, Massachusetts' version of the UCC states that any attempts to limit or exclude the implied warranties of merchantability or fitness for a particular purpose are "unenforceable."[114] This prohibition of such disclaimers makes Massachusetts a particularly attractive venue for implied warranty claims.

However, the UCC often does not apply to data breach lawsuits. Many data breach cases arise when customers sue online networks, banks, healthcare providers, and other companies that provide them with *services*. The UCC only applies to the sale of goods, while the common law (law created by centuries of court rulings) typically applies to the sale of services. Determining whether a data breach arises from a sale of good or a sale of services, however, can be tricky.

For instance, in the Sony Play Station Network data breach class action, among the plaintiffs' many claims was a breach of the implied warranty of fitness for a particular purpose under the Massachusetts UCC.[115] Because Sony

---

111 Uniform Commercial Code 2-315.
112 Uniform Commercial Code 2-316.
113 *Id.*
114 Mass. Gen. Law 2-316A(2).
115 *In re* Sony Gaming Networks and Customer Data Security Data Breach Litigation, 996 F. Supp.2d 942, 983 (S.D. Cal. 2014).

had disclaimed implied warranties, the Massachusetts statute appeared to be an attractive route for the plaintiffs to bring an implied warranty claim. However, the Court rejected the claim because it involved a breach of the online *services* that Sony provided via the Play Station Network. The Massachusetts version of the UCC defines "goods" as "all things ... which are movable at the time of identification to the contract for sale."[116] The Court concluded that even though the online services could only be accessed by the consumer's purchase of a Play Station Network game console, the "thrust, or purpose of the contract" was to provide access to the Play Station Network, which is not a movable "thing" as defined by the UCC. [117]

Similarly, in the *Hannaford* case,[118] a lawsuit arising from the breach of payment card information at a grocery store, the plaintiffs brought a breach of implied warranty claim under Maine's version of the Uniform Commercial Code. They alleged that the retailer's acceptance of card data rendered its electronic payment processing system a "good" that it implicitly guaranteed to securely process card transactions. The Court swiftly dismissed this claim, concluding that "goods" under the UCC would include the retailer's groceries but not the payment system that it uses to process card data.[119]

Many states also recognize *common law* implied warranty claims. Because these are not derived from the UCC, the warranties *do* apply to the sale of services, such as online accounts, but the common law in many states typically allows companies to use clear and prominent disclaimers to avoid being bound by implied warranties.

For instance, in the Sony Play Station Network case, the plaintiffs claimed that Sony breached implied warranties under the common law of Florida, Michigan, Missouri, and New York. Sony argued that these claims are invalid because it disclaimed all warranties both in the Play Station Network User Agreement and Privacy Policy. The user agreement stated:

> No warranty is given about the quality, functionality, availability or performance of Sony Online Services or any content or service offered on or though Sony Online Services. *All services and content are provided "AS IS" and "AS AVAILABLE" with all fault.* SNEA does not warrant that the service and content will be uninterrupted, error-free or without delays. In addition to the limita-

---

116 MASS. GEN. LAW 2-105(1).

117 *In re* Sony Gaming Networks and Customer Data Security Data Breach Litigation, 996 F. Supp.2d 942, 983 (S.D. Cal. 2014).

118 *In re* Hannaford Bros. Co. Customer Data Security Breach Litigation, 613 F.Supp.2d 108, 127 (D. Me. 2009), aff'd in part and rev'd in part on other grounds, Anderson v. Hannaford Bros. Co., 659 F. 3d 151 (1st Cir. 2011).

119 *Id*. at 120.

120 *In re* Sony Gaming Networks and Customer Data Security Data Breach Litigation, 996 F. Supp.2d 942, 981 (S.D. Cal. 2014). (emphasis added)

tions of liability in merchantability, warranty of fitness for a particular purpose and warranty of non-infringement, SCEA assumes no liability for any inability to purchase, access, download or use any content, data, or service.[120]

Likewise, the Play Station Network Privacy Policy stated:

> We take reasonable measures to protect the confidentiality, security, and integrity of the personal information collected from our website visitors … . Unfortunately, there is no such thing as perfect security. As a result, although we strive to protect personally identifying information, *we cannot ensure or warrant the security of any information transmitted to us through or in connection with our websites*, that we store on our systems or that is stored on our service providers' systems.[121]

The court granted Sony's motion to dismiss, reasoning that the two documents, when read together, sufficiently disclaim any guarantees that consumers' personal information will be secure.[122] It is unclear whether one of those documents, standing alone, would be sufficient to avoid all implied warranty lawsuits arising from the data breach. The disclaimer in the User Agreement satisfies the long-standing legal rule that disclaimers of warranties should state that goods and services are provided "as is." However, the Privacy Policy provides a clear disclaimer that Sony does not guarantee the safety of personal information. Had this language not been in the Privacy Policy, the plaintiffs would have had a strong argument that a reasonable consumer would not expect the User Agreement's "As Is" provision to apply to data security.

Common law implied warranty claims are not as common as UCC implied warranty lawsuits, and many state courts have not ruled on the exact scope of these implied warranties as applied to services such as computing and data storage. Courts have recognized common law implied warranties for construction[123] and the repair of goods that were sold by the merchant.[124] Courts decide whether to extend implied warranties to services on a case-by-case basis, assessing the public interest in recognizing such obligations.[125] Accordingly, it is likely that more precise rules for common law implied warranty claims in data breach cases will emerge over the next decade.

---

121 *Id*. (emphasis added)
122 *Id*. at 982.
123 *See, e.g.*, Spectro Alloys Corp. v. Fire Brick Engineers Co., 52 F. Supp. 3d 918 (D. Minn. 2014).
124 *See, e.g.*, Rocky Mountain Helicopters, Inc. v. Lubbock Cty. Hosp. Dist., 987 S.W.2d 50, 52–53 (Tex. 1998).
125 *Id*. at 53 ("[p]ublic policy does not justify imposing an implied warranty for service transactions in the absence of a demonstrated, compelling need" and "[t]here is no compelling need for an implied warranty when other adequate remedies are available to the consumer.").

In short, implied warranty claims probably are not the strongest route for plaintiffs in data breach lawsuits. Unless a related data breach loss arises from the plaintiff's purchase of a tangible good, it is unlikely that the UCC's implied warranties will apply. And it remains to be seen whether state supreme courts will conclude that recognizing common law implied warranties for data security is in the public interest. Even if a warranty does apply, many large companies easily address such risk with clear and conspicuous disclaimers.

2.2.5 Invasion of Privacy by Publication of Private Facts

In some data breach cases, plaintiffs bring a claim under the common-law tort of invasion of privacy due to publication of private facts. These claims will almost definitely fail, absent extraordinary circumstances.

Publication of private facts is one of four common-law privacy torts, and the most applicable to data breaches.[126] To state a claim for the publication of private facts, the plaintiff generally must prove "(1) the publication, (2) of private facts, (3) that are offensive, and (4) are not of public concern."[127] If plaintiffs' personal data are exposed due to a data breach, they could seek damages under this tort.

However, convincing a court to allow such a lawsuit is difficult, absent demonstration that the materially was widely circulated and the defendant was somehow involved in the publication. For instance, in *Galaria v. Nationwide Mutual Insurance Co.*,[128] plaintiffs filed a class action lawsuit against Nationwide Mutual Insurance, after a breach of Nationwide's computer systems allowed hackers to obtain personal information that the plaintiffs had provided to the insurer. The plaintiffs did not allege misuse of their personal information or identity theft. Among the claims in the plaintiffs' putative class action lawsuit was invasion of privacy due to publication of private facts. The district court dismissed this claim for two reasons. First, the court stated that even though the breach exposed their personally identifiable information, there was no allegation that Nationwide *disclosed* the data. Instead, the data was allegedly stolen from Nationwide.[129] This ruling suggests that only if the defendant in a breach case takes an affirmative action to disseminate information – such as posting it on a website – an invasion of privacy claim will not succeed. Second, the court held that even if Nationwide had disseminated the data, the plaintiffs did not allege publicity of the information. The plaintiffs

---

126 The other three torts are misappropriation of the plaintiff's name or likeness (i.e., using the plaintiff's name or likeness in an advertisement without permission), intrusion upon seclusion (i.e., spying on the plaintiff in her home), and false light (i.e., disclosing information, in a highly offensive manner, that places the plaintiff in a false light.).

127 Spilfogel v. Fox Broadcasting Co., 433 Fed. Appx. 724, 725 (11th Cir. 2011).

128 Galaria v. Nationwide Mutual Insurance Co., 998 F. Supp. 2d 646 (S.D. Ohio 2014).

129 *Id.* at 662.

would have needed to demonstrate "publicity to the public at large or to so many persons that the information is certain to become public knowledge."[130]

2.2.6 Unjust Enrichment

Even if a plaintiff cannot establish a breach of an express or implied contract due to a data breach or inadequate data security, the plaintiff may attempt to bring a similar type of claim under the theory of "unjust enrichment."

Unjust enrichment is a theory of recovering damages "when one person has obtained a benefit from another by fraud, duress, or the taking of an undue advantage."[131] As with other common law claims, the precise rules for unjust enrichment vary by state. The U.S. Court of Appeals for the Eleventh Circuit articulated a common framework for unjust enrichment in the AvMed data breach case.[132] Applying Florida law, the court held that a plaintiff must demonstrate "(1) the plaintiff has conferred a benefit on the defendant; (2) the defendant has knowledge of the benefit; (3) the defendant has accepted or retained the benefit conferred; and (4) the circumstances are such that it would be inequitable for the defendant to retain the benefit without paying fair value for it."[133] Applying these factors, the Eleventh Circuit concluded that the plaintiffs alleged a viable unjust enrichment claim. The court reasoned that the plaintiffs paid monthly premiums to the company, which AvMed should have used to cover the costs of adequate data security, and that the company failed to do so.[134]

Similarly, in the consumer class action against Target, the district court refused to dismiss the unjust enrichment claim against the retailer, reasoning that if the plaintiffs "can establish that they shopped at Target after Target knew or should have known of the breach, and that Plaintiffs would not have shopped at Target had they known about the breach, a reasonable jury could conclude that the money Plaintiffs spent at Target is money to which Target in equity and good conscience should not have received."[135] However, the court rejected the plaintiff's other unjust enrichment claim, in which they asserted that they were overcharged for their products because the goods that Target sold "included a premium for adequate data security."[136] The court found that this allegation did not support an unjust enrichment claim because Target charges the same price to customers who pay with credit cards as it charges to customers who pay with cash, and the customers who paid with cash were not harmed

---

130 *Id.*
131 Heldenfels Bros. v. City of Corpus Christi, 832 S.W.2d 39, 41 (Tex. 1992).
132 Resnick v. AvMed, Inc., 693 F.3d 1317 (11th Cir. 2012).
133 *Id.* at 1328 (quoting Della Ratta v. Della Ratta, 927 So.2d 1055, 1059 (Fla. Dist. Ct. App. 2006)).
134 *Id.*
135 *In re* Target Corp. Data Security Breach Litigation, 66 F. Supp. 1154, 1178 (D. Minn. 2014).
136 *Id.* at 1177.

by the data breach. This unjust enrichment claim, the Court concluded, might be more viable if Target charged a higher price to credit card customers.

Typically, unjust enrichment is not available to plaintiffs if another cause of action covers the same claim.[137] So, for example, if a plaintiff's unjust enrichment claim regarding a data breach arises primarily out of the defendant's failure to abide by the terms of a contract, then the unjust enrichment claim would not succeed.[138]

2.2.7 State Consumer Protection Laws

Besides the court-created common-law claims that companies face after data breaches, state consumer protection statutes provide plaintiffs with an additional cause of action. All fifty states and the District of Columbia have enacted consumer protection laws. Although the exact wording of the statutes – and courts' interpretations of them – varies by state, they generally prohibit unfair competition, unconscionable acts, and unfair or deceptive acts of trade or commerce. The state consumer protection laws are similar to Section 5 of the FTC Act, but unlike Section 5, most of the state consumer protection laws allow private plaintiffs to bring lawsuits.

State consumer protection law claims in data breach cases often allege that the defendant fraudulently misrepresented its data security practices. However, such claims typically will only succeed if the court concludes that the misrepresentations likely would deceive a reasonable person. For instance, in the Sony Play Station Network breach litigation, the plaintiffs brought claims under California consumer protection laws, alleging that Sony misrepresented the following aspects of its products and services:

- continual access to the Play Station Network was a feature of the game consoles;
- online connectivity was a feature of the game consoles;
- characteristics and quality of the security of the Sony Play Station Network; and
- Sony uses "reasonable security measures" to protect its consumers' personal information.[139]

---

137 *See, e.g.,* Goldman v. Metro. Life Ins. Co., 841 N.E.2d 742, 746-47 (N.Y. 2005) ("Given that the disputed terms and conditions fall entirely within the insurance contract, there is no valid claim for unjust enrichment.").

138 *See In re* Anthem, Inc. Data Breach Litigation (N.D. Cal. 2016) ("As the parties acknowledge, the viability of Plaintiffs' New York unjust enrichment claim depends largely upon the viability of Plaintiffs' breach of contract claims."); *In re* Sony Gaming Networks and Customer Data Security Data Breach Litigation, 996 F.Supp.2d 942, 984 (S.D. Cal. 2014) ("Under Florida, Massachusetts, Michigan, Missouri, New Hampshire, New York, Ohio, and Texas law a plaintiff may not recover for unjust enrichment where a "valid, express contract governing the subject matter of the dispute exists.").

139 *In re* Sony Gaming Networks and Customer Data Security Data Breach Litigation, 996 F. Supp.2d 942, 989–90 (S.D. Cal. 2014).

The court ruled that the first two alleged misrepresentations were not valid grounds for a consumer protection lawsuit because a reasonable consumer would not believe that Sony promised "continued and uninterrupted access" to its online services,[140] in part because its Terms of Service explicitly stated that Sony "does not warrant that the service and content will be uninterrupted, error-free or without delays." However, the Court concluded that the third and fourth statements provided a sufficient basis for consumer protection claims, as Sony's policies had promised "reasonable security" and "industry-standard" encryption".[141]

Common among the obstacles to cybersecurity-related consumer protection law claims is the demonstration that the consumer suffered a financial loss. For instance, in the Sony Play Station Network litigation, the plaintiffs also brought a claim under Florida's consumer protection statute, which requires consumers to demonstrate "actual damages." Florida state courts have defined "actual damages" as the "difference in the market value of the product or service in the condition in which it was delivered and its market value in the condition in which it should have been delivered according to the contract of the parties."[142] The Sony plaintiffs sought to recover three costs: (1) the amount that they overpaid for their game consoles, (2) the monthly premiums for the services when they were unavailable, and (3) the value of their breached personal information. The district court dismissed this claim, concluding that none of these claims constitutes actual damages under the Florida law. The plaintiffs failed to demonstrate that they overpaid for the consoles or the services because of Sony's alleged misrepresentations about its data security, the court concluded.[143] Moreover, the court concluded that personal information "does not have an apparent monetary value" and therefore is not a proper basis for a claim of actual damages under the Florida law.[144]

However, the injury requirement is surmountable for plaintiffs, particularly during the early stages of litigation. For example, in the Target consumer class action arising from the 2013 data breach, the plaintiffs alleged violations of the consumer protection laws of forty-nine states and the District of Columbia. They claimed that Target violated these laws by failing to implement adequate data security, failing to disclose its inadequate data security, failing to notify consumers of the breach, and continuing to accept credit and debit cards after it knew, or should have known, of the breach. Twenty-six of the consumer

---

140 *Id.* at 990.
141 *Id.*
142 Rollins, Inc. v. Heller, 454 So.2d 580, 585 (Fla. Dist. Ct. App. 1984) (internal citations omitted).
143 *In re* Sony Gaming Networks and Customer Data Security Data Breach Litigation, 996 F. Supp.2d 942, 994 (S.D. Cal. 2014).
144 *Id.* (quoting Burrows v. Purchasing Power, LLC, No. 1:12-cv-22800-UU, 2012 WL 9391827, at *3 (S.D. Fla. Oct. 18, 2012).

protection laws require economic injury, and Target argued that the claims under those statutes therefore should be dismissed. However, the district court denied this motion, concluding that plaintiffs alleged that they suffered fees for new credit cards, late fees, and other charges as a result of the breach.[145]

State consumer protection laws are primarily designed to be enforced by state officials, such as state attorney general, just as the FTC enforces Section 5 of the FTC Act. Accordingly, courts are hesitant to allow private lawsuits under consumer protection statutes when common-law remedies such as negligence are available. In the *Hannaford* grocery store data breach case, the plaintiffs brought a claim under the Maine Unfair Trade Practices Act, which provides that "[u]nfair methods of competition and unfair or deceptive acts or practices in the conduct of any trade or commerce are declared unlawful."[146] The provision of the statute creating a private right of action states that "[a]ny person who purchases or leases goods, services or property, real or personal, primarily for personal, family or household purposes and *thereby suffers any loss of money or property*, real or personal," due to the defendant's actions, may sue for damages and other relief.[147] The First Circuit affirmed the district court's dismissal of the claim under the Maine law, concluding that the substantial injury requirement, combined with the requirement that a plaintiff suffer a loss of money or property, requires a narrow reading of the Maine statute. Claims for breach of contract and negligence are more appropriate for the data breach in which the plaintiffs are not seeking damages for restitution.[148]

2.3 Class Action Certification in Data Breach Litigation

Even if plaintiffs demonstrate that they have standing *and* that they have stated a sufficient common-law or statutory claim, they usually face an additional hurdle: class certification. Most data breach complaints are filed as putative class action cases, in which the plaintiffs seek to represent all of the people who were harmed by a data breach.

This is largely a matter of economy. Assume that a breach of a retailer's payment card systems led to damages of $250 per consumer. It would make little sense for an attorney to take on the case on behalf of a single plaintiff, since the $250 that the plaintiff might eventually win in litigation would not come close to covering the costs of the attorney's time. A class action lawsuit allows the

---

145 *In re* Target Corporation Customer Data Security Breach Litigation, 66 F. Supp. 3d 1154, 1162 (D. Minn. 2014).
146 Me. Rev. Stat. tit. 5, 207.
147 Me. Rev. Stat. tit. 5, 213(1).
148 Anderson v. Hannaford Bros. Co., 659 F.3d 151 (1st Cir. 2011).

plaintiff's attorney to file a lawsuit on behalf of *all* similarly situated consumers. If the attorney sues on behalf of 100,000 customers whose data was compromised in the breach, then $25 million is at stake. Plaintiff's attorneys who work on contingency often recover one-third of a damages award *plus* costs, so, suddenly, this case is quite lucrative for the attorney. Because of the large number of individuals often affected by data breaches, breach litigation has become an increasingly popular form of class action litigation.

Class actions typically begin with a small group of plaintiffs – known as "class representatives" – who file a class action complaint on behalf of the entire class of affected individuals. If the judge does not grant the defendant's motion to dismiss or motion for summary judgment, the case may proceed to trial, which could lead to a verdict that is divided among all class members (minus attorney fees and costs, of course). However, if a court denies a defendant's motion to dismiss or for summary judgment, it is common for the plaintiffs and defendants to reach a settlement, avoiding trial altogether.

However, plaintiffs are not automatically entitled to receive damages – or settle – on behalf of similarly situated individuals. They first must meet a set of requirements known as "class certification." Since 2005, when Congress passed a law that makes it easier to bring class action litigation in federal courts,[149] most class action cases have been brought in federal courts, rather than state courts. To receive class certification in federal court, plaintiffs must convince the judge that they satisfy the requirements of Federal Rule of Civil Procedure 23.[150] Federal Rule of Civil Procedure is divided into two sections: 23(a) and 23(b).

Under Rule 23(a), plaintiffs must satisfy four prerequisites before being permitted to sue on behalf of a class:

1) *Numerosity.* "[T]he class is so numerous that joinder of all members is impracticable."[151]
2) *Commonality.* "[T]here are questions of law or fact common to the class."[152]
3) *Typicality.* "[T]he claims or defenses of the representative parties are typical of the claims or defenses of the class."[153]

---

149 Class Action Fairness Act of 2005, Pub. L. No. 109-2, 119 Stat. 4 (codified as amended in scattered sections of 28 U.S.C.).
150 Even if a class action lawsuit is brought in state court, the procedural requirements often mirror those in Federal Rule of Civil Procedure 23. *See* Thomas E. Willging & Shannon R. Wheatman, *Attorney Choice of Forum in Class Action Litigation: What Difference Does It Make?*, 81 NOTRE DAME L. REV. 591, 593 (2006) ("[T]here is little empirical evidence supporting the belief that state and federal courts differ generally in their treatment of class actions … . ").
151 FED. R. CIV. P. 23(a)(1).
152 FED. R. CIV. P. 23(a)(2).
153 FED. R. CIV. P. 23(a)(3).

4) *Adequacy.* "[T]he representative parties will fairly and adequately protect the interests of the class."[154]

Perhaps the biggest barrier under Rule 23(a) is demonstrating commonality, due to a 2011 United States Supreme Court opinion. In *Wal-Mart v. Dukes,*[155] a massive employment discrimination case, the Supreme Court held that three plaintiffs did not satisfy the commonality requirement to represent a class of 1.5 million female Wal-Mart employees who allegedly were denied promotion or equal pay because of their gender. The gist of the class action lawsuit was that Wal-Mart's "corporate culture" – and not an explicit corporate policy – leads to discrimination against female employees. Instead, the plaintiffs argued that the corporate policy of allowing local supervisors to have discretion in pay and promotions led to common discrimination throughout the company. Despite the plaintiffs' statistical evidence of companywide discrimination, the Supreme Court held that a policy that provides discretion to local supervisors is not enough to demonstrate commonality.[156] The Supreme Court noted that merely raising common questions is not sufficient: class action lawsuits must be able "to generate common *answers* apt to drive the resolution of the litigation."[157] Although an employment discrimination case is quite different from a standard data breach case, the *Wal-Mart* case is important for data security because it demonstrates that high bar that all class representative face in establishing commonality. For instance, if a company has suffered multiple data breaches, *Wal-Mart* makes it more difficult for class representatives whose data was compromised in Breach A to sue on behalf of plaintiffs whose data was compromised in Breaches B and C, unless the class representatives can demonstrate a common cause for all three of the breaches.

In addition to satisfying all four requirements of Section 23(a), the class representatives must demonstrate that their case falls into one of four categories provided in Rule 23(b). They are:

1) separate claims would possibly create "inconsistent or varying adjudications,"[158]
2) separate claims would "be dispositive of the interests of other members not parties to the individual adjudications or would substantially impair or impede their ability to protect their interest,"[159]

---

154 FED. R. CIV. P. 23(a)(4).
155 Wal-Mart Stores, Inc. v. Dukes, 131 S. Ct. 2541 (2011).
156 *Id.* at 2556–57 ("Because respondents provide no convincing proof of a companywide discriminatory pay and promotion policy, we have concluded that they have not established the existence of any common question.").
157 *Id.* at 2551.
158 FED. R. CIV. P. 23(b)(1)(A).
159 FED. R. CIV. P. 23(b)(1)(B).

3) the goal is declaratory or injunctive relief,[160] or

4) "questions of law or fact common to class members predominate" and "class action is superior to other available methods."[161]

The final type of Rule 23(b) claim, known as "predominance," is the most common avenue through which data breach plaintiffs seek class certification.

As with other areas of data breach litigation, courts vary in their approaches to class certification. Unlike environmental litigation and other common forms of class action lawsuits that have existed for decades, data breach litigation does not have the same depth of judicial precedent, causing widely different results. Some courts easily find that plaintiffs satisfy Rules 23(a) and 23(b) for all victims of a single data breach, while other courts are much more skeptical of certifying data breach class action lawsuits.

To understand how courts have applied the class certification standards to data breach cases, below are examples of two notable class certification opinions.

***In re Hannaford Bros. Co. Customer Data Security Breach Litigation*, No. 2:08-MD-1954 (D. Me. March 13, 2013)**   In this putative class action lawsuit, described above, the class representatives brought seven claims arising from a large data breach of a grocery store chain. The U.S. Court of Appeals for the First Circuit upheld the district court's dismissal of five claims, but allowed the plaintiffs to proceed on claims of negligence and breach of implied contract. The case returned to the district court, which then faced the task of deciding whether to certify the class.

The district court concluded that the plaintiffs satisfied all four of the Rule 23(a) requirements:

- ***Numerosity.***   The court relied on data from credit card issuers that showed that thousands of cardholders whose data was compromised purchased identity theft protection in the year after the breach, and thousands also were charged card replacement fees. The court acknowledged that it was impossible to determine whether the Hannaford breach was the cause of all of the expenses, but noted that it is permitted to draw "reasonable inferences" about numerosity. The judge noted that the case likely will result in "generous fees" for the lawyers representing the plaintiffs, and that he is concerned that "few class members will ultimately be interested in taking the time to file the paperwork necessary to obtain the very small amount of money that may be available if there is a recovery." However, the judge stated that such concerns are for Congress, and that he cannot consider such issues when ruling on numerosity.

---

160 FED. R. CIV. P. 23(b)(2).
161 FED. R. CIV. P. 23(b)(3).

- **Commonality.** Although the losses suffered by the individual class members may vary, the judge determined that the plaintiff satisfied the commonality requirement because all of the claims arise from the common question of whether Hannaford's actions caused the breach and remediation measures.
- **Typicality.** The judge concluded that the class representatives satisfied the typicality requirement because the interests of the class members and representatives are aligned: demonstrating that Hannaford was negligent and breached an implied contract. Hannaford argued that the alleged economic harm to class members varied; for example, some purchased credit monitoring and others paid fees for new cards. Because the claims differ, they require different evidence of causation, and therefore fail to satisfy the typicality requirement, the company asserted. The judge acknowledged that "there is some force" to this argument, but held that the customers' mitigation steps – whether by purchasing identity theft protection or ordering a new card – was mitigation from the same alleged action (or inaction) of Hannaford.
- **Adequacy.** To satisfy the adequacy requirement, class representatives must demonstrate: (1) there is not a potential conflict between the representatives and class members, and (2) the lawyers are qualified, experienced, and able to conduct the litigation. Hannaford argued that the class representatives chose to file a lawsuit rather than apply to the company for refund gift cards, but the judge concluded that this is not a conflict.

Although the court concluded that the plaintiffs satisfied all of the requirements of Rule 23(a), the court denied class certification because the plaintiffs failed to satisfy Rule 23(b). The plaintiffs argued that their lawsuit satisfies Rule 23(b)(3), a lawsuit in which common questions of law and fact **predominate** questions regarding individual class members *and* a class action is **superior** to other available methods. Accordingly, the court considered both (1) superiority and (2) predominance. The court had little difficulty finding that the class action is superior to individual lawsuits, since "[g]iven the size of the claims, individual class members have virtually no interest in individually controlling the prosecution of separate actions[.]"

However, the judge concluded that the plaintiffs did not satisfy the predominance requirement. Although the class members' alleged injuries arise from the same data breach, the types of injuries (lost card fees, identity theft protection, etc.) varies. The plaintiffs claimed that they could find expert witnesss to testify, based on industry statistics, about the proportion of the fees and costs that could be attributed to the Hannaford breach, and that class administrators would determine how to distribute any proceeds from the case. However, the plaintiffs had not presented the judge with an expert opinion about how the damages would be determined, and therefore, the judge ruled that the plaintiffs cannot prove total damages, and the alternative "is a trial involving individual issues for each class member as to what happened to his/her data and account, what he/she did about it, and why."

The Hannaford case demonstrates a key barrier to plaintiffs in achieving class certification for data breach cases. Even if all class members are affected by the same data breach, it is quite likely that at least some class members suffered different types of damage. Before seeking class certification, the plaintiff must be able to demonstrate to the court how it can accurately determine the damages that this wide range of class members have suffered.

In re Heartland Payment Systems, Inc. Customer Data Security Breach Litigation: Consumer Track Litigation, 851 F.Supp.2d 1040 (S.D. Tex. 2012)
Heartland, a large processor of payment card data, suffered a breach that exposed approximately 100 million customers' payment card data to hackers. A number of consumer lawsuits were filed across the nation, and they were consolidated into a case in Texas. As with many data breach cases, the parties reached a settlement. However, in order for the settlement to be binding on all of the approximately 100 million affected individuals, the court needed to determine whether to certify the class.

The judge concluded that the plaintiffs met all four requirements of Rule 23(a):

- **Numerosity.** In two sentences, the judge concluded that the 100 million-member nationwide class easily satisfied the numerosity requirement.
- **Commonality.** The judge concluded that the plaintiffs satisfied the commonality requirement, even under the more stringent *Wal-Mart* standard, because there is a common factual question regarding "what actions Heartland took before, during, and after the data breach to safeguard the Consumer Plaintiffs' financial information."
- **Typicality.** The judge ruled that the plaintiffs satisfied the typicality requirement because the outcome of the claims centers on Heartland's conduct, not the characteristics of any individual class member.
- **Adequacy.** The judge concluded that the plaintiffs satisfied the adequacy requirement. The plaintiffs' lawyers have "extensive experience" in class action litigation, and therefore provide adequate representation, the judge ruled, and the class representatives do not have any apparent conflicts with the proposed class members.

As in the *Hannaford* case, the plaintiffs here asserted that their lawsuit satisfies the "predominance" and "superiority" requirements of Rule 23(b)(3). The judge ruled that the plaintiffs satisfied both requirements. The class action is superior to individual litigation, the judge ruled. The judge concluded that common questions predominate individual issues. The judge noted that only one member of the 100 million-member proposed class objected. Even though there are some differences in the state laws at issue in the class action, the court concluded that those differences are not so large as to affect any class members' rights. Moreover, because the parties were seeking to settle, the judge concluded that it was unnecessary to be concerned about the manageability of a trial.

It is difficult to entirely square the results of *Hannaford* and *Heartland*. In both cases, it is likely that class members suffered different levels of harm from a breach, yet the class was certified in *Heartland* and denied in *Hannaford*. One explanation for the difference in results is that *Heartland* involved a class certification for the purposes of settlement. Therefore, the defendant was not opposing certification. In contrast, *Hannaford* involved a costly dispute that had been going on for many years, and the defendant vigorously opposed class certification.

2.4   Insurance Coverage for Cybersecurity Incidents

When facing these large class action lawsuits – which often carry the potential of break-the-company damages or settlements – companies often seek coverage from their insurance providers under their commercial general liability policies. Unfortunately, such coverage is far from certain, unless the company has purchased special additional cyber insurance. Even with specialized insurance, companies may not be fully covered for the many types of costs that are likely to arise after a cybersecurity incident.

Companies typically have commercial general liability insurance coverage, which covers the businesses for bodily injury, property damage, and other incidents that could cause harm to others and lead to litigation. These policies contain a number of limitations and exceptions to coverage.

Although each insurer determines the precise language of its commercial general liability policy, Insurance Services Office, Inc. offers a standard form, ISO CG, which typically is used as the starting point for insurers' policies. After data breaches, companies most often seek coverage under the policy's promise to pay certain expenses related to "personal and advertising injury," which the form policy defines as including "[o]ral or written publication, in any manner, of material that violates a person's right of privacy[.]"

Insurers often go to court to challenge companies' attempts to obtain coverage for data breaches under commercial general liability policies. The most common argument is that a data breach – often caused by an unknown hacker – does not constitute a "publication" by the covered company. Courts are divided on this issue.

Some courts easily conclude that any data breach constitutes a "publication" of personal information and therefore is covered under commercial general liability policies. For instance, in *Travelers Indemnity Company of America v. Portal Healthcare Solutions, LLC,*[162] customers had filed a class action lawsuit

---

162 Travelers Indemnity Company of America v. Portal Healthcare Solutions, LLC, No. 14-1944 (4th Cir. April 11, 2016) (unpublished).

against Portal, a healthcare company, arising from a data breach that allegedly exposed their medical records on the Internet. Portal sought coverage for the litigation from Travelers, its commercial general liability carrier. The policy required Travelers to pay money arising from Portal's "electronic publication of material that … gives unreasonable publicity to a person's private life[.]" Travelers then sued Portal, seeking a court judgment that it was not required to cover Portal's expenses for the breach. Travelers's primary argument was that the exposure does not constitute "publication." Travelers pointed to a dictionary definition of "publication as "to place before the public (as through a mass medium)." The insurer argued that no "publication" occurred because Portal had no intent to expose the information to the public, and also because there was no allegation that a third party viewed the information. The district court ordered the insurer to cover Portal, and the Fourth Circuit affirmed. The Fourth Circuit agreed with the district court's conclusion that such distinctions are irrelevant, and that the online exposure of a patient's medical records constitutes publication of material that gives unreasonable publicity to a person's private life.[163]

Other courts, however, have reached opposite conclusions about similar policy language. For instance, Sony sought coverage under its commercial general liability policy for the Play Station Network breach discussed earlier in this chapter. Its policy required the insurer, Zurich American Insurance, to cover Sony's costs related to "[o]ral or written publication, in any manner, of material that violates a person's right of privacy." A New York state trial judge indicated that he had a difficult time determining whether to require Zurich to cover Sony.[164] On the one hand, the judge stated during a court hearing, in the "electronic age," allowing exposure of data that a company had promised would be secure might constitute "publication." On the other hand, the judge ultimately concluded that the policy only covers "publication" by Sony, and because the information was acquired by outside hackers without any affirmative acts by Sony, Zurich was not required to cover Sony for the breach.

Even if personal information is exposed due to the actions of a policyholder, some courts still may conclude that the incident was not "publication" that triggers insurance coverage under commercial general liability policies. For instance, in *Creative Hospitality Ventures, Inc. v. United States Liability Insurance Co.*,[165] the policyholder had been sued for violating the Fair and Accurate Credit Card Transaction Act by printing more than the last five digits of consumers' credit card numbers on their receipts. The policyholder sought coverage from its insurer's commercial general liability policy. The U.S. Court

---

163 *Id.*
164 Zurich American Insurance Co. v. Sony Corp., No. 651982/2011 (N.Y. Sup. Ct. 2014).
165 Creative Hospitality Ventures, Inc. v. United States Liability Insurance Co., 444 Fed. Appx. 370 (11th Cir. Sept. 30, 2011).

of Appeals for the Eleventh Circuit denied coverage, reasoning that the receipts do not constitute "publication" under the policy. To define "publication," the Eleventh Circuit looked to a dictionary, which defined the term as "communication (as of news or information) to the public: public announcement" or "the act or process of issuing copies ... for general distribution to the public."[166] Although the policyholder allegedly communicated the credit card information on its receipts, it did not disclose the information to the general public, the Eleventh Circuit reasoned. Instead, the policyholder only provided the receipts to the customers. Therefore, the Court concluded, the alleged credit card disclosures do not constitute "publication" and the insurer was not required to cover the costs of litigation.[167]

Recognizing the uncertainty of coverage under commercial general liability policies, insurers are increasingly offering supplemental cybersecurity insurance policies to companies. These policies cover losses and expenses for a wide range of cyber-related incidents.

For instance, one of the leading cybersecurity insurance policies is CyberSecurity by Chubb, which the insurer marketed as "a flexible insurance solution designed by cyber risk experts to address the full breadth of risks associated with doing business in today's technology-dependent world." The policy's marketing materials state that it covers a liability for a wide range of harms to third parties, such as disclosure of private information, copyright and trademark infringement, reputational injury, system security failures that harm third-party systems, and injuries arising from systems outages.[168] The policy also covers a number of direct costs to the company, including data breach notification, crisis management, forensic consultants, and online vandalism.[169]

However, even if companies purchase broad cybersecurity-related policies, they may not be guaranteed coverage for all losses. For instance, restaurant chain P.F. Chang's had purchased the CyberSecurity by Chubb policy for approximately $134,000 a year. In 2014, it experienced a data breach that exposed approximately 60,000 customer credit card numbers. The insurer reimbursed P.F. Chang's more than $1.7 million for various costs, including a forensic investigation and defense of a lawsuit brought by customers. However, the insurer refused to pay more than $1.9 million in fees assessed by credit card companies due to the company's failure to comply with the Payment Card Industry Data Security Standards. The U.S. District Court for the District of Arizona concluded that the credit card company fees do not cover the types of "privacy injuries" that the cybersecurity insurance policy is intended to insure.

---

166 *Id.* at 375–76.
167 *Id.* at 376.
168 CyberSecurity by Chubb, *available at* http://www.chubb.com/businesses/csi/chubb10600.pdf.
169 *Id.*

The Court noted that the restaurant chain is "a sophisticated party," and if it had wanted coverage for such fees, it "could have bargained for that coverage."[170] The Court also concluded that the coverage was barred under an exclusion in the policy, which provides that the insurer is not responsible for any liability assumed by P.F. Chang's "under any contract or agreement."[171]

The P.F. Chang's case demonstrates the need for companies to carefully scrutinize cybersecurity insurance policies and, if necessary, attempt to bargain for coverage that they would expect from a cybersecurity policy. Cybersecurity is a particularly complex area of insurance because so many new types of liabilities may arise, many of which were unanticipated at the time that the policy was purchased.

Because of the unpredictability of insurance coverage for cybersecurity, many companies choose to self-insure by setting aside money to cover expenses in the event of a cyber incident.[172] Such a strategy has some significant upsides. Rather than being at the mercy of an insurance company – and perhaps paying significant attorney fees to resolve an insurance dispute – self-insurance provides a company with immediate funds to cover cybersecurity expenses. However, self-insurance is quite expensive. A company must have large cash reserves to set aside the amount required to cover breach-related costs. For

---

Questions to Ask When Shopping for Cybersecurity Insurance

- What cybersecurity incidents are already covered by my commercial general liability policy?
- Does the insurance place a cap on hourly fees for forensics experts and lawyers?
- Does the insurance only cover data breaches, or does it cover other types of attacks, like denial of service?
- Does the insurance cover disruption to business and reputational damage?
- Does the insurance cover credit monitoring services for consumers?
- Does the insurance apply to intellectual property-related risks?
- Does the insurance cover fees from credit card companies and other business partners that result from data breaches?
- Would it be less expensive to self-insure for cybersecurity incidents?

---

170 P.F. Chang's China Bistro, Inc. v. Federal Insurance Co., No. CV-15-01322-PHX-SMM (D. Ariz. May 26, 2016).

171 *Id.*

172 *See* National Protection and Programs Directorate, U.S. Department of Homeland Security, Cybersecurity Insurance Workshop Readout Report (Nov. 2012) at 42 ("Another insurer cautioned that self-insurance should not be discounted as a reasonable risk management strategy. When a company decides to self-insure, he stated, it typically knows about its cyber risks, however inexactly, and sets aside funding in the event of a loss.").

instance, P.F. Chang's costs from the 2014 data breach exceeded $3 million. Although its insurer only paid $1.7 million of those costs, it obtained that coverage by paying approximately $134,000 a year.

2.5 Protecting Cybersecurity Work Product and Communications from Discovery

As this chapter has demonstrated, businesses that experience data breaches face a number of legal claims from plaintiffs who often seek tens of millions of dollars.[173] Many of the legal claims described above depend on the specific facts of a data breach, such as:

- What steps did a company take to secure the data?
- Were those steps in line with other companies in the industry?
- Did executives have any advance warning that the data security measures were inadequate?
- Were executives aware of similar incidents?
- Did the company divert money from cybersecurity to other areas of the business?
- How did executives respond when they learned of the breach?

These are just some of the many questions that are bound to arise when plaintiffs are attempting to demonstrate that a company's negligence or other violation of a legal duty caused the plaintiffs' personal information to be exposed.

Unfortunately for companies, answers to many of these questions are readily available in the email inboxes of their executives and information technology staffers, as well as incident reports and assessments of security vulnerabilities. Indeed, companies increasingly hire cybersecurity forensics firms to prevent cybersecurity incidents from occurring. Companies engage cybersecurity professionals to perform penetration tests, which "prove (or disprove) real-world attack vectors against an organization's IT assets, data, humans, and/or physical security."[174] The results of these tests can help a company reconfigure its systems, policies, and processes to guard against security threats.[175]

Companies also increasingly hire consultants for the more urgent task of remediating and mitigating harm after a security incident has taken place.

---

173 Much of this section originally appeared in THE CYBERSECURITY PRIVILEGE, an article by this book's author in I/S: A JOURNAL OF LAW AND POLICY FOR THE INFORMATION SOCIETY (2016).

174 Eric Basu, *What is a Penetration Test and Why Would I Need One for My Company?* FORBES (Oct. 12, 2013) ("A penetration test is designed to answer the question: 'What is the *real-world* effectiveness of my existing security controls against an active, human, skilled attacker?'").

175 *Id.*

Cybersecurity professionals must immediately gain full access to a network to determine the extent of the intrusion, and the necessary steps to remediate any damage and prevent further unauthorized access.[176] The cybersecurity experts and lawyers must work together to determine whether they are legally required to notify state regulators or consumers of the breach under the state notification laws described in Chapter. Cybersecurity professionals also collaborate with public affairs departments and consultants to publicly explain the incident in a manner that is prompt, complete, and accurate.[177]

Cybersecurity professionals wear multiple hats, including auditor, technologist, policy maker, strategist, and spokesperson. To perform such wide-ranging duties, cybersecurity professionals must have broad and unfettered access to information that a company or organization may store in a variety of media and formats, and they must be able to candidly communicate with their clients.

Unfortunately for companies, there is strong possibility that cybersecurity professionals' reports and emails can be obtained by plaintiffs and used against them in litigation. In United States civil litigation, parties typically have a broad right of discovery, which allows them to obtain documents, depositions, and other relevant information from the opposing party and third parties. Courts generally have a strong presumption in favor of allowing parties to conduct discovery and present evidence to courts.[178] The only way to avoid this presumption in favor of disclosure is to demonstrate that an evidentiary privilege applies. Courts and legislatures have created evidentiary privileges for communications and work products of certain professionals for whom confidentiality is an integral part of their jobs. For instance, the United States recognizes evidentiary privileges, to varying degrees, for attorneys, psychotherapists, clergy, and journalists. No court or legislature has created a stand-alone privilege for the work of cybersecurity professionals, owing partly to the fact that the profession is so new, and evidentiary privileges are slow to develop.[179]

---

176 Nate Lord, *Data Breach Experts Share the Most Important Next Step You Should Take after a Data Breach in 2014–15 and Beyond*, DIGITAL GUARDIAN (May 4, 2015) ("By bringing in an unbiased, third-party specialist, you can discover exactly what has been accessed and compromised, identify what vulnerabilities caused the data breach, and remediate so the issue doesn't happen again in the future.").

177 Natalie Burg, *Five Lessons for Every Business From Target's Data Breach*, FORBES (Jan. 17, 2014) ("[A] security crisis can very quickly turn into a crisis of trust and loyalty if swift communications and responsive customer service aren't employed — even if the fault lies with the same weak credit card security used by so many other businesses.").

178 *See* University of Pennsylvania v. EEOC, 493 US 182, 189 (1990) ("We do not create and apply an evidentiary privilege unless it promotes sufficiently important interests to outweigh the need for probative evidence") (citations omitted) (internal quotation marks omitted).

179 *See* Wolfle v. United States, 291 U.S. 7, 12 (1934) (evidentiary privileges are "governed by common law principles as interpreted and applied by the federal courts in the light of reason and experience.").

Despite the lack of a stand-alone privilege for cybersecurity professionals, companies and their forensics experts still have a reasonable chance of getting at least some protection for their communications and reports. To shield this material from discovery, companies attempt to obtain three attorney-related evidentiary privileges. To do so, companies are increasingly hiring attorneys to supervise the work of cybersecurity consultants. The three privileges are (1) the attorney–client privilege, (2) the work product doctrine, and (3) the non-testifying expert privilege. As we will see, these privileges only offer limited protection, and are not always guaranteed to prevent confidential cybersecurity information from being obtained by plaintiffs.

2.5.1 Attorney–Client Privilege

The attorney–client privilege protects from discovery communications between attorneys and clients in the course of seeking and providing legal advice.[180] The privilege is nearly absolute and only contains a few limited exceptions, such as instances in which the attorney helped the client perpetrate crime or fraud,[181] or if the client disputes the attorney's competence or job performance.[182]

This broad privilege is intended "to encourage full and frank communication between attorneys and their clients and thereby promote broader public interests in the observance of law and administration of justice."[183] The privilege "exists to protect not only the giving of professional advice to those who can act on it but also the giving of information to the lawyer to enable him to give sound and informed advice."[184]

Although the attorney–client privilege is absolute, it only covers certain types of communications.[185] The specific elements of the privilege vary slightly by jurisdiction, but the following Ninth Circuit summary generally is an accurate illustration of the privilege's scope of coverage:

> (1) When legal advice of any kind is sought (2) from a professional legal adviser in his or her capacity as such, (3) the communications

---

180 Upjohn Co. v. United States, 449 U.S. 383, 388 (1981).

181 United States v. Zolin, 491 US 554, 563 (1989) ("It is the purpose of the crime-fraud exception to the attorney–client privilege to assure that the seal of secrecy between lawyer and client does not extend to communications made for the purpose of getting advice for the commission of a fraud or crime.") (citation omitted) (internal quotation marks omitted).

182 United States v. Pinson, 584 F.3d 972 (10th Cir. 2009) ("The theoretical basis for the assertion that raising an ineffective-assistance claim waives attorney–client privilege is the exception to the privilege that applies when a litigant chooses to place privileged communications directly in issue.").

183 *Upjohn*, 449 U.S. at 388.

184 *Id.* at 384.

185 *See generally* Mohawk Indus., Inc. v. Carpenter, 130 S. Ct. 599 (2009).

relating to that purpose, (4) made in confidence (5) by the client, (6) are, at the client's instance, permanently protected (7) from disclosure by the client or by the legal adviser (8) unless the protection be waived.[186]

The privilege, therefore, protects communications from the client to the attorney – or from the attorney to the client – that are exchanged for the purpose of rendering legal advice. The privilege protects *communications*, and does not protect the evidence underlying the communications. For instance, suppose that a company is reviewing its server logs and discovers an apparent breach. The company's CIO immediately emails a description of the apparent breach to the company's outside counsel. Although the CIO's email to the attorney may be privileged, the server's logs would not be privileged.

Additionally, the attorney–client privilege only applies to communications that seek or provide *legal* advice. For instance, if a company's lawyers advise on *and* help implement a business transaction, only the legal advice that they provide will be privileged. Any "business advice" likely will fall outside of the scope of the privilege, though courts may disagree as to whether a specific communication is legal or business advice.[187] Applying this framework, if a company emails a cybersecurity consultant with a question about network protection and merely CC's the company's lawyer, a court may find that the communication was unrelated to *legal* advice, and therefore not protected by the attorney–client privilege.

Moreover, if a third party receives the communication, a court may find that the attorney–client privilege does not apply in that situation.[188] However, communications may still be protected if they include nonlawyers who are assisting the lawyer in the representation. For instance, the communications of an accountant or translator working for a law firm may be protected by the privilege. As Judge Friendly wrote a half-century ago, "[w]hat is vital to the privilege is that the communication be made in confidence for the purpose of obtaining legal advice from the lawyer."[189] Similarly, the attorney–client privilege covers

---

186 United States v. Martin, 278 F.3d 988, 999 (9th Cir. 2002).
187 United States v. ChevronTexaco, 241 F. Supp. 2d 1065, 1069 (N.D. Cal. 2003) ("Because the purported privileged communications involve attorneys who apparently performed the dual role of legal and business advisor, assessing whether a particular communication was made for the purpose of securing legal advice (as opposed to business advice) becomes a difficult task."); Cuno, Inc. v. Pall Corp., 121 F.R.D. 198, 204 (E.D.N.Y. 1988) ("[w]here a lawyer mixes legal and business advice the communication is not privileged 'unless the communication is designed to meet problems which can fairly be characterized as predominantly legal'").
188 *See* Cavallaro v. United States, 284 F.3d 236, 237 (1st Cir. 2002) ("The presence of third parties during an attorney–client communication is often sufficient to undermine the 'made in confidence' requirement, or to waive the privilege[.]") (internal citations omitted).
189 United States v. Kovel, 296 F.2d 918, 922 (2d Cir. 1961).

consultants who perform work under the supervision of attorneys, if that work is conducted as part of the attorney's representation of clients.[190]

Accordingly, if a cybersecurity professional helps an attorney provide legal advice to a client, those communications may be covered by the attorney–client privilege. However, the attorney–client privilege is of limited use for a good deal of the work that cybersecurity professionals perform. Perhaps the largest obstacle for the purposes of cybersecurity consulting is the requirement that the communications relate to legal advice.[191] For instance, an email that describes the result of a network vulnerability test, for example, likely would not qualify as legal advice. Even if a cybersecurity professional is supervised by an attorney, there is no guarantee that the professional's communications with the attorney or client would be protected under the attorney–client privilege.

2.5.2 Work Product Doctrine

The work product doctrine is more likely to cover some cybersecurity work that is performed at the direction of attorneys, but the doctrine, unlike the attorney–client privilege, is not absolute.

The doctrine was first articulated in 1947, when the Supreme Court ruled in *Hickman v. Taylor*[192] that an attorney's notes and reports based on witness interviews could not later be discovered in litigation involving the attorney's client. Although the Court concluded that the attorney–client privilege does not protect the documents,[193] it nonetheless denied discovery, reasoning that the request was "an attempt to secure the production of written statements and mental impressions contained in the files and the mind of the attorney … without any showing of necessity or any indication or claim that denial of such production would unduly prejudice the preparation of petitioner's case or cause him any hardship or injustice."[194]

The *Hickman* work product doctrine was later codified in Federal Rule of Civil Procedure 26(b)(3).[195] That rule provides that "[o]rdinarily, a party may not discover documents and tangible things that are prepared in anticipation of

---

190 *See* Fed. Trade Comm'n v. TRW, Inc., 628 F.2d 207, 212 (D.C. Cir. 1980) ("[T]he attorney–client privilege can attach to reports of third parties made at the request of the attorney or the client where the purpose of the report was to put in usable form information obtained from the client.").

191 *See Kovel*, 296 F.2d at 922 ("If what is sought is not legal advice but only accounting service …, or if the advice sought is the accountant's rather than the lawyer's, no privilege exists.").

192 329 U.S. 495 (1947).

193 *Id.* at 508.

194 *Id.* at 509.

195 *See* United States v. Adlman, 134 F.3d 1194, 1197 (2d Cir. 1998) ("Rule 26(b)(3) codifies the principles articulated in *Hickman*.").

litigation or for trial by or for another party or its representative (including the other party's attorney, consultant, surety, indemnitor, insurer, or agent)."[196] However, the rule is not absolute: it allows discovery if "the party shows that it has substantial need for the materials to prepare its case and cannot, without undue hardship, obtain their substantial equivalent by other means"[197] or if a court otherwise finds good cause to order the disclosure of relevant work product.[198] If the Court orders disclosure of work product, "it must protect against disclosure of the mental impressions, conclusions, opinions, or legal theories of a party's attorney or other representative concerning the litigation."[199]

The work product doctrine covers more than just communications that are necessary for legal advice. The doctrine protects *work product* that is prepared in anticipation of litigation or trial. Moreover, Federal Rule of Civil Procedure 26 explicitly states that *consultants'* work product may be protected, provided that it is prepared in anticipation of litigation. Indeed, courts have held that the work product doctrine applies to materials prepared by environmental consultants,[200] medical device safety consultants,[201] and insurance claims investigators.[202] Similarly, a cybersecurity professional's report might be protected by the work product doctrine.[203]

However, the exceptions to the work product doctrine limit the extent of the protection that it provides to cybersecurity work. Perhaps most important is the requirement that the work product be prepared in anticipation of litigation or trial. The Second Circuit, reflecting a common approach to the doctrine, interpreted work product to have been created "in anticipation of litigation" if "in light of the nature of the document and the factual situation in the particular case, the document can fairly be said to have been prepared or obtained because of the prospect of litigation."[204] Although this approach is relatively

---

196 Fed. R. Civ. P. 26(b)(3).
197 Fed. R. Civ. P. 26(b)(3)(A)(ii).
198 Fed. R. Civ. P. 26(b)(3)(A)(i).
199 Fed. R. Civ. P. 26(b)(3)(B).
200 Martin v. Bally's Park Place Hotel & Casino, 983 F.2d 1252, 1260–62 (3d Cir. 1993).
201 Ebert v. C.R. Bard, Inc., 2014 WL 1632155 (E.D. Pa. April 24, 2014).
202 Carver v. Allstate Insurance Co., 94 F.R.D. 131 (S.D. Ga. 1982).
203 *See* Benjamen C. Linden et al., *Use Outside Counsel to Control Data Breach Loss,* BLOOMBERG BNA (Mar. 21, 2014) ("The work product doctrine may be an additional means to shield findings from a post-breach investigation during subsequent litigation. Whereas the attorney–client privilege applies only to communications, work product applies broadly to 'documents and tangible things that are prepared in anticipation of litigation or for trial by or for another party or its representative (including the other party's attorney, consultant, surety, indemnitor, insurer, or agent).' Thus, when investigative documents in the aftermath of a breach are prepared primarily in anticipation of litigation, the doctrine might protect them. However, when documents appear to be the product of a routine investigation and were not prepared primarily in anticipation of litigation, courts are much less likely to protect the work product doctrine.").
204 *See* United States v. Adlman, *supra* note 70 at 1202 (citations omitted) (internal quotation marks omitted).

broad and could encompass large swaths of documents, the party asserting the work product doctrine would need to demonstrate that the materials were created *because of* potential litigation. A consultant's report about the causes of a data breach likely would have a greater chance of being covered by the work product doctrine than the consultant's annual, routine assessment of a company's cybersecurity controls. The company would have a stronger argument that the consultant prepared the data breach report in response to a real threat of actual litigation. The annual, routine assessment, in contrast, is less likely to be likened to a real prospect of litigation. This creates a perverse result: companies likely receive *less* protection for taking proactive measures to *protect* their networks from attacks than they do for taking remedial measures *after* breaches have occurred.

Moreover, even if work product was prepared in anticipation of litigation, a court *still* could require its disclosure if the court concludes that the party requesting the materials has demonstrated a substantial need or other good cause for the discovery.[205] Routine work product is less likely to receive protection under the work product doctrine unless it is "core" or "opinion" work product related to an attorney's conclusions or impressions about particular litigation.[206] In the cybersecurity context, this means that a forensics expert's initial evaluation of a data breach most likely could be discovered in subsequent litigation if the opposing party demonstrates substantial need or good cause. In contrast, that consultant's analysis of claims in a pending complaint arising from the data breach is more likely to be protected under the work product doctrine. Again, this dichotomy results in cybersecurity professionals' work receiving less protection if it is not related to ongoing litigation.

Although the work product doctrine has a broader scope than the attorney–client privilege, the work product doctrine is not absolute. Because litigants could successfully argue that a good deal of the work performed by cybersecurity consultants falls within one of the doctrine's exceptions, companies cannot rely on the work product doctrine to prevent the compelled disclosure of cybersecurity material.

---

205 FED. R. CIV. P. 26(b)(3)(A)(i)–(ii).

206 *In re* Cendant Corp. Securities Litigation, 343 F. 3d 658 (3d Cir. 2003) ("Stated differently, Rule 26(b)(3) establishes two tiers of protection: first, work prepared in anticipation of litigation by an attorney or his agent is discoverable only upon a showing of need and hardship; second, 'core' or 'opinion' work product that encompasses the mental impressions, conclusions, opinion, or legal theories of an attorney or other representative of a party concerning the litigation is generally afforded near absolute protection from discovery.") (internal quotation marks omitted); *In re* San Juan Dupont Plaza Hotel Fire Litig., 859 F.2d 1007, 1015 (1st Cir. 1988) ("Courts typically afford ordinary work product only a qualified immunity, subject to a showing of substantial need and hardship, while requiring a hardier showing to justify the production of opinion work product.").

2.5.3 Non-Testifying Expert Privilege

A third, narrower privilege prevents the compelled disclosure of certain non-testifying experts. Federal Rule of Civil Procedure 26(b)(4)(D) states that "a party may not, by interrogatories or depositions, discover facts known or opinions held by an expert retained or specially employed by another party in anticipation of litigation or to prepare for trial and who is not expected to be called as a witness at trial," unless the party can demonstrate "exceptional circumstances under which it is impracticable for the party to obtain facts or opinions on the same subject by other means."[207] The non-testifying expert privilege is "designed to promote fairness by precluding unreasonable access to an opposing party's diligent trial preparation."[208]

The non-testifying expert privilege is quite strong, and courts have interpreted the "exceptional circumstances" exemption to be quite limited.[209] However, it has limited value for cybersecurity investigations. As the Ninth Circuit recently noted, the rule "shields only against disclosure through interrogatories and depositions[.]"[210] Accordingly, the rule would not prevent the disclosure of a report prepared by a cybersecurity expert; it would only prevent that expert from being subjected to interrogatories and depositions. Moreover, like the work product doctrine, the non-testifying expert privilege only applies to anticipated litigation or trial preparation.[211] A routine cybersecurity

	Attorney–client privilege	Work product doctrine	Non-testifying expert privilege
Type of material protected	Communications between attorneys and clients while providing legal advice	Documents and tangible things that are prepared in anticipation of litigation	Facts known or opinions held by a retained expert
Individuals to whom it applies	Attorneys and individuals who assist them (such as paralegals or consultants)	Attorney, consultant, surety, indemnitor, insurer, or agent	Expert retained in anticipation of litigation and who is not expected to be called as a witness
Scope	Absolute, with a few narrow exceptions	Qualified – may be overcome in exceptional circumstances	Qualified – may be overcome in exceptional circumstances

---

207 FED. R. CIV. P. 26(b)(4)(D).
208 Durflinger v. Artiles, 727 F.2d 888, 891 (10th Cir. 1984).
209 *In re* Shell Oil Refinery, 132 F.R.D. 437, 442 (E.D. La. 1990) ("The exceptional circumstances requirement has been interpreted by the courts to mean an inability to obtain equivalent information from other sources.").
210 Ibrahim v. Department of Homeland Sec., 669 F. 3d 983, 999 (9th Cir. 2012).
211 FED. R. CIV. P. 26(b)(4)(D).

investigation, therefore, likely would not be covered under this privilege. This privilege would, however, apply to an incident assessment that a cybersecurity professional prepares to assess the merits of pending litigation.

2.5.4 Applying the Three Privileges to Cybersecurity: *Genesco v. Visa*

Few published opinions have directly addressed the application of the attorney–client privilege, work product doctrine, and non-testifying expert privilege to the work of cybersecurity professionals. This is not surprising; discovery disputes often are settled orally in discussions between the parties and magistrate judges; therefore, there is not a written opinion documenting many of these disputes. The most extensive written discussion of the application of these privileges to cybersecurity was in *Genesco v. Visa*.[212]

In that case, hackers had accessed customer payment card information that was stored on the network of Genesco, a retail chain.[213] Genesco's general counsel, Roger Sisson retained Stroz Friedberg, a cybersecurity consulting firm.[214] Genesco's retention agreement with Stroz stated that the retention was "in anticipation of potential litigation and/or legal or regulatory proceedings."[215]

After consulting its own investigation, Visa assessed more than $13 million in fines and reimbursement assessments against two banks that processed Genesco's credit card purchases, claiming that Genesco's inadequate data security violated payment card data security standards and Visa's operating regulations.[216] Genesco, which had an indemnification agreement with the banks, sued Visa, asserting that the assessments lacked factual basis and violated various state laws.[217] In discovery, Visa subpoenaed Stroz for deposition testimony and its work product related to the investigation, and also requested to depose Sisson and that Sisson provide documents related to his investigation of the incident.[218]

The court largely denied Visa's discovery requests. The court first held that the requests for Stroz's deposition and work product is prohibited by the non-testifying expert privilege.[219] Visa argued that Stroz was a fact witness, but the court rejected this argument, concluding that "the Stroz representative would necessarily be applying his or her specialized knowledge," and that Visa had not

---

212 Genesco v. Visa U.S.A., 302 F.R.D. 168 (M.D. Tenn. 2014).
213 *Id.* at 171.
214 *Id.* at 180–81.
215 *Id.* at 181.
216 *Id.* at 170.
217 *Id.*
218 *Id.* at 181–82.
219 *Id.* at 189–90.

established the "extraordinary circumstances" needed to overcome the non-testifying expert privilege.[220]

The Court also held that the attorney–client privilege and the work product doctrine prevent the compelled disclosure of both the requests to Sisson and to Stroz.[221] The court held that "[a]ttorney's factual investigations 'fall comfortably within the protection of the attorney–client privilege,'"[222] and that the privilege "extends to the Stroz firm that assisted counsel in his investigation."[223] The court also recognized that the work product doctrine "attaches to an agent's work under counsel's direction."[224] The court held that the work product doctrine applies because "Genesco's affidavits satisfy that the Stroz firm was retained in contemplation of litigation, as reflected in the express language of the retainer agreement."[225]

In 2015, Visa subpoenaed IBM for work product regarding remedial security measures that IBM performed for Genesco after the breach.[226] In a brief order, the court rejected this request, concluding that because Genesco "retained IBM to provide consulting and technical services so as to assist counsel in rendering legal advice[,]" IBM's materials are protected by the attorney–client privilege and work product doctrine.[227]

Commentators hailed the *Genesco* rulings as a demonstration that cybersecurity work could be privileged, provided that they are conducted under the supervision of an attorney. Lawyers at one large law firm hailed the opinion as "a roadmap for confidentiality protections" that "underscores legal counsel's critical role in today's digital economy where the question is not 'if' but 'when,' an organization will be breached."[228] Lawyers at another firm advised that the decision "demonstrates how important it is for you to designate experienced privacy counsel to lead cybersecurity initiatives, including determining proactive privacy and security measures, directing forensic investigations, and spearheading data breach response efforts."[229] A news article declared that, in

---

220 *Id.* at 190 ("To accept that characterization would effectively eviscerate and undermine the core purpose of FED. R. CIV. P. 26(b)(4)(D).").

221 *Id.* at 195.

222 *Id.* at 190 (quoting Santra T.E. v. South Berwyn School Dist. 100, 600 F.3d 612, 619 (7th Cir. 2010)).

223 *Id.*

224 *Id.*

225 *Id.* at 193.

226 Genesco, Inc. v. Visa U.S.A., Inc., 2015 U.S. Dist. LEXIS 52314 (M.D. Tenn. Mar. 24, 2015).

227 *Id.*

228 Aravind Swaminathan et al., *Court Says Cyber Forensics Covered by Legal Privilege*, ORRICK (Apr. 24, 2015), *available at* https://www.orrick.com/Events-and-Publications/Pages/Court-Says-Cyber-Forensics-Covered-by-Legal-Privilege.aspx.

229 *Communications with Your Cybersecurity Consultant and Forensic Reports may Now be Protected*, MCDONALD HOPKINS (June 11, 2015), *available at* http://www.mcdonaldhopkins. com/alerts/data-privacy-and-cybersecurity-communications-with-your-cybersecurity-consultant-and-forensice-reports-may-now-be-protected.

light of the opinion, the "smart and most conservative proactive approach" to cybersecurity risk management is "to have the appropriate law firm take the lead, hire the required consultants, and have all reports, analysis, memos, plans and communications protected under the attorney–client and work product privileges."[230]

The commentators were correct, to an extent. The *Genesco* rulings extend the same protections to communications and work product of cybersecurity consultants as previous court opinions have extended to the work and communications of environmental consultants, product safety experts, and others retained and supervised by counsel for the purposes of providing legal advice or preparing for litigation. The 2015 order regarding IBM, in particular, is encouraging because IBM provided technical consulting to help remediate security flaws on Genesco's network. Although the court viewed these services as part of Genesco's legal strategy, remedial measures for a computer network could have longer lasting effects that help Genesco in the future, entirely unrelated to the Visa litigation.

That said, the *Genesco* case also illustrates the evidentiary privileges' limits for cybersecurity work. The gravamen of Genesco's argument throughout the discovery dispute was that Stroz and IBM were merely helping Genesco challenge the Visa fees or prepare for its defense in other claims related to the breach.[231] Genesco framed its arguments as such for good reason: had it not framed the IBM and Stroz work as part of a legal defense strategy, the communications and work product likely would have been discoverable, as reflected in the court's focus on the three attorney-related privileges.

---

230 Denis Kleinfeld, *Your Computer Will Be Hacked, It's Just a Question of When*, NEWSMAX (May 4, 2015), *available at* http://www.newsmax.com/Finance/Kleinfeld/Cybersecurity-Hack-Passcodes-Risk/2015/05/04/id/642323/.

231 Opp. Brief of Genesco, Genesco, Inc. v. Visa U.S.A., Inc., 2015 U.S. Dist. LEXIS 52314 (M.D. Tenn. Mar. 24, 2015) ("Here, it is undisputed that IBM prepared the PCI Gap Assessment pursuant to an engagement by Genesco's General Counsel for the purpose of assisting Genesco's General Counsel in providing legal advice to Genesco regarding its *legal* obligation to be PCI DSS compliant.").

3

Cybersecurity Requirements for Specific Industries

Chapters 1 and 2 covered the general data security obligations that all U.S. companies face under Section 5 of the FTC Act, state data security laws, and common law torts that could lead to class actions lawsuits and other litigation. These requirements apply equally to companies regardless of their industry.

In addition to these general data security requirements, companies that handle particularly sensitive information or operate in industries that carry particularly high national security risks face more stringent requirements. This chapter will cover six such prominent legal requirements for sensitive information: (1) the Gramm-Leach-Bliley Act Safeguards Rule for financial institutions, (2) the Red Flags Rule for information for certain creditors and financial institutions, (3) the Payment Card Industry Data Security Standard (PCI DSS) for credit and debit card information, (4) the Health Information Portability and Accountability Act Security Rule for certain health-related information, (5) Federal Energy Regulatory Agency guidelines for electric grid cybersecurity, and (6) Nuclear Regulatory Commission cybersecurity requirements for nuclear reactor licensees.

Keep in mind that the general cybersecurity requirements described in Chapters 1 and 2 *also* apply to these industries, unless there is an exception for companies that comply with industry-specific laws and regulations. Moreover, it is increasingly common for companies that provide highly sensitive information

Cybersecurity Law, First Edition. Jeff Kosseff.
© 2017 John Wiley & Sons, Inc. Published 2017 by John Wiley & Sons, Inc.
Companion Website: www.wiley.com/go/kosseff/cybersecurity

to certain contractors, such as law firms and accountants, to *contractually* require additional cybersecurity protections.

3.1 Financial Institutions: Gramm-Leach-Bliley Act Safeguards Rule

In 1999, Congress enacted the Gramm-Leach-Bliley Act, a comprehensive overhaul of financial regulation in the United States. Many of the most controversial portions of the act, which relaxed decades-old ownership restrictions on financial institutions, are outside of the scope of this book. For the purposes of cybersecurity, the most relevant section is known as the Safeguards Rule, which requires federal regulators to adopt data security standards for the financial institutions that they regulate.

The Gramm-Leach-Bliley Act requires the agencies to adopt administrative, technical, and physical safeguards:

1) to insure the security and confidentiality of customer records and information,
2) to protect against any anticipated threats or hazards to the security or integrity of such records, and
3) to protect against unauthorized access to or use of such records or information that could result in substantial harm or inconvenience to any customer.[1]

The statute only applies to "nonpublic personal information," which it defines as personally identifiable financial information that is (1) provided by a consumer to a financial institution, (2) resulting from any transaction with the consumer or any service performed for the consumer, or (3) otherwise obtained by the financial institution.[2]

A number of agencies regulate financial institutions, and they have taken slightly different approaches to developing regulations under the GLBA Safeguards Rule. The remainder of this section examines the primary regulations issued by the various agencies.

3.1.1 Interagency Guidelines

Agencies that regulate banks and related financial institutions have collaborated to develop Interagency Guidelines to implement the Safeguards Rule. The agencies that have adopted the Interagency Guidelines into their regulations, and the types of institutions that they regulate, are as follows:

- *Office of the Comptroller of the Currency.* Regulates national banks, federal branches and federal agencies of foreign banks, and any subsidiaries

---

1 15 U.S.C. § 6801(b).
2 15 U.S.C. § 6809(4).

of these entities (other than brokers, dealers, insurers, investment companies, and investment advisers).

- **Federal Reserve Board.** Regulates member banks, branches and agencies of foreign banks, commercial lending companies owned or controlled by foreign banks, Edge and Agreement Act Corporations, bank holding companies and their nonbank subsidiaries or affiliates (other than brokers, dealers, insurers, investment companies, and investment advisers).
- **Federal Deposit Insurance Corporation.** Regulates state nonmember banks, insured state branches of foreign banks, and any subsidiaries of such entities, except brokers, dealers, insurers, investment companies, and investment advisers.
- **Office of Thrift Supervision.** Regulates insured savings associations and any subsidiaries, except brokers, insurers, investment companies, and investment advisers.[3]

The Interagency Guidelines require covered institutions to implement a "comprehensive written information security program" to safeguard nonpublic personal information.[4] The agencies stated that financial institutions must take the following steps while developing and implementing their programs:

- **Involve the board of directors.** The board or a board committee should approve the security program and oversee its development, implementation, and maintenance.
- **Assess risk.** The institutions should conduct an "assessment of reasonably foreseeable risks" involving the security of customer information.
- **Manage and control risk.** The institutions should design their programs to control the risks by considering measures such as access controls, restrictions on physical locations where customer information is stored, encryption of information in transit and at rest, segregation of duties, background checks for employees, and system monitoring.

  - *Train employees on the information security program.*
  - *Maintain regular testing of controls and systems.*
  - *Properly dispose of customer information.*
  - *Provide adequate oversight of service providers' information security measures.*
  - *Adjust information security programs as new threats arise.*
  - *Report to board of directors any material matters related to the information security program at least once a year.*[5]

---

3 The National Credit Union Administration, which regulates credit unions, has adopted a Safeguards Rule that is largely identical to the Interagency Guidelines. 12 C.F.R. § 248.
4 Each participating agency has adopted a version of the Interagency Guidelines in its regulations. For ease of reference, this subsection will refer to the version of the Interagency Guidelines in the Federal Reserve's regulations, appendixes D-2 to 12 C.R.R. § 208.
5 *Id.*

The Interagency Guidelines further require financial institutions to maintain incident response programs for *sensitive* customer information, which the guidelines define as a customer's name, address, or phone number in combination with at least one of the following:

- Social Security number,
- driver's license number,
- account number,
- credit or debit card number, or
- personal identification number or password that permits access to a customer's account.

Sensitive customer information includes any additional information that would enable an unauthorized user to access a customer's account (i.e., username and password).

Incident response programs for sensitive information must contain procedures to:

- assess "the nature and scope of the incident and identification of what customer information has been accessed or misused";
- determine what information types have been accessed;
- notify its primary federal regulator (e.g., the Office of the Comptroller of the Currency) as soon as possible after the institution becomes aware of an incident;
- notify appropriate law enforcement authorities consistent with requirements to file Suspicious Activity Reports;
- take steps "to contain and control the incident to prevent further unauthorized access to or misuse of customer information, while preserving records and other evidence"; and
- notify the customer as soon as possible if the institution, after investigation, determines that sensitive customer information likely was misused, or that the unauthorized access likely will result in misuse or harm to individuals (the institution may delay notification if law enforcement provides a written request for a delay because notice would interfere with a law enforcement investigation).[6] Note that this requirement is similar to the state laws that take a "risk-of-harm" approach to notification requirements, as it allows financial institutions to conduct a balancing test to determine whether to issue notifications.

The notices must contain: a description, in general, of the data breach, the types of information that were accessed without authorization, and mitigation steps taken by the financial institution; a telephone number for further information about the breach; and a reminder to "remain vigilant" and report apparent identity theft. [7]

---

6 *Id.*
7 *Id.*

Although the Interagency Guidelines are comprehensive, the banking regulators have not focused on enforcement of their data security regulations as much as many other regulators, such as the Securities and Exchange Commission and the FTC.

3.1.2   Securities and Exchange Commission Regulation S-P

The Securities and Exchange Commission's Regulation S-P sets the GLBA Safeguards Rule requirements for brokers, dealers, investment companies, and investment advisers that are registered with the SEC.[8] The SEC's version of the Safeguards Rule is not as detailed as the Interagency Guidelines, though the SEC has been fairly aggressive in its enforcement of the rule in recent years.

The SEC's regulations broadly require institutions to adopt written information security policies and procedures that contain administrative, technical, and physical safeguards that meet the three goals of the GLBA Safeguards Rule: insuring security and confidentiality of customer information, protecting the information from anticipated threats or hazards, and protecting the information from unauthorized access that could substantially harm or inconvenience the customer.[9] Regulation S-P also requires institutions to properly dispose of consumer report information and take steps to protect against unauthorized access.[10]

Despite the relative lack of specificity in the SEC's version of the Safeguards Rule, the agency has indicated that cybersecurity is a high priority, and that it will use the regulation to pursue institutions that do not adequately protect customer information. In September 2015, the SEC announced a settlement of an administrative proceeding with R.T. Jones Capital Equities Management, an investment adviser that experienced a data breach, originating in China, and exposed the personal information of approximately 100,000 people.[11] Although R.T. Jones notified affected individuals and there were no reports of harm, the SEC brought the administrative action because the company did not have a written information security program. In the settlement order, the SEC noted that the company failed to conduct periodic risk assessments, use a firewall to protect the web server that contains client information, encrypt customer information, or develop an incident response plan.[12] The no-fault settlement

---

8 17 C.F.R. § 248.30.

9 *Id.*

10 *Id.*

11 *In re* R.T. Jones Capital Equities Management, Inc., Administrative Proceeding File No. 3-16827, Order Instituting Administrative and Cease-and-Desist Proceedings Pursuant to Sections 203(e) and 203(k) of the Investment Advisers Act of 1940, Making Findings, and Imposing Remedial Sanctions and a Cease-and-Desist Order.

12 *Id.*

required the company to cease future violations of the SEC's Safeguards Rule and to pay a $75,000 penalty. In announcing the settlement, Marshall S. Sprung, Co-Chief of the SEC Enforcement Division's Asset Management Unit, warned that firms "must adopt written policies to protect their clients' private information and they need to anticipate potential cybersecurity events and have clear procedures in place rather than waiting to react once a breach occurs."[13]

3.1.3 FTC Safeguards Rule

The FTC regulates financial institutions that are not regulated by one of the banking agencies or the SEC. Among the types of financial institutions that the FTC regulates are consumer reporting agencies, retailers that offer credit to customers, and mortgage brokers.

Like the SEC, the FTC did not pass an incredibly detailed Safeguards Rule. Nonetheless, the FTC has been quite aggressive in its enforcement of the Safeguards Rule, partly due to the key role that customer information plays for consumer reporting agencies and other financial institutions regulated by the FTC.

The FTC's Safeguards Rule, like those of the other agencies, requires financial institutions to develop, implement, and maintain a comprehensive written information security program that contains administrative, technical, and physical safeguards that meet the GLBA Safeguards Rule's three key objectives listed at the start of this chapter.

The FTC's regulations require information security programs to be carried out and protected as follows:

- Designate employees to coordinate the program.
- Identify "reasonably foreseeable internal and external risks to the security, confidentiality, and integrity of customer information." The assessment should consider, at minimum, workforce training, information systems, intrusion detection and prevention programs, and incident response plans.
- Based on this assessment, companies should implement safeguards, and conduct regular assessments of the strength and viability of those safeguards.
- Contractually require service providers to comply with the Safeguards Rule and oversee their compliance.
- Regularly evaluate and adjust information security policies and procedures.

The FTC has brought a number of enforcement actions against companies that failed to develop information security programs that meet these requirements. Typically, the FTC brings cases after a financial institution has experienced a data breach. The summaries that follow are a few of the most prominent

---

13 Press Release, Securities and Exchange Commission, SEC Charges Investment Adviser with Failing to Adopt Proper Cybersecurity Policies and Procedures Prior to Breach (Sept. 22, 2015).

settlements of enforcement actions that the FTC has brought under the Safeguards Rule.

In the Matter of ACRAnet, Inc., **Docket No. C-4331 (2011)**   Data breaches often trigger FTC scrutiny of a financial institution's compliance with the Safeguards Rule. ACRAnet assembles consumer reports for the three major consumer reporting agencies, Equifax, Experian, and TransUnion. The reports contain a great deal of sensitive and nonpublic information, such as consumer's names, addresses, Social Security numbers, birth dates, and work history. The company sells these reports to mortgage brokers, and therefore is a financial institution subject to FTC's Safeguards Rule. In 2007 and 2008, hackers accessed nearly 700 consumer reports due to vulnerabilities in the networks of ARCAnet's clients. After the breach, the FTC states that ACRANet did not take steps to prevent similar breaches by, for instance, requiring clients to demonstrate that their computer networks are free of security threats. The FTC asserted that ACRANet violated the Safeguards Rule by failing to:

- implement adequate customer information safeguards;
- test and monitor its information security controls;
- evaluate and adjust its information security program; and
- develop a comprehensive information security program.

In the Matter of James B. Nutter & Co., **Docket No. C-4258 (2009)**   James B. Nutter & Co. makes and services residential loans, and is therefore covered by the FTC Safeguards Rule. The company collects a great deal of highly sensitive information, including employment history, credit history, Social Security numbers, and driver's license numbers. It uses its website and computer network to obtain personal information from customers, store data, and otherwise conduct its lending business. An unauthorized individual managed to hack into the company's network and send spam. Although there was no evidence of theft of customer information, the FTC stated in its complaint that the hacker "could have accessed personal information without authorization." The FTC claimed that the company violated the Safeguards Rule by failing to:

- develop a comprehensive written information security program;
- identify risks to personal information;
- develop personal information risk controls;
- evaluate and adjust the information security program; and
- oversee service providers and contractually require them to implement personal information safeguards.

In the Matter of Superior Mortgage Corporation, **Docket C-4153 (2005)**   Superior Mortgage Corporation, a residential mortgage direct lender, collects during the mortgage application process sensitive information such as credit card account numbers and Social Security numbers. The FTC brought a complaint against the company for violating the Safeguards Rule. Although the complaint does not mention a specific data breach or other attack on the company's system, the complaint noted that the company's website only encrypted sensitive customer information while in transit, but not while it was at rest. The decrypted customer information allegedly was then emailed in clear text to the company's headquarters and branch offices. The company's online privacy policy claimed that "[a]ll information submitted is handled by SSL encryption[.]" The FTC alleged that Superior Mortgage violated the Safeguards Rule by, among other things, failing to:

- conduct a security risk assessment;
- implement adequate password policies for access to sensitive customer information;
- encrypt sensitive customer data; and
- oversee service providers' compliance with information security requirements.

In the Matter of Goal Financial, LLC, **Docket No. C-4216 (2008)** The FTC also expects companies to adequately oversee their employees' handling of personal information. In such a case, employees of Goal Financial, a marketer and originator of student loans, transferred more than 7000 consumer files to third parties. Additionally, a Goal Financial employee sold hard drives that had not yet been wiped of approximately 34,000 customers' sensitive personal information. In its complaint against Goal Financial, the FTC alleged that the company violated the Safeguards Rule by failing to: identify reasonably foreseeable risks, design and implement safeguards to control those risks, develop a written information security program, and require contractors to safeguard customer information.

3.2 Financial Institutions and Creditors: Red Flag Rule

In 2003, amid growing concern about identity theft, Congress passed the Fair and Accurate Credit Transaction Act of 2003. Among other provisions, the statute required banking regulators and the FTC to develop regulations that require financial institutions and creditors that offer covered accounts to develop "reasonable policies and procedures" to prevent identity theft of their account holders.[14]

The Red Flag Rule only applies to companies that (1) are financial institutions or creditors *and* (2) offer "covered accounts" to individuals. To determine whether the Red Flag Rule applies, companies must analyze the definition of both terms.

---

14 15 U.S.C. § 1681m.

What are Examples of Red Flags?

In a supplement to the Red Flag Rule regulations, the FTC provided an illustrative list of examples of red flags. Keep in mind that these are only examples, and there very well may be other indications of risk:

Alerts, notifications, or warnings from a consumer reporting agency

1) A fraud or active duty alert is included with a consumer report.
2) A consumer reporting agency provides a notice of credit freeze in response to a request for a consumer report.
3) A consumer reporting agency provides a notice of address discrepancy, as defined in § 641.1(b) of this part.
4) A consumer report indicates a pattern of activity that is inconsistent with the history and usual pattern of activity of an applicant or customer, such as:
   a) a recent and significant increase in the volume of inquiries,
   b) an unusual number of recently established credit relationships,
   c) a material change in the use of credit, especially with respect to recently established credit relationships, or
   d) an account that was closed for cause or identified for abuse of account privileges by a financial institution or creditor.

Suspicious documents

5) Documents provided for identification appear to have been altered or forged.
6) The photograph or physical description on the identification is not consistent with the appearance of the applicant or customer presenting the identification.
7) Other information on the identification is not consistent with information provided by the person opening a new covered account or customer presenting the identification.
8) Other information on the identification is not consistent with readily accessible information that is on file with the financial institution or creditor, such as a signature card or a recent check.
9) An application appears to have been altered or forged, or gives the appearance of having been destroyed and reassembled.

Suspicious personal identifying information

10) Personal identifying information provided is inconsistent when compared against external information sources used by the financial institution or creditor. For example:
    a) the address does not match any address in the consumer report, or
    b) the Social Security Number (SSN) has not been issued, or is listed on the Social Security Administration's Death Master File.

11) Personal identifying information provided by the customer is not consistent with other personal identifying information provided by the customer. For example, there is a lack of correlation between the SSN range and date of birth.

12) Personal identifying information provided is associated with known fraudulent activity as indicated by internal or third-party sources used by the financial institution or creditor. For example:

   a) the address on an application is the same as the address provided on a fraudulent application, or

   b) the phone number on an application is the same as the number provided on a fraudulent application.

13) Personal identifying information provided is of a type commonly associated with fraudulent activity as indicated by internal or third-party sources used by the financial institution or creditor. For example:

   a) the address on an application is fictitious, a mail drop, or a prison; or

   b) the phone number is invalid, or is associated with a pager or answering service.

14) The SSN provided is the same as that submitted by other persons opening an account or other customers.

15) The address or telephone number provided is the same as or similar to the address or telephone number submitted by an unusually large number of other persons opening accounts or by other customers.

16) The person opening the covered account or the customer fails to provide all required personal identifying information on an application or in response to notification that the application is incomplete.

17) Personal identifying information provided is not consistent with personal identifying information that is on file with the financial institution or creditor.

18) For financial institutions and creditors that use challenge questions, the person opening the covered account or the customer cannot provide authenticating information beyond that which generally would be available from a wallet or consumer report.

Unusual use of, or suspicious activity related to, the covered account

19) Shortly following the notice of a change of address for a covered account, the institution or creditor receives a request for a new, additional, or replacement card or a cell phone, or for the addition of authorized users on the account.

20) A new revolving credit account is used in a manner commonly associated with known patterns of fraud. For example:

   a) the majority of available credit is used for cash advances or merchandise that is easily convertible to cash (e.g., electronics equipment or jewelry), or

b) the customer fails to make the first payment or makes an initial payment but no subsequent payments.

21) A covered account is used in a manner that is not consistent with established patterns of activity on the account. There is, for example:

a) nonpayment when there is no history of late or missed payments,
b) a material increase in the use of available credit,
c) a material change in purchasing or spending patterns,
d) a material change in electronic fund transfer patterns in connection with a deposit account, or
e) a material change in telephone call patterns in connection with a cellular phone account.

22) A covered account that has been inactive for a reasonably lengthy period of time is used (taking into consideration the type of account, the expected pattern of usage, and other relevant factors).

23) Mail sent to the customer is returned repeatedly as undeliverable although transactions continue to be conducted in connection with the customer's covered account.

24) The financial institution or creditor is notified that the customer is not receiving paper account statements.

25) The financial institution or creditor is notified of unauthorized charges or transactions in connection with a customer's covered account.

Source: Federal Trade Commission.

How do Companies Implement the Red Flags Rule?

The regulations require the financial institution or creditor's board of directors or board committee to approve the initial Red Flag Rule program,[15] and to involve the board, a board committee, or a senior manager in the oversight, development, implementation, and administration of the program.[16] Companies are required to train their staff to implement the program[17] and to appropriately and effectively oversee service provider arrangements.[18]

The FTC has stated that it expects companies to take a variety of approaches to meeting their requirements under the Red Flag Rule, and that while "some businesses and organizations may need a comprehensive program to address a high risk of identity theft, a streamlined program may be appropriate for businesses facing a low risk."[19] In other words, the Red Flag Rule is not a one-size-fits-all program, and companies should adopt their own program relative to their company's needs and risks.

---

15 16 C.F.R. 681.1(e)(1).
16 16 C.F.R. 681.1(e)(2).
17 16 C.F.R. 681.1(e)(3).
18 16 C.F.R. 681.1(e)(4).
19 Federal Trade Commission, Fighting Identity Theft with the Red Flags Rule: A How-To Guide for Business (May 2013).

3.2.1 Financial Institutions or Creditors

The FTC and banking regulators issued their first iteration of the Red Flag regulations in 2007, but the regulations' implementation was delayed after an outcry from the business community about the lack of clarity in the regulations. Although "financial institution" is clearly defined, the regulations contained a broad definition of "creditor" that could have included professionals such as doctors and lawyers because they bill clients after they perform the services. Many such professionals argued that their operations do not pose a substantial risk of identity theft, and therefore they should not be required to develop comprehensive identity theft prevention programs.

Congress responded to the industry concerns in 2010 by passing the Red Flag Program Clarification Act of 2010.[20] The law defines "creditor" as a company that, in the ordinary course of business:

   i) obtains or uses consumer reports, directly or indirectly, in connection with a credit transaction;
   ii) furnishes information to consumer reporting agencies ... in connection with a credit transaction; or
   iii) advances funds to or on behalf of a person, based on an obligation of the person to repay the funds or repayable from specific property pledged by or on behalf of the person.[21]

The Clarification Act explicitly states that the term "creditor" does not include an entity that "advances funds on behalf of a person for expenses incidental to a service provided by the creditor to that person."[22]

The new definition clarifies that the Red Flag Rule applies to financial institutions; companies that obtain, use, or provide information for credit reports; or companies that lend money to people, provided that the loan is for something other than the lender's own services. Accordingly, under the clarified Red Flag Rule, a doctor or lawyer does not become subject to the Red Flag Rule merely by billing a customer after providing the service.

3.2.2 Covered Accounts

Not all financial institutions and creditors are covered by the Red Flag Rule. The requirements only apply if the company offers a "covered account." The Red Flag Rule regulations define "covered accounts" as including two types of accounts:

   i) [a]n account that a financial institution or creditor offers or maintains, primarily for personal, family, or household purposes,

---

20 P.L. 111-319.
21 *Id.*
22 *Id.*

that involves or is designed to permit multiple payments or transactions, such as a credit card account, mortgage loan, automobile loan, margin account, cell phone account, utility account, checking account, or savings account; and

ii) [a]ny other account that the financial institution or creditor offers or maintains for which there is a reasonably foreseeable risk to customers or to the safety and soundness of the financial institution or creditor from identity theft, including financial, operational, compliance, reputation, or litigation risks.[23]

To determine whether an account falls within either definition, the regulations instruct the financial institution or creditor to consider the methods that the company provides to open its accounts, the methods that the company provides to access the accounts, and the company's previous experience with identity theft.[24] Keep in mind that the regulations apply as long as the financial institution or creditor has at least *one* covered account.

In other words, financial institutions and creditors must conduct a balancing test to determine whether the risk of identity theft to its customers is reasonably foreseeable. They are only required to develop an identity theft prevention plan if they determine that the risk is reasonably foreseeable and, therefore, they offer covered accounts. The regulators expect the companies to periodically reassess this risk. Companies should make an honest assessment of the risk. If a company obtains highly sensitive personal information via an unencrypted Internet connection, it is difficult to conceive of how a company could find that there is not a reasonably foreseeable risk of identity theft. It is a best practice to document the reasoning behind the determination of whether a company offers a covered account.

3.2.3 Requirements for a Red Flag Identity Theft Prevention Program

The Red Flag regulations require financial institutions and creditors that offer at least one covered account to develop a *written* identity theft prevention program designed "to detect, prevent, and mitigate identity theft in connection with the opening of a covered account or any existing covered account."[25]

The written program must explain how the financial institution or creditor will accomplish four goals:

1) Identify "red flags," which the regulations define as a "pattern, practice, or specific activity that indicates the possible existence of identity theft."[26] Among the red flags that the regulators have stated companies should

---

23 16 C.F.R. § 681.1(b)(3).
24 16 C.F.R. § 681.1(c).
25 16 C.F.R. § 681.1(d)(1).
26 16 C.F.R. § 681.1(b)(9).

consider are risk factors (e.g., the types of covered accounts and the methods through which customers can access these accounts), the sources of the red flags, and categories of red flags (e.g., alerts that have been provided to the businesses by law enforcement agencies, victims, and others).

2) Detect the red flags that the financial institution or creditor has identified. Companies should obtain identifying information about and verify the identities of people opening covered accounts, authenticate those customers, monitor their transactions, and verify the validity of address change requests.

3) Appropriately respond to red flags that are detected to prevent and mitigate identity theft. The regulators wrote that appropriate responses may include continued monitoring of customers' accounts, contacting customers or law enforcement to inform them of red flags, modifying log-in credentials to customer accounts, or closing accounts that appear to have been compromised.[27]

4) Periodically update the Red Flag program to reflect changes in risk. When updating the program, the regulation states, financial institutions and creditors should consider, among other things, recent incidents of identity theft that the company has experienced, changes to identity theft mitigation practices, new types of identity theft, and changes to the company's structure or ownership that might increase the likelihood of identity theft.[28]

3.3 Companies that use Payment and Debit Cards: Payment Card Industry Data Security Standard (PCI DSS)

Companies that accept or use credit or debit cards (including, but not limited to retailers), are required to comply with the Payment Card Industry Data Security Standard (PCI DSS), an extensive set of operational and technical rules that are intended to protect payment card numbers and associated data. The goal of the rules is to reduce the chances of the data being stolen and used for identity theft.

The PCI DSS standards are adopted not by courts or legislatures but by an organization comprised of the major credit card companies (American Express, Discovery Financial Services, JCB, MasterCard, and Visa).

The PCI Security Standards Council has developed detailed technical guidance for businesses of varying sizes to comply with the standards, available on

---

27 Appendix A to 16 C.F.R. § 681.
28 16 C.F.R. § 681.1(d)(2) and Appendix A to Part 681.

its website, www.pcisecuritystandards.org. In short, PCI DSS consists of six goals and twelve requirements:

Build and maintain a secure network and systems.
Requirement 1: Install and maintain a firewall configuration to protect cardholder data.
Requirement 2: Do not use vendor-supplied defaults for system passwords and other security parameters.

Protect cardholder data.
Requirement 3: Protect stored cardholder data.
Requirement 4: Encrypt transmission of cardholder data across open, public networks.

Maintain a vulnerability management program.
Requirement 5: Protect all systems against malware and regularly update anti-virus software or programs.
Requirement 6: Develop and maintain secure systems and applications.

Implement strong access control measures.
Requirement 7: Restrict access to cardholder data by business need to know.
Requirement 8: Identify and authenticate access to system components.
Requirement 9: Restrict physical access to cardholder data.

Regularly monitor and test networks.
Requirement 10: Track and monitor all access to network resources and cardholder data.
Requirement 11: Regularly test security systems and processes.

Maintain an information security policy.
Requirement 12: Maintain a policy that addresses information security for all personnel.[29]

The credit card companies individually enforce these requirements by contractually imposing them on the banks, which in turn impose the requirements on the merchants and others that accept and use their credit cards. The credit card companies and banks can impose substantial fines on retailers that fail to comply with PCI DSS, but the amount of those fines is not publicly disclosed.

---

29 This list is provided courtesy of PCI Security Standards Council, LLC ("PCI SSC") and is protected by copyright laws. © PCI Security Standards Council, LLC. All rights reserved.

Additionally, two state laws refer to PCI DSS:

- Nevada requires merchants that conduct business in Nevada to comply with PCI DSS.[30]
- Washington State requires certain businesses to "take reasonable care to guard against unauthorized access" to payment card information, but exempts those businesses from liability if the information was encrypted or the business was "certified compliant with the payment card industry data security standards."[31] In 2016, Home Depot attempted to use this safe harbor to dismiss a class action filed by financial institutions after a data breach at the retailer, but the court denied the motion because the financial institutions' complaint alleged that Home Depot did not comply with PCI DSS.

Even in states that have not adopted laws that incorporate PCI DSS, the standards could help determine the general standard of care in common-law tort and contract claims. For example, in the *Hannaford* case discussed in Chapter 2, involving the breach of a grocery chain's payment card systems, the district court concluded that it is possible that retailers have an implied contract with their consumers to incorporate industry data security standards with their payment card data:

> If a consumer tenders a credit or debit card as payment, I conclude that a jury could find certain other implied terms in the grocery purchase contract: for example, that the merchant will not use the card data for other people's purchases, will not sell or give the data to others (except in completing the payment process), and will take reasonable measures to protect the information (which might include meeting industry standards), on the basis that these are implied commitments that are "absolutely necessary to effectuate the contract," and "indispensable to effectuate the intention of the parties." A jury could reasonably find that customers would not tender cards to merchants who undertook zero obligation to protect customers' electronic data. But in today's known world of sophisticated hackers, data theft, software glitches, and computer viruses, a jury could not reasonably find an implied merchant commitment against every intrusion under any circumstances whatsoever (consider, for example, an armed

---

30 NRS § 603A.215(1) ("If a data collector doing business in this State accepts a payment card in connection with a sale of goods or services, the data collector shall comply with the current version of the Payment Card Industry (PCI) Data Security Standard, as adopted by the PCI Security Standards Council or its successor organization, with respect to those transactions, not later than the date for compliance set forth in the Payment Card Industry (PCI) Data Security Standard or by the PCI Security Standards Council or its successor organization.").
31 WASH. REV. CODE § 19.255.020.

robber confronting the merchant's computer systems personnel at gunpoint).[32]

In short, PCI DSS has become the de facto standard of care for all companies – large and small – that accept, use, process, or store credit or debit card information. Companies are wise to keep informed about the PCI Council's latest guidance regarding PCI DSS compliance.

3.4 Health Providers: Health Insurance Portability and Accountability Act (HIPAA) Security Rule

Certain health-related providers and companies are required to comply with an extensive series of regulations for the security of health data. Under its authority from the Health Insurance Portability and Accountability Act, the Department of Health and Human Services has promulgated regulations known as the HIPAA Security Rule.

The HIPAA Security Rule applies to two types of entities: "covered entities" and "business associates." Other companies, even if they handle health information, are not subject to HIPAA, unless required by a contract. A "covered entity" is a health plan, healthcare clearinghouse, or a healthcare provider who transmits health information in electronic form. A "business associate" is a provider of "data transmission services" to a covered entity, a person who offers a personal health record to individuals on behalf of a covered entity, or a subcontractor that "creates, receives, maintains, or transmits protected health information on behalf of the business associate."[33] Examples of business associates include attorneys who require access to protected health information to provide services and medical transcriptionist services.

The HIPAA Security Rule only applies to "protected health information" that is collected from an individual and is created or received by a covered entity, and relates to "the past, present, or future physical or mental health or condition of an individual; the provision of health care to an individual; or the past, present, or future payment for the provision of health care to an individual."[34] Information is only protected health information if it directly identifies an individual or if there is a reasonable basis to believe that it could identify an individual.[35]

---

32 *In re* Hannaford Bros. Co. Customer Data Security Breach Litigation, 613 F.Supp.2d 108, 119 (D. Me. 2009), aff'd in part and rev'd in part on other grounds, Anderson v. Hannaford Bros. Co., 659 F. 3d 151 (1st Cir. 2011).
33 45 C.F.R. § 160.103.
34 45 C.F.R. § 160.103.
35 *Id.*

The HIPAA Security Rule requires covered entities and business associates to ensure the confidentiality, integrity, and availability of electronic protected health information and take steps to protect against reasonably anticipated threats. [36] As with the GLBA Safeguards Rule, the HIPAA Security Rule is not a one-size-fits-all approach, and instead states that covered entities and business associates may "use any security measures that allow the covered entity or business associate to reasonably and appropriately implement the standards and implementation specification[.]"[37] The regulations instruct covered entities and business associates to consider their size, complexity, and capabilities, technical infrastructure, costs of security measures, and likelihood and magnitude of potential information security risks. [38]

Despite its flexible approach, the HIPAA Security Rule imposes a number of administrative, physical, technical, and organizational standards that covered entities and business associates must adopt. The following are the requirements from the current HIPAA regulations, located at 45 CFR Part 164, edited here for clarity and brevity:

Administrative safeguards.[39]

- Manage security process to "prevent, detect, contain, and correct security violations." The entity must conduct an "accurate and thorough" assessment of potential risks and vulnerabilities, implement security procedures that reduce these risks, sanction noncompliant employees, and regularly review system activity.
- Designate an information security official.
- Develop authorization procedures to reduce the likelihood of unauthorized employees accessing electronic protected health information.
- Develop clearance procedures to determine whether employees should be entrusted with access to electronic protected health information.
- Develop procedures to terminate access to former employees or employees who are no longer eligible to access the information.
- If a healthcare clearinghouse is part of a larger entity, the clearinghouse "must implement policies and procedures that protect the electronic protected health information of the clearinghouse from unauthorized access by the larger organization."
- Develop policies and procedures to allow authorized users to access electronic protected health information.
- Develop a security awareness and training program for all employees. The program should include security reminders, information about protection

---

36 45 C.F.R. § 164.306(a).
37 45 C.F.R. § 164.306(b).
38 *Id.*
39 45 C.F.R. § 164.308.

from malicious software, log-in monitoring, and password management. The training should be tailored to the employees' job responsibilities. For instance, executives' training might differ from training for call center employees.

- Develop policies for security incident response and reporting.
- Develop a contingency plan for physical emergencies such as fires and other natural disasters.
- Periodically conduct technical and nontechnical evaluations of information security policies and procedures.

Physical safeguards.[40]

- Limit physical access to facilities and systems that store protected health information.
- Establish contingency operations and plans that allow restoration of lost data.
- Develop procedures and policies to physically safeguard the equipment that stores electronic protected health information.
- Develop procedures to prevent unauthorized physical access to facilities.
- Document repairs and modification to doors, locks, and other physical components that safeguard protected health information.
- Develop physical safeguards to "restrict access to authorized users" to all systems that contain electronic protected health information.
- Develop policies that restrict the physical removal and transit of devices that store electronic protected health information.

Technical safeguards.[41]

- Develop technical policies and procedures to allow only those who have been granted access rights. These technical safeguards include unique user identification, emergency access procedure, automatic logoff after a specified time of inactivity, and encryption and decryption of electronic protected health information.
- Develop mechanisms that routinely log activity on systems that store electronic protected health information.
- Develop policies and procedures that protect the integrity of electronic protected health information and prevent improper modifications.
- Develop procedures for verifying an individual's identity before providing that individual with access to protected health information.
- Implement technical safeguards for networks that carry electronic personal health information, with the goal of preventing unauthorized access.

---

40 45 C.F.R. § 164.310.
41 45 C.F.R. § 164.312.

- Prevent the improper modification of electronic protected health information.
- Encrypt electronic protected health information "whenever deemed appropriate." Although the HIPAA regulations do not explicitly require encryption in all circumstances, it is increasingly common for encryption to be default for sensitive information such as the health data that is covered by HIPAA.

Organizational safeguards.[42]

- A covered entity's contract with a business associate that has access to electronic protected health information must explicitly require the business associate to comply with HIPAA's security requirements.
- The business associate contract must "ensure that any subcontractors that create, receive, maintain, or transmit electronic protected health information on behalf of the business associate" also agree to comply with HIPAA's security requirements.
- Group health plans must include, in their plan documents, a statement that the sponsor of the plan "will reasonably and appropriately safeguard electronic protected health information created, received, maintained, or transmitted to or by the plan sponsor on behalf of the group health plan."

The Department of Health and Human Services also has developed a detailed set of regulations that require covered entities to notify affected individuals and regulators about data breaches of unsecured protected health information. If business associates experience a breach, they are required to notify the covered entity within sixty days, and the covered entity is obligated to inform individuals.[43]

The breach notification requirement does not apply if all of the protected health information has been "secured" pursuant to guidance from the Department of Health and Human Services or if there is a "low probability" of compromise.[44] The Department states that protected health information can be secured by an encryption method that has been validated by the National Institute of Standards and Technology, or if the media on which the protected health information has been properly destroyed (i.e., by shredding paper, film, or other hard copy media or destroying electronic media). Redaction alone does not constitute "securing" data, according to the Department.[45]

---

42 45 C.F.R. § 164.312.

43 45 § C.F.R. 164.410.

44 *See* DEPARTMENT OF HEALTH AND HUMAN SERVICES, GUIDANCE TO RENDER UNSECURED PROTECTED HEALTH INFORMATION UNUSABLE, UNREADABLE, OR INDECIPHERABLE TO UNAUTHORIZED INDIVIDUALS.

45 *Id.*

Unless law enforcement requests a delay for investigative purposes, covered entities must provide breach notifications to affected individuals without unreasonable delay and no later than sixty calendar days after first discovering the breach.[46]

HIPAA requires notices to contain many of the same elements as the notices required in the state data breach statutes, discussed in Chapter 1. Keep in mind that many of the state breach notice laws contain safe harbors that allow HIPAA-covered entities to satisfy the state breach notice requirements by complying with HIPAA's notice procedures. HIPAA breach notifications must contain the following:

- A description of the breach, including the date of the breach and date of discovery of the breach.
- A description of the types of unsecured protected health information that were involved (date of birth, diagnosis, etc.). Companies should be careful to avoid the inadvertent disclosure of personally identifiable information in their descriptions of the breach and the information involved.
- Steps that the individual should take to protect from harm, such as identity theft.
- A brief description of the covered entity's investigation and mitigation following the breach.
- Contact information for more questions, including a toll-free telephone number, email address, website, or mailing address.[47]

The notification must be provided in writing to each individual's last known mailing address, or to an email address if the individual had agreed to electronic notice and had not revoked consent.[48] If the covered entity is aware that the individual is deceased, and has a mailing address for the next of kin or personal representative of the affected individual, the covered entity should send the notification to that address via first-class mail.[49]

If there is not sufficient contact information to send written notifications to individuals via postal mail, covered entities may use a substitute notice process. If there is insufficient contact information for fewer than ten individuals, then covered entities can provide an alternative form of written notice, notice by telephone, or other means. If there is insufficient or out-of-date contact information for ten or more people, the substitute notification must (1) be a conspicuous posting on the covered entity's website for ninety days, or a conspicuous notice in major local print or broadcast media, *and* (2) include a toll-free number, active for at least ninety days, to provide individuals with more information about whether they were affected by the breach.[50]

---

46 45 C.F.R. § 164.404.
47 45 C.F.R. § 164.404(c).
48 45 C.F.R. § 164.404(d)(1).
49 *Id.*
50 45 C.F.R. § 164.404(d)(2).

If the covered entity determines that there is an urgent need to notify individuals, the entity may also notify the individuals by telephone and other means, in addition to written notice.[51]

If a breach involves the unsecured protected health information of more than 500 residents of a single state or jurisdiction, the covered entity must notify prominent outlets in the state or jurisdiction within sixty calendar days of discovery of the breach, and the content of the notification should be the same as in the individual notifications.[52]

The regulations also require notification to the Department of Health and Human Services. If the breach involves 500 or more individuals, a covered entity must inform the Department at the same time that it notifies individuals.[53] If the breach involves fewer than 500 individuals, the covered entity must maintain a log of breaches and, within sixty days after the end of each calendar year, provide the Department with the log of all breaches from the preceding calendar year.[54] The Department of Health and Human Services' website contains instructions for the manner in which to notify the department of both categories of breaches.[55]

The Department of Health and Human Services' Office of Civil Rights enforces the HIPAA privacy and security regulations. In 2014, the most recent year for which data was available, the Office investigated 427 data breaches, and required that covered entities take corrective action in 415 of those cases.

Unlike the FTC, the Department of Health and Human Services does not publicly release the full text of its investigative complaints and settlements. However, on its website, the Department summarized some cases without specifying the identities of the covered entities:

- A pharmacy chain's pseudoephedrine log books were visible to customers at the check-out counter. After a written analysis from the Department, the chain developed policies to safeguard the logs, and trained its staff on these policies.
- A local Medicaid-funded agency sent protected health information to vendors that had not signed business associate contracts (and had therefore not agreed to comply with the Security Rule). After an investigation by the Department, the agency developed procedures for disclosure of information only to its business associates and trained staff accordingly.
- A large health maintenance organization had a computer flaw that accidentally sent a customer's explanation of benefits to a family member who was not

---

51 *Id.*
52 45 C.F.R. § 164.406.
53 45 C.F.R. § 164.408.
54 *Id.*
55 *Id.*

authorized to receive them. After an investigation by the Department, the HMO corrected this flaw and reviewed all transactions over a six-month period for similar flaws.

3.5 Electric Utilities: Federal Energy Regulatory Commission Critical Infrastructure Protection Reliability Standards

Among the many concerns about potential cyber threats, attacks on the nation's electric grid is among the most frequently discussed. A cyberattack that causes large metropolitan areas to go dark could have devastating effects on national security and the economy.

Accordingly, the Federal Energy Regulatory Commission, which regulates national electric utilities, has increasingly focused on cybersecurity. In January 2016, FERC adopted seven critical infrastructure protection reliability standards that originated from the North American Electric Reliability Corp., a nonprofit organization. Unlike many of the other industry-specific laws and regulations, such as GLBA and HIPAA, the FERC standards are not only concerned with the confidentiality of data but also with preventing any disruptions due to cyberattacks.

This section contains a summary of key provisions of each of the seven standards, but utilities should review the complete standards to ensure compliance.

3.5.1 CIP-003-6: Cybersecurity – Security Management Controls

At least every fifteen months, utilities' senior managers should approve cybersecurity policies that address:

- employee training;
- electronic security perimeters, including remote access;
- cyber system physical security;
- system security management;
- incident response planning;
- incident recovery plans;
- configuration change management;
- information protection; and
- response to exceptional circumstances.

Utilities should name a responsible manager for leading the implementation of the cybersecurity standards, who is permitted to delegate authority to other employees, provided that this delegation has been approved by a senior manager of the utility. In practice, it is common for the responsible manager to be a Chief Information Security Officer or equivalent.

3.5.2 CIP-004-6: Personnel and Training

Utilities should implement quarterly training for security awareness that "reinforces cybersecurity practices (which may include associated physical security practices) for the [utilities'] personnel who have unauthorized electronic or authorized unescorted physical access" to the utilities' systems. These training sessions should be designed for individual jobs. For instance, a supervisor's training likely will differ from those of a line worker.

Utilities should review employees' criminal history at least once every seven years, and conduct other "personnel risk assessment" programs for individuals who need access to utilities' cyber systems.

In addition to training, utilities should ensure that employees do not have access to cyber systems when they no longer need to have access (e.g., if they leave their jobs). Utilities also should develop processes to timely revoke access to cyber systems.

3.5.3 CIP-006-6: Physical Security of Cyber Systems

This guideline requires utilities to develop a comprehensive plan for the physical security of facilities that house the utilities' cyber systems. These plans should include controls such as intrusion alarms and logs of physical entries. The policies should require "continuous escorted access of visitors" within the physical perimeter of the utility's facilities, except under exceptional circumstances.

3.5.4 CIP-007-6: Systems Security Management

To minimize the attack surface, when technically feasible, utilities should enable only the logical network accessible ports that are needed for the utilities' operations. The utilities also should implement a patch management process. At least once every thirty-five days, the utilities should evaluate new security patches and take other steps to reduce the likelihood of harm from malicious code.

CIP-007-6 suggests that utilities maintain audit logs of failed log-in attempts, malicious code, and other potential cybersecurity events. Utilities should develop a process that alerts them to such events.

The guidelines also require utilities to pay close attention to log-in credentials. Utilities should inventory user accounts, change default passwords, establish standards for minimum password length, and, when possible, require authorized users to change passwords at least once every fifteen months.

Utilities also should either impose a maximum number of failed login attempts, or implement a system that alerts the information security staff of unsuccessful login attempts.

3.5.5 CIP-009-6: Recovery Plans for Cyber Systems

CIP-009-6 provides a framework for utilities to create plans that enable them to respond to cyber incidents. Utilities should develop recovery plans that designate specific responsibilities for responders, describe how data will be stored, and provide plans for backing up and preserving data after an incident. At least once every fifteen months, utilities should test recovery plans by recovering from an incident that has occurred during that time period, conducting a paper drill or tabletop exercise, or conducting an operational exercise. The utilities should test the recovery plans at least once every thirty-six months through an "operational exercise of the recovery plans."

Within ninety days of a recovery plan test or actual recovery, utilities should document "lessons learned," update the recovery plan, and notify relevant individuals of the updates.

3.5.6 CIP-010-2: Configuration Change Management and Vulnerability Assessments

Utilities must develop configuration change management processes to "prevent unauthorized modifications" to cyber systems. Change management processes should include a "baseline configuration" that identifies operating systems, installed software, accessible ports, and security patches. The processes also should authorize and document any changes that fail to comply with this baseline configuration.

At least once every thirty-five days, utilities should monitor for deviations from the baseline configuration. At least once every fifteen months, they should conduct a vulnerability assessment to ensure proper implementation of cybersecurity controls. At least every thirty-six months, when feasible, the utility should assess the vulnerabilities, based on this baseline configuration.

Utilities should authorize the use of transient cyber assets (e.g., removable media), except in exceptional circumstances. The authorization should specify the users, locations, defined acceptable use, operating system, firmware, and software on the removable media. Utilities must determine how to minimize threats to these transient assets. Within thirty-five days before use of a transient cyber asset, utilities must ensure that security patches to all transient cyber assets are updated.

3.5.7   CIP-011-2: Information Protection

Utilities should implement information protection programs that include procedures for securely handling information regardless of whether the data is at rest and in transit. Utilities should prevent the "unauthorized retrieval" of information from their systems and ensure that information is securely disposed.

3.6   Nuclear Regulatory Commission Cybersecurity Regulations

Just as policy makers are concerned about a cyberattack threatening the electric grid, they also are deeply concerned about the prospect of a cyberattack on a U.S. nuclear power facility. Such an attack could have devastating national security implications. Accordingly, in 2009, the U.S. Nuclear Regulatory Commission adopted a thorough cybersecurity regulation for licensees of nuclear power reactors. In 2013, the NRC created a Cybersecurity Directorate, which oversees the cybersecurity of the nuclear industry and works with FERC, the Department of Homeland Security, and others that oversee the cybersecurity of the nation's power system.

The NRC's cybersecurity rule[56] requires nuclear licensees to protect their computer and communication systems with safety-related and important-to-safety functions, security functions, emergency preparedness functions, and support systems and equipment that, if compromised, would harm safety, security, or emergency preparedness.[57] The NRC regulations require nuclear licensees to protect these systems and networks from cyberattacks that would harm the integrity or confidentiality of data or software; deny access to the systems, services, or data; and harm the operation of the systems, network, and equipment.[58] The NRC's regulations broadly require nuclear operators to develop cybersecurity programs to implement security controls that protect nuclear facilities from cyberattacks, reduce the likelihood of cyber incidents, and mitigate harm caused by cyber incidents.[59] The regulations provide a great deal of flexibility for nuclear licensees to determine how to develop and draft these plans.

To implement the cybersecurity program, the NRC regulations require licensees to ensure that nuclear licensee employees and contractors receive appropriate cybersecurity training, properly manage cybersecurity risks, incorporate

---

56 10 C.F.R. § 73.54.
57 10 C.F.R. § 73.54(a)(1).
58 10 C.F.R. § 73.54(a)(2).
59 10 C.F.R. § 73.54(c).

cybersecurity into any considerations of modifications to cyber assets, and properly notify regulators of cybersecurity incidents.[60]

The NRC requires licensees to develop a written cybersecurity plan that implements the program. The plan must describe how the licensee will implement the program, and account for relevant site-specific conditions. The cybersecurity plan also must provide an incident response and recovery plan that describes the capability for detection and response, mitigation, correcting exploited vulnerabilities, and restoring affected systems.[61]

---

60 10 C.F.R. § 73.54(d).
61 10 C.F.R. § 73.54(e).

4

Cybersecurity and Corporate Governance

CHAPTER MENU

As cybersecurity vulnerabilities increasingly have threatened companies' bottom lines and operational abilities, boards of directors and top executives understandably are concerned about the protection of confidential information and ensuring uninterrupted business operations. A number of federal laws, regulations, and guidelines also require top management to ensure adequate cybersecurity, both as an ongoing part of business operations and as a prerequisite for certain corporate events, such as securities offerings, obtaining foreign investments, and exporting goods.

This chapter reviews some of the legal issues that often arise in these scenarios. First, the chapter reviews the Securities and Exchange Commission's (SEC) expectations for cybersecurity of publicly traded companies, as well as the general fiduciary duty that companies have to shareholders, and how that applies to cybersecurity. The chapter then examines the cybersecurity expectations of the Committee on Foreign Investment in the United States (CFIUS), which reviews foreign investments in U.S. companies. Last, the chapter reviews how export controls restrict cybersecurity research and information sharing.

The laws and regulations discussed in this chapter affect different areas of corporate governance and in some cases are not directly related. SEC regulations require companies to be transparent to investors about cybersecurity challenges and incidents. A fiduciary duty is imposed by courts when companies harm shareholders by egregiously failing to protect against cyber threats. The CFIUS regulations restrict foreign investments that raise cybersecurity

Cybersecurity Law, First Edition. Jeff Kosseff.
© 2017 John Wiley & Sons, Inc. Published 2017 by John Wiley & Sons, Inc.
Companion Website: www.wiley.com/go/kosseff/cybersecurity

concerns. The export controls could limit companies' ability to share urgent cyber-threat information. In all of these areas, the unique, real-time nature of cybersecurity intersects with the slower-paced world of government regulation of large corporations. In all of these cases, the rules are far from settled, creating great uncertainty for executives and boards of directors.

4.1 Securities and Exchange Commission Cybersecurity Expectations for Publicly Traded Companies

The Securities and Exchange Act of 1934, a Depression-era law intended to regulate publicly traded companies, provides the Securities and Exchange Commission with great discretion. Among its comprehensive regulations for publicly traded companies is Regulation S-K, which sets forth the requirements for regular public filings that companies must make with the SEC. Such filings include the 10-Q, a quarterly financial report, the 10-K, a more comprehensive annual financial report, and 8-Ks, which are issued at any time to inform the SEC – and investors – about any material developments. The goal of Regulation S-K – and the SEC's requirement for such filings – is to increase transparency so that investors can make informed decisions.

The SEC has long required companies to make these annual filings in an effort to provide transparency to investors and potential investors. By understanding a company's finances – including its key risks, the SEC believes that investors can make more informed decisions. In a 2016 statement, SEC Chair Mary Jo White explained the rationale for the SEC's requirements for quarterly and annual filings:

> The SEC's disclosure regime is central to our mission to protect investors and the integrity of our capital markets. Since 1934, our disclosure requirements have been designed to foster transparency, honesty, and confidence in the markets so that investors can make informed investment and voting decisions and companies can appropriately access the capital they need. In the modern era, Regulation S-K has become the key tool for furthering these goals and is a central repository for the Commission's rules covering the business and financial information that companies must provide in their filings, including information describing a company's business, risks that the company faces, and management's discussion and analysis of a company's financial condition and results of operations.[1]

---

1 Statement from Chair White on Regulation S-K Concept Release, Apr. 14, 2016.

In recent years, SEC officials have recognized that cybersecurity is among the risks that require greater transparency for investors. In a 2014 speech, White said that the "SEC's formal jurisdiction over cybersecurity is directly focused on the integrity of our market systems, customer data protection, and disclosure of material information."[2] SEC Commissioner Luis A. Aguilar, who has focused on the need for better cybersecurity among U.S. companies, encouraged companies to broadly disclose cybersecurity risks that could impact not only the company, but others. "It is possible that a cyber-attack may not have a direct material adverse impact on the company itself, but that a loss of customers' personal and financial data could have devastating effects on the lives of the company's customers and many Americans," Aguilar said. "In such cases, the right thing to do is to give these victims a heads-up so that they can protect themselves."[3]

Neither the Securities Exchange Act of 1934 nor Regulation S-K explicitly requires companies to disclose cybersecurity risks in their 10-Ks or other SEC filings. However, in October 2011, the SEC's Division of Corporation Finance issued CF Disclosure Guidance: Topic No. 2, Cybersecurity, nonbinding guidance in which it strongly encouraged companies to disclose a range of cybersecurity risks. In the Guidance, the SEC noted the many potential costs and negative consequences that could arise from a cyber incident, including increased costs resulting from remediation, cybersecurity incident preparation, litigation, and reputational harm. While the SEC does acknowledge that its regulations do not explicitly require cybersecurity disclosures, it nonetheless imposes a number of disclosure requirements that obligate registrants to disclose such risks and incidents, and that "material information regarding cybersecurity risks and cyber incidents is required to be disclosed when necessary in order to make other required disclosures, in light of the circumstances under which they are made, not misleading."[4]

In practice, companies typically disclose cybersecurity risks and vulnerabilities in four sections of their 10-K annual reports: (1) Risk factors; (2) Management's discussion and analysis of financial condition and results of operations (MD&A); (3) Description of business; and (4) Legal proceedings.

4.1.1   10-K Disclosures: Risk Factors

The commonly used 10-K section for cybersecurity disclosures is "Risk factors." Regulation S-K requires publicly traded companies to provide a "concise" and logically organized list of "the most significant factors that make

---

2 Opening Statement at SEC Roundtable on Cybersecurity, Chair Mary Jo White (Mar. 26, 2014).
3 Commissioner Luis A. Aguilar, Board of Directors, Corporate Governance and Cyber-Risks: Sharpening the Focus (June 10, 2014).
4 *Id.*

the offering speculative or risky."[5] Regulation S-K instructs companies to explain "how the risk affects the issuer or the securities being offered," and to "[s]et forth each risk factor under a subcaption that adequately describes the risk."[6]

In the 2011 Cybersecurity Guidance, the SEC stated that in determining whether to disclose a cybersecurity risk factor, companies should consider "all available relevant information, including prior cyber incidents and the severity and frequency of those incidents."[7] The SEC requires companies to consider the probability and magnitude of future cyber incidents. The Guidance instructs companies to consider not just the theft of consumer personal information, but also the loss of confidential corporate information and interruptions in business operations.[8]

The SEC's Guidance stated that disclosures under the Risk Factors section of the annual report can include the characteristics of the publicly traded company's business that causes significant cybersecurity risks. For instance, if a company regularly processes customer health information, it likely should note that fact in the Risk Factors section. If a company regularly uses outside service providers to process customer information, it also should consider noting that in the Risk Factors section, according to the SEC Guidance. Companies also should consider describing data breaches and other material cybersecurity incidents. The SEC instructs companies to consider describing "relevant insurance coverage," such as the supplemental cyber insurance discussed in Chapter 2 of this book.[9]

The SEC's Guidance warns companies to avoid "boilerplate" language in their cybersecurity risk factor disclosures, though it noted that companies are not legally required to provide information that would compromise their cybersecurity to hackers. "Instead, registrants should provide sufficient disclosure to allow investors to appreciate the nature of the risks faced by the particular registrant in a manner that would not have that consequence," the SEC wrote.[10]

The SEC's Guidance demonstrates the inherent conflict between the SEC's long-standing rule that companies should be transparent about risk factors, and the unfortunate reality in cybersecurity that information about vulnerabilities can quickly be used against companies by cybercriminals. Companies are still attempting to determine the necessary balance between the two demands,

---

5 17 C.F.R. 229.503.
6 *Id.*
7 SEC, CF Disclosure Guidance: Topic No. 2, Cybersecurity (Oct. 13, 2011).
8 *Id.*
9 *Id.*
10 *Id.*

and as will be seen later in this section, companies have developed a fairly wide range of disclosure practices.

4.1.2 10-K Disclosures: Management's Discussion and Analysis of Financial Condition and Results of Operations (MD&A)

Regulation S-K also requires 10-K filings to include a section entitled "Management's discussion and analysis of financial condition and results of operations" (MD&A), in which the company discusses its changes in its financial condition and the results of its operations.[11] Among the results that companies must describe are "any unusual or infrequent events or transactions or any significant economic changes that materially affected the amount of reported income from continuing operations[.]"[12]

In its Cybersecurity Guidance, the SEC states that companies should discuss cybersecurity in this section if cyber risks or incidents "represent a material event, trend, or uncertainty that is reasonably likely to have a material effect on the registrant's results of operations, liquidity, or financial condition or would cause reported financial information not to be necessarily indicative of future operating results or financial condition."[13]

Companies typically are much more likely to include information about such uncertainties in their discussions about risk factors, although the SEC has not explicitly stated which section should include information about cybersecurity. Often, companies that discuss cybersecurity threats in their MD&A section also have included similar information in the risk factors section.

4.1.3 10-K Disclosures: Description of Business

Regulation S-K requires companies to describe the "general development" of their business over the past five years.[14] In its Cybersecurity Guidance, the SEC states that companies should discuss cybersecurity here if "one or more cyber incidents materially affect a registrant's products, services, relationships with customers or suppliers, or competitive conditions[.]"[15] For instance, the SEC states that if a company's soon-to-be-released product is subject to a cyber vulnerability, it should consider reporting that under "Description of business." In practice, "Description of business" is a relatively rare 10-K section for cybersecurity disclosures, unless the company is in the technology sector and cybersecurity is an essential part of its business.

---

11 17 C.F.R. 229.303.
12 *Id.*
13 SEC, CF Disclosure Guidance: Topic No. 2, Cybersecurity (Oct. 13, 2011).
14 17 C.F.R. 229.101.
15 SEC, CF Disclosure Guidance: Topic No. 2, Cybersecurity (Oct. 13, 2011).

4.1.4   10-K Disclosures: Legal Proceedings

Regulation S-K requires companies to briefly describe "any material pending legal proceedings,"[16] though companies are not required to report "ordinary routine litigation incidental to the business[.]"[17] Regulation S-K states that companies must report legal proceedings if the total claim for damages (arising out of either a single lawsuit or multiple related lawsuits) exceeds 10 percent of the company's current assets.[18] The SEC's Cybersecurity Guidance states that if a data breach compromises a significant amount of customer information, the company "should disclose the name of the court in which the proceedings are pending, the date instituted, the principal parties thereto, a description of the factual basis alleged to underlie the litigation, and the relief sought."[19]

4.1.5   10-K Disclosures: Examples

To provide a better understanding of how companies interpret the SEC's expectation for cybersecurity disclosures, below are excerpts from 10-K filings from large publicly traded companies. As you can see, companies take a wide range of approaches. Some disclose threats and potential threats in detail, while others provide general statements about threats to confidential information and business operations.

4.1.5.1   Wal-Mart

Wal-Mart, the largest company on the Fortune 500 list of publicly traded U.S. companies, provides unusually extensive disclosures about its cybersecurity vulnerabilities. In its "Risk factors" section, Wal-Mart describes the general steps that it takes to guard against various cyberattacks, the impact that disruptions of its primary and back-up computer systems would have on Wal-Mart's operations, potential disruptions to its important e-commerce business, and the costs and reputational harm of data breaches that reveal customer information.

Excerpts from Wal-Mart 10-K Filing, March 30, 2016

> **We rely extensively on information systems to process transactions, summarize results and manage our business. Disruptions in both our primary and secondary (back-up) systems could harm our ability to conduct our operations.**
>
> Although we have independent, redundant and physically separate primary and secondary information systems, given the number of individual transactions we have each year, it is critical

---

16 17 C.F.R. 229.103.
17 *Id.*
18 *Id.*
19 SEC, CF Disclosure Guidance: Topic No. 2, Cybersecurity (Oct. 13, 2011).

that we maintain uninterrupted operation of our business-critical information systems. Our information systems, including our back-up systems, are subject to damage or interruption from power outages, computer and telecommunications failures, computer viruses, worms, other malicious computer programs, denial-of-service attacks, security breaches (through cyberattacks from cyber-attackers and sophisticated organizations), catastrophic events such as fires, tornadoes, earthquakes and hurricanes, and usage errors by our associates. If our information systems and our back-up systems are damaged, breached or cease to function properly, we may have to make a significant investment to repair or replace them, and we may suffer interruptions in our operations in the interim. Any material interruption in both our information systems and back-up systems may have a material adverse effect on our business or results of operations. In addition, we are pursuing complex initiatives to transform our information technology processes and systems, which will include, for many of our information systems, establishing common processes across our lines of business. The risk of system disruption is increased when significant system changes are undertaken, although we believe that our change management process will mitigate this risk. If we fail to integrate our information systems and processes, we may fail to realize the cost savings anticipated to be derived from these initiatives.

If the technology-based systems that give our customers the ability to shop with us online do not function effectively, our operating results, as well as our ability to grow our e-commerce business globally, could be materially adversely affected.

Many of our customers shop with us over our e-commerce websites and mobile commerce applications, including walmart.com and samsclub.com in the U.S. and our retail websites in 10 other countries, which are a part of our multi-channel sales strategy. Increasingly, customers are using computers, tablets, and smart phones to shop online and through mobile commerce applications with us and with our competitors and to do comparison shopping. We are increasingly using social media to interact with our customers and as a means to enhance their shopping experience. As a part of our multi-channel sales strategy, we offer "Walmart Pickup" and "Club Pickup" and in a growing number of locations, "Online Grocery" programs under which many products available for purchase online can be shipped to and picked up by the customer at his or her local Walmart store or Sam's Club, which provides additional customer traffic at such stores and clubs. Multi-channel retailing is a rapidly evolving part of the retail industry and of our operations in the U.S. and in a number of markets in which our Walmart International segment operates.

We must anticipate and meet our customers' changing expectations while adjusting for new developments and technology investments by our competitors through focusing on the building and delivery of a seamless shopping experience across all channels by each operating segment. Any failure on our part to provide attractive, user-friendly e-commerce platforms that offer a wide assortment of merchandise at competitive prices and with low cost and rapid delivery options and that continually meet the changing expectations of online shoppers and developments in online and mobile commerce application merchandising and related technology could place us at a competitive disadvantage, result in the loss of e-commerce and other sales, harm our reputation with customers, have a material adverse impact on the growth of our e-commerce business globally and could have a material adverse impact on our business and results of operations.

Any failure to maintain the security of the information relating to our company, customers, members, associates and vendors that we hold, whether as a result of cybersecurity attacks on our information systems or otherwise, could damage our reputation with customers, members, associates, vendors and others, could cause us to incur substantial additional costs and to become subject to litigation, and could materially adversely affect our operating results.

As do most retailers, we receive and store in our digital information systems certain personal information about our customers and members, and we receive and store personal information concerning our associates and vendors. We also utilize third-party service providers for a variety of reasons, including, without limitation, encryption and authentication technology, content delivery to customers, back-office support, and other functions. In addition, our online operations at www.walmart.com, www.samsclub.com and our websites in certain of our foreign markets depend upon the secure transmission of confidential information over public networks, including information permitting cashless payments. Each year, cyber-attackers make numerous attempts to access the information stored in our information systems. We maintain substantial security measures to protect, and to prevent unauthorized access to, such information and have security processes, protocols and standards that are applicable to our third-party service providers to protect information from our systems to which they have access under their engagements with us.

However, we or our third-party service providers may be unable to anticipate one or more of the rapidly evolving and increasingly sophisticated means by which cyber-attackers may attempt to defeat our security measures or those of our third-party service providers and breach our or our third-party service providers' information systems. During fiscal 2016, we were notified that a third-party service provider that hosts the online photo center for Walmart Canada suffered a security breach that compromised information of users of that company's site, including some Walmart Canada customers, which we believe has not had a material impact on Walmart Canada or the Company. Walmart Canada discontinued use of this third-party service provider. Sam's Club in the United States also used the same third-party service provider to host its online photo center through a different system than the one used by Walmart Canada. After the breach in Canada, Sam's Club suspended the operation of the online photo center until a security review could be completed by the third-party service provider. Once the security review was complete and new technology with enhanced security measures was implemented by the third-party service provider, along with a determination that the information of Sam's Club members was not compromised by the security breach, Sam's Club resumed the operation of the online photo center through the same third-party service provider.

Cyber threats are rapidly evolving and are becoming increasingly sophisticated. As cyber threats evolve and become more difficult to detect and successfully defend against, one or more cyber threats might defeat our security measures or those of our third-party service providers in the future like the incident referenced above and obtain the personal information of customers, members, associates and vendors that we hold or to which our third-party service providers have access, and we or our third-party service providers may not discover any security breach and loss of information for a significant period of time after the security breach occurs. Moreover, associate error or malfeasance, faulty password management or other irregularities may result in a defeat of our or our third-party service providers' security measures and breach our or our third-party service providers' information systems (whether digital or otherwise).

Any breach of our security measures or those of our third-party service providers and loss of our confidential information, which could be undetected for a period of time, or any failure by us to comply with applicable privacy and information security laws and regulations could cause us to incur significant costs to protect any customers and members whose personal data was compromised and to restore customer and member confidence in us and to make changes to our information systems and administrative processes to address security issues and compliance with applicable laws and regulations.

In addition, such events could materially adversely affect our reputation with our customers, members, associates, vendors and shareholders, as well as our operations, results of operations, financial condition and liquidity, could result in the release to the public of confidential information about our operations and financial condition and performance and could result in litigation against us or the imposition of penalties, fines, fees or liabilities, which may not be covered by our insurance policies. Moreover, a security breach could require us to devote significant management resources to address the problems created by the security breach and to expend significant additional resources to upgrade further the security measures that we employ to guard such important personal information against cyberattacks and other attempts to access such information and could result in a disruption of our operations, particularly our digital retail operations.

We accept payments using a variety of methods, including cash, checks, credit and debit cards, our private label cards and gift cards, and we may offer new payment options over time, which may have information security risk implications. By accepting debit and credit cards as a retailer for payment, we are subject to the Payment Card Industry Data Security Standard ("PCI DSS"), issued by the Payment Card Industry Security Standards Council. PCI DSS contains compliance guidelines and standards with regard to our security surrounding the physical and electronic storage, processing and transmission of individual cardholder data. The payment card industry set October 1, 2015 as the date on which it will shift liability for certain transactions to retailers who are not able to accept Europay, MasterCard, Visa (EMV) chip card credit and debit transactions. While we already accept many EMV cards, if we are unable to fully implement EMV as planned, we may incur increased costs associated with the liability shift. By accepting debit cards for payment, we are also subject to compliance with the American National Standards Institute encryption standards and payment network security operating guidelines. Even though we comply with these guidelines and standards and other information security measures, we cannot be certain that the security measures we maintain to protect all of our information technology systems are able to prevent, contain or detect any cyberattacks, cyber terrorism, or security breaches from known malware or malware that may be developed in the future. To the extent that any disruption results in the loss, damage or misappropriation of information, we may be materially adversely affected by claims from customers, financial institutions, regulatory authorities, payment card networks and others. In addition, the cost of complying with stricter privacy and information security laws and standards could be significant to us.

4.1.5.2 Berkshire Hathaway

Wal-Mart's extensive disclosures reflect, in part, the large amount of sensitive consumer data that it handles on a regular basis. Some large companies that do not deal directly with consumers tend to have more abbreviated cybersecurity disclosures. For instance, consider investment firm Berkshire Hathaway's "Risk factors" disclosure, which focuses primarily on potential harms to its operations.

Excerpts from Berkshire Hathaway 10-K Filing, Feb. 26, 2016

Cyber security risks

We rely on information technology in virtually all aspects of our business. A significant disruption or failure of our information technology systems could result in service interruptions, safety failures, security violations, regulatory compliance failures, an inability to protect information and assets against intruders, and other operational difficulties. Attacks perpetrated against our information systems could result in loss of assets and critical information and exposes us to remediation costs and reputational damage.

Although we have taken steps intended to mitigate these risks, including business continuity planning, disaster recovery planning and business impact analysis, a significant disruption or cyber intrusion could lead to misappropriation of assets or data corruption and could adversely affect our results of operations, financial condition and liquidity. Additionally, if we are unable to acquire or implement new technology, we may suffer a competitive disadvantage, which could also have an adverse effect on our results of operations, financial condition and liquidity.

Cyber attacks could further adversely affect our ability to operate facilities, information technology and business systems, or compromise confidential customer and employee information. Political, economic, social or financial market instability or damage to or interference with our operating assets, or our customers or suppliers may result in business interruptions, lost revenue, higher commodity prices, disruption in fuel supplies, lower energy consumption, unstable markets, increased security and repair or other costs, any of which may materially adversely affect us in ways that cannot be predicted at this time. Any of these risks could materially affect our consolidated financial results. Furthermore, instability in the financial markets as a result of terrorism, sustained or significant cyber attacks, or war could also materially adversely affect our ability to raise capital.

4.1.5.3 Target Corp

Companies that have experienced high-profile data breaches are more likely to report significant cybersecurity vulnerabilities in their 10-K reports. For instance, Target, which experienced a large data breach during the 2013 holiday shopping season, was still discussing the impact of the incident in the 10-K report that it filed in March 2016. In light of the high profile of the data breach, Target acknowledged that cybersecurity could affect not only costs of litigation and remediation, but also could reduce revenues by harming the retailer's reputation. Due to the high stakes of the various lawsuits that arose from the data breach, Target discussed cybersecurity not only in its "Risk factors" section, but it also specifically discussed the ongoing cost of the legal proceedings in a note to its consolidated financial statements.

Excerpts from Target 10-K Filing, March 11, 2016

Technology Investments and Infrastructure Risks

If our capital investments in technology, supply chain, new stores and remodeling existing stores do not achieve appropriate returns, our competitive position, financial condition and results of operations may be adversely affected.

Our business is becoming increasingly reliant on technology investments, and the returns on these investments can be less predictable than building new stores and remodeling existing stores. We are currently making, and will continue to make, significant technology investments to support our efforts to provide a consistent guest experience across all sales channels, implement improvements to our guest-facing technology, and evolve our supply chain and our inventory management systems, information processes, and computer systems to more efficiently run our business and remain competitive and relevant to our guests. These technology initiatives might not provide the anticipated benefits or may provide them on a delayed schedule or at a higher cost. We must monitor and choose the right investments and implement them at the right pace, which depends on our ability to accurately forecast our needs and is influenced by the amount and pace of investments by our competitors. In addition, our growth also depends, in part, on our ability to build new stores and remodel existing stores in a manner that achieves appropriate returns on our capital investment. We compete with other retailers and businesses for suitable locations for our stores. Many of our expected new store sites are smaller and non-standard footprints located in fully developed markets, which require changes to our supply chain practices and are generally more time-consuming, expensive and uncertain undertakings than expansion into undeveloped suburban and ex-urban markets. Targeting the wrong opportunities, failing to make the best investments, or making an investment commitment significantly above or below our needs could result in the loss of our competitive position and adversely impact our financial condition or results of operations.

A significant disruption in our computer systems and our inability to adequately maintain and update those systems could adversely affect our operations and our ability to maintain guest confidence.

We rely extensively on our computer systems to manage and account for inventory, process guest transactions, manage and maintain the privacy of guest data, communicate with our vendors and other third parties, service REDcard accounts, summarize and analyze results, and on continued and unimpeded access to the Internet to use our computer systems. Our systems are subject to damage or interruption from power outages, telecommunications failures, computer viruses and malicious attacks, security breaches and catastrophic events. If our systems are damaged or fail to function properly or reliably, we may incur substantial repair or replacement costs, experience data loss or theft and impediments to our ability to manage inventories or process guest transactions, engage in additional promotional activities to retain our guests, and encounter lost guest confidence, which could adversely affect our results of operations.

We continually make significant technology investments that will help maintain and update our existing computer systems. Implementing significant system changes increases the risk of computer system disruption. The potential problems and interruptions associated with implementing technology initiatives could disrupt or reduce our operational efficiency, and could negatively impact guest experience and guest confidence.

Data Security and Privacy Risks
If our efforts to protect the security of information about our guests, team members and vendors are unsuccessful, we may face additional costly government enforcement actions and private litigation, and our sales and reputation could suffer.

An important component of our business involves the receipt and storage of information about our guests, team members, and vendors. We have programs in place to detect, contain and respond to data security incidents. However, because the techniques used to obtain unauthorized access, disable or degrade service, or sabotage systems change frequently and may be difficult to detect for long periods of time, we may be unable to anticipate these techniques or implement adequate preventive measures. In addition, hardware, software, or applications we develop or procure from third parties may contain defects in design or manufacture or other problems that could unexpectedly compromise information security. Unauthorized parties may also attempt to gain access to our systems or facilities, or those of third parties with whom we do business, through fraud, trickery, or other forms of deceiving our team members, contractors, vendors, and temporary staff.

Until the data breach in the fourth quarter of 2013, all incidents we experienced were insignificant. The data breach we experienced in 2013 was significant and went undetected for several weeks. Both we and our vendors have experienced data security incidents subsequent to the 2013 data breach; however, to date these other incidents have not been material to our consolidated financial statements. Based on the prominence and notoriety of the 2013 data breach, even minor additional data security incidents could draw greater scrutiny. If we or our vendors experience additional significant data security breaches or fail to detect and appropriately respond to significant data security breaches, we could be exposed to additional government enforcement actions and private litigation. In addition, our guests could lose confidence in our ability to protect their information, which could cause them to discontinue using our REDcards or loyalty programs, or stop shopping with us altogether.

Note 19 to Consolidated Financial Statements

As previously reported, in the fourth quarter of 2013, we experienced a data breach in which an intruder stole certain payment card and other guest information from our network (the Data Breach), which resulted in a number of claims against us, several of which have been finally or preliminarily resolved as follows:

Payment Card Network Claims. Each of the four major payment card networks made a written claim against us regarding the Data Breach. During 2015 we entered into settlement agreements with all four networks.

Consumer Class Action. A class action suit was asserted on behalf of a class of guests whose information was compromised in the Data Breach. This action was settled and received Court approval during 2015, but is being appealed by several objecting parties. We believe the settlement terms will be maintained on appeal.

Financial Institutions Class Action. A class action was asserted on behalf of financial institution issuers of credit cards impacted by the Data Breach. This action was settled and received preliminary Court approval in the fourth quarter of 2015. A hearing for final Court approval of the settlement is scheduled for the second quarter of our fiscal 2016.

Actions related to the Data Breach that remain pending are: (1) one action previously filed in Canada; (2) several putative class action suits brought on behalf of shareholders; and (3) ongoing investigations by State Attorneys General and the Federal Trade Commission.

Our accrual for estimated probable losses is based on actual settlements reached to date and the expectation of negotiated settlements in the pending actions. We have not based our accrual on any determination that it is probable we would be found liable for the losses we have accrued were these claims to be litigated. While our estimates may change as new information becomes available, we do not believe any adjustments will be material.

We recorded $39 million of pretax Data Breach-related expenses during 2015. Along with legal and other professional services, expenses included an adjustment to the accrual based on refined estimates of our probable exposure. We recorded $191 million of Data Breach-related expenses, partially offset by expected insurance proceeds of $46 million, for net expenses of $145 million during 2014. These expenses were included in our Consolidated Statements of Operations as SG&A, but were not part of segment results.

Since the Data Breach, we have incurred $291 million of cumulative expenses, partially offset by expected insurance recoveries of $90 million, for net cumulative expenses of $201 million.

4.1.6 Disclosing Data Breaches to Investors

The 10-K is an annual report that requires publicly traded companies to disclose significant events of the past year and forward-looking risks. However, a data breach could have immediate consequences for a company's finances and, in some cases, viability. It is becoming increasingly common for companies to file an "8-K" form (known as a "current report") to notify investors soon after a data breach occurs.

In its cybersecurity guidance, the SEC provided little direction as to when such updates are necessary, merely stating that companies should consider whether it is necessary to file 8-K reports "to disclose the costs and other consequences of material cyber incidents."[20] The form 8-K merely states that companies may choose to file 8-K's of "other events" that the company "deems of importance to security holders."

In many cases, investors already are well aware of high-profile data breaches, due to the state data breach reporting requirements discussed in Chapter 1 of this book. Without any clear guidance on the topic from the SEC, companies have developed different approaches. Some do not disclose cyber incidents on separate 8-K's, either mentioning the incidents in their 10-K report or determining that the incidents are not material. Some companies file 8-K reports around the same time that they disclose incidents to state regulators and consumers. And other companies delay their notifications.

Target, for instance, publicly disclosed its large data breach on December 19, 2013. It did not immediately file an 8-K report, and began to receive substantial criticism. On January 30, 2014, lawyers published a commentary piece in which they questioned the lack of an 8-K, writing, "Target's securities lawyers may believe that the breach is not 'important to security holders,' or is not sufficiently material enough to the roughly $38 billion company to warrant an 8-K filing, but 70 million to 110 million affected customers is hardly immaterial, even for Target."[21] Sen. Jay Rockefeller chimed in, sending a letter to Target's chief executive, asking why the company "appears to be ignoring SEC rules that require you to disclose to the SEC and your investors the costs and business consequences of this recent data breach."[22]

On February 26, 2014 – more than two months after the initial public disclosure – Target filed an 8-K in which it disclosed the breach to investors. The filing amended the risk factors section of its 10-K, and stated, in part:

> The data breach we experienced in 2013 has resulted in government inquiries and private litigation, and if our efforts to protect the security of personal information about our guests and team members are unsuccessful, future issues may result in additional costly government enforcement actions and private litigation and our sales and reputation could suffer.
>
> A significant disruption in our computer systems and our inability to adequately maintain and update those systems could adversely affect our operations and our ability to maintain guest confidence.
>
> We experienced a significant data security breach in the fourth quarter of fiscal 2013 and are not yet able to determine the full extent of its impact and the impact of government investigations

---

20 SEC, CF Disclosure Guidance: Topic No. 2, Cybersecurity (Oct. 13, 2011).
21 Cynthia J. Larose, *To 8-K or Not – For Target, That is Indeed the Question*, Law 360 (Jan. 30, 2014).
22 *Id.*

and private litigation on our results of operations, which could be material.[23]

The widespread criticism of Target's failure to more promptly notify investors has caused an increasing number of companies to file 8-Ks soon after they publicly report data breaches. Although the SEC has not explicitly stated that companies must do so, there always is a risk that regulators may eventually expect such reporting, as the 8-K requirements are ambiguous. Moreover, prompt disclosure of cyber incidents to shareholders weakens potential claims in shareholder derivative lawsuits, as discussed below.

Some companies file 8-Ks about major data breaches in a much more expeditious manner. For instance, on September 2, 2014, Home Depot began investigating blog reports of a data breach on its systems. Home Depot soon discovered that hackers accessed approximately 56 million payment card numbers of its retail customers from April to September 2014.[24] On September 18, 2014, Home Depot publicly announced its findings. On the same day, Home Depot filed an 8-K with the SEC, in which it stated, in part:

> The investigation into a possible breach began on Tuesday morning, September 2, immediately after The Home Depot received reports from its banking partners and law enforcement that criminals may have breached its systems.
>
> Since then, the Company's IT security team has been working around the clock with leading IT security firms, its banking partners and the Secret Service to rapidly gather facts, resolve the problem and provide information to customers.
>
> The Company's ongoing investigation has determined the following:
>
> > Criminals used unique, custom-built malware to evade detection. The malware had not been seen previously in other attacks, according to Home Depot's security partners. The cyber-attack is estimated to have put payment card information at risk for approximately 56 million unique payment cards.
> > The malware is believed to have been present between April and September 2014.
>
> To protect customer data until the malware was eliminated, any terminals identified with malware were taken out of service, and the Company quickly put in place other security enhancements. The

---

23 Target Corp., 8-K Filing, Feb. 26, 2014.
24 Brian Krebs, *Home Depot: 56M Cards Impacted, Malware Contained*, KREBS ON SECURITY (Sept. 18, 2014).

hackers' method of entry has been closed off, the malware has been eliminated from the Company's systems, and the Company has rolled out enhanced encryption of payment data to all U.S. stores.

There is no evidence that debit PIN numbers were compromised or that the breach has impacted stores in Mexico or customers who shopped online at HomeDepot.com or HomeDepot.ca.

The Home Depot is offering free identity protection services, including credit monitoring, to any customer who used a payment card at a Home Depot store in 2014, from April on.[25]

Home Depot's filing is a model for prompt and responsible disclosure of a cybersecurity incident. Although the SEC does not have a threshold requirement for 8-K filings regarding data breaches, it is clear that the breach of more than 50 million customers' credit and debit card information will lead to significant legal liability (and Home Depot quickly faced multiple lawsuits). Home Depot's 8-K clearly describes what its investigation uncovered, and the steps that Home Depot has taken to mitigate damage. Home Depot provided enough detail to paint a useful picture of the situation for investors, but it did not "over-disclose" and provide information that hackers could use to further exploit its network and systems.

4.2 Fiduciary Duty to Shareholders and Derivative Lawsuits Arising from Data Breaches

If a data breach causes significant harm to a company, shareholders may attempt to bring a suit, known as "derivative litigation," against company officers who they allege were responsible for the harm. The lawsuits often arise under the state laws of Delaware, where many large U.S. corporations are incorporated.

Derivative lawsuits often arise when shareholders claim that directors breached their "fiduciary duty" of care to the company by allowing serious harm to occur. Delaware courts have stated that such a breach occurs when the directors caused or "allowed a situation to develop and continue which exposed to corporation to enormous legal liability and that in doing so they violated a duty to be active monitors of corporate performance."[26] The Delaware Court of Chancery stated that among the harms that could be the basis of derivative suits are: "regulatory sanctions, criminal or civil fines, environmental disasters, accounting restatements, misconduct by officers or employees, massive business losses, and innumerable other potential calamities."[27] Typically, boards of directors will not approve a lawsuit against their own officials. In that case, plaintiffs file a derivative lawsuit, seeking permission to sue the officials on behalf of the company.

---

25 Home Depot, 8-K Filing (Sept. 16, 2014).
26 *In re* Caremark Int'l Inc. Deriv. Litig., 698 A.2d 959, 967 (Del.Ch. 1996).
27 Louisiana Municipal Police v. Pyott, 46 A.3d 313, 2012 (Del. Ct. Chancery 2012).

Shareholders must meet a high hurdle before being permitted to sue on behalf of the company, as courts typically presume that directors and officers make decisions that they believe, in good faith, to be in the companies' best interests.[28] To defeat this presumption, known as the business judgment rule, plaintiffs must demonstrate that the board's refusal to sue was made in "bad faith" or "based on an unreasonable investigation."[29]

To demonstrate that a board refused to bring a suit in bad faith, the plaintiffs must establish that the board utterly failed to meet its obligations to the corporation and shareholders. Among the scenarios that Delaware courts have concluded would constitute bad faith:

- the directors intentionally acted with a purpose that was not intended to advance the company's best interests;
- the directors intentionally violated the law; or
- the directors intentionally failed "to act in the face of a known duty to act, demonstrating a conscious disregard" for their duties.[30]

The third scenario could be the basis of a data breach related derivative lawsuit. Shareholders claim that the directors failed to adequately monitor a company's data security, therefore causing harm to the company.[31]

There have been few published court opinions regarding derivative lawsuits arising from data breaches. In 2014, a New Jersey federal court (applying Delaware law) dismissed a lawsuit against Wyndham Worldwide Corporation officials arising from the data breach discussed in Chapter 1.[32] The court rejected two attempts by the plaintiffs to overcome the business judgment rule. First, the plaintiffs argued that the board did not act in good faith because it was represented by the same counsel in the FTC action and the shareholder demand for a lawsuit.[33] The court held that counsel's duties were not conflicting; rather, in both instances, it was responsible for acting in Wyndham's best interests.[34] Second the plaintiffs argued that the board failed to reasonably

---

28 *See* Stone ex rel. AmSouth Bancorporation v. Ritter, 911 A.2d 362, 364, 373 (Del. 2006) ("[D]irectors' good faith exercise of oversight responsibility may not invariably prevent employees from violating criminal laws, or from causing the corporation to incur significant financial liability, or both.").

29 *In re* Merrill Lynch & Co., 773 F. Supp. 2d 330, 351 (S.D.N.Y. 2011).

30 *In re* Walt Disney Co. Deriv. Litig., 906 A.2d 27, 67 (Del.2006) (quoting *In re* Walt Disney Co. Deriv. Litig., 907 A.2d 693, 755-56 (Del.Ch.2005), aff'd, 906 A.2d 27 (Del.2006)).

31 *See* Stone ex rel. AmSouth Bancorporation v. Ritter, 911 A.2d 362, 364, 369 (Del.2006) ("The third of these examples describes, and is fully consistent with, the lack of good faith conduct that the *Caremark* court held was a "necessary condition" for director oversight liability, i.e., "a sustained or systematic failure of the board to exercise oversight – such as an utter failure to attempt to assure a reasonable information and reporting system exists.").

32 Palkon ex. Rel. Wyndham Worldwide Corp. Civil Action No. 2:14-CV-01234 (SRC) (D. N.J. Oct. 20, 2014).

33 *Id.*

34 *Id.*

investigate the demand to bring a lawsuit. The court similarly rejected this argument, reasoning that board members had discussed the breaches at fourteen board meetings between October 2008 and August 2012, and that the board's audit committee routinely discussed the breaches, and therefore, those investigations alone "would indicate that the Board had enough information when it assessed Plaintiff's claim."[35] The Wyndham case demonstrates the difficulty of bringing a viable shareholder derivative claim even in cases in which the company likely was not providing adequate oversight of its cybersecurity.

Although shareholders have not yet been successful in data breach-related derivative lawsuits, that very well may change as data breaches increasingly put the viability of publicly traded companies at risk. While cybercrime and breaches were at one point a minor annoyance that resulted in some negative publicity, they now can put a company's future at risk, due to the sophistication of the attacks. Accordingly, companies should be aware of the very real possibility that, in the future, shareholders could succeed in a lawsuit against corporate officials due to a serious data breach.

4.3 Committee on Foreign Investment in the United States and Cybersecurity

Cybersecurity also has become a significant concern when foreign investors seek to invest money in U.S. companies. Policy makers worry that foreign control of U.S. technology companies could expose the United States to national security vulnerabilities.

All investments that would result in foreign control of a U.S. business must first be reviewed by the Committee on Foreign Investment in the United States (CFIUS). CFIUS is an interagency committee that is chaired by the Secretary of Treasury, and also includes the Attorney General, Secretary of Homeland Security, Secretary of Commerce, Secretary of Defense, Secretary of State, Secretary of Energy, U.S. Trade Representative, and Director of the White House Office of Science and Technology Policy.

In recent years, Congress and CFIUS have been concerned that the attempts of investors in some countries – in particular, China – to acquire U.S. technology companies could undercut U.S. security. In a report to Congress for 2014, CFIUS wrote that it believes that "there may be an effort among foreign governments or companies to acquire U.S. companies involved in research, development, or production of critical technologies for which the United States is a leading producer."[36]

---

35 *Id.*
36 Committee on Foreign Investment in the United States, Annual Report to Congress, CY 2014 at 29.

Among the highest profile cybersecurity-related concerns in a CFIUS matter was Japan-based SoftBank's acquisition of a majority interest in Sprint Nextel Corp. Congressman Mike Rogers, then-Chairman of the House Intelligence Committee, raised concerns that Softbank would require Sprint to use equipment from China-based Huawai Technologies in its U.S. telecommunications network, a move that could compromise the security of U.S. communications.[37] In a report issued by Rogers' committee the previous year, his staff investigated national security concerns related to Huawei and ZTE, the two largest China-based telecommunications equipment makers. The report concluded that the "risks associated with Huawei's and ZTE's provision of equipment to U.S. critical infrastructure could undermine core U.S. national-security interests."[38] The House Committee urged CFIUS to block any acquisitions involving Huawei and ZTE. To obtain CFIUS approval, Sprint and SoftBank agreed that they would not use Huawei equipment, and that the U.S. government could veto any new equipment purchased by Sprint for use on its network.[39] The quick response and agreement to provide the U.S. government such leeway over the company's operations demonstrated a renewed focus on cybersecurity by CFIUS, as well as a recognition by industry that CFIUS has significant leverage in such deals.

CFIUS conducts much of its review proceedings confidentially, so therefore there is not significant guidance as to exactly what cybersecurity measures U.S. companies must take in order to satisfy CFIUS. However, in November 2008, CFIUS revised its operating regulations to require applicants to include a copy of its cybersecurity plan, if any, "that will be used to protect against cyber attacks on the operation, design, and development of the U.S. business' services, networks, systems, data storage, and facilities."[40] In its commentary to the 2008 regulations, CFIUS noted that this requirement applies to all companies – not just technology businesses – and that the regulations do not require a particular form of cybersecurity plan to satisfy CFIUS.

In practice, companies are less likely to face cybersecurity-related obstacles with CFIUS if they provide a thorough description of their access and authorization procedures, cybersecurity safeguards, internal security organization, incident response plan, and other standard cybersecurity safeguards. Moreover, companies are more likely to face CFIUS-related cybersecurity scrutiny if they provide critical infrastructure (e.g., a cellular phone carrier or electric utility) or have a direct relationship to national security (e.g., a defense contractor).

---

37 Elizabeth Wasserman and Todd Shields, *Softbank, Sprint Pledge Not to Use Huawei, Lawmaker Says*, BLOOMBERG TECHNOLOGY (Mar. 28, 2013).

38 HOUSE PERMANENT SELECT COMMITTEE ON INTELLIGENCE, INVESTIGATIVE REPORT ON THE U.S. NATIONAL SECURITY ISSUES POSED BY CHINESE TELECOMMUNICATIONS COMPANIES HUAWEI AND ZTE (Oct. 8, 2012).

39 Alina Selyukh and Nathan Layne, *Spring, SoftBank Reach Deal with U.S. over Security Concerns*, REUTERS (May 28, 2013).

40 31 C.F.R. 800.402.

4.4 Export Controls and the Wassenaar Arrangement

Countries around the world have long participated in informal agreements to control the export of guns, military aircraft, missiles, and other weapons that can harm national security. In recent years, there has been growing concern that these controls could constrain companies' ability to implement cybersecurity protections and share information about vulnerabilities.

The United States and forty other nations participate in the Wassenaar Arrangement, under which they agree to broad categories of export controls. The Wassenaar Arrangement is not a formal treaty, and nations are not legally bound by its terms. However, the United States and other participating nations traditionally have enacted regulations to comply with the Wassenaar Arrangement, in an effort to create an international set of norms for this important national security issue.

In recent years, many participating nations have been concerned about dictatorial governments' use of surveillance technology to suppress dissenting voices. In December 2013, to address these concerns, the United Kingdom successfully led a campaign to amend the Wassenaar Arrangement to add certain types of "intrusion software" to the list of technologies that should be subject to export controls.[41]

The Wassenaar Arrangement's 2013 amendments broadly define "intrusion software" in this way:

> "Software" specially designed or modified to avoid detection by 'monitoring tools', or to defeat 'protective countermeasures', of a computer or network capable device, and performing any of the following:
>
> a. The extraction of data or information, from a computer or network capable device, or the modification of system or user data; or
> b. The modification of the standard execution path of a program or process in order to allow the execution of externally provided instructions.

---

41 *See* Written Testimony of Cristin Flynn Goodwin, Microsoft Corporation, Oversight and Government Reform Subcommittee on Information Technology, Homeland Security Subcommittee on Cybersecurity, Infrastructure Protection, and Security Technologies, Joint Subcommittee on Wassenaar: Cybersecurity & Export Control (Jan. 12, 2016) at 2–3 ("Although many Wassenaar proceedings are confidential, Microsoft understand that the original intent behind these controls was to restrict the export of sophisticated surveillance systems to authoritarian governments. Such systems, like those developed and sold by companies like Gamma Group (owner of FinFisher) and Hacking Team are reportedly used to spy on or otherwise repress political dissidents and other citizens. These sophisticated turnkey systems are claimed to permit the targeting and monitoring of an individual's phone calls, emails, and other communications.").

The Wassenaar Arrangement then adds the following types of technologies to the export control list:

4. A. 5. Systems, equipment, and components therefore, specially designed or modified for the generation, operation or delivery of, or communication with, "intrusion software."

4. D. 4. "Software" specially designed or modified for the generation, operation or delivery of, or communication with, "intrusion software."

4. E. 1. c. "Technology" for the "development" of "intrusion software."

4. D. 1. a. "Software" specially designed or modified for the "development" or "production" of equipment or "software" specified by 4.A. or 4.D.

4. E. 1. "Technology" according to the General Technology Note, for the "development," "production" or "use" of equipment or "software" specified by 4.A. or 4.D.

The Wassenaar Arrangement notes that the export controls do not apply to technology that is "the minimum necessary for the installation, operation, maintenance (checking) or repair of those items which are not controlled or whose export has been authorized," nor do they apply to technology that is in the public domain or for "basic scientific research." Despite these exceptions, a number of advocacy groups worried that this definition of "intrusion software" is so broad that it could effectively prohibit the international sharing of tools that are used in cybersecurity research.[42]

The advocacy groups – and many large technology companies – became even more concerned in 2015, when the U.S. Department of Commerce proposed rules to implement the 2013 amendments to the Wassenaar Arrangement. The U.S. proposal would have added the following technologies to the list of U.S. export controls:

Systems, equipment, components and software specially designed for the generation, operation or delivery of, or communication with, intrusion software include network penetration testing products that use intrusion software to identify vulnerabilities of computers and network-capable devices.

---

42 *See* Nate Cardozo and Eva Galperin, *What is the U.S. doing about Wassenaar, and Why do We Need to Fight It?* Electronic Frontier Foundation (May 28, 2015) ("We have significant problems with even the narrow Wassenaar language; the definition risks sweeping up many of the common and perfectly legitimate tools used in security research.").

> Technology for the development of intrusion software includes proprietary research on the vulnerabilities and exploitation of computers and network-capable devices.[43]

Advocacy groups and technology companies united in fierce opposition to the U.S. proposal, stating that it was even more sweeping than the Wassenaar Arrangement, and would effectively prohibit technology companies from sharing legitimate information about emerging cybersecurity threats.[44] Rather than collaborating in real time to fight urgent cybersecurity threats, the companies and researchers would be required to seek a license from regulators. A Microsoft attorney told a congressional committee that, due to the Wassenaar Arrangement, a cybersecurity conference in Japan was canceled.[45]

In light of the strong opposition to the Wassenaar Arrangement and the U.S. proposal to implement the controls on intrusion software, the Obama administration announced in February 2016 that it would attempt to renegotiate the Wassenaar Arrangement to prevent a negative impact on cybersecurity research.[46] In light of the widespread concern about authoritarian regimes' surveillance, it is unclear as of the publication of this book whether U.S. efforts to renegotiate the Wassenaar Arrangement will be successful.

The widespread concern over the Wassenaar Arrangement – and the strong opposition of consumer advocacy groups and technology companies – demonstrates the difficulty that governments and companies have when attempting to fight real-time cybersecurity threats while at the same time preserving national security. Perhaps more than most other national security threats,

---

43 Department of Commerce, Bureau of Industry and Security, Wassenaar Arrangement 2013 Plenary Agreements Implementation: Intrusion and Surveillance Items 80 Fed. Reg. 28853 (May 20, 2015).

44 *See, e.g.,* Prepared Testimony and Statement for the Record of Cheri F. McGuire, Vice President, Global Government Affairs & Cybersecurity Policy, Symantec Corporation, Before the House Committee on Homeland Security, Subcommittee on Cybersecurity, Infrastructure Protection, and Security Technologies (Jan. 12, 2016) at 1 ("These restrictions would devastate the U.S. cybersecurity industry itself and harm the security of nearly every U.S. multinational company. This rule is not an export control on a few specific tools. It is a stringent new regulation on the entire cybersecurity industry and its customers that would harm the economic and national security of the U.S. Ultimately, it would leave every American less protected against cybercriminals and cyber terrorists.").

45 *See* Written Testimony of Cristin Flynn Goodwin, Microsoft Corporation, Oversight and Government Reform Subcommittee on Information Technology, Homeland Security Subcommittee on Cybersecurity, Infrastructure Protection, and Security Technologies, Joint Subcommittee on WASSENAAR: CYBERSECURITY & EXPORT CONTROL (Jan. 12, 2016) at 4–5 ("The prospect of untangling a web of export filings for a cadre of international security researchers working in real-time to create security solutions to challenging problems simply stifled the research altogether.").

46 *See* Katie Bo Williams, *Obama Administration to Renegotiate Rules for "Intrusion Software,"* THE HILL (Feb. 29, 2016).

cybersecurity relies heavily on the private sector – including large corporations – to develop solutions. Such reliance requires trust, and, in some cases, a relaxation on onerous regulations that could prevent the private sector from doing its job. As seen in the heated battle over export controls, governments around the world are having a difficult time adjusting to this new view of national security in the cyber age. Moreover, companies must pay careful attention to government regulations and proposals that could undermine their legitimate and important cybersecurity activities.

5

Anti-Hacking Laws

CHAPTER MENU

U.S. legislators have passed statutes to address what they view as the increasingly large threat of computer hacking. This chapter looks at some of the commonly used laws to prosecute people who access computers, software, or data without authorization or in excess of authorization: the Computer Fraud and Abuse Act, state computer hacking laws, section 1201 of the Digital Millennium Copyright Act, and the Economic Espionage Act. Section 2701 of the Stored Communications Act, which penalizes individuals for hacking stored communications, such as email, is discussed in Chapter 7, along with the rest of the Electronic Communications Privacy Act.

The laws discussed in this chapter provide government prosecutors with the ability to bring criminal charges against individuals who hack computers without authorization. In some cases, conviction on a single count of these laws can result in a prison sentence of ten or more years, as well as severe fines. The laws also allow the victims of computer hacking to bring civil suits to recover damages from the hackers and obtain injunctions to prevent further damage.

Unfortunately, some anti-hacking laws were written before the arrival of many technologies that are now commonplace in computer networks and systems. Accordingly, in many cases there are disagreements about the reach of the laws, and what constitutes illegal "hacking" that should lead to criminal sentences and civil liability.

Some prosecutors, plaintiffs, and courts have adopted particularly broad views of these anti-hacking laws. Many of these statutes prohibit not only traditional unauthorized access but the unauthorized use or transfer of information, or circumvention of access controls. Indeed, the laws often present

Cybersecurity Law, First Edition. Jeff Kosseff.
© 2017 John Wiley & Sons, Inc. Published 2017 by John Wiley & Sons, Inc.
Companion Website: www.wiley.com/go/kosseff/cybersecurity

barriers to cybersecurity researchers who are seeking to identify software bugs and other flaws in order to help companies improve the security of their products and services. At the same time, companies that often are the victims of hacking argue that the laws are not strong enough to deter the worst behavior. Anti-hacking legislation is particularly a concern for companies that experience widespread theft of their trade secrets and other confidential information.

In short, there is little agreement about the scope and reach of computer hacking laws. For that reason, many of the laws discussed in this chapter are still controversial, and a number of key political players have long called for significant amendments to the laws.

5.1 Computer Fraud and Abuse Act

The Computer Fraud and Abuse Act is the primary U.S. federal statute that prohibits and penalizes certain forms of computer hacking. The statute imposes both criminal and civil penalties for actions taken by an individual who either lacks authorization to access a computer or exceeds authorized access to that computer.

5.1.1 Origins of the CFAA

Congress passed the CFAA due to a growing concern about computers becoming increasingly networked and subject to unauthorized access, compromising sensitive data such as credit card numbers. The modern version of the CFAA is based on a 1986 amendment to a 1984 law, the Counterfeit Access Device and Computer Fraud and Abuse Act, which was focused primarily on hacking financial institutions and the federal government. Rather than only addressing particular types of sensitive information, Congress chose to regulate the *method* by which people access all information without proper authorization. As the 1984 House Judiciary Committee Report accompanying the initial bill noted, experts testified in committee hearings "that we need to shift attention in our statutes from concepts such as 'tangible property' and credit and debit instruments to concepts of 'information' and 'access to information.'"[1]

The Judiciary Committee acknowledged that computer fraud was neglected in federal and state laws because it was seen as a "white collar" crime. This neglect was a mistake, the House Report concluded, because "an attack on white collar crime can often be much more productive, economically, to this country than the more publicized emphasis on violent crime."[2] For instance, the Committee cited a decline in highway construction costs of between 25

---

1 H. Rep. 98-894 (July 24, 1984) at 4.
2 *Id*. at 4–5.

and 35 percent, and attributed that change to successful federal prosecutions for bid-fixing in that industry.[3] In other words, increased penalties for white collar crime will result in significant economic benefits for society by reducing white collar crime.

Congress was particularly concerned about the possibility of white collar criminals using the rapidly developing computer technology to carry out economic crimes. In 1983, the Judiciary Committee noted, personal computer sales were estimated at $1.5 billion, up from "virtually zero" in 1976.[4] The Committee heard extensive testimony that "criminal elements gained access to computers in order to perpetuate crimes," and that the criminals "possess the capability to access and control high technology processes vital to our everyday lives[.]"[5] The criminal justice system at the time was "largely uninformed concerning the technical aspects of computerization, and bound by traditional legal machinery which in many cases may be ineffective against unconventional criminal operations," the Committee wrote.[6] The Committee was particularly concerned that a new crime, known as "hacking," did not fit easily into existing criminal laws. The Committee reasoned that the general public fails to appreciate the harm that can be caused by hacking: "People can relate to mugging a little old lady and taking her pocketbook, but the perception is that perhaps there is not something so wrong about taking information by use of a device called a computer even if it costs the economy millions now and potentially billions in the future."[7] This proved to be quite prescient: a 2014 study conducted by the Center for Strategic and International Studies estimated that cybercrime costs the U.S. economy approximately $100 billion annually.

To address these concerns, Congress passed in 1984 the Counterfeit Access Device and Computer Fraud and Abuse Act,[8] which created felonies and misdemeanors for certain computer hacking and counterfeit access device crimes. It has been amended six times since its initial passage and is now known as the Computer Fraud and Abuse Act. The statute currently criminalizes seven different categories of behavior, each outlined in sections (a)(1) through (a)(7) of the CFAA. It is useful to think of each of these sections as a stand-alone crime because alleged hackers often are charged under multiple sections of the CFAA.

5.1.2 Access without Authorization and Exceeding Authorized Access

The seven subsections of the CFAA primarily apply to acts that individuals commit when they use a computer either without "authorization" to access the

---

3 *Id.* at 5.
4 *Id.* at 8.
5 *Id.* at 9.
6 *Id.*
7 *Id.* at 12.
8 18 U.S.C. § 1030.

computer or "exceeding authorized access" to the computer. Some of the CFAA sections only apply if the defendant did not have authorization, and others apply either if the defendant didn't have authorization *or* if the defendant exceeded authorized access.

At the outset, it is important to understand the forms of "access" that trigger the protections of the CFAA. The CFAA does not define "access," though one court, relying on the dictionary definition of the word, stated that the transitive verb "access" means "to gain access to," and the noun "access" means "to exercise the freedom or ability to make use of something."[9] Regardless of the exact definition of the term, courts generally require the defendant to have played an active role in entering the computer and either obtaining information or causing damage. Passively *receiving* information – and nothing more – does not constitute access under the CFAA. For example, in *Role Models America, Inc. v. Jones*,[10] an academy for high school dropouts sued its former principal, alleging that he used his access to the academy's computer systems to disclose proprietary information to Nova Southeastern University, where he was completing his dissertation. The academy in fact sued the former principal and Nova, alleging that they both violated the CFAA. The district court granted Nova's motion to dismiss, reasoning that even if the academy's allegations were true, Nova did nothing more than receive information to which the principal was not entitled. The court wrote that in the context of the CFAA, "access" is an "active verb: it means 'to gain access to,' or 'to exercise the freedom or ability to make use of something.'"[11]

The more difficult question to answer is: was this act without authorization or in excess of authorized access? Among the most common defenses in CFAA cases surrounds the definition of "authorization" or "exceeds authorized access." The statute does not provide an incredibly clear definition of either term. "Authorization" is not defined in the statute, and the statute defines "exceeds authorized access" as "to access a computer with authorization and to use such access to obtain or alter information in the computer that the accesser is not entitled so to obtain or alter."[12] Unfortunately, this definition does not specifically address whether specific types of access exceed authorization, leading to a great deal of uncertainty in CFAA cases. In fact, whether a user has exceeded authorized access or accessed a computer without authorization is among the most frequently litigated issues in CFAA cases.

The issue is frequently disputed in cases in which a defendant had previously been authorized to access a computer, but either obtains information that the defendant was not entitled to access or uses the information in a way unin-

---

9 America Online, Inc. v. National Health Care Discount, Inc., 121 F. Supp. 2d 1255 (N.D. Iowa 2000) (internal quotations and ellipses omitted).
10 Role Models America, Inc. v. Jones, 305 F. Supp. 2d 564 (D. Md. 2004).
11 *Id*. at 566–67.
12 18 U.S.C. § 1030(e)(6).

tended by the owner of that information. Typically, in these cases, the government or a civil plaintiff argues that the defendant exceeded authorized access, though there are some cases in which prosecutors and plaintiffs have argued that the defendant no longer had any authorization to access a computer, and therefore was acting "without authorization."[13] There is a good deal of uncertainty as to whether accessing "without authorization" or "exceeding authorized access" includes actions that violate a website's terms of use or a company's internal information technology policies.

Some commentators have proposed three primary ways in which the CFAA could be violated. "Code-based" CFAA violations occur when the defendant circumvents computer software code in order to access a computer without authorization or in excess of authorized access.[14] "Contract-based" CFAA violations occur when the defendant's access is in violation of an agreement, policy, or terms of service.[15] "Norms-based" CFAA violations occur when the defendant's access is contrary to general societal expectations.[16] There is little dispute that code-based violations fall within the scope of the CFAA. However, there is great disagreement as to whether contract-based and norms-based violations are covered by the statute.

A narrow reading of the statute would lead to the conclusion that you only violate the CFAA if you commit a code-based violation. A broader reading of the statute would allow prosecutors and plaintiffs to bring CFAA cases not only arising from code-based violations but also contract-based and norms-based violations. Federal courts currently are split as to how broadly to interpret the CFAA, as will be discussed in detail below.

5.1.2.1 Narrow View of "Exceeds Authorized Access" and "Without Authorization"

The more restrictive reading of the CFAA is seen in *United States v. Nosal*,[17] a 2012 decision of the United States Court of Appeals for the Ninth Circuit, sitting en banc. David Nosal, a former employee of an executive search firm, convinced his ex-coworkers to use their access to the firm's computer systems to provide him with confidential information. The ex-coworkers had access to this data, which Nosal planned to use to start a competing search firm. Nosal

---

13 *See* JUSTICE DEPARTMENT, PROSECUTING COMPUTER CRIMES at 6 ("Prosecutors rarely argue that a defendant accessed a computer 'without authorization' when the defendant had some authority to access that computer. However, several civil cases have held that defendants lost their authorization to access computers when they breached a duty of loyalty to the authorizing parties, even if the authorizing parties were unaware of the breach.").
14 Orin Kerr, *Obama's Proposed Changes to the Computer Hacking Statute: A Deep Dive*, WASH. POST, Volokh Conspiracy blog (Jan. 14, 2015).
15 *Id.*
16 *Id.*
17 United States v. Nosal, 676 F. 3d 854 (9th Cir. 2012) (en banc).

was indicted under numerous criminal laws, including section (a)(4) of the CFAA (discussed in depth below). The government charged that Nosal aided and abetted his ex-coworkers in exceeding their authorized access to the network with intent to defraud.[18]

Nosal moved to dismiss the CFAA charges, arguing that he did not violate the CFAA because he did not exceed authorized access. According to Nosal, the CFAA only covers hackers, and not those who misuse information to which they had lawful access.[19] The Ninth Circuit agreed with Nosal and adopted his restrictive reading of "exceeds authorized access." The court concluded that "[i]f Congress meant to expand the scope of criminal liability to everyone who uses a computer in violation of computer use restrictions — which may well include everyone who uses a computer — we would expect it to use language better suited to that purpose."[20] The court reasoned that the government's proposed broad interpretation of "exceeds authorized access" would enable the government to bring federal criminal charges against individuals who innocuously violated workplace computer policies. Such broad governmental discretion, the court reasoned, would lead to truly absurd results:

> Employees who call family members from their work phones will become criminals if they send an email instead. Employees can sneak in the sports section of the New York Times to read at work, but they'd better not visit ESPN.com. And sudoku enthusiasts should stick to the printed puzzles, because visiting www.dailysudoku.com from their work computers might give them more than enough time to hone their sudoku skills behind bars.
>
> The effect this broad construction of the CFAA has on workplace conduct pales by comparison with its effect on everyone else who uses a computer, smart-phone, iPad, Kindle, Nook, X-box, Blu-Ray player or any other Internet-enabled device. The Internet is a means for communicating via computers: Whenever we access a web page, commence a download, post a message on somebody's Facebook wall, shop on Amazon, bid on eBay, publish a blog, rate a movie on IMDb, read www.NYT.com, watch YouTube and do the thousands of other things we routinely do online, we are using one computer to send commands to other computers at remote locations. Our access to those remote computers is governed by a series of private agreements and policies that most people are only dimly aware of and virtually no one reads or understands.[21]

---

18 *Id.* at 856.
19 *Id.*
20 *Id.* at 857.
21 *Id.* at 860.

The Ninth Circuit's *Nosal* holding is the most forceful articulation of the narrow approach to interpreting CFAA's "exceeds authorized access" provision. One commentator stated that the opinion "is a huge victory for those of us who have urged the courts to adopt a narrow construction of the CFAA."[22]

In fact, less than a year after the Ninth Circuit issued the *Nosal* opinion, the U.S. Court of Appeals for the Fourth Circuit adopted the Ninth Circuit's reasoning in a civil CFAA case. In *WEC Carolina Energy Solutions LLC v. Miller*, WEC,[23] an energy services company, brought a CFAA lawsuit against Mike Miller, a former employee. WEC alleged that before leaving the company, Miller used his access to the company's servers and Intranet to download confidential documents about the company's projects, and later took a job at a WEC competitor and used the confidential information to make a presentation to a potential customer.[24]

WEC claimed that this violated sections (a)(2), (a)(4), and (a)(5) of the CFAA because Miller used the information without authorization or in excess of authorized access. Although (a)(2) and (a)(4) apply to acts that are *either* without authorization or exceeding authorized access, (a)(5) only applies to acts that are without authorization. The Fourth Circuit observed that "the distinction between these terms is arguably minute[.]"[25] The court concluded that, based on the ordinary meaning of the terms, "authorization" means that "an employee is authorized to access a computer when his employer approves or sanctions his admission to that computer," and therefore "without authorization" means that the employee "gains admission to a computer without approval."[26] The court concluded that "exceeds authorized access" means that the employee "has approval to access a computer, but uses his access to obtain or alter information that falls outside the bounds of his approved access."[27] Importantly, the court reasoned that neither "without authorization" nor "exceeds authorized access" can be read to include "the improper *use* of information validly accessed."[28]

Imposing liability on individuals based on an individual's use of information – even if they had lawful access – would lead to absurd results, the Fourth Circuit reasoned. For instance, the court stated, this interpretation "would impute liability to an employee who with commendable intentions disregards his employer's policy against downloading information to a personal computer

---

22 Orin Kerr, *Ninth Circuit Hands down En banc Decision in United States v. Nosal, Adopting Narrow Interpretation of Computer Fraud and Abuse Act*, Volokh Conspiracy (Apr. 10, 2012).
23 WEC Carolina Energy Solutions LLC v. Miller, 687 F.3d 199 (4th Cir. 2012).
24 *Id.* at 202.
25 *Id.* at 204.
26 *Id.*
27 *Id.*
28 *Id.* (emphasis in original).

so that he can work at home and make headway in meeting his employer's goals."[29]

Most recently, the U.S. Court of Appeals for the Second Circuit adopted the *Nosal* reasoning in *United States v. Valle*.[30] In that case, Gilberto Valle, a New York City Police Department officer, was charged with crimes arising from online communications in which he discussed committing sexual violence against women he knew. Among the charges was a CFAA violation because he allegedly used his access to law enforcement databases to obtain home addresses, birth dates, and other information about the women who were named in his violent fantasies.[31] Prosecutors charged that this violated the CFAA because Valle knew of the NYPD's policy that the information was strictly limited to use for official police business.[32]

The Second Circuit held that Valle did not violate the CFAA. It relied in part on the legislative history of the 1986 amendments to the CFAA.[33] The Senate Committee Report to these amendments explained that Congress did not intend to impose liability for those "who inadvertently stumble into someone else's computer file or computer data," and that such a scenario was "particularly true in those cases where an individual is authorized to sign onto and use a particular computer, but subsequently exceeds his authorized access by mistakenly entering another computer or data file that happens to be accessible from the same terminal."[34] The court reasoned that this legislative history "consistently characterizes the evil to be remedied—computer crime—as 'trespass' into computer systems or data, and correspondingly describes 'authorization' in terms of the portion of the computer's data to which one's access rights extend."[35] The Second Circuit acknowledged that the terms "authorization" and "exceeds authorized access" are ambiguous, but ultimately decided that it is required to adopt the narrower, less punitive version under the "rule of lenity," a principle of statutory interpretation that requires courts to interpret ambiguous criminal statutes in favor of criminal defendants, based on the principle that it is the duty of Congress, and not the courts, to create laws that punish criminals.[36]

Under the narrow interpretation of "without authorization" and "exceeds authorized access," as articulated in *Nosal*, *WEC*, and *Valle*, individuals are only liable for CFAA violations if their initial *access* to the system or data was not permitted. Therefore, how the individual *used* the data is irrelevant.

---

29 *Id.* at 206.
30 *United States v. Valle*, 807 F.3d 508 (2d Cir. 2015).
31 *Id.* at 512–13.
32 *Id.* at 513.
33 *Id.* at 525.
34 *Id.*, quoting S. Rep. No. 99-432, at 2480 (1986) (internal quotation marks omitted).
35 *Id.*
36 *Id.* at 526–27.

5.1.2.2 Broader View of "Exceeds Authorized Access" and "Without Authorization"

Some other courts have adopted a broader reading of the CFAA, in which individuals may be liable for misusing information to which they initially had lawful access. Typically, courts that adopt the broad approach to the CFAA will hold that violations of contracts, terms of use, and other rules or agreements constitute acting either without authorization or in excess of authorization. In other words, the broader view of the CFAA allows liability not only for code-based violations but also for contract-based violations.[37]

The first federal appellate court to examine the scope of "exceeds authorized access" and "without authorization" was the U.S. Court of Appeals for the First Circuit, in the 2001 civil CFAA case, *EF Cultural Travel BV v. Explorica*.[38] In that case, a company, EF, brought a CFAA claim against a competitor and the competitors' employees for using an automated software program to scrape pricing information from the company's publicly available website. The employees had previously worked for EF, and had entered into a confidentiality agreement in which they agreed to not disclose or use any confidential information for any third party's benefit or against EF's interests.[39] The plaintiffs presented evidence that the former employee used his knowledge of confidential EF information to develop the scraping tool. The defendants requested that the court dismiss the lawsuit, contending that they did not "exceed" authorized access. The First Circuit rejected this argument, concluding that the defendants "would face an uphill battle trying to argue that it was not against EF's interests for appellants to use the tour codes to mine EF's pricing data."[40] This is a particularly broad interpretation of the term "exceeds authorized access" because there was not even an allegation that the scraping program violated an explicit terms of use or other policy on a user agreement.

Violations of terms of use and workplace policies are more common for charges of exceeding authorized access under the CFAA. For instance, in *United States v. Rodriguez*,[41] the government brought CFAA charges against Roberto Rodriguez, a former Social Security Administration customer service representative. SSA's policies prohibited its employees from obtaining information "without a business reason." Rodriguez refused to sign forms acknowledging the policy, and accessed the Social Security records of seventeen

---

37 *See* Matthew Gordon, *A Hybrid Approach to Analyzing Authorization in the Computer Fraud and Abuse Act*, 21 B.U.J. Sci & Tech. L. (2015) ("The contract-based approach has the benefit of not being as restrictive as the code-based approach. The contract-based approach provides protection even when information is not protected by a password. This is useful when the information needs to be protected from an insider who would have the password[.]").
38 EF Cultural Travel BV v. Explorica, Inc., 274 F. 3d 577 (1st Cir. 2001).
39 *Id*. at 581.
40 *Id*. at 583.
41 United States v. Rodriguez, 628 F.3d 1258 (11th Cir. 2010).

individuals without a business reason, and without the individuals' knowledge. Among the individuals whose records were accessed was Rodriguez's ex-wife.[42] Rodriguez was convicted of violating the CFAA, and on appeal to the U.S. Court of Appeals for the Eleventh Circuit, he argued that he did not "exceed authorized access" because his access was limited to the databases that he was permitted to access due to his job requirements.[43]

The court rejected Rodriguez's argument and held that he exceeded his authorized access by accessing the information for reasons unrelated to his job.[44] The court reasoned that this constituted a CFAA violation because the Social Security Administration had explicitly told him that he was not permitted to *obtain* the information for reasons that were unrelated to business purposes. In other words, the court concluded, the violation occurred not because Rodriguez *misused* the information, but because he *obtained* the information in violation of the Social Security Administration's policy.

Rodriguez also argued that he did not exceed authorized access because he did not *use* the information in a criminal manner (e.g., for identity theft). The court quickly disregarded this argument, concluding that the manner in which he *used* the information is not relevant to deciding whether he violated the CFAA; the inquiry for the court was whether he *obtained* the information in violation of the statute.[45] The *Rodriguez* case is an example of a broad reading of the CFAA, in which the focus of the court's inquiry is not merely whether the initial access was authorized, but whether the access was used to further unauthorized activities.

Similarly, in *United States v. John*,[46] Dimetriace Eva-Lavon John, a Citigroup employee, used her credentials to provide information about corporate customers' financial accounts to her half-brother, who used the information to commit fraud.[47] John was charged and convicted on a number of counts, including the CFAA. On appeal, she argued that she did not exceed authorized access because she was authorized to access and view the corporate customer account information. The U.S. Court of Appeals for the Fifth Circuit rejected this argument, concluding that "authorized access" may include use limitations that are placed on the information, "at least when the user knows or reasonably should know that he or she is not authorized to access a computer and information obtainable from that access in furtherance of or to perpetrate a crime."[48] For instance, the court wrote, if an employer authorizes employees "to utilize

---

42 *Id.* at 1260.
43 *Id.* at 1263.
44 *Id.*
45 *Id.* at 1263.
46 United States v. John, 597 F.3d 263 (5th Cir. 2010).
47 *Id.* at 269.
48 *Id.* at 271.

computers for any lawful purpose but not for unlawful purposes and only in furtherance of the employer's business," the company's employees would exceed authorized access if they "used that access to obtain or steal information as part of a criminal scheme."[49]

Applying this definition of authorized access to the charges against John, the Fifth Circuit concluded that she clearly violated the CFAA. The court noted that Citigroup's internal policy, which was presented to John at employee training sessions, explicitly barred employees from misusing confidential information. "Despite being aware of these policies," the court concluded, "John accessed account information for individuals whose accounts she did not manage, removed this highly sensitive and confidential information from Citigroup premises, and ultimately used this information to perpetrate fraud on Citigroup and its customers."[50] Key to the court's decision was evidence that John had actually been trained on the policies that prohibited such access.

In short, the broad interpretation of CFAA includes not only code-based violations, but also violations based on contract and norms.

5.1.2.3 Attempts to Find a Middle Ground

Courts nationwide have recognized the clear split between the *Nosal/WEC/Valle* narrow reading of the CFAA and the *John/Rodriguez* broad reading. Some courts, rather than selecting one definition, have attempted to distinguish the two lines of thinking and find a middle ground in which the facts of each case determine which reading of the CFAA to apply.

For instance, in 2015, the U.S. District Court for the District of Columbia reasoned that the reading of the CFAA depends in part on whether the defendant *knowingly* violated the law or an agreement. In *Roe v. Bernabei & Wachtel PLLC*,[51] the plaintiff had secretly recorded her employer allegedly sexually harassing her. She allowed a coworker to copy the video. The coworker, along with other colleagues, later sued the employer. They also allegedly provided the media with copies of the video.[52] The plaintiff sued the former coworkers and their law firm for, among other things, violating various provisions of the CFAA by intentionally accessing a protected computer while exceeding authorization, and obtaining information from that computer and furthering intended fraud.[53]

The defendants moved to dismiss this claim, arguing that a CFAA violation did not exist because the plaintiff had voluntarily allowed her coworker to copy the video. The judge recognized that courts have different interpretations of

---

49 *Id.*

50 *Id.* at 272.

51 Roe v. Bernabei & Wachtel PLLC, 85 F. Supp. 3d 89 (D. DC 2015).

52 *Id.* at 94.

53 *Id.*

the term "exceeds authorized access." The judge ultimately concluded that the narrower version, as articulated in *Nosal*, applied to this case, and dismissed the CFAA claims. The judge reasoned that the more expansive view, as stated in cases such as *Rodriguez*, involves "circumstances in which employees knowingly violated internal employer policies related to the use of data, either unlawfully, or in violation of their employment agreement."[54] In this case, there was no allegation of an explicit agreement or law that prohibited the defendants from sharing this information. Although the court adopted the *Nosal* line of reasoning for this case, it is possible that, had the coworkers violated an explicit agreement, the court would have sustained the CFAA claims.

As courts continue to apply both interpretations of the CFAA to a wide set of fact patterns, it will be increasingly difficult for courts to find such a middle ground; the interpretations clearly conflict with each other. Quite simply, the federal courts are split as to whether an individual can be found guilty of violating the CFAA merely by misusing information to which the individual had proper access. Unless the United States Supreme Court eventually resolves the issue, federal courts will continue to apply different definitions of "without authorization" and "exceeds authorized access." A court's decision about which interpretation to use will inevitably affect the fate of any CFAA criminal prosecution or civil lawsuit.

5.1.3 The Seven Sections of the CFAA

Although courts exert a great deal of effort determining whether a CFAA defendant has accessed a computer without authorization or exceeded authorized access, that determination is only the beginning of their inquiry under the CFAA. Individuals only violate the CFAA if, while acting without authorization or in excess of authorization, their behavior falls into one of seven categories specified by the CFAA, such as obtaining information or damaging a computer. Below is an overview of the seven subsections of the CFAA, and the types of behavior that courts have held constitutes – and does not constitute – violations of the law. For all seven of these subsections, the CFAA imposes criminal penalties not only on the commission of these acts *but also* on conspiracies and attempts to commit the acts.[55]

> **The Seven Prohibited Acts under the Computer Fraud and Abuse Act**
>
> Section (a)(1): ***Hacking to commit espionage.*** Knowingly accessing a computer without authorization or exceeding authorized access, and by means of such conduct having obtained classified information, with reasons to believe

---

54 *Id.* at 103.
55 18 U.S.C. § 1030(b).

that the information could be used to the injury of the United States or to the advantage of any foreign nation, willfully communicating or otherwise delivering the information to a person not entitled to receive it, or willfully retaining the information and failing to deliver it to the individual entitled to receiving it.

Section (a)(2): *Hacking to obtain information.* Intentionally accessing a computer without authorization, or exceeding authorized access, and thereby obtaining information in a financial record of a financial institution, card issuer, or consumer reporting agency; information from any department or agency of the United States; or information from any computer that is used in or affecting interstate or foreign commerce.

Section (a)(3): *Hacking a federal government computer.* Intentionally, without authorization to access any nonpublic computer of a department or agency of the United States, accessing a computer that is exclusively for the use of the government of the United States, or, in the case of a computer not exclusively for government use, is used by or for the U.S. government and such conduct affects that use.

Section (a)(4): *Hacking to commit fraud.* Knowingly and with intent to defraud, accessing a protected computer without authorization, or exceeding authorized access, and by means of such conduct furthering the intended fraud and obtaining anything of value, unless the object of the fraud and the thing obtained consists only of the use of the computer and the value of the use is not more than $5000 in any one-year period.

Section (a)(5): *Hacking to commit damage.* (A) Knowingly causing the transmission of a program, information, code, or command, and as a result of such conduct, intentionally causing damage without authorization, to a computer used in or affecting interstate or foreign commerce; (B) intentionally accessing without authorization a computer used in or affecting interstate or foreign commerce, and as a result of such conduct, recklessly causing damage; or (C) intentionally accessing without authorization a computer used in or affecting interstate or foreign commerce, and as a result of such conduct, causing damage and loss.

Section (a)(6): *Trafficking in passwords.* Knowingly and with intent to defraud trafficking in any password or similar information if the trafficking affects interstate or foreign commerce or the computer is used by or for the U.S. government.

Section (a)(7): *Threats of hacking.* With intent to extort money or other things of value, transmitting in interstate or foreign commerce any communication containing any: (A) threat to damage a computer used in or affecting interstate or foreign commerce; (B) threat to obtain information from a computer

> used in or affecting interstate or foreign commerce without authorization or in excess of authorization or to impair the confidentiality of information obtained from such a computer without authorization or by exceeding authorized access; or (C) demand or request for money or other thing of value in relation to damage a computer used in or affecting interstate or foreign commerce, where such damage was caused to facilitate the extortion.

5.1.3.1 CFAA Section (a)(1): Hacking to Commit Espionage

Section (a)(1) prohibits individuals from knowingly accessing a computer without authorization or exceeding authorized access, and obtaining classified information, and willfully communicating, delivering, transmitting, or causing the communication, delivery, or transmission to any person who is not authorized to receive the information.[56] The statute also prohibits the willful retention of the data, and failure to deliver it to the U.S. employee who is entitled to receive it. Section (a)(1) only applies if the individual had reason to believe that the information could be used to injure the United States or to the advantage of a foreign nation.

No published court opinion interprets this subsection, largely because it is rare for prosecutions to be brought under this subsection. That likely is because the federal government typically brings espionage-related hacking prosecutions under the Espionage Act,[57] which criminalizes many forms of unauthorized access, use, and disclosure of classified information.

Violations of Section (a)(1) are felonies, and violations carry prison terms of up to ten years and fines. If an individual violates Section (a)(1) after having been convicted of another CFAA violation, the prison term can be up to twenty years.

5.1.3.2 CFAA Section (a)(2): Hacking to Obtain Information

Section (a)(2) of the CFAA prohibits individuals from intentionally accessing computers without authorization or in excess of authorized access, and obtaining (1) information contained in a financial record of a financial institution, card issuer, or consumer reporting agency; (2) information from any federal government department or agency; or (3) information from any "protected computer," which the CFAA defines as a computer that is either used by a financial institution or the federal government, or is used in or affecting interstate or foreign commerce.[58]

Because it is relatively easy to demonstrate that companies' computers affect interstate or foreign commerce, Section (a)(2) is a frequent basis for CFAA

---

56 18 U.S.C. § 1030(a)(1).
57 18 U.S.C. § 791 *et seq.*
58 18 U.S.C. § 1030(a)(2).

criminal prosecutions and civil litigation. Indeed, the CFAA had initially only applied to computers that are used in interstate commerce, but in 2008, Congress amended the statute to include computers that affect interstate commerce because it recognized the need to "address the increasing number of computer hacking crimes that involve computers located within the same state[.]"[59] Under this incredibly broad definition of "protected computer," it is difficult to imagine any U.S. companies whose computers do not qualify as "protected computers" that are covered by the CFAA. Indeed, one federal court in California stated that the requirement for a "protected computer" will "always be met when an individual using a computer contacts or communicates with an Internet website."[60] Moreover, in 2001, Congress amended the CFAA to clarify that it applies not only to actions that affect interstate commerce but also *foreign* commerce. As the U.S. Justice Department observed, this amendment "addresses situations where an attacker within the United States attacks a computer system located abroad and situations in which individuals in foreign countries route communications through the United States as they hack from one foreign country to another."[61]

The act covered by Section (a)(2) – obtaining information – is quite broad. In the Senate report accompanying the 1986 amendments to CFAA that established Section (a)(2), the legislators wrote that "obtaining information" includes "mere observation of the data."[62] The legislators clarified that, for the government or a litigant to demonstrate that an individual obtained information under Section (a)(2), they need not prove that the defendant had been "physically removing the data from its original location or transcribing the data[.]"[63] In the three decades since this report, there has been little dispute that "obtaining information" under Section (a)(2) does not necessarily include the actual removal of the data. Observation of data – such as by hacking into a company's website – is sufficient to establish that the individual "obtained" the information. However, there are some limits to the breadth of this definition. Merely accessing a computer without authorization or in excess of authorization – and not actually viewing or otherwise obtaining any information – will not constitute a Section (a)(2) violation.

Perhaps the most significant barrier to charges or claims under Section (a)(2) is the requirement that the act of obtaining information be intentional.

---

59 153 Cong. Rec. S14570 (Oct. 16, 2007) (remarks of Sen. Leahy).
60 United States v. Drew, 259 F.R.D. 449, 457 (C.D. Cal. 2009); *see also* Paradigm Alliance v. Celeritas Technologies, LLC, 248 F.R.D. 598, 602 (D. Kan. 2008) ("The essence of defendants' CFAA claim is that Paradigm repeatedly accessed or attempted to access Celeritas' password protected 'web-based' application after being told that access was no longer permitted. As a practical matter, a computer providing a web-based application accessible through the internet would satisfy the interstate communication requirement.").
61 Justice Department, Prosecuting Computer Crimes at 5.
62 S.Rept. 99-432 at 6 (1986).
63 *Id*. at 6–7.

Congress intentionally set this higher standard in its 1986 amendments to the CFAA. The initial 1984 version of the CFAA applied to acts that were committed "knowingly." In 1986, Congress replaced "knowingly" with "intentionally." In the report accompanying the 1986 amendments, the Senate committee members wrote that "intentional acts of unauthorized access – rather than mistaken, inadvertent, or careless ones – are precisely what the Committee intends to proscribe."[64] The Committee analyzed Supreme Court precedent that interpreted the term "knowingly," and reasoned that the "knowingly" standard could apply to acts that apply whenever the individual is "aware that the result is practically certain to follow from his conduct, whatever his desire may be as to that result."[65] Although this broad definition of "knowingly" might be appropriate for other crimes, the Committee reasoned that it is not appropriate for computer hacking because it "might not be sufficient to preclude liability on the part of those who inadvertently 'stumble into' someone else's computer file or computer data."[66]

Replacing "knowingly" with "intentionally," the Committee concluded, "is designed to focus Federal criminal prosecutions on those whose conduct evinces a clear intent to enter, without proper authorization, computer files or data belonging to another."[67] The Committee, relying on earlier interpretations of the term "intentional," stated that it "means more than one voluntarily engaged in conduct or caused a result. Such conduct or the causing of the result must have been the person's conscious objective."[68]

The limits imposed by the word "intentionally" were evident in a 2006 federal court opinion in the District of Columbia, arising from a civil action against IBM.[69] Butera & Andres, a DC law firm, alleged that its servers were hacked, and the attacker's IP addresses were located at an IBM facility in North Carolina. The law firm sued IBM and the anonymous individual – whom the firm alleged to be an employee of IBM – under a variety of causes of action, including a violation of Section (a)(2) of the CFAA. IBM moved to dismiss the claims, arguing that the plaintiff's complaint failed to allege that IBM acted intentionally.[70] The district court granted IBM's motion to dismiss, agreeing that the complaint failed to allege that IBM acted with any intent. The court reasoned that the mere allegation that the hacker's IP addresses were located in IBM's facilities did not permit an inference that IBM *participated* in the alleged hacking.[71] "Far from pleading any intentional conduct on the part of IBM," the

---

64 *Id.* at 5.
65 *Id.* at 6.
66 *Id.*
67 *Id.*
68 *Id.*
69 Butera & Andrews v. Intern. Business Machines, 456 F. Supp. 2d 104 (D.D.C. 2006).
70 *Id.* at 107–08.
71 *Id.* at 110.

court observed, "the plaintiffs' position appears directed, at most, at establishing the likelihood that an individual employed at the IBM facility in Durham is responsible for the alleged attacks."[72] Such an allegation does not rise to the level of "intentional" hacking, the court concluded.[73]

Demonstrating intent under Section (a)(2), however, is not an insurmountable task. Indeed, courts generally have held that for the government or a civil plaintiff to establish a Section (a)(2) violation, they only need to prove that the defendant intended to obtain information by accessing a computer without authorization or exceeding authorized access. It is unnecessary to demonstrate that the defendant intended for the information to be used in any particular way.

For example, in a 2007 case, *United States v. Willis*,[74] defendant Todd A. Willis, an employee of an Oklahoma City debt collection business, had access to a proprietary database of individuals' personal information, and was explicitly prohibited from obtaining the information for personal reasons.[75] A law enforcement investigation revealed that Willis provided his drug dealer with a coworker's credentials, and the credentials were later used to commit identity theft.[76] Willis was charged with aiding and abetting a violation of Section (a)(2), convicted by jury, and sentenced to forty-one months in prison.[77] On appeal to the U.S. Court of Appeals for the Tenth Circuit, Willis argued that his conviction was invalid because he did not have the intent to defraud when he provided the credentials. The Tenth Circuit rejected this argument after reviewing the legislative history of the 1986 amendments to CFAA, and concluded that the government did not have an obligation to demonstrate that Willis intended to use the information in any particular way; the inquiry for the court was whether his intentional *access* and obtaining of the information violated the CFAA.[78]

---

72 *Id.* at 111.

73 *Id.* at 112 ("The plaintiff does not allege that the complained-of attacks were committed by the John Doe defendant to 'further[] his employer's interests,' even assuming that the Doe defendant was employed by IBM. Rather, all the plaintiff alleges is that 'John Doe in his capacity as IBM employee or agent[.]'" (internal citation omitted).

74 United States v. Willis, 476 F.3d 1121 (10th Cir. 2007).

75 *Id.* at 1123.

76 *Id.*

77 *Id.* at 1124.

78 *Id.* at 1125 ("A plain reading of the statute reveals that the requisite intent to prove a violation of § 1030(a)(2)(C) is not an intent to defraud (as it is under (a)(4)), it is the intent to obtain unauthorized access of a protected computer.... That is, to prove a violation of (a)(2)(C), the Government must show that the defendant: (1) intentionally accessed a computer, (2) without authorization (or exceeded authorized access), (3) and thereby obtained information from any protected computer if the conduct involved an interstate or foreign communication. The government need not also prove that the defendant had the intent to defraud in obtaining the information or that the information was used to any particular ends.").

Similarly, in *Thayer Corporation v. Reed*,[79] Thayer Corporation filed a civil lawsuit against its former Chief Financial Officer, David Reed. Among the many counts in the complaint was a CFAA claim under Section (a)(2). Thayer alleged that for approximately a week after Reed's employment ceased, he forwarded Thayer human resources emails to his personal email account. Reed asserted that the email transfers were the result of a mistake by his phone provider, and that as soon as he saw that he was receiving the Thayer emails, he directed the phone company to fix the issue. The court rejected this argument, reasoning that the complaint alleged that Reed "intercepted, read, deleted and forwarded emails from Thayer's human resources director," explained that Reed created Thayer's password system, and alleged that Reed "knew of discussions regarding his severance package, information that only could have been obtained from the human resources manager's emails." Assuming that the allegations in the complaint were true, the court concluded, "Mr. Reed could not have unintentionally done any of these things; each requires the intent to access, intercept, and use Thayer's email system without authorization, causing harm."[80]

These cases have a consistent theme: to satisfy the "intentional" requirement of Section (a)(2), the government or civil plaintiff must establish that the defendant knew that they were obtaining the information through unauthorized hacking. However, they need not establish that the defendant intended to cause harm, defraud, or support the commission of another crime.

Section (a)(2) violations may be charged as felonies or misdemeanors. If a violation is charged as a misdemeanor, the defendant could be punished by a fine and up to one year in prison. A violation of Section (a)(2) may be charged as a felony, punishable by a fine and up to five years in prison, if one of the following is true: (1) the offense was committed for commercial advantage or private financial gain; (2) the office was committed in furtherance of any criminal or tortious act that violates the U.S. Constitution or any federal or state laws; or (3) the information obtained is valued at more than $5000. Additionally, if an individual violates Section (a)(2) after having previously been convicted of a CFAA violation, that individual can be charged with a felony punishable by a fine and up to ten years in prison.

5.1.3.3 CFAA Section (a)(3): Hacking a Federal Government Computer

Section (a)(3) prohibits individuals from intentionally accessing nonpublic federal government computers without authorization. This prohibition applies to both computers that are "exclusively for the use of the Government of the United States," and computers that are "used by or for the Government of the United States and such conduct affects that use by or for the Government of the United States."[81]

---

79 Thayer Corp. v. Reed, Case No. 2:10-cv-00423-JAW (D. Me. July 11, 2011).
80 *Id.*
81 18 U.S.C. 1030(a)(3).

At first glance, one might wonder why Section (a)(3) is necessary, since Section (a)(2) also explicitly prohibits certain hacks of federal government computers. Section (a)(3) differs because it prohibits the mere act of intentionally *accessing* a federal government computer without authorization, regardless of whether the defendant actually obtained any information. This provision was conceived two years after the initial CFAA was enacted, members of Congress indicated a desire to "balance its concern for Federal employees and other authorized users against the legitimate need to protect Government computers against abuse by 'outsiders.'"[82] Congress addressed this balance by amending the CFAA to create this separate prohibition on unauthorized access to federal computers. According to the Senate report accompanying the amendments, this section was drafted in response to the U.S. Justice Department's concerns about whether Section (a)(2) "covers acts of mere trespass," that is, unauthorized access, or whether it requires a further showing that the information perused was "used, modified, destroyed, or disclosed."[83] Congress stated that it intended for Section (a)(3) to create "a simple trespass offense" that applies "to persons without authorized access to Federal computers."[84] In this respect, Section (a)(3) is significantly broader than Section (a)(2).

However, Section (a)(3) also is narrower than Section (a)(2) in one important area: while Section (a)(2) applies to *both* access without authorization *and* exceeding authorized access, Section (a)(3) only applies to access without authorization. Congress intentionally excluded "exceeding authorized access" from Section (a)(3) due to its belief that "government employees and others who are authorized to use a Federal Government computer would face prosecution for acts of computer access and use that, while technically wrong, should not rise to the level of criminal conduct," according to the 1986 Senate report.[85] The legislators concluded that if an employee "briefly exceeds his authorized access and peruses data belonging to the department that he is not supposed to look at," the employee should be subject to administrative sanctions, but not criminal penalties.[86]

Section (a)(3) does not apply to unauthorized access of *any* federal government computer. In 1996, Congress amended Section (a)(3) to clarify that it only applies to unauthorized access of *nonpublic* federal government computers. In the Senate report accompanying the 1996 amendment, Congress warned that despite the new restriction of Section (a)(3) to nonpublic federal government computers, "a person who is permitted to access publicly available Government computers, for example, via an agency's World Wide Web site,

---

82 S. Rept. 99-432 at 7 (1986).
83 *Id.*
84 *Id.*
85 *Id.*
86 *Id.*

may still be convicted under (a)(3) for accessing without authority any nonpublic Federal Government computer."[87]

There have been few prosecutions under Section (a)(3). Among the few was a recent criminal case against Jerry Wang, the chief executive officer of two universities in California. The government alleged that Wang provided one of his employees with Wang's access to the Department of Homeland Security's Student and Exchange Visitor Information System, which processes the information that DHS uses to determine whether universities are complying with student immigration laws. The government alleges that this unauthorized employee filed forged documents. Among the fifteen counts was a charge that Wang violated Section(a)(3). Wang moved to dismiss this count, arguing that providing log-in credentials to an employee to input data does not violate Section (a)(3). The court denied this motion, concluding that the indictment sufficiently alleged a violation of the statute.[88]

The U.S. Department of Justice's manual on computer crimes attributes the lack of prosecutions under Section (a)(3) to the fact that a first-time violation of Section (a)(3) is a misdemeanor, while a first-time violation of Section (a)(2) may be charged as a felony, with greater penalties.[89] Accordingly, if an act falls under both Section(a)(2) and Section (a)(3), prosecutors may have greater incentive to bring the charges under Section (a)(2).

If, however, an individual is charged under Section (a)(3) after having previously been convicted of a CFAA violation, the crime can be charged as a felony with a fine and up to ten years in prison.

5.1.3.4   CFAA Section (a)(4): Hacking to Commit Fraud

Section (a)(4) prohibits individuals from knowingly and with intent to defraud accessing a protected computer without authorization, or exceeding authorization, and furthering the intended fraud and obtaining anything of value. This provision does not apply if the object of the fraud and the thing obtained consists only of the use of the computer, and the value of that use is not more than $5000 during any one-year period.[90]

Section (a)(4) is similar to the federal mail fraud and wire fraud statutes. But when Congress enacted this provision in the 1986 amendments to CFAA, it expressed a desire to ensure that fraud conducted over a computer – rather than the mails or wires – be covered explicitly under a criminal law. According to the Senate report accompanying the amendments, for a prosecution under Section (a)(4), "the use of the computer must be more directly linked to the intended fraud," meaning that it "must be used by an offender without

---

87 S.R. 304-357 (1996).
88 United States v. Wang, Case No.: 5:12-CR-00581-EJD, 2014 U.S. Dist. LEXIS 25525 (N.D. Cal. Feb. 26, 2014).
89 U.S. Department of Justice, Prosecuting Computer Crimes at 25.
90 18 U.S.C. § 1030(a)(4).

authorization or in excess of his authorization to obtain property of another, which property furthers the intended fraud."[91]

Courts generally have been willing to conclude that a wide range of types of improper access "further" the intended fraud, as required by Section (a)(4). For instance, in *United States v. Lindsley,*[92] the defendant was charged with violations of Section (a)(4) and other statutes for using his personal computer to illegally access Sprint's internal computer system and steal customers' calling card numbers. His co-defendants allegedly sold the calling card numbers, and the government alleged that the total losses that Lindsley caused exceeded $1.8 million. Lindsley pleaded guilty and was sentenced to forty-one months in prison. The large prison sentence was primarily due to a sentencing enhancement that was triggered by the large losses. Lindsley appealed the sentence and argued that it was not reasonably foreseeable that his co-defendants would resell the card numbers. The U.S. Court of Appeals for the Fifth Circuit, in an unpublished opinion, affirmed the sentence, concluding that the loss was foreseeable and therefore was properly foreseeable to Lindsley.[93]

Similarly, in *United States v. Bae,*[94] the defendant, a retailer whose store sold lottery tickets, pleaded guilty to a Section (a)(4) violation. He was charged with using his lottery terminal to generate more than $500,000 in tickets for himself. The tickets were redeemable for more than $296,000 and the defendant redeemed them for approximately $224,000. When calculating his sentence, the district court attributed $503,650 in losses, equal to the total value of the tickets after subtracting the commission that the defendant would have received as a retailer. The defendant appealed the sentence, arguing that the market price does not reflect the actual cost to the lottery system, and that therefore the district court should have calculated his sentence based on the redemption value of the tickets. The U.S. Court of Appeals for the D.C. Circuit rejected this argument and affirmed his sentence, concluding that the proper measure of damage under Section (a)(4) is the fair market value of the property *at the time* that it was illegally acquired.[95]

Although both the *Lindsley* and *Bae* opinions dealt with the narrow issue of criminal sentencing, the courts' reasoning indicates a willingness to broadly attribute subsequent fraud to an initial illegal access. In other words, even if the eventual fraud is attenuated from the initial access, the defendant still may be liable under Section (a)(4).

Perhaps the largest barrier to Section(a)(4) cases is the requirement to demonstrate that the defendant obtained something "of value" that is worth more than $5000. Consider the prosecution of Richard Czubinski, a customer service

---

91 S. Rept. 99-432 at 9 (1986).
92 United States v. Lindsley, 2001 U.S. App. LEXIS 32209 (5th Cir. May 3, 2001) (unpublished).
93 *Id.*
94 United States v. Bae, 250 F.3d 774 (D.C. Cir. 2001).
95 *Id.*at 776.

employee at the Internal Revenue Service. The federal government brought charges against Czubinski under numerous statutes, including Section (a)(4), alleging that he used his credentials to search the tax records of a number of people for whom he had no legitimate business reason to be querying, including political staffers, a state prosecutor who handled a case against his father, his brother's instructor, and a woman whom Czubinski had dated.[96] At trial, there was evidence that he only mentioned his access to the data to one acquaintance, and there was no further evidence that he had shared or otherwise used any of the information that he viewed.[97] He was convicted by a jury on thirteen counts, and appealed.

In 1997, the U.S. Court of Appeals for the First Circuit reversed his Section (a)(4) conviction. (At the time, Section (a)(4) required proof that the hacker obtained something of value, but did not have a $5000 minimum value.) At issue in the appeal was whether the taxpayer IRS information qualifies as something of "value," even though there was no evidence that Czubinski used it in any way. The court concluded that in this case, the government failed to demonstrate that the information had any value to Czubinski. Instead, the court reasoned, he accessed the data merely to satisfy his "idle curiosity."[98] In other words, viewing confidential information – and not doing anything with that knowledge – does not constitute obtaining a thing "of value" in violation of Section (a)(4). The mere act of accessing information on a computer without authorization or in excess of authorization more easily fits under Section (a)(2).

Section (a)(4)'s intent requirement is more specific than other sections of the CFAA: the violation must not only be done knowingly, but it must be done with intent to defraud. One of the few courts that has interpreted this phrase in the context of the CFAA took a fairly broad approach. In *Shurgard Storage Centers v. Safeguard Self Storage*,[99] the plaintiff, a self-storage company, alleged that one of its managers emailed confidential business information to its competitor, and was later hired by the competitor. The plaintiff sued the competitor alleging a number of claims, including violation of Section (a)(4). The competitor moved to dismiss the complaint, arguing that the complaint did not adequately allege that the competitor intended to defraud the plaintiff.[100] At common law, to demonstrate that fraud occurred, a plaintiff must demonstrate nine elements, including a representation of fact that was false, and the plaintiff's reliance on this false statement. Requiring a Section (a)(4) plaintiff (or a government prosecutor) to demonstrate common-law fraud would make it exceptionally difficult to bring a case under this provision. The court rejected

---

96 United States v. Czubinski, 106 F.3d 1069, 1072 (1st Cir. 1997).
97 *Id.*
98 *Id.* at 1078.
99 Shurgard Storage Centers, Inc. v. Safeguard Self Storage, Inc., 119 F. Supp. 2d 1121 (W.D. Wash. 2000).
100 *Id.* at 1125.

this reading of Section (a)(4), agreeing with the plaintiff that, in the context of Section (a)(4), "defraud" means "wronging one in his property rights by dishonest methods and schemes."[101] The court reasoned that Section (a)(4) does not require proof of common-law fraud, and only requires demonstration of a "wrongdoing."[102]

A federal judge in Iowa later adopted the broad definition of "defraud" as articulated in *Shurgard Storage Centers*. In *NCMIC Finance Corporation v. Artino*,[103] a company alleged that a former executive violated Section (a)(4) when he used his access to the company's computer systems to obtain confidential customer information. The judge concluded that these actions constituted an intent to defraud for the purposes of Section (a)(4) because they harmed the plaintiff's property rights.[104]

Violations of Section (a)(4) are charged as felonies punishable by a fine or imprisonment of up to five years. If the defendant had previously been convicted of violating the CFAA, the prison term can be up to ten years.

5.1.3.5 CFAA Section (a)(5): Hacking to Damage a Computer

Section (a)(5) of the CFAA prohibits three types of behavior, all related to damaging computers through hacking: (1) knowingly causing the transmission of a program, information, code, or command, and, as a result of such conduct, intentionally causing damage without authorization, to a protected computer; (2) intentionally accessing a protected computer without authorization, and as a result of such conduct, recklessly causing damage; or (3) intentionally accessing a protected computer without authorization, and as a result of such conduct, causes damage and loss.[105]

Section (a)(5) is among the more commonly prosecuted and litigated provisions of the CFAA, as it covers a wide range of actions, including the deployment of viruses and malware, denial-of-service attacks, and deletion of data. The three subsections of (a)(5) are quite different, and therefore we will examine each separately.

5.1.3.5.1 *CFAA Section (a)(5)(A): Knowing Transmission that Intentionally Damages a Computer Without Authorization*

Section (a)(5)(A) requires prosecutors (or private plaintiff) to demonstrate four general elements: that the defendant (1) knowingly caused the transmission of a program, information, code, or command; (2) and as a result of such conduct, *intentionally* caused (3) damage to a protected computer; (4) without authorization.

---

101 *Id.*
102 *Id.*
103 NCMIC Finance Corporation v. Artino, 638 F. Supp. 2d 1042 (S.D. Iowa 2009).
104 *Id.* at 1062.
105 18 U.S.C. 1030(a)(5).

The first element requires a demonstration that the plaintiff knowingly caused the transmission of program, information, code, or command. The biggest hurdle for satisfying this element is a demonstration that a transmission occurred, though courts generally have interpreted this to cover a fairly wide range of activities. For instance, in *International Airport Centers, LLC v. Citrin*,[106] a company filed a Section (a)(5)(A) civil claim against a former employee who allegedly deleted proprietary company data from his laptop before quitting and starting his own business.[107] The former employee also installed a secure-erasure program that ensured that the files could not be recovered.[108] The former employee argued that the claim should be dismissed because merely deleting a file does not constitute a "transmission" under the CFAA. The U.S. Court of Appeals for the Seventh Circuit agreed it might be "stretching the statute too far" to hold that merely pressing "delete" – and nothing more – constitutes "transmission." However, the court allowed the claim to proceed because the installation of the secure-erasure program did constitute "transmission."[109] The *Citrin* opinion, which has been widely cited in other CFAA cases, demonstrates that, although courts consider many types of acts to be "transmission," there are some limits to the term's scope.

The second element requires the government or plaintiff to demonstrate that as a result of the knowing transmission, the defendant *intended* to damage a protected computer. It is important to keep in mind that this requirement is separate from the first element; not only must the government or plaintiff establish a *knowing* transmission, it also must demonstrate *intentional* damage. Although the CFAA does not define "intentional," courts generally have held that it requires a greater showing than a "knowing" act. For instance, the U.S. Court of Appeals for the Third Circuit has defined "intentionally," in the context of Section (a)(5), as "performing an act deliberately and not by accident."[110] In perhaps the most extensive discussion of the requirement to demonstrate intentional causation of damage, the U.S. Court of Appeals for the Sixth Circuit considered a civil lawsuit by a homebuilder against a labor union that organized an extensive email campaign, which the company claimed clogged employee inboxes and brought business to a standstill.[111] Relying on the dictionary definition, the Sixth Circuit, in *Pulte Homes, Inc. v. Laborers' International Union of North America*, concluded that in the context of the CFAA, "intentionally" means acting "with the conscious purpose of causing damage (in a statutory sense)" to a computer system.[112]

---

106 International Airport Centers, LLC v. Citrin, 440 F. 3d 418 (7th Cir. 2006).
107 *Id*. at 419.
108 *Id*.
109 *Id*.
110 United States v. Carlson, 209 Fed. Appx. 181, 185 (3d Cir. Dec. 22 2006) (unpublished).
111 Pulte Homes, Inc. v. Laborers' International Union of North America, 648 F.3d 295 (6th Cir. 2011).
112 *Id*. at 303.

Applying that definition, the court reasoned that the union acted intentionally because it instructed thousands of union members to email three of the company's executives and urged union members to "fight back." The court reasoned that such language "suggests that such a slow-down was at least one of its objectives."[113] These opinions suggest that as long as there is some credible evidence that the defendant committed the act with the purpose of causing damage, courts will conclude that the "intentional" requirement is satisfied.

The third element requires the government or plaintiff to demonstrate that the defendant caused *damage* to a protected computer. The CFAA defines "damage" as "any impairment to the integrity or availability of data, a program, a system, or information."[114] A federal court in Illinois, after reviewing nationwide CFAA cases, concluded that "damage" includes "the destruction, corruption, or deletion of electronic files, the physical destruction of a hard drive, or any diminution in the completeness or usability of the data on a computer system."[115] Although this is a fairly broad definition, it has some limits. For instance, in *New South Equipment Mats, LLC v. Keener*,[116] a federal judge in Mississippi dismissed a Section (a)(5) claim against a former employee who allegedly copied confidential business information but did not delete or modify the data on the company's computers.[117] The court concluded that because the company did not allege anything more than merely copying the information, it could not demonstrate that the former employee caused damage.[118] In contrast, in the *Pulte* case, the Sixth Circuit concluded that the email campaign *did* cause damage to Pulte because it disrupted the company's operations and prevented it from fully using its computer systems.[119] Although there is little binding precedent on the exact definition of "damage," these court opinions suggest that any harm to the original data or computer system, including an inability to access, likely will qualify as "damage," but merely copying data will not.

The fourth and final element is that the damage must have occurred without authorization. This typically does not present a significant issue in claims

---

113 *Id.*
114 18 U.S.C. § 1030(e)(8).
115 TriTeq Lock & Sec. LLC v. Innovative Secured Solutions, LLC, Civ. Action No. 10 CV 1304, 2012 WL 394229, at *6 (N.D.Ill. Feb. 1, 2012).
116 New South Equipment Mats, LLC v. Keener, 989 F. Supp. 2d 522 (S.D. Miss. 2013).
117 *Id.* at 524–25.
118 *Id.* at 530 ("[T]here is nothing in the complaint's factual allegations to indicate that Keener did more than copy files and transmit information. There is no allegation that he deleted files.").
119 Pulte Homes, Inc. v. Laborers' International Union of North America, 648 F.3d 295, 301–302 (6th Cir. 2011) ("Because Pulte alleges that the transmissions diminished its ability to send and receive calls and e-mails, it accordingly alleges an impairment to the integrity or availability of its data and systems—i.e., statutory damage.").

under Section (a)(5)(A) because the government or plaintiff must only demonstrate that the *damage* – not the access – was not authorized.[120]

5.1.3.5.2 CFAA Section (a)(5)(B): Intentional Access Without Authorization that Recklessly Causes Damage

Section (a)(5)(B) requires prosecutors to demonstrate three general elements: (1) intentional access of a protected computer; (2) without authorization; and (3) as a result of the access, recklessly causes damage. This is a very different crime from Section (a)(5)(A). In short, Section (a)(5)(B) focuses on whether the *access* was intentional and unauthorized, while Section (a)(5)(A) focuses on whether the *damage* was intentional and unauthorized.

The first element, intentional access of a protected computer, focuses on whether the *access* was intentional. In contrast, Section (a)(5)(A) only applies if the defendant intended to *cause damage*. In other words, the inquiry into intent under Section (a)(5)(B) is whether the defendant intentionally accessed a protected computer. Whether the defendant intended to cause damage is irrelevant to a prosecution or civil action under Section (a)(5)(B).

The second element requires a demonstration that the intentional access was without authorization. Again, this differs from Section (a)(5)(A), which focuses on whether the *damage* was authorized. Section (a)(5)(B)'s authorized access requirement also is narrower than the access provisions of other sections of the CFAA. Other sections, such as Section (a)(2), apply to acts that are done *either* without authorization *or* exceeding authorized access, but Section (a)(5) only applies to the first category. These terms are discussed more generally in Section 5.1.2 of this chapter, but they have special significance for this provision of the CFAA because it does not apply to exceeding authorized access. One court concluded that "without authorization" only applies to people who have "no rights, limited or otherwise, to access the computer in question."[121] The Sixth Circuit in *Pulte*, which, as discussed above, had ruled that the company had stated a viable claim under Section (a)(5)(A), dismissed the company's claim under Section (a)(5)(B).[122] The court reasoned that because the company allows the general public to contact its employees via email, it could not allege that the union encouraged people to access its computer systems without authorization.[123]

The third element requires the government or plaintiff to demonstrate that the intentional, unauthorized access recklessly caused damage. The definition

---

120 *See* Shamrock Foods Co. v. Gast, 535 F. Supp. 2d 962, 967 n.1 (D. Ariz. 2008) (explaining the difference between provisions in the CFAA that "define violation in terms of accessing a protected computer without authorization" and those that are "violated by causing damage without authorization").

121 LVRC Holdings LLC v. Brekka, 581 F.3d 1127, 1133 (9th Cir. 2009).

122 Pulte Homes, Inc. v. Laborers' International Union of North America, 648 F.3d 295, 304 (6th Cir. 2011).

123 *Id.*

of "damage" generally is the same as was discussed above for Section (a)(5)(A). The key difference is that for a claim under Section (a)(5)(B), the damage must have been caused *recklessly*. The CFAA does not define "recklessly," nor is there a significant discussion of the term in precedential CFAA cases. The Model Penal Code, which many states have adopted as the framework for their criminal laws, states that a person acts recklessly "when he consciously disregards a substantial and unjustifiable risk that the material element exists or will result from his conduct."[124] Applying this definition to Section (a)(5)(B), a person recklessly causes damage if she consciously disregards a large risk of damage created by her unauthorized, intentional access to a computer system.

Often, individuals will be found to have violated *both* Sections (a)(5)(A) and (a)(5)(B) with a single act. For instance, in the *Citrin* case described above, in which the Seventh Circuit concluded that the defendant violated Section (a)(5)(A) by deleting his former employers' files and installing a secure erasure program to permanently wipe the memory, the court concluded that the defendant *also* violated Section (a)(5)(B). The court concluded that he did not have authorized access after his employment terminated, and that his intentional access recklessly caused damage because "he resolved to destroy files that incriminated himself and other files that were also the property of his employer, in violation of the duty of loyalty that agency law imposes on an employee."[125]

5.1.3.5.3 CFAA Section (a)(5)(C): Intentional Access Without Authorization that Causes Damage and Loss

Section (a)(5)(C) requires prosecutors to demonstrate three general elements: (1) intentional access of a protected computer; (2) without authorization; and (3) as a result of the access, causes damage and loss.

Section (a)(5)(C) is quite similar to Section (a)(5)(B), with two key differences: Section (a)(5)(C) applies even if the damage was not recklessly caused, therefore allowing it to apply to a wider range of actions. However, Section (a)(5)(C) only applies if the defendant caused both damage *and* loss, while Section (a)(5)(B) only requires a showing of damage. "Loss" under the CFAA includes any reasonable costs to the victim, though courts have a wide range of opinions as to what costs qualify as "losses" under the CFAA. The next subsection, which covers the requirements for misdemeanors and felony convictions under Section (a)(5), explains how courts have defined "loss" for the purposes of CFAA cases.

---

124 MODEL PENAL CODE § 2.02(2)(c). The Model Penal Code elaborates that "[t]he risk must be of such a nature and degree that, considering the nature and purpose of the actor's conduct and the circumstances known to him, its disregard involves a gross deviation from the standard of conduct that a law-abiding person would observe in the actor's situation."
125 International Airport Centers, LLC v. Citrin, 440 F. 3d 418, 420 (7th Cir. 2006).

5.1.3.5.4 *CFAA Section (a)(5): Requirements for Felony and Misdemeanor Cases*

Congress has repeatedly amended the maximum criminal penalties under Section (a)(5), and it currently is among the most complex sentencing structures under the CFAA. Any violation of Section (a)(5) can be charged as a misdemeanor, punishable by a fine and up to a year in prison. However, if prosecutors seek more than a year in prison, they must charge the defendant with a felony. Section (a)(5) only allows felony charges in certain situations.

First-Time Violations of Sections (a)(5)(A) or (A)(5)(B), without Aggravating Factors To convict a defendant of a felony under Sections (a)(5)(A) and (a)(5)(B), if the defendant had not been convicted under the CFAA before committing the act, prosecutors must demonstrate that the offense caused one of the following:

- loss to one or more persons during a single year, totaling at least $5000 in value;
- the "modification or impairment, or potential modification or impairment, of the medical examination, diagnosis, treatment, or care of at least one individual";
- physical injury;
- a threat to public health or safety;
- damage to a federal government computer "in furtherance of the administration of justice, national defense, or national security"; or
- damage to ten or more protected computers during a single year.[126]

If the government can establish one of these forms of harm, it can seek a fine and imprisonment of up to ten years under Section (a)(5)(A), and a fine and imprisonment of up to five years under Section (a)(5)(B). If the government cannot establish one of those forms of harm, these violations are punishable as misdemeanors, with a fine and up to a year in prison.

According to the Justice Department's Computer Crime manual, felonies under Sections (a)(5)(A) and (a)(5)(B) are most often charged under the first scenario: causing a loss to one or more persons of at least $5000 over a one-year period.[127]

When courts determine whether a Section (a)(5) charge is punishable as a felony due to a loss, they must decide whether the government has adequately alleged at least $5000 in losses. Until 2001, the CFAA did not explicitly define "loss," leading courts to develop a fairly wide range of definitions. Congress's 2001 amendments that defined "loss" were modeled after an opinion issued a year earlier by the U.S. Court of Appeals for the Ninth Circuit, *United*

---

126 18 U.S.C. § 1030(c)(4)(A)(i).
127 U.S. Justice Department, PROSECUTING COMPUTER CRIMES at 42.

States v. Middleton.[128] The government brought a Section (a)(5)(A) charge against Nicholas Middleton, the former employee of an Internet service provider. After leaving the ISP, he accessed an administrative account to create new accounts, change administrative passwords, modify the computer's registry, and delete the ISP's billing system and other databases.[129] The ISP devoted significant staff time to repairing the damage that Middleton caused, and purchased new software. At his criminal trial, the judge denied his request to instruct the jury as to the meaning of "damage," and he was convicted of a Section (a)(5)(A) violation.

On appeal, Middleton argued that the government had not demonstrated that he caused at least $5000 in damages. The government had alleged that he caused approximately $10,000 in damages, and it arrived at this estimate by calculating the amount of time that each employee spent on remediation, and multiplying it by their hourly rates, and adding the costs of the consultant and the new software.[130] Middleton asserted that this method was incorrect because at least one of the employees was paid on a fixed salary and therefore did not pay any additional amount for the employee to fix the damage. The Ninth Circuit agreed with the government's calculation, and concluded that whether the employee is hourly or salaried is irrelevant; the proper question is "whether the amount of time spent by the employees and their imputed hourly rates were reasonable for the repair tasks that they performed[.]"[131] Applying that definition to Middleton's case, the Ninth Circuit concluded that the jury was reasonable to find that Middleton's actions caused at least $5000 in losses.[132]

The 2001 amendments to the CFAA, based on *Middleton* and included in the USA Patriot Act, define "loss" as "any reasonable cost to any victim, including the cost of responding to an offense, conducting a damage assessment, and restoring the data, program, system, or information to its condition prior to the offense, and any revenue lost, cost incurred, or other consequential damages incurred because of interruption of service."[133] Few published opinions in Section (a)(5) criminal cases have interpreted this definition, partly because it is so broad that there is little dispute as to what sorts of harms are covered. However, there has been some dispute about its application in CFAA civil cases, which are discussed in Section 5.1.4 of this chapter.

---

128 United States v. Middleton, 231 F.3d 1207 (9th Cir. 2000). Until Congress amended the CFAA in 2008 to add a Section (a)(5)(A) misdemeanor provision, the government only had the option of charging Section (a)(5)(A) violations as a felony.
129 *Id.* at 1209.
130 *Id.* at 1214.
131 *Id.*
132 *Id.*
133 18 U.S.C. § 1030(e)(11).

First-Time Violations of Section (a)(5)(C) Unlike the two other crimes in Section (a)(5), Section (A)(5)(C) does not provide for felony charges for first-time offenders. If a defendant has not been convicted of any other CFAA crime before violating Section (a)(5)(C), the government can only charge the defendant with a misdemeanor, punishable by a fine and up to a year in prison.

Repeat Violations under Section (a)(5) If the defendant had been convicted of a CFAA crime before violating Section (a)(5), the penalties will be higher (and, in the cases of Sections (a)(5)(A) and (a)(5)(B), do not require proof of at least $5000 in losses or the five other scenarios described above). A defendant previously convicted of a CFAA crime can be sentenced to a fine and up to twenty years in prison for violations of Section (a)(5)(A) and (a)(5)(B), and a fine and up to ten years in prison for violations of Section (a)(5)(C).

Aggravating Factors In certain cases, an individual convicted of a Section (a)(5)(A) violation can receive a greater sentence, regardless of whether it is a first-time offense or the size of the losses caused by the hacking. If the defendant attempted to cause or knowingly or recklessly caused serious bodily injury via a Section (a)(5)(A) violation, she may be sentenced to a fine or up to twenty years in prison. If the defendant attempted to cause or knowingly or recklessly caused death via a Section (a)(5)(A) violation, she can be sentenced to a fine and up to a life term in prison.

5.1.3.6 CFAA Section (a)(6): Trafficking in Passwords

Section (a)(6) of the CFAA prohibits individuals from knowingly, and with the intent to defraud, trafficking in passwords or similar information through which a computer can be accessed without authorization, provided that the trafficking either affects interstate or foreign commerce, or the computer is used by or for the federal government. Because of the relatively small penalties attached to Section (a)(6), it is among the less commonly prosecuted and litigated sections of the CFAA.

Congress added Section (a)(6) to the CFAA in 1986, out of concern that hackers were using "pirate bulletin boards" to share victims' passwords.[134]

Section (a)(6) is intended to broadly define the term "password," and cover a wide range of information that can be used to access a computer. The Senate Judiciary Committee's report accompanying the 1986 bill clarified that the legislators intended to not only protect the single string of characters commonly thought of as a "password" but also intended to cover "longer more detailed explanations on how to access others' computers."

In the rare instances in which courts have written opinions interpreting Section (a)(6), there occasionally has been a dispute about the meaning of "trafficking."

---

134 H. Rept. 99-612 at 7 (1986).

Section (a)(6) defines "traffic" as "transfer, or otherwise to dispose of, to another, or obtain control of with intent to transfer or dispose of." This is a fairly broad definition of "traffic," and it does not require evidence that the defendant sold the password or information for money. However, the defendant will not be liable for *receiving* passwords. For instance, in *State Analysis v. American Financial Services*,[135] a federal judge dismissed a Section (a)(6) civil lawsuit filed by a database provider against a company that allegedly received a password for the database from another source. The court reasoned that such behavior does not qualify as "trafficking" for the purposes of the CFAA.[136]

Even if the defendant trafficked in passwords, Section (a)(6) only applies if the prosecutor or plaintiff can demonstrate that the defendant did so with an intent to defraud. In *AtPac, Inc. v. Aptitude Solutions, Inc.*,[137] Nevada County, California was transitioning software service providers, from AtPac to Aptitude Solutions. To make the transition easier, Nevada County requested that AtPac provide Aptitude with a user account, allowing Aptitude to access the county's data. Nevertheless, a county employee created a log-in account on AtPac's system and provided it to Aptitude. AtPac sued the county and Aptitude for violating Section (a)(6). The district court swiftly dismissed this claim. The court noted that merely providing another person with a password is not prohibited by Section (a)(6). That provision only applies, the court noted, if the defendant intended to defraud. Although the County employee's actions might have violated AtPac's license agreement, the court reasoned, there was no evidence that the County intended to defraud AtPac. The County's actions were "not the sort of fraud Congress envisioned when it made password trafficking subject to criminal penalties," the court wrote.[138]

Moreover, Section (a)(6) only applies if the traffic password allows a computer to be accessed without authorization. The *AtPac* court concluded that this also provided it with a reason to dismiss the lawsuit. The court determined that under the CFAA, "a person cannot access a computer 'without authorization' if the gatekeeper has given them permission to use it."[139] AtPac had already given the County permission to log in to the server. The court wrote that it "cannot conclude that Congress intended to impose criminal liability on third parties just because a computer licensee violates a license agreement."[140]

If the defendant has not been convicted of a CFAA violation before violating Section (a)(6), the defendant can be sentenced to a fine and no more than a

---

135 State Analysis v. American Financial Services, 621 F. Supp. 2d 309 (E.D. Va. 2009).
136 *Id.* at 317 ("The Complaint does not allege that KSE transferred, or otherwise disposed of, AFSA's passwords; rather, it alleges that KSE received them from AFSA and used them without authorization.").
137 AtPac, Inc. v. Aptitude Solutions, Inc., 730 F. Supp. 2d 1174 (E.D. Cal. 2010).
138 *Id.* at 1183.
139 *Id.* at 1180.
140 *Id.* at 1183.

year in prison. If the defendant had been convicted of a CFAA violation before violating Section (a)(6), the defendant can be sentenced to a fine and up to ten years in prison.

5.1.3.7 CFAA Section (a)(7): Threatening to Damage or Obtain Information from a Computer

Section (a)(7) prohibits individuals from transmitting in interstate or foreign commerce any communication containing three types of threats or demands: (1) a threat to damage a protected computer; (2) a threat to obtain information from a protected computer without authorization or in excess of authorization or to "impair the confidentiality of information obtained from a protected computer without authorization or by exceeding authorized access"; or (3) a demand or request for "money or other thing of value in relation to damage to a protected computer, where such damage was caused to facilitate the extortion."[141] Section (a)(7) only applies if the defendant was acting with intent to extort from any person any money or other thing of value.

Unlike Sections (a)(1)–(a)(5), Section (a)(7)'s applicability does not depend on whether the defendant *actually* accessed, damaged, or obtained information from a computer. Instead, Section (a)(7) applies to the defendant's *attempt* to extort money from a victim by threatening a computer crime.

Section (a)(7) addresses a similar crime that is prohibited by the Hobbs Act, a 1948 federal extortion law. That statute imposes a sentence of a fine and up to twenty years in prison on any individual who "threatens physical violence to any person or property."[142] In the 1996 Senate Report accompanying the CFAA amendments, Section (a)(7)'s authors wrote that Section (a)(7) was necessary because the term "property" in the Hobbs Act "does not clearly include the operation of a computer, the data or programs stored in a computer or its peripheral equipment, or the decoding keys to encrypted data."[143] The government likely could attempt that computers, networks, and data are property under the Hobbs Act, but it wanted a more direct route to prosecute online extortionists that would present less legal uncertainty. In fact, defendants who are charged with violating Section (a)(7) often also are charged with violating the Hobbs Act.

Section (a)(7) is relatively new to the CFAA. Congress added the provision in 1996, after the U.S. Justice Department reported that hackers had increasingly made threats to penetrate computer systems. In the Senate report accompanying the 1996 amendments to the CFAA, the legislators expressed a desire to "address a new and emerging problem of computer-age blackmail."[144]

---

141 18 U.S.C. § 1030(a)(7).
142 18 U.S.C. § 1951.
143 S.R. 104-367 (1996) at 12.
144 S.R. 104-367 (1996) at 12.

In fact, Congress's motivations for amending the CFAA appear to be quite prescient more than two decades later. As Congress explained:

> One can imagine situations in which hackers penetrate a system, encrypt a database and then demand money for the decoding key. This new provision would ensure law enforcement's ability to prosecute modern-day blackmailers, who threaten to harm or shut down computer networks unless their extortion demands are met.[145]

Sound familiar? Twenty years after Congress enacted Section (a)(7), ransomware became among the most concerning trends in cybersecurity. Theoretically, Section (a)(7) provides a very direct mechanism to bring criminal and civil actions against hackers that have used ransomware to attempt to extort money from companies and individuals. However, many of the most egregious ransomware distributors hide behind well-masked anonymity, making prosecutions and civil lawsuits quite difficult. They use Bitcoin as the payment currency, further cloaking their identity and the ability to be tracked by law enforcement.

Ransomware – and other extortion attempts – often originate from other countries. Congress contemplated this problem in 1996 when it drafted Section (a)(7), and explicitly stated that it covers threats used in both interstate *and* foreign commerce. The government used this ability to prosecute foreign extortionists in *United States v. Ivanov*.[146] Aleksey Ivanov allegedly hacked into the computer system of a Connecticut company that processes online retailers' credit card transactions. While he was located in Russia or another former Soviet bloc country, Ivanov emailed the company to inform them that he obtained its system administrator root passwords, threatened to destroy its database, and demanded $10,000.[147] Among the email messages that he sent was the following:

> [name redacted], now imagine please Somebody hack you network (and not notify you about this), he download Atomic software with more than 300 merchants, transfer money, and after this did 'rm-rf/' and after this you company be ruined. I don't want this, and because this i notify you about possible hack in you network, if you want you can hire me and im allways be check security in you network. What you think about this?[148]

Ivanov was indicted in federal court in Connecticut on eight counts, including a violation of Section (a)(7). Ivanov filed a motion to dismiss the indictment,

---

145 *Id.*
146 United States v. Ivanov, 175 F. Supp. 2d 367 (D. Conn. 2001).
147 *Id.* at 369.
148 *Id.*

arguing that because he was in Russia or another Soviet bloc country at the time of the alleged email threats, the CFAA and other statutes could not apply to him. The district court denied this motion for two reasons. First, it reasoned that if an individual violates a law with the intent to cause effects within the United States, then U.S. courts have jurisdiction to hear criminal cases involving that action.[149] Ivanov allegedly transmitted a threat to a company located in Connecticut, and threatened to further damage its computers, also located in Connecticut.[150] Second, the court concluded that Section (a)(7)'s explicit reference to computers used in "foreign" commerce demonstrated an intent of Congress to apply the statute extraterritorially.[151]

Courts have generally required a Section (a)(7) indictment or civil claim to provide proof of an explicit threat. Merely hacking to cause damage or obtain information will not sustain a Section (a)7) claim, even if that action violates other parts of the CFAA. In Ivanov's case, the email was clear proof of an explicit threat that violates Section (a)(7).

In other cases, however, the evidence of a threat is not as compelling. In *Vaquero Energy v. Herda*,[152] Vaquero Energy, an oil and gas collection and installations company, hired Jeff Herda to provide information technology support. Vaquero Energy alleges that Herda and his company changed the passwords to critical SCADA systems and devices without Vaquero Energy's permission.[153] Vaquero Energy claimed that it asked Herda to provide all of its log-ins and passwords, but Herda provided incomplete information, and that he later stopped providing services to the company. Vaquero Energy claimed that its lack of password information left its systems vulnerable and insecure, and sued Herda under a number of statutes, including Section (a)(7) of the CFAA. In a preliminary injunction order, the court concluded that the Section (a)(7) claim was unlikely to succeed on the merits because Vaquero Energy did not allege that Herda made a threat or demand. Although Vaquero Energy's lawyer demanded that Herda provide the passwords, and Herda responded, the court concluded that this exchange did not constitute a demand or threat made by Herda.[154] Moreover, the court found that the claim also failed because there was no allegation that Herda changed the password in order to extort money. The *Vaquero Energy* case demonstrates the need for prosecutors and civil litigants to allege a specific threat and intent to extort money.

A defendant is convicted of a violation of Section (a)(7) faces a fine and up to five years in prison. If the defendant had been convicted of a CFAA offense

---

149 *Id.* at 370.
150 *Id.* at 372.
151 *Id.* at 374.
152 Vaquero Energy v. Herda, Case No. 1:15-cv-00967 JLT, 2015 U.S. Dist. LEXIS 126122 (E.D. Cal. Sept. 25, 2015).
153 *Id.* at *3.
154 *Id.* at *13.

before violating Section (a)(7), the defendant faces a fine and up to ten years in prison.

5.1.4 Civil Actions under the CFAA

Although the CFAA is primarily a criminal statute that is enforced by federal prosecutors, the statute allows certain private parties that have suffered a damage or loss by CFAA violations to bring civil actions against the violators. Indeed, many of the CFAA cases discussed in this section involve civil litigation between two private parties. This is partly due to the nature of the acts that constitute CFAA violations: obtaining information or causing damage without proper authorization. These actions often cause significant harm to companies, and they understandably seek compensation. Moreover, private CFAA claims often arise in larger disputes with former employees who later work for a competitor.

CFAA lawsuits must be brought within two years of the harmful act, or the date of discovery of the damage.[155] The statute prohibits private CFAA lawsuits that arise from the negligent design or manufacture of hardware, software, or firmware.

The CFAA only allows private litigants to sue if they have suffered a "damage" or "loss." The CFAA defines "damage" as "any impairment to the integrity or availability of data, a program, a system, or information,"[156] and defines "loss" as "any reasonable cost to any victim, including the cost of responding to an offense, conducting a damage assessment, and restoring the data, program, system, or information to its condition prior to the offense, and any revenue lost, cost incurred, or other consequential damages incurred because of interruption of service."[157]

Courts generally have applied broad definitions of these terms, and allowed a fairly wide range of plaintiffs to sue. For instance, in the *Shurgard Storage Centers* case, discussed in Section 5.1.3.4 of this chapter, the plaintiff alleged that its former employees' use of its computer systems to send trade secrets to the defendant, its competitor, caused damages under the CFAA.[158] The defendant contended that these actions did not constitute "damage" because there was not any *impairment* to the integrity or availability of the data or information, as required in the statute.[159] The court acknowledged that the term "integrity," in this context, is ambiguous. To resolve the dispute, the court

---

155 18 U.S.C. § 1030(g).
156 18 U.S.C. § 1030(e)(8).
157 *Id.*
158 Shurgard Storage Centers, Inc. v. Safeguard Self Storage, Inc., 119 F. Supp. 2d 1121 (W.D. Wash. 2000).
159 *Id.* at 1126.

looked to the Senate report accompanying the 1996 CFAA amendments, which changed the definition of "damage." The Senate wrote that it intended the term "damage" to include the theft of information – such as passwords – even if the original data was not altered or rendered inaccessible. Applying this broad definition of "damage" to Shurgard Storage's claims, the court concluded that even though the confidential business information remained intact and unharmed on the company's computers, the data's integrity was impaired because it was stolen. Therefore, the court held that the plaintiffs had sufficiently alleged damages under CFAA.[160]

Even if private parties have suffered a damage or loss, they may only bring CFAA lawsuits in certain circumstances. To establish the right to file a civil action, the plaintiff must allege that the CFAA violation resulted in one of the following:

- loss to at least one person, totaling at least $5000 in value during a one-year period;
- the actual or potential modification or impairment of the medical examination, diagnosis, treatment, or care of at least one individual;
- physical injury;
- a threat to public health or safety; or
- damage affecting a federal government computer in furtherance of the administration of justice, national defense, or national security.[161]

If the lawsuit alleges only a loss to a person that totals at least $5000 in damages, the plaintiff may only recover economic damages. However, if the lawsuit alleges any of the four other types of harms arising from the CFAA violation, the plaintiff may obtain compensatory damages, injunctive relief, and other equitable relief.[162]

In some CFAA civil actions seeking economic damages for losses, courts have grappled with what constitutes at least "$5000 in value." The statute provides a right to economic damages if the offense caused "loss to 1 or more persons during any 1-year period (and, for purposes of an investigation, prosecution, or other proceeding brought by the United States only, loss resulting from a related course of conduct affecting 1 or more other protected computers) aggregating at least $5,000 in value."[163]

For instance, in *Creative Computing v. Getloaded.com LLC*,[164] the Ninth Circuit considered a civil action under Section (a)(4) that the operator of an online trucking services website, Creative Computing, filed against a competitor, Getloaded.com. Creative Computing alleged that Getloaded.com used its

---

160 *Id.* at 1126–27.
161 18 U.S.C. § 1030(g); 18 U.S.C. § 1030(c)(4)(A)(i).
162 18 U.S.C. 1030(g).
163 18 U.S.C. § 1030(c)(4).
164 Creative Computing v. Getloaded.com LLC, 386 F.3d 930 (9th Cir. 2004).

customers' credentials to log in to Creative Computing's website and obtain information. Creative Computing also alleged that Getloaded.com's officers hacked Creative Computing's website code, and hired a Creative Computing employee, who downloaded customer data and other confidential information.[165] With all of this data, Creative Computing alleged, Getloaded.com attempted to replicate Creative Computing's website and business model. Getloaded.com sought to dismiss the lawsuit, arguing that the CFAA only allows civil damages if the plaintiff suffered at least $5000 in damages from *each* instance of unauthorized access.[166] The Ninth Circuit rejected this reading of the statute, holding that the $5000 minimum "applies to how much damage or loss there is to the victim over a one-year period, not from a particular intrusion."[167] In other words, if Company A hacks Company B's website 10,000 times during a year, each time causing $1 in damage, Company B could sue Company A for CFAA violations. If, however, each hack caused 25 cents in damage, Company B could not sue Company A because the total damage would be less than $5000.

5.1.5 Criticisms of the CFAA

Companies, government agencies, and advocacy groups have criticized the CFAA for not effectively presenting many proposals to amend – and in some cases, repeal – the CFAA. Some argue that the CFAA is far too punitive in light of the relatively minor acts that it prohibits, while others argue that it does not effectively prevent some of the most pressing cybersecurity threats.

Among the most prominent criticisms of the CFAA comes from advocacy groups and some legislators, who argue that the CFAA imposes significant criminal penalties on technical violations of the CFAA that do little or no harm to people or property. Perhaps their most compelling argument comes from the case of Aaron Swartz, who as a teenager helped develop Reddit and the technology underlying RSS news feeds. Throughout his teens and twenties, Swartz was an active member of the CopyLeft, movement, which challenged the ability of companies to control the distribution of their materials on the Internet.

In 2010, Swartz, while working at a laboratory at Harvard, connected a computer to the Massachusetts Institute of Technology's network and, without the school's approval, downloaded millions of academic articles via the school's access to JSTOR, a proprietary database. In 2011, Swartz was arrested, and later indicted in federal court for eleven counts under CFAA Sections (a)(2), (a)(4), and (a)(5), as well as two counts of wire fraud, exposing Swartz to up to

---

165 *Id.* at 932.
166 *Id.* at 933.
167 *Id.* at 934.

thirty-five years in prison.[168] In 2013, at age 26, Swartz committed suicide. A number of critics used this tragedy to highlight what they viewed as significant problems with the CFAA.

Justin Peters, in Slate, wrote that the Swartz suicide demonstrates the "disproportionate" nature of U.S. computer crime laws, and "the laxity with which these laws have been conceived and amended – and the increasing severity of their corresponding penalties – has had serious consequences."[169] Sen. Ron Wyden introduced Aaron's Law, which would make the following changes to the CFAA:

- explicitly adopt the narrower *Nosal* reading of "exceeds authorized access" and clarify that merely violating an agreement does not trigger the CFAA;
- prevent a defendant from being liable for multiple CFAA counts arising from a single incident; and
- prevent the prosecution for a single act under both the CFAA and state hacking laws.[170]

Cybersecurity researchers also are among the most vocal critics of the CFAA.[171] They argue that the rigid requirements of many CFAA sections have a chilling effect on researchers who seek to help companies find and patch vulnerabilities in their systems and networks. Zach Lanier, a cybersecurity researcher, told the *Guardian* newspaper in 2014 that after he informed a device maker of a security vulnerability that he discovered, he received a response from the device maker's lawyer, who claimed that Lanier violated the CFAA. Lanier said that this threat caused him to abandon the research on this flaw. "The looming threat of CFAA as ammunition for anyone to use willy-nilly was enough," Lanier told the *Guardian*, "and had a chilling effect on our research."[172]

Cybersecurity professionals also criticize the CFAA for limiting their ability to engage in active defense of their computers and networks (also known as "hacking back"). Consider a company that is barraged with attacks from a specific set of IP addresses. That company's information security professionals might be tempted to counterattack, in an attempt to knock the adversary

---

168 Superseding Indictment, United States v. Swartz, Crim. No. 11-CR-10260-NMG (Sept. 12, 2012).

169 Justin Peters, *Congress has a Chance to Fix its Bad 'Internet Crime' Law*, SLATE (Apr. 24, 2015).

170 S.1030, 114th Congress.

171 *See* Kaveh Waddell, *Aaron's Law Reintroduced as Lawmakers Wrestle over Hacking Penalties*, The Atlantic (Apr. 21, 2015) ("The CFAA in its current form is harmful to computer security researchers—who hack into devices and networks to find and expose vulnerabilities—according to the Electronic Frontier Foundation, because it exposes researchers to liability and punishment at the same level as malicious hackers.").

172 Tom Brewster, *U.S. Cybercrime Laws being used to Target Security Researchers*, THE GUARDIAN (May 29, 2014).

offline. Unfortunately for the company, such responses pose a very real risk of violating Section (a)(5) of the CFAA. Critics of "hacking back" assert that it is difficult to attribute the source of an attack with 100 percent certainty, and therefore the retaliatory actions could hurt innocent bystanders. For instance, Robert M. Lee, co-founder of Dragos Security LLC, said that if "organizations cannot effectively run defense programs and tackle the security basics, they cannot run an effective offensive program."[173] They argue that the CFAA correctly prohibits individuals and companies from taking the law into their own hands.

On the other side of the spectrum, some critics argue that the CFAA does not adequately protect the United States against emerging threats, such as botnets and the 2014 attack by North Korea on Sony Pictures Entertainment. In 2015, President Obama responded to these concerns by introducing a bill to update the CFAA. His proposal would explicitly criminalize the sale of "means of access," such as botnets, and increase the penalties for certain CFAA violations. The proposal also would define "exceeds authorized access" as occurring when an individual accesses, obtains, or alters information if the individual "is not entitled to obtain or alter," *or* "for a purpose that the accesser knows is not authorized by the computer owner."

Neither Aaron's Law nor the White House proposal had been enacted by Congress as of the publication of this book, though it is likely that there will be continued efforts to amend the CFAA.

The Story of Megan Meier, Lori Drew, and the CFAA

Among the highest profile CFAA cases in recent years was the U.S. government's unsuccessful attempt to prosecute Lori Drew under the statute. The story of Drew's prosecution demonstrates the limits of the CFAA in the increasingly complex world of social media and always-on connectivity.

Megan Meier, a 13-year-old Missouri girl, was contacted via MySpace by an individual calling himself "Josh Evans," a 16-year-old boy who appeared to be interested in pursuing a relationship with Meier. After flirting with Meier for a few weeks, Josh Evans told her that the world would be a better place without her in it. That same day, Meier committed suicide.

Josh Evans was not a teenage boy. Rather, he was a fictional character created by Lori Drew, Meier's adult neighbor, Drew's teenage daughter, and an employee of Drew. The suicide – and the revelation that an adult was behind a deadly prank – grabbed national attention. However, Missouri prosecutors did not have sufficient evidence to bring charges against Drew under state law.

---

173 Taylor Armerding, *Hack the Hackers? The Debate Rages On*, CSO (May 1, 2015).

> Federal prosecutors in California, where MySpace is headquartered, decided to take matters into their own hands. They charged Drew with violating Section (a)(2) of the CFAA, alleging that she violated MySpace's terms of service to obtain information about Meier, therefore exceeding authorized access. After trial, the jury found her not guilty of three CFAA felony counts (which required a demonstration that she violated Section (a)(2) in furtherance of the tort of intentional infliction of emotional distress), but found her guilty of a misdemeanor count under Section (a)(2), which did not require a link to the emotional distress tort.
>
> The district court judge set aside the jury's misdemeanor conviction of Drew, concluding that it would be unconstitutionally vague to convict someone based on the violation of a website's terms of service. The court reasoned that "if any conscious breach of a website's terms of service is held to be sufficient by itself to constitute intentionally accessing a computer without authorization or in excess of authorization, the result will be that section 1030(a)(2)(C) becomes a law that affords too much discretion to the police and too little notice to citizens who wish to use the Internet." The government did not appeal this decision.
>
> The difficulty of convicting Drew of what was indisputably a horrendous act demonstrates the difficulty of applying the 1980s-era Computer Fraud and Abuse Act to many of the emerging social issues that arise online. In recent years, victims' rights groups have proposed many laws that create new civil and criminal remedies for online harassment.

5.2 State Computer Hacking Laws

Most states also have similar anti-hacking laws that apply to hacking that occurs within their boundaries.[174] Some state laws predate the CFAA, and often prohibit activities that are not addressed by the CFAA. Therefore, if you are considering the legal implications of computer fraud or hacking, you must consider not only the CFAA but the state law.

To illustrate the requirements of some state computer hacking laws – and the key differences with the CFAA, it is useful to examine California Penal Code 502, one of the most prominent and commonly prosecuted state computer crime laws. California Penal Code 502 explicitly penalizes 154 types of computer-related actions. California Penal Code 502, edited slightly below for clarity and brevity, prohibits any of the following acts, provided that they were committed knowingly:

1) Accessing and without permission altering, damaging, deleting, destroying, or otherwise using any data, computer, computer system, or computer

---

174 For a complete list of the state anti-hacking laws, visit the National Conference of State Legislatures website, which contains a list of the state laws and links to the full text of the laws. The website is *available at* http://www.ncsl.org/research/telecommunications-and-information-technology/computer-hacking-and-unauthorized-access-laws.aspx.

network in order to either (a) devise or execute any scheme or artifice to defraud, deceive, or extort, or (b) wrongfully control or obtain money, property, or data.

2) Accessing and without permission taking, copying, or making use of any data from a computer, computer system, or computer network, or taking or copying any supporting documentation, whether existing or residing internal or external to a computer, computer system, or computer network.

3) Without permission using or causing to be used computer services.

4) Accessing and without permission adding, altering, damaging, deleting, or destroying any data, computer software, or computer programs that reside or exist internal or external to a computer, computer system, or computer network.

5) Without permission disrupting or causing the disruption of computer services or denies or causes the denial of computer services to an authorized user of a computer, computer system, or computer network.

6) Without permission providing or assisting in providing a means of accessing a computer, computer system, or computer network.

7) Without permission accessing or causing to be accessed any computer, computer system, or computer network.

8) Introducing any computer contaminant into any computer, computer system, or computer network.

9) Without permission using the Internet domain name or profile of another individual, corporation, or entity in connection with the sending of one or more electronic mail messages or posts and thereby damages or causes damage to a computer, computer data, computer system, or computer network.

10) Without permission disrupting or causing the disruption of government computer services or denying or causing the denial of government computer services to an authorized user of a government computer, computer system, or computer network.

11) Accessing and without permission adding, altering, damaging, deleting, or destroying any data, computer software, or computer programs that reside or exist internal or external to a public safety infrastructure computer system computer, computer system, or computer network.

12) Without permission disrupting or causing the disruption of public safety infrastructure or denying or causing the denial of computer services to an authorized user of a public safety infrastructure computer system computer, computer system, or computer network.

13) Without permission providing or assisting in providing a means of accessing a computer, computer system, or public safety infrastructure computer system computer, computer system, or computer network in violation of this section.

14) Introducing any computer contaminant into any public safety infrastructure computer system computer, computer system, or computer network.[175]

---

175 Cal. Penal Code § 502(c).

Like the CFAA, California Penal Code 502 provides hacking victims with the ability to sue individuals who violate this statute and cause damage or loss.[176]

The most striking difference between Cal. Penal Code 502 and the CFAA is that the California law enumerates twice as many prohibited acts. However, the statutes prohibit many of the same types of actions, though the California law is more specific, in part because it has been amended six times since 2000 and more directly addresses new technological issues. For instance, sections 4, 5, 10, 11, 12, and 14 all involve damage to computers, systems, or data, and many of these acts likely could fall under the broader umbrella of CFAA Section (a)(5).

The California hacking law also covers actions that the CFAA does not explicitly address. For instance, the prohibition in section 3 of the California law – related to the use of computer services without permission – criminalizes the theft of services such as email and cloud storage. The CFAA does not directly address such a crime, though in some cases it could be covered under Section (a)(2)'s prohibitions regarding obtaining information. Likewise, Section 9 of the California law explicitly prohibits hacking Internet domain names to send spam. Although the CFAA does not address spam, there is a reasonable argument that in some cases, such activities cause damage in violation of Section (a)(5) of the CFAA.

Perhaps the largest overall difference between the California law and the CFAA is the type of access required to trigger the law's prohibition. As discussed above, the CFAA applies to acts that are done either without authorization or exceeding authorized access. In contrast, the California hacking law applies to access that is done knowingly and "without permission."

Unfortunately, the definition of "without permission" is not entirely clear. The statute does not define the term, and the California Supreme Court – which has the final authority in interpreting California state laws – has not weighed in on the issue. However, federal judges interpreting the California statute in civil cases have reached opposite conclusions.

In a 2007 case, *Facebook, Inc. v. ConnectU*,[177] a California federal judge held that ConnectU, a Facebook competitor, violated Section 502 by accessing the email addresses of millions of Facebook users, in violation of Facebook's terms of use. ConnectU argued that private companies such as Facebook should not be permitted to dictate terms of service that could lead to criminal penalties. The judge rejected this argument, reasoning that "[t]he fact that private parties are free to set the conditions on which they will grant such permission does not mean that private parties are defining what is criminal and what is not."[178]

---

176 CAL. PENAL CODE § 502(e).
177 Facebook, Inc. v. ConnectU, 489 F. Supp. 2d 1087, 1089 (N.D. Cal. 2007).
178 *Id.* at 1091.

A different judge from the same court rejected that reasoning in a 2010 case, *Facebook, Inc. v. Power Ventures, Inc.*,[179] concluding that "allowing violations of terms of use to fall within the ambit of the statutory term 'without permission' does essentially place in private hands unbridled discretion to determine the scope of criminal liability recognized under the statute. If the issue of permission to access or use a website depends on adhering to unilaterally imposed contractual terms, the website or computer system administrator has the power to determine which actions may expose a user to criminal liability." Rather than looking at the terms of use to determine whether access was without permission, the judge stated that access without permission is that which "circumvents technical or code-based barriers that a computer network or website administrator erects to restrict the user's privileges within the system, or to bar the user from the system altogether."[180]

If the California Supreme Court were to eventually adopt the *ConnectU* reasoning, Cal. Penal Code 502 would be just as broad – if not broader – than even the most expansive interpretations of the CFAA. However, the *Power Ventures* interpretation of Cal. Penal Code 502 is even more restrictive than the narrow interpretations of the CFAA. For now, there is little certainty for individuals and companies in California, as neither interpretation is binding on any other judge in California.

5.3 Section 1201 of the Digital Millennium Copyright Act

Since the founding of the United States, laws have provided the authors of creative works and expressions with a copyright, which gives them a limited right to control the distribution, publication, and performance of their works. The U.S. Constitution encourages such protection, providing Congress with the ability to "promote the progress of science and useful arts, by securing for limited times to authors and inventors the exclusive right to their respective writings and discoveries."[181] For more than two centuries, copyright law has been an integral part of the economic framework for producing books, newspapers, music, movies, and other creative expression. U.S. copyright law provides the creators of content with certain exclusive rights to control the republication, performance, and other uses of their content for a limited duration. Over the past two decades, as content such as books, music, and videos has increasingly

---

179 Facebook, Inc. v. Power Ventures, Inc., C 08-05780 JW, 2010 U.S. Dist. LEXIS 93517 (N.D. Cal. July 20, 2010).
180 *Id.* at *11.
181 U.S. Const. art. I, § 8.

moved online, Congress and regulators have grappled with determining how to apply copyright law to the Internet.

Section 1201 of the Digital Millennium Copyright Act restricts the ability of individuals to circumvent access controls that protect copyrighted material. Unlike other provisions in U.S. copyright law, which protect the rights of copyright owners to control the distribution, performance, copying, and other use of their protected works, Section 1201 protects the technology that companies use to control access to their works. Because of this close nexus with technology, Section 1201 is deeply intertwined with cybersecurity. Like the CFAA, it restricts the ability of individuals to access digital materials. However, it also has received a great deal of criticism by making it more difficult to perform vulnerability testing and other security research on any products, software, or services that contain access controls.

5.3.1 Origins of Section 1201 of the DMCA

In 1996, members of the World Intellectual Property Organization – including the United States – finalized the WIPO Copyright Treaty, which set common legal rules for copyright protection in the digital age. Among the provisions in the treaty was a requirement that participating nations "provide adequate legal protection and effective legal remedies against the circumvention of effective technological measures that are used by authors in connection with the exercise of their rights."[182]

In 1998, Congress enacted the Digital Millennium Copyright Act, which significantly amended U.S. copyright laws to implement the WIPO Copyright Treaty and, more generally, "to make digital networks safe places to disseminate and exploit copyrighted materials."[183] The law contains many important and noteworthy provisions, such as Section 512, which establishes a process by which websites and other online services may be notified of infringing content on their services, and must remove that content to avoid being sued for copyright infringement. For the purposes of cybersecurity, however, the most relevant DMCA provision is Section 1201.

Section 1201 of the DMCA is intended to satisfy the WIPO Copyright Treaty's requirement regarding circumvention. In the Senate report accompanying the DMCA, legislators stated that they intended to punish the circumvention of measures that are intended to protect copyrighted works, such as passwords, if the "primary purpose" of that circumvention is to break the

---

182 WIPO Copyright Treaty, art. 11.
183 S. Rep. 105-190 (1998) at 1; *see also* H.R. Rep. No. 105-551, pt. 1, at 17 (1998) ("Copyright laws have struggled through the years to keep pace with emerging technology from the struggle over music played on a player piano roll in the 1900's to the introduction of the VCR in the 1980's. With this constant evolution in technology, the law must adapt in order to make digital networks safe places to disseminate and exploit copyrighted materials.").

control. The report states that such prohibitions are analogous to "making it illegal to break into a house using a tool, the primary purpose of which is to break into houses."[184]

5.3.2 Three Key Provisions of Section 1201 of the DMCA

Section 1201 of the DMCA has three primary provisions that each restrict certain actions regarding access controls:

- Section (a)(1) prohibits the act of **circumventing** technology that controls access to copyrighted material.
- Section (a)(2) prohibits **trafficking** in technology that facilitate circumvention of access control measures.
- Section (b)(1) prohibits **trafficking** in technology that facilitate circumvention of measures that protect against copyright infringement.

This subsection examines each of these restrictions, and how courts have interpreted them.

5.3.2.1 DMCA Section 1201(a)(1)

Section (a)(1) of the DMCA is perhaps the most direct and least controversial of the three sections. It prohibits individuals from circumventing "a technological measure that effectively controls access to a work" that is protected by copyright law.[185]

Congress included Section (a)(1) because, at the time the DMCA was passed, "the conduct of circumvention was never before made unlawful," according to the Senate report accompanying the DMCA.[186]

At the outset, it is important to note that Section (a)(1) focuses solely on whether the defendant *circumvented* technology that protects a copyrighted work. As legislators stated when they drafted the DMCA, the types of actions prohibited by Section (a)(1) are analogous to "breaking into a locked room in order to obtain a copy of a book."[187] Section (a)(1) does *not* restrict subsequent use, performance, or distribution of the copyrighted materials that are obtained via this circumvention; those activities are protected in other provisions in U.S. copyright law.[188]

---

184 S. Rep. 105-190 at 11.
185 17 U.S.C. § 1201(a)(1).
186 S. Rep. 105-190 (1998) at 12.
187 H.R. Rep. No. 105-551, pt. 1, at 17 (1998).
188 *See* Universal City Studios, Inc. v. Corley, 273 F.3d 429, 443 (2d Cir. 2001) ("[T]he DMCA targets the circumvention of digital walls guarding copyrighted material (and trafficking in circumvention tools), but does not concern itself with the use of those materials after circumvention has occurred."); H.R. Rep. No. 105-551, pt. 1, at 18 ("Paragraph (a)(1) does not apply to the subsequent actions of a person once he or she has obtained authorized access to a copy of a work protected under Title 17, even if such actions involve circumvention of additional forms of technological protection measures.").

The statute explicitly states that a technological measure "effectively controls access to a work" if the measure, "in the ordinary course of its operation, requires the application of information, or a process or a treatment, with the authority of the copyright towner, to gain access to the work."[189] Courts generally have broadly included many types of controls under this definition, and they typically do not require a high degree of technological sophistication for a control to qualify as a technological measure. For instance, in *IMS Inquiry Management Systems, LTD v. Berkshire Information Systems, Inc.,*[190] the plaintiff, which offered a web-based system that companies use to track magazine advertising, alleged that its competitor accessed its service without authorization and copied content for use on its competing service. The plaintiff alleged that the competitor obtained the log-in credentials from a third party, in violation of the user agreement.[191] The court concluded that the plaintiff's password protection constitutes an effective technological measure under Section (a)(1) because to access the plaintiff's service, "a user in the ordinary course of operation needs to enter a password, which is the application of information."[192]

The more difficult question under Section (a)(1), however, is whether the defendant circumvented a technological measure. Alleging that the defendant infringed the copyright of a work that is protected by a technological measure is not, by itself, sufficient to sustain a Section (a)(1) claim.[193] The statute defines "circumvent a technological measure" as "to descramble a scrambled work, to decrypt an encrypted work, or otherwise to avoid, bypass, remove, deactivate, or impair a technological measure, without the authority of the copyright owner."[194] In the *IMS* case, the court concluded that the plaintiff failed to allege that the defendants circumvented a technological measure.[195] The court reasoned that the plaintiff merely accused the defendant of using a valid password to access the site, and the defendant "is not said to have avoided or bypassed the deployed technological measure in the measure's gatekeeping capacity."[196] Avoiding permission to use the password, the court reasoned, is not the same

---

189 17 U.S.C. § 1201(3)(B).

190 IMS Inquiry Management Systems, LTD v. Berkshire Information Systems, Inc., 307 F. Supp. 2d 521 (S.D.N.Y. 2004).

191 *Id.* at 523.

192 *Id.* at 531.

193 Dish Network, LLC v. World Cable, Inc., 893 F. Supp. 2d 452, 463 (E.D.N.Y. 2012) ("[M]erely alleging that a defendant 'accessed' a copyrighted work that is protected by a technological measure is not enough to state a claim for a violation of the DMCA. Rather, the plain language of the statute ... requires a plaintiff alleging circumvention (or trafficking) to prove that the defendant's access was unauthorized.") (internal citation and quotation marks omitted).

194 17 U.S.C. § 1201(3)(A).

195 IMS Inquiry Management Systems, LTD v. Berkshire Information Systems, Inc., 307 F. Supp. 2d 521, 532 (S.D.N.Y. 2004).

196 *Id.*

as actively circumventing the password technology. The court noted that unlike the CFAA, which prohibits access based on whether it is authorized and injurious, the DMCA is focused on circumventing *technology* that protects copyrighted content.[197]

Indeed, courts have made clear that Section (a)(1) violations do not occur merely because a user violates an agreement. For instance, in *Auto Inspection Services, Inc. v. Flint Auto Auction*,[198] the plaintiff, Auto Inspection Services, developed software for automobile inspections. One of its former customers, Flint Auto Auction (FAA), developed very similar software. One of the former FAA employees who helped develop the competing software testified that FAA provided him with a printout of Auto Inspection Services's software interface, and instructed him to design the software based on that interface.[199] Auto Inspection Services sued FAA for, among other things, a violation of Section (a)(1), and sought a preliminary injunction to effectively block the use of FAA's software.[200] The district court denied this request, concluding that Auto Inspection Services failed to provide any evidence that FAA circumvented a technological measure. Using a printout of a software interface to design competing software, the court held, is not the same thing as accessing source code, modifying the source code, or otherwise creating a derivative software program.[201]

Courts also require Section (a)(1) plaintiffs to allege in their complaints the *specific* technology that the defendant circumvented, and how that circumvention occurred. For instance, in *LivePerson, Inc. v. 24/7 Customer, Inc.*,[202] LivePerson, which makes real-time interaction software for ecommerce companies, filed a number of claims against 24/7 Customer, a competitor. The two companies had worked together to provide services to some companies, and at one point LivePerson provided 24/7 Customer with a license to use LivePerson's software to serve customers. LivePerson alleges that 24/7 Customer developed competing technology, in part by accessing LivePerson's backend system and copying LivePerson's technology. In its complaint, LivePerson alleged that 24/7 used its access to LivePerson's systems to "observe, penetrate, and manipulate the operation of LivePerson's technology and download extensive data … in order … to reverse engineer and copy LivePerson's technology."[203] The court noted that LivePerson's complaint does not allege that 24/7 used reverse engineering to circumvent LivePerson's security measures but rather that "LivePerson believes that 24/7 breached its security measures in an effort to

197 *Id.*
198 Auto Inspection Services, Inc. v. Flint Auto Auction, Inc., Case No. 06-15100, 2006 U.S. Dist. LEXIS 83056 (E.D. Mich. Dec. 4, 2006).
199 *Id.* at *4.
200 *Id.* at *6.
201 *Id.* at *10.
202 LivePerson, Inc. v. 24/7 Customer, Inc., 83 F. Supp. 3d 501 (S.D.N.Y. 2015).
203 *Id.* at 510.

reverse engineer and misappropriate the proprietary technology and method-ologies that LivePerson pioneered," an allegation that the court concluded was not specific enough to constitute circumvention under the DMCA.[204] The court also rejected LivePerson's assertion that 24/7's alleged mimicking of LivePerson in order to gain access to its system was a violation of Section (a)(7).[205] In the cases in which courts have allowed Section (a)(1) claims to pro-ceed, the court noted, the complaints explicitly described the technology that was designed to prevent unauthorized access to a copyrighted material. Merely alleging the circumvention of technology intended to protect copyrighted works, without specifying the technology and how it was circumvented, is insufficient to support a Section (a)(1) claim.

Unlike the CFAA and other statutes, Section (a)(1) does not explicitly require the defendant to have acted in a specific mental state (e.g., "knowingly" or "intentionally") in order for the statute to apply to that conduct. However, courts generally will not allow a Section (a)(1) claim to move forward unless there is evidence that the defendant *actively* circumvented a technological measure that was designed to protect copyrighted material. If, for instance, the defendant accessed copyrighted material because the technological measure is not functioning properly, the plaintiff's claim likely will not succeed. In *Healthcare Advocates, Inc. v Harding, Earley, Follmer & Frailey*,[206] a law firm used the Internet Archive's Wayback Machine, www.archive.org, to investigate Healthcare Advocates, a company that was suing the firm's client for trade-mark infringement. The Wayback Machine archives old versions of publicly available websites. To access the archived content, users type in the web address, and are presented with the dates for which the site has been archived. Healthcare Advocates had placed a robots.txt file on its website, which was intended to prevent the Wayback Machine from archiving its old content. However, due to a malfunction with the Wayback Machine's servers, the previ-ous versions of the Healthcare Advocates website were available when the law firm searched for them. Healthcare Advocates sued the law firm under Section (a)(1), alleging that the firm obtained the archived websites by "hacking."[207] The district court agreed with the plaintiff that, in this context, the robots.txt file constituted a technological measure, as it was intended to prevent public access to archived screenshots of the company's website. However, the court disagreed with Healthcare Advocates – and dismissed the Section (a)(1) claim on summary judgment – because Healthcare Advocates did not provide any evidence that the law firm circumvented the robots.txt file. The court reasoned

---

204 *Id.*
205 *Id.*
206 Healthcare Advocates, Inc. v Harding, Earley, Follmer & Frailey, 497 F. Supp. 2d 627 (E.D. Pa. 2007).
207 *Id.* at 632.

that the law firm employees had no reason to know that Healthcare Advocates used robots.txt, and therefore "they could not avoid or bypass any protective measure, because nothing stood in the way of them viewing these screenshots."[208]

Another common dispute that arises in Section (a)(1) cases is whether the access control that was circumvented protects materials that are covered by U.S. copyright law. A good illustration of this inquiry can be seen in the Eighth Circuit's decision, *Davidson & Associates v. Jung.*[209] The plaintiff, a video game creator, offered an online gaming site, Battle.net, which allowed users to play the CD-ROMs that they purchased in the stores with other players online. To play games with other users on Battle.net, users were required to enter a "CD Key" that was included with CD-ROM games.[210] The defendants organized the bnetd project, a nonprofit project that emulates Battle.net and allows users to play online. To make their alternative site compatible with the plaintiff's games, they used reverse engineering of the plaintiff's software to test the interoperability.[211] Users were able to access the plaintiff's games on bnetd even if they did not have a valid CD Key.[212] The plaintiff sued the bnetd developers and organizers under Sections (a)(1) and (a)(2). The plaintiff alleged that the defendants violated Section (a)(1) by circumventing the CD Key requirement, which controlled access to the plaintiff's games.[213] The defendants argued that Battle.net is a functional process that is not protected by copyright because it does not constitute creative expression.[214] The Eighth Circuit rejected this argument and affirmed the district court's ruling that the defendants violated Section (a)(1), reasoning that the only way that the appellants could have accessed the copyrighted material provided through Battle.net was by reverse engineering and circumventing the site.[215]

Section (a)(1) cases often are not as complex as cases involving the other two subsections of the DMCA because the scope is relatively clear. As the U.S. Court of Appeals for the Second Circuit noted in 2001, Section (a)(1) differs from the other two DMCA subsections "in that it targets the use of a circumvention technology, not the trafficking in such a technology."[216] As we will see next, the inquiry becomes much more complicated – and courts disagree more frequently – when the alleged DMCA violations arise from trafficking in circumvention technology.

---

208 *Id.* at 644.
209 Davidson & Associates v. Jung, 422 F. 3d 630 (8th Cir. 2005).
210 *Id.* at 634–35.
211 *Id.* at 636.
212 *Id.*
213 *Id.* at 640.
214 *Id.* at 641.
215 *Id.*
216 Universal City Studios, Inc. v. Corley, 273 F.3d 429, 441 (2d Cir. 2001).

5.3.2.2 DMCA Section 1201(a)(2)

Section 1201(a)(2) states that no person "shall manufacture, import, offer to the public, provide, or otherwise traffic in any technology, product, service, device, component, or part thereof," that:

a) "is primarily designed or produced for the purpose of circumventing a technological measure that effectively controls access" to a copyrighted work;
b) "is primarily designed or produced for the purpose of circumventing a technological measure that effectively controls access" to a copyrighted work; **or**
c) "is marketed by that person or another acting in concert with that person with that person's knowledge for use in circumventing a technological measure that effectively controls access" to a copyrighted work"[217]

In short, Section (a)(2) prohibits the *trafficking* of technology that is used to circumvent controls that protect copyrighted works.[218] In contrast, Section (a)(1) prohibits the actual act of circumvention of those controls. In the Senate report accompanying the DMCA, the legislators stated that Section (a)(2) would provide a cause of action against a company that manufactured a device that was designed to circumvent a control that only allowed authorized individuals to access the plain text of a copyrighted work.[219]

The primary legal dispute that arises in Section (a)(2) cases is whether the technology trafficked actually facilitates copyright infringement or other violations of rights protected by the Copyright Act. The DMCA does not directly address this issue, though Section 1201(c)(1), somewhat cryptically, states that "[n]othing in this section shall affect rights, remedies, limitations, or defenses to copyright infringement, including fair use, under this title."[220] Section 1201(c)(1) can be read to merely prevent the anti-circumvention provisions from abrogating existing rights that owners and consumers have under the copyright act, but it also can be read to limit Section 1201's scope only to cases that involve circumvention that leads to actual copyright infringement.

Courts have taken two very different approaches to interpreting the scope and reach of Section (a)(2). Some courts have taken a narrow approach, requiring a nexus between the access that is violated and the protection of copyright. Other courts, in contrast, have held that Section (a)(2) applies to technology that circumvents controls that are used to protect copyrighted content, regardless of whether that technology is *actually* used to access copyrighted content.

---

217 17 U.S.C. § 1201(a)(2).
218 *See* H.R. Rep. No. 105-551 at 18 ("In order to provide meaningful protection and enforcement of the copyright owner's right to control access to his or her copyrighted work, this paragraph supplements the prohibition against the act of circumvention in paragraph (a)(1) with prohibitions on creating and making available certain technologies, products and services used, developed or advertised to defeat technological protections against unauthorized access to a work.").
219 S. Rep. 105-190 (1998) at 12.
220 17 U.S.C. § 1201(c)(1).

5.3.2.2.1 Narrow Interpretation of Section (a)(2): Chamberlain Group v. Skylink Technologies

The U.S. Court of Appeals for the Federal Circuit took the narrow approach to interpreting Section (a)(2) in a 2004 case, *Chamberlain Group v. Skylink Technologies.*[221] Chamberlain makes a garage door opener that uses a copyrighted "rolling code" software that constantly alters the radio frequency signal that is needed for the transmitter to open the garage door.[222] Skylink manufactures a fixed-code transmitter, Model 39, that circumvents the rolling code but nonetheless enables users to open garage doors that are connected to Chamberlain's garage door openers.[223] Chamberlain argues that rolling code openers are more secure because they prevent burglars from grabbing the signal and using it later. Chamberlain did not claim that Skylink infringed Chamberlain's copyright in the code. Instead, Chamberlain claimed that the rolling code software protects itself, and therefore, by selling a transmitter that circumvents Chamberlain's rolling code, Skylink is violating Section (a)(2) by trafficking in a product that circumvents technology that protects copyrighted content.[224]

The Federal Circuit rejected Chamberlain's interpretation of Section (a)(2), concluding that for a plaintiff to state a valid Section(a)(2) claim, there must be a link between the access that is being circumvented and the *infringement* of copyrighted content. The court reasoned that Chamberlain's interpretation of the DMCA "ignores the significant differences between defendants whose accused products enable copying and those, like Skylink, whose accused products enable only legitimate uses of copyrighted software."[225] In other words, Section (a)(2) does not create a broad new property right; instead, it protects circumvention that is reasonably related to a property right that is currently provided by the Copyright Act. The court articulated this Section (a)(2) interpretation in a six-element test:

> A plaintiff alleging a violation of § 1201(a)(2) must prove: (1) ownership of a valid *copyright* on a work, (2) effectively controlled by a *technological measure*, which has been circumvented, (3) that third parties can now access (4) *without authorization*, in a manner that (5) infringes or facilitates infringing a right protected by the Copyright Act, because of a product that (6) the defendant either (i) *designed or produced* primarily for circumvention; (ii) made available despite only *limited commercial significance* other than circumvention; or (iii) *marketed* for use in circumvention of the controlling technological measure. A plaintiff incapable of

---

221 Chamberlain Group v. Skylink Technologies, 381 F.3d 1178 (Fed. Cir. 2004).
222 *Id.* at 1183.
223 *Id.*
224 *Id.* at 1185.
225 *Id.* at 1198.

establishing any one of elements (1) through (5) will have failed to prove a prima facie case. A plaintiff capable of proving elements (1) through (5) need prove only one of (6)(i), (ii), or (iii) to shift the burden back to the defendant.[226]

Although the Federal Circuit's six-part test largely relies on the statute's wording, the Federal Circuit clearly emphasizes the need to demonstrate that the trafficked product helps circumvent access in order to violate an *existing* right under the copyright laws. Elaborating on this framework, the court concluded that it *necessarily* requires a link between the access circumvention and a violation of existing copyright law, and that Chamberlain failed to demonstrate such a link, and therefore failed to prove the fifth element of the six-part test:

> The DMCA does not create a new property right for copyright owners. Nor, for that matter, does it divest the public of the property rights that the Copyright Act has long granted to the public. The anticircumvention and anti-trafficking provisions of the DMCA create new grounds of liability. A copyright owner seeking to impose liability on an accused circumventor must demonstrate a reasonable relationship between the circumvention at issue and a use relating to a property right for which the Copyright Act permits the copyright owner to withhold authorization—as well as notice that authorization was withheld. A copyright owner seeking to impose liability on an accused trafficker must demonstrate that the trafficker's device enables either copyright infringement or a prohibited circumvention. Here, the District Court correctly ruled that Chamberlain pled no connection between unauthorized use of its copyrighted software and Skylink's accused transmitter. This connection is critical to sustaining a cause of action under the DMCA.[227]

Soon after the Federal Circuit issued its opinion in *Chamberlain*, courts quickly adopted its narrow interpretation of Section (a)(2). For instance, in 2005, the U.S. District Court for the Northern District of Illinois rejected a Section (a)(2) claim by the distributor of more than 3300 copyrighted fonts against Adobe Systems, arising out of a feature on Adobe Acrobat that allowed users to select among the plaintiff's fonts when completing a PDF form.[228] The plaintiffs claimed that this feature was only possible by adding code that circumvented the fonts' embedding bits, which impose licensing restrictions in fonts and indicate to software programs (e.g., Reader) how a font may be used.

---

226 *Id*. at 1203 (emphasis in original).
227 *Id*. at 1204.
228 Agfa Monotype Corp. v. Adobe Systems, Inc., 404 F. Supp. 2d 1030 (N.D. Ill. 2005).

However, embedding bits do not actually prevent users from accessing the fonts, which are available for free online.[229] The primary issue here arose from the second prong of the *Chamberlain* test, whether the embedding bits constituted a technological measure that effectively controlled access to the copyrighted fonts. The court concluded that the embedding bits did not satisfy this requirement, reasoning that an embedding bit "is a passive entity that does nothing by itself," and that the fonts had long been available to the public for free download. The court focused on the lack of technological restrictions placed on the fonts, reasoning that the plaintiffs' embedding bits are neither encrypted nor authenticated, and software such as Acrobat "need not enter a password or authorization sequence to obtain access to the embedding bits or the specification for the TrueType font."[230] Although the outcome of this case focused on the nature of the technological control, the overall approach was quite similar to that of *Chamberlain*, which was decided based on whether the control prevented copyright infringement. In both opinions, the court's broader inquiry was whether the technology actually protected against rights provided in U.S. copyright law.

5.3.2.2.2 Broad Interpretation of Section (a)(2): MDY Industries, LLC v. Blizzard Entertainment, Inc.

For more than five years, *Chamberlain* was viewed as the prevailing interpretation of Section (a)(2), and many district courts applied its relatively restrictive six-part test to claims under the statute. This changed in 2010, when the U.S. Court of Appeals for the Ninth Circuit issued its opinion in *MDY Industries, LLC v. Blizzard Entertainment, Inc.*[231] That case arose from Glider, a game-playing bot that enabled World of Warcraft players to automatically win early levels of the game, allowing them to focus on the more advanced stages. The developer of Glider, Michael Donnelly, started a company, MDY Industries, which earned approximately $3.5 million from licensing Glider.[232]

In response to Glider, World of Warcraft's developer, Blizzard Entertainment, launched Warden, a technology that is designed to prevent players who use third-party software, such as bots, from accessing the World of Warcraft servers and playing the game.[233] Warden contained a "resident" component that occasionally scans a user computer's RAM while it is playing World of Warcraft to determine whether there are any activities that indicate the presence of an auto-playing bot. Warden also used scan.dll, a software module, to scan a computer's RAM before allowing a connection to World of Warcraft's servers.

---

229 *Id.* at 1031.
230 *Id.* at 1036.
231 MDY Industries, LLC v. Blizzard Entertainment, Inc., 629 F.3d 928 (9th Cir. 2010).
232 *Id.* at 935–36.
233 *Id.* at 942.

If scan.dll detected a user was running a program such as Glider, it would not permit the player to access its servers. MDY responded to this feature by only allowing Glider to launch *after* scan.dll scanned the RAM for bots. MDY promoted its ability to circumvent World of Warcraft's detection systems.[234] Blizzard requested that MDY cease and desist, threatening to sue, and MDY responded by filing its own lawsuit, asking the court to declare that it did not violate the anti-circumvention provisions of Section 1201 of the DMCA.

Once the *Blizzard* case reached the U.S. Court of Appeals for the Ninth Circuit, the court refused to adopt the narrow interpretation of Section (a)(2) as stated in *Chamberlain*. Flatly rejecting the Federal Circuit's conclusion that Section 1201 does not create a new property right, the Ninth Circuit held that Section (a)(2) "creates a new anti-circumvention right distinct from the traditional exclusive rights of a copyright owner."[235] In short, the Ninth Circuit criticized the *Chamberlain* approach as ignoring the plain language of Section (a)(2). Although the *Chamberlain* court reasoned that its construction of the statute was more logical and sound public policy, the Ninth Circuit concluded that such considerations should not be a factor when the plain language of a statute is clear.[236]

Moreover, the Ninth Circuit noted that Section 1201(b)(1) (discussed below) already explicitly links a violation to copyright infringement.[237] Section (a)(2) applies when the defendant "circumvent[s] a technological measure," and the statute defines that term by providing two examples: descrambling scrambled work or decrypting an encrypted work. The court noted that these acts "do not necessarily result in someone's reproducing, distributing, publicly performing, or publicly displaying the copyrighted work, or creating derivative works based on the copyrighted work."[238] In contrast, Section (b)(1) applies to defendants who "circumvent protection afforded by a technological measure," that "effectively protects the right of a copyright owner" under U.S. copyright law. Distinguishing between Sections (a)(2) and (b)(1) "ensures that neither section is rendered superfluous," the court wrote.[239] The court also recognized that the Senate Judiciary Report accompanying the DMCA stated that Sections (a)(2) and (b)(1) were "designed to protect two distinct rights and to target two

---

234 *Id.* at 936.
235 *Id.* at 950.
236 *Id.* at 951 ("As a threshold matter, we stress that such considerations cannot trump the statute's plain text and structure.").
237 *Id.* at 950. *See also id.* at 944 ("[I]n contrast to § 1201(a), § 1201(b)(1) prohibits trafficking in technologies that circumvent technological measures that effectively protect 'a right of a copyright owner.' Section 1201(b)(1)'s prohibition is thus aimed at circumventions of measures that protect the copyright itself: it entitles copyright owners to protect their existing exclusive rights under the Copyright Act.").
238 *Id.* at 945.
239 *Id.* at 946.

distinct classes of devices," and that "many devices will be subject to challenge only under one of the subsections."[240]

Like the Federal Circuit, the Ninth Circuit articulated a six-element test that plaintiffs must satisfy in order to succeed on a Section (a)(2) claim. The tests differ, however, in that the Ninth Circuit does not require a *link* between the control measure and preventing copyright infringement. The Ninth Circuit stated that the plaintiff must demonstrate that the defendant:

> (1) traffics in (2) a technology or part thereof (3) that is primarily designed, produced, or marketed for, or has limited commercially significant use other than (4) circumventing a technological measure (5) that effectively controls access (6) to a copyrighted work.[241]

Applying this broader interpretation of Section (a)(2) to the World of Warcraft dispute, the Ninth Circuit considered three types of components of World of Warcraft: (1): the literal elements, which is the source code that resides on customers' computers; (2) the individual nonliteral elements, which are the individual, discrete audio and visual elements of the computer game, such as an individual sound or picture; and (3) the dynamic nonliteral elements, which it described as "real-time experience of traveling through different worlds, hearing their sounds, viewing their structures, encountering their inhabitants and monsters, and encountering other players."[242]

The Ninth Circuit concluded that under its definition of Section (a)(2), Glider does not violate Section (a)(2) regarding the computer game's literal elements and individual nonliteral elements because "Warden does not effectively control access to these [World of Warcraft] elements."[243] The literal element, which is the computer game's code, resides on the player's hard drive, and not on the server.[244] Similarly, World of Warcraft users can access the individual nonliteral elements – such as a single sound or image – even if they do not connect to Blizzard's server.[245] Warden only blocks users from accessing the servers to play World of Warcraft online with other users; it does not prevent players from accessing the code, images, and sounds that are stored on their computers.

The Ninth Circuit, however, concluded that MDY violated Section(a)(2) regarding the dynamic nonliteral elements of the game, that is, the overall experience of playing the game and encountering other players.[246] The gist of

---

240 *Id.* at 946–47, quoting S. Rep. No. 105-190, at 12 (1998).
241 *Id.* at 953.
242 *Id.* at 942–43.
243 *Id.* at 952.
244 *Id.*
245 *Id.*
246 *Id.* at 953–54.

the court's reasoning is that Warden controlled access to the overall display of the game online, which is protected by copyright law, and MDY trafficked in a technology – Glider – that it marketed as a means to circumvent Warden.[247] The ruling on the dynamic nonliteral elements illustrates the significant difference between the Federal Circuit's approach to Section (a)(2) in *Chamberlain*, and the Ninth Circuit's approach in this case. If the Ninth Circuit had adopted the Federal Circuit's analytical framework for Section (a)(2), it is highly unlikely that it would have found that MDY violated the statute. Glider was not intended to help users *infringe* the copyright of World of Warcraft, by copying or redistributing it; instead, Glider merely allowed users to advance through early stages of the game.

The fact that this broad view of Section (a)(2) was reached in the Ninth Circuit is particularly important because the Ninth Circuit covers the western United States, including California, which is home to many large technology companies that are more likely to bring anti-circumvention complaints. Unless the Ninth Circuit reverses its interpretation of Section (a)(2), or the United States Supreme Court decides to hear an anti-circumvention case and adopts the Federal Circuit's approach, the *MDY* interpretation of Section (a)(2) will remain binding precedent throughout the Ninth Circuit.

In a 2015 case in the U.S. District Court for the Central District of California, *NNG, KFT. V. AVA Enterprises, Inc.*,[248] plaintiff NNG, which makes navigation software, alleged that navigation device maker AVA violated Section (a)(2). NNG claimed that AVA installed pirated copies of NNG's software on its devices, along with software code that circumvents the authentication code that NNG uses to prevent unauthorized use of its software.[249] AVA moved to dismiss the complaint, contending that the authentication does not control the access to the copyright-protected code or files, but rather it simply validates whether the device is authorized to run NNG's software.[250] The authentication code only controls access to the dynamic nonliteral elements – namely the experience of using the software. Because NNG did not allege that AVA infringed the copyright of the dynamic nonliteral elements, AVA argued, NNG could not claim a Section (a)(2) violation. In other words, AVA argued that the court should limit Section (a)(2) claims to the circumvention of access controls that leads to copyright infringement. The district court rejected this argument, concluding that it "would be correct in other Circuits, but not here." The court recognized that because it is located in the Ninth Circuit, it is bound by the *MDY* holding that a Section (a)(2) claim does not necessarily need to be linked

---

247 *Id.*
248 NNG, KFT. v. Ava Enterprises, Inc., Case No. 2:14-cv-00220-ODW(AJW), 2015 U.S. Dist. LEXIS 88742 (C.D. Cal. July 8, 2015).
249 *Id.* at *3.
250 *Id.* at *4.

to an allegation of copyright infringement.[251] Applying *MDY* to the allegations in the lawsuit, the court reasoned that it is "undisputed that the technological measure in this case, the Authentication Code, effectively controls access to one element of NNG's copyrighted computer software – the dynamic non-literal elements."[252] NNG's failure to allege that AVA infringed the dynamic non-literal elements "is of no consequence," the court concluded.[253]

The *NNG* case clearly demonstrates the huge divide among circuits in their interpretation of the scope of Section (a)(2). In the courts that adopt *Chamberlain's* ruling, Section (a)(2) only protects rights that are already provided in the copyright law, such as the ability to control the copying and distribution of copyrighted works. In the courts that adopt the *MDY* reading of the statute, Section (a)(2) creates a new right to prevent companies from distributing products that circumvent access controls. The *MDY* reading is particularly relevant to the cybersecurity profession because it creates a fairly powerful legal remedy for companies to pursue those that assist in bypassing technological controls.

5.3.2.3 DMCA Section 1201(b)(1)

Section (b)(1) states that no person:

> shall manufacture, import, offer to the public, provide, or otherwise traffic in any technology, product, service, device, component, or part thereof that–
>
> a) is primarily designed or produced for the purpose of circumventing protection afforded by a technological measure that effectively protects a right of a copyright owner under this title in a work or a portion thereof;
> b) has only limited commercially significant purpose or use other than to circumvent protection afforded by a technological measure that effectively protects a right of a copyright owner under this title in a work or a portion thereof; or
> c) is marketed by that person or another acting in concert with that person with that person's knowledge for use in circumventing protection afforded by a technological measure that effectively protects a right of a copyright owner under this title in a work or a portion thereof.[254]

---

251 *Id.* at *10.
252 *Id.* at *11.
253 *Id.* at *13. The Court did grant AVA's motion to dismiss the Section (a)(2) claim, but on different grounds. The Court concluded that AVA's devices did not satisfy the statute's requirements because they are not "primarily designed to circumvent any technological measure and do not conduct the actual circumventing," rather, they "merely house the alleged pirated software to which 'access … has already been obtained.'" *Id.*
254 17 U.S.C. § 1201(b)(1).

Section (b)(1) defines "circumvent protection afforded by a technological measure" as "avoiding, bypassing, removing, deactivating, or otherwise impairing a technological measure."[255] The statute states that a technological measure "effectively protects a right of a copyright owner under this title" if the measure, "in the ordinary course of its operation, prevents, restricts, or otherwise limits the exercise of a right of a copyright owner under this title."[256]

Section (b)(1) appears to be quite similar to Section (a)(2), as both prohibit trafficking in technology that circumvents technological measures. The primary difference between the two sections is that Section (a)(2) applies to technology that circumvents technological measures that control access to copyrighted works, while Section (b)(1) is narrower, and only applies to technology that circumvents a technological measure that *protects against violations of copyright owners' rights* – that is, copyright infringement.[257] Under the narrow *Chamberlain* interpretation of Section (a)(2), there is not a substantial difference between Sections (a)(2) and (b)(1), as both sections require a direct link to copyright infringement. However, under the Ninth Circuit's more expansive view of Section (a)(2), the two sections are significantly different, with Section (a)(2) applying broadly to circumvention of technology that protects copyrighted works, regardless of whether the circumvention aids infringement. The Senate Commerce Committee's report accompanying the DMCA indicated its intention for Section (b)(1) to be more narrowly focused on technology that aids copyright infringement.[258]

Indeed, in *MDY*, the Ninth Circuit concluded that even though the plaintiff had sufficiently alleged a violation of Section (a)(2) under the court's broad reading of that statute, the plaintiff did not prevail on its claim under Section (b)(1). The court reasoned that its Warden software does not protect against infringement or any other violation of copyright laws, and therefore the circumvention could not violate Section (b)(1).[259]

---

255 17 U.S.C. § 1201(b)(2)(A).

256 17 U.S.C. § 1201(b)(2)(B).

257 *See* Ticketmaster LLC v. RMG Technologies, Inc., 507 F. Supp. 2d 1096 (C.D. Cal. 2007) ("Sections 1201(a)(2) and 1201(b)(1) differ only in that 1201(a)(2), by its terms, makes it wrongful to traffic in devices that circumvent technological measures that *control access to protected works*, while 1201(b)(1) makes it wrongful to traffic in devices that circumvent technological measures that *protect rights of a copyright owner in a work.*") (emphasis in original).

258 S. Rep. 105-190 at 29 ("Subsection (b) applies to those technological measures employed by a copyright owner that effectively protect his or her copyright rights in a work, as opposed to those technological protection measures covered by subsection (a), which prevent unauthorized access to a copyrighted work. Unlike subsection (a), which prohibits the circumvention of access control technologies, subsection (b) does not, by itself, prohibit the circumvention of effective technological copyright protection measures.").

259 MDY Industries, LLC v. Blizzard Entertainment, Inc., 629 F. 3d 928, 954-55 ("[A]lthough WoW players can theoretically record game play by taking screen shots, there is no evidence that Warden detects or prevents such allegedly infringing copying. This is logical, because Warden was designed to reduce the presence of cheats and bots, not to protect WoW's dynamic non-literal elements against copying.").

If a court finds that a defendant has violated Section (b)(1), the court likely will also find that the defendant has violated Section (a)(2). For example, in *Craigslist, Inc. v. Naturemarket, Inc.,* [260]online classified advertising website Craigslist alleged that defendant Naturemarket developed and distributed software that enabled Naturemarket customers to automatically post multiple ads on Craigslist and to harvest Craigslist user email addresses in order to send spam email messages. Both acts violate Craigslist terms of service, and Craigslist attempts to prevent such automatic posting and harvesting by using a CAPTCHA program and telephone verification, which requires the user to enter a unique code, in an effort to prevent automated programs from accessing the site.[261] Craigslist alleged that Naturemarket copied portions of Craigslist's website in order to operate and develop its autoposter software. Naturemarket did not respond to Craigslist's complaint, and the district court granted default judgment to Craigslist, concluding that Craigslist's complaint stated valid claims under both Sections (a)(2) and (b)(1). Naturemarket violated Section (a)(2), the court concluded, applying the Ninth Circuit's broad interpretation of the statute, because they trafficked in a product that circumvented CAPTCHA and telephone verification, which "enabled unauthorized access to and copies of copyright-protected portions of Plaintiff's website."[262] The court concluded that because CAPTCHA protected plaintiff's copyright rights in the website, Craigslist stated a viable claim that Naturemarket violated Section (b)(1).[263]

In short, regardless of the circuit in which a Section 1201 dispute is adjudicated, a plaintiff who successfully states a Section (b)(1) claim typically also will prevail under Section (a)(2). However, the reverse is not always true. A successful Section (a)(2) claim, particularly in a jurisdiction that adopts the broad *MDY* reading of the statute, does not necessarily mean that the defendant also violated Section (b)(1), since Section (a)(2) does not require a link to copyright infringement.

5.3.3 Section 1201 Penalties

Violators of Section 1201 can face both civil actions and criminal prosecutions. Any person who is injured by a Section 1201 violation can bring a civil action against the violator in federal court. The plaintiff can seek injunctions preventing the circumvention or trafficking, impounding of a device used to violate Section 1201, damages, costs, attorney's fees, and the modification or destruction of a device used to violate the law.[264]

---

260 Craigslist, Inc. v. Naturemarket, Inc., 694 F. Supp. 2d 1039 (N.D. Cal. 2010).
261 *Id*. at 1048.
262 *Id*. at 1056.
263 *Id*.
264 17 U.S.C. § 1203(b).

If the plaintiff in a Section 1201 case can seek either actual damages or statutory damages. Actual damages are the actual costs that the Section 1201 violation caused for the plaintiff, along with any profits that the violator earned due to the illegal act, provided that they are not already taken account for in the other actual damages.[265] Statutory damages are a fixed amount per violation, set by the court as it "considers just." Violations of Section 1201 carry statutory damages between $200 and $2500 per act of circumvention.[266] If the violator demonstrates that it "was not aware and had no reason to believe that its acts constituted a violation," the court is permitted to reduce or remit the damages award.[267]

Section 1201 violations also can trigger criminal prosecutions, but only if the violator did so "willfully and for purposes of commercial advantage or private financial gain."[268] The maximum sentence for a first offense is a $500,000 fine or five years in prison, and the maximum sentence for subsequent offense is a $1 million fine or ten years in prison.[269] The statute of limitations for criminal prosecutions is five years.

5.3.4 Section 1201 Exemptions

Section 1201 has attracted a great deal of criticism from the cybersecurity community and consumer rights groups, who argue that the statute is not in the public interest because it prevents researchers from discovering vulnerabilities in software. As the Center for Democracy and Technology stated, the anti-circumvention provisions of Section (a)(1) "means a researcher who uncovers a software vulnerability by circumventing, for example, digital rights management (DRM) software, is breaking the law."[270] Critics also assert that Section 1201's prohibition on the distribution of tools that facilitate circumvention has had a chilling effect on online discussion about cybersecurity because publishers and ISPs fear that such discussions could lead to DMCA liability.[271]

Congress attempted to address these concerns by including a number of limited exceptions to the anti-circumvention provisions, though many critics say

---

265 17 U.S.C. § 1203(c)(2).
266 17 U.S.C. § 1203(c)(3).
267 17 U.S.C. § 1203(c)(5).
268 17 U.S.C. § 1204(a).
269 *Id.*
270 Erik Stallman, Center for Democracy and Technology, *Improve Cybersecurity by Allowing Vulnerability Research* (Feb. 13, 2015).
271 *See* Electronic Frontier Foundation, Unintended Consequences: Fifteen Years under the DMCA (March 2013) ("Bowing to DMCA liability fears, online service providers and bulletin board operators have censored discussions of copy-protection systems, programmers have removed computer security programs from their websites, and students, scientists and security experts have stopped publishing details of their research.").

that these exceptions are not sufficient to address their concerns about the effects that Section 1201 has on cybersecurity, researchers, and consumers.

The most prominent – and flexible – exception allows the Librarian of Congress to temporarily exempt particular classes of works from Section (a)(1)'s anti-circumvention provisions, provided that the Librarian determines that the users of those works are "adversely affected by virtue of such prohibition in their ability to make noninfringing uses of that particular class of works[.]"[272] In making this determination, the Librarian is required to consider the availability of copyrighted works for use; the availability for use of works for non-profit archival, preservation, and educational purposes; the impact that a Section 1201 prohibition would have on "criticism, comment, news reporting, teaching, scholarship, or research"; whether circumvention affects the market value of copyrighted works; and other factors that the Librarian considers appropriate.[273]

These Librarian-granted exceptions are somewhat limited. The Librarian can only grant them in a rulemaking proceeding that occurs once every three years. The exceptions are temporary, and expire after three years. Perhaps most important, the temporary exceptions *only* apply to the anti-circumvention provision of Section (a)(1); they do *not* apply to the anti-trafficking provisions of Sections (a)(2) and (b)(1).[274]

In October 2015, the Librarian of Congress issued its most recent triennial rulemaking for Section (a)(1) exemptions. Among the ten classes of users and works that the Librarian exempted from Section (a)(1) are the following:

- Motion pictures, where circumvention is undertaken only to make use of "short portions" of the motion pictures for the purpose of criticism or comment in specific instances, such as for use in documentary filmmaking, non-commercial videos, and nonfiction multimedia e-books offering film analysis.
- Computer programs that enable smart televisions to "execute lawfully obtained software applications," provided that circumvention is accomplished for the sole purpose of enabling interoperability of such applications with the smart television's software programs.
- Certain lawfully acquired video games, provided that the copyright owner does not provide access to an external computer server that is necessary to authenticate local gameplay. This exception only applies for certain purposes, such as restoring access for personal gameplay.[275]

---

272 17 U.S.C. § 1201(a)(1)(B).
273 17 U.S.C. § 1201(a)(1)(C).
274 *See* 17 U.S.C. § 1201(a)(1)(E) ("Neither the exception under subparagraph (B) from the applicability of the prohibition contained in subparagraph (A), nor any determination made in a rulemaking conducted under subparagraph (C), may be used as a defense in any action to enforce any provision of this title other than this paragraph.").
275 37 C.F.R. § 201.40.

> **Classes of Works that did not Receive Section1201 Exemptions in 2015**
>
> Although the Librarian of Congress granted a number of high-profile exemptions to the DMCA in 2015, some exemption applications were denied. They include:
>
> - **Space-shifting and format-shifting of videos and electronic books.** Consumer groups asked the Librarian to allow the circumvention of technological measures that prevent consumers from viewing purchased movies and books on alternate devices.
> - **Jailbreaking e-readers.** This exception would have allowed individuals to circumvent technological measures that prevent ebook readers from running lawfully acquired applications or software.
> - **Jailbreaking video game consoles.** An individual requested an exemption to allow a number of uses for home video game consoles, including the installation of alternative operating systems.

Some advocacy groups offered tempered praise for the wide range of exceptions that the Librarian of Congress granted in the 2015 rulemaking, but they criticized the office for delaying the effective date of the exceptions by twelve months, resulting in the exceptions only being effective for two years.[276] Advocacy groups also criticized the complexity of the exceptions, and noted that a temporary Library of Congress rulemaking is perhaps not the best way to address the concerns of cybersecurity researchers and others.[277] Advocacy groups also asserted that the Librarian of Congress attempted to reach a middle ground among the users and rights holders, leading to unnecessarily complex exemptions that are difficult to implement in the real world.[278] Critics of Section 1201 have long expressed these concerns. In 1999, a year after Congress passed the DMCA, University of California-Berkeley law professor Pamela

---

276 Erik Stallman, Center for Democracy and Technology, A Qualified Win for Cybersecurity Researchers in DMCA Triennial Rulemaking (Oct. 27, 2015) ("Given that the exemption lasts for only three years, a one-year delay means that after spending the next year in legal limbo, researchers will have only two years to perform any research that relies on the exemption. That limitation will force researchers and academic institutions to lower their horizons and may also create obstacles in funding their work.").

277 *Id.* ("The sheer complexity of some of the granted exemptions – and the need to re-request them every three years – suggests that DMCA rulemaking proceedings are simply not the best vehicle for industrial policymaking where copyright infringement is, at most, a tangential concern.").

278 Kendra Albert, Electronic Frontier Foundation, The New DMCA Section 1201 Exemption for Video Games: A Closer Look (Nov. 13, 2015) ("The Register made a number of compromises on many of the exemptions, designed to find a middle ground between proponents and opponents. That eliminates much of the legal clarity that the exemptions are meant to provide.").

Samuelson wrote that "because none of the Librarian's findings last for more than a three-year period, copyright industry lobbyists will have multiple opportunities to carve back or eliminate any user-friendly exceptions that the Librarian might have the temerity to recommend."[279]

In addition to the temporary exemptions that the Librarian of Congress grants every three years, the DMCA includes some permanent – but very narrow – exceptions to Section (a)(1) for specified uses. As with the Librarian's temporary exceptions, these do not apply to the trafficking provisions of Sections (a)(2) or (b)(1) unless specified:

- *Nonprofit libraries, archives, and educational institutions.* Section 1201(d) exempts nonprofit libraries, archives, or educational institutions from Section (a)(1)'s anti-circumvention requirements in order to determine, in good faith, whether to lawfully acquire a copy of a copyrighted work.[280] If a nonprofit library, archive, or educational institution circumvents access controls to make this determination, it may not retain the copy longer than necessary to determine whether to acquire the work, nor may it use the copy for purposes other than making this determination. This exception is not available if the organization already has an identical copy that is reasonably available. The exemption is not available to libraries or archives that are closed to the public or only available to affiliated researchers.

- *Law enforcement and intelligence activities.* Under Section 1201(e), legal activities of federal, state, and local law enforcement, security, and intelligence agencies are not subject to *any* of the prohibitions in Section 1201 (Sections (a)(1), (a)(2), and (b)(1)). This includes the agencies' information security activities, which the statute defines as "activities carried out in order to identify and address the vulnerabilities of a government computer, computer system, or compute network."[281]

- *Reverse engineering for interoperability.* Section 1201(f) allows individuals who lawfully obtain the right to use a copy of a computer program to circumvent an access control technology without violating Section 1201, provided that the *only* purpose for which they circumvent the control is to identify and analyze the elements that are necessary to achieve interoperability with another program, and those elements have not been available to the user through other means.[282] Section 1201 defines "interoperability" as "the ability of computer programs to exchange information, and of such programs mutually to use the information which has been exchanged."

---

279 Pamela Samuelson, *Intellectual Property and the Digital Economy: Why the Anti-Circumvention Regulations Need to be Revised*, 14 BERKELEY TECH. L. J. 1, 41 n. 208 (1999).
280 17 U.S.C. § 1201(d).
281 17 U.S.C. § 1201(e).
282 17 U.S.C. § 1201(f).

- *Encryption research.* Section 1201(g) allows encryption researchers to circumvent an access control if (1) the researcher lawfully obtained the encrypted content, (2) the circumvention is necessary to conduct encryption research, (3) the researcher made a good-faith effort to obtain authorization to circumvent the control, and (4) the circumvention does not independently constitute copyright infringement or a violation of the CFAA. The exemption also allows researchers to provide the technological means of circumvention to a collaborating researcher.[283]

To determine whether the researcher qualifies for this exemption, the statute lists three factors: (1) the manner in which the information derived from the research is circumvented, and whether it is reasonably calculated to advance the state of knowledge or development of encryption; (2) whether the researcher has an appropriate background, training, and experience in encryption technology; and (3) whether the researcher provides the results of the research to the copyright owner.[284]

Some researchers have criticized this exemption for not providing the certainty necessary to conduct encryption research. In a petition to the Librarian of Congress, Johns Hopkins computer scientist Matthew D. Green wrote that the exemption includes "complex multifactor tests that cannot be evaluated *ex ante*, potential restrictions on the dissemination of research results, and requirements to seek authorization in advance of performing research."[285]

- *Preventing minors from accessing the Internet.* Section 1201(h) instructs courts, when applying Sections (a)(1) and (a)(2) to a component or part, to consider the necessity for the component's or part's intended and actual incorporation in technology that does not violate the copyright law and has the "sole purpose" of preventing minors from accessing material on the Internet.[286] This is a relatively vague provision that does not give clear guidance as to the exact types of activities that are exempt from 1201 liability. The legislative history of the DMCA indicates that Congress intended to ensure that parents could install technology on their home computers that restrict their children's access to harmful material on the Internet.[287]
- *Protection of personally identifying information.* Section 1201(i) allows an individual to circumvent controls on copyrighted works in order to

---

283 17 U.S.C. § 1201(g).
284 *Id.*
285 Matthew D. Green, Petition for Exemption: Applied Cryptography, Security, and Reverse Engineering Research, Docket No. 2014-07.
286 17 U.S.C. § 1201(h).
287 H.R. Rep. No. 105-551, part 2 at 45 (expressing concern that the DMCA's anti-circumvention protections "might inadvertently make it unlawful for parents to protect their children from pornography and other harmful material available on the Internet, or have unintended legal consequences for manufacturers of products designed solely to enable parents to protect their children in this fashion.").

protect the individual's privacy, but only if the company that possesses the data failed to conspicuously disclose the collection and dissemination and provide the individual with the chance to opt out. An individual may circumvent access controls without violating Section(a)(1), provided that all of the following four conditions are met: (1) the access control or the content that it protects is capable of collecting or disseminating personally identifiable information that reflects the online activities of a person who seeks to access the protected work; (2) in the normal course of business, the access control, or the work it protects, collects and disseminates information about the person who seeks to access the protected work, without providing conspicuous notice of the collection or dissemination to that person, and without providing the person the ability to opt out of the collection or dissemination; (3) the circumvention has the "sole effect" of identifying and disabling the collection nor dissemination of the personally identifying information; and (4) the circumvention is *only* conducted to prevent the collection or dissemination of the personally identifying information.[288] The legislative history of the provision indicates that Congress intended this exception to apply only in cases when companies did not provide transparency and choice regarding personal information.[289]

- *Security testing.* Section 1201(j) creates an exemption to Section (a)(1) for certain forms of security testing, which the statute defines as accessing a computer "solely for the purpose of good faith testing, investigating, or correcting, a security flaw or vulnerability, with the authorization of the owner or operator" of the computer.[290] The statute provides the following two factors for consideration when determining whether the exemption applies: (1) whether the information obtained through testing was used "solely to promote the security of the owner or operator of the computer," or shared with the developer; and (2) whether the information was used in a way that facilitates copyright infringement or the violation of privacy or data security laws.

Security researchers have identified three primary shortfalls that render this exemption relatively toothless for their work. First, the exemption, by its very terms, only applies if the researcher has obtained prior approval from the owner or operator of the computer, system, or network. Companies often do not want unaffiliated parties to independently test their security, fearing negative publicity or legal exposure. Second, as with the encryption research exemption, there is no certainty that a court

---

288 17 U.S.C. § 1201(i).
289 H.R. Rep. No. 105-551, part 2 at 45 ("Only if there is no disclosure of privacy-related practices, or instances where consumers are left without the capability to disable the gathering of personal information, could a consumer circumvent a technological protection measure to protect his or her own privacy.").
290 17 U.S.C. § 1201(j).

would agree that the two factors weigh in favor of the exemption. Therefore, researchers risk exposure to DMCA liability without any guarantee that the exemption applies. Third, Section 1201(j) explicitly states that the exemption does not apply if the testing violates another law, such as the CFAA. In light of the broad view of the CFAA in some courts, discussed above in Section 5.1.2.2, there is a reasonable chance that this exception would not apply merely because a security test is viewed by a court as exceeding authorization.[291]

In sum, the seven permanent statutory exemptions to Section 1201 often do not provide cybersecurity researchers and consumers with the certainty that is necessary to circumvent access controls, even if they have a good-faith reason to believe that the exception applies. Violating the DMCA could result in significant civil damages and, in some cases, criminal charges. The multi-factor balancing tests are applied by a court, only after the individual is accused of violating the DMCA. Therefore, it is impossible for the person to have certainty *before* circumventing an access control.

5.3.5 The First Amendment and DMCA Section 1201

In light of the uncertainty that Section 1201 has created for a number of researchers who work on encryption, cybersecurity, and related fields, some critics assert that the statute violates the First Amendment's guarantee of freedom of speech. The gist of their argument is that software code is speech, and by prohibiting the distribution or discussion of certain types of code, Section 1201 censors speech and therefore violates the First Amendment.

In 2015 comments to the United States Copyright Office, a group of leading cybersecurity researchers expressed the primary First Amendment concerns with Section 1201:

> Academic and other research institutions can be risk-averse, advising faculty and students to steer clear of research with unclear liability; faculty advise students to work in areas less fraught with potential legal and public-relations challenges; and peer review may look unfavorably upon researchers whose work treads too closely to legal lines. Funders may be reluctant to support certain kinds of research. Academic publication venues are forced to wrestle with questions regarding the legality of research, despite its public value.[292]

---

291 Erik Stallman, Center for Democracy and Technology, The Current DMCA Exemption Process is a Computer Security Vulnerability (Jan. 21, 2015) ("[A] researcher arguably violates the CFAA simply by exceeding the authorization given. Accordingly, a researcher who exceeds that authorization may be subject to liability under both the CFAA and the DMCA. Unsurprisingly, there is no reported case upholding a claim of good-faith security testing under this exception.").

292 Comments of Ben Adida, et al. to the United States Copyright Office (May 21, 2015).

In short, cybersecurity researchers say that fear of criminal prosecution and civil litigation under Section 1201 makes it incredibly difficult for them to conduct research on vulnerabilities in software and systems. The restrictions, they say, also make it difficult for them to communicate their findings via publications and conferences, having a chilling effect on speech. Researchers have raised these First Amendment objections to Section 1201 in a handful of court cases. To date, courts have not invalidated Section 1201 due to these concerns.

Among the highest profile of these cases emerged in 2001, when a group of academic researchers discovered a flaw in the copyright protection system that was used on audio CDs. The researchers had planned to present their findings at a large computer science conference, but they withdrew from the conference after receiving a threat from the RIAA, asserting that the publication of the research would violate the DMCA. The researchers then sued the recording industry, seeking a judgment from the court declaring that publication of the research would not violate Section 1201, and even if it did, applying the DMCA in that manner would violate the First Amendment. "In chilling publication and presentation of scientific research," they wrote in their complaint, "the DMCA wreaks havoc in the marketplace of ideas, not only the right to speak, but the right to receive information – the right to learn."[293] The court dismissed the case for lack of standing, and did not rule on the broader statutory and First Amendment arguments. The researchers did not appeal this ruling.

Later that year, however, the U.S. Court of Appeals for the Second Circuit did rule on the constitutionality of Section 1201 in another case. In *Universal City Studios, Inc. v. Corley*,[294] major movie studios sued Eric Corley, who published "DeCSS" code on his computer hacker website, 2600.com. He also linked to other sites that hosted DeCSS. DeCSS circumvents CSS, an encryption format that the major movie studios use to prevent unauthorized copying of their DVDs. The major movie studios sued Corley under Section (a)(2), seeking a permanent injunction to prevent him from both *posting* the DeCSS code and *linking* to other sites that host the code. After trial, the district court judge granted the permanent injunction. Corley appealed to the Second Circuit, primarily arguing that Section 1201, as applied to this case, violated the First Amendment.[295]

To understand how the court assessed this claim, it is necessary to know general framework for First Amendment analysis. First, it is necessary to ask whether the law regulates speech. If the law regulates an activity other than speech, the First Amendment's free speech protections will not apply. Second, if a law does, in fact, regulate speech, then it is necessary to determine whether

---

293 First Amended Complaint, Felten v. Recording Industry Association of America, Case No. CV-01-2660 (GEB) (June 26, 2001).
294 Universal City Studios, Inc. v. Corley, 273 F. 3d 429 (2d Cir. 2001).
295 *Id.* at 441–42.

the law is *content-based* or *content-neutral*. If the law is content-based, then it will only survive a First Amendment challenge if the government demonstrates that it serves compelling governmental interests by the least restrictive means that are available. If the law is *content-neutral*, then a court will allow it if it furthers a substantial government interest that is unrelated to suppressing free expression, and the law is narrowly tailored so that it does not burden substantially more speech than necessary. The content-neutral analysis is a much lower bar than the requirements for content-based restrictions. Accordingly, the constitutionality of a statute that restricts speech often hinges on whether a court classifies it as content-based or content-neutral.

Applying the First Amendment framework to the DeCSS case, the Second Circuit first determined that computer programs and code constitute "speech" that is protected by the First Amendment.[296] Acknowledging that computer code is different from more traditional forms of speech, such as literature, the court concluded that courts have long provided First Amendment protection to "dry information, devoid of advocacy, political relevance, or artistic expression."[297] The court likened programmers' communication via code to musicians' communication via musical notes.[298]

The next step in the analysis is to determine whether Section 1201's restrictions on publication of DeCSS and linking to other sites is content-based or content neutral. The court reasoned that both restrictions are content-neutral. Corley argued that Section 1201's trafficking restrictions are content-based because they are specifically directed at communications regarding a particular topic: access control circumvention. The court disagreed, reasoning that Section 1201 and the district court's injunction target only the "non-speech" aspects of DeCSS: decrypting CSS.[299] Section 1201, as applied to DeCSS, is content-neutral, the Second Circuit reasoned, because it is not "concerned with whatever capacity DeCSS might have for conveying information to a human being."[300]

Applying the more lenient First Amendment test for content-neutral laws, the court concluded that Section 1201, as applied to this case, is constitutional. Prohibiting the posting of DeCSS code, the court ruled, serves a substantial government interest by "preventing unauthorized access to encrypted copyrighted material," and the government's actions are unrelated to suppressing free speech because it regulates DeCSS distribution "regardless of

---

296 *Id.* at 446.
297 *Id.*
298 *Id.* at 448 ("Limiting First Amendment protection of programmers to descriptions of computer code (but not the code itself) would impede discourse among computer scholars, just as limiting protection for musicians to descriptions of musical scores (but not sequences of notes) would impede their exchange of ideas and expression.").
299 *Id.* at 454.
300 *Id.*

whether DeCSS code contains any information comprehensible by human beings that would qualify as speech."[301] The prohibition on posting DeCSS code does not burden substantially more speech than necessary, the court concluded. Although the court acknowledged that the unconditional prohibition on posting the code "is not absolutely necessary to preventing unauthorized access to copyrighted materials," Corley failed to demonstrate that the injunction burdens *substantially* more speech than is necessary. Had the court concluded that the injunction was content-based, it is unlikely that the injunction would have survived this challenge, since the government would have needed to demonstrate that the injunction is the *least* restrictive means to accomplish protect CSS-encrypted movies. The court suggested that the injunction's prohibition on *linking* to DeCSS code raises more difficult First Amendment issues, but ultimately it upheld the constitutionality of that prohibition as well.[302]

In more recent years, litigants have mounted similar First Amendment challenges to various aspects of Section 1201, but they have faced similar skepticism from courts.[303] Because the United States Supreme Court has not directly ruled on whether Section 1201 comports with the First Amendment, it is possible – though unlikely – that a court could invalidate the use of Section 1201 based on a First Amendment challenge.

5.4 Economic Espionage Act

The Economic Espionage Act prohibits the theft of U.S. companies' trade secrets, either to benefit a foreign government or to economically benefit anyone other than the owner. The statute was passed in 1996 to impose criminal penalties for both foreign and corporate espionage, and amended significantly in 2016 to allow companies to bring civil suits for trade secret theft. The evolution – and growing importance – of the Economic Espionage Act demonstrates the increasingly grave threat that trade secrets pose in the United States.

---

301 *Id.* at 454.

302 *Id.* at 457–58.

303 *See, e.g.,* United States v. Elcom Ltd., 203 F. Supp. 2d 1111 (N.D. Cal. 2002) ("[T]he DMCA does not burden substantially more speech than is necessary to achieve the government's asserted goals of promoting electronic commerce, protecting copyrights, and preventing electronic piracy."); 321 Studios v. Metro Goldwyn Mayer Studios, Inc., 307 F. Supp. 2d 1085 (N.D. Cal. 2004) ("Congress determined that the DMCA was needed to protect copyrights and intellectual property rights; this Court finds that the challenged provisions further important and substantial government interests unrelated to the suppression of free expression, and that the incidental restrictions on First Amendment freedoms are no greater than essential to the furtherance of those interests.").

> ## Overview of Key Provisions of the Economic Espionage Act
>
> **Section 1831: *Economic espionage*.** Prohibits individuals from stealing, copying, receiving, or possessing trade secrets without authorization, if the individuals intended or knew that the offense would benefit any foreign government, foreign instrumentality, or foreign agent. Imposes fines and prison time of up to fifteen years.
>
> **Section 1832: *Theft of trade secrets*.** Prohibits individuals from stealing, copying, receiving, or possessing trade secrets without authorization, if the individuals acted with intent to convert a trade secret, that is related to a product or service used in or intended for use in interstate or foreign commerce, to the economic benefit of anyone other than the trade secret's owner, and intending or knowing that the offense will injury the owner. Imposes fines and prison time of up to ten years.
>
> **Section 1836: *Civil actions*.** Allows victims of trade secret misappropriation to file civil lawsuits, seeking injunctions to prevent further misappropriation and monetary damages to recover the amount lost due to the misappropriation. In extraordinary circumstances, the victims can file emergency requests for courts to seize property to prevent misappropriation.

5.4.1 Origins of the Economic Espionage Act

At first glance, economic espionage and the theft of trade secrets may not appear to be of particular concern for cybersecurity professionals. However, the Economic Espionage Act is one of the first U.S. laws that was crafted with cybersecurity in mind. When Congress passed the Economic Espionage Act in 1996, companies were just beginning to consider how to integrate the Internet into their daily business operations. The companies also were taking greater advantage of computers and data centers for warehousing data that had long been contained only on paper and stored in folders and drawers.

As an increasing amount of data is stored on computers and in remote data centers, espionage and theft of trade secrets has become common, causing great economic risk for companies. Indeed, many executives view the theft of trade secrets as an even greater threat than the theft of personal information, because the theft of confidential business information such as trade secrets could undercut a company's entire economic model.

Companies have long protected their nontangible assets – information – with intellectual property laws. However, those laws only provide limited protection for much of the information that companies seek to keep confidential. Copyright law only protects creative expressions that are fixed in a medium. While, for example, an email or report may be protected by copyright, the information contained in that report is not protected. Patent law only offers protection if the

United States Patent and Trademark Office has approved a patent. The patent approval process is long and complex, and requires the applicant to demonstrate that the invention is nonobvious, useful, and new. A great deal of confidential business information, such as financial projections, sales statistics, and business plans, often is not covered under federal intellectual property laws.

The most likely source of protection for confidential corporate data are the many state laws that protect trade secrets. However, most of these laws do not provide sufficient penalties to deter corporate espionage. Moreover, the laws generally provide only for private civil litigation, so they rely on the victimized companies to investigate and litigate claims against the perpetrators.

Recognizing the need for a federal law to deter corporate espionage in the emerging information age, Congress drafted and enacted the Economic Espionage Act. In its report accompanying the bill, the House Judiciary Committee noted the rapidly increasing espionage threats that companies were facing as their data was stored on computers and servers:

> Computer technology enables rapid and surreptitious duplications of the information. Hundreds of pages of information can be loaded onto a small computer diskette, placed into a coat pocket, and taken from the legal owner. This material is a prime target for theft precisely because it costs so much to develop independently, because it is so valuable, and because there are virtually no penalties for its theft.[304]

The Judiciary Committee noted the particular dangers of espionage that arise from insider threats. "A great deal of the theft is committed by disgruntled individuals or employees who hope to harm their former companies or line their own pockets," the Committee wrote.[305]

5.4.2 Criminal Prohibitions on Economic Espionage and Theft of Trade Secrets

The Economic Espionage Act contains two separate prohibitions: Section 1831 prohibits economic espionage for a foreign government or entity, and Section 1832 prohibits the theft of trade secrets to benefit one company at the expense of another company.

The two sections differ primarily regarding the purpose and intent behind the defendant's trade secret theft, as described in more detail below.

---

304 H.R. Rep. 104-788 at 5 (1996).
305 *Id.*

Both sections, however, require the defendant to have committed one of the five following acts:

- Stealing, or without authorization appropriating, taking, carrying away, or concealing, or by fraud, artifice, or deception obtaining a trade secret.
- Without authorization copying, duplicating, sketching, drawing, photographing, downloading, uploading, altering, destroying, photocopying, replicating, transmitting, delivering, sending, mailing, communicating, or conveying a trade secret.
- Receiving, buying, or possessing a trade secret, knowing the same to have been stolen or appropriated, obtained, or converted without authorization.
- Attempting to commit any of the aforesaid offenses.
- Conspiring with at least one other person to commit any of the first three offenses, and one or more of the conspirators do any act to effect the object of the conspiracy.[306]

Violations of Section 1831 carry prison time of up to fifteen years and a fine of up to $5 million for an individual. Organizations that violate Section 1831 face a fine of up to $10 million or three times the value of the stolen trade secret, whichever is greater. Violations of Section 1832 carry prison time of up to ten years or a fine. Organizations that violate Section 1832 face a fine of up to $5 million, or three times the value of the stolen trade secret, whichever is greater.

Sections 1831 and 1832 apply to conduct that occurs outside of the United States, if either an act in furtherance of the violation was committed in the United States, or if the offender is a U.S. citizen or permanent resident alien, or an organization that is organized under U.S. laws.[307]

5.4.2.1 Definition of "Trade Secret"

Both Sections 1831 and 1832 only apply if the information at issue constitutes a "trade secret." The Economic Espionage Act broadly defines "trade secret" as:

> all forms and types of financial, business, scientific, technical, economic, or engineering information, including patterns, plans, compilations, program devices, formulas, designs, prototypes, methods, techniques, processes, procedures, programs, or codes, whether tangible or intangible, and whether or how stored, compiled, or memorialized physically, electronically, graphically, photographically, or in writing if—
>
> a) the owner thereof has taken reasonable measures to keep such information secret; and

---

306 18 U.S.C. § 1831 and 1832.
307 18 U.S.C. § 1837.

b) the information derives independent economic value, actual
   or potential, from not being generally known to, and not
   being readily ascertainable through proper means by, another
   person who can obtain economic value from the disclosure
   or use of the information.[308]

Congress modeled the Economic Espionage Act's definition of "trade secret" after the definition in the Uniform Trade Secrets Act, intending for the definition to broadly encompass many types of confidential information.[309]

In some cases, defendants argue that information is not a trade secret because the owner failed to take "reasonable measures" to keep the information secret. Although there is not a precise checklist to determine whether companies have taken sufficiently reasonable measures, courts consider a wide range of factors, such as the number of people authorized to access the information, the security of the storage of the information, confidentiality agreements, and the company's information security and document destruction policies.[310]

Despite this broad definition of trade secrets, defendants often seek to dismiss Economic Espionage Act cases by arguing that the government failed to demonstrate that the company took reasonable measures to ensure secrecy. For example, in a 2008 criminal trial in Los Angeles, Tien Shiah was tried for violating Section 1832.[311] Shiah, who was born in Taiwan and raised and educated in Canada, worked at a California company, and had accepted a job at another company. Before leaving his first employer, he gathered a number of confidential electronic files on a laptop, as well as hard copies. He believed this was a "toolkit" that was a record of his work at the first employer.[312] Two years later, Shiah left his second employer, and created another "toolkit" of a number of confidential documents, including many regarding pricing and business strategy.[313]

At trial, the judge concluded that his employer had taken reasonable steps to keep the information secret. The judge first noted that it is unnecessary to demonstrate that the company prevented even its own employees from seeing the data, as that would threaten internal productivity.[314] The proper inquiry

---

308 18 U.S.C. § 1839(3).
309 *See* H. Rept. 104-788(1996) at 12 ("These general categories of information are included in the definition of trade secret for illustrative purposes and should not be read to limit the definition of trade secret. It is the Committee's intent that this definition be read broadly.").
310 *See* United States v. Chung, 659 F.3d 815, 825-26 (9th Cir. 2011).
311 United States v. Shiah, CASE NO. SA CR 06-92 DOC, 2008 U.S. Dist. LEXIS 11973 (C.D. Cal. Feb. 19, 2008).
312 *Id.* at *3.
313 *Id.* at *16.
314 *Id.* at *60–61.

is whether the company took reasonable steps to prevent *outsiders* from accessing the data. Among the steps that the company took to safeguard the data:

- Requiring every employee to sign a confidentiality agreement.
- Using firewalls, intrusion detection software, strong passwords, layered protection between the Intranet and Internet, and selective storage of files.
- Requiring nondisclosure agreements before sharing information with outside entities.
- Marking documents as confidential.
- Strengthening the physical security of its facilities.

However, the judge noted a few areas in which the employer could have improved its efforts to maintain secrecy of the data:

- Explain the confidentiality agreement to employees, and provide them with a copy for their records.
- Implement a comprehensive system to designate confidentiality of documents.
- Refer employees to the confidentiality agreement during their exit interviews.
- Ask employees at exit interview whether they copied any files.
- Inspect employee's computer upon termination to determine whether the employee has taken any confidential information.[315]

On balance, the court concluded, the employer's confidentiality practices were "generally effective," and the deficiencies "were not so extensive to qualify as unreasonable."[316] The court's well-reasoned analysis in this case provides an example of the factors that courts will weigh when determining whether companies took reasonable steps to protect confidential information. Keep in mind that another court could have just as easily found that the employer did not take reasonable steps, depending on the weight that the court were to accord to each protective measure. Accordingly, companies that seek to ensure that their information constitutes a trade secret for the purposes of the Economic Espionage Act should attempt to take as many protective measures as possible.

Defendants also argue that information does not constitute a trade secret because the information does not derive independent economic value from not being known to another person who can obtain economic value from the

---

315 *Id.* at *61–66.
316 *Id.* at *68.

disclosure or use of the information.[317] To make this determination, courts typically consider "the degree to which the secret information confers a competitive advantage on its owner."[318] In general, courts have been willing to find that confidentiality of information creates independent value, and they typically do not require proof of an actual increase in value due to the confidentiality. In part, that is because the statute allows the economic value to be actual *or* potential.[319]

For instance, in the *Shiah* criminal prosecution, the court concluded that the information that Shiah copied has independent economic value due to its confidentiality. The pricing information, for instance, "would allow competitors to compete more effectively with respect to price by undermining [the employer's] pricing structure and also obtain more favorable terms from their suppliers."[320] Disclosure of information about the company's unreleased products would hurt the company's research and development efforts, the court reasoned.[321] Revealing the confidential customer information could harm the company's relationships with its customers, the court wrote.[322] The court recognized that some of the information in the files that Shiah copied were not confidential, such as information that already was publicly available, and Congress did not intend to accord trade secret status to such data.[323] Nonetheless, the information constituted a trade secret because at least *some* of it derived value from remaining confidential.[324]

---

317 Until 2016, the statute required proof that "the information derives independent economic value, actual or potential, from not being generally known to, and not being readily ascertainable through proper means by, *the public*." (emphasis added). The Defend Trade Secrets Act of 2016 replaced "the public" with "another person who can obtain economic value from the disclosure or use of the information." The House Report accompanying the 2016 bill stated that this was a minor revision intended to bring the statute's definition in line with that in the Uniform Trade Secrets Act. H.R. Rep. 114-529 at 13–14 (2016). As of publication of this book, no court applied this new definition in a written opinion, but it is likely that this minor change would affect the outcome of the leading Economic Espionage Act cases discussed in this chapter.

318 United States v. Chung, 659 F.3d 815, 826-27 (9th Cir. 2011).

319 *See* United States v. Jin, 733 F.3d 718 (7th Cir. 2013) ("The government doesn't have to prove that the owner of the secret actually lost money as a result of the theft. For remember that the 'independent economic value' attributable to the information's remaining secret need only be 'potential' as distinct from 'actual.'").

320 *Id.* at *58.

321 *Id.*

322 *Id.*

323 *Id.* at *59.

324 *Id.* ("Each of these files contained some information that derived value from not being generally known to the public, which is sufficient to satisfy the first prong of the trade secret test beyond a reasonable doubt.")

5.4.2.2 "Knowing" Violations of the Economic Espionage Act

Both Sections 1831 and 1832 apply only to acts that are done "knowingly." Congress added this additional state-of-mind requirement to limit the application of the Economic Espionage Act to people who are aware that they are handling trade secrets. In the Senate Judiciary Committee's report accompanying the Economic Espionage Act, the legislators wrote that to knowingly commit an act in violation of the Economic Espionage Act requires "(1) an awareness of the nature of one's conduct, and (2) an awareness of or a firm belief in or knowledge to a substantial certainty of the existence of a relevant circumstance, such as whether the information is proprietary economic information as defined by this statute."[325]

Prosecutors need not demonstrate that the defendant knew that the act was illegal, nor do they need to be aware that the information legally qualifies as a trade secret.[326] Instead, prosecutors only must prove that the defendants were aware that the information was proprietary.[327]

5.4.2.3 Purpose and Intent Required under Section 1831: Economic Espionage

As mentioned above, Sections 1831 (Economic Espionage) and 1832 (Theft of Trade Secrets) apply to the same five acts involving the theft, copying, receipt, or purchase of trade secrets. The difference between the two sections is the purpose and intent behind these acts. Section 1831 involves a violation that is motivated by the desire to help a foreign government, while Section 1832 involves a violation that is motivated by the desire to help one company succeed and harm the victim. It is possible to see a defendant charged under *both* sections, if the act is intended to both help another country as well as a company in that country.

Section 1831 applies if the defendant knowingly committed the offense "intending or knowing that the offense will benefit any foreign government, foreign instrumentality, or foreign agent[.]"[328] Section 1831 explicitly states

---

325 S. Rep. 104-359 at 16 (1996).

326 *Id.* ("The statute does not require proof that the actor knew that his conduct violated Federal law. The Committee intends that the knowing state of mind requirement may be satisfied by proof that the actor was aware of a high probability of the existence of the circumstance, although a defense should succeed if it is proven that the actor actually and reasonably believed that the circumstance did not exist.").

327 *See* United States v. Roberts, No. 3:08-CR-175, 2009 WL 5449224, at *6–7 (E.D. Tenn. Nov. 17, 2009) ("a defendant must know that the information he or she seeks to steal is proprietary, meaning belonging to someone else who has an exclusive right to it, but does not have to know that it meets the statutory definition of a trade secret.").

328 18 U.S.C. § 1831.

that it only applies if the foreign instrumentalities[329] and agents[330] are linked to a foreign government. Accordingly, an offense that is intended to violate a foreign private company – and not the government – will not qualify as a Section 1831 violation (though it might fall under Section 1832).

For instance, Hanjuan Jin was indicted under both Sections 1831 and 1832 for allegedly stealing trade secrets from her former employer, Motorola, and moved to China with plans to work for a competing company. The judge conducted a bench trial (which is a trial that is decided by the judge, not a jury), and determined that although Jin violated Section 1832, there was insufficient evidence to convict her of economic espionage under Section 1831. The government argued that by providing the trade secrets to a Chinese company, Jin intended to benefit the People's Republic of China. The district court rejected this argument, concluding that "[t]here is certainly plenty of speculative proof that the PRC may have benefited from Jin's conduct, but such speculation does not equate to proof beyond a reasonable doubt."[331] The *Jin* case demonstrates the difficulty of proving a Section 1831 violation. The government faces the heavy burden of demonstrative *beyond a reasonable doubt* that the defendant not only stole trade secrets but did so with the intent or knowledge that the action would benefit a foreign government.

That is not to say that it is impossible to demonstrate that the defendant stole trade secrets with the intent of benefiting a foreign government. Consider a 2011 case from the U.S. Court of Appeals for the Ninth Circuit, *United States v. Chung*.[332] Dongfan Chung, a former Boeing engineer, was charged with violating Section 1831 because he provided Boeing trade secrets to China. Chung, who was born in China, worked in Boeing facilities in the United States for more than three decades before retiring in 2002. During the 2005 search of the home of another criminal suspect, federal agents found a letter to Chung, from a Chinese government official, thanking Chung for providing information to China and requesting additional information about airplanes and space shuttles. This letter provided the agents with reason to further investigate Chung. In 2006, with his consent, they searched his home and found more than 300,000 pages of Boeing documents, many relating to space shuttle design.[333] They also learned that he gave a presentation about Boeing space shuttles to Chinese engineers. Chung was convicted at trial on violations of Section 1831, as well as other crimes.

---

329 18 U.S.C. § 1839(1) ("the term 'foreign instrumentality' means any agency, bureau, ministry, component, institution, association, or any legal, commercial, or business organization, corporation, firm, or entity that is substantially owned, controlled, sponsored, commanded, managed, or dominated by a foreign government.").

330 18 U.S.C. § 1839(2) ("the term 'foreign agent' means any officer, employee, proxy, servant, delegate, or representative of a foreign government").

331 United States v. Jin, 833 F. Supp. 2d 977, 1020 (N.D. Ill. 2012); aff'd on other grounds at 733 F.3d 718 (7th Cir. 2013).

332 United States v. Chung, 659 F.3d 815 (9th Cir. 2011).

Chung appealed the 1831 conviction. The Ninth Circuit held that there is "ample evidence" that Chung possessed the trade secrets with the intent of benefiting the Chinese government. "Defendant intended to benefit China by providing technical information responsive to requests from Chinese officials and by delivering presentations to Chinese engineers," the court wrote.[334] The *Chung* case shows court's willingness to conclude that a Section 1831 defendant intended to benefit a foreign government based on compelling circumstantial evidence. Possessing the documents, and nothing more, probably would not have satisfied Section 1831's intent requirements. However, Chung's ongoing contacts with Chinese officials, coupled with his possession of trade secrets, was enough for the court to affirm his Section 1831 conviction.

5.4.2.4 Purpose and Intent Required under Section 1832: Theft of Trade Secrets

In recent years, prosecutors have brought a number of high-profile cases under Section 1832, likely owing to the fact that employees are increasingly transferring large amounts of data from their current employer to a future employer. The abundance of portable digital media and unrestricted workplace Internet access makes such theft remarkably easy.

Section 1832 applies if the defendant knowingly commits one of the five offenses related to trade secrets "with intent to convert a trade secret, that is related to a product or service used in or intended for use in interstate or foreign commerce, to the economic benefit of anyone other than the owner thereof, and intending or knowing that the offense will injure any owner of that trade secret[.]"[335]

The requirement of "intent to convert a trade secret" simply means that the defendant intended to transfer the trade secret to an individual or entity other than the legally authorized owner. This is based on the common law tort of conversion, which courts typically define as an "unauthorized assumption and exercise of the right of ownership over goods or personal chattels belonging to another, to the alteration of their condition or the exclusion of an owner's rights."[336] In the cyber realm, if an employee downloads thousands of pages of confidential sales documents, hoping to use them in a future job with a competitor, the employee intends to convert trade secrets.

Perhaps the most contentious – and complex – requirement is that the trade secret be related to a product or service used in or intended for use in interstate or foreign commerce. In fact, Congress has changed the precise wording of this requirement over the years as it has struggled to determine the scope of Section 1832.

---

333 *Id.* at 819.
334 *Id.* at 828.
335 18 U.S.C. § 1832(a).
336 Variety Wholesalers v. Salem Logistics, 723 SE 2d 744 (N.C. 2012).

When the Economic Espionage Act was initially introduced in the Senate, it did not require that the trade secret have any link to interstate or foreign commerce; instead, it imposed criminal penalties on any individual who steals "proprietary economic information having a value of not less than $100,000."[337] The House added an interstate or foreign commerce requirement, which applied to the conversion of any trade secret "that is related to or included in a product that is produced for or placed in interstate or foreign commerce." That limitation was included in the bill that was enacted in 1996, and remained in effect until 2012.

That interstate commerce provision, however, raised some significant challenges for prosecutors and uncertainty for courts. What did it mean for a product to be produced for or placed in interstate commerce? And what if the trade secret related to a service, rather than a product? The limitations of this definition became apparent in a 2012 opinion from the U.S. Court of Appeals for the Second Circuit. In *United States v. Aleynikov,*[338] Sergey Aleynikov, a Goldman Sachs computer programmer, was charged with violating Section 1832. Prosecutors alleged that he stole source code for Goldman's high-frequency trading system, and had accepted a job with another company that was developing its own high-frequency trading system.[339] Aleynikov was convicted, and he appealed, arguing that Goldman's high-frequency trading system was not a product that is produced for or placed in interstate commerce. Aleynikov argued that the high-frequency trading system was strictly for Goldman's internal use, and the company had no plans to sell or license the system. The Second Circuit agreed with Aleynikov and reversed his Section 1832 conviction. Even though the software helped Goldman *engage* in interstate and foreign commerce, the Second Circuit concluded that the statutory provision is far more limited, and only applies to products that are in the stream of commerce or are intended to be placed in the stream of commerce.[340]

The *Aleynikov* decision quickly set off alarms throughout corporate America.[341] Corporations develop a great deal of proprietary technology that is intended strictly for internal use. The court's opinion suggested that

---

337 S. 1556, 104th Cong (1996).
338 United States v. Aleynikov, 676 F.3d 71 (2d Cir. 2012).
339 *Id.* at 73–74.
340 *Id.* at 26–27: "Because the HFT system was not designed to enter or pass in commerce, or make something that does, Aleynikov's theft of source code relating to that system was not an offense under the EEA."
341 *See* Trade Secrets Institute, Case Report: United States v. Aleynikov ("The February 2012 reversal of Aleynikov's conviction of trade secrets theft – especially the Second Circuit's ruling that Aleynikov was wrongly charged with espionage, since the code was not a product designed for interstate or foreign commerce – called into question the government's ability to prosecute theft of internal trading systems or other internal financial instruments under the Economic Espionage Act.").

employees would not be liable under the Economic Espionage Act for the theft of this valuable data. Within months of the Second Circuit's decision members of Congress introduced the Theft of Trade Secrets Clarification Act of 2012. The bill's sponsors stated their intent to prevent future decisions such as *Aleynikov,* and the legislation passed without controversy.[342] The bill expanded the reach of Section 1832, applying to trade secrets that are "related to a product or service used in or intended for use in interstate or foreign commerce." This amendment significantly broadened the reach of Section 1832, allowing it to apply not only to products that are sold or licensed, but to products *and* services that are used in interstate or foreign commerce. For instance, while Goldman's high-frequency trading system did not fall within the scope of the older version of Section 1832, it clearly is covered by the current version because the software is used in interstate and foreign commerce.

Section 1832 also is limited by the requirement that the act be "for the economic benefit" of anyone other than the owner. Courts have held that an employee does not violate Section 1832 merely by gaining skills and expertise at Employer A, quitting, and using those skills at Employer B. Individuals only violate Section 1832 if they use *confidential information* for the benefit of themselves or others, such as a new employer.[343]

5.4.3 Civil Actions for Trade Secret Misappropriation: The Defend Trade Secrets Act of 2016

Until 2016, the Economic Espionage Act was enforceable only by federal prosecutors. If a company wanted to obtain an injunction or recover damages for the theft of trade secrets, its only recourse was filing a lawsuit in state court under one of the forty-eight state trade secret misappropriation laws. Companies often were unable to effectively use state trade secrets laws because the process was overly burdensome. Trade secret theft often affected a company's operations in all states, and bringing separate suits in each state would be impractical. Moreover, state courts often do not operate at the fast pace that is necessary to address trade secret theft involving a multinational company.

Recognizing the limitations of state trade secret laws, members of Congress in 2014 began to propose legislation to amend the Economic Espionage Act to allow companies to bring trade secret misappropriation lawsuits in federal

---

342 *See* 158 Cong. Rec. S6978-03 (statement of Sen. Leahy) ("clarifying legislation that the Senate will pass today corrects the court's narrow reading to ensure that our federal criminal laws adequately address the theft of trade secrets").

343 United States v. Martin, 228 F.3d 1, 11 (1st Cir.2000) ("1832(a) was not designed to punish competition, even when such competition relies on the know-how of former employees of a direct competitor. It was, however, designed to prevent those employees (and their future employers) from taking advantage of confidential information gained, discovered, copied, or taken while employed elsewhere.").

court. They succeeded in 2016, when President Obama signed the Defend Trade Secrets Act of 2016.

The primary component of the bill is a new civil remedy for trade secret misappropriation, allowing companies to directly sue under federal law if their trade secrets have been stolen. In the House Judiciary Committee report accompanying the bill, legislators expressed a desire to provide a "single, national standard for trade secret misappropriation with clear rules and predictability for everyone involved."[344] Congress recognized the close link between trade secret theft and cybersecurity, and noted that despite companies' efforts to improve their security measures, such theft has increasingly taken a toll on the U.S. economy.[345]

5.4.3.1 Definition of "Misappropriation"

The Defend Trade Secrets Act of 2016 allows companies to bring a federal civil suit if they have been the victims of misappropriation, a term that had not been previously used in the Economic Espionage Act. The bill provides two definitions for "misappropriation":

a) acquisition of a trade secret of another by a person who knows or has reason to know that the trade secret was acquired by improper means; or

b) disclosure or use of a trade secret of another without express or implied consent by a person who –

   i) used improper means to acquire knowledge of the trade secret;

   ii) at the time of disclosure or use, knew or had reason to know that the knowledge of the trade secret was –

      i) derived from or through a person who had used improper means to acquire the trade secret;

      ii) acquired under circumstances giving rise to a duty to maintain the secrecy of the trade secret or limit the use of the trade secret; or

      iii) derived from or through a person who owed a duty to the person seeking relief to maintain the secrecy of the trade secret or limit the use of the trade secret; or

   iii) before a material change of the position of the person, knew or had reason to know that –

      i) the trade secret was a trade secret; and

      ii) knowledge of the trade secret had been acquired by accident or mistake.[346]

---

344 H.R. Rep. 114-529 at 6 (2016).
345 *Id*. at 4.
346 18 U.S.C. § 1839(5).

The term "improper means" is defined to include "theft, bribery, misrepresentation, breach or inducement of a breach of a duty to maintain secrecy, or espionage through electronic or other means[.]"[347] The term does not include lawful means of acquisition, including reverse engineering or independent derivation.[348]

The House Judiciary Committee report states that this definition is largely identical to that which is in the Uniform Trade Secrets Act, which is the basis for the forty-eight state trade secret laws. Congress used the state laws' definition "to make clear that this Act is not intended to alter the balance of current trade secret law or alter specific court decisions."[349]

The Defend Trade Secrets Act provides three general types of relief that misappropriation victims may seek: (1) civil seizures, (2) injunctions and other equitable relief, and (3) damages.

5.4.3.2 Civil Seizures

In certain extraordinary circumstances, a company may go to federal court to seek an order for the seizure of property, if the seizure is necessary to prevent propagation or dissemination of the trade secret that has been misappropriated.[350] The company may apply for the seizure through an *ex parte* process, meaning that the other party need not be present to litigate the request. The House Judiciary Committee stated that it only intends the civil seizure process to be used "in instances in which a defendant is seeking to flee the country or planning to disclose the trade secret to a third party immediately or is otherwise not amenable to the enforcement of the court's orders."[351]

For a court to grant a civil seizure motion, it must find the following to be clearly true:

- Other equitable relief would be inadequate.
- Denying the seizure would result in an "immediate and irreparable injury."
- The harm of denying the seizure outweighs the harm caused by the seizure.
- The applicant likely will succeed in demonstrating trade secret misappropriation.
- The person whose property is being seized actually has the trade secret.
- The application describes the matter to be seized and the circumstances with reasonable particularity.
- The person against whom the seizure is being ordered, or other people, would make the property inaccessible to the court if notified.
- The applicant has not publicized the request for seizure.[352]

---

347 18 U.S.C. § 1839(6).
348 *Id.*
349 *Id.* at 14.
350 18 U.S.C. § 1836(b)(2)(A)(i).
351 H.R. Rep. 114-529 at 9–10 (2016).
352 18 U.S.C. § 1836(b)(2)(A)(ii).

If a court issues a seizure order, it must set a hearing within seven days after the order has been issued. At the hearing, the applicant for the order has the burden of proof of proving the facts that support the order. If the court determines that the applicant has not met that burden, the seizure order will be immediately dissolved.[353]

Any party that has an interest in the matter seized may request an immediate hearing, which can be *ex parte*, to encrypt the seized material.[354]

5.4.3.3 Injunctions

A company that has been the victim of trade secret misappropriation may request an injunction to prevent actual or threatened misappropriation. Injunctions under this act may block threatened misappropriation, provided that they do not entirely prevent an individual from starting a new job. The injunction allows conditions to be placed on employment to be based on evidence of threatened misappropriation, but not only on information that the person knows. Such injunctions also may not conflict with state laws regarding restraints on trades or businesses.[355] The House Judiciary Committee stated that it added these limits on injunctive relief to "protect employee mobility," consistent with employment protection laws in many states.[356]

Injunctions also may require parties to take affirmative actions to protect a trade secret. And in exceptional circumstances, injunctions may condition future use of a trade secret on the payment of a reasonable royalty, for a limited period of time.[357]

5.4.3.4 Damages

The Defend Trade Secrets Act also enables plaintiffs to recover compensatory damages from the defendants. The Act allows plaintiffs to recover damages for actual loss caused by the misappropriation, as well as damages for unjust enrichment that are not included in the actual loss total.[358]

Alternatively, plaintiffs can seek to recover compensatory damages by imposing a "reasonable royalty" for the defendant's unauthorized disclosure or use of the trade secret.[359] The House Judiciary Committee stated that it does not intend to encourage the use of reasonable royalties, and prefers alternative remedies.[360] If the court determines that the defendant "willfully and

---

353 18 U.S.C. § 1836(b)(2)(F).
354 18 U.S.C. § 1836(b)(2)(H).
355 18 U.S.C. § 1836(b)(3)(A).
356 H.R. Rep. 114-529 at 12 (2016).
357 18 U.S.C. § 1836(b)(3)(A).
358 18 U.S.C. § 1836(b)(3)(B)(i).
359 18 U.S.C. § 1836(b)(3)(A).
360 H.R. Rep. 114-529 at 12 (2016).

maliciously" misappropriated the trade secret, the plaintiff may recover exemplary damages of up to twice as much of the compensatory damages awarded.[361]

5.4.3.5 Statute of Limitations
Plaintiffs must bring Economic Espionage Act civil actions within three years of the date the misappropriation was discovered or should have been discovered through exercise of reasonable diligence.[362] This requirement is identical to the statute of limitations in the Uniform Trade Secrets Act.[363]

---

361 H.R. Rep. 114-529 at 12 (2016).
362 18 U.S.C. § 1836(d).
363 H.R. Rep. 114-529 at 12 (2016).

6

Public–Private Cybersecurity Partnerships

Much of this book focuses on the consequences that a company may face for inadequate cybersecurity, such as enforcement actions or lawsuits by the Federal Trade Commission or state attorneys general. However, the federal government's role in private-sector cybersecurity is not merely one of a regulator. The government also operates a number of programs that are designed to help companies battle the ever-evolving field of cybersecurity threats. Cyberspace is unique in that it involves both public and private infrastructure, and therefore the federal government recognizes that it has a role in securing the Internet. Moreover, the federal government can act as a central repository of cybersecurity information.

This chapter first reviews the increasingly centralized civilian cybersecurity operations, many of which are located within the Department of Homeland Security. It next examines DHS's cybersecurity information-sharing program, created by the Cybersecurity Act of 2015, and a similar program that the U.S. Energy Department operates for electric utilities. The chapter then reviews the voluntary Cybersecurity Framework developed by the National Institute of Standards and Technology. Finally, the chapter examines the U.S. military's ability to protect civilian networks and systems, and the limits placed on these activities under the Posse Comitatus Act.

Cybersecurity Law, First Edition. Jeff Kosseff.
© 2017 John Wiley & Sons, Inc. Published 2017 by John Wiley & Sons, Inc.
Companion Website: www.wiley.com/go/kosseff/cybersecurity

6.1 U.S. Government's Civilian Cybersecurity Organization

The U.S. federal government does not have a single agency or department that is responsible for nationwide cybersecurity, as it does for health, education, housing, and other key policy issues. Due to the unique nature of cybersecurity, the responsibilities are scattered throughout the federal government.

Much of the federal government's proactive cybersecurity programs are centered in the U.S. Department of Homeland Security (DHS), which has primary responsibility for the civilian (nonmilitary) cybersecurity. Over the years, statutes and presidential orders have increasingly consolidated civilian cybersecurity responsibilities within DHS.

DHS's cybersecurity operations are housed in the Office of Cybersecurity and Communications, which is part of DHS's National Protection and Programs Directorate (a broad organization that also includes programs to protect federal property and critical infrastructure from terrorism and natural disasters). The Office of Cybersecurity and Communications operates EINSTEIN, a broad program that protects civilian federal government computers from cybersecurity threats, by monitoring and deterring threats in real time. The Office also operates the National Cybersecurity and Communications Integration Center (NCCIC). Within NCCIC is the U.S. Computer Emergency Readiness Team (US-CERT), which provides round-the-clock monitoring for emerging cybersecurity threats, and issues alerts about significant cybersecurity issues that it has detected.

In recent years, Congress and other officials have made clear that DHS plays a central role in coordinating civilian cybersecurity. In 2015, Congress passed the Cybersecurity Act of 2015, which, as described below, provided limited legal immunity to encourage the private sector to share information about cybersecurity threats and defensive measures with the federal government. A lesser-publicized provision in that law significantly expanded the cybersecurity authorities of NCCIC. The provision, entitled the National Cybersecurity Protection Advancement Act of 2015, centralized the responsibility for cyber-threat information sharing within NCCIC. The statute also provides NCCIC and DHS with significant responsibility for nationwide cybersecurity planning.

DHS, however, is far from the only federal agency or department that has taken some ownership of cybersecurity. For instance, in 2016, President Obama formed the White House's Commission on Enhancing National Cybersecurity, which is comprised of public and private sector representatives and is charged with advising the government on cybersecurity.[1] The President also has advisers dedicated to cybersecurity, as does the President's National Security Council.

The U.S. State Department has additionally a cybersecurity coordinator who is dedicated to representing the nation on international cybersecurity issues. Among the issues that the State Department frequently discusses with other nations are export controls (discussed in Chapter 4 of this book), international cybercrime standards, and cyber-threat sharing and incident response programs.

The U.S. Department of Commerce also is quite involved in helping U.S. businesses reduce the risk of data breaches and other incidents. The Commerce Department's National Institute of Standards and Technology has developed a number of voluntary, nonbinding cybersecurity standards, including the Cybersecurity Framework discussed later in this chapter.

The U.S. Justice Department's Computer Crimes and Intellectual Property Section leads the government's efforts on prosecuting cybercrimes. Among the many responsibilities of the section is partnering with the private sector and educating the sector about emerging cybercrime issues.

Departments that focus on a particular industry often have attempted to help those industries ensure that they have adequate cybersecurity. For instance, the Food and Drug Administration has issued guidelines for the cybersecurity of medical devices, an issue that has long been seen as a serious national security concern. The U.S. Energy Department, discussed later in this chapter, has listed cybersecurity of the electric grid among its top priorities, and has started a threat-sharing information exchange for utilities. The Federal Communications Commission has offered cybersecurity resources to assist telecommunications providers in shoring up their network security. The National Highway Traffic Safety Administration, part of the U.S. Department of Transportation, has been researching the cybersecurity risks associated with connected automobiles.

6.2 Department of Homeland Security Information Sharing under the Cybersecurity Act of 2015

DHS has long operated the NCCIC and US-CERT, but the private sector has been hesitant to provide real-time threat information to the federal government because of concerns about liability under a wide range of laws, including antitrust

---

1 *See* White House, Fact Sheet, Cybersecurity National Action Plan (Feb. 9, 2009) ("The Commission will make recommendations on actions that can be taken over the next decade to strengthen cybersecurity in both the public and private sectors while protecting privacy; maintaining public safety and economic and national security; fostering discovery and development of new technical solutions; and bolstering partnerships between Federal, State, and local government and the private sector in the development, promotion and use of cybersecurity technologies, policies, and best practices.").

and privacy. Recognizing this barrier, after years of heated debate, Congress in late 2015 passed, and President Obama signed, the Cybersecurity Act of 2015. The Cybersecurity Act has a number of components, including the creation of new processes by which companies can monitor and defend their networks, provisions that are discussed in Chapter 7 of this book. The new law also creates a greatly expanded platform by which private companies and the government can exchange information about cyber-threat indicators and defensive measures.

The information sharing – and limited immunity – applies only for the sharing or receipt of cyber-threat indicators or defensive measures. The statute broadly defines "cyber-threat indicator" as information that is necessary to describe or identify:

- malicious reconnaissance, including anomalous patterns of communications that appear to be transmitted for the purpose of gathering technical information related to a cybersecurity threat or security vulnerability;
- a method of defeating a security control or exploitation of a security vulnerability;
- a security vulnerability, including anomalous activity that appears to indicate the existence of a security vulnerability;
- a method of causing a user with legitimate access to an information system or information that is stored on, processed by, or transiting an information system to unwittingly enable the defeat of a security control or exploitation of a security vulnerability;
- malicious cyber command and control;
- the actual or potential harm caused by an incident including a description of the information exfiltrated as a result of a particular cybersecurity threat;
- any other attribute of a cybersecurity threat, if disclosure of such attribute is not otherwise prohibited by law; or
- any combination thereof.

Examples of Cyber-Threat Indicators

In a June 2016 Guidance for non-federal entities that seek to participate in the information-sharing program established under the Cybersecurity Act of 2015, the U.S. Department of Homeland Security provided these examples of cyber-threat indicators that the private sector could share with the government:
- A company could report that its web server log files show that a particular IP address has sent web traffic that appears to be testing whether the company's content management system has not been updated to patch a recent vulnerability.
- A security researcher could report on her discovery of a technique that permits unauthorized access to an industrial control system.

- A software publisher could report a vulnerability it has discovered in its software.
- A managed security service company could report a pattern of domain name lookups that it believes correspond to malware infection.
- A manufacturer could report unexecuted malware found on its network.
- A researcher could report on the domain names or IP addresses associated with botnet command and control servers.
- An engineering company that suffers a computer intrusion could describe the types of engineering files that appear to have been exfiltrated, as a way of warning other companies with similar assets.
- A newspaper suffering a distributed denial of service attack to its website could report the IP addresses that are sending malicious traffic.

Source: Department of Homeland Security, Department of Justice, Guidance to Assist Non-Federal Entities to Share Cyber Threat Indicators and Defensive Measures with Federal Entities under the Cybersecurity Information Sharing Act of 2015 (June 15, 2016).

The statute defines "defensive measure" as "an action, device, procedure, signature, technique, or other measure applied to an information system or information that is stored on, processed by, or transiting an information system that detects, prevents, or mitigates a known or suspected threat or security vulnerability." The statute explicitly states that "defensive measure" does not include "a measure that destroys, renders unusable, provides unauthorized access to, or substantially harms an information system or information stored on, processed by, or transiting such information system" that is neither owned by the private entity that is operating the defensive measure or another entity that is "authorized to provide consent and has provided consent to that private entity for operation of the measure."

To encourage sharing of information regarding cyber-threat indicators and defensive measures, the law provides limited immunity for companies that share information with the federal government, via specific procedures promulgated by the Attorney General and Secretary of Homeland Security. If a private entity complies with the requirements of the Cybersecurity Act of 2015 and accompanying regulations, it will not be held liable for monitoring its systems for cyber threats. Moreover, private entities are not liable for properly sharing or receiving cyber-threat indicators under the Cybersecurity Act of 2015.

The immunity only applies for sharing information for a "cybersecurity purpose," which the statute defines as "the purpose of protecting an information system or information that is stored on, processed by, or transiting an information system from a cybersecurity threat or security vulnerability." The statute defines "cybersecurity threat" as "an action, not protected by the First Amendment to the Constitution of the United States, on or through an information system that may result in an unauthorized effort to adversely impact the security, availability, confidentiality, or integrity of an information system or information that is stored on, processed by, or transiting an information system." "Cybersecurity threat" does not include a violation of a consumer terms of service or licensing agreement. This relatively narrow definition is intended to ensure that companies cannot gather and share private information with the government for reasons entirely unrelated to cybersecurity.

The limited immunity only applies if the private companies comply with DHS procedures – required under the Cybersecurity Act of 2015 – to adequately secure the information from unauthorized access, and to review cyber-threat indicators *before sharing* and remove any information that is not directly related to the cybersecurity threat. For instance, imagine that a retailer has seen a specific type of attack resulting in the theft of its customers' payment card information. That retailer should not actually transmit to DHS the list of compromised customer names and payment card numbers, as it is difficult to imagine that such information would be directly related to the cybersecurity threat. Instead, the company should either describe the attack, or redact the personally identifiable information from the data that it sends to DHS.

The Cybersecurity Act of 2015 explicitly states that it does not create a duty for the private sector to share cyber threats, nor does it create a duty for the private sector to warn or act due to its receipt of cyber-threat information.[2] The Cybersecurity Act of 2015 requires DHS to create an information system that:

- accepts cyber-threat indicators and defensive measures from any non-federal entity;
- ensures that federal entities receive the cyber-threat indicators in real time; and
- ensures that the sharing protects privacy rights and complies with other regulations.

In 2016, DHS unveiled its Automated Indicator Sharing (AIS) system, operated by NCCIC and US-CERT as required by the new cybersecurity law. Private entities voluntarily receive and share indicators through AIS, typically anonymously unless they choose to have their name associated with the cyber-threat indicator. DHS states that it does not validate the cyber-threat indicators; instead, it shares indicators based on the volume and velocity of the tips that it receives, as quickly as possible.

DHS does not require companies to go through an extensive vetting process to use AIS. Instead, they must agree to a Terms of Use and connect to DHS's managed system.

As required by the Cybersecurity Act of 2015, DHS has built in a number of functions to protect privacy in AIS. Among the protections are:

- using automated technology to delete unnecessary personally identifiable information;

---

2 Sec. 106 of the Cybersecurity Act of 2015.

- using human review of certain data to ensure privacy and proper functions;
- minimizing the data that DHS includes in cyber-threat indicator reports;
- only retaining the information that is necessary to combat cyber threats; and
- only collecting information that is used either for network defense or law enforcement.

Even if companies do not participate in AIS, they may share cyber-threat indicators and defensive measures with DHS via its website or email.

Because the law was recently added to the books, as of publication of this book, we do not have any court opinions that interpret the terms "cyber-threat indicator" or "cybersecurity threat." However, the broad language of the definitions suggest that if a service provider reasonably believes that email messages or other Internet traffic might help companies understand a cybersecurity threat, such as malware, then the service provider would be immune from lawsuits under the SCA – or any other federal or state laws, for that matter.

6.3   Energy Department's Cyber-Threat Information Sharing

A frequent concern that cybersecurity experts and policy makers raise relates to an attack on the U.S. electric grid. Such an attack could not only cause widespread economic disruption, not to mention the potential for serious physical harm.

The primary challenge for cybersecurity in the power grid is that the grid is comprised of the infrastructure of a number of private companies. The grid is interconnected, so a cyberattack on one company could have a spiral attack across the grid, even if some of the other utilities had taken steps that would have prevented such an attack.

In 2013, the U.S. Department of Energy attempted to address this, in part, with the Cybersecurity Risk Information Sharing Program (CRISP), a voluntary program through which utilities could share classified and unclassified cyber-threat data, with the Energy Department as the intermediary. The Energy Department operates CRISP with the Electricity Sector Information Sharing and Analysis Center, an industry group that also exchanges cyber-threat data.

Much of the CRISP data is classified, so it is difficult to know how effective CRISP has been so far. In a 2014 letter to the North American Electric Reliability Corporation, Patricia Hoffman, the U.S. Assistant Secretary for the Energy Department's Office of Electricity Delivery and Energy Reliability, stated that the Department envisions CRISP eventually being operated by the private sector, collaborating with the government, to "serve as the primary communications channel for the Electricity Subsector and enhance the ability of the sector to prepare for and respond to cyber and physical threats, vulnerabilities, and incidents."

The Energy Department's deep involvement in the development and roll-out of an industry-specific threat-sharing program demonstrates the grave threat that cyberattacks on the power grid could pose for the nation. Rather than simply delegating responsibility to the private sector or assuming that DHS would handle electric grid cyber threats through US-CERT, the Energy Department recognized the special need for industry-specific information sharing with government involvement.

6.4 Critical Infrastructure Executive Order and the National Institute of Standards and Technology's Cybersecurity Framework

Over the past decade, policy makers have become increasingly concerned that companies have not developed adequate procedures and policies to guard against cyber threats. This is particularly concerning because private companies operate a great deal of the power grids, communications networks, and other infrastructure that is central to the U.S. economy and national security.

In 2013, President Obama recognized this concern in an executive order regarding the cybersecurity of "critical infrastructure," which he broadly defined as "systems and assets, whether physical or virtual, so vital to the United States that the incapacity or destruction of such systems and assets would have a debilitating impact on security, national economic security, national public health or safety, or any combination of those matters."[3]

In the Executive Order, President Obama articulated a national policy "to enhance the security and resilience of the Nation's critical infrastructure and to maintain a cyber environment that encourages efficiency, innovation, and economic prosperity while promoting safety, security, business confidentiality, privacy, and civil liberties." The Executive Order calls for achieving those goals through a "partnership" with the private sector. This overall approach is noteworthy because it does not call for new regulations or laws to force companies to adopt specific safeguards. The Executive Order appears to recognize that strong cybersecurity is in companies' best interests, and that the government can help companies achieve those goals.

The Executive Order directed the Attorney General, Secretary of Homeland Security, and Director of National Intelligence to establish a process for sharing information about cyber threats – a process that was later codified and expanded upon in the Cybersecurity Act of 2015 information-sharing program (described above). The executive order also directed the Commerce Department's National Institute of Standards and Technology (NIST) to

---

3 Executive Order – Improving Critical Infrastructure Cybersecurity (Feb. 12, 2013).

develop a voluntary cybersecurity framework for operators of critical infrastructure. The Executive Order directs NIST to incorporate industry feedback and align "policy, business and technological approaches to address cyber risks."

In February 2014, in response to the Executive Order, NIST released the Framework for Improving Critical Infrastructure Cybersecurity. The 39-page document draws on a number of existing security standards. The NIST Framework does not proscribe specific technological solutions; rather, as its drafters state, it "provides organization and structure to today's multiple approaches to cybersecurity by assembling standards, guidelines, and practices that are working effectively in industry today." NIST emphasizes that its Framework is not a "one-size-fits-all" cybersecurity solution, and that companies have a wide range of risks and are best suited to "determine activities that are important to critical service delivery and can prioritize investments to maximize the impact of each dollar spent."

The NIST Framework core consists of five key principles for cybersecurity risk management. Below are the principles as stated by NIST, along with the implementation factors listed in the Framework, edited slightly. The NIST Framework is presented in multiple charts; this book consolidates those principles into a single list for clarity and brevity:

- *Identify.* Understand the organization and the cybersecurity risks to its systems, assets, data, and capabilities. Among the components of this function:
  o Inventory software platforms and physical devices and systems.
  o Map organizational communications and data flows.
  o Catalogue external information systems.
  o Prioritize hardware, devices, data, and software based on their classification, criticality, and business value.
  o Establish cybersecurity roles and responsibilities for the workforce and third-party stakeholders, such as suppliers and customers.
  o Identify and communicate the organization's role in the supply chain, critical infrastructure, and industry sector.
  o Establish and communicate priorities for organizational mission, objectives, and activities.
  o Establish dependencies and critical functions for delivery of critical services.
  o Establish resilience requirements to support delivery of critical services.
  o Establish organizational information security policy.
  o Coordinate information security roles and responsibilities with internal roles and external partners.
  o Understand and manage legal and regulatory requirements for cybersecurity, including privacy.
  o Address cybersecurity risks in governance and risk management processes.

o Document and identify asset vulnerabilities.

o Receive threat and vulnerability information from information-sharing forums.

o Identify and document threats.

o Identify potential business impacts.

o Use threats, vulnerabilities, likelihoods, and impacts to determine risk.

o Identify and prioritize risk responses.

o Establish and run risk management processes.

o Determine and clearly express organizational risk tolerance, in considering the organization's role in critical infrastructure and its sectoral risks.

- **Protect.** Implement safeguards to deliver services:

o Manage identities and credentials for authorized devices, physical access to assets, and remote access.

o Manage access permissions, with the principles of least privilege and separation of duties.

o Protect network integrity, incorporating network segregation when possible.

o Inform and train all users, and ensure that privileged users, senior executives, security personnel and third-party stakeholders understand roles and responsibilities.

o Protect data at rest and in transit.

o Formally manage assets throughout removal, transfers, and disposition.

o Maintain adequate capacity to ensure data availability.

o Implement protections against data leaks.

o Use integrity-checking mechanisms to verify software, firmware, and information integrity.

o Separate development and testing from the protection environment.

o Create and maintain a baseline configuration of information technology and industrial control systems.

o Implement a system development life cycle.

o Implement configuration change control processes.

o Periodically conduct, maintain, and test backups of information.

o Meet policy and regulations regarding physical operating environment.

o Destroy data according to policy.

o Continuously improve protection processes.

o Share effectiveness of protection technologies with appropriate parties.

o Implement, manage, and test response and recovery plans.

o Include cybersecurity in human resources practices.

o Develop and implement a vulnerability management plan.

o Perform and log maintenance and repair of assets, and approve remote maintenance in a manner that prevents unauthorized access.

o Develop and review audit logs.

o Protect and restrict use of removable media.

o Control access to systems according to the principle of least functionality.

o Protect communications and control networks.

- *Detect.* Continuously monitor the organization's systems and networks to more quickly become aware of cybersecurity incidents:
  o Establish and manage a baseline of network operations and expected data flows.
  o Analyze detected events to understand attack targets and methods.
  o Aggregate and correlate event data from multiple sources.
  o Determine impact of events.
  o Establish incident alert thresholds.
  o Monitor network, physical environment, and personnel activity to detect cybersecurity events.
  o Detect malicious code and unauthorized mobile code.
  o Monitor external service provider activity.
  o Monitor for unauthorized personnel, connections, devices, and software.
  o Perform vulnerability scans.
  o Define roles and responsibilities to ensure accountability.
  o Ensure that detection activities comply with all applicable requirements.
  o Test detection processes.
  o Communicate event detection information to appropriate parties.
  o Continuously improve detection processes.
- *Respond.* Develop and implement a cybersecurity incident response program:
  o Execute response plan during or after an event.
  o Ensure that personnel know their roles and order of operations when a response is needed.
  o Report events consistent with established criteria.
  o Share information consistent with response plans.
  o Coordinate with stakeholders consistent with response plans.
  o Voluntarily share information with external stakeholders.
  o Investigate notifications from detection systems.
  o Understand the impact of an incident.
  o Perform forensics.
  o Categorize incidents consistent with response plans.
  o Contain and mitigate incidents.
  o Mitigate and document newly identified vulnerabilities as accepted risks.
  o Incorporate lessons learned into response plans and update response strategies.
- *Recover.* Develop and implement a plan to restore networks and systems after a cybersecurity incident:
  o Execute a recovery plan during or after an event.
  o Incorporate lessons learned into a response plan and update recovery strategy.
  o Manage public relations.
  o Repair reputation after an event.
  o Communicate recovery activities to internal stakeholders and executive and management team.

NIST Cybersecurity Framework Implementation Tiers

The NIST Cybersecurity Framework provides four "implementation tiers" that evaluate a company's "rigor and sophistication" in cybersecurity risk management. Tier 1 is the lowest level of rigor and sophistication, and Tier 4 is the highest. However, NIST recognizes that Tier 4 simply is not possible for all organizations. NIST suggests that companies determine the desirable tier, based on feasibility of implementation and risk tolerance. The following is NIST's description of each of the implementation tiers:

Tier 1: Partial

- *Risk management process.* Organizational cybersecurity risk management practices are not formalized, and risk is managed in an ad hoc and sometimes reactive manner. Prioritization of cybersecurity activities may not be directly informed by organizational risk objectives, the threat environment, or business/mission requirements.
- *Integrated risk management program.* There is limited awareness of cybersecurity risk at the organizational level and an organization-wide approach to managing cybersecurity risk has not been established. The organization implements cybersecurity risk management on an irregular, case-by-case basis due to varied experience or information gained from outside sources. The organization may not have processes that enable cybersecurity information to be shared within the organization.
- *External participation.* An organization may not have the processes in place to participate in coordination or collaboration with other entities.

Tier 2: Risk Informed

- *Risk management process.* Risk management practices are approved by management but may not be established as organizational-wide policy. Prioritization of cybersecurity activities is directly informed by organizational risk objectives, the threat environment, or business/mission requirements.
- *Integrated risk management program.* There is an awareness of cybersecurity risk at the organizational level but an organization-wide approach to managing cybersecurity risk has not been established. Risk-informed, management-approved processes and procedures are defined and implemented, and staff has adequate resources to perform their cybersecurity duties. Cybersecurity information is shared within the organization on an informal basis.
- *External participation.* The organization knows its role in the larger ecosystem but has not formalized its capabilities to interact and share information externally.

Tier 3: Repeatable

- *Risk management process.* The organization's risk management practices are formally approved and expressed as policy. Organizational cybersecurity practices are regularly updated based on the application of risk management processes to changes in business/mission requirements and a changing threat and technology landscape.
- *Integrated risk management program.* There is an organization-wide approach to manage cybersecurity risk. Risk-informed policies, processes, and procedures are defined, implemented as intended, and reviewed. Consistent methods are in place to respond effectively to changes in risk. Personnel possess the knowledge and skills to perform their appointed roles and responsibilities.
- *External participation.* The organization understands its dependencies and partners and receives information from these partners that enables collaboration and risk-based management decisions within the organization in response to events.

Tier 4: Adaptive

- *Risk management process.* The organization adapts its cybersecurity practices based on lessons learned and predictive indicators derived from previous and current cybersecurity activities. Through a process of continuous improvement incorporating advanced cybersecurity technologies and practices, the organization actively adapts to a changing cybersecurity landscape and responds to evolving and sophisticated threats in a timely manner.
- *Integrated risk management program.* There is an organization-wide approach to managing cybersecurity risk that uses risk-informed policies, processes, and procedures to address potential cybersecurity events. Cybersecurity risk management is part of the organizational culture and evolves from an awareness of previous activities, information shared by other sources, and continuous awareness of activities on their systems and networks.
- *External participation.* The organization manages risk and actively shares information with partners to ensure that accurate, current information is being distributed and consumed to improve cybersecurity before a cybersecurity event occurs.

Source: National Institute of Standards and Technology, Framework for Improving Critical Infrastructure Cybersecurity (Feb. 12, 2014).

Keep in mind that the NIST Cybersecurity Framework is entirely voluntary, even for operators of the most critical infrastructure. NIST did not intend to create binding requirements, nor does it have the authority to do so.

However, companies are increasingly adopting the Framework, in the manner they see fit, to strengthen their cybersecurity processes. The Cybersecurity

Framework is increasingly becoming a de facto standard of care that companies expect their business partners to follow. Accordingly, it is in a company's best interests to demonstrate that it complies, to some extent, with the general principles articulated in the Framework. Moreover, if a company experienced a breach or other cybersecurity incident, and subsequently faces a lawsuit or regulatory action, it might reduce the likelihood of liability if it could demonstrate the steps that it took to integrate the NIST Cybersecurity Framework into its operations.

Government agencies have recognized the value of the Cybersecurity Framework and have integrated it into their operations. For instance, in October 2015, the federal Office of Management and Budget, which is partly responsible for setting government-wide information technology policies, required federal agencies and departments to adopt the Framework. Similarly, in 2014, the state of Virginia began requiring its agencies to adopt the Framework. The Cybersecurity Framework is a good example of a public–private partnership that seeks to improve cybersecurity in the private sector without imposing regulations or the fear of costly litigation.

6.5 U.S. Military Involvement in Cybersecurity and the Posse Comitatus Act

This chapter has focused on *civilian* government agencies, such as DHS and NIST, that assist the private sector with cybersecurity. However, some of the most skilled government cybersecurity experts are in the military. Due to centuries-old restrictions, these experts face significant limits on their ability to help companies and individuals defend their systems and networks.

The National Security Agency, which is part of the U.S. Defense Department, specializes in signals intelligence – that is, intercepting foreign intelligence information. The NSA employs some of the world's leading code-breakers, who seek to intercept and decode foreign intelligence communications. That process is known as signals intelligence, and is believed to be the largest component of NSA. NSA also operates an Information Assurance Directorate, which is charged with protecting the security of national security information.

Headquartered in the same location as NSA – and run by the same individual – is U.S. Cyber Command, which organizationally is located within U.S. Strategic Command. As of publication of this book, policy makers were discussing a proposal to separate NSA and Cyber Command. The Cyber Command is charged with leading the Defense Department's defense of its information networks, and to conduct cyber operations on behalf of the U.S. military. Each of the military services has cyber commands that are part of the U.S. Cyber Command: Army Cyber Command, Fleet Cyber Command, Air Force Cyber Command, and Marine Forces Cyber Command. The U.S. Department of Defense has three primary cyber missions:

- Defend Department of Defense networks, systems, and information.
- Provide cyber support to military operational and contingency plans.
- Defend the U.S. homeland and U.S. national interests against cyberattacks of significant consequence.[4]

The third mission has the most significance for the private sector. In the Department of Defense's 2015 strategic report on cyber, it stated that the department "must work with its interagency partners, the private sector, and allied and partner nations to deter and if necessary defeat a cyberattack of significant consequence on the U.S. homeland and U.S. interests."[5]

Such a mission is sound, as the Defense Department has deep expertise in cyber, and protecting national security is clearly within the Department of Defense's missions. However, a long-standing legal rule known as posse comitatus presents a significant limit on such actions.

The Posse Comitatus Act, passed in 1878, prohibits the use of the U.S. military to enforce the laws. It states:

> Whoever, except in cases and under circumstances expressly authorized by the Constitution or Act of Congress, willfully uses any part of the Army or the Air Force as a posse comitatus or otherwise to execute the laws shall be fined under this title or imprisoned not more than two years, or both.[6]

Congress passed the law after the Civil War, in response to concerns of the former confederacy that the federal government would use its military to create a police state. Although the statute only mentions the Army and Air Force, regulations also apply the prohibition to the Navy and Marines. The Posse Comitatus Act does not apply to state National Guard forces or the U.S. Coast Guard.

For the U.S. military to support domestic cyber defense, it must fall under an exception to the Posse Comitatus Act. Military cyber operations that enforce domestic laws must fall under another statute that provides an exception to the Posse Comitatus Act. For instance, the Insurrection Act, which was passed in 1807, before the Posse Comitatus Act, allows the President to use the armed forces to enforce laws or suppress rebellion if "unlawful obstructions, combinations, or assemblages, or rebellion against the authority of the United States, make it impracticable to enforce the laws of the United States in any State by the ordinary course of judicial proceedings."[7] Additionally, a group of statutes known as Defense Support of Civil Authorities allow the Defense Secretary to

---

4 DEPARTMENT OF DEFENSE CYBER STRATEGY (April 2015).
5 *Id.* at 14.
6 18 U.S.C. § 1385.
7 10 U.S.C. § 332.

provide law enforcement with relevant information collected during military training or operations.[8]

In its September 2015 update to its manual on defense support of civil operations, the Department of Defense for the first time addressed the types of cyber incidents that might allow the U.S. military to provide domestic government agencies with support. The Defense Department wrote that "[l]arge-scale cyber incidents may overwhelm government and private-sector resources by disrupting the internet and taxing critical infrastructure information systems," and that complications from these incidents "may threaten lives, property, the economy, and national security."[9] In such cases, the Department wrote, its services "support the remediation, restoration, and protection of critical emergency telecommunication networks and infrastructure," and that "[c]yberspace technical assistance may be provided in response to a request from a lead federal agency."[10]

The Defense Department's 2015 manual indicates the Department's willingness to help protect civilian networks in a wide range of cases that would threaten national security. The Posse Comitatus Act places some limits on these goals, but if the government can demonstrate that a significant threat to national security exists, it likely could justify the use of the military in the defense of private networks and systems.

---

8 10 U.S.C. 371.
9 Defense Department, Multi-Service Tactics, Techniques, and Procedures for Defense Support of Civil Authorities (Sept. 2015).
10 *Id.*

7

Surveillance and Cyber

CHAPTER MENU
Fourth Amendment 260
Electronic Communications Privacy Act 275
Communications Assistance for Law Enforcement Act (CALEA) 293
Encryption and the All Writs Act 294

Any examination of cybersecurity law would be incomplete without an examination of the constraints that both the government and private companies have on monitoring networks and sharing information. From the Fourth Amendment's prohibition on unreasonable searches and seizures to the Cybersecurity Act of 2015, both the government and companies face significant constraints on monitoring electronic traffic, even if the intentions are to protect networks and users.

As discussed throughout this book, cybersecurity involves more than just preventing viruses and malware from infecting systems or flooding networks with denial of service attacks. Cybersecurity involves efforts by both the private and public sector to secure the Internet and computer systems and to fight cybercrime. This chapter focuses on the tools – and limits – that U.S. government entities have to conduct cyber operations.

This chapter first examines U.S. legal restrictions on government and private sector surveillance. We first begin with a discussion of the Fourth Amendment's application to electronic content, and the general prohibition on warrantless searches and seizures by the government and government agents. We then examine the Electronic Communications Act and its three components: (1) the Stored Communications Act, which restricts government and private sector access to communications and data that are stored on servers and in the cloud; (2) the Wiretap Act, which restricts governments' and the private sectors' ability to monitor data while it is in transit; and (3) the Title III/pen register statute, which restricts the ability of the government to obtain "noncontent" information, such as the to/from lines of email addresses.

Cybersecurity Law, First Edition. Jeff Kosseff.
© 2017 John Wiley & Sons, Inc. Published 2017 by John Wiley & Sons, Inc.
Companion Website: www.wiley.com/go/kosseff/cybersecurity

The section then examines the Communications Assistance for Law Enforcement Act, which requires telecommunications carriers and equipment makers to assist U.S. law enforcement with lawful surveillance. Finally, we examine the All Writs Act, and the government's attempts to use the eighteenth-century law to compel smartphone manufacturers to help the government access encrypted information.

This chapter demonstrates that both constitutional and statutory restrictions on cyber surveillance and operations are still developing and that courts often are unsure what limits are appropriate on government cyber operations. The complexities are compounded because many of the restrictions are drawn from decades-old statutes that did not contemplate cloud computing, social media, and other technologies.

7.1 Fourth Amendment

The government's electronic surveillance may be restricted by the Fourth Amendment. The Fourth Amendment is among the greatest constitutional limits on the government's ability to exercise power over individuals. If the government obtains evidence of a crime in a manner that violates the Fourth Amendment, all evidence gathered during that search or seizure cannot be admitted as evidence in the criminal trial of the individual whose rights were violated (though there are a few exceptions to this rule, as we'll discuss later). This section examines the Fourth Amendment's application to government surveillance and other actions in cyberspace.

The Fourth Amendment states:

> The right of the people to be secure in their persons, houses, papers, and effects, against unreasonable searches and seizures, shall not be violated, and no Warrants shall issue, but upon probable cause, supported by Oath or affirmation, and particularly describing the place to be searched, and the persons or things to be seized.

Since our nation's founding, the United States Supreme Court and lower courts have developed a wide range of factors and balancing tests that they apply to determine whether a government search or seizure has violated the Fourth Amendment. For the purposes of this book, we will focus primarily on the cases that involved government access to *information*. There is a long line of court cases assessing government access to physical objects (e.g., whether a police office can search a car due to the smell of marijuana smoke). This chapter only reviews such cases to the extent that they are useful in understanding how the Fourth Amendment limits government cyber operations.

To best understand how courts analyze the Fourth Amendment, we have broken up the analysis into six questions. This is *not* the only way to conduct a

Fourth Amendment analysis; indeed, courts approach these issues in a variety of ways and not necessarily in this order. Some of the questions have very easy answers, while others are far from settled:

1) Was the search or seizure conducted by a government entity (e.g., a police department) or government agent (e.g., a government contractor)?
2) Did the search or seizure intrude upon an individual's privacy interests?
3) Did the government have a warrant?
4) If the government did not have a warrant, did an exception to the warrant requirement apply?
5) Was the search or seizure reasonable under the totality of the circumstances?

7.1.1   Was the Search or Seizure Conducted by a Government Entity or Government Agent?

The Fourth Amendment only restricts searches and seizures that are conducted *by a government* entity or by a *government agent* that is acting for the government. Like the other constitutional rights, the Fourth Amendment is subject to what is known as the state action doctrine: it only restricts the actions of the government, and not of a private party. For instance, the government likely would violate the First Amendment by prohibiting Internet service providers from allowing their users to promote certain politicians on their websites. However, if the Internet service provider chose to prohibit its users from posting that content on their websites, the users would not be able to challenge that prohibition as a violation of the First Amendment. That is because the Internet service provider, acting independently, is not a state actor.[1] The logic holds for the Fourth Amendment.

It is fairly simple to determine whether a government entity has conducted a search or seizure. In the United States, any federal, state, or local government agency or department is fully subject to the limits of the Fourth Amendment. For instance, if law enforcement officers obtain the email of a Los Angeles resident, they are subject to the Fourth Amendment regardless of whether they work for the Los Angeles Police Department, the California State Police, or the Federal Bureau of Investigation.

The more difficult question arises when a criminal defendant alleges that a *government agent* conducted a search. This is a particularly tricky task in cyber-related Fourth Amendment cases, since cyber infrastructure often is controlled by private companies that, at times, work with the government. In 1989, the United Supreme Court ruled that "[a]lthough the Fourth Amendment

---

1 *See* United States v. Jarrett, 338 F.3d 339, 344 (4th Cir.2003) (holding that the Fourth Amendment does not apply to searches that are conducted "by private individuals acting in a private capacity.").

does not apply to a search or seizure, even an arbitrary one, effected by a private party on his own initiative, the Amendment protects against such intrusions if the private party acted as an instrument or agent of the Government."[2]

The Supreme Court has not defined precisely what it means to be an "instrument or agent" of the government. Lower courts have confronted the issue, and although their definitions vary somewhat, they generally have held that courts should consider the following factors when determining whether a private party acted as a government agent in conducting a search:

- If the government instigated the private party's search of the individual.
- The degree to which the government participated in the search.
- The degree of control that the government exercised over the search.
- Whether the private party was motivated by its own business interests or by the government.[3]

The "government agent" issue arises frequently in government prosecutions for online child pornography crimes. This is because the government often gathers evidence through a system established by federal law, which involves the participation of Internet service providers, the government, and a nonprofit organization, the National Center for Missing and Exploited Children (NCMEC).

If online service providers (e.g., email services or Internet service providers) obtain actual knowledge that a customer appears to have violated federal child pornography laws, they are required by federal law to file a report with NCMEC.[4] NCMEC then reviews the report, as well as the apparent child pornography content, and if it determines that the content is in fact child pornography, it provides information to local, state, or federal law enforcement agencies. The federal law also provides legal immunity to the online service providers for their fulfillment of this duty, so that they cannot be sued for filing a NCMEC report if a customer appears to be exchanging child pornography on their services.[5]

Online service providers are not required to take any affirmative steps to look for child pornography. They are only required to file reports if they discover it on their services. Many service providers, however, voluntarily use automated hash scanning in an attempt to prevent their use of services for illegal content. Often, the online services compare hash values of all user content with a NCMEC database of the hash values of known child pornography images.

---

2 Skinner v. Railway Labor Executives' Assn., 489 U.S. 602 (1989).
3 United States v. Silva, 554 F.3d 13, 16 (1st Cir. 2009).
4 18 U.S.C. § 2258A.
5 18 U.S.C. § 2258C.

When these automated searches lead to criminal prosecutions under federal child pornography laws, criminal defendants often challenge the admissibility of the evidence. They argue that the online service provider and NCMEC conducted a search of their private email or other online content, and that the warrantless search violated the Fourth Amendment. Courts typically have rejected such arguments, but occasionally have been open to hearing defendants' Fourth Amendment claims in such cases.

For instance, in *United States v. Richardson*,[6] AOL used its image detection and filtering process (IDFP) to automatically scan hashes of customers' email content with NCMEC's database of hashes from known child pornography images. AOL detected a match for the email of its customer, Thomas McCoy Richardson, and filed a NCMEC report, as required by federal law. NCMEC provided the information to North Carolina state police, who investigated and eventually discovered dozens of child pornography images and videos on Richardson's computer, leading Richardson to admit to police that he viewed child pornography. Richardson was charged with federal child pornography crimes, and moved to suppress both the images and his statements, arguing that they were obtained due to a warrantless search of his AOL account. The gravamen of his argument was that AOL acted as a government agent when it scanned his account and reported the images to NCMEC, and therefore violated the Fourth Amendment by conducting the search without a warrant. The U.S. Court of Appeals for the Fourth Circuit concluded that AOL was not a government agent and therefore was not subject to the Fourth Amendment warrant requirement. First, the court reasoned, the government agents had absolutely no control over AOL's search, and noted that no government agent even asked AOL to conduct the search of Richardson's email.[7] Relatedly, the court reasoned, Richardson presented no evidence that AOL conducted the search with the intent to help the government in a child pornography investigation. Richardson argued that the mandatory reporting requirement in federal law effectively transformed AOL into a government agent. The Fourth Circuit rejected this argument, reasoning that the law does not, in any way, obligate AOL to conduct the search in the first place. In fact, the statute explicitly states that providers are *not* obligated to conduct such searches.

In similar Fourth Amendment challenges in child pornography cases, other courts reached similar conclusions in cases in which the defendants have claimed that Internet service providers were government agents. Courts routinely hold that service providers have legitimate business interests – independent of the

---

6 United States v. Richardson, 607 F. 3d 357 (4th Cir. 2010).
7 *Id.* at 364–65.

government – to automatically scan content and keep their services free of child pornography.[8]

A more difficult question arises when child pornography defendants argue not only that the online service providers acted as government agents, but that NCMEC also is a government agent. That is a tougher call, because NCMEC receives federal government funding and operates for the primary purpose of protecting children from exploitation. In *United States v. Keith*,[9] David Keith sought to suppress evidence collected in a search of his home and computer. The warrant for the search was supported, in part, by evidence of child pornography detected by AOL via its automated scanning of customer email accounts and included in a NCMEC report, which was used by state police in an investigation that eventually led to federal child pornography charges. Unlike other defendants, who only argued that their ISP acted as a government agent, Keith argued that both AOL *and* NCMEC were government agents and therefore subject to the Fourth Amendment. The federal court swiftly dismissed Keith's claim that AOL was a government agent, concluding that "AOL is motivated by its own wholly private interests in seeking to detect and deter the transmission of child pornography through its network facilities."[10] However, the court agreed with Keith's argument that NCMEC was a government agent. The court noted that the statute authorizing the NCMEC reporting program refers to the program as a "partnership" between NCMEC and the government, and that its examination of the files provided by AOL was "conducted for the sole purpose of assisting the prosecution of child pornography crimes."[11] Although AOL acted as a private party in scanning the content, the court reasoned, NCMEC was a government agent when it expanded on the search. However, the court did not suppress the evidence collected in the search of his home because warrant also relied on evidence of child pornography provided by Staples employees who incidentally discovered child pornography images while repairing Keith's laptop.

The *Keith* opinion quickly set off alarms in the community of law enforcement, advocacy groups, and technology companies that seek to prevent the use of online services to distribute child pornography. For now, the *Keith* opinion is an outlier, but it serves as an important reminder that if private entities work too closely with the government on cybercrime issues, they could be subject to the Fourth Amendment warrant requirement.

---

8 *See, e.g.*, United States v. Cameron, 699 F. 3d 621, 638 (1st Cir. 2012) ("[T]here is no evidence that the government instigated the search, participated in the search, or coerced Yahoo! to conduct the search. Thus, if Yahoo! chose to implement a policy of searching for child pornography, it presumably did so for its own interests.").

9 United States v. Keith, 980 F. Supp. 2d 33 (D. Mass. 2013).

10 *Id.* at 40.

11 *Id.* at 41.

7.1.2 Did the Search or Seizure Intrude Upon an Individual's Privacy Interests?

If a government entity or government agency conducted a search or seizure, the Fourth Amendment applies only if the search or seizure invaded the individual's privacy interests. In other words, did the individual have a reasonable expectation of privacy?

For electronic surveillance, the answer to this question traces back to a 1967 United States Supreme Court case, *Katz v. United States.*[12] FBI agents, acting without a search warrant, installed a wiretap on a public payphone and heard the defendant discussing his illegal wagering operations. The defendant argued that his conviction was invalid because the FBI needed a warrant to conduct the surveillance. Until this decision, courts generally had focused on the physical characteristics of a search when determining whether the government invaded a constitutionally protected interest. In this case, the government argued that the defendant had no reasonable expectation of privacy because the defendant made the phone call from a public phone booth that was partly glass, so that he could be seen by passersby while he was making the call. However, the Court found this argument unpersuasive, reasoning that "what he sought to exclude when he entered the booth was not the intruding eye – it was the uninvited ear."[13] The government also argued that the Fourth Amendment did not apply to the wiretap because the FBI did not physically penetrate the phone booth. The Court rejected this argument as well, concluding that "the Fourth Amendment protects people—and not simply 'areas'—against unreasonable searches and seizures," and that "the reach of that Amendment cannot turn upon the presence or absence of a physical intrusion into any given enclosure."[14] The Court reversed the defendant's conviction, concluding that the Fourth Amendment did, in fact, apply to electronic surveillance:

> The Government's activities in electronically listening to and recording the petitioner's words violated the privacy upon which he justifiably relied while using the telephone booth and thus constituted a "search and seizure" within the meaning of the Fourth Amendment. The fact that the electronic device employed to achieve that end did not happen to penetrate the wall of the booth can have no constitutional significance.[15]

The conclusion in the *Katz* case is among the most significant developments in Fourth Amendment history because it took the Fourth Amendment out of

---

12 Katz v. United States, 389 U.S. 347 (1967).
13 *Id.* at 352.
14 *Id.* at 353.
15 *Id.*

the exclusively physical realm, and recognized that individuals could have a reasonable expectation of privacy in *information*. *Katz* set the groundwork for the modern Fourth Amendment disputes involving government surveillance of telephones, email, and other electronic communications.

It is important to note that the Supreme Court in *Katz* did not conclude that individuals automatically have a reasonable expectation of privacy in *all* electronic communications. In an oft-cited concurrence in *Katz*, Justice Harlan articulated a two-prong test to determine whether a reasonable expectation of privacy exists for Fourth Amendment purposes:

1) whether the individual "exhibited an actual (subjective) expectation of privacy,"[16] and
2) whether that subjective expectation of privacy is "one that society is prepared to recognize as 'reasonable.'"[17]

In other words, under this two-pronged test, the Fourth Amendment only protects an individual if that individual *actually* expected privacy *and* that expectation is reasonable. In *Katz*, the Court concluded that the defendant expected that his phone conversation would be private, and that objectively, this expectation was reasonable.

For electronic surveillance, among the biggest obstacles to finding a reasonable expectation of privacy is the third-party doctrine. Under this doctrine, individuals do not have a Fourth Amendment reasonable expectation of privacy in information once they have disclosed that information to an outside party. For instance, if John tells Jane a secret, and then Jane voluntarily provides that secret information to the police, John cannot claim that the police violated his Fourth Amendment rights by obtaining the information without a warrant. Of course, in the context of electronic surveillance, the third-party doctrine often is more difficult to parse.

The third-party doctrine, in the electronic surveillance realm, emerged in a 1979 United States Supreme Court case, *Smith v. Maryland*.[18] In that case, the telephone company, at the request of the police, installed a pen register at its offices to document the numbers that were called by a robbery suspect. The police did not obtain a warrant for the pen register. Based on the information collected through the pen register, the police obtained a warrant to search the defendant's home, and he eventually was convicted of robbery. The United States Supreme Court distinguished this case from *Katz*, because the pen registers only obtain lists of phone numbers, and not the *contents* of the communications. This distinction is crucial, the Court reasoned, because people understand that they are voluntarily conveying the phone number that they are calling to the phone

---

16 *Id.* at 361 (Harlan, J., concurring).
17 *Id.*
18 Smith v. Maryland, 442 U.S. 735 (1979).

company. Therefore, under the first prong of Justice Harlan's *Katz* test, they should not have an actual expectation that the phone number is private:

> All telephone users realize that they must "convey" phone numbers to the telephone company, since it is through telephone company switching equipment that their calls are completed. All subscribers realize, moreover, that the phone company has facilities for making permanent records of the numbers they dial, for they see a list of their long-distance (toll) calls on their monthly bills.[19]

Moreover, the Court reasoned, even if individuals had a subjective expectation that the phone numbers that they dialed would remain private, such an expectation would be objectively unreasonable:

> When he used his phone, petitioner voluntarily conveyed numerical information to the telephone company and "exposed" that information to its equipment in the ordinary course of business. In so doing, petitioner assumed the risk that the company would reveal to police the numbers he dialed. The switching equipment that processed those numbers is merely the modern counterpart of the operator who, in an earlier day, personally completed calls for the subscriber.[20]

Smith v. Maryland is perhaps the most significant limit on the Fourth Amendment rights created by *Katz*. It has been used by advocates of the National Security Agency to justify its bulk metadata collection program – though the United States Supreme Court has not yet ruled on that issue. Under the doctrinal rule of *Smith v. Maryland*, NSA's program of collecting certain noncontent information of email and phone calls should similarly be exempt from Fourth Amendment scrutiny (and therefore not subject to a warrant requirement). But NSA critics argue that the Supreme Court, in 1979, did not anticipate the bulk collection of millions of sets of metadata when it decided *Smith v. Maryland*.

A more difficult issue arises when individuals use an intermediary to communicate electronic information, such as email. Does the protective rule of *Katz* apply? Or does *Smith*'s third-party doctrine prevent the application of the Fourth Amendment to government attempts to obtain stored email?

The United States Supreme Court has not addressed the issue directly. However, in 2010, the U.S. Court of Appeals for the Sixth Circuit addressed the

---

19 *Id.* at 742.
20 *Id.* at 744.

issue in *United States v. Warshak*.[21] In that case, the government obtained thousands of emails from the ISP of a corporate executive, to help bring a fraud case against the executive. The government had not obtained a search warrant for the emails; instead, it used a simple subpoena, and the defendant did not receive notice until more than a year after the email was disclosed. The Sixth Circuit held that although the Stored Communications Act (discussed below) did not require a warrant for the emails at issue, the Fourth Amendment did. The Court reasoned that the government must obtain a warrant to obtain paper mail delivered via the postal service, and "[g]iven the fundamental similarities between email and traditional forms of communication, it would defy common sense to afford emails lesser Fourth Amendment protection."[22] Due to the *Warshak* decision, law enforcement in the Sixth Circuit – Kentucky, Michigan, Ohio, and Tennessee – is required under the Fourth Amendment to obtain warrants before compelling the disclosure of emails, regardless of the length of time it has been stored. But *Warshak* is not binding in other parts of the United States. Since *Warshak*, federal prosecutors and law enforcement have been more likely to seek warrants for all emails, but they maintain that they are not required to do so.[23]

Other newer forms of surveillance technologies demonstrate the difficulty of applying the third-party doctrine. A number of courts have been asked to suppress evidence that law enforcement obtained via the warrantless collection of cell site information. Such information may enable law enforcement to pinpoint a suspect's location at a particular time, often providing probable cause for an arrest or a warrant to search a residence. At issue in these cases is whether the individual had a reasonable expectation of privacy in the cell site information. In recent years, courts have overwhelmingly held that, under the third-party doctrine, the Fourth Amendment does not require warrants for such searches. The U.S. Court of Appeals for the Sixth Circuit – which issued the *Warshak* opinion protecting email content from warrantless searches – declined to extend Fourth Amendment protections to cell site data.[24] As with the call logs in *Smith*, the Court reasoned, cell site data does not reveal information about *content* and therefore is not subject to the Fourth Amendment:

> Instead the records include routing information, which the wireless providers gathered in the ordinary course of business. Carriers necessarily track their customers' phones across different cell-site sectors to connect and maintain their customers' calls. And carriers keep records of these data to find weak spots in their network

---

21 631 F.3d 266 (2010).
22 *Id.* at 285-86.
23 Declan McCullagh, *DOJ: We don't Need Warrants for E-Mail, Facebook Chats*, C-Net (May 8, 2013).
24 *United States v. Carpenter* (6th Cir. 2016).

and to determine whether roaming charges apply, among other purposes. Thus, the cell-site data – like mailing addresses, phone numbers, and IP addresses – are information that facilitate personal communications, rather than part of the content of those communications themselves. The government's collection of business records containing these data therefore is not a search.[25]

There is a growing movement to reconsider the third-party doctrine because it makes little sense in the cyber age. Notably, in *United States v. Jones*,[26] the United States Supreme Court reversed the conviction of a criminal defendant because the evidence used against him was obtained via the warrantless installation of a GPS tracking device on his car. The majority opinion focused on the physical intrusion caused by the government's installation of the device on his property. Perhaps even more notable than the majority opinion was Justice Sotomayor's concurrence, in which she suggested that the Court should reconsider the third-party doctrine altogether:

> This approach is ill suited to the digital age, in which people reveal a great deal of information about themselves to third parties in the course of carrying out mundane tasks. People disclose the phone numbers that they dial or text to their cellular providers; the URLs that they visit and the e-mail addresses with which they correspond to their Internet service providers; and the books, groceries, and medications they purchase to online retailers … [W]hatever the societal expectations, they can attain constitutionally protected status only if our Fourth Amendment jurisprudence ceases to treat secrecy as a prerequisite for privacy. I would not assume that all information voluntarily disclosed to some member of the public for a limited purpose is, for that reason alone, disentitled to Fourth Amendment protection.[27]

Justice Sotomayor's concurrence was noteworthy because, if it eventually is adopted by the majority, it would undercut decades of Fourth Amendment jurisprudence and expose a wide range of information to Fourth Amendment protection, even if it was disclosed to third parties.

7.1.3 Did the Government have a Warrant?

If a government entity or government agent has conducted a search that invades a protected interest (i.e., where the individual had a reasonable

---

25 *Id.*
26 132 S. Ct. 945 (2012).
27 *Id.* at 957 (Sotomayor, J., concurring).

expectation of privacy), the government typically must have a warrant supported by probable cause in order to comply with the Fourth Amendment. A warrant must be issued by a "neutral magistrate," who in some cases may be a judge, but also may be a magistrate whose primary job is to determine whether law enforcement has presented probable cause that the search will yield evidence that a crime has or will be committed. Typically, the neutral magistrate bases the probable cause determination on an affidavit that law enforcement submits along with the search warrant request.

The United States Supreme Court has stated that the purpose of a warrant is to assure the citizen "that the intrusion is authorized by law, and that it is narrowly limited in its objectives and scope."[28] The "detached scrutiny" of a neutral magistrate "ensures an objective determination whether an intrusion is justified in any given case," the Court has stated.[29]

Generally, if a neutral magistrate issues a search warrant, it is very difficult for a defendant to later seek to suppress evidence gathered from the search on Fourth Amendment grounds. In *United States v. Leon*,[30] a criminal defendant in a drug case sought to suppress evidence that was collected under a search warrant that he claimed to not be supported by probable cause. The United States Supreme Court declined to suppress the evidence, even though the warrant was not supported by probable cause. Because the police conducted the search in good faith pursuant to a warrant that they believed to be valid, the Court concluded that it should not suppress the evidence gathered by the search. The "good-faith" exception makes it incredibly difficult to challenge a magistrate's probable cause determination, absent extreme recklessness or deceptive behavior by law enforcement.

One barrier to the use of warrants, however, is the "particularity" requirement. If a magistrate judge issues a warrant, the warrant must satisfy the Fourth Amendment's explicit requirement for *particularity*, describing the place to be searched as well as the persons or things to be seized.[31] This does not necessarily mean that the warrant describe the precise evidence that law enforcement expects to collect.[32] In determining whether a warrant satisfied the particularity requirement, courts consider "(1) whether probable cause exists to seize all items of a particular type described in the warrant; (2) whether the warrant sets out objective standards by which executing officers can differentiate items subject to seizure from those which are not; and (3) whether the government

---

28 Skinner v. Railway Labor Executives' Assn., 489 U.S. 602, 621–22 (1989).
29 *Id.* at 622.
30 United States v. Leon, 468 U.S. 897 (1984).
31 *See* Massachusetts v. Sheppard, 468 U.S. 981, 988, n. 5 (1984) ("[A] warrant that fails to conform to the particularity requirement of the Fourth Amendment is unconstitutional").
32 *See* United States v. Spilotro, 800 F. 2d 959, 963 (9th Cir.1986). ("Warrants which describe generic categories of items are not necessarily invalid if a more precise description of the items subject to seizure is not possible.").

was able to describe the items more particularly in light of the information available to it at the time the warrant was issued."[33]

Courts have recognized the difficulty of applying the particularity requirement to cyber searches, and generally are deferential to law enforcement and magistrates. For instance, in *United States v. Adjani*,[34] the U.S. Court of Appeals for the Ninth Circuit refused to suppress evidence collected under a warrant that allowed the search and seizure of, among other things, "[a]ny computer equipment and storage device capable of being used to commit, further, or store evidence of the offense listed above."[35] The defendants argued that rather than allowing a "wholesale search" of their email, the warrant should have specified search terms. The court sympathized with this argument, but ultimately concluded that to "require such a pinpointed computer search, restricting the search to an email program or to specific search terms, would likely have failed to cast a sufficiently wide net to capture the evidence sought."[36] The court reasoned that computer files "are easy to disguise or rename," and therefore an overly limited search warrant would prevent law enforcement from collecting evidence.[37] Although search warrants for email and other electronic evidence must have some particularity, courts recognize that law enforcement needs some leeway to conduct legitimate searches of the vast amounts of electronic data.

7.1.4   If the Government did not have a Warrant, did an Exception to the Warrant Requirement Apply?

If the government entity or a government agent conducts a *warrantless* search or seizure that invades a protected interest, the government must demonstrate that an exception to the warrant requirement applies. If the government does convince the court that an exception applies, the evidence collected as a result of the search will be suppressed.

The courts have articulated a number of exceptions to the warrant requirement. Among the most commonly cited exceptions are:

- the individual provided consent for the search;[38]
- the evidence is in plain view (i.e., from the street, the police could see marijuana plants in the defendant's yard);[39]

---

33 *Id.* at 963 (internal citations omitted).
34 United States v. Adjani, 452 F. 3d 1140 (9th Cir. 2006).
35 *Id.* at 1144.
36 *Id.* at 1149–50.
37 *Id.* at 1150.
38 *See* Schneckloth v. Bustamonte, 412 U.S. 218, 222 (1973) ("[A] search authorized by consent is wholly valid.").
39 *See* Payton v. New York, 445 U.S. 573, 586–87 (1980) ("The seizure of property in plain view involves no invasion of privacy and is presumptively reasonable, assuming that there is probable cause to associate the property with criminal activity.").

- police have probable cause to search an automobile (a recognition that given the mobility of cars, it is difficult to obtain a warrant before searching them);[40]
- exigent circumstances;[41]
- programmatic searches and special needs unrelated to routine law enforcement purposes (i.e., drunk driving checkpoints, border searches, searches of students' lockers in schools, searches of parolees, and searches at large public gatherings to reduce the risk of terrorism);[42] and
- searches incident to a lawful arrest, if the search is necessary to prevent the destruction of evidence or detainees escape, or harm to the police officer.[43]

In 2014, the United States Supreme Court issued its opinion in *Riley v. California*.[44] The decision, involving the search incident to lawful arrest exception, has had a significant impact on cyber-related searches. When David Leon Riley was lawfully arrested for firearms possession, the police seized his smartphone, searched the text messages on the phone, and found messages that indicated that Riley was associated with a street gang. Riley was convicted for various gang-related offenses, and sought to overturn his conviction, arguing that the police conducted a warrantless search of his phone. The Court agreed with Riley and reversed his conviction, concluding that the search incident to lawful arrest exception did not apply to cell phones. The exception applies when there is a concern that the arrestee will harm officers or destroy evidence; the Court reasoned that neither concern is present in the case of a cell phone. The police could seize the cell phone, and obtain a warrant to search it. There was no danger that the data would be destroyed. Particularly notable about the majority opinion, written by Chief Justice Roberts, was the strong language that the Court used to caution law enforcement against warrantless searches of data:

> Our cases have recognized that the Fourth Amendment was the founding generation's response to the reviled "general warrants"

---

40 *See* Cardwell v. Lewis, 417 U.S. 583, 589 (1974) (plurality opinion) ("[T]he Court has recognized a distinction between the warrantless search and seizure of automobiles or other movable vehicles, on the one hand, and the search of a home or office, on the other. Generally, less stringent warrant requirements have been applied to vehicles.").
41 *See* Chambers v. Maroney, 399 U.S. 42, 51 (1970) ("As a general rule, it has also required the judgment of a magistrate on the probable-cause issue and the issuance of a warrant before a search is made. Only in exigent circumstances will the judgment of the police as to probable cause serve as a sufficient authorization for a search.").
42 *See* United States v. Martinez-Fuerte, 428 U.S. 543, 566–67 (1976) ("[S]tops for brief questioning routinely conducted at permanent checkpoints are consistent with the Fourth Amendment and need not be authorized by warrant. The principal protection of Fourth Amendment rights at checkpoints lies in appropriate limitations on the scope of the stop.").
43 *See* New York v. Belton, 453 U.S. 454, 460 (1981) ("[W]hen a policeman has made a lawful custodial arrest of the occupant of an automobile, he may, as a contemporaneous incident of that arrest, search the passenger compartment of that automobile.").
44 Riley v. California, 134 S. Ct. 2473 (2014).

and "writs of assistance" of the colonial era, which allowed British officers to rummage through homes in an unrestrained search for evidence of criminal activity. Opposition to such searches was in fact one of the driving forces behind the Revolution itself. In 1761, the patriot James Otis delivered a speech in Boston denouncing the use of writs of assistance. A young John Adams was there, and he would later write that "[e]very man of a crowded audience appeared to me to go away, as I did, ready to take arms against writs of assistance." According to Adams, Otis's speech was "the first scene of the first act of opposition to the arbitrary claims of Great Britain. Then and there the child Independence was born."

Modern cell phones are not just another technological convenience. With all they contain and all they may reveal, they hold for many Americans "the privacies of life." The fact that technology now allows an individual to carry such information in his hand does not make the information any less worthy of the protection for which the Founders fought. Our answer to the question of what police must do before searching a cell phone seized incident to an arrest is accordingly simple — get a warrant.[45]

The *Riley* opinion likely will have impacts that reach far beyond cases involving searches incident to lawful arrests. It is perhaps the Supreme Court's strongest statement, since *Katz*, in opposition to the government's warrantless searches of criminal suspects' information. *Riley* is a clear indication that the Supreme Court believes that the Fourth Amendment applies just as much to electronic information as it does to physical objects. Although the case involved a relatively narrow issue related to the search of an arrestee, it likely will have a large impact on a wide range of future cyber-related Fourth Amendment cases.

7.1.5 Was the Search or Seizure Reasonable under the Totality of the Circumstances?

The Fourth Amendment protects individuals against "unreasonable" searches and seizures. If the government obtains a warrant, it is generally presumed to be reasonable.[46] If, however, a warrantless search is conducted under an exception to the warrant requirement, the government still must demonstrate that the search was "reasonable" and therefore did not violate the Fourth Amendment.[47]

---

45 *Id.* at 2494–95 (internal citations omitted).

46 "[S]earches pursuant to a warrant will rarely require any deep inquiry into reasonableness," Illinois v. Gates, 462 U.S. 213, 267 (1983) (White, J., concurring in judgment).

47 *See* Maryland v. King, 133 S. Ct. 1958, 1970 (2013) ("Even if a warrant is not required, a search is not beyond Fourth Amendment scrutiny; for it must be reasonable in its scope and manner of execution.").

To assess reasonableness of a search, courts conduct a "totality of the circumstances" analysis of the search, in which they evaluate "on the one hand, the degree to which it intrudes upon an individual's privacy and, on the other, the degree to which it is needed for the promotion of legitimate governmental interests."[48]

Courts have great leeway in determining the weight that they will accord to these often-competing values. A recent application, relevant to cyber searches, arose in the case of Jamshid Muhtorov, a legal permanent resident of the United States who was charged with providing material support to a designated terrorist organization. The government notified Muhtorov that it planned to use evidence that it collected under Section 702 of the FISA Amendments Act of 2008, a program (colloquially known as "PRISM") that allows federal intelligence agencies to conduct electronic surveillance of targets who are believed to be located outside of the United States *and* are not United States citizens. Although Muhtorov was located within the United States, the target of the surveillance apparently was not believed to be in the United States, and therefore the communications were collected under Section 702 (the contents of the communications was classified and not included in the court opinion). Muhtorov asked the court to suppress the evidence collected under Section 702, arguing that it violated his Fourth Amendment rights.

A Colorado federal judge denied Muhtorov's motion to suppress. After concluding that foreign intelligence gathering falls within the "special needs" exception to the warrant requirement (a conclusion reached by many other federal courts, but never addressed directly by the United States Supreme Court), the Colorado judge concluded that under the totality of the circumstances, the search was reasonable. The judge concluded both that Section 702, on its face, is constitutional, and that it was constitutionally applied to Muhtorov. Key to the judge's ruling was an extensive set of "minimization procedures" that the government uses to weed out information that is not related to foreign intelligence and to reduce the likelihood of searches being conducted of people who are either U.S. citizens or located in the United States. "I conclude on the record before me that a proper and supported application was filed, and that the targeting and minimization procedures forwarded were tailored to the government's legitimate foreign intelligence purposes and took into account the privacy interests of individuals whose communications would be incidentally acquired," the judge wrote.[49]

Ultimately, unless the Supreme Court has explicitly found a specific government practice to be reasonable or unreasonable, courts have a great deal of leeway under the totality of the circumstances framework. Whether the government's needs outweigh the individual's privacy interests ultimately is a

---

48 Wyoming v. Houghton, 526 U.S. 295, 300 (1999).
49 United States v. Muhtorov, Criminal Case No. 12-cr-00033-JLK (D. Colo. Nov. 19, 2015).

value judgment that likely will vary by court and judge. Accordingly, it often is difficult to predict, with certainty, whether a government search or seizure comports with the Fourth Amendment. This is particularly true with cyber searches, which often involve novel factual issues that have not yet been addressed by other courts.

7.2 Electronic Communications Privacy Act

In satisfying the Fourth Amendment's requirements, the government *also* must ensure that it isn't violating any statutes that restrict the ability of the government's ability to conduct electronic surveillance. The Electronic Communications Privacy Act (ECPA) is the most comprehensive U.S. law relating to cyber surveillance. ECPA limits the ability of government agencies, such as law enforcement, to obtain emails, monitor networks, and obtain Internet traffic logs. ECPA also imposes strict boundaries on the ability of service providers (e.g., phone companies and email service providers) from providing other private parties or the government with access to customer emails and other records.

ECPA is so central to cybersecurity because it severely limits the ability of both the government and the private sector to monitor networks for cybersecurity vulnerabilities and threats and to share the information. Moreover, it restricts the ability of law enforcement to monitor communications for kinetic threats (e.g., terrorist plots).

Congress passed much of ECPA in 1986. Although it has been amended since then, the heart of the law remains the same today as when it was passed more than three decades ago. This has led a number of critics to call for a full-scale overhaul of the statute.[50]

For now, however, ECPA remains the law of the land, and it shapes the cyber decisions of many companies and government agencies. This chapter provides an overview of the three sections of ECPA: the Stored Communications Act, the Wiretap Act, and the Pen Register Act. The Stored Communications Act regulates the ability of governments to compel – and service providers to disclose – stored communications such as email messages and cloud content. The Wiretap Act restricts the ability of the government to monitor communications while they are in transit. The Pen Register Act restricts the ability of government agencies and private parties to obtain noncontent information about telephone and email communications, such as phone numbers dialed and the to/from headers on email messages. The entire text of ECPA is reprinted in Appendix E. This section is intended to provide an overview of the key concepts necessary to understanding how ECPA applies to cybersecurity.

---

50 *See, e.g.*, Elena Schneider, *Technology Companies are Pressing Congress to Bolster Privacy Protections*, NEW YORK TIMES (May 26, 2014).

7.2.1 Stored Communications Act

Data that is stored on a computer, server, or the cloud – such as email and files – may be covered by the Stored Communications Act (SCA). As the U.S. Court of Appeals for the Ninth Circuit observed, the SCA "reflects Congress's judgment that users have a legitimate interest in the confidentiality of communications in electronic storage at a communications facility."[51]

The SCA, passed in 1986, covers three general categories: (1) access to stored communications;[52] (2) voluntary disclosure of stored communications by service providers;[53] and (3) law enforcement agency's attempts to compel service providers to disclose stored communications.[54]

The first category can be seen as a supplement to the Computer Fraud and Abuse Act, which is described in Chapter 5. Indeed, criminal charges against computer hackers often are brought under both the SCA and CFAA. The second category involves the restrictions placed on a service provider's ability to disclose its users' information. In many ways, this is analogous to a privacy law. The third category limits the government's ability to require service providers to provide users' information. This section will consider each of these SCA categories in turn.

Before examining each of these three categories, it is important to understand the scope of the SCA's applicability. The SCA applies to two types of services: electronic communications services (ECS) and remote computing services (RCS). The definitions of these services are important, because the SCA imposes different requirements depending on whether a service is classified as an ECS or RCS. In many cases, a service provider may be both an ECS and an RCS.[55]

The SCA defines ECS as "any service which provides to users thereof the ability to send or receive wire or electronic communications,"[56] which are the "transfer of signs, signals, writing, images, sounds, data, or intelligence of any nature transmitted in whole or in part by a wire, radio, electromagnetic, photoelectric or photooptical system that affects interstate or foreign commerce."[57] Many courts have held that unopened emails stored on servers or the cloud fall within the definition of ECS.[58] Similarly, a secured website that is

---

51 Theofel v. Farey-Jones, 359 F. 3d 1066 (9th Cir. 2004).
52 18 U.S.C. § 2701.
53 18 U.S.C. § 2702.
54 18 U.S.C. § 2703.
55 *See In re U.S.*, 665 F. Supp. 2d 1210, 1214 (D. Or. 2009) ("Today, most ISPs provide both ECS and RCS; thus, the distinction serves to define the service that is being provided at a particular time (or as to a particular piece of electronic communication at a particular time), rather than to define the service provider itself.").
56 18 U.S.C. §§ 2510 (15); 2711(1).
57 18 U.S.C. §§ 2510 (12), 2711(1).

used to communicate has been held to be an ECS.[59] Moreover, courts have held that Internet access, provided by Internet service providers, are an ECS,[60] as are cell phone service providers.[61]

The SCA defines RCS as "the provision to the public of computer storage or processing services by means of an electronic communications system," which it defines as "(A) any temporary, intermediate storage of a wire or electronic communication incidental to the electronic transmission thereof; and (B) any storage of such communication by an electronic communication service for purposes of backup protection of such communication."[62] Keep in mind that Congress passed the SCA in 1986 – long before the modern era of cloud computing. When passing the SCA, the Senate issued a report in which it provided the following explanation of its reasons for explicitly covering RCS:

> In the age of rapid computerization, a basic choice has faced the users of computer technology. That is, whether to process data inhouse on the user's own computer or on someone else's equipment. Over the years, remote computer service companies have developed to provide sophisticated and convenient computing services to subscribers and customers from remote facilities. Today businesses of all sizes — hospitals, banks and many others — use remote computing services for computer processing. This processing can be done with the customer or subscriber using the facilities of the remote computing service in essentially a time-sharing arrangement, or it can be accomplished by the service provider on the basis of information supplied by the subscriber or customer. Data is most often transmitted between these services and their customers by means of electronic communications.[63]

Although information technology habits have changed since 1986, the Senate's general explanation of the use of "remote facilities" continues to apply to the definition of RCS. Services such as cloud computing and data centers – in which data is stored remotely for long-term use – fall under the definition of

---

58 *See* Theofel v. Farey-Jones, 359 F. 3d 1066 (9th Cir. 2004) (holding that email services are ECS); U.S. v. Warshak, 631 F. 3d 266 (6th Cir. 2010) (same); Bohach v. City of Reno, 932 F. Supp. 1232 (D. Nev. 1996) (same); Special Markets Insurance Consultants. v. Lynch (N.D. Ill. 2012) ("The cases cited by the parties and those located by this court's research have consistently held that Yahoo, AOL, and similar services are, indeed, the "electronic communication services" contemplated by the SCA.").
59 *See* Konop v. Hawaiian Airlines, Inc., 302 F. 3d 868 (9th Cir. 2002).
60 *In re* DoubleClick Inc. Privacy Litigation, 154 F. Supp. 2d 497 (S.D.N.Y. 2001).
61 *In re* App. of US for an Order for Prosp. Cell, 460 F. Supp. 2d 448 (S.D.N.Y. 2006).
62 18 U.S.C. §§ 2510 (17); 2711(1).
63 S. Rep. No. 99–541, at 2–3 (1986), U.S. CODE CONG. & ADMIN. NEWS 1986, pp. 3555, 3556–57.

RCS. In some cases, it may not be entirely clear whether a service is an ECS or RCS.[64] For instance, email that is opened and then stored for many years – as is common practice – has been argued to be both RCS or ECS. The confusion largely is due to the fact that the SCA was enacted in 1986, a time when remote storage was limited, and it therefore was inconceivable to remotely store opened email for a long period of time. But the distinction between RCS and ECS is vital. As we will see, the designation may play an important role in determining the privacy protections that the SCA affords to a service's users.

7.2.1.1 Section 2701: Third-Party Hacking of Stored Communications

Section 2701 of the SCA makes it a criminal offense to access an individual's email (or other ECS) without authorization. The statute also allows victims of unauthorized access to bring civil claims. Think of this section as a restriction on the ability of outside parties to hack a stored communication.

The statute imposes criminal penalties on any individual who "(1) intentionally accesses without authorization a facility through which an electronic communication service is provided" or "(2) intentionally exceeds an authorization to access that facility," and, through either of those actions, "thereby obtains, alters, or prevents authorized access to a wire or electronic communication while it is in electronic storage in such a system[.]"[65] Individuals who are convicted of this crime face fines and up to ten years in prison. The law allows service providers and individuals to file civil actions against violators.[66]

A significant limitation on this criminal provision is the application only to a *facility* through which an ECS is provided. Courts generally have held that hacking an individual's computer or smartphone does not constitute a violation of the SCA because that individual device is not a "facility"; instead, the unauthorized access must be of an email account, cloud service, or other ECS facility.[67] For instance, in 2012, a California federal judge dismissed a

---

64 *See* Orin Kerr, *A User's Guide to the Stored Communications Act – and a Legislator's Guide to Amending it*, G.W. L. Rev. (2004). ("There are closer cases, however, and some of these closer cases are important ones. In particular, the proper treatment of opened e-mail is currently unclear. The traditional understanding has been that a copy of opened e-mail sitting on a server is protected by the RCS rules, not the ECS rules. The thinking is that when an e-mail customer leaves a copy of an already-accessed e-mail stored on a server, that copy is no longer 'incident to transmission' nor a backup copy of a file that is incident to transmission: rather, it is just in remote storage like any other file held by an RCS.")

65 18 U.S.C. § 2701.

66 18 U.S.C. § 2707.

67 *See, e.g.*, Freedom Banc Mortg. Servs., Inc. v. O'Harra, No. 11–1073, 2012 WL 3862209, at *9 (S.D. Ohio Sept. 5, 2012) ("[T]he relevant facilities' that the SCA is designed to protect are not computers that enable the use of an electronic communication service, but instead are facilities that are operated by electronic communication service providers and used to store and maintain electronic storage."); Cousineau v. Microsoft Corporation (W.D. Wash. 2014) ("In this situation, Plaintiff's phone did not provide location services to other users in a server-like fashion, but instead received the relevant services from Microsoft.").

Section 2701 class action lawsuit against Apple, alleging that its iOS devices violated plaintiffs' privacy rights by allowing third-party applications to collect information about users. The judge noted that although "the computer systems of an email provider, a bulletin board system, or an ISP are uncontroversial examples of facilities that provide electronic communications services to multiple users," individuals' computers, laptops and mobile devices do not constitute "facilities."[68]

Another significant limitation on this statute is the requirement that the access to the facility be "without authorization" or in excess of authorization. As with the CFAA, discussed in Chapter 5, it often is difficult for the government or civil plaintiffs to demonstrate that access was entirely without authorization or in excess of authorization. For instance, in a 2000 case in Michigan, a company accused its former manufacturer's representative of continuing to access the company's confidential sales information, which was stored on the network of one of its retailers, Kmart. The company alleged that the representative's continued access to the information, even after its termination, constituted a Section 2701 violation.[69] The district court disagreed and dismissed the lawsuit. Even though the manufacturer's representative continued to access the sales information after its termination – and it arguably had no need to do so – the court reasoned that Kmart continued to provide the representative with access to its network. "Where a party consents to another's access to its computer network, it cannot claim that such access was unauthorized," the court concluded.

In contrast, the next year, a court allowed a Section 2701 class action lawsuit to proceed against Intuit, which the plaintiffs allege used website cookies to violate their privacy rights. The court reasoned that, unlike the Michigan case, "Plaintiffs here allege that they did not authorize Defendant to access data contained in the cookies it implanted on Plaintiffs' computers."[70]

7.2.1.2 Section 2702: Restrictions on Service Providers' Ability to Disclose Stored Communications and Records to the Government and Private Parties

Section 2702 of the SCA restricts the ability of *both* ECS and RCS providers to voluntarily disclose both communications contents and consumer records. Disputes under this section commonly arise during discovery in civil cases; parties to litigation often subpoena service providers for emails, logs, and other

---

68 *In re* iPhone Application Litigation, 844 F. Supp. 2d 1040 (N.D. Cal. 2012).
69 Sherman & Co. v. Salton Maxim Housewares, Inc., 94 F. Supp. 2d 817 (E.D. Mich. 2000).
70 In re Intuit Privacy Litigation, 138 F. Supp. 2d 1272 (C.D. Cal. 2001).

records. Importantly, Section 2702 does not have an exception that allows RCS and ECS providers to turn over information in civil discovery.[71]

The statute prohibits a public ECS provider from knowingly divulging to either the government *or* private parties "the contents of a communication while in electronic storage by that service."[72] Public RCS providers are prohibited from divulging contents of communications that are maintained on the service on behalf of – and received via electronic transmission from – a subscriber or customer. RCS providers also may not disclose contents of communications that are stored on their services, unless the customer has provided authorization (e.g., by creating a public folder on the cloud). The statute broadly defines "contents" to include "any information concerning the substance, purport, or meaning of that communication."[73]

Keep in mind that Section 2702 only applies to ECS and RCS services that are provided *to the public.* This generally has been interpreted to include service providers that have customers; a purely internal email system (e.g., a private company's email and document storage server) likely would not be considered to be provided "to the public." For instance, in a 1998 case, an Illinois federal judge rejected the argument that Section 2702 applies to an ECS provider "even if that provider maintains the system primarily for its own use and does not provide services to the general public."[74] The court concluded that "the statute covers any entity that provides electronic communication service (e.g., e-mail) to the community at large."[75]

Section 2702 contains a number of exceptions that allows service providers to disclose communications content under limited circumstances:

- *To the intended recipient of the communications content.*[76] For example, Gmail can deliver the email to the address that is in the "to" line of the email).
- *If law enforcement obtains a warrant or other valid process that is authorized under another statute.*[77] For instance, Section 2703 of the SCA, discussed below, provides a few mechanisms for law enforcement to obtain valid process to compel service providers to disclose communications content. If the service providers receive this process, they will not be held liable for disclosure.

---

71 *See* Mintz v. Mark Bartelstein & Associates, Inc., 885 F. Supp. 2d 987 ("The SCA does not contain an exception for civil discovery subpoenas."); Flagg v. City of Detroit, 252 F.R.D. 346, 350 (E.D. Mich. 2008) ("[A]s noted by the courts and commentators alike, § 2702 lacks any language that explicitly authorizes a service provider to divulge the contents of a communication pursuant to a subpoena or court order.").

72 18 U.S.C. § 2702.

73 18 U.S.C. §§ 2510 (8); 2711(1).

74 Andersen Consulting LLP v. UOP, 991 F. Supp. 1041 (N.D. Ill. 1998).

75 *Id.*

76 18 U.S.C. § 2702(b)(1).

77 18 U.S.C. § 2702(b)(2).

- *If the originator or addressee of the information consents to the disclosure.*[78]
- *To deliver the communications to its destination.*[79]   An example is an email provider that has to transmit a message through a third-party service provider in order for it to reach its intended destination.
- *As is "necessarily incident to the rendition of the service or to the protection of the rights or to the protection of the rights or property of the provider of the service."*[80]   This is one of the more controversial exceptions to Section 2702. For instance, in 2006, Apple contended that if it did not comply with a civil subpoena for a customer's communications content, the company could face court sanctions, and therefore providing the information protects Apple's rights or property. The California Court of Appeal rejected this argument, concluding that the "effect of such an interpretation would be to permit disclosure whenever someone threatened the service provider with litigation."[81] However, few courts have directly addressed this exception, so it is not entirely clear exactly what types of disclosure *would* fall under this exception.
- *To the National Center for Missing and Exploited Children, in connection with a child pornography investigation.*[82]   As discussed in the Fourth Amendment section above, 18 U.S.C. 2258A requires all ECS and RCS providers to file a report with the National Center for Missing and Exploited Children if the providers obtain actual knowledge of an apparent violation of federal child pornography laws. Filing this report is explicitly exempt from the SCA.
- *If the contents were inadvertently obtained by the service provider and appear to pertain to the commission of a crime.*   No published court opinion has interpreted this provision, but based on court rulings regarding other exceptions to the SCA, for this exception to apply, a service provider likely would have to present substantial evidence that it obtained the contents "inadvertently."
- *To a governmental entity, if the provider, in good faith, believes that "an emergency involving danger of death or serious physical injury to any person requires disclosure without delay of communications relating to the emergency."*[83]   For instance, one court suggested in nonbinding dicta to a case that if a service provider obtains credible evidence of potential child

---

78 18 U.S.C. § 2702(b)(3).
79 18 U.S.C. § 2702(b)(4).
80 18 U.S.C. § 2702(b)(5).
81 O'Grady v. Superior Court, 44 Cal. Rptr. 3d 72 (Cal. Ct. App. 2006).
82 18 U.S.C. § 2702(b)(6).
83 18 U.S.C. § 2702(b)(7).

abuse, it is authorized to provide communications content to a government social services agency.[84]

Section 2702 allow RCS and ECS providers to divulge "a record or other information pertaining to a subscriber to or customer of such service" to non-governmental entities, provided that the record does *not* include the *contents* of communications. Such records include subscriber names, addresses, and social security numbers.[85] However, RCS and ECS providers still are prohibited from disclosing customer records to government entities, unless (1) otherwise authorized by Section 2703; (2) with the customer's consent; (3) necessarily incident to render the service or protect the service provider's rights or property; (4) to the government, if the provider believes in good faith that an emergency exists; or (5) to NCMEC in connection with a child pornography investigation.

Individuals who believe that their SCA rights have been violated can file a civil action for actual and punitive damages.[86]

7.2.1.2.1 The Cybersecurity Act of 2015: Allowing Service Providers to Disclose Cybersecurity Threats to the Government

A recently enacted law expands the ability of RCS and ECS providers to disclose communications content and customer records to the government. In December 2015, Congress passed the Cybersecurity Act of 2015, which is intended to promote collaboration between the private sector and federal government on cybersecurity.

The Cybersecurity Act of 2015, described above, may significantly expand the ability of operators of computer networks and systems to monitor for cybersecurity threats without facing liability under the Stored Communications Act. The Cybersecurity Act allows private entities to monitor their own information systems – as well as information systems of other entities with consent – for "cybersecurity purposes."[87] It defines "cybersecurity purpose" as "the purpose of protecting an information system or information that is stored on, processed by, or transiting an information system from a cybersecurity threat or security vulnerability."[88]

---

84 United States v. D'Andrea, 497 F. Supp. 2d 117 (D. Mass. 2007); Kerr, supra note 14 at 25 ("The SCA gives greater privacy protection to content information for reasons that most people find intuitive: actual contents of messages naturally implicate greater privacy concerns than information (much of it network-generated) about those communications.").

85 See, e.g., United States v. Hambrick, 55 F. Supp. 2d 504 (W.D. Va. 1999) ("this court does not find that the ECPA has legislatively determined that an individual has a reasonable expectation of privacy in his name, address, social security number, credit card number, and proof of Internet connection.").

86 18 U.S.C. 2707.

87 6 U.S.C. § 1503(a).

88 6 U.S.C. § 1501(4).

The Act broadly defines "cybersecurity threat" as "an action, not protected by the First Amendment to the Constitution of the United States, on or through an information system that may result in an unauthorized effort to adversely impact the security, availability, confidentiality, or integrity of an information system or information that is stored on, processed by, or transiting an information system."[89] Cybersecurity threats do not include actions that merely violate a customer terms of service or licensing agreement. The Act defines "security vulnerability" as "any attribute of hardware, software, process, or procedure that could enable or facilitate the defeat of a security control."[90]

Because the law was recently enacted, we do not yet know how broadly courts will interpret key terms such as "cybersecurity threat" and "security vulnerability." However, the plain language of the statute appears to be fairly broadly worded, increasing the likelihood that courts will apply it to a wide variety of attempts to investigate past cyber incidents and prevent future incidents. If that is the case, then the Cybersecurity Act may enable private parties to monitor their own systems and networks – and the systems and networks of others who have provided consent.

The statute also allows private companies to operate "defensive measures" for "cybersecurity purposes." However, the statute's definition of "defensive measures" is rather narrow, and explicitly excludes "hacking back" at a network that the company believes had attacked its network. The statute defines "defensive measure" as "an action, device, procedure, signature, technique, or other measure applied to an information system or information that is stored on, processed by, or transiting an information system that detects, prevents, or mitigates a known or suspected threat or security vulnerability."[91] The statute explicitly states that "defensive measure" does not include "a measure that destroys, renders unusable, provides unauthorized access to, or substantially harms an information system or information stored on, processed by, or transiting such information system" that is neither owned by the private entity that is operating the measure or another entity that is "authorized to provide consent and has provided consent to that private entity to operate the measure."[92]

Examples of Defensive Measures under the Cybersecurity Act of 2015

In June 2016, the U.S. Department of Homeland Security released guidance for the implementation of the Cybersecurity Act of 2015. It listed the following as illustrative examples of "defensive measures" under the statute:
- A computer program that identifies a pattern of malicious activity in web traffic flowing into an organization.

---

89 6 U.S.C. § 1501(5).
90 6 U.S.C. § 1501(17).
91 6 U.S.C. § 1501(7).
92 *Id.*

- A signature that could be loaded into a company's intrusion detection system in order to detect a spear phishing campaign with particular characteristics.
- A firewall rule that disallows a type of malicious traffic from entering a network.
- An algorithm that can search through a cache of network traffic to discover anomalous patterns that may indicate malicious activity.
- A technique for quickly matching, in an automated manner, the content of an organization's incoming Simple Mail Transfer Protocol (SMTP, a protocol commonly used for email) traffic against a set of content known to be associated with a specific cybersecurity threat without unacceptably degrading the speed of email delivery to end users.

Source: DEPARTMENT OF HOMELAND SECURITY AND DEPARTMENT OF JUSTICE: GUIDANCE TO ASSIST NON-FEDERAL ENTITIES TO SHARE CYBER THREAT INDICATORS AND DEFENSIVE MEASURES WITH FEDERAL ENTITIES UNDER THE CYBERSECURITY INFORMATION SHARING ACT of 2015.

7.2.1.3   Section 2703: Government's Ability to Force Service Providers to Turn Over Stored Communications and Customer Records

Section 2703 of the SCA restricts the government's ability to compel ECS and RCS providers to disclose communications content and records. As we will see, this is not the only restriction on the government; in addition to the Section 2703 requirements, the government also must satisfy the requirements of the Fourth Amendment of the U.S. Constitution. In some cases, even if the SCA allows the government to compel disclosure, the Fourth Amendment may prevent it.

Section 2703's restrictions for the disclosure of communications content depend on whether the provider is an ECS or RCS provider, and the length of time the communications content has been stored. In short, electronic communications in electronic storage with ECS providers for 180 days or less receive more protection than older ECS communications (or any RCS communications). This distinction is a relic of the mid-1980s, when most electronic communications were immediately downloaded onto individuals' computers and rarely stored for the long term on a service provider.

Despite a widespread consensus that the 180-day distinction is arcane and wholly inapplicable to modern technology, the 1986 law remains the law of the land for now. Here is how it works: The government must obtain a court-issued warrant, supported by probable cause, to compel communications content from an ECS provider if that content has been "in electronic storage in an electronic communications system for one hundred and eighty days or less."[93]

---

93 18 U.S.C. § 2703; *see* United States v. Weaver, 636 F. Supp. 2d 769 (C.D. Ill. 2009) ("Thus, for emails less than 181 days old, the question of whether a warrant is necessary turns on whether the emails are 'in electronic storage' or are 'held or maintained … solely for the purpose of providing storage or computer processing services to [the] subscriber or customer.' … If the emails the Government requested here are in electronic storage, Microsoft need not produce them without a warrant, but if they are held or maintained solely to provide the customer storage or computer processing services, Microsoft must comply with the Government's subpoena.").

Some courts have concluded that once emails are open, they are no longer in electronic storage – and therefore, not subject to the warrant requirement[94] – while others have reached an opposite conclusion and required a warrant for any emails stored with ECS providers, as long as they are no more than 180 days old.[95]

To obtain communications content stored with an ECS provider for more than 180 days – or stored with an RCS provider – the government has a few options.

First, it could go to court and obtain a warrant supported by probable cause, just as it would for ECS content that is stored for 180 days or less. But that is a fairly high burden to meet, and the SCA allows two other options.

Second, it could use an administrative subpoena that is authorized by a federal or state statute, or a federal or state grand jury or trial subpoena. The rules differ depending on jurisdiction, but the government typically does not need to come anywhere close to demonstrating probable cause; however, the material sought must be relevant and related to the investigation or trial.[96]

Third, the government may obtain what is known as a "(d) order," which is because it is a mechanism created by subsection (d) of Section 2703 of the SCA. A federal or state court may issue a (d) order if the government "offers specific and articulable facts showing that there are reasonable grounds to believe that the contents of a wire or electronic communication, or the records or other information sought, are relevant and material to an ongoing criminal investigation."[97] Although this requires the government to provide some specific facts, this showing, as with a subpoena, is much lower than the probable cause required to obtain a warrant. A court can quash or modify a (d) order only if the service provider files a motion that demonstrates that "the information or records requested are unusually voluminous in nature or compliance with such order otherwise would cause an undue burden on such provider."[98]

To obtain communications via an administrative subpoena or (d) order, the government must provide prior notice to the subscriber or customer, unless it

---

94 United States v. Weaver, 636 F. Supp. 2d 769 (C.D. Ill. 2009) ("Previously opened emails stored by Microsoft for Hotmail users are not in electronic storage, and the Government can obtain copies of such emails using a trial subpoena. Microsoft must comply with the Government's subpoena here.").

95 Theofel v. Farey-Jones, 359 F.3d 1066, 1075 (9th Cir. 2004) ("The ISP copy of the message functions as a "backup" for the user. Notably, nothing in the Act requires that the backup protection be for the benefit of the ISP rather than the user. Storage under these circumstances thus literally falls within the statutory definition.").

96 *See, e.g.,* Fed. R. Crim. P. 17(c)(2) (allowing a court to quash or modify a criminal subpoena "if compliance would be unreasonable or oppressive").

97 18 U.S.C.§ 2703(d).

98 18 U.S.C. 2703(d).

convinces a court to delay notice because "there is reason to believe that notification of the existence of the court order may have an adverse result[.]"[99]

A number of critics say the 180-day distinction has become outdated and is often unworkable for modern communications. For this reason, members of both parties in Congress have long been attempting to amend the SCA to provide for the same level of protection regardless of the amount of time that a communication has been in storage. "In 2015, it is absurd that the government is free to rifle through Americans' emails that are older than six months," Sen. Ron Wyden, a sponsor of one such amendment, said in 2015. "Because of this arcane law, as technology advances, Americans' civil liberties are eroding."[100]

Moreover, as discussed in Section 7.1, some courts are beginning to hold that the Fourth Amendment requires a warrant for the government to obtain all communications, regardless of the length of time that they are stored. As of the publication of this book in 2016, momentum was building in Congress for an amendment to the Stored Communications Act that would eliminate the 180-day distinction and require the government to obtain a warrant for stored communications regardless of the length of time that they had been stored.

7.2.2 Wiretap Act

As its name suggests, the Stored Communications Act restricts the disclosure and procurement of communications that are stored on a medium (e.g., a server). In contrast, the Wiretap Act[101] restricts the ability for the government and private parties to intercept communications as they are in transit.

The Wiretap Act was passed as Title III of the Omnibus Crime Control and Safe Streets Act of 1968 in response to the United States Supreme Court's ruling in *Katz v. United States*[102] that the Fourth Amendment restricts the government's use of wiretaps to eavesdrop on telephone calls.[103]

The Wiretap Act contains a broad, general prohibition on the intentional interception, procurement, and use of electronic, wire, or oral communications.[104] The statute also prohibits the intentional interception or disclosure of

---

99 18 U.S.C. § 2705(1)(A).
100 Grant Gross, *U.S. Lawmakers Introduce Two Bills to Protect Email Privacy*, PC WORLD (Feb. 12, 2015).
101 18 U.S.C. §§ 2510–22.
102 389 U.S. 347 (1967).
103 Gelbard v. United States, 408 U.S. 41, 78 (1972) (Rehnquist, J., dissenting).("Congress undertook to draft comprehensive legislation both authorizing the use of evidence obtained by electronic surveillance on specified conditions, and prohibiting its use otherwise.").
104 18 U.S.C. § 2511.

the contents of unlawfully intercepted communications.[105] As the U.S. Court of Appeals for the Eleventh Circuit accurately summarized, a typical claim of a Wiretap Act violation consists of a demonstration that the defendant "(1) intentionally (2) intercepted, endeavored to intercept or procured another person to intercept or endeavor to intercept (3) the contents of (4) an electronic communication (5) using a device."[106] The Wiretap Act uses the same definition of "contents" as the SCA: "any information concerning the substance, purport, or meaning of that communication."[107] Courts generally have broadly interpreted this definition to include personally identifiable information such as names and birthdates.[108] However, data automatically generated about the call, such as the call time and duration, is not considered "content" that is covered by the Wiretap Act.[109]

Violations of the Wiretap Act carry criminal fines and prison time of up to five years. The statute also allows the victims of Wiretap Act violations to file civil lawsuits for damages and equitable relief.[110]

The Wiretap Act's broad prohibitions contain a number of exceptions.

First, the Wiretap Act does not prohibit an employee of a communications provider from intercepting, disclosing, or using communications for any activity "which is a necessary incident to the rendition of his service or to the protection of the rights or property of the provider of that service."[111] As one court noted, this exception "has been repeatedly interpreted by Courts to authorize telephone companies to intercept and monitor calls placed over their facilities in order to combat fraud and theft of service."[112] Similarly, this exception enables employers to monitor employee email accounts without facing Wiretap Act charges.[113]

Second, communications providers may provide information to the government as authorized by the Foreign Intelligence Surveillance Act, which sets the framework for collection of foreign intelligence information from U.S. infrastructure.[114]

---

105 *Id.*
106 *In re* Pharmatrak, 329 F. 3d 9 (1st Cir. 2003).
107 18 U.S.C. § 2510(8).
108 *See In re* Pharmatrak, 329 F.3d 9 (1st Cir. 2003).
109 *See* United States v. Reed, 575 F.3d 900, 917 (9th Cir. 2009), *In re* iPhone Application Litigation, 844 F. Supp. 2d 1040, 1061 (N.D. Cal. 2012) ("'[C]ontent' is limited to information the user intended to communicate, such as the words spoken in a phone call.").
110 18 U.S.C. § 2520.
111 18 U.S.C. § 2511(2)(a)(i).
112 United States v. Villanueva, 32 F. Supp. 2d 635 (S.D.N.Y. 1998).
113 *In re* Information Management Services, Inc. Derivative Litigation, 81 A.3d 278 (Del. Ct. Chancery) ("Employers monitor email (or reserve the right to do so) in large part to protect their property and to guard against potential liability.").
114 18 U.S.C. § 2511(2)(a)(ii).

Third, a law enforcement officer who is party to a communication is not subject to the Wiretap Act's prohibitions.[115] Relatedly, the Wiretap Act does not restrict law enforcement if at least one party to the communication has provided consent.[116] In other words, if one of the parties to a phone conversation or email exchange is an undercover officer, or a private party acting on behalf of law enforcement, then the Wiretap Act would not restrict the government's interception of that phone call.

Fourth, a private individual may intercept a communication if that individual is a party to the communication, or if the person is party to the communication, or if one of the parties provided consent.[117] However, this exception does not apply if the interception is conducted to commit a criminal or tortious act that violates a state or federal law. For instance, some states have imposed "two-party consent" laws that require consent from all parties to a communication before wiretapping is permitted.[118]

The most significant exception to the Wiretap Act, for government purposes, allows law enforcement to seek a court order for the interception of wire, oral, or electronic communications.[119] Under this exception, law enforcement must fulfill a number of requirements before obtaining an order that allows them to intercept communications.

Applications for wiretap orders must contain the identity of the officer seeking the information, a "full and complete statement of the facts," including:

> (i) details as to the particular offense that has been, is being, or is about to be committed, (ii) [when possible] a particular description of the nature and location of the facilities from which or the place where the communication is to be intercepted, (iii) a particular description of the type of communications sought to be intercepted, (iv) the identity of the person, if known, committing the offense and whose communications are to be intercepted.[120]

The application also must describe whether other investigative procedures have been attempted, the period of time for which interception has been attempted, and a statement concerning previous applications for wiretaps.[121]

After reviewing the application, the judge may grant the order only after finding that there is probable cause to believe that the target of the wiretap is

---

115 18 U.S.C. § 2511(2)(c).

116 *Id.*

117 18 U.S.C. § 2511(2)(d).

118 For a complete list of these state laws, *see* REPORTER'S COMMITTEE FOR FREEDOM OF THE PRESS, REPORTER'S REPORTING GUIDE, *available at* https://www.rcfp.org/rcfp/orders/docs/RECORDING.pdf.

119 18 U.S.C. § 2518.

120 *Id.*

121 *Id.*

committing, has committed, or soon will commit a particular serious criminal offense *and* that there is probable cause to believe that communications concerning the offense will be obtained via the wiretap.[122] The court also must find that normal investigative procedures that do not require a wiretap either have failed or reasonably appear unlikely to result in information about the offense.[123] The court also generally must find that there is probable cause to believe that the Internet connection or other communications facility that is being wiretapped is being used by the target of the investigation.[124]

In short, before a court will grant a wiretap order, it must determine that probable cause exists for three different elements: (1) that the target has committed, is committing, or soon will commit a crime; (2) that the wiretap will lead to information about this crime; and (3) that the target will use the communications facilities specified in the wiretap application. This is a relatively high standard to meet. As one court held, probable cause for a wiretap application requires a "reasonable and common sense" evaluation of all of the facts:

> Under this standard, the question that must be decided in issuing a warrant is whether there is probable cause to believe that evidence of a crime will be uncovered. Obviously, certainty is not required at this stage, and the exact quantum of support required has frequently been described as "a fair probability," but more than a "mere suspicion," that such evidence will be discovered. Facts can amount to a fair probability without being proof beyond a reasonable doubt or even a prima facie showing.[125]

In other words, although a court need not be certain that the wiretap will uncover evidence of a crime, law enforcement must make a substantial showing in order to obtain a wiretap order.

A wiretap order may be authorized for no longer than thirty days.[126] If law enforcement needs an extension, then it must seek an extension of up to thirty days. As one federal appeals court stated, the Wiretap Act intends law enforcement "to adopt minimization techniques to reduce to a practical minimum the interception of conversations unrelated to the criminal activity under investigation."[127]

Although the Wiretap Act traditionally applied to the interception of phone calls, it also limits the ability of private parties and law enforcement to intercept

---

122 18 U.S.C. § 2518(3).
123 *Id.*
124 *Id.*
125 United States v. Alfano, 838 F. 2d 158, 161–62 (6th Cir. 1988).
126 18 U.S.C. § 2518(5).
127 United States v. Carey, No. 14–50222 (9th Cir. Sept. 7, 2016) (internal quotation marks and citation omitted).

electronic communications while in transit. Accordingly, the Wiretap Act applies not only to phone calls, but to email messages, instant messages, text messages, and other communications that are intercepted while in transit.[128]

The Cybersecurity Act of 2015, discussed above, has the potential to significantly enhance the ability of private entities to monitor systems and networks for cybersecurity threats. As discussed above, the Cybersecurity Act allows organizations to monitor their systems and networks – and the systems and networks of others who have provided consent – for "cybersecurity purposes," which is intended to protect systems from a cybersecurity threat or security vulnerability.

Consider a large Internet service provider that constantly confronts malware that slows down its systems and threatens the online security of its customers. The Cybersecurity Act of 2015 enables the ISP to monitor the email and other communications of its users, to the extent that this monitoring is conducted exclusively for "cybersecurity purposes." Because the law was recently passed, we do not yet have clear guidance from courts as to how they will interpret the phrases "cybersecurity purpose," "cybersecurity threat," and "security vulnerability." Even if courts do adopt a broad interpretation of the phrase, companies must ensure that *all* scanning is conducted for that purpose, and that cybersecurity is not merely a pretext for another reason for monitoring.

7.2.3 Pen Register Act

As described in Section 7.1, the United States Supreme Court has held that the Fourth Amendment does not restrict the government's use of pen registers to obtain noncontent information, such as logs of telephone numbers and other metadata. In response to this ruling, Congress in 1986 passed Chapter 206 of ECPA, known as the Pen Register Act.

The Pen Register Act restricts the collection of noncontent communications data by the government and private parties. The statute applies to "pen registers," which it defines as devices or processes that record "dialing, routing, addressing, or signaling information" of a wire or electronic communication.[129] It also applies to "trap and trace devices," which record the metadata of incoming communications.[130]

The Pen Register Act does not apply to the contents of communications – those are regulated under the Stored Communications Act and Wiretap Act. In 2001, as part of the PATRIOT Act, Congress amended the Pen Register Act to clarify that it applies to the metadata of electronic communications, such as email. However, the subject line of emails is typically considered to be content, and therefore is not covered by the Pen Register Act.

---

128 *See* Luis v. Zang, No. 14–3601 (6th Cir. Aug. 16, 2016).
129 18 U.S.C. § 3127.
130 *Id.*

The Pen Register Act imposes a general prohibition[131] on the use of pen register and trap and trace devices, with a few key exceptions:

- if the pen register or trap and trace device is related to the "operation, maintenance, and testing" of a communications service;[132]
- if the pen register or trap and trace device is related to the protection of the communications providers or their users to keep the service fee of abuse or unlawful service use;[133]
- if the user has consented;[134] or
- if the government has obtained a court order under Section 3123 of the Pen Register Act.[135]

Section 3123 does *not* require the government to demonstrate probable cause that a crime has occurred or will occur. Instead, law enforcement must satisfy the more lenient requirement of demonstrating that "information likely to be obtained by such installation and use is relevant to an ongoing criminal investigation."[136]

A Section 3123 order must specify the identity of the person to whom a telephone line or facility is leased, the identity of the person who is the subject of the investigation, the attributes of the communications to which the order applies, and a statement of the offense to which the information likely to be obtained by the device relates.[137] The orders may not exceed sixty days and may be extended by new court order for up to sixty days.[138] Communications providers are prohibited from disclosing the existence of a pen register or trap and trace order unless directed by the issuing court.[139]

7.2.4 National Security Letters

Among the most controversial aspects of the 2001 USA PATRIOT Act, passed after the September 11, 2001, terrorist attacks, was an expansion of the government's ability to issue national security letters. National security letters are administrative subpoenas that allow the government to secretly obtain certain information relevant to national security investigations. It has since been amended modestly to address some concerns of privacy advocates.

---

131 18 U.S.C. § 3121.
132 18 U.S.C. § 3121(b)(1).
133 18 U.S.C. § 3121(b)(2).
134 18 U.S.C. § 3121(b)(3).
135 18 U.S.C. § 3121(a).
136 18 U.S.C. § 3123(a)(1).
137 18 U.S.C. § 3123(b)(1).
138 18 U.S.C. § 3123(c).
139 18 U.S.C. § 3123(d).

The National Security Letter provision of the Stored Communications Act[140] allows the Federal Bureau of Investigation to provide a wire or electronic communication service provider with a name, phone number, or account number and request the associated name, address, length of service, and local and long-distance toll billing records of that person or account. Rather than obtain court approval, an FBI official need only certify in writing that "the name, address, length of service, and toll billing records sought are relevant to an authorized investigation to protect against international terrorism or clandestine intelligence activities."[141] If the request does not include local and long-distance toll billing records, the FBI need only certify that the *information* sought is relevant to an authorized investigation to protect against international terrorism or clandestine intelligence activities. The national security letter may not be issued solely due to an individual's First Amendment protected activities (e.g., organizing a lawful protest).[142]

The National Security Letter statute prohibits communications service providers from revealing the existence of a national security letter to any person, provided that the FBI certifies that the absence of a disclosure prohibition would result in a danger to U.S. national security, interference with a criminal, counterterrorism, or counterintelligence investigation, interference with diplomatic relations, or danger to the life or physical safety of any person.[143] If a communications provider receives such a nondisclosure order, it is permitted to disclose the existence of the national security letter to people to whom disclosure is necessary for compliance, an attorney to receive legal advice, or others approved by the FBI.[144] Individuals to whom the providers have disclosed the existence of a national security letter also are bound by the gag order.[145]

In 2006 and 2015, Congress amended the National Security Letter statute to allow for a limited form of judicial review.[146] If a service provider receives a nondisclosure order associated with a national security letter, it may notify the government that it wishes to have a court review the order, or filed a petition for review in federal court. Within thirty days of receiving notification, the government must ask a federal court for an order prohibiting disclosure.[147] The application must include a certification from a senior Justice Department

---

140 18 U.S.C. § 2709. The PATRIOT Act also amended the Gramm-Leach-Bliley Act to allow national security letters for financial records, 12 U.S.C. § 3414(a)(5)(A), and the Fair Credit Reporting Act to allow national security letters for consumer reports, 15 U.S.C. § 1681u.
141 18 U.S.C. § 2709(b)(1).
142 18 U.S.C. § 2709(b)(2).
143 18 U.S.C. § 2709(c)(1).
144 18 U.S.C. § 2709(c)(2).
145 *Id.*
146 18 U.S.C. § 3511.
147 18 U.S.C. § 3511(b)(1)(B).

or FBI official explaining why an absence of a prohibition on disclosure may result in a danger to U.S. national security, interference with a criminal, counterterrorism, or counterintelligence investigation, interference with diplomatic relations, or danger to the life or physical safety of any person.[148] The federal court will approve the nondisclosure order only if it agrees with the government's allegations in its application.[149]

7.3 Communications Assistance for Law Enforcement Act (CALEA)

This chapter has examined the limits on the government's ability to obtain information about individuals' communications. If the government is permitted to obtain the information, it still must have cooperation from communications providers, such as phone companies and Internet service providers.

That's where the Communications Assistance for Law Enforcement Act (CALEA)[150] comes in. The statute, passed in 1994, requires telecommunications carriers to assist law enforcement in conducting electronic surveillance under lawful warrants and court orders.

The Federal Communications Commission, which enforces CALEA, has broadly applied CALEA's requirements not only to traditional phone companies like AT&T and Verizon but also to Voice Over Internet Protocol and broadband service providers.[151]

CALEA requires telecommunications providers that "provide a customer or subscriber with the ability to originate, terminate, or direct communications" to ensure that their systems and networks are capable of expeditiously assisting the government in conducting lawfully authorized electronic surveillance.[152]

CALEA also requires telecommunications providers to secure their law enforcement assistant technology to "ensure that any interception of communications or access to call-identifying information effected within its switching premises can be activated only in accordance with a court order or other lawful authorization and with the affirmative intervention of an individual officer or employee of the carrier acting in accordance with regulations prescribed by the Commission."[153]

---

148 *Id.*
149 *Id.*
150 47 U.S.C. §§ 1001–10.
151 In the Matter of Communications Assistance for Law Enforcement Act and Broadband Access and Services, ET Docket No. 04–295 (May 12, 2006).
152 47 U.S.C. § 1002.
153 47 U.S.C. § 1004.

The FCC has stated that telecommunications are free to develop their own solutions to ensure that their systems comply with CALEA's requirements.[154]

CALEA's requirements are limited to telecommunications providers. The requirements do not apply to information services or telecommunications equipment.[155] Nor does CALEA require telecommunications carriers to help the government decrypt communications, unless the carrier provided the encryption and possesses the key or other information necessary to decrypt.[156]

7.4   Encryption and the All Writs Act

Among the most prominent cyber-related surveillance disputes in recent years has involved government access to encrypted communications. This is not a new debate; indeed, in the 1990s, the government failed in its attempt to require technology companies to include a "backdoor" to allow law enforcement access to encrypted communications. The debate re-emerged in 2016, as encryption was the default setting on a number of smartphones and mobile apps. The FBI and state and local law enforcement increasingly became concerned that even if they had a lawful warrant, supported by probable cause, to search a mobile device, they would be unable to do so because the data was encrypted.

The issue received national prominence in early 2016, during the government's investigation of a San Bernardino shooting that killed fourteen people. The government sought to obtain information from the iPhone of one of the two shooters, Syed Riswan Farook, who had died during the shooting. The phone was owned by Farook's employer, and the FBI obtained a search warrant for the phone. However, the government was unable to access the content on the phone because it was locked with a passcode. Normally, the FBI could circumvent this passcode by using a "brute force" attack that automatically enters all combinations of numbers until it gains access. However, this iPhone operating system is equipped with a function that automatically wipes data from a device after ten unsuccessful attempts at entering a password. The government requested that a California federal court order Apple to assist it in disabling the auto-wipe function from the device.

---

154 *See* Federal Communications Commission, Communications Assistance for Law Enforcement Act website ("A telecommunications carrier may comply with CALEA in different ways. First, the carrier may develop its own compliance solution for its unique network. Second, the carrier may purchase a compliance solution from vendors, including the manufacturers of the equipment it is using to provide the service. Third, the carrier may purchase a compliance solution from a trusted third party (TPP).").
155 47 U.S.C. § 1002(b)(2).
156 47 U.S.C. § 1002(b)(3).

No statute explicitly requires Apple to assist the government with carrying out a search warrant, as there is not an equivalent of CALEA for device makers. Rather, the government sought this order under the All Writs Act, a statute that states that "all courts established by Act of Congress may issue all writs necessary or appropriate in aid of their respective jurisdictions and agreeable to the usages and principles of law."[157] The United States Supreme Court has stated that this statute is "a residual source of authority to issue writs that are not otherwise covered by statute."[158] In other words, the government sought to use the All Writs Act as a catchall statute to order Apple to help it carry out a search warrant.

No binding appellate court ruling had explicitly required a company such as Apple to help the government defeat encryption. The government relied largely on a 1977 United States Supreme Court case, *United States v. New York Telephone Co.*,[159] in which the Court held that the All Writs Act requires a phone company to assist the FBI with carrying out a pen register order. The Court concluded that the Act extends "to persons who, though not parties to the original action or engaged in wrongdoing, are in a position to frustrate the implementation of a court order or the proper administration of justice, ... and encompasses even those who have not taken any affirmative action to hinder justice."[160] Courts also have held that the All Writs Act requires, among other things, credit card companies to provide records to law enforcement[161] and landlords to provide law enforcement with security camera footage.[162]

Apple vigorously opposed the federal government's attempts to require it to assist in breaking the security protections on the San Bernardino shooter's iPhone. Apple argued that the FBI's request goes beyond just asking for passive assistance in carrying out a pen register order; the government's request would require that Apple write software code to circumvent a security protection. That type of compelled speech, Apple argued, would violate the First Amendment. The California court never had an opportunity to rule on the dispute because in March 2016, the federal government withdrew its request for a court order. The government stated that a third party had assisted the FBI in accessing the content on the device, though it did not provide further details.

Although the California court never ruled on the high-profile dispute, a federal judge in Brooklyn ruled in 2016 that the All Writs Act does not require Apple to assist law enforcement in accessing an iPhone. In that case, the

---

157 28 U.S.C. § 1651(a).
158 Pennsylvania Bureau of Correction v. United States Marshals Service, 474 U.S. 34, 43 (1985).
159 United States v. New York Telephone Co., 434 U.S. 159 (1977).
160 *Id.* at 174.
161 United States v. Hall, 583 F. Supp. 717 (E.D. Va. 1984).
162 *In re* Application of United States for an Order Directing X to Provide Access to Videotapes, No. 03–89 (D. Md. Aug. 22, 2003) (unpublished).

federal Drug Enforcement Agency received a warrant to search the residence of a drug-trafficking suspect. Among the items that the agents obtained in the search was an iPhone 5s.[163] The government then obtained a warrant to search the iPhone. The government requested Apple's technical assistance to unlock the phone, and Apple said that it would only provide the assistance if it was ordered to do so by a court. The government requested a court order under the All Writs Act, and Apple opposed the request, arguing that the statute does not require Apple to write code to help circumvent the device's security features.

The U.S. District Court for the Eastern District of New York rejected the government's application for an order compelling Apple's assistance. Central to the court's ruling was the fact that Congress passed CALEA, which requires telecommunications carriers to assist law enforcement in carrying out search warrants but explicitly excludes "information service providers" such as Apple. If Congress had intended to require companies such as Apple to assist law enforcement, the court reasoned, Congress would have explicitly included the companies within the scope of CALEA or a similar statute. The court reasoned that if it were to adopt the government's broad reading of the All Writs Act, it would transform the statute "from a limited gap-filling statute that ensures the smooth functioning of the judiciary itself into a mechanism for upending the separation of powers by delegating to the judiciary a legislative power bounded only by Congress's superior ability to prohibit or preempt."[164]

The court noted that the All Writs Act was enacted by the First Congress in 1789, during a time when the Founders carefully divided powers among the three branches of government. The court stated that it was difficult to imagine the Founders passing the All Writs Act with the intention of providing the executive branch with such broad powers. "The government's interpretation of the breadth of authority the AWA confers on courts of limited jurisdiction thus raises serious doubts about how such a statute could withstand constitutional scrutiny under the separation of power's doctrine," the court wrote. "It would attribute to the First Congress an anomalous diminishment of its own authority (to deny a request to increase the executive's investigative powers it deemed inadvisable simply by declining to enact it) as well as an equally implausible intention to confer essentially unlimited legislative powers on the judiciary."[165]

The Eastern District of New York opinion, while emphatic, is not binding on any court. Accordingly, there is a chance that another court – including an

---

163 *In re* Order Requiring Apple, Inc. to Assist in the Execution of a Search Warrant Issued by This Court, No. 15-MC-1902 (JO) (E.D.N.Y. Feb. 29, 2016).
164 *Id.*
165 *Id.*

appellate court, which issues binding opinions – could view the All Writs Act in a more expansive light. Moreover, many law enforcement advocates are pushing Congress to pass a CALEA-like law that would explicitly require companies such as Apple to assist law enforcement with unlocking devices. In short, it is likely that the debate about technology companies' compelled assistance to law enforcement will continue to be a hotly debated issue in the judicial, legislative, and executive branches.

8

Cybersecurity and Federal Government Contractors

Federal government contracting is a multi-billion-dollar industry in the United States. Companies provide a wide range of services to the federal government, ranging from information technology to janitorial services to management consulting. To the extent that any of these businesses exchange data with the federal government, they must comply with a wide range of cybersecurity laws and regulations.

In recent years, Congress and federal agencies have intensified their scrutiny of contractors' cybersecurity practices, in the aftermath of contractor Edward Snowden's leak of massive volumes of classified National Security Agency documents and the breach of millions of Americans' security clearance applications with the Office of Personnel Management. This chapter provides a broad overview of the laws and regulations that are most likely to affect the cybersecurity of government contractors.

In short, cybersecurity requirements for government contractors depend on the types of information they handle. All contractors that handle federal government information systems must comply with the recently overhauled Federal Information Security Management Act and the National Institute of Standards and Technology's *Special Publication 800-53*, which sets baseline requirements for cybersecurity of government information. Contractors that handle classified information must comply with much more stringent requirements set by the Defense Security Service in the *National Industrial Security Program Operating Manual* (*NISPOM*). Recently, government regulators have created new requirements for contractors that handle information that, while not classified, is considered sensitive enough to warrant protections beyond those in

Cybersecurity Law, First Edition. Jeff Kosseff.
© 2017 John Wiley & Sons, Inc. Published 2017 by John Wiley & Sons, Inc.
Companion Website: www.wiley.com/go/kosseff/cybersecurity

Special Publication 800-53. This new category, known as controlled unclassified information (CUI), likely will result in many federal contractors being required to significantly strengthen their cybersecurity practices.

8.1 Federal Information Security Management Act

In 2002, Congress passed the Federal Information Security Management Act (FISMA),[1] which established a framework for agencies to manage their information security. In 2014, in light of the tremendously more complex web of cybersecurity threats, Congress overhauled FISMA with the passage of the Federal Information Security Modernization Act of 2014.[2] FISMA's requirements affect not only the information security of government agencies but also their contractors and subcontractors.

FISMA delegates a great deal of responsibility for cybersecurity to individual federal departments and agencies, but it also centralizes many cybersecurity functions within the Office of Management and Budget and Department of Homeland Security. The Office of Management and Budget is charged with developing government-wide information security policies, standards, and guidelines, requiring agencies to adopt adequate information security protections, and coordinating with the National Institute of Standards and Technology on standards and guidelines (discussed below).[3] The Department of Homeland Security is responsible for developing government-wide requirements on reporting security incidents, for annual agency cybersecurity reports, for risk mitigation requirements, for monitoring agency information security, and for providing operational and technical assistance to agencies.[4]

The updated FISMA also requires federal agency heads to take a number of steps to increase their agencies' cybersecurity. Among the responsibilities of each agency head are the following:

- Implementing information security protections that are commensurate "with the risk and magnitude of the harm resulting from unauthorized access, use, disclosure, disruption, modification, or destruction of" information collected, used, or maintained by the agency or a contractor.
- Ensuring that senior agency officials conduct information security risk assessments, implement necessary protections, and periodically test and evaluate information security controls.
- Delegating information security compliance authority to agency chief information officers.

---

1 44 U.S.C. 3552 *et seq.*
2 P.L. 113-283.
3 44 U.S.C. 3553.
4 *Id.*

- Overseeing agency information security training.
- Annually reporting on the effectiveness of agency information security controls.
- Holding all personnel accountable for complying with an agency-wide information security program.[5]

FISMA requires each agency to develop a comprehensive information security program that contains the following elements:

- Periodic risk assessments.
- Policies and procedures that are based on the risk assessments.
- Subordinate plans for information security.
- Security training for agency employees and contractors.
- Annual testing and evaluation of information security policies and procedures.
- Remedial action to correct security flaws.
- Security incident detection, reporting, and response procedures.
- Continuity of operations plans for information systems.[6]

Notably, the updated FISMA requires agencies to "expeditiously" notify the House and Senate Judiciary Committees of data breaches.[7] The notices must be provided within thirty days of discovery of the breach, and must include:

- a general description of the breach,
- an estimate of the number of individuals whose information was disclosed,
- an assessment of the risk of harm to those individuals,
- a description of any circumstances that require a delay in notifying affected individuals, and
- an estimate of when the agency will notify individuals.[8]

8.2 NIST Information Security Controls for Government Agencies and Contractors

FISMA delegates responsibility for specific information security standards to the National Institute of Standards and Technology (NIST), an agency within the U.S. Department of Commerce. NIST has produced a number of detailed standards for various aspects of information security at government agencies and their contractors. Perhaps the two most influential NIST documents are

---

5 44 U.S.C. 3354.
6 *Id.*
7 44 U.S.C. 3358.
8 *Id.*

Federal Information Processing Standards 200 and *NIST Special Publication 800-53 (SP 800-53)*, which set baseline requirements for information security controls. These documents constitute the baseline information security standard for the federal government and its contractors and subcontractors that operate federal information systems. More sensitive information, such as classified information and defense information, is covered by even more stringent requirements, discussed later in the chapter.

Under *FIPS 200*, agencies and contractors must implement minimum information security requirements. To implement these minimum information security requirements, agencies and contractors must select from security controls that are listed in *SP 800-53*. *SP 800-53* is nearly 500 pages, and details dozens of security controls. Organizations select from the menu of controls based on whether their information systems are classified as low-impact, moderate-impact, or high-impact (with higher impact systems receiving the more stringent controls). Below is a list of the seventeen minimum information security requirements from *FIPS 200*, along with some of the corresponding categories of security controls as stated in *SP 800-53*:

- *Access control.* Agencies and contractors must ensure that only authorized users, processes, and devices are permitted to access information systems. Security control categories include the following:
  - Access control policy and procedures
  - Account management
  - Access enforcement
  - Information flow enforcement
  - Separation of duties
  - Least privilege
  - Unsuccessful log-on attempts
  - System use notification
  - Previous logon notification
  - Concurrent session control
  - Session lock
  - Session termination
  - Supervision and review of access control
  - Permitted actions without identification or authentication
  - Security attributes
  - Remote access
  - Wireless access
  - Mobile access
  - External information system use
  - Information sharing
  - Publicly accessible content
  - Data mining protection

- *Awareness and training.* Agencies and contractors must ensure that managers and personnel are adequately trained regarding information security. Security control categories include the following:
  - Security awareness and training policy and procedures
  - Role-based security training
  - Security training records
  - Contacts with security groups and associations
- *Audit and accountability.* System audit records must enable monitoring, analysis, investigation, and reporting of unauthorized activity on an information system. Actions must be traceable to individual users. Security control categories include the following:
  - Audit and accountability policy and procedures
  - Audit events
  - Content of audit records
  - Audit storage capacity
  - Response to audit processing failures
  - Audit review, analysis, and reporting
  - Time stamps
  - Protection of audit information
  - Nonrepudiation
  - Session audit
  - Cross-organizational audit
- *Certification, accreditation, and security assessments.* Periodic assessments of security controls will determine whether the current systems are effective and suggest corrections for deficiencies. Security control categories include the following:
  - Security assessments
  - System interconnections
  - Security certification
  - Continuous monitoring
  - Penetration testing
- *Configuration management.* Federal agencies and contractors must establish and maintain baseline inventories and configurations of hardware, software, firmware, and other information systems. Security control categories include the following:
  - Baseline configuration
  - Configuration change control
  - Security impact analysis
  - Least functionality
  - Information system component inventory
  - Software usage restrictions
  - User-installed software
- *Contingency planning.* Agencies and contractors are required to develop plans for operating information systems during emergencies, such as natural

disaster, to ensure continuity of operations. Security control categories include the following:
- Contingency plan
- Contingency training
- Contingency plan testing
- Alternate storage site
- Information system backup

- ***Identification and authentication.*** Authorized users (and their devices and processes) must be accurately identified in order to prevent unauthorized access. Security control categories include the following:
  - Identification and authentication of organizational users
  - Device identification and authentication
  - Identifier management
  - Service identification and authentication

- ***Incident response.*** Agencies and contractors must develop comprehensive plans to detect, contain, and respond to information security incidents and to report incidents to the appropriate officials and authorities. Security control categories include the following:
  - Incident response training
  - Incident response testing
  - Incident handling
  - Incident monitoring
  - Incident reporting
  - Incident response plan

- ***Maintenance.*** Agencies and contractors must regularly maintain their information systems and security controls. Security control categories include the following:
  - Maintenance tools
  - Maintenance personnel
  - Timely maintenance

- ***Media protection.*** Agencies and contractors must limit access to information system media to authorized users and permanently wipe information systems media before disposal. Security control categories include the following:
  - Media access
  - Media storage
  - Media sanitization
  - Media use
  - Media downgrading

- ***Physical and environmental protection.*** Physical access to information systems must be restricted to authorized individuals. Organizations also must protect their information systems from environmental hazards and ensure that they have adequate environmental controls in the physical

facilities that contain information systems. Security control categories include the following:
- Physical access authorization
- Monitoring physical access
- Visitor access records
- Emergency power
- Fire protection
- Temperature and humidity controls
- Water damage protection
- ***Planning.***   Information security plans must describe the security controls that the agency or contractor has implemented as well as the rules of behavior for those who access the information systems. Security control categories include the following:
  - System security plan
  - Rules of behavior
  - Privacy impact assessment
  - Central management
- ***Personnel security.***   Agencies and contractors must take steps to ensure that employees and service providers who have access to information systems are trustworthy and meet specified security criteria. The organizations also should ensure that when an employee or service provider is transferred or terminated, the information systems are protected, and that personnel are formally sanctioned for failing to comply with information security policies and procedures. Security control categories include the following:
  - Personnel screening
  - Access agreements
  - Third-party personnel security
- ***Risk assessment.***   Agencies and contractors must periodically conduct assessments of their information security, considering their operations, assets, and individuals. Security control categories include the following:
  - Security categorization
  - Vulnerability scanning
  - Technical surveillance countermeasures survey
- ***System and services acquisition.***   Agencies and contractors must ensure that they have sufficient resources for information security, use a system development life cycle process for information security, restrict use and installation of software, and ensure that their third-party providers maintain adequate information security. Security control categories include the following:
  - Allocation of resources
  - Acquisition process
  - Software usage restrictions
  - User-installed software

– Developer configuration management
– Tamper resistance and detection

- *System and communications protection.* Organizations must monitor and protect their information systems at external boundaries and key internal boundaries, and employ architectural designs, software development techniques, and systems engineering principles that promote information security. Security control categories include the following:
  – Security function isolation
  – Denial of service protection
  – Boundary protection
  – Transmission confidentiality
  – Cryptographic key establishment and management
  – Session authenticity
  – Covert channel analysis

- *System and information integrity.* Agencies and contractors are required to identify, report, and correct flaws in the information system; protect information systems from malicious code; and monitor security alerts and advisories and respond appropriately. Security control categories include the following:

  – Flaw remediation
  – Malicious code protection
  – Information system monitoring
  – Software, firmware, and information integrity
  – Predictable failure prevention

8.3 Classified Information Cybersecurity

In addition to the general cybersecurity requirements of *FIPS 200* and *SP 800-53*, contractors face heightened requirements if they are dealing with sensitive government information. The most restrictive requirements apply to contractors that handle classified information.

Cybersecurity requirements for contractors that handle classified government information are set by the Defense Security Service (DSS). DSS publishes the *National Industrial Security Program Operating Manual* (*NISPOM*), which sets the rules for industry's access to classified information.

Chapter 8 of *NISPOM* establishes the information security requirements for contractor information systems that are used to capture, create, store, process, or distribute classified information. Among the key requirements of Chapter 8 are the following:

- *Information security program.* The contractor must maintain a risk-based set of management, operational, and technical controls, including policies and procedures to reduce security risks, information security training for all users, testing and evaluation of all security policies and procedures, incident detection and response plans, continuity of operations plans, and a self-inspection plan.

- *System security plan.* The contractor must have a system security plan that documents its information security protections and controls, and includes supporting documentation (e.g., a risk assessment, plan of action, and configuration checklist).

- *IS security manager.* The contractor must designate a qualified IS security manager who is responsible for implementing the IS program, monitoring compliance, verifying self-inspections, certifying in writing that the system security plan has been implemented and controls are in place, briefing users on their information security responsibilities and ensuring necessary training.

- *Information system users.* All users are required to comply with the security program, be accountable for their actions on an information system, not share authentication mechanisms, protect authentication mechanisms at the highest classification level and most restrictive category of information to which that mechanism permits access, and be subject to monitoring of activity on a classified network.

- *Assessment and authorization.* Contractors must work with the government agency to assess security controls in order to receive an authorization to handle classified information. A contractor will be re-evaluated for authorization to handle classified information at least once every three years. All security-related changes must be approved in advance by the government agency.

- *Systems and services controls.* Contractors must allocate "sufficient resources" to information security. As part of their routine assessment and self-inspection, contractors must assess and monitor security controls.

- *Risk assessment.* Contractors must conduct a comprehensive risk assessment, categorizing the potential impact level for confidentiality based on the information's classification, and monitoring changes to the information system that may affect security.

- *Personnel security.* Employees who access classified systems must meet the security requirements (e.g., a clearance). Once an employee no longer requires access to the system, the authentication credentials must be disabled. The contractor must review audit logs to determine whether any employees fail to comply with security policies.

- *Physical and environmental protection.* Contractors must limit physical access to information systems, protect the physical plant, and protect against environmental hazards.

- *Configuration management.* Contractors must implement baseline configurations and information system inventories.

- *Maintenance.* Contractors must perform necessary maintenance, such as patch management, and provide controls on the tools and personnel used for the maintenance
- *Integrity.* Contractors must protect systems from malicious code.
- *Media protection.* Contractors must mark all media with level of authorization until a classification review is conducted, and limit access to the classified information.
- *Incident response.* Contractors must implement incident detection processes and immediately report any incidents to government agencies.
- *Authentication and access.* Contractors must identify users, authenticate them, and limit access to authorized users, accounting to the types of transactions and functions to which each user is permitted access.
- *Audit and accountability.* Contractors must create audit records to enable monitoring of activity on their systems.
- *System and communications protection.* Contractors must monitor, control, and protect organizational communications.

In 2011, as cyber threats to classified information increased in frequency and magnitude, President Obama issued Executive Order 13587, entitled Structure Reforms to Improve the Security of Classified Networks and the Responsible Sharing and Safeguarding of Classified Information. The executive order seeks to "ensure coordinated interagency development and reliable implementation of policies and minimum standards regarding information security, personnel security, and systems security; address both internal and external security threats and vulnerabilities; and provide policies and minimum standards for sharing classified information both within and outside the Federal Government."

The executive order requires all agencies that operate or access classified computer networks to designate a senior official for classified information sharing and safeguarding, implement an insider threat detection and prevention program, and perform self-assessments of compliance. In response to the executive order, DSS amended *NISPOM* in May 2016 to require contractors that handle classified information to create an insider threat program. Contractors must create an insider threat program plan that describes:

- the contractor's capability to gather relevant insider threat information;
- the contractor's procedures to report that an individual potentially poses an insider threat; to deter employees from becoming insider threats; and to mitigate insider threat risks; and
- corporate-wide plans to address requirements for cleared facilities.

Contractors must conduct annual self-inspections and certifications of their insider threat programs, and they must report behaviors that indicate insider threats. They also must implement a system or process that identifies negligence or carelessness in handling classified information. Contractors are further required to provide insider threat awareness training to all cleared employees at least once a year.

8.4 Covered Defense Information and Controlled Unclassified Information

Even if information is not classified, it may be subject to more stringent cyber-security requirements if it is sufficiently sensitive. In 2010, President Obama issued Executive Order 13556, which called for adequate safeguards of "controlled unclassified information" (CUI), which it defined as "unclassified information throughout the executive branch that requires safeguarding or dissemination controls[.]" The National Archives and Records Administration (NARA) is responsible for implementing the safeguards throughout the executive branch, and as of publication of this book was finalizing its rules for handling of CUI.

Additionally, in 2015, the Defense Department overhauled its contractor cybersecurity rules for its sensitive, yet unclassified information.[9] The rules apply to agencies and contractors that handle "covered defense information," which is the Defense Department's version of CUI. The Defense Department's regulations define "covered defense information" as unclassified information that falls into one of the following categories:

- Controlled technical information, which is defined as "technical information with military or space application that is subject to controls on the access, use, reproduction, modification, performance, display, release disclosure, or dissemination."
- Critical information, which are specific facts identified through operations security process about "friendly intentions, capabilities, and activities vitally needed by adversaries for them to plan and act effectively so as to guarantee failure or unacceptable consequences for friendly mission accomplishment."
- Export control of unclassified information regarding items, commodities, technology, or software "whose export could reasonably be expected to adversely affect the United States national security and nonproliferation objectives."
- Other information identified in the contract "that requires safeguarding or dissemination controls pursuant to and consistent with laws, regulations, and Governmentwide policies."

---

9 DEPARTMENT OF DEFENSE, DEFENSE ACQUISITION REGULATIONS SUPPLEMENT: NETWORK PENETRATION REPORTING AND CONTRACTING FOR CLOUD SERVICES, 80 Fed. Reg. 51739 (Aug. 26, 2015).

In practice, "covered defense information" is so broad that it can include virtually all aspects of a defense contractor's business, even its contract with the Defense Department. Even if a defense contractor does not handle any classified information, it likely is covered by these new cybersecurity rules. For that reason, the new regulations were met with significant consternation among the defense contracting community.

The two primary requirements of the new Defense Department regulations are an expedited security incident reporting requirement and compliance with a more stringent NIST security framework for sensitive but unclassified information. Under the new regulations, contractors and subcontractors that handle covered defense information are required to "rapidly report" cyber incidents to the Defense Department within 72 hours of discovery.[10] This is among the shortest breach reporting requirements in the United States, and it puts significant pressure on defense contractors to quickly gather the necessary information after discovering an incident.

The regulations broadly define "cyber incident" as "actions taken through the use of computer networks that result in an actual or potentially adverse effect on an information system and/or the information residing therein."[11] Accordingly, the reporting requirement applies not only to data breaches, but any attacks or incidents that could harm covered defense information on the contractor's network or systems.

The new regulations also require contractors and subcontractors handling covered defense information to comply with NIST's *Special Publication 800-171 (SP 800-171), Protecting Controlled Unclassified Information in Nonfederal Information Systems and Organizations.* As seen below, *SP 800-171*'s requirements are far more extensive than the general contractor requirements under *SP 800-53*. After defense contractors voiced a great deal of concern regarding compliance with *SP 800-171*, the Defense Department agreed to allow contractors until December 31, 2017, to get into compliance with the new standard.

NARA's proposed rule would require contractors that handle CUI also to comply with *SP 800-171*. Moreover, in August 2015, the Office of Management and Budget issued proposed guidance in which it instructs agencies to require contractors that handle CUI to comply with *SP 800-171*. In short, *SP 800-171* will eventually become the de facto cybersecurity standard for many federal contractors.

Below are the key security requirements of the new standard for contractors that handle covered defense information, as stated in *SP 800-171*:

- *Access control.*
  - Limit information system access to authorized users, processes acting on behalf of authorized users, or devices (including other information systems).

---

10 48 C.F.R. 252.204-7012.
11 *Id.*

- Limit information system access to types of transactions and functions that authorized users are permitted to execute.
- Control the flow of (controlled unclassified information, or "CUI") in accordance with approved authorizations.
- Separate the duties of individuals to reduce the risk of malevolent activity without collusion.
- Employ the principle of least privilege, including for specific security functions and privileged accounts.
- Use nonprivileged accounts or roles when accessing nonsecurity functions.
- Prevent nonprivileged users from executing privileged functions and audit the execution of such functions.
- Limit unsuccessful logon attempts.
- Provide privacy and security notices consistent with applicable CUI rules.
- User session lock with pattern-hiding displays to prevent access/viewing of data after period of inactivity.
- Terminate (automatically) a user session after a defined condition.
- Monitor and control remote access sessions.
- Employ cryptographic mechanisms to protect confidentiality of remote access sessions.
- Route remote access via managed access control points.
- Authorize remote execution of privileged commands and remote access to security-relevant information.
- Authorize wireless access prior to allowing such connections.
- Protect wireless access using authentication and encryption.
- Control connection of mobile devices.
- Encrypt CUI on mobile devices.
- Verify and control/limit connections to and use of external information systems.
- Limit use of organizational portable storage devices on external information systems.
- Control information posted or processed on publicly accessible information systems.
- *Awareness and training.*
  - Ensure that managers, systems administrators, and users of organizational information systems are made aware of the security risks associated with their activities and of the applicable policies, standards, and procedures related to the security of organizational information systems.
  - Ensure that organizational personnel are adequately trained to carry out their assigned information security-related duties and responsibilities.
  - Provide security awareness training on recognizing and reporting potential indicators of insider threat.
- *Audit and accountability.*
  - Create, protect, and retain information system audit records to the extent needed to enable the monitoring, analysis, investigation, and

reporting of unlawful, unauthorized, or inappropriate information system activity.
- Ensure that the actions of individual information system users can be uniquely traced to those users so that they can be held accountable for their actions.
- Review and update audited events.
- Alert in the event of an audit process failure.
- Correlate audit review, analysis, and reporting processes for investigation and response to indications of inappropriate, suspicious, or unusual activity.
- Provide audit reduction and report generation to support on-demand analysis and reporting.
- Provide an information system capability that compares and synchronizes internal system clocks with an authoritative source to generate time stamps for audit records.
- Protect audit information and audit tools from unauthorized access, modification, and deletion.
- Limit management of audit functionality to a subset of privileged users.
- *Configuration management.*
  - Establish and maintain baseline configurations and inventories of organizational information systems (e.g., hardware, software, firmware, and documentation) throughout the respective system development life cycles.
  - Establish and enforce security configuration settings for information technology projects employed in organizational information systems.
  - Track, review, approve/disapprove, and audit changes to information systems.
  - Analyze the security impact of changes prior to implementation.
  - Define, document, approve, and enforce physical and logical access restrictions associated with changes to the information system.
  - Employ the principle of least functionality by configuring the information system to provide only essential capabilities.
  - Restrict, disable, and prevent the use of nonessential programs, functions, ports, protocols, and services.
  - Apply denial-by-exception (blacklist) policy to prevent the use of unauthorized software or deny-all, permit-by-exception (whitelisting) policy to allow the execution of authorized software.
  - Control and monitor user-installed software.
- *Identification and authentication.*
  - Identify information system users, processes acting on behalf of users, or devices.
  - Authenticate (or verify) the identities of those users, processes, or devices, as a prerequisite to allowing access to organizational information systems.

- Use multifactor authentication for local and network access to privileged accounts and for network access to nonprivileged accounts. Employ replay-resistant authentication mechanisms for network access to privileged and nonprivileged accounts.
- Prevent reuse of identifiers for a defined period.
- Disable identifiers after a defined period of inactivity. Enforce a minimum password complexity and change of characters when new passwords are created.
- Prohibit password reuse for a specified number of generations.
- Allow temporary password use for system log-ons with an immediate change to a permanent password.
- Store and transmit only encrypted representation of passwords. Obscure feedback of authentication information.

- *Incident response.*
  - Establish an operational incident-handling capability for organizational information systems that includes adequate preparation, detection, analysis, containment, recovery, and user response activities.
  - Track, document, and report incidents to appropriate officials and/or authorities both internal and external to the organization.
  - Test the organizational incident response capability.

- *Maintenance.*
  - Perform maintenance on organizational information systems.
  - Provide effective controls on the tools, techniques, mechanisms, and personnel used to conduct information system maintenance.
  - Ensure equipment removed for off-site maintenance is sanitized of any CUI.
  - Check media containing diagnostic and test programs for malicious code before the media are used in the information system.
  - Require multifactor authentication to establish nonlocal maintenance sessions via external network connections and terminate such connections when nonlocal maintenance is complete.
  - Supervise the maintenance activities of maintenance personnel without required access authorization.

- *Media protection.*
  - Protect (i.e., physically control and securely store) information system media containing CUI, both paper and digital.
  - Limit access to CUI on information system media to authorized users.
  - Sanitize or destroy information system media containing CUI before disposal or release for reuse.
  - Mark media with necessary CUI markings and distribution limitations.
  - Control access to media containing CUI and maintain accountability for media during transport out of controlled areas.
  - Implement cryptographic mechanisms to protect the confidentiality of CUI stored on digital media during transport unless otherwise protected by alternative physical safeguards.

- Control the use of removable media on information system components.
- Prohibit the use of portable storage devices when such devices have no identifiable owner.
- Protect the confidentiality of backup CUI at storage locations.

- *Personnel security.*
  - Screen individuals prior to authorizing access to information systems containing CUI.
  - Ensure that CUI and information systems containing CUI are protected during and after personnel actions such as terminations and transfers.

- *Physical protection.*
  - Limit physical access to organizational information systems, equipment, and the respective operating environments to authorized individuals.
  - Protect and monitor the physical facility and support infrastructure for those information systems.
  - Escort visitors and monitor physical activity.
  - Maintain audit logs of physical access.
  - Control and manage physical access devices.
  - Enforce safeguarding measures for CUI at alternate work sites (e.g., telework sites).

- *Risk assessment.*
  - Periodically assess the risk to organizational operations (mission, functions, image, or reputation, etc.), organizational assets, and individuals, resulting from the operation of organizational information systems and the associated processing, storage, or transmission of CUI.
  - Scan for vulnerabilities in the information system and applications periodically and when new vulnerabilities affecting the system are identified.
  - Remediate vulnerabilities in accordance with assessments of risk.

- *Security assessment.*
  - Periodically assess the security controls in organizational information systems to determine if the controls are effective in their application. Develop and implement plans of action designed to correct deficiencies and reduce or eliminate vulnerabilities in organizational information systems.
  - Monitor information system security controls on an ongoing basis to ensure the continued effectiveness of the controls.

- *System and communications protection.*
  - Monitor, control, and protect organizational communications (i.e., information transmitted or received by organizational information systems) at the external boundaries and key internal boundaries of the information systems.
  - Employ architectural designs, software development techniques, and systems engineering principles that promote effective information security within organizational information systems.
  - Separate user functionality from information system management functionality.

– Prevent unauthorized and unintended information transfer via shared system resources.
– Implement subnetworks for publicly accessible system components that are physically or logically separated from internal networks.
– Deny network communications traffic by default and allow network communications traffic by exception (i.e., deny-all, permit-by-exception).
– Prevent remote devices from simultaneously establishing nonremote connections with the information system and communicating via some other connection to resources in external networks.
– Implement cryptographic mechanisms to prevent unauthorized disclosure of CUI during transmission unless otherwise protected by alternative physical safeguards.
– Terminate network connections associated with communications sessions at the end of the sessions or after a defined period of inactivity.
– Establish and manage cryptographic keys for cryptography when used to protect the confidentiality of CUI.
– Prohibit remote activation of collaborative computing devices, and provide indication of devices in use to users present at the device.
– Control and monitor the use of mobile code.
– Control and monitor the use of Voice over Internet Protocol (VoIP) technologies.
– Protect the authenticity of communications sessions.
– Protect the confidentiality of CUI at rest.

- *System and information integrity.*

– Identify, report, and correct information and information system flaws in a timely manner.
– Provide protection from malicious code at appropriate locations within organizational information systems.
– Monitor information system security alerts and advisories and take appropriate actions in response.
– Update malicious code protection mechanisms when new releases are available.
– Perform periodic scans of the information system and real-time scans of files from external sources as files are downloaded, opened, or executed.
– Monitor the information system including inbound and outbound communications traffic, to detect attacks and indicators of potential attacks.
– Identify unauthorized use of the information system.

9

Privacy Laws

Thus far we have focused primarily on laws that affect the security of data, systems, and networks, and the ability of the government and the private sector to conduct surveillance on this infrastructure to prevent cybercrime and other harms. However, an examination of cybersecurity law would be incomplete without an overview of privacy law.

Privacy law limits companies' collection, use, sharing, and retention of personal information. While data security laws provide the safeguards that companies must have in place to prevent hackers from accessing customer data, privacy law restricts companies' ability to use customer data. For instance, privacy law may prevent a company from selling customer web-browsing activities to third-party marketers, building customer profiles based on the videos they view online, or using facial recognition.

Some might argue that privacy law is outside of the scope of cybersecurity law, and they may be correct. At least under some conceptions of cybersecurity law, it is irrelevant how companies choose to legitimately use customer data. However, cybersecurity is an emerging field and there is not a single, settled definition. Nevertheless, privacy does often intersect with cybersecurity, and, consequently, all cybersecurity professionals should have a basic understanding of privacy legal principles.

Any examination of cybersecurity law would be incomplete without an overview of the legal restrictions on the use and disclosure of personal information.

Cybersecurity Law, First Edition. Jeff Kosseff.
© 2017 John Wiley & Sons, Inc. Published 2017 by John Wiley & Sons, Inc.
Companion Website: www.wiley.com/go/kosseff/cybersecurity

As with data security, the Federal Trade Commission regulates privacy under Section 5 of the FTC Act, which prohibits unfair and deceptive trade practices. However, the United States, unlike other jurisdictions, such as the European Union and Canada, does not have a general privacy law that applies to all companies. Instead, privacy regulation in the United States, like data security regulation, is a web of federal and state laws, some of which focus on specific industries or types of data. This chapter provides an overview of the regulation of privacy under Section 5 of the FTC Act, as well as the most prominent federal and state privacy laws that restrict the private sector's cyber-related use and disclosure of personal information.[1]

9.1   Section 5 of the FTC Act and Privacy

As described more thoroughly in Chapter 1, Section 5 of the Federal Trade Commission Act declares illegal "unfair or deceptive acts or practices in or affecting commerce."[2] The statute states that "unfair" practices are those that cause or are likely to cause "substantial injury to consumers which is not reasonably avoidable by consumers themselves and not outweighed by countervailing benefits to consumers or to competition."[3]

As with data security, the FTC has not promulgated privacy regulations under Section 5. Rather, it takes a case-by-case approach to determine whether a company's privacy practices are unfair or deceptive. In general, the FTC expects companies to disclose material aspects of the manner in which they handle personal data (i.e., if they share information with third parties) and to be honest in their statements about data processing (i.e., not to lie in their privacy policies). Transparency, full disclosure, and honesty are among the most important principles in complying with the FTC's privacy expectations. Unlike data protection regulators in other countries, the FTC does not impose a specific set of data privacy requirements on all companies.

The FTC most clearly articulated its privacy expectations in March 2012, when it issued a 73-page report, entitled *Protecting Consumer Privacy in an Era of Rapid Change.*[4] Although the report is not legally binding, it provides the best guidance to date as to the types of actions that companies can take to

---

1 This chapter is limited to privacy laws that impact *private sector* cybersecurity. This chapter does not cover privacy laws that apply primarily to government entities or schools (e.g., the Family Educational Rights and Privacy Act) or to practices that typically do not involve cyber (e.g., the Telephone Consumer Protection Act).

2 15 U.S.C. § 45(a)(1).

3 15 U.S.C. § 45(n).

4 FEDERAL TRADE COMMISSION, PROTECTING CONSUMER PRIVACY IN AN ERA OF RAPID CHANGE: RECOMMENDATIONS FOR BUSINESSES AND POLICYMAKERS (Mar. 2012).

reduce the chances of facing FTC enforcement actions regarding their privacy practices. The following are the principles in the FTC's report:

- ***Privacy by design.*** Companies should integrate privacy into every element of their organizations, products, and services. When developing new products and services, privacy and data security should be considered from the very start. Companies should consider limits on data collection, retention policies, data disposal practice, and data accuracy.
- ***Simplified consumer choice.*** A company must obtain affirmative consent from consumers if the company collects sensitive data or plans to use consumer data in a manner that is materially different from the manner in which the company claimed it would be used when it collected the data. However, the FTC does not believe that companies *always* need to obtain affirmative consent. If its practices "are consistent with the context of the transaction or the company's relationship with the consumer, or are required or specifically authorized by law," the company is not required to obtain consent, the FTC wrote.
- ***Privacy notices.*** The FTC recognizes the value in disclosing privacy practices via privacy notices (often known as "privacy policies" on websites). However, the Commission noted its concerns that privacy policies often are long and complex, and therefore not particularly useful to consumers. The FTC urged companies to make their privacy notices "clearer, shorter, and more standardized to enable better comprehension and comparison of privacy practices." The FTC urged companies to consider using some "standardized elements" to enable easier comparison.
- ***Access.*** The FTC believes that consumers should have reasonable access to the data that companies maintain regarding them, allowing the consumers to correct errors. The Commission stated that "consumer access should be proportional to the sensitivity and the intended use of the data at issue." If data is used only for marketing purposes, the FTC is less likely to conclude that consumers should be permitted to access it, as the costs of access likely would outweigh the consumer benefits. However, if the data is used to make individual determinations about a consumer's employability or creditworthiness, the FTC believes that consumers should have a right to access the data.
- ***Consumer education.*** Companies should educate consumers about their privacy practices. In particular, the FTC urges companies to provide consumers with information from the FTC's privacy and security websites and resources.

The FTC followed up on its Privacy Report in February 2013, when the FTC staff issued a report with best practices for mobile app privacy.[5] The mobile report contained privacy recommendations for app platforms (e.g., the iTunes store and mobile operating systems) and app developers (the creators of the

---

5 FTC Staff Report, Mobile Privacy Disclosures, Building Trust through Transparency (Feb. 2013).

apps). Although the report does not constitute binding law, it provides a good indication of the FTC's privacy expectations for mobile apps.

In the mobile report, the FTC staff stated that the app platforms should consider the following features for its apps and privacy disclosures:

- Just-in-time disclosures and opt-in consent before allowing apps to collect sensitive information such as geolocation data.
- A one-stop "dashboard" allowing customers to review the types of content accessed by apps that they have downloaded.
- Privacy best practices so that developers can be required to make privacy disclosures.
- Clear disclosures about extent to which apps are reviewed for privacy before they are made available on platform.
- A "Do Not Track" mechanism for smartphone users, allowing consumers to prevent ad networks from tracking them.

The FTC recommended that app developers consider the following:

- Posting a privacy policy that is easily accessible through app stores.
- Just-in-time-disclosures and opt-in consent for collecting and sharing sensitive information.
- Coordinating with ad networks and other third parties to provide accurate disclosures to consumers.
- Self-regulatory programs to provide guidance on uniform, short-form privacy notices.

Transparency is perhaps the FTC's most important expectation for companies' privacy practices. The FTC provides companies with tremendous flexibility in determining how to collect, use, and share customers' personal information, but it expects that companies will accurately disclose these practices to consumers. If a company does not disclose a material practice – or, even worse, misrepresents it – the FTC may bring an enforcement action.

For example, in August 2012, the FTC announced a $22.5 million civil penalty against Google for violating a previous privacy-related consent order. The FTC alleged that Google surreptitiously placed advertising tracking cookies in consumers' Safari web browsers. These cookies allowed targeted advertising via Google's DoubleClick advertising network. However, Google informed Safari users that they did not need to take any actions to opt out of targeted advertisements because Safari's default setting effectively prevents such cookies. Typically, the FTC settles privacy and data security cases by entering into consent orders that require a company take specific remedial actions, and it does not fine them initially. However, the FTC imposed the $22.5 million because Google already was operating under a 2011 consent order, arising from alleged misrepresentation of its privacy practices on a social network, Google Buzz. In a statement accompanying the $22.5 million fine, the FTC stated that the penalty "signals to Google and other companies that the Commission will vigorously enforce its orders."

Similarly, in 2011, the FTC announced a settlement and consent decree with Facebook arising from allegations about the social network's privacy practices. Among other things, the FTC alleged that Facebook made users' friends lists public without providing them with advance warning. Additionally, the FTC alleged that Facebook's "Friends Only" setting still allowed user content to be shared with third-party application used by the users' friends.

Companies that tout their privacy protections in their marketing to consumers must ensure that their products and services live up to those promises. For instance, in May 2014, the FTC reached a settlement with Snapchat, a mobile messaging application that marketed the fact that messages sent via the service would "disappear forever" after a designated time period. The FTC brought the complaint because users could circumvent this requirement, and store the messages beyond the expiration date.

The FTC in recent years has increasingly focused on particularly sensitive data collected by new technologies, such as geolocation. For instance, in December 2013, it announced a settlement with Goldenshores Technologies, the creator of a popular flashlight app for Android. The FTC alleged that the company provided third parties, including ad networks, with users' precise location and unique device identifiers, but it failed to disclose this sharing in its privacy policy. Moreover, the FTC states that when customers first opened the app, they had an option to "accept" or "refuse" the end user licensing agreement, but that this presented a "false choice" because the information already had been sent to third parties after the app was downloaded.

The White House Consumer Privacy Bill of Rights

In February 2012, shortly before the FTC released its privacy report, President Obama's White House released a Consumer Privacy Bill of Rights. The document, which is entirely nonbinding, demonstrates the Obama White House's core beliefs in flexible but clear privacy requirements for the private sector. Many of these values also are seen in the FTC privacy report. The White House proposed incorporating this policy into binding law, but Congress never enacted the legislation. Although the White House Consumer Privacy Bill of Rights is not binding, it is a good reflection of state and federal regulators' expectations for companies that handle customers' personal information. Below is the full text of the Consumer Privacy Bill of Rights:

The Consumer Privacy Bill of Rights applies to *personal data*, which means any data, including aggregations of data, which is linkable to a specific individual. Personal data may include data that is linked to a specific computer or other device. The Administration supports Federal legislation that adopts the principles of the Consumer Privacy Bill of Rights. Even without legislation, the Administration will convene multistakeholder processes that use these rights as a template for codes of conduct that are enforceable by the Federal Trade Commission. These elements – the Consumer Privacy Bill of Rights, codes of conduct, and strong enforcement – will increase interoperability between the U.S. consumer data privacy framework and those of our international partners.

1) **Individual Control: Consumers have a right to exercise control over what personal data companies collect from them and how they use it.** Companies should provide consumers appropriate control over the personal data that consumers share with others and over how companies collect, use, or disclose personal data. Companies should enable these choices by providing consumers with easily used and accessible mechanisms that reflect the scale, scope, and sensitivity of the personal data that they collect, use, or disclose, as well as the sensitivity of the uses they make of personal data. Companies should offer consumers clear and simple choices, presented at times and in ways that enable consumers to make meaningful decisions about personal data collection, use, and disclosure. Companies should offer consumers means to withdraw or limit consent that are as accessible and easily used as the methods for granting consent in the first place.

2) **Transparency: Consumers have a right to easily understandable and accessible information about privacy and security practices.** At times and in places that are most useful to enabling consumers to gain a meaningful understanding of privacy risks and the ability to exercise Individual Control, companies should provide clear descriptions of what personal data they collect, why they need the data, how they will use it, when they will delete the data or de-identify it from consumers, and whether and for what purposes they may share personal data with third parties.

3) **Respect for Context: Consumers have a right to expect that companies will collect, use, and disclose personal data in ways that are consistent with the context in which consumers provide the data.** Companies should limit their use and disclosure of personal data to those purposes that are consistent with both the relationship that they have with consumers and the context in which consumers originally disclosed the data, unless required by law to do otherwise. If companies will use and disclose personal data for other purposes, they should provide heightened Transparency and Individual Control by disclosing these other purposes in a manner that is prominent and easily actionable by consumers at the time of data collection. If, subsequent to collection, companies decide to use or disclose personal data for purposes that are inconsistent with the context in which the data was disclosed, they must provide heightened measures of Transparency and Individual Choice. Finally, the age and familiarity with technology of consumers who engage with a company are important elements of context. Companies should fulfill the obligations under this principle in ways that are appropriate for the age and sophistication of consumers. In particular, the

principles in the Consumer Privacy Bill of Rights may require greater protections for personal data obtained from children and teenagers than for adults.

4) **Security: Consumers have a right to secure and responsible handling of personal data.** Companies should assess the privacy and security risks associated with their personal data practices and maintain reasonable safeguards to control risks such as loss; unauthorized access, use, destruction, or modification; and improper disclosure.

5) **Access and Accuracy: Consumers have a right to access and correct personal data in usable formats, in a manner that is appropriate to the sensitivity of the data and the risk of adverse consequences to consumers if the data is inaccurate.** Companies should use reasonable measures to ensure they maintain accurate personal data. Companies also should provide consumers with reasonable access to personal data that they collect or maintain about them, as well as the appropriate means and opportunity to correct inaccurate data or request its deletion or use limitation. Companies that handle personal data should construe this principle in a manner consistent with freedom of expression and freedom of the press. In determining what measures they may use to maintain accuracy and to provide access, correction, deletion, or suppression capabilities to consumers, companies may also consider the scale, scope, and sensitivity of the personal data that they collect or maintain and the likelihood that its use may expose consumers to financial, physical, or other material harm.

6) **Focused Collection: Consumers have a right to reasonable limits on the personal data that companies collect and retain.** Companies should collect only as much personal data as they need to accomplish purposes specified under the Respect for Context principle. Companies should securely dispose of or de-identify personal data once they no longer need it, unless they are under a legal obligation to do otherwise.

7) **Accountability: Consumers have a right to have personal data handled by companies with appropriate measures in place to assure they adhere to the Consumer Privacy Bill of Rights.** Companies should be accountable to enforcement authorities and consumers for adhering to these principles. Companies also should hold employees responsible for adhering to these principles. To achieve this end, companies should train their employees as appropriate to handle personal data consistently with these principles and regularly evaluate their performance in this regard. Where appropriate, companies should conduct full audits. Companies that disclose personal data to third parties should at minimum ensure that the recipients are under enforceable contractual obligations to adhere to these principles, unless they are required by law to do otherwise.

Source: WHITE HOUSE, CONSUMER DATA PRIVACY IN A NETWORKED WORLD: A FRAMEWORK FOR PROTECTING PRIVACY AND PROMOTING INNOVATION IN THE GLOBAL DIGITAL ECONOMY (Feb. 2012), app. A.

9.2   Health Insurance Portability and Accountability Act

Although the FTC has not enacted specific privacy regulations for all companies, some sectors are legally required to abide detailed privacy regulations. Among the most restrictive is healthcare, owing in part to the sensitive nature of health records.

Chapter 3 described the data security and breach notification requirements of the Health Insurance Portability and Accountability Act (HIPAA), enforced by the U.S. Department of Health and Human Services.[6] Also under HIPAA, the Department has adopted a Privacy Rule, which limits the ability of health plans, healthcare providers, healthcare clearinghouses, and their business associates to use and disclose "protected health information," which is information that relates to an individual's physical or mental health or condition, the provision of healthcare to the individual, or the individual's payments for healthcare.[7] The Privacy Rule only applies if the information identifies the individual; it does not apply to the use or disclosure of de-identified information.

The Privacy Rule allows covered entities to use and disclose protected health information:

- To the individual.
- For treatment, payment, or healthcare.
- Incidental to a permitted use or disclosure.
- If the individual has authorized the use or disclosure.
- For use in a facility directory or to notify family or friends of care, provided that the individual has the opportunity to agree or object (if the individual is incapacitated, the use or disclosure may be deemed to be in the individual's best interests).
- If the use or disclosure is in the public interest, which the law defines as one of the following categories: (1) required by law; (2) for public health activities; (3) regarding victims of abuse, neglect, or domestic violence; (4) for health oversight activities, such as criminal investigations of a health provider; (5) for judicial and administrative proceedings; (6) for law enforcement purposes; (7) information about decedents; (8) for cadaveric organ, eye, or tissue donation purposes; (9) for research purposes; (10) to avert a serious threat to health or safety; (11) for specialized government functions, such as military and national security activities; and (12) for workers compensation.[8]

---

6 Pub. L. No. 104-191, 110 Stat. 1936 (1996).
7 45 C.F.R. § 160.103.
8 45 C.F.R. §§ 164.502-164.514.

If the use or disclosure is not explicitly covered by one of the exemptions above, the covered entity or business associate is required to obtain the individual's *written* authorization, which specifically allows the use and disclosure. For instance, in order for a healthcare provider to be permitted to use an individual's protected health information for marketing purposes, the written authorization must explicitly give permission to use the data for marketing.[9]

When covered entities and business associates use or disclose protected health information, they typically must make "reasonable efforts" to only use or disclose the "minimum necessary" information for the intended purpose. In other words, if a health insurer needs the healthcare provider's records of a patient's most recent physical in order to process its payment, the healthcare provider should not provide the insurer with records from the patient's ten most recent visits. The "minimum necessary" limit does not apply in a few select cases – notably if needed for treatment, disclosed to the individual who is the subject of the information, or if disclosed under an authorization by the individual.[10]

Covered entities also must fulfill a number of administrative requirements under the Privacy Rule. They must designate a privacy official responsible for implementation of its privacy policies and procedures. Covered entities also must train all of their employees regarding protected health information.[11] HIPAA further imposes a number of data security requirements, which are discussed in Chapter 3.

The HIPAA Privacy Rule also requires covered entities to provide consumers with "adequate notice of the uses and disclosures of protected health information that may be made by the covered entity, and of the individual's rights and the covered entity's legal duties with respect to protected health information."[12] If the covered entity has a direct treatment relationship with the individual, it must make a good-faith effort to obtain a written acknowledgment that the customer has received the privacy notice.[13]

In addition to restricting the use and disclosure of protected health information, HIPAA provides individuals with a relatively broad right of access to their information.[14] Individuals do not, however, have a right to access psychotherapy notes or information that is compiled in reasonable anticipation of, or for use in, a civil, criminal, or administrative action or proceeding.[15]

---

9 45 C.F.R. § 164.508.
10 45 C.F.R. § 164.502(b).
11 45 C.F.R. § 164.530.
12 45 C.F.R. § 520.
13 *Id.*
14 45 C.F.R. § 164.524.
15 *Id.*

9.3 Gramm-Leach-Bliley Act and California Financial Information Privacy Act

As with health information, nonpublic financial data also receives special protection under U.S. law. The Gramm-Leach-Bliley Act (GLBA), whose data security requirements were discussed in Chapter 3, also imposes privacy requirements on financial institutions. GLBA's privacy requirements, known as the Privacy Rule, generally are less burdensome than the HIPAA requirements that healthcare providers face, owing in part to the greater sensitivity of healthcare data.

GLBA imposes two general requirements: notice and choice. Under the notice requirement, a financial institution generally must provide customers with privacy notices at the time that the relationship with the customer is formed and at least once a year after that.[16] The notices must provide "clear and conspicuous disclosure" of the institution's privacy practices, including its policies for disclosing nonpublic personal information to nonaffiliated third parties, the categories of persons to whom the information may be disclosed, the categories of nonpublic personal information that the financial institution collects, the institution's confidentiality and security policies, and other disclosures.[17] Financial regulators have developed model privacy notices that could satisfy this requirement.[18] In 2014, the Consumer Financial Protection Bureau adopted a new regulation that allows certain institutions to satisfy this requirement by posting the notices online, provided that they do not share nonpublic personal information with unaffiliated third parties.[19]

GLBA's Privacy Rule also requires financial institutions to allow users to choose whether to permit certain types of information sharing. If the financial institution is sharing information with a nonaffiliated third party that is performing services for the financial institution (e.g., marketing the institution's services), the institution does not need to provide the user with choice before sharing the data. However, if the financial institution intends to disclose nonpublic personal information to nonaffiliated third parties for other purposes (e.g., to market another company's services), the institution first must clearly and conspicuously notify the individual of the planned sharing and provide the individual with an opportunity to opt out *before* the institution shares the information.[20]

---

16 15 U.S.C. § 6803.

17 *Id.*

18 The FTC's model privacy notice is available at https://www.ftc.gov/system/files/documents/rules/privacy-consumer-financial-information-financial-privacy-rule/privacymodelform_optout.pdf. The model form developed by banking regulators and the SEC is available at https://www.sec.gov/rules/final/2009/34-61003_modelprivacyform.pdf.

19 12 C.F.R. § 1016.

20 15 U.S.C . § 6802.

A California law imposes more restrictive choice requirements on financial institutions. The California Financial Information Privacy Act, also known as SB-1,[21] requires companies to receive *opt-in* consent from consumers before sharing their data with most unaffiliated third parties (unless the sharing is necessary to provide the financial services to the customers). This opt-in requirement is significantly more restrictive than GLBA's opt-out requirement because opt-in requires the customer to provide explicit consent before the sharing occurs. In contrast, under the opt-out system, if a customer does nothing after receiving notice, the information sharing is permitted. The California Financial Information Privacy Act also restricts financial institutions' ability to share information with *affiliated* entities. To do so under the California law, customers must obtain opt-out consent. This also is more restrictive than the GLBA Privacy Rule, which does not restrict financial institutions' sharing of data among affiliated companies.

9.4 CAN-SPAM Act

In the early 2000s, as email was becoming an important component of business and personal lives, policy makers focused on the increasing volume of junk "spam" email messages that were flooding inboxes around the nation. States began to develop their own patchwork of anti-spam laws, and in 2003, Congress passed a single national restriction on spam, the Controlling the Assault of Non-Solicited Pornography and Marketing Act of 2003 (CAN SPAM Act).[22] The law is enforced by the Federal Trade Commission and Federal Communications Commission. The statute has been criticized by some consumer groups because it preempts more stringent state laws and prevents consumers from bringing private lawsuits against spammers.

Among the key requirements of the CAN SPAM Act are the following:

- **Prohibition of false or misleading transmission information.** The CAN SPAM Act prohibits the senders of commercial email messages from using false header information, including email addresses or IP addresses. The statute states that header information is misleading "if it fails to identify accurately a protected computer used to initiate the message because the person initiating the message knowingly uses another protected computer to relay or retransmit the message for purposes of disguising its origin."[23]

---

21 CAL. FIN. CODE 4050–60.
22 15 U.S.C. 7704.
23 *Id.*

- *Prohibition of deceptive subject headings.* Senders of commercial email messages may not use a subject line that "would be likely to mislead a recipient, acting reasonably under the circumstances, about a material fact regarding the contents or subject matter of the message[.]"[24]
- *Return address or opt-out.* Senders of commercial email must include a return email address or other mechanism (e.g., a link) that allows recipients to request not to receive commercial emails in the future. Once a sender receives such a request, it must stop sending commercial emails to that address within ten business days.
- *Identification of email as advertisement.* Commercial email must contain a "clear and conspicuous identification" that the email is an advertisement or solicitation, a notice of the opportunity to decline to receive further email, and a valid *physical* mailing address of the sender.

Companies that violate the CAN SPAM Act can face FTC penalties of up to $16,000 *per email.*

9.5 Video Privacy Protection Act

The Video Privacy Protection Act (VPPA),[25] passed in 1988 in an effort to protect the privacy of video cassette rental information, has had a surprisingly large impact on the data processing abilities of websites and apps that deliver online video content.

Congress passed the VPPA in response to a newspaper's publication of the video rental records of Judge Robert Bork, who had been nominated to the United States Supreme Court. The VPPA prevents "video tape service providers" from knowingly disclosing an individual's personally identifiable video requests or viewing habits, unless the individual has provided informed, written consent. The requirement is rather broad, though it contains a few exceptions, including disclosures that are incidental to the ordinary course of business for the service provider (debt collection activities, order fulfillment, request processing, and the transfer of ownership) and to law enforcement under a warrant, subpoena, or court order. Companies may use opt-out consent to share only customers' names and addresses, providing that their video viewing information is not disclosed.

Why should websites and apps be concerned about a law that restricts the ability of "video tape service providers" to share information? The statute rather broadly defines "video tape service providers" as "any person, engaged

---

24 *Id.*
25 18 U.S.C. 2710.

in the business, in or affecting interstate or foreign commerce, of rental, sale, or delivery of prerecorded video cassette tapes or similar audio visual materials[.]"[26] This definition is broad enough to encompass not only video rental stores, but websites and apps that provide video (whether it be streaming movies, television shows, or news clips). For instance, in 2012, a federal court ruled that Hulu's online movie streaming is covered by the VPPA because Hulu provides "similar audio visual materials."[27]

VPPA disputes often arise when websites or apps provide individually identifiable video viewing information to third-party analytics companies. Unless companies can convince a court that they are not covered by the VPPA or an exception applies, they must obtain a very specific form of consent from the consumer in order to share the data. The VPPA requires the request for consent be "separate and distinct" from any other legal or financial notice. For instance, to obtain a consumer's consent online, the provider must use a separate online pop-up ad seeking consent to disclose video viewing information, and the customer must take an affirmative act, such as clicking "I agree." The notice may not be buried in a larger privacy policy or terms of service. Once a website or app obtains consent, it may share video viewing information for two years, or until the consumer revokes consent.

Companies have good reason to care about compliance with the VPPA. The statute allows damages of at least $2500 *per violation*. This large amount makes the VPPA a particularly attractive tool for class action plaintiffs' lawyers. Imagine that a newspaper's website shared the video viewing information of 100,000 registered users with its online analytics provider and did not obtain proper consent. A VPPA class action lawsuit could recover $250 million. For this reason, it is important that companies take extra precautions to ensure that they obtain adequate consent before sharing video viewing information.

A number of states have enacted statutes that are similar to the VPPA. One notable state law is the Michigan Video Rental Privacy Act, which is broader than the VPPA. The Michigan law restricts information sharing by companies that are "engaged in the business of selling at retail, renting, or lending books or other written materials, sound recordings, or video recordings."[28] In 2014, a federal court ruled that this includes not only online video providers but also magazines that share information about their subscribers.[29] Accordingly, at least for Michigan subscribers, companies must be careful about sharing subscriber information not only for videos but for virtually all forms of online content.

---

26 *Id.*

27 In re Hulu Privacy Litigation, No. C 11–03764 LB, 2012 WL 3282960 (N.D. Cal. Aug. 10, 2012).

28 MICH. COMP. LAWS § 445.1712

29 Kinder v. Meredith Corp., Case No. 14-cv-11284 (E.D. Mich. Aug. 26, 2014).

9.6   Children's Online Privacy Protection Act

The Children's Online Privacy Protection Act (COPPA)[30] restricts the online collection of personal information from minors who are under 13 years old. The Federal Trade Commission has promulgated regulations[31] under COPPA and enforces the law.

COPPA applies to two types of website and online services: (1) those that are directed to children under 13 and (2) those that have actual knowledge that they are collecting or maintaining information from children under 13. To determine whether a website or online service is directed to children under 13, the FTC's regulations state that the Commission considers:

- subject matter;
- visual content;
- use of animated characters or child-oriented activities and incentives, music or other audio content;
- age of models;
- presence of celebrities who appeal to children
- language or other characteristics of the service; and
- whether advertising promoting or appearing on the website or online service is directed to children.[32]

Websites and online services that are covered under COPPA must provide clear notice on their sites about the information that they collect from children, how they use the information, and their disclosure practices for this information. The websites and services must obtain "verifiable parental consent" before collecting, using, or disclosing any personal information from children under 13. The FTC broadly defines personal information as including:

- first and last name;
- physical mailing address;
- online contact information;
- screen or user name that functions as online contact information;
- telephone number;
- social security number;
- persistent identifier "that can be used to recognize a user over time and across different websites or online services";
- photograph, video, or audio file, where such file contains a child's image or voice;

---

30 15 U.S.C. §§ 6501–05.
31 16 C.F.R. § 312.
32 16 C.F.R. § 312.2

- geolocation information that can identify the street and city or town; or
- information regarding the child or the child's parents, collected along with an identifier described above.[33]

To obtain verifiable parental consent, the regulations state, websites and online services must use methods that are "reasonably calculated, in light of available technology, to ensure that the person providing consent is the child's parent."[34] Included among the examples of such methods listed in the regulations are:

- requiring parent to sign a consent form and return it by postal mail, fax, or electronic scan;
- requiring parent to use a credit or debit card or other payment system that notifies the account holder of a transaction;
- having parent call a toll-free number;
- having parent connect to company via video-conference; and
- checking a form of government-issued identification against databases of such information (as long as the parent's identification is promptly deleted after verification).[35]

If a website or online service is collecting personal information only for internal operations, and will not disclose it to any outside party, it also can obtain parental consent using the "email plus" method, in which the parent provides consent via a return email message, provided that the website or online service also take an additional confirming step, either (1) requesting in the initial message that the parent include a phone number or mailing address to which the operator send a confirming phone call or letter, or (2) after a "reasonable" delay, the operator sends another email confirming consent.[36]

Even if a website or online service has obtained verifiable parental consent, it must provide parents with an ongoing opportunity to access the personal information collected from their children, delete the information, and prevent further use or collection of the information. The websites and online services also are required to maintain the confidentiality, security, and integrity of information that they collect from children, though the regulations do not specify particular data security safeguards that the companies must enact.

If the FTC determines that a website or online service has violated COPPA, it can bring an enforcement action in court, seeking damages of up to $16,000 per violation. The largest COPPA enforcement action to date resulted in a $3 million settlement. Playdom, which develops online multi-player games, operated a website called Pony Stars, a virtual online world directed to children.

---

33 *Id.*
34 16 C.F.R. § 312.5(b).
35 *Id.*
36 *Id.*

The FTC alleged that from 2006 to 2010, hundreds of thousands of children registered for Pony Stars, even though Playdom did not properly obtain verifiable parental consent, nor did it properly post a COPPA-compliant privacy policy.

9.7 California Online Privacy Laws

Some of the most stringent online privacy laws were adopted not by Congress but by the California legislature. Although the laws only apply to California residents, they have become de facto requirements for most companies that conduct business in the United States. In addition to the California Financial Information Privacy Act, described above, California has imposed requirements on companies via the California Online Privacy Protection Act (CalOPPA), the California Shine the Light law, and the California "Eraser Button" law.

9.7.1 California Online Privacy Protection Act (CalOPPA)

Until 2004, many U.S. websites did not contain privacy policies. The general rule had been that companies do not need to post a privacy policy, but if they did, the policy must accurately reflect the company's data processing practices. This rule changed in 2004, when CalOPPA went into effect. The statute requires all operators of commercial websites or online services that collect personally identifiable information about California customers to "conspicuously" post a privacy policy.[37] The privacy policy must, at minimum, contain the following elements:

- The categories of personally identifiable information collected about individual consumers.
- The categories of third parties with whom the website or service may share the personally identifiable information.
- A description of any process that the website or service maintains for consumers to "review and request changes" to their personally identifiable information.
- A description of the process by which the website or service notifies customers of "material changes" to their privacy policies.
- The effective date of the privacy policy.
- A description of the website or service's response to web browser "Do Not Track" signals or similar mechanisms.

---

37 CAL. BUS. AND PROF. CODE § 22575.

- A disclosure of whether other parties may collect personally identifiable information about a consumer's online activities "over time and across different websites" when the consumer uses the website or service.[38]

CalOPPA defines personally identifiable information as individually identifiable information including:

- first and last name
- home or other physical address
- email address
- phone number
- social security number
- any other identifier that permits physical or online contacting of an individual
- information collected by the website or service that is maintained in a personally identifiable form in combination with one of the identifiers above.[39]

Since it went into effect, CalOPPA has effectively set a nationwide requirement that all companies post a privacy policy describing how they handle customers' personal information. The California Attorney General aggressively enforces the policy, and in recent years has taken the position that CalOPPA also requires mobile apps to post privacy policies.

9.7.2 California Shine the Light Law

In 2005, the California Shine the Light law[40] went into effect, adding additional privacy requirements for websites. The statute applies to businesses that have established business relationships with customers and have disclosed their personal information in the past calendar year to third parties for direct marketing.

The following are the categories of personal information under the California Shine the Light law:

- name and address
- email address
- age
- date of birth
- children's names
- email or other addresses of children
- number of children
- age or gender of children

---

38 *Id.*
39 *Id.*
40 CAL. CIVIL CODE § 1798.83.

- height
- weight
- race
- religion
- occupation
- phone number
- education
- political party affiliation
- medical condition
- drugs, therapies, or medical products or equipment used
- kind of product the customer purchased, leased, or rented
- real property purchased, leased, or rented
- kind of service provided
- social security number
- bank account number
- credit card number
- debit card number
- bank or investment account, debit card, or credit card balance
- payment history
- information regarding an individual's creditworthiness, assets, income, or liabilities

Upon request from a customer, a business that is covered by this statute must provide the following information to the customer, for free:

- A list of the categories of personal information that the business has disclosed to third parties for direct marketing purposes.
- The names and addresses of all third parties that received personally identifiable information for direct marketing purposes.
- Examples of products or services marketed, if the nature of the third parties' business cannot be reasonably determined by their names.

Businesses that are required to comply with the California Shine the Light law must designate mailing and email addresses (or, at their discretion, a toll-free phone or fax number), to which customers may direct requests for information. Businesses must take one of the following steps to ensure compliance with the law:

- Notify all agents and supervisors of employees who have regular contact with customers of the designated addresses or phone numbers or the means to obtain that information. The businesses must instruct those employees to inform customers of that contact information if customers inquire about their compliance with the California Shine the Light law;
- From the website home page, include a link to a page entitled "Your Privacy Rights" or add a section entitled "Your Privacy Rights" to the larger privacy policy. The section must describe the customer's rights under the California

Shine the Light law and provide the necessary contact details to obtain the information; or

- Make the address and phone number, or means to obtain the contact information, "readily available upon request" at every place of business in California where the business or its agents regularly have contact with customers.[41]

Businesses also may comply with this requirement by stating in their privacy policy that either (1) they do not disclose personal information of customers to third parties for the third parties' direct marketing purposes unless the customer opts in or (2) that the business will not disclose personal information to third parties for the third parties' direct marketing purposes if the customer opts out (provided that the customer is notified of this right and provided with a cost-free method to exercise that right).

Companies that receive requests under the Shine the Light law must respond within 30 days. If the request is received in a manner other than the designated addresses or phone numbers, the business generally must respond within 150 days.

Businesses with fewer than twenty full-time or part-time employees are exempt from the California Shine the Light law, and businesses are not required to respond to a single customer more than once per calendar year.

9.7.3 California Minor "Eraser Law"

California's later endeavor into privacy law went into effect in 2015. Known as the "eraser law,"[42] the statute imposes a number of restrictions on websites, online services, and apps that are directed to minors. Unlike the federal COPPA, which only applies to minors under 13, the California law applies if the website, service, or app is targeted at minors under 18.

A website, service, or app is considered to be "directed to minors" and therefore covered by the statute if it "is created for the purpose of reaching an audience that is predominately comprised of minors, and is not intended for a more general audience comprised of adults."[43] The statute is known as the "eraser law" because it provides minors with a limited ability to request the removal of certain information.

The statute requires covered websites, services, and apps to allow minors who are registered users to request and obtain removal of content and information that the minor posted on the service. The sites must notify minor registered users of the instructions to remove the data.[44]

---

41 *Id.*
42 Cal. Bus. and Prof. Code § 22580–81.
43 *Id.*
44 *Id.*

Covered websites, services, and apps are not required to remove content or information under any of the following circumstances:

- Another state or federal law requires the service to maintain the content or information.
- The content or information was stored or posted by a third party other than the minor.
- The content or information is anonymized so that the minor is not individually identifiable.
- The minor does not follow the instructions for requesting removal of content.
- The minor has been compensated for providing the content.[45]

This statute received a great deal of media attention because it allows users to request the removal of certain content. However, the right is limited. First, it only applies if the minor was a registered user, and it only covers content that the *minor* provided. If, for example, the minor's friend posted personal information about the minor on a social media site, the minor would not have a right to request removal.

Less discussed in the media coverage, but perhaps more significant, are the restrictions that the statute places on online marketing. It prohibits covered websites, services, and apps from marketing the certain categories of products and services:

- alcoholic beverages
- firearms or handguns
- ammunition or reloaded ammunition
- handgun safety certificates
- aerosol container of paint that is capable of defacing
- property
- etching cream that is capable of defacing property
- tobacco, cigarette, or cigarette papers, or blunt wraps, or any other preparation of tobacco; any other instrument or paraphernalia that is designed for the smoking or ingestion of tobacco; products prepared from tobacco, or any controlled substance
- BB device
- dangerous fireworks
- tanning in an ultraviolet tanning device
- dietary supplement products containing ephedrine group alkaloids
- tickets or shares in a lottery game

---

45 *Id.*

- *Salvia divinorum* or Salvinorin A, or any substance or material containing *Salvia divinorum* or Salvinorin A
- body branding
- permanent tattoo
- drug paraphernalia
- electronic cigarette
- obscene matter
- a less lethal weapon

9.8   Illinois Biometric Information Privacy Act

The Illinois Biometric Information Privacy Act[46] is being increasingly used by plaintiffs' lawyers to limit online services' use of facial recognition and other new technologies. The statute prohibits companies from obtaining or disclosing "biometric identifiers or biometric information" unless the companies first obtain the individuals' opt-in consent.

The statute broadly defines "biometric identifier" to include "a retina or iris scan, fingerprint, voiceprint, or scan of hand or face geometry." The statute excludes a number of types of information from the definition of "biometric identifier," including photographs, writing samples, and physical descriptions of individuals. The statute defines "biometric information" as "any information, regardless of how it is captured, converted, stored, or shared, based on an individual's biometric identifier used to identify an individual."

Private parties can bring lawsuits under the statute for $5000 *per violation*. As with other statutes, this can lead to significant, bet-the-company damages if a plaintiff brings a class action lawsuit on behalf of thousands of customers.

The statute received significant attention in May 2016 when a federal judge refused to dismiss a class action lawsuit under the statute against Facebook. The plaintiffs claimed that Facebook violated the Illinois law with its "Tag Suggestions" program, in which Facebook scans photos uploaded by users and uses facial recognition to suggest that the users tag the photo subjects by name. Facebook moved to dismiss the lawsuit, claiming that the statute does not apply because it explicitly states that it does not cover photographs. The court disagreed and denied the motion to dismiss, reasoning that Facebook's facial recognition technology constitutes a "scan of face geometry," which is covered by the statute. The court reasoned that the exclusion for photographs is "better

---

46 740 ILCS 14.

understood to mean paper prints of photographs, not digitized images stored as a computer file and uploaded to the Internet."[47]

The Facebook decision was significant because it broadly applies the Illinois law to facial recognition technologies. Companies must ensure that they obtain adequate consent before using facial recognition or other new technologies, or they could find themselves on the hook for significant penalties under the Illinois law.

---

47 *In re* Facebook Biometric Information Privacy Litigation, Case No. 15-cv-03747-JD (N.D. Cal. May 5, 2016).

10

International Cybersecurity Law

The preceding chapters focused primarily on the cybersecurity obligations that U.S. companies face within the United States. However, many U.S. companies must worry not only about U.S. laws and regulations but about the laws and regulations of other nations. In this chapter, we review the primary cybersecurity laws of the five largest U.S. trading partners: the European Union, Canada, China, Mexico, and Japan.

As this chapter demonstrates, other jurisdictions have more clearly articulated a comprehensive data security and privacy legal framework than the United States has done. The U.S. cybersecurity and privacy laws often vary by sector (and, in some cases, by state), while other large countries have adopted across-the-board laws that severely restrict the collection, storage, use, and disclosure of personal information.

At the outset, many of the other jurisdictions' laws, unlike many of those in the United States, focus on the terms "data controller" and "data processor." This is a key distinction that, under many of these laws, affects the legal responsibilities of companies. The definitions vary by jurisdiction, but the easiest way to generally view this distinction is that data controllers help determine precisely how data is used, distributed, shared, collected, or otherwise processed, while data processors merely follow instructions from the data controllers. For instance, an employer that collects tax information from its employees is a data controller. The third-party payroll company that issues the employer's paychecks likely is a data processor. In many countries, the data controller is responsible for the practices of the data processor.

Cybersecurity Law, First Edition. Jeff Kosseff.
© 2017 John Wiley & Sons, Inc. Published 2017 by John Wiley & Sons, Inc.
Companion Website: www.wiley.com/go/kosseff/cybersecurity

This chapter is intended to be a high-level overview of the cybersecurity legal frameworks in these countries, to provide U.S. businesses with a general understanding of their obligations. In some cases, the chapter is based on English translations of laws and regulations that are published primarily in foreign languages. Moreover, there may be additional local and regional laws that alter a particular company's responsibilities. Accordingly, companies should consult with local counsel about the legal requirements.

10.1 European Union

In 2016, the European Union replaced its 1995 privacy law, Directive 95/46/EC of the European Parliament, and replaced it with the General Data Protection Regulation (GDPR). The GDPR, like the 1995 Directive, sets the general framework for privacy and data security laws that member states must eventually adopt.

Europe views privacy as a fundamental human right, and therefore its requirements for privacy and data security generally are more stringent than those in the United States. This section first will outline the key components of the GDPR, and then it will examine the methods by which U.S. companies can obtain legal approval to process the data of EU residents.

GDPR applies to the processing (i.e., collecting, using, storing, or disclosing) of "personal data" of EU residents, regardless of whether that processing occurs in the European Union or another jurisdiction. GDPR broadly defines "personal data" as "any information that is relating to an identified or identifiable natural person ('data subject'); an identifiable natural person is one who can be identified, directly or indirectly, in particular by reference to an identifier such as a name, an identification number, location data, an online identifier or to one or more factors specific to the physical, physiological, genetic, mental, economic, cultural or social identity of that natural person[.]"[1] In other words, information may be personal data even if it does not contain the individual's name, provided that the individual could be identified by that data. For instance, information about the income of an individual who lives at a particular address likely would be considered personal data, even if the individual's name was not used, because that information could be traced to the individual who lives at that address.

The GDPR applies to two general types of companies: controllers (the entity that "determines the purposes and means of the processing of personal data") and processors (the entity that "processes personal data on behalf of the controller."). Controllers are responsible for ensuring that their processors provide "sufficient guarantees to implement appropriate technical and organisational

---

1 G.D.P.R., art. 4(1).

measures in such a manner that processing will meet the requirements" of the GDPR.[2]

GDPR imposes the following general principles for the processing of personal data:

- *Lawfulness, fairness, and transparency.* Companies must employ lawful, fair, and transparent processing of personal data.
- *Purpose limitation.* Companies must collect personal information for legitimate and specific purposes. Companies must explicitly state the purposes for which they are collecting personal data, and may not expand upon those uses.
- *Data minimization.* Companies must collect only what is necessary for the stated purposes.
- *Accuracy.* Companies must take "every reasonable step" to ensure accurate and updated personal data.
- *Storage limitation.* Companies must allow only identification of data subjects as long as necessary to achieve the stated purposes.
- *Integrity and confidentiality.* Companies must protect data from unauthorized access, loss, or destruction via "appropriate technical or organizational measures."[3]

Processing of personal data is lawful only if one of the following conditions is satisfied:

- The individual has provided consent to processing the personal data. If the data subject provides consent via a written declaration, that consent must be "clearly distinguishable" from other issues, intelligible, and easily accessible. Individuals must be able to revoke their consent at any time. Parents must provide consent for children under 16.
- The individual is subject to a contract for which processing is necessary.
- Processing is necessary for the controller of the data to comply with a legal obligation.
- Processing is necessary to protect "the vital interests of the data subject or of another natural person."
- Processing is necessary to perform a task in the public interest or under the data controller's official authority.
- Processing is necessary for the legitimate interests of the data controller or a third party, provided that those interests do not override the fundamental rights and freedoms of the data subject.[4]

---

2 G.D.P.R., art. 28.
3 G.D.P.R., art. 5(1).
4 G.D.P.R., arts. 6–8.

GDPR imposes additional restrictions on the processing of "special categories" of particularly sensitive data, which it defines as data that reveals "racial or ethnic origin, political opinions, religious or philosophical beliefs, or trade union membership, and the processing of genetic data, biometric data for the purpose of uniquely identifying a natural person, data concerning health or data concerning a natural person's sex life or sexual orientation[.]"[5] Typically, the data may be processed only if the individual has provided explicit consent for the processing of that sensitive data, or if another narrow exception applies.[6]

The processing of personal data must further be "transparent." If the personal data is collected from the data subject, the company must clearly and intelligibly provide the data subject with the following information:

- The contact information for the data controller and, if applicable, its data protection officer.
- The purposes for the processing and legal basis, and, if applicable, the legitimate interests that the controller or a third party is pursuing.
- The recipients or categories of recipients of the personal data.
- If the data controller plans to transfer the personal data to another jurisdiction.
- The length of time the personal data will be stored.
- The right to request access to and erasure of personal data.
- The right to withdraw consent under certain circumstances.
- The right to complain to a supervisory authority.
- Whether the provision of the personal data is required by statute or contract and the consequences of the data subject's failure to provide the personal data.
- Existence of automated decision-making, such as profiling.[7]

Among the most discussed provisions of the GDPR is Article 17, which provides a "right to be forgotten." Under this provision, data subjects have a qualified right to request that data controllers erase personal data if they can demonstrate that one of the following circumstances exists:

- The personal data is no longer necessary to serve the purposes for which it was collected or processed.
- The data subject has withdrawn the consent that allowed the personal data to be collected and there are no other grounds for processing.
- The data subject objects and the controller fails to demonstrate "compelling legitimate grounds for the processing which override the interests, rights

---

5 G.D.P.R., art. 9.
6 *Id.*
7 G.D.P.R., art. 13.

and freedoms of the data subject or for the establishment, exercise or defence of legal claims."

- The personal data was processed unlawfully.
- The EU or member state requires erasure under a different law.
- The personal data was collected from a child under 16 for information services.[8]

The GDPR states that controllers are not required to delete data if processing is necessary "for exercising the right of freedom of expression and information."[9] This reflects the EU belief that the right to be forgotten request must balance, on one hand, the right of individual privacy and, on the other hand, the right to free speech.

The GDPR does not explicitly state the specific data security measures that companies must implement for personal data. Rather, it instructs controllers and processors to "implement appropriate technical and organizational measures to ensure a level of security appropriate to the risk." Among the considerations that the GDPR suggests that companies apply when making these determinations are:

- pseudonymization and encryption of personal data;
- safeguarding the ongoing confidentiality, integrity, availability and resilience of processing systems and services;
- guaranteeing to restore the availability and access to personal data in a timely manner in the event of a physical or technical incident; and
- regularly testing of technical and organizational security measures.[10]

Significant among the additions in the GDPR is a data breach notification requirement (long a feature of U.S. law, as discussed in Chapter 1). If a company experiences a breach of personal data, the controller must without undue delay, and, if feasible, within seventy-two hours, notify government regulators.[11] If the controller fails to notify the government within seventy-two hours, it must provide a reason for the delay.

The notification to regulators must contain the following information:

- Nature of the data breach.
- Categories and number of data subjects.
- Categories and number of personal data records involved.
- Name and contact details of the controller's data protection officer and other contact points.
- Likely consequences of the breach.
- Measures taken to mitigate the adverse effects of the breach.[12]

---

8 G.D.P.R., art. 17.
9 *Id.*
10 G.D.P.R., art. 32.
11 G.D.P.R., art. 33.
12 *Id.*

Controllers also are required to notify individuals of data breaches if they determine that the breach "is likely to result in a high risk to the rights and freedoms of the individuals."[13] The GDPR does not require the notices to be sent within a specified time period, but rather states that individuals should be notified "without undue delay." The individual notices must contain all of the information that must be sent to regulators, except for the description of the nature of the breach and categories and number of data subjects and personal data records.[14]

Notification to individuals is not required under one of the following circumstances:

- The controller had implemented encryption or other safeguards that render the personal data unintelligible.
- The controller took subsequent measures that "ensure that the high risk to the rights and freedoms of data subjects" likely will not materialize.
- The individual notices would "involve disproportionate effort." In this case, the controller must provide the notice via a public communication.[15]

For U.S. companies, perhaps the biggest concern in the GDPR (as in the earlier 1995 Directive) is the restriction of transfers of Europeans' personal data to third countries. Europeans' personal information may only be transferred to a company outside of the United States if one of the following circumstances exists:

- The nation to which the data is being transferred has been deemed by the European Commission to have "adequate" protection for personal data. The Commission makes this determination based on its evaluation of the nation's rule of law, respect for human rights, data protection regulation, and international commitments regarding personal data. The European Commission has set a very high bar for adequacy and, as of 2016, has only found the following jurisdictions to be adequate: Andorra, Argentina, Canada, Faeroe Islands, Guernsey, Israel, Isle of Man, Jersey, New Zealand, Switzerland, and Uruguay.
- The foreign company has adopted binding corporate rules that impose significant restrictions (similar to those in the GDPR) on personal data processing.
- The foreign company agrees to handle the Europeans' data pursuant to standard contractual clauses that have been adopted by the European Commission.
- The foreign company agrees to "binding and enforceable commitments" regarding safeguards and data subjects' rights via an approved code of conduct or certification mechanism.

---

13 G.D.P.R., art. 34.
14 *Id.*
15 *Id.*

Many U.S. companies had long used a certification program known as "Safe Harbor" to process data of European residents. The Safe Harbor framework, which was negotiated by U.S. and EU officials, required U.S. companies to self-certify that they complied with specified data protection principles. However, in October 2015, the Court of Justice of the European Union struck down the Safe Harbor program,[16] concluding that U.S. government foreign intelligence surveillance programs revealed by Edward Snowden rendered the Safe Harbor's protections inadequate.

Because so many U.S. companies relied on the Safe Harbor framework to conduct business with Europe, government officials throughout the United States and European Union quickly began negotiating a new certification framework to replace Safe Harbor. The result is a new arrangement known as the Privacy Shield, which the European Commission approved in July 2016.

The Privacy Shield requires participating U.S. companies to adhere to the following privacy principles:

- *Notice.* Companies must inform data subjects about the type of data collected, purposes, right of access, choice, and other elements regarding the processing.[17]
- *Data integrity and purpose limitation.* Companies must limit their processing of personal data to the stated purpose.
- *Choice.* Individuals must have an opportunity to opt out of processing that is materially different from the original purpose. Individuals must be provided opt-in choices for sensitive information.
- *Data integrity and purpose limitation.* Companies may not maintain information that identifies an individual once the data no longer serves the stated purpose.
- *Security.* Companies must implement "reasonable and appropriate" security measures and contractually require service providers to do the same.
- *Access.* Data subjects have the right to access their personal information, though this access may be limited "in exceptional circumstances." Individuals may correct, amend or delete inaccurate information.
- *Recourse, enforcement, and liability.* Companies must ensure compliance with the Privacy Shield and annually certify their compliance. Companies also must implement redress procedures to handle complaints about their personal data processing. This compliance is subject to investigation and enforcement by U.S. regulators.

---

16 Schrems v. Data Protection Commissioner (Case C-362/14).
17 Commission Implementing Decision of 12.7.2016 pursuant to Directive 95/46/EC of the European Parliament and of the Council on the adequacy of the protection provided by the EU–U.S. Privacy Shield.

- *Accountability for onward transfer.* Before transferring Europeans' data to another country, the U.S. company must ensure that adequate protections are in place to guarantee the same level of protection as the Privacy Shield.[18]

To address the concerns about U.S. government surveillance that led to the invalidation of the Safe Harbor agreement, the United States agreed to limits on and oversight of its surveillance programs, and to a redress mechanism for EU residents.

10.2 Canada

Canada's primary privacy and data security law is the Personal Information and Electronic Documents Act (PIPEDA). Unlike the U.S. patchwork of industry-specific privacy and data security laws, PIPEDA sets a national standard for the use, disclosure, and protection of identifiable information about a Canadian resident.

PIPEDA's requirements are divided into ten principles:

- *Accountability.* Companies must designate privacy and data security compliance with specified employees (e.g., chief privacy officers and chief information security officers), and provide the identity of these employees upon request. Companies must contractually require that their service providers protect Canadians' personal information. Companies also are required to develop procedures to protect personal information and respond to complaints and inquiries, train staff regarding these procedures, and explain the company's personal information policies and procedures.[19]
- *Identifying purposes.* Companies must identify the purposes for which they collect personal information at or before the time of collection. PIPEDA allows companies to communicate the purpose orally or in writing. To use information for a new purpose that was not identified at collection, companies must obtain the individual's consent for the new purpose.[20]
- *Consent.* With some exceptions, companies must obtain knowing consent of individuals before collecting, using, or disclosing their personal information. Companies generally should obtain consent at the time of data collection. The law allows companies to obtain consent via a number of methods, including an application form, a checkoff box, orally, or at the time that the individuals use the company's product or service. PIPEDA

---

18 *Id.* at 2.1.
19 Sec. 4.1 of PIPEDA.
20 Sec. 4.2 of PIPEDA.

allows limited exceptions to the consent requirement, including legal, medical, and security reasons.[21]

- *Limiting collection.* Companies may only collect personal information that is "necessary for the purposes identified by the organization." This applies both to the volume and types of information that companies collect. For instance, if a company collects personal information in order to provide telecommunications services, it likely cannot justify collecting customers' health information. Companies also must collect information by "fair and lawful means." In other words, they cannot deceive customers to obtain the information, and they must comply with all other legal requirements.[22]

- *Limiting use, disclosure, and retention.* Companies may only disclose and use personal information for the stated purposes. For example, if a retailer obtains a customer's address in order to process a purchase, it may not sell that information to a third-party marketing firm unless that purpose was explicitly stated (and consent was obtained). Companies also must dispose of personal information once it is no longer necessary.[23]

- *Accuracy.* Companies must ensure that the personal information that they maintain is updated, complete, and accurate. This principle is intended to reduce the likelihood that a decision about an individual (e.g., an employment offer or credit approval) is made based on inaccurate information.[24]

- *Safeguards.* While many of the principles focus more on privacy concerns with personal information, this principle is more directly targeted toward data security. The principle generally requires companies to protect personal information with security safeguards that are "appropriate to the sensitivity of the information." Companies should implement three types of safeguards: (1) physical measures (e.g., limiting access to offices where personal information is stored), (2) organizational measures (e.g., requiring background checks for employees who have access to particularly sensitive personal information), and (3) technological measures (e.g., encryption). The statute requires companies to ensure that employees understand that they must protect the confidentiality of all personal information.[25]

---

21 Sec. 4.3 of PIPEDA. ("For example, legal, medical, or security reasons may make it impossible or impractical to seek consent. When information is being collected for the detection and prevention of fraud or for law enforcement, seeking the consent of the individual might defeat the purpose of collecting the information. Seeking consent may be impossible or inappropriate when the individual is a minor, seriously ill, or mentally incapacitated. In addition, organizations that do not have a direct relationship with the individual may not always be able to seek consent. For example, seeking consent may be impractical for a charity or a direct-marketing firm that wishes to acquire a mailing list from another organization. In such cases, the organization providing the list would be expected to obtain consent before disclosing personal information.").
22 Sec. 4.4 of PIPEDA.
23 Sec. 4.5 of PIPEDA.
24 Sec. 4.6 of PIPEDA.
25 Sec. 4.7 of PIPEDA.

The Privacy Commissioner of Canada, which oversees PIPEDA's implementation, stated that the following are examples of "reasonable" safeguards:
- Risk management
- Security policies
- Human resources security
- Physical security
- Technical security
- Incident management
- Business continuity planning.[26]

The Privacy Commissioner suggests that companies consider the following factors when assessing the reasonableness of security safeguards:
- Sensitivity of the personal information
- Foreseeable risks
- Likelihood of damage occurring
- Medium and format of the record containing the personal information
- Potential harm that could be caused by an incident
- Cost of preventative measures.[27]

- *Openness.* Companies must openly tell individuals how they handle personal information. The statute encourages companies to use a "generally understandable" form that includes: the contact information for the employee who is responsible for personal information policies and practices and receives complaints; how to access personal information; a description of the categories of personal information that the company maintains, and how it uses that information; any brochures or other documents that describe personal information policies at the company; and the personal information that is provided to related organizations. The notice about its privacy practices may be made online, provided over the phone, communicated via a brochure, or other methods.[28]
- *Individual access.* If a Canadian resident requests the personal information that a company has maintained, used, or disclosed about that resident, the company must provide that information to the individual, providing the individual to challenge the information's accuracy and completeness. The statute allows some exception to this requirement, such as instances in which it would be "prohibitively costly" to provide the personal information to the individual, if there are legal restrictions on the disclosure, or if the information contains personal information about other individuals. The individual

---

26 OFFICE OF THE PRIVACY COMMISSIONER OF CANADA, SECURITY PERSONAL INFORMATION: A SELF-ASSESSMENT TOOL FOR ORGANIZATIONS.
27 *Id.*
28 Sec. 4.8 of PIPEDA.

has the opportunity to challenge the completeness and accuracy of the data, and if the company fails to satisfactorily resolve the individual's concerns, the company must document those concerns and transmit them to any third parties that have access to the personal information.[29]

- **Challenging compliance.** Canada provides individuals with the rights to challenge companies' compliance with PIPEDA. This is a marked difference from many U.S. federal privacy laws, such as Section 5 of the FTC Act and HIPAA, which are enforceable only by federal agencies. In Canada, companies must implement a complaint process and make those procedures easily available to individuals. Companies are required to investigate all complaints and take appropriate measures to rectify any valid concerns.[30]

In 2015, Canada amended PIPEDA to require data breach notifications. If a company determines that a data breach "creates a real risk of significant harm to an individual," it must file a report with the Privacy Commissioner and notify the individual.[31] PIPEDA defines "significant harm" as including "bodily harm, humiliation, damage to reputation or relationships, loss of employment, business or professional opportunities, financial loss, identity theft, negative effects on the credit record and damage to or loss of property."[32] In determining whether a real risk of significant harm arose from a data breach, PIPEDA instructs companies to consider the sensitivity of the breached personal information, the probability that the information has been or will be misused, and any other prescribed factors.[33]

The breach notice must "contain sufficient information to allow the individual to understand the significance to them of the breach and to take steps, if any are possible, to reduce the risk of harm that could result from it or to mitigate that harm."[34] Notice must be provided "as soon as feasible" after the company determines that a breach has occurred.

Three provinces – Alberta, Quebec, and British Columbia – are not covered by PIPEDA because they have passed separate privacy and data security laws. These laws are substantially similar to PIPEDA and rely on the same basic concepts such as purpose limitation, consent, and openness.[35]

---

29 Sec. 4.9 of PIPEDA.
30 Sec. 4.10 of PIPEDA.
31 Sec. 10.1 of PIPEDA.
32 *Id.*
33 *Id.*
34 *Id.*
35 *See* Office of the Privacy Commissioner of Canada, Legal Information Related to PIPEDA, Substantially Similar Provincial Legislation ("Several provincial statutes have also been deemed substantially similar to PIPEDA. Under paragraph 26(2)(b) of PIPEDA, the Governor in Council can exempt an organization, a class of organizations, an activity or a class of activities from the application of PIPEDA with respect to the collection, use or disclosure of personal information that occurs within a province that has passed legislation deemed to be substantially similar to the PIPEDA.").

10.3 China

Although China has enacted some privacy and data security laws, it is unclear how aggressively the government or courts will enforce those laws, as China does not have the government regulators that are as dedicated to data protection and privacy as those in the European Union and Canada. Indeed, China has long faced criticism for the restrictions that it places on individuals' use of the Internet.[36] Nonetheless, there are a number of privacy and data security laws that apply to companies doing business in China, and the government has proposed further restrictions.

In 2012, a significant statement about privacy from the Chinese government came from the Standing Committee of the National People's Congress. The Standing Committee issued the Decision on Strengthening Network Information Protection, which imposed new privacy obligations on certain companies.[37] It is unclear precisely how broadly the decision is intended to apply. According to an unofficial English translation, the Decision applies to "internet service providers and other enterprises and institutions that collect or use citizens' personal electronic information in the course of their business."[38] The Decision requires these companies to "abide by the principles of legality, legitimacy, and necessity," and to "clearly indicate the objective, methods, and scope of collection and use of information, and obtain agreement from the person whose data is collected[.]"[39] The Decision also requires covered companies to "strictly preserve the secrecy of citizens' individual electronic information they collect in their business activities," and states that companies may not "divulge, distort, or damage" the data or "sell or illegally provide" the data to other persons. Covered companies are required to "adopt technological measures and other necessary measures to ensure information security and prevent [...] citizens' individual electronic information collected during business activities [from being] divulged, damaged, or lost."[40]

In a 2015 report, European privacy experts criticized the "easily evident" shortcomings of the 2012 China decision, as compared with the EU data protection regime: "[I]t is lacking in scope (Internet only), in enforcement mechanism (none whatsoever), in basic data subject rights (none whatsoever), as well as, in its principle-setting (their list does not include all of the principles in the

---

36 HUMAN RIGHTS WATCH, WORLD REPORT 2015: China ("The Chinese government targeted the Internet and the press with further restrictions in 2014. All media are already subject to pervasive control and censorship. The government maintains a nationwide Internet firewall exclude politically unacceptable information.").

37 NATIONAL PEOPLE'S CONGRESS STANDING COMMITTEE DECISION CONCERNING STRENGTHENING NETWORK INFORMATION PROTECTION (as translated on the China Copyright and Media blog, chinacopyrightandmedia.wordpress.com) (Dec. 29, 2012).

38 *Id.*

39 *Id.*

40 *Id.*

EU data protection approach)."[41] The EU report did, however, concede that if the China Decision is seen as a "first attempt" at data protection, "then the Decision does present certain merits, mostly in the form of basic data protection elements that may be found in its text."[42]

In 2013, China amended its Consumer Protection Law to reiterate the privacy principles of the Standing Committee's 2012 Decision restrictions on companies that collect and use the personal information of Chinese residents. According to an unofficial translation, the amendment states, in relevant part:

> Proprietors collecting and using consumers' personal information shall abide by principles of legality, propriety and necessity, explicitly stating the purposes, means and scope for collecting or using information, and obtaining the consumers' consent. Proprietors collecting or using consumers' personal information shall disclose their rules for their collection or use of this information, and must not collect or use information in violation of laws, regulations or agreements between the parties.
>
> Proprietors and their employees must keep consumers' personal information they collect strictly confidential and must not disclose, sell, or illegally provide it to others. Proprietors shall employ technical measures and other necessary measures to ensure information security, and to prevent consumers' personal information from being disclosed or lost. In situations where information has been or might be disclosed or lost, proprietors shall immediately adopt remedial measures.
>
> Proprietors must not send commercial information to consumers without their consent or upon their request of consumers, or where they have clearly refused it.[43]

These amendments to the Consumer Protection Law impose fairly stringent general restrictions on companies that handle personal information, similar to the principles in the European Union's GDPR. However, some commentators have questioned how aggressively this law can be enforced, as China does not have data protection authorities similar to those in the European Union.[44]

---

41 EUROPEAN PARLIAMENT, DIRECTORATE-GENERAL FOR INTERNAL POLICIES, POLICY DEPARTMENT, CITIZENS' RIGHTS AND CONSTITUTIONAL AFFAIRS, THE DATA PROTECTION REGIME IN CHINA (2015).

42 *Id.*

43 Art. 29 of CONSUMER PROTECTION LAW (as translated by China Law Translate).

44 EUROPEAN PARLIAMENT, DIRECTORATE-GENERAL FOR INTERNAL POLICIES, POLICY DEPARTMENT, CITIZENS' RIGHTS AND CONSTITUTIONAL AFFAIRS, THE DATA PROTECTION REGIME IN CHINA (2015) ("[I]f judged from a data protection point of view the amended Chinese consumer law could not possibly amount to a data protection regime, because it is missing both in scope (purpose of the legislation as well as in principles, rights and enforcement mechanism.").

In 2013, China expanded on its expectations for Internet and telecommunications companies' handling of personal information when China's Ministry of Industry and Information Technology released the Information Security Technology Guidelines for Personal Information Protection on Public and Commercial Service Information Systems.[45] According to an unofficial English translation, the Guidelines define "personal information" as "[c]omputer data that is handled in computer systems that are related to a specific natural person, and that can be used independently or in combination with other information to distinguish that specific natural person."[46] The voluntary guidelines present eight principles that also look similar to those of the European Union:

- *Clear purpose.* Companies must have a "specific, clear, and reasonable purpose" to handle personal information, and they may not alter that purpose unless the data subject is first made aware of the change.
- *Least sufficient use.* Companies may only use "the smallest amount of information related to the purpose" that is necessary to accomplish the purpose, and must delete personal information "in the shortest time."
- *Open notification.* Companies must properly notify data subjects of their handling of personal information in "clear, easily understandable, and appropriate ways."
- *Individual consent.* Companies must obtain consent from data subjects *before* handling their personal information.
- *Quality guarantee.* Companies must guarantee that they will keep personal information "secret, intact, and usable."
- *Security guarantee.* Companies must implement sufficient administrative and technical safeguards "that are suited to the possibility and gravity of harm to personal information, protecting personal information security, preventing retrieval or disclosure of information without the authorization of the personal information, and the loss, leakage, destruction, and alteration of personal information."
- *Honest implementation.* Companies must abide by the promises that they made regarding the handling of personal information.
- *Clear responsibilities.* Companies must clarify the responsibilities for handling personal information and record handling processes so that they can be easily traced.[47]

Because these guidelines are voluntary, it is unclear what effect, if any, it will have at moving China toward an EU-style data protection regime.

---

45 INFORMATION SECURITY TECHNOLOGY GUIDELINES FOR PERSONAL INFORMATION PROTECTION ON PUBLIC AND COMMERCIAL SERVICE INFORMATION SYSTEMS (as translated on the China Copyright and Media blog, chinacopyrightandmedia.wordpress.com) (Aug. 9, 2013).
46 *Id.*
47 *Id.*

Recently, the Standing Committee of the National People's Congress has proposed a more comprehensive cybersecurity law. A development at the time of publication of this book was a June 2016 release of a Second Reading Draft of the law. The Standing Committee was still taking public comments, and therefore the legislation is subject to further change.

According to an unofficial English translation of the Second Draft of the Cybersecurity Law,[48] the Standing Committee intends to "ensure network security, to preserve cyberspace sovereignty, national security and the societal public interest, to protect the lawful rights and interests of citizens, legal persons and other organizations, and to promote the healthy development of economic and social information."[49] The most pertinent requirement of the draft proposal is for the personal information of Chinese citizens, along with "other important business data gathered or produced by critical infrastructure operators," to be stored within mainland China.[50] The draft law also would require companies to take a number of general steps after a data breach, including an assessment, adoption of safeguards, and public notification, though the draft law does not specify details of those requirements.

10.4 Mexico

In 2010, Mexico enacted the Federal Law on the Protection of Personal Data Possessed by Private Persons. Many of the laws restrictions and rights are similar to those in the EU data protection regime, though they are not identical. A key difference is that unlike the European Union, Mexico does not restrict the export of personal information only to countries with "adequate" privacy protections. Additionally, Mexico's law places a greater responsibility on data controllers, even when the data is in the hands of a third party.

Mexico's privacy law broadly applies to all privacy companies' processing and handling of Mexican residents' "personal data," which the statute defines as "[a]ny information concerning an identified or identifiable individual."[51] Mexico's law requires data controllers to adhere to the following principles:

- *Legality/legitimacy.* Controllers may not violate any legal restrictions on the collection and processing of personal data.[52]
- *Consent.* In general, controllers must obtain consent from data subjects before their personal data is collected or processed. Consent may be inferred

---

48 China Law Translate, Cybersecurity Law (Draft) (Second Reading)
49 *Id.*
50 *Id.*
51 Official English Translation of the Federal Law on Protection of Personal Data Held by Private Parties.
52 *Id.* at art. 7.

if the individual receives a privacy notice disclosing the processing and does not object. Otherwise, Mexico's law requires express consent, and it allows consent to be provided verbally, in writing, electronically, via other technology, or "by unmistakable indications." Consent for financial or asset data processing must be provided expressly. Individuals may revoke consent at any time.[53]

– *Consent for sensitive personal data.* The statute imposes more stringent consent requirements for the processing of "sensitive personal data," which is defined as personal data "touching on the most private areas of the data owner's life, or whose misuse might lead to discrimination or involve a serious risk for said data owner." Among the categories of personal data that the statute categorizes as sensitive are those that reveal race, ethnicity, health status, genetic information, religious beliefs, union membership, political views, and sexual preferences. For such sensitive personal data, controllers must obtain express written consent from the data owner via a signature, electronic signature, "or any authentication mechanism established for such purpose."[54]

– *Exceptions to consent.* The statute does not require consent in the following circumstances: (1) any law allows processing without consent, (2) the personal data is publicly available, (3) the data is subject to a "prior dissociation procedure," (4) the processing fulfills a legal relationship between the data owner and controller, (5) an emergency situation that could harm an individual's person or property, (6) the processing is necessary for health treatment, or (7) a competent authority issues a resolution.

• *Notice/information.* Controllers must provide a privacy notice that informs individuals "what information is collected on them and why."[55] Notices must contain (1) identity and domicile of the controller; (2) purposes for the processing of personal information; (3) options for data subjects to limit use or disclosure of the data; (4) procedures for individuals to exercise rights of access, rectification, cancellation, or objection; (5) if applicable, where the data will be transferred; and (6) how individuals will be notified of changes to the privacy notice.[56]

• *Quality.* The controller is responsible for ensuring that the personal data is correct, up-to-date, and relevant. Once the data is no longer necessary for the purposes stated in the privacy notice, it must be deleted.[57]

• *Purpose.* Personal data may only be processed for the purposes articulated in the privacy notice.[58]

---

53 *Id.* at art. 8.
54 *Id.* at art. 9.
55 *Id.* at art. 15.
56 *Id.* at art. 16.
57 *Id.* at art. 11.
58 *Id.* at art. 12.

- *Fidelity/loyalty.* The law presumes a "reasonable expectation of privacy" in all instances in which personal data is processed, recognizing "the trust any one person places in another for personal data provided to be treated pursuant to any agreement of the parties in the terms established by this Law."[59] The law prohibits companies from obtaining data deceptively or fraudulently.[60]
- *Proportionality.* Personal data may only be processed "as necessary, appropriate and relevant with relation to the purposes set out in the privacy notice." The statute explicitly requires controllers to "make reasonable efforts to limit the processing period" of sensitive personal data to the minimum required.[61]
- *Accountability.* Data controllers are responsible for ensuring compliance with Mexico's privacy laws, even if the data is processed by a third party at the controller's request. The statue requires the controller to take "all necessary and sufficient action" to ensure that all third parties respect the privacy notice that has been provided to the individual.[62]

In addition to these general privacy-related principles, Mexico's privacy law requires all processors of personal data to implement physical, technical, and administrative data security safeguards.[63] Although Mexico's privacy statute does not specify the necessary safeguards, the Ministry of the Economy has elaborated on the security requirements in regulations that implemented the statute.[64]

According to the regulations, data controllers must consider the following factors when determining security measures for personal data:

- "Inherent risk" for the type of data
- Sensitivity of the data
- Technological development
- Potential consequences for the individuals if the security is violated[65]

Controllers also should attempt to account for the number of data subjects whose personal information is stored, previous vulnerabilities that the controllers have encountered, the risk based on the value that the personal data might have to an unauthorized third party, and other factors that impact risk or result from other laws or regulations.[66]

---

59 *Id.* at art. 7.
60 *Id.*
61 *Id.* at art. 13.
62 *Id.* at art. 14.
63 *Id.* at art. 19.
64 Official English Translation of Regulations to the Federal Law on the Protection of Personal Data Held by Private Parties (Dec. 21, 2011).
65 *Id.* at art. 60.
66 *Id.*

The regulations state that controllers must take the following actions, at minimum, to secure personal data:

- Inventory all processing systems and personal data.
- Determine duties of personal data processors.
- Conduct a risk analysis for personal data.
- Establish security measures for personal data evaluate the implementation of these measures.
- Conduct a gap analysis to determine the necessary security measures that are missing.
- Develop plan to fill the gaps identified in the gap analysis.
- Conduct security reviews and audits.
- Provide data security training for all personnel who process personal data.
- Maintain records of personal data storage media.[67]

Controllers are required to document all of these security measures, and to update them.[68]

If a breach occurs, the controller must undertake an "exhaustive review of the magnitude of the breach[.]"[69] If the review concludes that the breach significantly prejudices the data subjects' property or rights, the controller is required to issue a breach notification to the data subject "without delay[.]"[70] The notice must include, at minimum, (1) a description of the breach, (2) an inventory of the types of personal data that potentially were compromised, (3) recommendations for the data subject to protect his or her interests, (4) corrective actions that the data controller implemented immediately, and (5) instructions to obtain more information about the breach.[71] The controller also is required to conduct a thorough analysis of the cause of the breach and implement "corrective, preventative, and improvement steps" to avoid another breach in the future.[72]

10.5 Japan

In Japan, privacy and data security law largely is governed by a 2003 statute, the Act on the Protection of Personal Information (APPI).[73] The statute is more similar to the comprehensive EU approach to data regulation, and certainly is

---

67 *Id.* at art. 61.
68 *Id.* at art. 61–62.
69 *Id.* at art. 61.
70 *Id.*
71 *Id.* at art. 65.
72 *Id.* at art. 66.
73 Unofficial English Translation of the Act on the Protection of Personal Information (Act No. 57 of 2003).

more stringent than the U.S. sectoral approach. Indeed, Japan's privacy and data security protections are among the most comprehensive in Asia.

However, Japan's privacy law also lacks some of the features of Europe's. For instance, Japan does not impose additional restrictions on "sensitive" personal information. Moreover, unlike the European data protection regime, the APPI does not distinguish between controllers and processors. Japan's law also does not require other countries' data protection laws to be "adequate" before allowing a foreign data transfer.

Among the notable features of APPI is its relatively broad definition of "personal information" that is protected by the statute. APPI defines "personal information" as "information about a living individual which can identify the specific individual by name, date of birth or other description contained in such information (including such information as will allow easy reference to other information and will enable the identification of the specific individual."[74] In other words, Japan considers personal information not only to be data that could help identify an individual, but it also includes data that could lead to *other* data that could help identify an individual. The restrictions apply to all "business operators" that handle personal information.[75]

In 2015, Japan's legislature amended APPI, with the goal of implementing the new provisions by the end of 2017. Because some of the details of the implementation of the amended law have yet to be finalized and the English language translation of the amendments are not yet available, below is a summary of the 2003 law, followed by an overview of reported changes.

Japan's privacy and data security laws, like those of Europe, suggest that personal information protection is a human right. APPI sets for a general "basic principle" that companies should cautiously handle Japanese residents' personal information "under the philosophy of respecting the personalities of individuals[.]"[76]

The following are among the key duties that 2003 APPI imposes on business operators that handle Japanese residents' personal information:

- **Purpose of utilization.** Business operators must specify the "purpose of utilization" when they handle personal information, and they may not unreasonably change the scope of that purpose. Business operators must obtain *prior consent* to handle personal information beyond the initial scope stated in the purpose of utilization.[77]
- **Proper acquisition.** Business operators may not use "deception or other wrongful means" to acquire personal information.[78]

---

74 *Id*. at art. 2.
75 *Id*.
76 *Id*. at art. 3.
77 *Id*. at art. 15–16.
78 *Id*.at art. 17.

- *Notice.* At the time that a business operator obtains personal information, it must "promptly notify" the individual of the purpose of utilization (either directly or via a public announcement). The notice requirement does not apply if the notice could harm individuals or property or the rights or legitimate interests of the business operator. The notice requirement also does not apply when it is necessary to comply with law enforcement or if the purpose "is clear in consideration of the circumstances of the acquisition."[79]

- *Accuracy.* Business operators must "endeavor to maintain" accurate and up-to-date personal information that is necessary to achieve the purpose of utilization.[80]

- *Security controls.* The statute requires business operators to "take necessary and proper measures for the prevention of leakage, loss, or damage, and for other security control of the personal data."[81] The statute does not specify the particular safeguards that businesses must implement to satisfy this requirement.

- *Employee supervision.* Business operators must "exercise necessary and appropriate supervision" to ensure that employees properly handle personal information.[82]

- *Transfers to third parties.* Business operators generally may not provide personal information to third parties without prior consent from the data subjects. This prohibition does not apply in a few exceptional cases: (1) if the transfer is based on laws or regulations, (2) if the transfer is necessary to protect individuals or property and consent is difficult to obtain, (3) if public health or child welfare and consent is difficult to obtain, and (4) if it is necessary to cooperate with government.[83]

- *Public privacy notice.* Business operators must post a publicly accessible document that contains the following information: (1) the name of the business operator who is handling the personal information, (2) the purpose of utilization for retained personal data, (3) procedures for handling requests regarding personal information from data subjects, and (4) any other information required by Cabinet Order.[84]

- *Correction of data.* Business operators generally must correct, add, or delete personal data at the request of the data subject.[85]

In September 2015, the Japanese Diet passed a bill that contained the first significant amendments to APPI since its passage more than a decade earlier.

---

79 *Id.* at art. 18.
80 *Id.* at art. 19.
81 *Id.* at art. 20.
82 *Id.* at art. 21.
83 *Id.* at art. 23.
84 *Id.* at art. 24.
85 *Id.* at art. 26.

The changes will go into effect by the end of 2017. Below are some of the significant changes:[86]

- Allowing companies to share certain data with third parties unless the data subject "opts out" (a more lenient standard than the 2003 law's "opt in" requirement.
- Under certain circumstances, disclosure of anonymized or pseudonymous data will not require individual consent.
- Restrictions on the transfer of personal data outside of Japan.
- Additional protection for "sensitive information," similar to the European Union.
- The Creation of a Privacy Protection Commission, which will enforce Japan's privacy law. The Commission, which was formed in August 2016, will determine many of the details of the implementation of the amended law.

---

86 Brian Caster, DLA Piper, *New Amendments to Japanese Privacy Law*, Sept. 26, 2015; Eric Kosinski, White and Case, *Transfer of Personal Data under Japan's Amended Personal Information Protection Act*, Oct. 3, 2015.

Appendix A

Text of Section 5 of the FTC Act

Section 5 of the Federal Trade Commission Act, described in Chapter 1, is the primary law under which the federal government regulates data security. Although the statute does not explicitly mention data security or cybersecurity, the FTC has long interpreted its prohibition on unfair and deceptive trade practices as authority for the Commission to penalize companies for particularly egregious data security practices.

Text of Section 5 of the Federal Trade Commission Act, 15 U.S.C. § 45

a) Declaration of unlawfulness; power to prohibit unfair practices; inapplicability to foreign trade

1) Unfair methods of competition in or affecting commerce, and unfair or deceptive acts or practices in or affecting commerce, are hereby declared unlawful.

2) The Commission is hereby empowered and directed to prevent persons, partnerships, or corporations, except banks, savings and loan institutions described in section 57a(f)(3) of this title, Federal credit unions described in section 57a(f)(4) of this title, common carriers subject to the Acts to regulate commerce, air carriers and foreign air carriers subject to part A of subtitle VII of title 49, and persons, partnerships, or corporations insofar as they are subject to the Packers and Stockyards Act, 1921, as amended [7 U.S.C. 181 *et seq*.], except as provided in section 406(b) of said Act [7 U.S.C. 227(b)], from using unfair methods of competition in or affecting commerce and unfair or deceptive acts or practices in or affecting commerce.

Cybersecurity Law, First Edition. Jeff Kosseff.
© 2017 John Wiley & Sons, Inc. Published 2017 by John Wiley & Sons, Inc.
Companion Website: www.wiley.com/go/kosseff/cybersecurity

3) This subsection shall not apply to unfair methods of competition involving commerce with foreign nations (other than import commerce) unless—

A) such methods of competition have a direct, substantial, and reasonably foreseeable effect—
   i) on commerce which is not commerce with foreign nations, or on import commerce with foreign nations; or
   ii) on export commerce with foreign nations, of a person engaged in such commerce in the United States; and

B) such effect gives rise to a claim under the provisions of this subsection, other than this paragraph.

If this subsection applies to such methods of competition only because of the operation of subparagraph (A)(ii), this subsection shall apply to such conduct only for injury to export business in the United States.

4)

A) For purposes of subsection (a), the term "unfair or deceptive acts or practices" includes such acts or practices involving foreign commerce that—
   i) cause or are likely to cause reasonably foreseeable injury within the United States; or
   ii) involve material conduct occurring within the United States.

B) All remedies available to the Commission with respect to unfair and deceptive acts or practices shall be available for acts and practices described in this paragraph, including restitution to domestic or foreign victims.

b) Proceeding by Commission; modifying and setting aside orders

Whenever the Commission shall have reason to believe that any such person, partnership, or corporation has been or is using any unfair method of competition or unfair or deceptive act or practice in or affecting commerce, and if it shall appear to the Commission that a proceeding by it in respect thereof would be to the interest of the public, it shall issue and serve upon such person, partnership, or corporation a complaint stating its charges in that respect and containing a notice of a hearing upon a day and at a place therein fixed at least thirty days after the service of said complaint. The person, partnership, or corporation so complained of shall have the right to appear at the place and time so fixed and show cause why an order should not be entered by the Commission requiring such person, partnership, or corporation to cease and desist from the violation of the law so charged in said complaint. Any person, partnership, or corporation may make application, and upon good cause shown may be allowed by the Commission to intervene and appear in said proceeding by counsel or in person. The testimony in any such proceeding shall be reduced to writing and filed in the office of the Commission. If upon such hearing the Commission shall be of the opinion that the method of competition or the act or practice in question is prohibited by this subchapter, it shall make a report in writing in which it shall state its findings as to the facts and shall issue and cause to be served on such person, partnership, or corporation an order requiring such person, partnership, or corporation to cease and desist from using such method of competition or such act or practice. Until the expiration of the time allowed for filing a petition for review, if no such petition has been duly filed within such time, or, if a petition for review has been filed within such time then until the record in the proceeding has been filed in a court of appeals of the United States, as hereinafter provided, the Commission may at any time, upon such notice and in such manner as it shall deem proper, modify or set aside, in whole or in part, any report or any order made or issued by it under this section. After the expiration of the time allowed for filing a petition for review, if no such petition has been duly filed within such time, the Commission may at any time, after notice and opportunity for hearing, reopen and alter, modify, or set aside, in whole or in part any report or order made or issued by it under this section, whenever in the opinion of the Commission conditions of fact or of law have so changed as to require such action or if the public interest shall so require, except that (1) the said person, partnership, or corporation may, within sixty days after service upon him or it of said report or order entered after such a reopening, obtain a review thereof in the appropriate court of appeals of the United States, in the manner provided in subsection (c) of this section; and (2) in the case of an order, the Commission shall reopen any such order to consider whether such order (including any affirmative relief provision contained in such order) should be altered, modified, or set aside, in whole or in part, if the person, partnership, or corporation involved files a request with the Commission which makes a satisfactory showing that changed conditions of law or fact require such order to be altered, modified, or set aside, in whole or in part. The Commission shall determine whether to alter, modify, or set aside any order of the Commission in response to a request made by a person, partnership, or corporation under paragraph [1] (2) not later than 120 days after the date of the filing of such request.

c) Review of order; rehearing

Any person, partnership, or corporation required by an order of the Commission to cease and desist from using any method of competition or act or practice may obtain a review of such order in the court of appeals of the United States, within any circuit where the method of competition or the act or practice in question was used or where such person, partnership, or corporation resides or carries on business, by filing in the court, within sixty days from the date of the service of such order, a written petition praying that the order of the Commission be set aside. A copy of such petition shall be forthwith transmitted by the clerk of the court to the Commission, and thereupon the Commission shall file in the court the record in the proceeding, as provided in section 2112 of title 28. Upon such filing of the petition the court shall have jurisdiction of the proceeding and of the question determined therein concurrently with the Commission until the filing of the record and shall have power to make and enter a decree affirming, modifying, or setting aside the order of the Commission, and enforcing the same to the extent that such order is affirmed and to issue such writs as are ancillary to its jurisdiction or are necessary in its judgement to prevent injury to the public or to competitors pendente lite. The findings of the Commission as to the facts, if supported by evidence, shall be conclusive. To the extent that the order of the Commission is affirmed, the court shall thereupon issue its own order commanding obedience to the terms of such order of the Commission. If either party shall apply to the court for leave to adduce additional evidence, and shall show to the satisfaction of the court that such additional evidence is material and that there were reasonable grounds for the failure to adduce such evidence in the proceeding before the Commission, the court may order such additional evidence to be taken before the Commission and to be adduced upon the hearing in such manner and upon such terms and conditions as to the court may seem proper. The Commission may modify its findings as to the facts, or make new findings, by reason of the additional evidence so taken, and it shall file such modified or new findings, which, if supported by evidence, shall be conclusive, and its recommendation, if any, for the modification or setting aside of its original order, with the return of such additional evidence. The judgment and decree of the court shall be final, except that the same shall be subject to review by the Supreme Court upon certiorari, as provided in section 1254 of title 28.

d) Jurisdiction of court

Upon the filing of the record with it the jurisdiction of the court of appeals of the United States to affirm, enforce, modify, or set aside orders of the Commission shall be exclusive.

e) Exemption from liability

No order of the Commission or judgement of court to enforce the same shall in anywise relieve or absolve any person, partnership, or corporation from any liability under the Antitrust Acts.

f) Service of complaints, orders and other processes; return

Complaints, orders, and other processes of the Commission under this section may be served by anyone duly authorized by the Commission, either (a) by delivering a copy thereof to the person to be served, or to a member of the partnership to be served, or the president, secretary, or other executive officer or a director of the corporation to be served; or (b) by leaving a copy thereof at the residence or the principal office or place of business of such person, partnership, or corporation; or (c) by mailing a copy thereof by registered mail or by certified mail addressed to such person, partnership, or corporation at his or its residence or principal office or place of business. The verified return by the person so serving said complaint, order, or other process setting forth the manner of said service shall be proof of the same, and the return post office receipt for said complaint, order, or other process mailed by registered mail or by certified mail as aforesaid shall be proof of the service of the same.

g) Finality of order:

An order of the Commission to cease and desist shall become final—

1) Upon the expiration of the time allowed for filing a petition for review, if no such petition has been duly filed within such time; but the Commission may thereafter modify or set aside its order to the extent provided in the last sentence of subsection (b).

2) Except as to any order provision subject to paragraph (4), upon the sixtieth day after such order is served, if a petition for review has been duly filed; except that any such order may be stayed, in whole or in part and subject to such conditions as may be appropriate, by—
   A) the Commission;
   B) an appropriate court of appeals of the United States, if (i) a petition for review of such order is pending in such court, and (ii) an application for such a stay was previously submitted to the Commission and the Commission, within the 30-day period beginning on the date the application was received by the Commission, either denied the application or did not grant or deny the application; or
   C) the Supreme Court, if an applicable petition for certiorari is pending.

3) For purposes of subsection (m)(1)(B) and of section 57b(a)(2) of this title, if a petition for review of the order of the Commission has been filed—
   A) upon the expiration of the time allowed for filing a petition for certiorari, if the order of the Commission has been affirmed or the petition for review has been dismissed by the court of appeals and no petition for certiorari has been duly filed;
   B) upon the denial of a petition for certiorari, if the order of the Commission has been affirmed or the petition for review has been dismissed by the court of appeals; or
   C) upon the expiration of 30 days from the date of issuance of a mandate of the Supreme Court directing that the order of the Commission be affirmed or the petition for review be dismissed.

4) In the case of an order provision requiring a person, partnership, or corporation to divest itself of stock, other share capital, or assets, if a petition for review of such order of the Commission has been filed—

   A) upon the expiration of the time allowed for filing a petition for certiorari, if the order of the Commission has been affirmed or the petition for review has been dismissed by the court of appeals and no petition for certiorari has been duly filed;

   B) upon the denial of a petition for certiorari, if the order of the Commission has been affirmed or the petition for review has been dismissed by the court of appeals; or

   C) upon the expiration of 30 days from the date of issuance of a mandate of the Supreme Court directing that the order of the Commission be affirmed or the petition for review be dismissed.

h) Modification or setting aside of order by Supreme Court

If the Supreme Court directs that the order of the Commission be modified or set aside, the order of the Commission rendered in accordance with the mandate of the Supreme Court shall become final upon the expiration of thirty days from the time it was rendered, unless within such thirty days either party has instituted proceedings to have such order corrected to accord with the mandate, in which event the order of the Commission shall become final when so corrected.

i) Modification or setting aside of order by Court of Appeals

If the order of the Commission is modified or set aside by the court of appeals, and if (1) the time allowed for filing a petition for certiorari has expired and no such petition has been duly filed, or (2) the petition for certiorari has been denied, or (3) the decision of the court has been affirmed by the Supreme Court, then the order of the Commission rendered in accordance with the mandate of the court of appeals shall become final on the expiration of thirty days from the time such order of the Commission was rendered, unless within such thirty days either party has instituted proceedings to have such order corrected so that it will accord with the mandate, in which event the order of the Commission shall become final when so corrected.

j) Rehearing upon order or remand

If the Supreme Court orders a rehearing; or if the case is remanded by the court of appeals to the Commission for a rehearing, and if (1) the time allowed for filing a petition for certiorari has expired, and no such petition has been duly filed, or (2) the petition for certiorari has been denied, or (3) the decision of the court has been affirmed by the Supreme Court, then the order of the Commission rendered upon such rehearing shall become final in the same manner as though no prior order of the Commission had been rendered.

k) "Mandate" defined

As used in this section the term "mandate", in case a mandate has been recalled prior to the expiration of thirty days from the date of issuance thereof, means the final mandate.

l) Penalty for violation of order; injunctions and other appropriate equitable relief

Any person, partnership, or corporation who violates an order of the Commission after it has become final, and while such order is in effect, shall forfeit and pay to the United States a civil penalty of not more than $10,000 for each violation, which shall accrue to the United States and may be recovered in a civil action brought by the Attorney General of the United States. Each separate violation of such an order shall be a separate offense, except that in a case of a violation through continuing failure to obey or neglect to obey a final order of the Commission, each day of continuance of such failure or neglect shall be deemed a separate offense. In such actions, the United States district courts are empowered to grant mandatory injunctions and such other and further equitable relief as they deem appropriate in the enforcement of such final orders of the Commission.

m) Civil actions for recovery of penalties for knowing violations of rules and cease and desist orders respecting unfair or deceptive acts or practices; jurisdiction; maximum amount of penalties; continuing violations; de novo determinations; compromise or settlement procedure

1)

   A) The Commission may commence a civil action to recover a civil penalty in a district court of the United States against any person, partnership, or corporation which violates any rule under this subchapter respecting unfair or deceptive acts or practices (other than an interpretive rule or a rule violation of which the Commission has provided is not an unfair or deceptive act or practice in violation of subsection (a)(1)) with actual knowledge or knowledge fairly implied on the basis of objective circumstances that such act is unfair or deceptive and is prohibited by such rule. In such action, such person, partnership, or corporation shall be liable for a civil penalty of not more than $10,000 for each violation.

   B) If the Commission determines in a proceeding under subsection (b) that any act or practice is unfair or deceptive, and issues a final cease and desist order, other than a consent order, with respect to such act or practice, then the Commission may commence a civil action to obtain a civil penalty in a district court of the United States against any person, partnership, or corporation which engages in such act or practice—

1) after such cease and desist order becomes final (whether or not such person, partnership, or corporation was subject to such cease and desist order), and

2) with actual knowledge that such act or practice is unfair or deceptive and is unlawful under subsection (a)(1) of this section.

   In such action, such person, partnership, or corporation shall be liable for a civil penalty of not more than $10,000 for each violation.

C) In the case of a violation through continuing failure to comply with a rule or with subsection (a)(1), each day of continuance of such failure shall be treated as a separate violation, for purposes of subparagraphs (A) and (B). In determining the amount of such a civil penalty, the court shall take into account the degree of culpability, any history of prior such conduct, ability to pay, effect on ability to continue to do business, and such other matters as justice may require.

2) If the cease and desist order establishing that the act or practice is unfair or deceptive was not issued against the defendant in a civil penalty action under paragraph (1)(B) the issues of fact in such action against such defendant shall be tried de novo. Upon request of any party to such an action against such defendant, the court shall also review the determination of law made by the Commission in the proceeding under subsection (b) that the act or practice which was the subject of such proceeding constituted an unfair or deceptive act or practice in violation of subsection (a).

3) The Commission may compromise or settle any action for a civil penalty if such compromise or settlement is accompanied by a public statement of its reasons and is approved by the court.

n) Standard of proof; public policy considerations

The Commission shall have no authority under this section or section 57a of this title to declare unlawful an act or practice on the grounds that such act or practice is unfair unless the act or practice causes or is likely to cause substantial injury to consumers which is not reasonably avoidable by consumers themselves and not outweighed by countervailing benefits to consumers or to competition. In determining whether an act or practice is unfair, the Commission may consider established public policies as evidence to be considered with all other evidence. Such public policy considerations may not serve as a primary basis for such determination.

Appendix B

Summary of State Data Breach Notification Laws

Section 1.2 of this book describes the common requirements of the data breach notification laws in forty-seven states and the District of Columbia. These summaries focus on the obligations of private companies; government agencies also often face separate notice obligations if they experience data breaches. For ease of reference, particularly for companies that are dealing with a data breach, this appendix summarizes key provisions of each of these forty-eight laws, including the types of personal information that trigger the breach notice requirement, significant exceptions to that requirement, and notice and format of breach notices.

Note that most state notification laws allow electronic notice; in all of these cases, consent to receive notices electronically must be consistent with the federal E-SIGN Act.

For ease of reference, this appendix includes many of the most important parts of the state laws, rather than merely reprinting the statutes in full. However, the state laws do have additional requirements that are specific to the state. Moreover, the breach notification laws could have been amended since the publication of this book; indeed, typically a few states each year amend their breach notice laws. Accordingly, it always is prudent for legal counsel to review the current version of the applicable breach notice laws to confirm requirements.

Alaska

Alaska Stat. §§ 45.48.010 *et seq.*

Types of personal information covered: An individual's first name or first initial and last name, in combination with at least one of the following elements: Social Security number, driver's license or state ID card number, credit card or debit card number and personal code if applicable, and passwords or PINS or other access codes for financial accounts.

Exceptions to notice requirement: (1) If all of the personal information was encrypted, provided that the encryption key was not also disclosed; and (2) if after an appropriate investigation and a written notification to the Alaska Attorney General, the company determines that "there is not a reasonable likelihood that harm to consumers whose personal information has been acquired has resulted or will result from the breach," but the company must retain this documentation for five years.

Timing of notice to individuals: Disclosure must be made "in the most expeditious time possible and without unreasonable delay" unless a delay is necessary for law enforcement or to determine the scope of the breach and restore the system's integrity.

Form of notice to individuals: Three options: (1) written document sent to most recent known mailing address; (2) email if that is company's primary method of communication with the individual; or (3) substitute notice if the cost of providing notice would exceed $150,000, the affected class in the state exceeds 300,000, or the company does not have sufficient information to provide notice. Substitute notice consists of email if the address is known, conspicuously posting disclosure on company's website, and notice to major statewide media.

Notice to state regulators or credit bureaus: The State Attorney General must be notified if company determines that there is not a risk of harm and therefore individual notice is unnecessary. Notice to credit bureaus is required if more than 1000 Alaska residents are notified, but this requirement does not apply if the company is subject to the Gramm-Leach-Bliley Act.

Arizona

Ariz. Rev. Stat. § 44-7501

Types of personal information covered: An individual's first name or first initial and last name in combination with at least one of the following: (1) Social Security number; (2) driver's license or state ID number; or (3) financial account or credit card or debit card number in combination with required security code, access code, or passcode (if necessary for access).

Exceptions to notice requirement: The notice requirement does not apply to (1) information that is encrypted or redacted; (2) if after reasonable investigation the company determines that the breach does not pose a reasonable likelihood of substantial economic loss; (3) if the company is subject to the requirements of GLBA or HIPAA; (4) if the company complies with the notification requirements of its "primary or functional federal regulator," or (5) if it follows its own notification procedures as part of an information security policy.

Timing of notice to individuals: Companies must provide notice "in the most expedient manner possible and without unreasonable delay subject to the needs of law enforcement" and any measure needed for the company to determine the scope of the breach, identify-affected individuals, and restore the system's integrity.

Form of notice to individuals: (1) Written notice; (2) electronic notice if that is the primary method of communicating with the company; (3) telephonic notice; or (4) substitute notice if the cost of other notice would exceed $50,000, more than 100,000 Arizona residents would be notified, or the company does not have sufficient contact information. Substitute notice consists of (1) email notice when available, (2) conspicuous posting of the notice on the company's website, and (3) notification to major statewide media.

Notice to state regulators or credit bureaus: Not required.

Arkansas

Ark. Code §§ 4-110-103, et seq.

Types of personal information covered: First name or first initial and last name in combination with one or more of the following: (1) Social Security number; (2) driver's license or state ID number; (3) financial account number, credit card number or debit card number in combination, with any code or password necessary to access financial account; or (4) medical information.

Exceptions to notice requirement: (1) If personal information is encrypted or redacted; (2) if after a reasonable investigation the company determines there is not a "reasonable likelihood of harm" to customers; (3) if other state or federal laws require equal or greater disclosure of data breaches; or (4) if the business "maintains its own notification procedures as part of an information security policy" and is otherwise consistent with the law's timing requirements, provided that the company follows its internal policies.

Timing of notice to individuals: Individual notice must be made "in the most expedient time and manner possible and without unreasonable delay," consistent with the needs of law enforcement and to determine the scope of the breach and restore the system's integrity.

Form of notice to individuals: (1) Written notice; (2) email notice; or (3) substitute notice if the cost of notifying would exceed $250,000, more than 500,000 residents of Arkansas would need to be notified, or the company does not have sufficient contact information. Substitute notice consists of email notice when an address is available, conspicuous posting of the notice on the company's website, and notification by statewide media.

Notice to state regulators or credit bureaus: Not required.

California

Cal. Civ. Code § 1798.82

Types of personal information covered: (1) An individual's first name or first initial and last name in combination with at least one of the following: (a) Social Security number; (b) driver's license or state ID card number; (c) financial account number, credit or debit card number, in combination with any required code or password; (d) medical information; (e) health insurance information; or (f) information collected through an automated license plate recognition system;

or

(2) a user name or email address, in combination with a password or Social Security question and answer that would permit access to an online account.
Exceptions to notice requirement: (1) If the data is encrypted; or (2) if a company complies with its internal information security policy notification procedures, consistent with the timing requirements of the statute. If a HIPAA-covered entity complies with HIPAA's breach notice requirements, it is not required to follow the California breach notice law's requirements for specific content to be included in the notification (described below).
Timing of notice to individuals: In the "most expedient time possible and without unreasonable delay," consistent with needs of law enforcement or to determine scope of the breach and restore system integrity.
Form of notice to individuals: (1) Written notice; (2) email notice; or (3) substitute notice, if the company demonstrates that the cost of notice would exceed $250,000, that more than 500,000 Californians would need to be notified, or the company does not have sufficient contact information. Substitute notice consists of email notice when available, conspicuous posting of the notice on the company's website, for at least thirty days; and (3) notification to major statewide media.

If the breach only involved the credentials for an online account, the company should send password-reset credentials. It should not email the notice to the breached email account.

The notice must be "written in plain language" and be titled "Notice of Data Breach."

The notice must contain: (1) name and contact information of company; (2) list of categories of personal information compromised; (3) if possible, the date or estimated date or ranges of the breach; (4) date of notice; (5) whether notice was delayed due to law enforcement investigation, if possible; (6) general description of the data breach, if possible; (7) toll-free phone numbers and addresses of major credit reporting agencies, and an offer for 12 months of free identity theft prevention and mitigation services, if Social Security or ID card number was exposed.

Companies also may choose to provide information about what they have done to protect consumers from harm arising from the breach and advice on how the consumers may take steps to protect themselves.

This notice should be presented under the following headings: "What Happened," "What Information Was Involved," "What We are Doing," "What You Can Do," and "For More Information."

Notice to state regulators or credit bureaus: If a company notifies more than 500 California residents due to a single data breach, the company must submit a single sample copy of the notice to the California Attorney General. Note that these sample copies are made publicly available on the California Attorney General's website.

Colorado

Colo. Rev. Stat. § 6-1-716

Types of personal information covered: First name or first initial and last name in combination with at least one of the following: (1) Social Security number; (2) driver's license or ID card number; or (3) account number or credit or debit card number, along with code or password necessary to access financial account.

Exceptions to notice requirement: (1) Encrypted or redacted personal information; (2) if the company follows its internal notification procedures "as part of an information security policy for the treatment of personal information" and is consistent with the statute's timing requirements; (3) if a company that is regulated by another state or federal law and follows that system's notification rules; or (4) if after an investigation the company concludes that misuse of the information "has not occurred and is not reasonably likely to occur."

Timing of notice to individuals: Disclosure must be provided "in the most expedient time possible and without unreasonable delay," subject to the needs of law enforcement and to determine the scope of the breach and restore the system's integrity.

Form of notice to individuals: (1) Written notice to mailing address listed in company's records; (2) telephonic notice; (3) electronic notice, if that is the company's primary method of communicating with the individual; or (4) substitute notice if the company demonstrates that the cost of notice exceeds $250,000, at least 250,000 Colorado residents would need to be notified, or the company does not have sufficient contact information. Substitute notice consists of email notice when available, conspicuous posting of the notice on the company's website, and notification to major statewide media.

Notice to state regulators or credit bureaus: Notice to state regulators not required. Notice to credit reporting agencies required, provided that more than 1000 Colorado residents are notified, and the company is not covered by the Gramm-Leach-Bliley Act. The notice to credit reporting agencies must state the date that the notice will be provided and the number of Colorado residents who will receive the notices.

Connecticut

Conn. Gen. Stat. § 36A-701b

Types of personal information covered: An individual's first name or first initial and last name in combination with at least one of the following: (1) Social Security number; (2) driver's license or state ID card number; or (3) account number, credit or debit card number, in combination with any required code or password to access the financial account.

Exceptions to notice requirement: (1) Encrypted information; (2) if, after investigation and consultation with relevant law enforcement agencies, the company determines that breach will not "likely result in harm" to individuals whose information was exposed; (3) if the company follows the notification procedures of its internal information security policies, provided that it complies with the statute's timing requirements and notifies the Connecticut Attorney General; and (4) if a company maintains a breach procedure under the rules of the Gramm-Leach-Bliley Act, provided that the company notifies the individuals and the Connecticut Attorney General.

Timing of notice to individuals: Individuals must be notified without unreasonable delay, and within ninety days of discovery of the incident, subject to needs of law enforcement, to identify individuals, and restore system integrity.

Form of notice to individuals: (1) Written notice; (2) telephone notice; (3) electronic notice; or (4) substitute notice, if the costs of notification would exceed $250,000, more than 500,000 people would be notified, or the company does not have sufficient contact information. Substitute notice consists of email when the address is available, conspicuous posting of the notice on the company's website, and notification to major statewide media, including newspapers, radio, and television.

Companies must provide "appropriate identity theft protection services, and, if applicable, identity theft mitigation services" for at least twelve months.

Notice to state regulators or credit bureaus: If any Connecticut residents are notified, the Connecticut Attorney General also must receive notification at the same time or earlier.

Delaware

Del. Code tit. 6 § 12B-101, et seq.

Types of personal information covered: An individual's first name or first initial and last name along with at least one of the following: (1) Social Security number; (2) driver's license or state ID card number; or (3) account or credit or debit card number, along with any required code or password.

Exceptions to notice requirement: (1) If the personal information was encrypted; (2) if, after a good faith and reasonable and prompt investigation, the company determines that misuse of Delaware residents' information has not occurred and is not "reasonably likely to occur"; (3) a company that follows the notification requirements of its information security policy and the timing is consistent with this statute; or (4) a company regulated by state or federal law and maintains notice procedures that are consistent with the rules of its primary regulator.

Timing of notice to individuals: Notice must be provided "in the most expedient time possible and without unreasonable delay," except as needed legitimately for law enforcement, to determine scope of the breach, and to restore the system's integrity.

Form of notice to individuals: (1) Written notice; (2) telephonic notice; (3) electronic notice; or (4) substitute notice, if the total cost of notification will exceed $75,000, more than 100,000 Delaware residents must be notified, or the company does not have sufficient contact information. Substitute notice consists of email notice if the company has email addresses, conspicuous posting of the notice on the company's website, and notice to major statewide media.

Notice to state regulators or credit bureaus: Not required.

District of Columbia

D.C. Code §§ 28-3851 et seq.

Types of personal information covered: (1) Individual's first name or first initial and last name, or phone number, or address, and at least one of the following: (a) Social Security number; (b) driver's license or D.C. ID card number; or (c) credit card or debit card number;

or

(2) any other number or code or combination of numbers or codes that allows access to or use of a financial or credit account.

Exceptions to notice requirement: (1) If the data is "rendered secure, so as to be unusable by an unauthorized third party" (i.e., encryption); (2) A company that notifies pursuant to notice procedures in its information security policy, provided that the timing is consistent with this law; or (3) a company that notifies pursuant to the Gramm-Leach-Bliley Act.

Timing of notice to individuals: Notice is required in the "most expedient time possible and without unreasonable delay," consistent with legitimate needs of law enforcement and with the need to determine scope of the breach and restore system integrity.

Form of notice to individuals: (1) Written notice; (2) electronic notice; or (3) substitute notice, if the company's total cost of notification would exceed $50,000, the number of DC residents requiring notification exceeds 100,000, or the company does not have sufficient contact information. Substitute notice consists of email notice when an address is available, conspicuous posting of the notice on the website of the company, and notice to major local and, if applicable, national media.

Notice to state regulators or credit bureaus: No notice to D.C. regulators required. Notice to credit reporting agencies required if more than 1000 D.C. residents are notified. The credit reporting agency notices must describe the "timing, distribution and content" of the individual notices.

Florida

Fla. Stat. § 501.171

Types of personal information covered: An individual's first name or first initial and last name in combination with any one or more of the following: (1) Social Security number; (2) driver's license or ID card number, passport number, military ID number, or similar number on a government document used to verify identity; (3) financial account or credit or debit card number, in combination with required code or password; (4) information regarding medical history, mental or physical condition, or medical treatment or diagnosis by healthcare professional; or (5) health insurance policy number or subscriber ID number and any unique identifier used by health insurer to verify identity.

Separately, Florida's notification law covers a user name or email address, in combination with a password or security question and answer that would permit access to an online account. The notification requirement applies even if the individual's name is not disclosed.

Exceptions to notice requirement: (1) If the information was encrypted; (2) if after investigation and consulting with law enforcement, the company "reasonably determines that the disclosure has not and will not likely result in identity theft or any other financial harm" to individuals, provided that the company documents this determination, provides the written documentation to the Florida Department of Legal Affairs within thirty days, and retains the determination for five years; or (3) if the entity follows the breach notice provisions for its primary or functional federal regulator and provides a copy of this notice to the Florida Department of Legal Affairs.

Timing of notice to individuals: Notice must be made "as expeditiously as practicable and without unreasonable delay," but no longer than thirty days after determination of a breach or reason to believe the breach has occurred, unless there is a written request from a law enforcement agency.

Form of notice to individuals: (1) Written notice; (2) email notice; or (3) substitute notice if cost of notifying exceeds $250,000, more than 500,000 Florida residents would need to be notified, or the company does not have contact information. Substitute notice consists of a conspicuous notice on the company's website and notice in print and broadcast media, including major media in urban and rural areas where the affected individuals reside.

Notices to individuals must include the date, estimated date, or date range of the breach, a description of the personal information at issue in the breach, and contact information for the company.

Third-party agents that suffer a data breach must notify the company whose customers' information is breached within ten days of the breach. When the company receives a notice from a third-party agent, the company should provide the required individual notices.

Notice to state regulators or credit bureaus: If more than 500 Florida residents' personal information is compromised, companies must inform the Florida Department of Legal Affairs within thirty days after a breach is discovered. The written notice must include a synopsis of the events surrounding the breach, the number of Floridians affected, services offered for free to individuals related to the breach, a copy of the individual notice, and the name, address, phone number, and email address of the company for more information about the breach.

Companies must provide written notice to credit reporting agencies if more than 1000 Florida residents' personal information is compromised.

Georgia

Ga. Code §§ 10-1-910 *et seq.*

Types of personal information covered: Note that Georgia's breach notice law only applies to breaches of the systems of "information brokers" or companies that maintain data on behalf of information brokers. The statute defines "information broker" as "any person or entity who, for monetary fees or dues, engages in whole or in part in the business of collecting, assembling, evaluating, compiling, reporting, transmitting, transferring, or communicating information concerning individuals for the primary purpose of furnishing personal information to nonaffiliated third parties, but does not include any governmental agency whose records are maintained primarily for traffic safety, law enforcement, or licensing purposes."

The statute defines "personal information" as an individual's first name or first initial and last name in combination with at least one of the following: (1) Social Security number; (2) driver's license or state ID card number; (3) financial account number or credit card or debit card number, along with any required access codes or passwords; (4) account passwords or personal ID numbers or other access codes; or (5) any of the previous for items when not in connection with individual's name if the information would be sufficient to conduct identity theft.

Exceptions to notice requirement: (1) Encrypted information; or (2) an information broker that provides notice pursuant to its information security policy, provided that the notice is consistent with this statute's timing requirements.

Timing of notice to individuals: Notice must be provided in the "most expedient time possible and without unreasonable delay," consistent with needs of law enforcement and needs to determine the scope of the breach and to restore the reasonable integrity, security, and confidentiality of the system.

Form of notice to individuals: (1) Written notice; (2) electronic notice; or (3) substitute notice, if the cost of providing notice would exceed $250,000, more than 500,000 Georgia residents would be notified, or the information broker does not have sufficient contact information. Substitute notice consists of email notice if addresses are available, conspicuous posting on the information broker's webpage, and notification to major statewide media.

Notice to state regulators or credit bureaus: If more than 10,000 Georgia residents are notified, the information broker must also notify the credit reporting agencies.

Hawaii

Haw. Rev. Stat. §§ 487N-1 *et seq.*

Types of personal information covered: A person's first name or first initial and last name in combination with at least one of the following: (1) Social Security number; (2) driver's license number or state ID card number; or financial account number, credit or debit card number, access code, or password.

Exceptions to notice requirement: (1) If the information was encrypted, and the key was not accessed; (2) if the information was redacted; (3) if the company determines that "illegal use" of the personal information, creating a risk of harm to the person, has not occurred and is not reasonably likely to occur; (4) if the company is a financial institution subject to the federal Interagency Guidance on Response Programs for Unauthorized Access to Customer Information and Customer Notice; or (5) a HIPAA-covered entity that complies with HIPAA's breach notice requirements.

Timing of notice to individuals: Notice should be made "without unreasonable delay," consistent with needs of law enforcement and with measures necessary to determine contact information and scope of the breach, and to restore the reasonable integrity, security, and confidentiality of the system.

Form of notice to individuals: (1) Written notice to last available address on record; (2) electronic notice; (3) telephone notice as long as contact is made directly with affected person; or (4) substitute notice if the cost of notice would exceed $100,000, the company would need to notify more than 200,000 Hawaii residents, or the business does not have sufficient contact information. Substitute notice consists of email if addresses are available, conspicuous posting of the notice on the company's website, and notification to major statewide media.

Notice must describe the incident in general terms, along with the type of personal information that was breached, the steps the company took to prevent further access, a telephone number for more information, and advice to "remain vigilant by reviewing financial account records and monitoring free credit reports."

Notice to state regulators or credit bureaus: If the company notifies more than 1000 Hawaii residents, it also must notify the Hawaii Office of Consumer Protection and the major credit reporting agencies. The notices should disclose the timing, distribution, and content of the notice.

Idaho

Idaho Code §§ 28-51-104 *et seq.*

Types of personal information covered: An individual's first name or first initial and last name in combination with at least one of the following: (1) Social Security number; (2) driver's license or state ID card number; or (3) financial account number, or credit or debit card number, along with any required code or password.

Exceptions to notice requirement: (1) If the information is encrypted; (2) if an investigation determines that misuse of information has not occurred and is not "reasonably likely to occur"; (3) if the company follows the security breach notification procedures of its information security policy, consistent with this statute's timing requirements; or (4) a company regulated by state or federal law that maintains procedures for data breach notification, provided that the company complies with those procedures.

Timing of notice to individuals: Notice must be provided to individuals in the "most expedient time possible and without unreasonable delay," consistent with needs of law enforcement, measures necessary to determine scope of the breach and identify affected individuals, and to restore the system's reasonable integrity.

Form of notice to individuals: (1) Written notice; (2) telephonic notice; (3) electronic notice; and (4) substitute notice, if the cost of notice would exceed $25,000, that more than 50,000 Idaho residents would need to be notified, or the company does not have sufficient contact information. Substitute notice consists of email notice to available addresses, conspicuous posting on the company's website, and notice to major statewide media.

Notice to state regulators or credit bureaus: Not required

Illinois

815 Ill. Comp. Stat. §§ 530/1 *et seq.*

Types of personal information covered: An individual's first name or first initial and last name in combination with at least one of the following: (1) Social Security number; (2) driver's license or state ID card number; or (3) financial account number or credit or debit card number, along with any required code or password.

Exceptions to notice requirement: (1) If data is encrypted or redacted; or (2) if the company follows the security breach notification procedures of its information security policy, consistent with this statute's timing requirements.

Timing of notice to individuals: Notice must be provided in the "most expedient time possible and without unreasonable delay," consistent with measures necessary to restore system integrity, confidentiality, and security.

Form of notice to individuals: (1) Written notice; (2) electronic notice; or (3) substitute notice, if the cost of providing notice would exceed $250,000, affected Illinois residents exceeds 500,000 people, or the company does not have sufficient contact information. Substitute notice must be provided via email if an address is available, conspicuous posting on the company's website, and notification to statewide media.

The notice must include toll-free phone numbers for the credit reporting agencies, toll-free phone number, address, and web address for the FTC, and a statement that these sources can provide information about fraud alerts and credit freezes. The notice must not include the number of Illinois residents whose data was compromised.

Notice to state regulators or credit bureaus: Not required.

Indiana

Ind. Code §§ 24-4.9-1-1 *et seq.*

Types of personal information covered: First name or first initial and last name, along with at least one of the following: (1) driver's license or state ID card number; (2) credit card number; or (3) financial account number or debit card number in combination with a security code, password, or access code. Separately, an unencrypted and unredacted Social Security number is considered to be personal information, even if it is not disclosed with an individual's name.

Exceptions to notice requirement: (1) If the information was redacted or encrypted and the key had not been acquired; (2) if the company does not know or should not have known that the breach "resulted in or could result in identity deception, … identity theft, or fraud"; (3) companies that maintain disclosure procedures under the USA PATRIOT Act, Executive Order 13224, Driver's Privacy Protection Act, Fair Credit Reporting Act, GLBA, or HIPAA; or (4) a financial institution that complies with the Interagency Guidance.

Timing of notice to individuals: Notice is required without unreasonable delay. A delay is reasonable if necessary to restore system integrity or discovery scope of breach, or in response to a request from the attorney general or a law enforcement agency.

Form of notice to individuals: (1) Written notice; (2) telephonic notice; (3) fax notice; (4) email; or (5) substitute notice, if the total cost of notice exceeds $250,000 or more than 500,000 Indiana residents would be notified. Substitute notice must be provided via a conspicuous posting on the company's website and notice to major news reporting media in the geographic area where Indiana residents affected by the data breach reside.

Notice to state regulators or credit bureaus: If any individuals are notified, the company must notify the Indiana Attorney General. If more than 1000 Indiana residents are notified, the company also must notify the major credit reporting agencies.

Iowa

Iowa Code §§715c.1 *et seq.*

Types of personal information covered: An individual's first name or first initial in combination with at least one of the following: (1) Social Security number; (2) driver's license or government identification number; (3) financial account number, credit card number or debit card number, along with any required code or password; (4) "unique electronic identifier or routing code," combined with any required security code, access code, or password that would enable access to a financial account; or (5) unique biometric data (i.e., retinal image or fingerprint).

Exceptions to notice requirement: (1) If data is encrypted and key is not accessed, or if the data is redacted; (2) the company complies with disclosure requirements of its primary or functional federal regulator, provided that the requirements at least provide equal protection as the state law; (3) the company is covered by GLBA and complies with its notice requirements; or (4) after investigation or consulting with law enforcement, the company determines there is "no reasonable likelihood of financial harm" to the affected individuals, provided that the company documents this determination in writing and retains the documentation for five years.

Timing of notice to individuals: In the "most expeditious manner possible and without unreasonable delay," consistent with legitimate law enforcement needs and measures that are necessary to determine the breach's scope, identify affected individuals, and restore the data's integrity, security, and confidentiality.

Form of notice to individuals: (1) Written notice; (2) electronic notice; or (3) substitute notice, if the cost of providing notice would exceed $250,000, more than 350,000 Iowa residents would need to be notified, or the company does not have sufficient contact information. Substitute notice consists of email to available addresses, conspicuous posting of the notice on the company's website, and notification to major statewide media.

Notices must contain a description of the breach, the approximate date of the breach, the type of personal information breached, contact information for consumer reporting agencies, and advice to the consumer to report suspected identity theft to local law enforcement or the Iowa Attorney General.

Notice to state regulators or credit bureaus: If 500 or more Iowa residents are notified, the company must notify the director of the consumer protection division of the Iowa Attorney General's office within five business days of notifying the Iowa residents. The law does not require notification of credit bureaus.

Kansas

Kansas Stat. §§ 50-7a01 *et seq.*

Types of personal information covered: An individual's first name or first initial and last name along with at least one of the following: (1) Social Security number; (2) driver's license or state ID card number; or (3) financial account or credit or debit card number, along with any required code or password.

Exceptions to notice requirement: (1) If the information is encrypted; (2) if an investigation determines that misuse of information has not occurred and is not "reasonably likely to occur"; (3) if the company follows the security breach notification procedures of its information security policy, consistent with this statute's timing requirements; or (4) a company regulated by state or federal law that maintains procedures for data breach notification, provided that the company complies with those procedures.

Timing of notice to individuals: In the "most expedient time possible and without unreasonable delay," consistent with legitimate law enforcement needs and measures that are necessary to determine the breach's scope and restore the system's integrity.

Form of notice to individuals: (1) Written notice; (2) electronic notice; or (3) substitute notice, if the cost of providing notice would exceed $100,000, more than 5000 Kansas residents would need to be notified, or the company does not have sufficient contact information. Substitute notice consists of email to available addresses, conspicuous posting of the notice on the company's website, and notification to major statewide media.

Notice to state regulators or credit bureaus: A company must notify credit reporting agencies of the timing, content, and distribution of notices if the company notified more than 1000 Kansas residents.

Kentucky

Ky. Rev. Stat. § 365.732

Types of personal information covered: An individual's first name or first initial and last name along with at least one of the following: (1) Social Security number; (2) driver's license or state ID card number; or (3) financial account or credit or debit card number, along with any required code or password.

Exceptions to notice requirement: (1) If the information is encrypted; (2) if an investigation determines that identity theft or fraud has not occurred and is not reasonably likely to occur; (3) if the company follows the security breach notification procedures of its information security policy, consistent with this statute's timing requirements; or (4) a company subject to HIPAA or GLBA.

Timing of notice to individuals: In the "most expedient time possible and without unreasonable delay," consistent with legitimate law enforcement needs and measures that are necessary to determine the breach's scope and restore the system's integrity.

Form of notice to individuals: (1) Written notice; (2) electronic notice; or (3) substitute notice, if the cost of providing notice would exceed $250,000, more than 500,000 Kentucky residents would need to be notified, or the company does not have sufficient contact information. Substitute notice consists of email to available addresses, conspicuous posting of the notice on the company's website, and notification to major statewide media.

Notice to state regulators or credit bureaus: A company must notify credit reporting agencies of the timing, content, and distribution of notices if the company notified more than 1000 Kentucky residents.

Louisiana

La. Rev. Stat. §§ 51:3071 *et seq.*

Types of personal information covered: An individual's first name or first initial and last name along with at least one of the following: (1) Social Security number; (2) driver's license or state ID card number; or (3) account or credit or debit card number, along with any required code or password.

Exceptions to notice requirement: (1) If the information is encrypted or redacted; (2) if a "reasonable investigation" determines there is not a "reasonable likelihood of harm to customers"; (3) if the company follows the security breach notification procedures of its information security policy, consistent with this statute's timing requirements; or (4) a financial institution subject to and in compliance with Interagency Guidance.

Timing of notice to individuals: In the most expedient time possible and without unreasonable delay, consistent with legitimate law enforcement needs and measures that are necessary to determine the breach's scope, prevent further disclosure, and restore the system's integrity.

Form of notice to individuals: (1) Written notice; (2) electronic notice; or (3) substitute notice, if the cost of providing notice would exceed $250,000, more than 500,000 Louisiana residents would need to be notified, or the company does not have sufficient contact information. Substitute notice consists of email to available addresses, conspicuous posting of the notice on the company's website, and notification to major statewide media.

Notice to state regulators or credit bureaus: A company must notify the Consumer Protection Section of the Office of the Louisiana Attorney General within ten days of notifying Louisiana residents. The notice should include the names of all Louisiana citizens who were notified of the breach.

Maine

Me. Rev. Stat. tit. 10 §§ 1346 *et seq.*

Types of personal information covered: An individual's first name or first initial and last name along with at least one of the following: (1) Social

Security number; (2) driver's license or state ID card number; (3) financial account or credit or debit card number, along with any required code or password; or (4) account passwords or PIN numbers or other access codes. Alternatively, any of those four data elements, without the individual's name, if the information "would be sufficient to permit a person to fraudulently assume or attempt to assume the identity of the person whose information was compromised."

Exceptions to notice requirement: (1) If the information is encrypted or redacted; (2) if an investigation determines that misuse of information has not occurred and is not reasonably likely to occur (though this exception does not apply to information brokers); (3) if the company follows the security breach notification procedures established by federal or Maine law, provided they are at least as protective as the requirements of this statute.

Timing of notice to individuals: In the most expeditious manner possible and without unreasonable delay, consistent with legitimate law enforcement needs and measures that are necessary to determine the breach's scope and restore the system's integrity.

Form of notice to individuals: (1) Written notice; (2) electronic notice; or (3) substitute notice, if the cost of providing notice would exceed $5000, more than 1000 Maine residents would need to be notified, or the company does not have sufficient contact information. Substitute notice consists of email to available addresses, conspicuous posting of the notice on the company's website, and notification to major statewide media.

Notice to state regulators or credit bureaus: A company that notifies Maine residents must notify the Maine Department of Professional and Financial Regulation or the Maine Attorney General. If the company notified more than 1000 Maine residents, the company must notify credit reporting agencies of the breach date, estimated number of people affected, and date of individual notification.

Maryland

Md. Code, Com. Law §§ 14-3501 *et seq.*

Types of personal information covered: An individual's first name or first initial and last name along with at least one of the following: (1) Social Security number; (2) driver's license or state ID card number; (3) financial account or credit or debit card number, along with any required code or password; or (4) an individual taxpayer identification number.

Exceptions to notice requirement: (1) If the information is encrypted or redacted; (2) if an investigation determines there is not a reasonable likelihood of misuse of the information, provided that the company retains written documentation of this determination for three years; (3) if the company is subject to rules of a primary or functional federal or state regulator; or (4) a financial institution subject to GLBA.

Timing of notice to individuals: Notification should be provided "as soon as reasonably practicable," consistent with legitimate law enforcement needs and measures that are necessary to determine the breach's scope, the company must identify individuals whose data was breached, and restore the system's integrity.

Form of notice to individuals: (1) Written notice; (2) electronic notice; (3) telephone notice; or (4) substitute notice, if the cost of providing notice would exceed $100,000, more than 175,000 Maryland residents would need to be notified, or the company does not have sufficient contact information. Substitute notice consists of email to available addresses, conspicuous posting of the notice on the company's website, and notification to major state-wide media.

Notices must contain descriptions of the types of data breached, the company's contact information, the toll-free phone numbers and addresses for the credit reporting agencies, the toll-free telephone number, addresses, and websites for the FTC and Maryland Attorney General, and a statement that individuals can obtain information about identity theft from these sources.

Notice to state regulators or credit bureaus: A company must notify the Maryland Attorney General **before** notifying Maryland residents. If more than 1000 Maryland residents are notified, credit bureaus also should be notified, and, the notice should state the timing, content, and distribution of the individual notices.

Massachusetts

Mass. Gen. Laws ch. 93H

Types of personal information covered: An individual's first name or first initial and last name along with at least one of the following: (1) Social Security number; (2) driver's license or state ID card number; or (3) financial account or credit or debit card number, along with any required code or password.

Exceptions to notice requirement: (1) If the information is encrypted with at least a 128-bit process and the key was not accessed; or (2) if the company follows the security breach notification procedures required by federal laws or regulations, provided that they notify Massachusetts residents and Massachusetts officials.

The statute does not have the standard risk-of-harm exception. Instead, it requires notification if a company "(1) knows or has reason to know of a breach of security or (2) when the person or agency knows or has reason to know that the personal information of such resident was acquired or used by an unauthorized person or used for an unauthorized purpose."

Timing of notice to individuals: Notification must be provided "as soon as practicable and without unreasonable delay."

Form of notice to individuals: (1) Written notice; (2) electronic notice; or (3) substitute notice, if the cost of providing notice would exceed $250,000, more than 500,000 Massachusetts residents would need to be notified, or the company does not have sufficient contact information. Substitute notice consists of email to available addresses, conspicuous posting of the notice on the company's website, and notification to major statewide media.

The notice must include the consumer's right to obtain a police report, instructions to request a security freeze, including fees paid to consumer reporting agencies. The notice must **not** describe the nature of the breach or the number of Massachusetts residents affected.

Notice to state regulators or credit bureaus: A company must notify the Massachusetts Attorney General and Director of Consumer Affairs and Business Regulation. The notice should describe the breach, the number of affected Massachusetts residents, and steps taken to remediate harm.

Michigan

Mich. Comp. Laws §§ 445.63, 445.72

Types of personal information covered: An individual's first name or first initial and last name along with at least one of the following: (1) Social Security number; (2) driver's license or state ID card number; or (3) financial account or credit or debit card number, along with any required code or password.

Exceptions to notice requirement: (1) If the personal information was encrypted and the key was not disclosed; (2) if the company determines that the breach "has not or is not likely to cause substantial loss or injury to, or result in identity theft of" a Michigan resident; (3) a financial institution that is subject to, and has notification procedures that are subject to examination by regulators for compliance with, the Interagency Guidance; or (4) an entity subject to and in compliance with HIPAA.

Timing of notice to individuals: Notice must be provided "without unreasonable delay," except as needed legitimately for law enforcement, to determine scope of the breach, and to restore the system's reasonable integrity.

Form of notice to individuals: (1) Written notice; (2) telephonic notice, subject to consent and format restrictions specified in the statute; (3) electronic notice, subject to consent and format restrictions specified in the statute; or (4) substitute notice, if the total cost of notification will exceed $250,000, more than 500,000 Michigan residents must be notified, or the company does not have sufficient contact information. Substitute notice consists of email notice if the company has email addresses; conspicuous posting of the notice on the company's website, and notice to major state-wide media that includes a telephone number to obtain assistance and information.

Notices must be written in a "clear and conspicuous manner," describe the breach in general terms, describe the type of personal information that is the subject of the unauthorized access or use, if applicable, describe remediation steps to prevent further breaches, include phone number for additional information, and remind recipients of the need to remain vigilant for identity theft and fraud.

Notice to state regulators or credit bureaus: Notice to major credit reporting agencies required if more than 1000 Michigan residents receive breach notices (though this does not apply to GLBA-covered companies). The notice must state the date of the notices that were sent to individuals.

Minnesota

Minn. Stat. §§ 325E.61, et seq.

Types of personal information covered: An individual's first name or first initial and last name along with at least one of the following: (1) Social Security number; (2) driver's license or state ID card number; or (3) financial account or credit or debit card number, along with any required code or password.

Exceptions to notice requirement: (1) if the personal information was encrypted, as long as the key was not accessed; (2) a company that follows the notification requirements of its information security policy and the timing is consistent with this statute; or (3) a company that qualifies as a "financial institution" under GLBA.

Timing of notice to individuals: Notice must be provided "in the most expedient time possible and without unreasonable delay," except as needed legitimately for law enforcement, to determine scope of the breach, identify affected individuals, and to restore the system's integrity.

Form of notice to individuals: (1) Written notice; (2) electronic notice; or (3) substitute notice, if the total cost of notification will exceed $250,000, more than 500,000 Minnesota residents must be notified, or the company does not have sufficient contact information. Substitute notice consists of email notice if the company has email addresses; conspicuous posting of the notice on the company's website, and notice to major statewide media.

Notice to state regulators or credit bureaus: If a company determines that more than 500 Minnesota residents must be notified, the company must notify the major consumer reporting agencies, within forty-eight hours of the determination, of the timing, distribution, and content of the notices.

Mississippi

Miss. Code § 75-24-29

Types of personal information covered: An individual's first name or first initial and last name along with at least one of the following: (1) Social Security number; (2) driver's license or state ID card number; or (3) financial account or credit or debit card number, along with any required code or password.

Exceptions to notice requirement: (1) If the personal information was encrypted or rendered unreadable or unusable by any other method or technology; (2) if after "appropriate investigation," the company "reasonably determines that the breach will not likely result in harm to the affected individuals"; (3) a company that follows the notification requirements of its information security policy and the timing is consistent with this statute; or (4) a company that maintains a breach procedure under the rules of GLBA.

Timing of notice to individuals: Notice must be provided "without unreasonable delay," except as needed legitimately for law enforcement, to determine scope of the breach, identify affected individuals, and to restore the system's integrity.

Form of notice to individuals: (1) Written notice; (2) telephone notice; (3) electronic notice; or (4) substitute notice, if the total cost of notification will exceed $5000, more than 5000 Mississippi residents must be notified, or the company does not have sufficient contact information. Substitute notice consists of email notice if the company has email addresses; conspicuous posting of the notice on the company's website, and notice to major statewide media, including newspapers, radio, and television.

Notice to state regulators or credit bureaus: Not required

Missouri

Mo. Rev. Stat. § 407.1500

Types of personal information covered: An individual's first name or first initial and last name along with at least one of the following: (1) Social Security number; (2) driver's license or state ID card number; (3) financial account or credit or debit card number, along with any required code or password; (4) "unique electronic identifier or routing code," along with any required code or password to access a financial account; (5) medical information; or (6) health insurance information.

Exceptions to notice requirement: (1) If the personal information was encrypted or redacted; (2) if after an "appropriate investigation" or consultation with law enforcement, the company "determines that a risk of identity theft or other fraud to any consumer is not reasonably likely to occur as a result of the breach," provided that the company documents this finding in writing and maintains it for five years; (3) a company that follows the notification requirements of its information security policy and the timing is consistent with this statute; or (4) a company that notifies consumers in accordance with mandated procedures of its functional state or federal regulator; (5) a financial institution subject to the Interagency Guidance, GLBA, or the National Credit Union Administration regulations.

Timing of notice to individuals: Notice must be provided "without unreasonable delay," except as needed legitimately for law enforcement, to determine scope of the breach, identify affected individuals, and to restore the system's integrity.

Form of notice to individuals: (1) Written notice; (2) electronic notice; (3) telephone notice, if affected customers are directly contacted, or (4) substitute notice, if the total cost of notification will exceed $100,000, more than 5000 Missouri residents must be notified, or the company does not have sufficient contact information. Substitute notice consists of email notice if the company has email addresses; conspicuous posting of the notice on the company's website, and notice to major statewide media.

The notice should contain a description of the incident "in general terms," the type of personal information obtained, a phone number for further information and assistance, if one exists, contact information for consumer reporting agencies, and advice that the consumer should "remain vigilant by reviewing account statements and monitoring free credit reports."

Notice to state regulators or credit bureaus: If a company determines that more than 1000 Missouri residents must be notified, the company must notify the Missouri Attorney General's office and the major consumer reporting agencies of the timing, distribution, and content of the notices.

Montana

Mont. Code §§ 30-14-1701 *et seq.*

Types of personal information covered: An individual's first name or first initial and last name along with at least one of the following: (1) Social Security number; (2) driver's license or state ID card number; (3) financial account or credit or debit card number, along with any required code or password; (4) medical record information; (5) taxpayer identification number; or (6) IRS-issued identity protection personal identification number.

Exceptions to notice requirement: (1) If the information is encrypted; (2) if the breach did not cause and is not "reasonably believed to cause" loss or injury to a Montana resident; or (3) if the company follows the security breach notification procedures of its information security policy, and does not unreasonably delay notice.

Timing of notice to individuals: Notice must be provided "without unreasonable delay," consistent with legitimate law enforcement needs and measures that are necessary to determine the breach's scope and restore the system's reasonable integrity.

Form of notice to individuals: (1) Written notice; (2) electronic notice; (3) telephone notice; or (4) substitute notice, if the cost of providing notice would exceed $250,000, more than 500,000 Montana residents would need to be notified, or the company does not have sufficient contact information. Substitute notice consists of email to available addresses, conspicuous posting of the notice on the company's website, and notification to major statewide media.

Notice to state regulators or credit bureaus: When a company notifies Montana residents of a breach, it must simultaneously submit an electronic copy of the notice and a statement with the date and method of distribution of the individual notices to the Montana Attorney General's consumer protection office. The copy must not contain any personally identifiable information about the individual notice recipients. The statute does not require reports to the consumer reporting bureaus, but if the individual notices state that individuals may obtain copies of their files from the bureaus, the company must coordinate with the bureau on the timing, content, and distribution of the individual notices. The coordination cannot unreasonably delay individual notices.

Nebraska

Neb. Rev. Stat. §§ 87-801 *et seq.*

Types of personal information covered: (a) An individual's first name or first initial and last name along with at least one of the following: (1) Social Security number; (2) driver's license or state ID card number; (3) financial account or credit or debit card number, along with any required code or password; (4) unique electronic identification number or routing code, in combination with any required security code, access code, or password; or (5) "unique biometric data," such as a fingerprint, voice print, or retinal or iris image, or other unique physical representation;

or

(b) a user name or email address, along with the password or security question that allows access to an online user account.

Exceptions to notice requirement: (1) If the information is encrypted, provided that the key was not accessed, or if the information was redacted;

(2) if an investigation determines that use of information about a Nebraska resident for an unauthorized purpose has not occurred and is not "reasonably likely" to occur; (3) if the company follows the security breach notification procedures of its information security policy, consistent with this statute's timing requirements; or (4) a company regulated by state or federal law that requires procedures for data breach notification, provided that the company complies with those procedures.

Timing of notice to individuals: Notice must be made "as soon as possible and without unreasonable delay," consistent with legitimate law enforcement needs and measures that are necessary to determine the breach's scope and restore the system's reasonable integrity.

Form of notice to individuals: (1) Written notice; (2) electronic notice; (3) telephone notice, or (4) substitute notice, if the cost of providing notice would exceed $75,000, more than 100,000 Nebraska residents would need to be notified, or the company does not have sufficient contact information. Substitute notice consists of email to available addresses, conspicuous posting of the notice on the company's website, and notification to major statewide media.

If the company has ten or fewer employees and the cost of notice would exceed $10,000, substitute notice consists of (1) email to known addresses; (2) notification by a paid advertisement in a local newspaper in the geographic area in which the company is located, provided that the ad covers at least a quarter of a page in the newspaper and is published at least once a week for three consecutive weeks; (3) conspicuous posting on the company's website; and (4) notification to major media outlets in the geographic area in which the company is located.

Notice to state regulators or credit bureaus: If a company notifies Nebraska residents of a data breach, it must also notify the Nebraska Attorney General concurrently or before it notifies the individuals.

Nevada

Nev. Rev. Stat. §§ 603A.010 *et seq.*

Types of personal information covered: First name or first initial and last name in combination with one or more of the following: (1) Social Security number (not including last four digits of number); (2) driver's license or state ID number; (3) financial account number, credit card number, or debit card number, in combination with any code or password necessary to access financial account; (4) medical identification number or health insurance identification number; or (5) a "user name, unique identifier or electronic mail address in combination with a password, access code or security question and answer that would permit access to an online account."

Exceptions to notice requirement: (1) If personal information is encrypted; (2) if the company is subject to and complies with GLBA's breach notice requirements; or (3) if the business maintains its own notification procedures as part of an information security policy and is otherwise consistent with the law's timing requirements, provided that the company follows its internal policies.

Timing of notice to individuals: Individual notice must be made in the "most expedient time possible and without unreasonable delay," consistent with the needs of law enforcement or needs to determine scope of the breach or restore reasonable integrity of the system data.

Form of notice to individuals: (1) Written notice; (2) electronic notice; or (3) substitute notice if the cost of notifying would exceed $250,000, more than 500,000 residents of Nevada would need to be notified, or the company does not have sufficient contact information. Substitute notice consists of email notice when an address is available, conspicuous posting of the notice on the company's website, and notification to major statewide media.

Notice to state regulators or credit bureaus: If more than 1000 Nevada residents are notified for one incident, the company must notify the major consumer reporting agencies of the time the notification was distributed and the content of the notification.

New Hampshire

N.H. Rev. Stat. §§ 359-C:19 *et seq.*

Types of personal information covered: First name or first initial and last name in combination with one or more of the following: (1) Social Security number; (2) driver's license or state ID number; or (3) financial account number, credit card number, or debit card number, in combination with any code or password necessary to access financial account.

Exceptions to notice requirement: (1) If personal information is encrypted; (2) if the company determines that misuse of the information has not occurred and is not "reasonably likely" to occur; or (3) a company subject to NH RSA 358-A:3 (e.g., a financial institution) and maintains procedures consistent with rules issued by a state or federal regulator.

Timing of notice to individuals: Individual notice must be made "as quickly as possible" after the company determines there is a risk of harm.

Form of notice to individuals: (1) Written notice; (2) telephone notice; (3) electronic notice, if it was primary means of communication with individual; (4) substitute notice if the cost of notifying would exceed $5000, more than 1000 residents of New Hampshire would need to be notified, or the company does not have sufficient contact information. Substitute notice consists of email notice when an address is available, conspicuous posting of the notice on the company's website, and notification to major statewide media; or (5) notice under the company's internal notification procedures maintained as part of an information security program.

The notice must include a description of the incident "in general terms," the approximate date of the breach, the type of personal information obtained due to the breach, and the telephone contact information for the company.

Notice to state regulators or credit bureaus: If the company notifies any individuals in New Hampshire, it also must notify the New Hampshire attorney general's office of the anticipated date of the individual notice and the approximate number of New Hampshire residents who will be notified. The statute does not require companies to provide names of affected residents. Companies subject to RSA 358-A:3 (e.g., financial institutions) should notify their primary regulator rather than the New Hampshire Attorney General's office.

If more than 1000 New Hampshire residents are notified for one incident, the company must notify the major consumer reporting agencies of the time the notification was distributed and the content of the notification. (Companies subject to GLBA need not notify credit bureaus.)

New Jersey

N.J. Stat. §§ 56:8-161 *et seq.*

Types of personal information covered: An individual's first name or first initial and last name along with at least one of the following: (1) Social Security number; (2) driver's license or state ID card number; or (3) financial account or credit or debit card number, along with any required code or password. "Dissociated" data that, if linked, would be personal information is considered to be personal information "if the means to link the dissociated data were accessed in connection with access to the dissociated data."

Exceptions to notice requirement: (1) If the information is encrypted; (2) if the company concludes that the information was not, or is not "reasonably believed" to have been, accessed by an "unauthorized person"; or (3) if the company follows the security breach notification procedures of its information security policy, provided that the procedures are "otherwise consistent with the requirements" of the New Jersey law.

Timing of notice to individuals: Notification must be provided "in the most expedient time possible and without unreasonable delay," consistent with legitimate law enforcement needs and measures that are necessary to determine the breach's scope and restore the system's integrity.

Form of notice to individuals: (1) Written notice; (2) electronic notice; or (3) substitute notice, if the cost of providing notice would exceed $250,000, more than 500,000 New Jersey residents would need to be notified, or the company does not have sufficient contact information. Substitute notice consists of email to available addresses, conspicuous posting of the notice on the company's website, and notification to major statewide media.

Notice to state regulators or credit bureaus: A company must notify the New Jersey Division of State Police **before** notifying individuals. If a company notifies more than 1000 New Jersey residents, it should, without unreasonable delay, notify all consumer reporting agencies of the timing, distribution, and content of the notices.

New York

N.Y. Gen. Bus. Law § 899-aa

Types of personal information covered: Any "information concerning a natural person which, because of name, number, personal mark, or other identifier, can be used to identify such natural person" along with at least one of the following: (1) Social Security number; (2) driver's license or state ID card number; or (3) financial account or credit or debit card number, along with any required code or password.

Exceptions to notice requirement: (1) If the personal information was encrypted and the key was not accessed; (2) if the company determines that the unauthorized acquisition did not compromise "the security, confidentiality, or integrity of personal information," after considering the following factors: (a) indications that the information is in the "physical possession and control of an unauthorized person"; (b) indications that "the information has been downloaded or copied"; and (c) indications that the information was "used by an unauthorized person, such as fraudulent accounts opened or instances of identity theft reported."

Timing of notice to individuals: Notice must be provided in the "most expedient time possible and without unreasonable delay," except as needed legitimately for law enforcement, to determine scope of the breach, identify affected individuals, and to restore the system's integrity.

Form of notice to individuals: (1) Written notice; (2) telephone notice; (3) electronic notice; or (4) substitute notice, if the total cost of notification will exceed $250,000, more than 500,000 New York residents must be notified, or the company does not have sufficient contact information. Substitute notice consists of email notice if the company has email addresses, conspicuous posting of the notice on the company's website, and notice to major statewide media.

The notice must include contact information for the company, and a description of the categories of information believed to have been acquired.

Notice to state regulators or credit bureaus: Any time that New York residents are notified of a data breach, the company should notify the New York Attorney General, the New York Department of State, and the New York Division of State Police of the timing, content, and distribution of the notices and the approximate number of New York residents affected. The notice must not delay notification of individuals.

If more than 5000 New York residents are notified at one time, the company must notify the consumer reporting agencies of the timing, content, and distribution of the notices and approximate number of New York residents affected.

North Carolina

N.C. Gen. Stat §§ 75-61, 75-65

Types of personal information covered: An individual's first name or first initial and last name along with at least one of the following: (1) Social Security number; (2) driver's license or state ID card number; or (3) checking account number; (4) savings account number; (5) credit card number; (6) debit card number; (7) personal identification code; (8) electronic identification numbers, electronic mail names or addresses, Internet account numbers, or Internet identification names; (9) digital signatures; (10) any other numbers or information that can be used to access a person's financial resources; (11) biometric data; (12) fingerprints; (13) passwords; or (14) parent's legal surname prior to marriage.

Exceptions to notice requirement: (1) If the personal information was encrypted and the key has not been accessed; (2) if the company "reasonably determines" that consumers have not been harmed and likely will not be harmed by the incident; or (3) a financial institution that complies with the Interagency Guidance.

Timing of notice to individuals: Notice must be provided "without unreasonable delay," except as needed legitimately for law enforcement, to determine scope of the breach, identify affected individuals, and to restore the system's integrity, security, and confidentiality.

Form of notice to individuals: (1) Written notice; (2) telephone notice; (3) electronic notice; or (4) substitute notice, if the total cost of notification will exceed $250,000, more than 500,000 North Carolina residents must be notified, or the company does not have sufficient contact information. Substitute notice consists of email notice if the company has email addresses; conspicuous posting of the notice on the company's website, and notice to major statewide media.

The notice must contain a description of the incident "in general terms," a description of the categories of personal information that were subject to unauthorized access, a description of the steps the business took to prevent further unauthorized access, a phone number for further information and assistance, advice to "remain vigilant by reviewing account statements and monitoring free credit reports," toll-free numbers and addresses for the major consumer reporting agencies, and toll-free numbers, addresses, and website addresses for the FTC and North Carolina Attorney General's office, along with a statement that the individual "can obtain information from these sources about preventing identity theft."

Notice to state regulators or credit bureaus: If any North Carolina residents are notified, the company must notify the North Carolina Attorney General's Consumer Protection Division, without unreasonable delay, of the nature of the breach, the number of consumers affected, steps taken to investigate the breach, steps taken to prevent a similar breach in the future, and information regarding the timing, distribution, and content of the notice.

If a company notifies more than 1000 North Carolina residents at once, the company must notify the consumer reporting agencies of the timing, distribution, and content of the individual notices.

North Dakota

N.D. Cent. Code §§ 51-30-01 *et seq.*

Types of personal information covered: An individual's first name or first initial and last name along with at least one of the following: (1) Social Security number; (2) driver's license or state ID card number; (3) financial account or credit or debit card number, along with any required code or password; (4) date of birth; (5) mother's maiden name; (6) medical information; (7) health insurance information; (8) employee identification number along with any required code or password; or (9) digitized or other electronic signature.

Exceptions to notice requirement: (1) If the information is encrypted or otherwise rendered unreadable or unusable; (2) a financial institution that complies with the Interagency Guidance; or (3) if the company follows the security breach notification procedures of its information security policy, consistent with this statute's timing requirements.

Timing of notice to individuals: In the "most expedient time possible and without unreasonable delay," consistent with legitimate law enforcement needs and measures that are necessary to determine the breach's scope and restore the system's integrity.

Form of notice to individuals: (1) Written notice; (2) electronic notice; or (3) substitute notice, if the cost of providing notice would exceed $250,000, more than 500,000 individuals would need to be notified, or the company does not have sufficient contact information. Substitute notice consists of email to available addresses, conspicuous posting of the notice on the company's website, and notification to major statewide media.

Notice to state regulators or credit bureaus: If a company notifies more than 250 individuals of a data breach, it must disclose the breach to the North Dakota Attorney General by mail or email.

Ohio

Ohio Rev. Code §§ 1349.19 *et seq.*

Types of personal information covered: First name or first initial and last name in combination with at least one of the following: (1) Social Security number; (2) driver's license or ID card number; or (3) account number or credit or debit card number, along with code or password necessary to access financial account. Personal information does not include information that already had lawfully been made publicly available by or to the news media.

Exceptions to notice requirement: (1) Encrypted or redacted personal information; (2) if the company is a financial institution, trust company, or credit union or affiliate of such, and is required by federal law to issue breach notices to affected customers; (3) if the company is a covered entity or business associate under HIPAA; or (4) if the company does not "reasonably believe" that the breach will cause a "material risk of identity theft or other fraud" to Ohio residents.

Timing of notice to individuals: Disclosure must be provided in the "most expedient time possible," but no later than forty-five days after discovery or notification of the breach, subject to legitimate needs of law enforcement and consistent with any measures necessary to determine the scope of the breach and to restore system integrity.

Form of notice to individuals: (1) Written notice; (2) telephonic notice; (3) electronic notice, if that is the company's primary method of communicating with the individual; or (3) substitute notice if the company demonstrates that the cost of notice exceeds $250,000, at least 500,000 Ohio residents would need to be notified, or the company does not have sufficient contact information. Substitute notice consists of email notice when available, conspicuous posting of the notice on the company's website, and notification to major media outlets, with the cumulative total readership, viewing audience, or listening audience combined is equal to at least 75 percent of Ohio's population.

Separately, Ohio allows a separate form of substitute notice if the company has ten or fewer employees and the cost of notice would exceed $10,000. In this case, the substitute notice must include (1) notice by a paid advertisement in a local newspaper that is distributed in the area in which the company is located, with the advertisement covering at least one-quarter of a page and published at least weekly for three consecutive weeks; (2) conspicuous posting of the notice on the company's website; and (3) notice to major media outlets in the company's geographic area.

Notice to state regulators or credit bureaus: Notice to state regulators not required. Notice to credit reporting agencies required, provided that more than 1000 Ohio residents are notified. The notice to credit reporting agencies must describe the timing, distribution, and content of the individual breach notices.

Oklahoma

Okla. Stat. tit. 24 §§ 161–165

Types of personal information covered: First name or first initial and last name in combination with at least one of the following: (1) Social Security number; (2) driver's license or ID card number; or (3) financial account number or credit or debit card number, along with code or password necessary to access financial account.

Exceptions to notice requirement: (1) Encrypted personal information, provided that the key was not accessed; (2) redacted personal information; (3) if the company follows its internal notification procedures and is consistent with the statute's timing requirements; (3) if a company that is regulated by another state or federal law and follows that system's notification rules; (4) a financial institution that complies with the federal Interagency Guidance on response programs; (5) a company that complies with notification procedures established by its primary or functional federal regulator; or (6) if the breach did not cause and is not reasonably believed to cause "identity theft or other fraud."

Timing of notice to individuals: Disclosure must be provided "without unreasonable delay," though delay is permitted for law enforcement purposes or to determine the scope of the breach and restore reasonable integrity to the system.

Form of notice to individuals: (1) Written notice to postal address listed in company's records; (2) telephonic notice; (3) electronic notice; (4) substitute notice if the company demonstrates that the cost of notice exceeds $50,000, at least 100,000 Oklahoma residents would need to be notified, or the company does not have sufficient contact information. Substitute notice consists of email notice when available, conspicuous posting of the notice on the company's website, and notification to major statewide media.

Notice to state regulators or credit bureaus: Notice to state regulators or credit bureaus is not required.

Oregon

Or. Rev. Stat. §§ 646A.600 *et seq.*

Types of personal information covered: First name or first initial and last name in combination with at least one of the following: (1) Social Security number; (2) driver's license or ID card number; (3) passport number or other identification number issued by the United States; (4) financial account number or credit or debit card number, along with code or password necessary to access financial account; (5) data from "automatic measurements of a consumer's physical characteristics" (e.g., fingerprint or retinal scans) that are used to authenticate a consumer's identity for a transaction; (6) health insurance policy number or health insurance subscriber identification number in combination with unique identifiers used by health insurers; or (7) information about medical history, medical or physical condition, medical diagnosis, or treatment. These seven categories of information – without an individual's name – still could be considered personal information if they would enable identity theft.

Exceptions to notice requirement: (1) Encrypted or redacted personal information; (2) if the company follows its internal notification procedures and is consistent with the statute's timing requirements; (3) if a company follows notification rules from its primary or functional federal regulator – or a state or federal law – provided that they provide greater protection to personal information and contain disclosure requirements that are "at least as thorough" as those in the Oregon law; (4) the company is a financial institution that complies with Gramm-Leach-Bliley; or (5) if, after an appropriate investigation or consultation with law enforcement, the company "reasonably determines" that the consumers are "unlikely to suffer harm." This determination must be documented in writing and retained for at least five years.

Timing of notice to individuals: Disclosure must be provided in the most "expeditious manner possible" and "without unreasonable delay," consistent with legitimate needs of law enforcement and measures necessary to determine contact information for affected consumers, the scope of the breach, and restore reasonable integrity, security, and confidentiality of the personal information

Form of notice to individuals: (1) Written notice; (2) telephonic notice, if the company directly contacts the consumer; (3) electronic notice, if that is the company's customary method of communicating with the individual; or (4) substitute notice if the company demonstrates that the cost of notice exceeds $250,000, at least 350,000 Oregon residents would need to be notified, or the company does not have sufficient contact information. Substitute notice consists of email notice when available, conspicuous posting of the notice on the company's website, and notification to major statewide television and media.

Notice must contain a description of the data breach "in general terms," the approximate date of the breach, the type of personal information that was subject to the breach, contact information for the company that was subject to the breach, contact information for credit bureaus, and advice to report suspected identity theft to law enforcement, including the Attorney General and the Federal Trade Commission.

Notice to state regulators or credit bureaus: If the number of affected Oregon residents exceeds 250, the company, either in writing or electronically, must provide the Oregon Attorney General with the same notice provided to consumers. Notice to credit reporting agencies without unreasonable delay is required, provided that more than 1000 Oregon residents are affected. The notice to credit bureaus should include the notice provided to individuals, and any police report number assigned to the data breach.

Pennsylvania

73 Pa. Stat. §§ 2301 *et seq*.

Types of personal information covered: First name or first initial and last name in combination with at least one of the following: (1) Social Security number; (2) driver's license or ID card number; or (3) financial account number or credit or debit card number, along with code or password necessary to access financial account.

Exceptions to notice requirement: (1) Encrypted information, if the key was not accessed; (2) redacted information; (3) if the company follows its internal notification procedures; (4) if a company complies with the notification requirements of its primary or functional federal regulator; (5) if the company is a financial institution that complies with the Interagency Guidance procedures; or (6) if the company does not "reasonably" believe that the breach has caused or will cause "loss or injury" to a Pennsylvania resident.

Timing of notice to individuals: Disclosure must be provided "without unreasonable delay," except to determine the scope of the breach and restore the reasonable integrity of the data system, or at the written request of law enforcement.

Form of notice to individuals: (1) Written notice to the last known postal address; (2) telephonic notice, if the individual can be reasonably expected to receive it and the notice clearly and conspicuously describes the incident generally and verifies personal information but does not require the customer to provide personal information, and the customer is provided with a phone number or website for further information or assistance; (3) electronic notice, if a prior business relationship exists and the company has a valid email address for the individual; or (4) substitute notice if the company demonstrates that the cost of notice exceeds $100,000, at least 175,000 Pennsylvania residents would need to be notified, or the company does not have sufficient contact information. Substitute notice consists of email notice when available, conspicuous posting of the notice on the company's website, and notification to major statewide media.

Notice to state regulators or credit bureaus: Notice to state regulators not required. Notice to credit reporting agencies required, provided that more than 1000 Pennsylvania residents are notified. The notice to credit reporting agencies must state the timing, distribution, and number of individual notices.

Rhode Island

R.I. Gen. Laws § 11-49.2-1 *et seq*.

Types of personal information covered: First name or first initial and last name in combination with at least one of the following: (1) Social Security number; (2) driver's license or ID card number; (3) financial account number or credit or debit card number, along with code or password necessary to access financial account; (4) medical or health insurance information; or (5) email address with any required security code, access code, or password that would permit access to an individual's personal, medical, insurance, or financial account.

Exceptions to notice requirement: (1) Encrypted personal information (using at least 128-bit process); (2) if the company follows its internal notification procedures and is consistent with the statute's timing requirements; (3) if a company follows a breach notification procedures under the rules of its primary or functional regulator; (4) the company is a financial institution that complies with the Interagency Guidelines; (5) the company is a health-related company that complies with HIPAA's breach notification procedures; or (6) if the company determines that the breach does not pose "a significant risk of identity theft" to Rhode Island residents.

Timing of notice to individuals: Disclosure must be provided in the "most expedient time possible" but no later than forty-five days after confirmation of the breach and the ability to ascertain the information required to fulfill the notice requirements, subject to the needs of law enforcement.

Form of notice to individuals: (1) Written notice; (2) electronic notice; or (3) substitute notice if the company demonstrates that the cost of notice exceeds $25,000, at least 50,000 Rhode Island residents would need to be notified, or the company does not have sufficient contact information.

Substitute notice consists of email notice when available, conspicuous posting of the notice on the company's website, and notification to major statewide media.

The individual notices should contain (1) a "general and brief description" of the breach, including how it occurred and the number of affected individuals; (2) the type of information that was breached; (3) date (or estimated date) of the breach; (4) date of discovery of the breach; (5) description of remediation services, including toll-free phone numbers and websites for credit reporting agencies, remediation service providers, and the Rhode Island Attorney General; and (6) a "clear and concise" description of the consumer's ability to file or obtain a police report regarding the data breach, how the individual can request a security freeze on financial accounts, and the fees that consumers may be required to pay to credit bureaus for these remedies.

Notice to state regulators or credit bureaus: Notice to the Attorney General and the major credit bureaus is required if more than 500 Rhode Island residents are notified. The notices should describe the timing, content, and distribution of the individual notices and the approximate number of affected individuals. These notices are not grounds to delay individual notifications.

South Carolina

S.C. Code § 39-1-90

Types of personal information covered: First name or first initial and last name in combination with at least one of the following: (1) Social Security number; (2) driver's license or ID card number; (3) financial account number or credit or debit card number, along with code or password necessary to access financial account; or (4) "other numbers or information which may be used to access a person's financial accounts or numbers or information issued by a governmental or regulatory entity that uniquely will identify an individual."

Exceptions to notice requirement: (1) Encrypted or redacted personal information; (2) if the company follows its internal notification procedures; (3) if a company is a financial institution or bank subject to the Gramm-Leach-Bliley Act; (4) if the company is a financial institution subject to and complying with the Interagency Guidance; or (5) if the company concludes that illegal use of the information has not occurred, is "not reasonably likely to occur," and does not create a "material risk of harm" to a South Carolina resident.

Timing of notice to individuals: Disclosure must be provided in the "most expedient time possible and without unreasonable delay," subject to the needs of law enforcement and to determine the scope of the breach and restore system integrity.

Form of notice to individuals: (1) Written notice; (2) telephonic notice; (3) electronic notice, if that is the company's primary method of communicating with the individual; or (4) substitute notice if the company demonstrates that the cost of notice exceeds $250,000, at least 500,000 South Carolina residents would need to be notified, or the company does not have sufficient contact information. Substitute notice consists of email notice when available, conspicuous posting of the notice on the company's website, and notification to major statewide media.

Notice to state regulators or credit bureaus: If more than 1000 South Carolina residents are notified, the company must notify without unreasonable delay the Consumer Protection Division of the South Carolina Department of Consumer Affairs and the major credit bureaus of the timing, distribution, and content of the notices to individuals.

Tennessee

Tenn. Code § 47-18-2107(a)

Types of personal information covered: First name or first initial and last name in combination with at least one of the following: (1) Social Security number; (2) driver's license or ID card number; or (3) account number or credit or debit card number, along with code or password necessary to access financial account.

Exceptions to notice requirement: (1) If the company is a financial institution subject to the Gramm-Leach-Bliley Act; (2) if the company is subject to HIPAA; (3) if the company complies with its internal notification procedures and is consistent with this statute's timing requirements; or (4) if the company determines that the breach did not "materially" compromise the security, confidentiality, or integrity of personal information.

Note that Tennessee is the only jurisdiction that does not exempt encrypted information from its breach notification law. However, a company would have a strong argument that encryption eliminates the possibility that the breach "materially" compromised the security, confidentiality, or integrity of the information.

Timing of notice to individuals: Disclosure must be provided immediately, but no later than forty-five days from the discovery or notification of the breach, unless the legitimate needs of law enforcement require a delay.

Form of notice to individuals: (1) Written notice; (2) electronic notice; or (3) substitute notice if the company demonstrates that the cost of notice exceeds $250,000, at least 500,000 Tennessee residents would need to be notified, or the company does not have sufficient contact information.

Substitute notice consists of email notice when available, conspicuous posting of the notice on the company's website, and notification to major statewide media.

Notice to state regulators or credit bureaus: Notice to state regulators not required. Notice to credit reporting agencies required, provided that more than 1000 Tennessee residents are notified. The notice to credit reporting agencies must describe the timing, distribution, and content of the individual notices.

Texas

Tex. Bus. & Comm. Code §§ 521.001 *et seq.*

Types of personal information covered: The Texas statute applies to "sensitive personal information," which includes two general categories: First name or first initial and last name in combination with at least one of the following: (1) Social Security number; (2) driver's license or ID card number; or (3) financial account number or credit or debit card number, along with code or password necessary to access financial account;

> or

information that identifies an individual and relates to (1) the physical or mental health or condition of the individual; (2) the provision of health care to the individual; or (3) payment for the provision of healthcare to the individual.

Some commentators have suggested that the Texas statute could be read to suggest that it requires companies to provide notice even if the individuals do not live in Texas, though no court has ruled on this issue.

Exceptions to notice requirement: (1) Encrypted data, provided that the accessor does not have the key or (2) if the company follows its internal notification procedures and is consistent with the statute's timing requirements.

Timing of notice to individuals: Disclosure must be made "as quickly as possible," except if a delay is requested by law enforcement or is necessary to determine the scope of the breach and restore the data system's reasonable integrity.

Form of notice to individuals: (1) Written notice to last known address; (2) electronic notice; or (3) substitute notice if the company demonstrates that the cost of notice exceeds $250,000, at least 250,000 people would need to be notified, or the company does not have sufficient contact information. Substitute notice consists of email notice when available, conspicuous posting of the notice on the company's website, and notification published in or broadcast on major statewide media.

Notice to state regulators or credit bureaus: Notice to state regulators is not required. Notice to credit reporting agencies is required, provided that more than 10,000 people are notified under this law. The notice to credit reporting agencies must state the timing, distribution, and content of the individual notices.

Utah

Utah Code §§ 13-44-101 *et seq.*

Types of personal information covered: First name or first initial and last name in combination with at least one of the following: (1) Social Security number; (2) driver's license or ID card number; or (3) financial account number or credit or debit card number, along with code or password necessary to access financial account.

Exceptions to notice requirement: (1) If the personal information is encrypted or protected by another method that renders the data unreadable or unusable; (2) if the company follows its internal notification procedures and is consistent with the statute's timing requirements; (3) if a company that is regulated by another state or federal law and follows that system's notification rules; or (4) if a good-faith, reasonable, and prompt investigation determines that identity theft or fraud has not occurred and is not "reasonably likely to occur."

Timing of notice to individuals: Disclosure must be provided in "the most expedient time possible and without unreasonable delay," subject to the needs of law enforcement and to determine the scope of the breach and restore system integrity.

Form of notice to individuals: (1) Written notice via first-class mail to the individual's most recent address; (2) telephonic notice, including via automatic dialing technology that is not legally prohibited; (3) electronic notice, if that is the company's primary method of communicating with the individual; or (4) publishing a notice in a general circulation newspaper.

Notice to state regulators or credit bureaus: Notice to state regulators or credit bureaus is not required.

Vermont

9 V.S.A. §§ 2430, *et seq.*

Types of personal information covered: First name or first initial and last name in combination with at least one of the following: (1) Social Security number; (2) driver's license or ID card number; (3) financial account number or credit or debit card number, along with code or password necessary to access financial account; or (4) account passwords, PINS, or other codes that could access a financial account.

Exceptions to notice requirement: (1) Encrypted or redacted personal information; (2) if a company is a financial institution that is subject to the Interagency Guidance; or (3) the company determines that misuse of personal information is "not reasonably possible" and notifies the Vermont Attorney General or Vermont Department of Financial Regulation of this determination.

Timing of notice to individuals: Disclosure must be provided "in the most expedient time possible and without unreasonable delay," but not later than forty-five days after the discovery or notification, subject to the needs of law enforcement and to determine the scope of the breach and restore systems integrity.

Form of notice to individuals: (1) Written notice to the individual's residence; (2) telephonic notice, provided that telephonic contact is made directly with each affected individual and not via a prerecorded message; (3) electronic notice, if the company has a valid email address; or (4) substitute notice if the company demonstrates that the cost of notice exceeds $5,000, at least 5000 Vermont residents would need to be notified, or the company does not have sufficient contact information. Substitute notice consists of conspicuous posting of the notice on the company's website and notification to major statewide and regional media.

Individual notices must contain (1) a description of the breach; (2) the type of personal information that was breached; (3) the steps that the company took to protect against further unauthorized access; (4) a toll-free number for more information; (5) advice to "remain vigilant" by reviewing account statements and free credit reports; and (6) date of the breach.

Notice to state regulators or credit bureaus:

Vermont requires two forms of notice to state regulators.

First, the Vermont Attorney General or Department of Financial Regulation must be notified of the dates of the breach and discovery, along with a preliminary description, within fourteen business days, consistent with the needs of law enforcement. Companies must notify state regulators no later than when they notify consumers. In other words, if a company notifies consumers seven days after discovering a breach, it must notify Vermont regulators at the same time that it notifies consumers, even though the fourteen-day period has not elapsed. If, before the breach occurs, the company swears in writing to the Attorney General that it maintains written security policies and procedures and responds to breaches in a manner consistent with Vermont law, they need only notify state regulators of the date of the breach and discovery of the breach before they notify individuals.

Second, when companies notify Vermont residents of data breaches, they also must provide Vermont regulators with a copy of the individual notice and the number of Vermont residents who were notified.

If more than 1000 consumers are notified, the company shall notify credit bureaus, without unreasonable delay, of the timing, distribution, and content of the notice.

Virginia

Va. Code § 18.2-186.6

Types of personal information covered: First name or first initial and last name in combination with at least one of the following: (1) Social Security number; (2) driver's license or ID card number; or (3) financial account number or credit or debit card number, along with code or password necessary to access financial account.

Exceptions to notice requirement: (1) Encrypted or redacted personal information; (2) if the company follows its internal notification procedures and is consistent with the statute's timing requirements; (3) if the company is subject to and complies with the notification requirements of the Gramm-Leach-Bliley Act or the requirements of its primary or functional state or federal regulator; or (4) if the company does not reasonably believe that the breach "has caused or will cause identity theft or other fraud" to a Virginia resident.

Timing of notice to individuals: Disclosure must be provided "without unreasonable delay," subject to the needs of law enforcement and to determine the scope of the breach and restore system integrity.

Form of notice to individuals: (1) Written notice to the last known postal address listed in the company's records; (2) telephonic notice; (3) electronic notice; or (4) substitute notice if the company demonstrates that the cost of notice exceeds $50,000, at least 100,000 Virginia residents would need to be notified, or the company does not have sufficient contact information. Substitute notice consists of email notice when available, conspicuous posting of the notice on the company's website, and notification to major statewide media.

Notice must describe: (1) the incident "in general terms"; (2) the categories of personal information subject to the breach: (3) the general steps taken to protect the information from further unauthorized access; (4) a phone number for more information, if one exists; and (5) advice to remain vigilant by reviewing account statements and free credit reports.

Notice to state regulators or credit bureaus: Notice to the Virginia Attorney General is required "without unreasonable delay" if any Virginia residents are notified. Notice to credit reporting agencies of the timing, distribution, and content of individual notices is required, provided that more than 1000 Virginia residents are notified.

Washington State

Wash. Rev. Code § 19.255.010

Types of personal information covered: First name or first initial and last name in combination with at least one of the following: (1) Social Security number; (2) driver's license or ID card number; or (3) financial account number or credit or debit card number, along with code or password necessary to access financial account.

Exceptions to notice requirement: (1) Personal information is encrypted (meeting NIST standards or similar technological guidelines) or otherwise modified to be rendered unreadable, unusable, or undecipherable by the unauthorized accessor; (2) if the company follows its internal notification procedures and is consistent with the statute's timing requirements; (3) if the company is subject to and complies with the notification requirements of HIPAA or the financial institution Interagency Guidelines; or (4) if the company determines that the breach is "not reasonably likely to subject consumers to a risk of harm."

Timing of notice to individuals: Disclosure must be provided in the "most expedient time possible and without unreasonable delay," and no later than forty-five days after discovery of the breach, subject to the needs of law enforcement and to determine the scope of the breach and restore system integrity.

Form of notice to individuals: (1) Written notice; (2) electronic notice; or (3) substitute notice if the company demonstrates that the cost of notice exceeds $250,000, at least 500,000 Washington state residents would need to be notified, or the company does not have sufficient contact information. Substitute notice consists of email notice when available, conspicuous posting of the notice on the company's website, and notification to major statewide media.

Notices must be written in plain language and include (1) name and contact information of the company, a list of the categories of personal information at issue, and toll-free telephone numbers of the major credit reporting agencies if personal information was exposed.

Notice to state regulators or credit bureaus: If a company is required to notify more than 500 Washington state residents of a breach, it must electronically submit a sample copy of that notification, without personally identifiable information, to the Washington State Attorney General, along with the number of Washington State residents affected (or an estimate if the exact number is unknown). Credit bureau notification is not required

West Virginia

W. Va. Code §§ 46A-2A-101 *et seq.*

Types of personal information covered: First name or first initial and last name in combination with at least one of the following: (1) Social Security number; (2) driver's license or ID card number; or (3) financial account number or credit or debit card number, along with code or password necessary to access financial account.

Exceptions to notice requirement: (1) Encrypted or redacted personal information; (2) if the company follows its internal notification procedures and is consistent with the statute's timing requirements; (3) if a company is subject to and follows the financial institution Federal Intergency Guidance for notifications or the notification requirements of its primary or functional regulator; or (4) if the company does not "reasonably believe that the breach has caused or will cause identity theft or other fraud" to a West Virginia resident.

Timing of notice to individuals: Disclosure must be provided "without unreasonable delay," subject to the needs of law enforcement and to determine the scope of the breach and restore system integrity.

Form of notice to individuals: (1) Written notice to postal address of the individual; (2) telephonic notice; (3) electronic notice; or (4) substitute notice if the company demonstrates that the cost of notice exceeds $50,000, at least 100,000 West Virginia residents would need to be notified, or the company does not have sufficient contact information. Substitute notice consists of email notice when available, conspicuous posting of the notice on the company's website, and notification to major statewide media.

Notice to state regulators or credit bureaus: Notice to state regulators not required. If more than 1000 West Virginia residents are notified, the company also must notify the credit reporting agencies of the timing, distribution, and content of the notices. This requirement does not apply to financial institutions that are subject to the GLBA.

Wisconsin

Wis. Stat. § 134.98

Types of personal information covered: First name or first initial and last name in combination with at least one of the following: (1) Social

Security number; (2) driver's license or ID card number; (3) financial account number or credit or debit card number, along with code or password necessary to access financial account; (4) DNA profile; or (5) unique biometric data, including fingerprint, voice print, retinal or iris image, or other unique physical representation.

Exceptions to notice requirement: (1) Encrypted or redacted personal information; (2) if a company is subject to and follows the financial institution Federal Interagency Guidance for notifications or HIPAA's notification procedures; or (3) if the breach "does not create a material risk of identity theft or fraud to the subject of the personal information."

Timing of notice to individuals: Disclosure must be provided "within a reasonable time," not to exceed forty-five days after the company learns of the breach. Reasonableness determinations should consider the number of notices required and methods of communication available. Notice may be delayed at the request of law enforcement.

Form of notice to individuals: The notice must be provided by mail or the method the company has previously used to communicate with the individual. If, with reasonable diligence, the company cannot determine the individual's mailing address and has not previously communicated with the individual, the company must use a "method reasonably calculated to provide actual notice to the subject of the personal information."

The individual notice should indicate that the company knows of a breach of personal information pertaining to the individual

Notice to state regulators or credit bureaus: Notice to state regulators not required. If more than 1000 Wisconsin residents are notified, the company also must notify the credit reporting agencies of the timing, distribution, and content of the notices.

Wyoming

Wyo. Stat. §§ 40-12-501 *et seq.*

Types of personal information covered: First name or first initial and last name in combination with at least one of the following: (1) Social Security number; (2) driver's license number; (3) financial account number, credit card number, or debit card number in combination with any security code or password that would allow access to a financial account; (4) tribal identification card; (5) federal or state government issued ID card; (6) shared secrets or security tokens that are known to be used for data based authentication; (7) username or email address in combination with a password; (8) birth or marriage certificate; (9) medical information; (10) health insurance information; (10) unique biometric data; and (11) individual taxpayer ID number.

Exceptions to notice requirement: (1) Redacted personal information; (2) if the company follows its internal notification procedures and is consistent with the statute's timing requirements; (3) if a company is subject to and follows the financial institution Federal Interagency Guidance for notifications; or (4) if an investigation determines that misuse of the personal information has not occurred and is not "reasonably likely to occur."

Timing of notice to individuals: Disclosure must be provided in the "most expedient time possible and without unreasonable delay," consistent with legitimate needs of law enforcement and measures necessary to determine the scope of the breach and restore reasonable integrity of the data system.

Form of notice to individuals: (1) Written notice; (2) electronic notice; or (3) substitute notice if the company demonstrates that the cost of notice exceeds $10,000 for Wyoming-based businesses or $250,000 for other businesses; at least 10,000 Wyoming residents would need to be notified if the company is Wyoming based, or 500,000 Wyoming residents would be notified if the company is not Wyoming based; or the company does not have sufficient contact information. Substitute notice consists of, conspicuous posting of the notice on the company's website, and notification to major statewide media.

Individual notices must contain, at minimum, (1) a toll-free phone number to contact the company and learn the contact information for major credit bureaus; (2) the types of personal information that were reasonably believed to have been breached; (3) a general description of the breach; (4) the approximate date of the breach, if determinable; (5) the steps taken by the company to prevent further harm; (6) advice to remain vigilant by reviewing account statements and monitoring credit reports; and (7) whether notification was delayed due to a law enforcement investigation, if that is possible to determine at the time of the notice.

Notice to state regulators or credit bureaus: Notice to state regulators and credit bureaus is not required.

Appendix C

Text of Section 1201 of the Digital Millennium Copyright Act

Section 1201 of the Digital Millennium Copyright Act, examined in Chapter 5, restricts the circumvention of controls that protect copyrighted materials. In practice, this can create significant obstacles for cybersecurity researchers who seek to test software for vulnerabilities. Below is the full text of Section 1201:

17 U.S.C. § 1201

a) Violations Regarding Circumvention of Technological Measures.—
1)
    A) No person shall circumvent a technological measure that effectively controls access to a work protected under this title. The prohibition contained in the preceding sentence shall take effect at the end of the 2-year period beginning on the date of the enactment of this chapter.
    B) The prohibition contained in subparagraph (A) shall not apply to persons who are users of a copyrighted work which is in a particular class of works, if such persons are, or are likely to be in the succeeding 3-year period, adversely affected by virtue of such prohibition in their ability to make noninfringing uses of that particular class of works under this title, as determined under subparagraph (C).
    C) During the 2-year period described in subparagraph (A), and during each succeeding 3-year period, the Librarian of Congress, upon the recommendation of the Register of Copyrights, who shall consult with the Assistant Secretary for Communications and Information of the Department of Commerce and report and comment on his or her views in making such recommendation, shall make the determination in a rulemaking proceeding for purposes of subparagraph (B) of whether persons who are users of a copyrighted work are, or are likely to be in the succeeding 3-year period, adversely affected by the prohibition under subparagraph (A) in their ability to make noninfringing

Cybersecurity Law, First Edition. Jeff Kosseff.
© 2017 John Wiley & Sons, Inc. Published 2017 by John Wiley & Sons, Inc.
Companion Website: www.wiley.com/go/kosseff/cybersecurity

uses under this title of a particular class of copyrighted works. In conducting such rulemaking, the Librarian shall examine—

i) the availability for use of copyrighted works;

ii) the availability for use of works for nonprofit archival, preservation, and educational purposes;

iii) the impact that the prohibition on the circumvention of technological measures applied to copyrighted works has on criticism, comment, news reporting, teaching, scholarship, or research;

iv) the effect of circumvention of technological measures on the market for or value of copyrighted works; and

v) such other factors as the Librarian considers appropriate.

D) The Librarian shall publish any class of copyrighted works for which the Librarian has determined, pursuant to the rulemaking conducted under subparagraph (C), that noninfringing uses by persons who are users of a copyrighted work are, or are likely to be, adversely affected, and the prohibition contained in subparagraph (A) shall not apply to such users with respect to such class of works for the ensuing 3-year period.

E) Neither the exception under subparagraph (B) from the applicability of the prohibition contained in subparagraph (A), nor any determination made in a rulemaking conducted under subparagraph (C), may be used as a defense in any action to enforce any provision of this title other than this paragraph.

2) No person shall manufacture, import, offer to the public, provide, or otherwise traffic in any technology, product, service, device, component, or part thereof, that—

A) is primarily designed or produced for the purpose of circumventing a technological measure that effectively controls access to a work protected under this title;

B) has only limited commercially significant purpose or use other than to circumvent a technological measure that effectively controls access to a work protected under this title; or

C) is marketed by that person or another acting in concert with that person with that person's knowledge for use in circumventing a technological measure that effectively controls access to a work protected under this title.

3) As used in this subsection—

A) to "circumvent a technological measure" means to descramble a scrambled work, to decrypt an encrypted work, or otherwise to avoid, bypass, remove, deactivate, or impair a technological measure, without the authority of the copyright owner; and

B) a technological measure "effectively controls access to a work" if the measure, in the ordinary course of its operation, requires the application of information, or a process or a treatment, with the authority of the copyright owner, to gain access to the work.

b) Additional Violations.—

1) No person shall manufacture, import, offer to the public, provide, or otherwise traffic in any technology, product, service, device, component, or part thereof, that—

   A) is primarily designed or produced for the purpose of circumventing protection afforded by a technological measure that effectively protects a right of a copyright owner under this title in a work or a portion thereof;

   B) has only limited commercially significant purpose or use other than to circumvent protection afforded by a technological measure that effectively protects a right of a copyright owner under this title in a work or a portion thereof; or

   C) is marketed by that person or another acting in concert with that person with that person's knowledge for use in circumventing protection afforded by a technological measure that effectively protects a right of a copyright owner under this title in a work or a portion thereof.

2) As used in this subsection—

   A) to "circumvent protection afforded by a technological measure" means avoiding, bypassing, removing, deactivating, or otherwise impairing a technological measure; and

   B) a technological measure "effectively protects a right of a copyright owner under this title" if the measure, in the ordinary course of its operation, prevents, restricts, or otherwise limits the exercise of a right of a copyright owner under this title.

c) Other Rights, Etc., Not Affected.—

1) Nothing in this section shall affect rights, remedies, limitations, or defenses to copyright infringement, including fair use, under this title.

2) Nothing in this section shall enlarge or diminish vicarious or contributory liability for copyright infringement in connection with any technology, product, service, device, component, or part thereof.

3) Nothing in this section shall require that the design of, or design and selection of parts and components for, a consumer electronics, telecommunications, or computing product provide for a response to any particular technological measure, so long as such part or component, or the product in which such part or component is integrated, does not otherwise fall within the prohibitions of subsection (a)(2) or (b)(1).

4) Nothing in this section shall enlarge or diminish any rights of free speech or the press for activities using consumer electronics, telecommunications, or computing products.

d) Exemption for Nonprofit Libraries, Archives, and Educational Institutions.—

1) A nonprofit library, archives, or educational institution which gains access to a commercially exploited copyrighted work solely in order to make a good faith determination of whether to acquire a copy of that work for the sole purpose of engaging in conduct permitted under this title shall not be in violation of subsection (a)(1)(A). A copy of a work to which access has been gained under this paragraph—
   A) may not be retained longer than necessary to make such good faith determination; and
   B) may not be used for any other purpose.

2) The exemption made available under paragraph (1) shall only apply with respect to a work when an identical copy of that work is not reasonably available in another form.

3) A nonprofit library, archives, or educational institution that willfully for the purpose of commercial advantage or financial gain violates paragraph (1)—
   A) shall, for the first offense, be subject to the civil remedies under section 1203; and
   B) shall, for repeated or subsequent offenses, in addition to the civil remedies under section 1203, forfeit the exemption provided under paragraph (1).

4) This subsection may not be used as a defense to a claim under subsection (a)(2) or (b), nor may this subsection permit a nonprofit library, archives, or educational institution to manufacture, import, offer to the public, provide, or otherwise traffic in any technology, product, service, component, or part thereof, which circumvents a technological measure.

5) In order for a library or archives to qualify for the exemption under this subsection, the collections of that library or archives shall be—
   A) open to the public; or
   B) available not only to researchers affiliated with the library or archives or with the institution of which it is a part, but also to other persons doing research in a specialized field.

e) Law Enforcement, Intelligence, and Other Government Activities.—
This section does not prohibit any lawfully authorized investigative, protective, information security, or intelligence activity of an officer, agent, or employee of the United States, a State, or a political subdivision of a State, or a person acting pursuant to a contract with the United States, a State, or a political subdivision of a State. For purposes of this subsection, the term "information security" means activities carried out in order to identify and address the vulnerabilities of a government computer, computer system, or computer network.

f) Reverse Engineering.—

1) Notwithstanding the provisions of subsection (a)(1)(A), a person who has lawfully obtained the right to use a copy of a computer program may circumvent a technological measure that effectively controls access to a particular portion of that program for the sole purpose of identifying and analyzing those elements of the program that are necessary to achieve interoperability of an independently created computer program with other programs, and that have not previously been readily available to the person engaging in the circumvention, to the extent any such acts of identification and analysis do not constitute infringement under this title.

2) Notwithstanding the provisions of subsections (a)(2) and (b), a person may develop and employ technological means to circumvent a technological measure, or to circumvent protection afforded by a technological measure, in order to enable the identification and analysis under paragraph (1), or for the purpose of enabling interoperability of an independently created computer program with other programs, if such means are necessary to achieve such interoperability, to the extent that doing so does not constitute infringement under this title.

3) The information acquired through the acts permitted under paragraph (1), and the means permitted under paragraph (2), may be made available to others if the person referred to in paragraph (1) or (2), as the case may be, provides such information or means solely for the purpose of enabling interoperability of an independently created computer program with other programs, and to the extent that doing so does not constitute infringement under this title or violate applicable law other than this section.

4) For purposes of this subsection, the term "interoperability" means the ability of computer programs to exchange information, and of such programs mutually to use the information which has been exchanged.

g) Encryption Research.—

1) Definitions.—For purposes of this subsection—

   A) the term "encryption research" means activities necessary to identify and analyze flaws and vulnerabilities of encryption technologies applied to copyrighted works, if these activities are conducted to advance the state of knowledge in the field of encryption technology or to assist in the development of encryption products; and

   B) the term "encryption technology" means the scrambling and descrambling of information using mathematical formulas or algorithms.

2) Permissible acts of encryption research.—Notwithstanding the provisions of subsection (a)(1)(A), it is not a violation of that subsection for a

person to circumvent a technological measure as applied to a copy, phonorecord, performance, or display of a published work in the course of an act of good faith encryption research if—

A) the person lawfully obtained the encrypted copy, phonorecord, performance, or display of the published work;

B) such act is necessary to conduct such encryption research;

C) the person made a good faith effort to obtain authorization before the circumvention; and

D) such act does not constitute infringement under this title or a violation of applicable law other than this section, including section 1030 of title 18 and those provisions of title 18 amended by the Computer Fraud and Abuse Act of 1986.

3) Factors in determining exemption.—In determining whether a person qualifies for the exemption under paragraph (2), the factors to be considered shall include—

A) whether the information derived from the encryption research was disseminated, and if so, whether it was disseminated in a manner reasonably calculated to advance the state of knowledge or development of encryption technology, versus whether it was disseminated in a manner that facilitates infringement under this title or a violation of applicable law other than this section, including a violation of privacy or breach of security;

B) whether the person is engaged in a legitimate course of study, is employed, or is appropriately trained or experienced, in the field of encryption technology; and

C) whether the person provides the copyright owner of the work to which the technological measure is applied with notice of the findings and documentation of the research, and the time when such notice is provided.

4) Use of technological means for research activities.—Notwithstanding the provisions of subsection (a)(2), it is not a violation of that subsection for a person to—

A) develop and employ technological means to circumvent a technological measure for the sole purpose of that person performing the acts of good faith encryption research described in paragraph (2); and

B) provide the technological means to another person with whom he or she is working collaboratively for the purpose of conducting the acts of good faith encryption research described in paragraph (2) or for the purpose of having that other person verify his or her acts of good faith encryption research described in paragraph (2).

5) Report to Congress.—Not later than 1 year after the date of the enactment of this chapter, the Register of Copyrights and the Assistant Secretary for Communications and Information of the Department of

Commerce shall jointly report to the Congress on the effect this subsection has had on—

A) encryption research and the development of encryption technology;

B) the adequacy and effectiveness of technological measures designed to protect copyrighted works; and

C) protection of copyright owners against the unauthorized access to their encrypted copyrighted works.

The report shall include legislative recommendations, if any.

h) Exceptions Regarding Minors.—In applying subsection (a) to a component or part, the court may consider the necessity for its intended and actual incorporation in a technology, product, service, or device, which—

1) does not itself violate the provisions of this title; and

2) has the sole purpose to prevent the access of minors to material on the Internet.

i) Protection of Personally Identifying Information.—

1) Circumvention permitted.—Notwithstanding the provisions of subsection (a)(1)(A), it is not a violation of that subsection for a person to circumvent a technological measure that effectively controls access to a work protected under this title, if—

A) the technological measure, or the work it protects, contains the capability of collecting or disseminating personally identifying information reflecting the online activities of a natural person who seeks to gain access to the work protected;

B) in the normal course of its operation, the technological measure, or the work it protects, collects or disseminates personally identifying information about the person who seeks to gain access to the work protected, without providing conspicuous notice of such collection or dissemination to such person, and without providing such person with the capability to prevent or restrict such collection or dissemination;

C) the act of circumvention has the sole effect of identifying and disabling the capability described in subparagraph (A), and has no other effect on the ability of any person to gain access to any work; and

D) the act of circumvention is carried out solely for the purpose of preventing the collection or dissemination of personally identifying information about a natural person who seeks to gain access to the work protected, and is not in violation of any other law.

2) Inapplicability to certain technological measures.—

This subsection does not apply to a technological measure, or a work it protects, that does not collect or disseminate personally identifying information and that is disclosed to a user as not having or using such capability.

j) Security Testing.—

1) Definition.—

For purposes of this subsection, the term "security testing" means accessing a computer, computer system, or computer network, solely for the purpose of good faith testing, investigating, or correcting, a security flaw or vulnerability, with the authorization of the owner or operator of such computer, computer system, or computer network.

2) Permissible acts of security testing.—

Notwithstanding the provisions of subsection (a)(1)(A), it is not a violation of that subsection for a person to engage in an act of security testing, if such act does not constitute infringement under this title or a violation of applicable law other than this section, including section 1030 of title 18 and those provisions of title 18 amended by the Computer Fraud and Abuse Act of 1986.

3) Factors in determining exemption.—In determining whether a person qualifies for the exemption under paragraph (2), the factors to be considered shall include—

A) whether the information derived from the security testing was used solely to promote the security of the owner or operator of such computer, computer system or computer network, or shared directly with the developer of such computer, computer system, or computer network; and

B) whether the information derived from the security testing was used or maintained in a manner that does not facilitate infringement under this title or a violation of applicable law other than this section, including a violation of privacy or breach of security.

4) Use of technological means for security testing.—

Notwithstanding the provisions of subsection (a)(2), it is not a violation of that subsection for a person to develop, produce, distribute or employ technological means for the sole purpose of performing the acts of security testing described in subsection (2),[1] provided such technological means does not otherwise violate section [2] (a)(2).

k) Certain Analog Devices and Certain Technological Measures.—

1) Certain analog devices.—

A) Effective 18 months after the date of the enactment of this chapter, no person shall manufacture, import, offer to the public, provide or otherwise traffic in any—

i) VHS format analog video cassette recorder unless such recorder conforms to the automatic gain control copy control technology;

ii) 8mm format analog video cassette camcorder unless such camcorder conforms to the automatic gain control technology;

iii) Beta format analog video cassette recorder, unless such recorder conforms to the automatic gain control copy control technology, except that this requirement shall not apply until there are 1,000 Beta format analog video cassette recorders sold in the United States in any one calendar year after the date of the enactment of this chapter;

iv) 8mm format analog video cassette recorder that is not an analog video cassette camcorder, unless such recorder conforms to the automatic gain control copy control technology, except that this requirement shall not apply until there are 20,000 such recorders sold in the United States in any one calendar year after the date of the enactment of this chapter; or

v) analog video cassette recorder that records using an NTSC format video input and that is not otherwise covered under clauses (i) through (iv), unless such device conforms to the automatic gain control copy control technology.

B) Effective on the date of the enactment of this chapter, no person shall manufacture, import, offer to the public, provide or otherwise traffic in—

i) any VHS format analog video cassette recorder or any 8mm format analog video cassette recorder if the design of the model of such recorder has been modified after such date of enactment so that a model of recorder that previously conformed to the automatic gain control copy control technology no longer conforms to such technology; or

ii) any VHS format analog video cassette recorder, or any 8mm format analog video cassette recorder that is not an 8mm analog video cassette camcorder, if the design of the model of such recorder has been modified after such date of enactment so that a model of recorder that previously conformed to the four-line colorstripe copy control technology no longer conforms to such technology.

Manufacturers that have not previously manufactured or sold a VHS format analog video cassette recorder, or an 8mm format analog cassette recorder, shall be required to conform to the four-line colorstripe copy control technology in the initial model of any such recorder manufactured after the date of the enactment of this chapter, and thereafter to continue conforming to the four-line colorstripe copy control technology. For purposes of this subparagraph, an analog video cassette recorder "conforms to" the four-line colorstripe copy control technology if it records a signal that, when played back by the playback function of that recorder in the normal viewing mode, exhibits, on a reference display device, a display containing distracting visible lines through portions of the viewable picture.

2) Certain encoding restrictions.—No person shall apply the automatic gain control copy control technology or colorstripe copy control technology to prevent or limit consumer copying except such copying—

A) of a single transmission, or specified group of transmissions, of live events or of audiovisual works for which a member of the public has exercised choice in selecting the transmissions, including the content of the transmissions or the time of receipt of such transmissions, or both, and as to which such member is charged a separate fee for each such transmission or specified group of transmissions;

B) from a copy of a transmission of a live event or an audiovisual work if such transmission is provided by a channel or service where payment is made by a member of the public for such channel or service in the form of a subscription fee that entitles the member of the public to receive all of the programming contained in such channel or service;

C) from a physical medium containing one or more prerecorded audiovisual works; or

D) from a copy of a transmission described in subparagraph (A) or from a copy made from a physical medium described in subparagraph (C).

In the event that a transmission meets both the conditions set forth in subparagraph (A) and those set forth in subparagraph (B), the transmission shall be treated as a transmission described in subparagraph (A).

3) Inapplicability.—This subsection shall not—

A) require any analog video cassette camcorder to conform to the automatic gain control copy control technology with respect to any video signal received through a camera lens;

B) apply to the manufacture, importation, offer for sale, provision of, or other trafficking in, any professional analog video cassette recorder; or

C) apply to the offer for sale or provision of, or other trafficking in, any previously owned analog video cassette recorder, if such recorder was legally manufactured and sold when new and not subsequently modified in violation of paragraph (1)(B).

4) Definitions.—For purposes of this subsection:

A) An "analog video cassette recorder" means a device that records, or a device that includes a function that records, on electromagnetic tape in an analog format the electronic impulses produced by the video and audio portions of a television program, motion picture, or other form of audiovisual work.

B) An "analog video cassette camcorder" means an analog video cassette recorder that contains a recording function that operates through a camera lens and through a video input that may be connected with a television or other video playback device.

C) An analog video cassette recorder "conforms" to the automatic gain control copy control technology if it—

    i) detects one or more of the elements of such technology and does not record the motion picture or transmission protected by such technology; or

    ii) records a signal that, when played back, exhibits a meaningfully distorted or degraded display.

D) The term "professional analog video cassette recorder" means an analog video cassette recorder that is designed, manufactured, marketed, and intended for use by a person who regularly employs such a device for a lawful business or industrial use, including making, performing, displaying, distributing, or transmitting copies of motion pictures on a commercial scale.

E) The terms "VHS format", "8mm format", "Beta format", "automatic gain control copy control technology", "colorstripe copy control technology", "four-line version of the colorstripe copy control technology", and "NTSC" have the meanings that are commonly understood in the consumer electronics and motion picture industries as of the date of the enactment of this chapter.

5) Violations.—

Any violation of paragraph (1) of this subsection shall be treated as a violation of subsection (b)(1) of this section. Any violation of paragraph (2) of this subsection shall be deemed an "act of circumvention" for the purposes of section 1203(c)(3)(A) of this chapter.

Appendix D

Text of the Computer Fraud and Abuse Act

The Computer Fraud and Abuse Act, described in Chapter , is the primary law by which the federal government prosecutes computer hacking. The CFAA also allows hacking victims to bring civil suits against hackers in certain circumstances. Many states have their own computer hacking laws, which are modeled after the CFAA but are not identical.

Text of the Computer Fraud and Abuse Act, 18 U.S.C. § 1030

a) Whoever—

1) having knowingly accessed a computer without authorization or exceeding authorized access, and by means of such conduct having obtained information that has been determined by the United States Government pursuant to an Executive order or statute to require protection against unauthorized disclosure for reasons of national defense or foreign relations, or any restricted data, as defined in paragraph y. of section 11 of the Atomic Energy Act of 1954, with reason to believe that such information so obtained could be used to the injury of the United States, or to the advantage of any foreign nation willfully communicates, delivers, transmits, or causes to be communicated, delivered, or transmitted, or attempts to communicate, deliver, transmit or cause to be communicated, delivered, or transmitted the same to any person not entitled to receive it, or willfully retains the same and fails to deliver it to the officer or employee of the United States entitled to receive it;

2) intentionally accesses a computer without authorization or exceeds authorized access, and thereby obtains—

A) information contained in a financial record of a financial institution, or of a card issuer as defined in section 1602(n) of title 15, or contained in a file of a consumer reporting agency on a consumer, as

Cybersecurity Law, First Edition. Jeff Kosseff.
© 2017 John Wiley & Sons, Inc. Published 2017 by John Wiley & Sons, Inc.
Companion Website: www.wiley.com/go/kosseff/cybersecurity

such terms are defined in the Fair Credit Reporting Act (15 U.S.C. 1681 *et seq.*);

B) information from any department or agency of the United States; or

C) information from any protected computer;

3) intentionally, without authorization to access any nonpublic computer of a department or agency of the United States, accesses such a computer of that department or agency that is exclusively for the use of the Government of the United States or, in the case of a computer not exclusively for such use, is used by or for the Government of the United States and such conduct affects that use by or for the Government of the United States;

4) knowingly and with intent to defraud, accesses a protected computer without authorization, or exceeds authorized access, and by means of such conduct furthers the intended fraud and obtains anything of value, unless the object of the fraud and the thing obtained consists only of the use of the computer and the value of such use is not more than $5,000 in any 1-year period;

5)

A) knowingly causes the transmission of a program, information, code, or command, and as a result of such conduct, intentionally causes damage without authorization, to a protected computer;

B) intentionally accesses a protected computer without authorization, and as a result of such conduct, recklessly causes damage; or

C) intentionally accesses a protected computer without authorization, and as a result of such conduct, causes damage and loss.

6) knowingly and with intent to defraud traffics (as defined in section 1029) in any password or similar information through which a computer may be accessed without authorization, if—

A) such trafficking affects interstate or foreign commerce; or

B) such computer is used by or for the Government of the United States;

7) with intent to extort from any person any money or other thing of value, transmits in interstate or foreign commerce any communication containing any—

A) threat to cause damage to a protected computer;

B) threat to obtain information from a protected computer without authorization or in excess of authorization or to impair the confidentiality of information obtained from a protected computer without authorization or by exceeding authorized access; or

C) demand or request for money or other thing of value in relation to damage to a protected computer, where such damage was caused to facilitate the extortion;

shall be punished as provided in subsection (c) of this section.

b) Whoever conspires to commit or attempts to commit an offense under subsection (a) of this section shall be punished as provided in subsection (c) of this section.

c) The punishment for an offense under subsection (a) or (b) of this section is—

1)
  A) a fine under this title or imprisonment for not more than ten years, or both, in the case of an offense under subsection (a)(1) of this section which does not occur after a conviction for another offense under this section, or an attempt to commit an offense punishable under this subparagraph; and
  B) a fine under this title or imprisonment for not more than twenty years, or both, in the case of an offense under subsection (a)(1) of this section which occurs after a conviction for another offense under this section, or an attempt to commit an offense punishable under this subparagraph;

2)
  A) except as provided in subparagraph (B), a fine under this title or imprisonment for not more than one year, or both, in the case of an offense under subsection (a)(2), (a)(3), or (a)(6) of this section which does not occur after a conviction for another offense under this section, or an attempt to commit an offense punishable under this subparagraph;
  B) a fine under this title or imprisonment for not more than 5 years, or both, in the case of an offense under subsection (a)(2), or an attempt to commit an offense punishable under this subparagraph, if—
    i) the offense was committed for purposes of commercial advantage or private financial gain;
    ii) the offense was committed in furtherance of any criminal or tortious act in violation of the Constitution or laws of the United States or of any State; or
    iii) the value of the information obtained exceeds $5,000; and
  C) a fine under this title or imprisonment for not more than ten years, or both, in the case of an offense under subsection (a)(2), (a)(3) or (a)(6) of this section which occurs after a conviction for another offense under this section, or an attempt to commit an offense punishable under this subparagraph;

3)
  A) a fine under this title or imprisonment for not more than five years, or both, in the case of an offense under subsection (a)(4) or (a)(7) of this section which does not occur after a conviction for another offense under this section, or an attempt to commit an offense punishable under this subparagraph; and

B) a fine under this title or imprisonment for not more than ten years, or both, in the case of an offense under subsection (a)(4),[4] or (a)(7) of this section which occurs after a conviction for another offense under this section, or an attempt to commit an offense punishable under this subparagraph;

4)

A) except as provided in subparagraphs (E) and (F), a fine under this title, imprisonment for not more than 5 years, or both, in the case of—

   i) an offense under subsection (a)(5)(B), which does not occur after a conviction for another offense under this section, if the offense caused (or, in the case of an attempted offense, would, if completed, have caused)—

      I) loss to 1 or more persons during any 1-year period (and, for purposes of an investigation, prosecution, or other proceeding brought by the United States only, loss resulting from a related course of conduct affecting 1 or more other protected computers) aggregating at least $5,000 in value;

      II) the modification or impairment, or potential modification or impairment, of the medical examination, diagnosis, treatment, or care of 1 or more individuals;

      III) physical injury to any person;

      IV) a threat to public health or safety;

      V) damage affecting a computer used by or for an entity of the United States Government in furtherance of the administration of justice, national defense, or national security; or

      VI) damage affecting 10 or more protected computers during any 1-year period; or

   ii) an attempt to commit an offense punishable under this subparagraph;

B) except as provided in subparagraphs (E) and (F), a fine under this title, imprisonment for not more than 10 years, or both, in the case of—

   i) an offense under subsection (a)(5)(A), which does not occur after a conviction for another offense under this section, if the offense caused (or, in the case of an attempted offense, would, if completed, have caused) a harm provided in subclauses (I) through (VI) of subparagraph (A)(i); or

   ii) an attempt to commit an offense punishable under this subparagraph;

C) except as provided in subparagraphs (E) and (F), a fine under this title, imprisonment for not more than 20 years, or both, in the case of—

   i) an offense or an attempt to commit an offense under subparagraphs (A) or (B) of subsection (a)(5) that occurs after a conviction for another offense under this section; or

   ii) an attempt to commit an offense punishable under this
   subparagraph;
   D) a fine under this title, imprisonment for not more than 10 years, or
   both, in the case of—
   i)   an offense or an attempt to commit an offense under subsection
        (a)(5)(C) that occurs after a conviction for another offense under
        this section; or
   ii) an attempt to commit an offense punishable under this
       subparagraph;
   E) if the offender attempts to cause or knowingly or recklessly causes
   serious bodily injury from conduct in violation of subsection (a)(5)
   (A), a fine under this title, imprisonment for not more than 20 years,
   or both;
   F) if the offender attempts to cause or knowingly or recklessly causes
   death from conduct in violation of subsection (a)(5)(A), a fine
   under this title, imprisonment for any term of years or for life, or
   both; or
   G) a fine under this title, imprisonment for not more than 1 year, or
   both, for—
   i)   any other offense under subsection (a)(5); or
   ii) an attempt to commit an offense punishable under this
       subparagraph.

d)

1) The United States Secret Service shall, in addition to any other agency
   having such authority, have the authority to investigate offenses under
   this section.

2) The Federal Bureau of Investigation shall have primary authority to
   investigate offenses under subsection (a)(1) for any cases involving espionage, foreign counterintelligence, information protected against unauthorized disclosure for reasons of national defense or foreign relations,
   or Restricted Data (as that term is defined in section 11y of the Atomic
   Energy Act of 1954 (42 U.S.C. 2014(y)), except for offenses affecting the
   duties of the United States Secret Service pursuant to section 3056(a) of
   this title.

3) Such authority shall be exercised in accordance with an agreement which
   shall be entered into by the Secretary of the Treasury and the Attorney
   General.

e) As used in this section—

1) the term "computer" means an electronic, magnetic, optical, electro-
   chemical, or other high speed data processing device performing logical,
   arithmetic, or storage functions, and includes any data storage facility or
   communications facility directly related to or operating in conjunction

with such device, but such term does not include an automated typewriter or typesetter, a portable hand held calculator, or other similar device;

2) the term "protected computer" means a computer—
   A) exclusively for the use of a financial institution or the United States Government, or, in the case of a computer not exclusively for such use, used by or for a financial institution or the United States Government and the conduct constituting the offense affects that use by or for the financial institution or the Government; or
   B) which is used in or affecting interstate or foreign commerce or communication, including a computer located outside the United States that is used in a manner that affects interstate or foreign commerce or communication of the United States;

3) the term "State" includes the District of Columbia, the Commonwealth of Puerto Rico, and any other commonwealth, possession or territory of the United States;

4) the term "financial institution" means—
   A) an institution, with deposits insured by the Federal Deposit Insurance Corporation;
   B) the Federal Reserve or a member of the Federal Reserve including any Federal Reserve Bank;
   C) a credit union with accounts insured by the National Credit Union Administration;
   D) a member of the Federal home loan bank system and any home loan bank;
   E) any institution of the Farm Credit System under the Farm Credit Act of 1971;
   F) a broker-dealer registered with the Securities and Exchange Commission pursuant to section 15 of the Securities Exchange Act of 1934;
   G) the Securities Investor Protection Corporation;
   H) a branch or agency of a foreign bank (as such terms are defined in paragraphs (1) and (3) of section 1(b) of the International Banking Act of 1978); and
   I) an organization operating under section 25 or section 25(a)1 of the Federal Reserve Act;

5) the term "financial record" means information derived from any record held by a financial institution pertaining to a customer's relationship with the financial institution;

6) the term "exceeds authorized access" means to access a computer with authorization and to use such access to obtain or alter information in the computer that the accesser is not entitled so to obtain or alter;

7) the term "department of the United States" means the legislative or judicial branch of the Government or one of the executive departments enumerated in section 101 of title 5;

8) the term "damage" means any impairment to the integrity or availability of data, a program, a system, or information;

9) the term "government entity" includes the Government of the United States, any State or political subdivision of the United States, any foreign country, and any state, province, municipality, or other political subdivision of a foreign country;

10) the term "conviction" shall include a conviction under the law of any State for a crime punishable by imprisonment for more than 1 year, an element of which is unauthorized access, or exceeding authorized access, to a computer;

11) the term "loss" means any reasonable cost to any victim, including the cost of responding to an offense, conducting a damage assessment, and restoring the data, program, system, or information to its condition prior to the offense, and any revenue lost, cost incurred, or other consequential damages incurred because of interruption of service; and

12) the term "person" means any individual, firm, corporation, educational institution, financial institution, governmental entity, or legal or other entity.

f) This section does not prohibit any lawfully authorized investigative, protective, or intelligence activity of a law enforcement agency of the United States, a State, or a political subdivision of a State, or of an intelligence agency of the United States.

g) Any person who suffers damage or loss by reason of a violation of this section may maintain a civil action against the violator to obtain compensatory damages and injunctive relief or other equitable relief. A civil action for a violation of this section may be brought only if the conduct involves 1 of the factors set forth in subclauses (I), (II), (III), (IV), or (V) of subsection (c)(4)(A)(i). Damages for a violation involving only conduct described in subsection (c)(4)(A)(i)(I) are limited to economic damages. No action may be brought under this subsection unless such action is begun within 2 years of the date of the act complained of or the date of the discovery of the damage. No action may be brought under this subsection for the negligent design or manufacture of computer hardware, computer software, or firmware.

h) The Attorney General and the Secretary of the Treasury shall report to the Congress annually, during the first 3 years following the date of the enactment of this subsection, concerning investigations and prosecutions under subsection (a)(5).

i)

1) The court, in imposing sentence on any person convicted of a violation of this section, or convicted of conspiracy to violate this section, shall order, in addition to any other sentence imposed and irrespective of any provision of State law, that such person forfeit to the United States—

   A) such person's interest in any personal property that was used or intended to be used to commit or to facilitate the commission of such violation; and

   B) any property, real or personal, constituting or derived from, any proceeds that such person obtained, directly or indirectly, as a result of such violation.

2) The criminal forfeiture of property under this subsection, any seizure and disposition thereof, and any judicial proceeding in relation thereto, shall be governed by the provisions of section 413 of the Comprehensive Drug Abuse Prevention and Control Act of 1970 (21 U.S.C. 853), except subsection (d) of that section.

j) For purposes of subsection (i), the following shall be subject to forfeiture to the United States and no property right shall exist in them:

1) Any personal property used or intended to be used to commit or to facilitate the commission of any violation of this section, or a conspiracy to violate this section.

2) Any property, real or personal, which constitutes or is derived from proceeds traceable to any violation of this section, or a conspiracy to violate this section.

Appendix E

Text of the Electronic Communications Privacy Act

The Electronic Communications Privacy Act (ECPA), discussed in Chapter 7, is actually a combination of three different provisions. Title I, known as the Wiretap Act, restricts interception of communications while in transit. Title II, known as the Stored Communications Act, restricts the disclosure of communications contents that are stored on a server or in the cloud. Title III, known as the Pen Register Statute, limits the government's ability to obtain non-content communications data (e.g., a list of phone numbers dialed or the to/from lines of email messages).

<u>Title I, Wiretap Act, 18 U.S.C. 2510–2522</u>

§2510. Definitions

As used in this chapter –

1) "wire communication" means any aural transfer made in whole or in part through the use of facilities for the transmission of communications by the aid of wire, cable, or other like connection between the point of origin and the point of reception (including the use of such connection in a switching station) furnished or operated by any person engaged in providing or operating such facilities for the transmission of interstate or foreign communications or communications affecting interstate or foreign commerce;

2) "oral communication" means any oral communication uttered by a person exhibiting an expectation that such communication is not subject to interception under circumstances justifying such expectation, but such term does not include any electronic communication;

3) "State" means any State of the United States, the District of Columbia, the Commonwealth of Puerto Rico, and any territory or possession of the United States;

Cybersecurity Law, First Edition. Jeff Kosseff.
© 2017 John Wiley & Sons, Inc. Published 2017 by John Wiley & Sons, Inc.
Companion Website: www.wiley.com/go/kosseff/cybersecurity

4) "intercept" means the aural or other acquisition of the contents of any wire, electronic, or oral communication through the use of any electronic, mechanical, or other device.

5) "electronic, mechanical, or other device" means any device or apparatus which can be used to intercept a wire, oral, or electronic communication other than –

   a) any telephone or telegraph instrument, equipment or facility, or any component thereof, (i) furnished to the subscriber or user by a provider of wire or electronic communication service in the ordinary course of its business and being used by the subscriber or user in the ordinary course of its business or furnished by such subscriber or user for connection to the facilities of such service and used in the ordinary course of its business; or (ii) being used by a provider of wire or electronic communication service in the ordinary course of its business, or by an investigative or law enforcement officer in the ordinary course of his duties;

   b) a hearing aid or similar device being used to correct subnormal hearing to not better than normal;

6) "person" means any employee, or agent of the United States or any State or political subdivision thereof, and any individual, partnership, association, joint stock company, trust, or corporation;

7) "Investigative or law enforcement officer" means any officer of the United States or of a State or political subdivision thereof, who is empowered by law to conduct investigations of or to make arrests for offenses enumerated in this chapter, and any attorney authorized by law to prosecute or participate in the prosecution of such offenses;

8) "contents", when used with respect to any wire, oral, or electronic communication, includes any information concerning the substance, purport, or meaning of that communication;

9) "Judge of competent jurisdiction" means –

   a) a judge of a United States district court or a United States court of appeals; and

   b) a judge of any court of general criminal jurisdiction of a State who is authorized by a statute of that State to enter orders authorizing interceptions of wire, oral, or electronic communications;

10) "communication common carrier" has the meaning given that term in section 3 of the Communications Act of 1934;

11) "aggrieved person" means a person who was a party to any intercepted wire, oral, or electronic communication or a person against whom the interception was directed;

12) "electronic communication" means any transfer of signs, signals, writing, images, sounds, data, or intelligence of any nature transmitted in whole or in part by a wire, radio, electromagnetic, photoelectronic or photooptical system that affects interstate or foreign commerce, but does not include –

   A) any wire or oral communication;

B) any communication made through a tone-only paging device;

C) any communication from a tracking device (as defined in section 3117 of this title); or

D) electronic funds transfer information stored by a financial institution in a communications system used for the electronic storage and transfer of funds;

13) "user" means any person or entity who –

A) uses an electronic communication service; and

B) is duly authorized by the provider of such service to engage in such use;

14) "electronic communications system" means any wire, radio, electromagnetic, photooptical or photoelectronic facilities for the transmission of wire or electronic communications, and any computer facilities or related electronic equipment for the electronic storage of such communications;

15) "electronic communication service" means any service which provides to users thereof the ability to send or receive wire or electronic communications;

16) "readily accessible to the general public" means, with respect to a radio communication, that such communication is not –

A) scrambled or encrypted;

B) transmitted using modulation techniques whose essential parameters have been withheld from the public with the intention of preserving the privacy of such communication;

C) carried on a subcarrier or other signal subsidiary to a radio transmission;

D) transmitted over a communication system provided by a common carrier, unless the communication is a tone only paging system communication; or

E) transmitted on frequencies allocated under part 25, subpart D, E, or F of part 74, or part 94 of the Rules of the Federal Communications Commission, unless, in the case of a communication transmitted on a frequency allocated under part 74 that is not exclusively allocated to broadcast auxiliary services, the communication is a two-way voice communication by radio;

17) "electronic storage" means –

A) any temporary, intermediate storage of a wire or electronic communication incidental to the electronic transmission thereof; and

B) any storage of such communication by an electronic communication service for purposes of backup protection of such communication;

18) "aural transfer" means a transfer containing the human voice at any point between and including the point of origin and the point of reception;

19) "foreign intelligence information", for purposes of section 2517(6) of this title, means –

A) information, whether or not concerning a United States person, that relates to the ability of the United States to protect against –

i) actual or potential attack or other grave hostile acts of a foreign power or an agent of a foreign power;

ii) sabotage or international terrorism by a foreign power or an agent of a foreign power; or

iii) clandestine intelligence activities by an intelligence service or network of a foreign power or by an agent of a foreign power; or

B) information, whether or not concerning a United States person, with respect to a foreign power or foreign territory that relates to –

i) the national defense or the security of the United States; or

ii) the conduct of the foreign affairs of the United States;

20) "protected computer" has the meaning set forth in section 1030; and

21) "computer trespasser" –

A) means a person who accesses a protected computer without authorization and thus has no reasonable expectation of privacy in any communication transmitted to, through, or from the protected computer; and

B) does not include a person known by the owner or operator of the protected computer to have an existing contractual relationship with the owner or operator of the protected computer for access to all or part of the protected computer.

§2511. Interception and disclosure of wire, oral, or electronic communications prohibited

1) Except as otherwise specifically provided in this chapter any person who –

a) intentionally intercepts, endeavors to intercept, or procures any other person to intercept or endeavor to intercept, any wire, oral, or electronic communication;

b) intentionally uses, endeavors to use, or procures any other person to use or endeavor to use any electronic, mechanical, or other device to intercept any oral communication when –

i) such device is affixed to, or otherwise transmits a signal through, a wire, cable, or other like connection used in wire communication; or

ii) such device transmits communications by radio, or interferes with the transmission of such communication; or

iii) such person knows, or has reason to know, that such device or any component thereof has been sent through the mail or transported in interstate or foreign commerce; or

iv) such use or endeavor to use (A) takes place on the premises of any business or other commercial establishment the operations of which affect interstate or foreign commerce; or (B) obtains or is for the purpose of obtaining information relating to the operations of any business or other commercial establishment the operations of which affect interstate or foreign commerce; or

v) such person acts in the District of Columbia, the Commonwealth of Puerto Rico, or any territory or possession of the United States;

c) intentionally discloses, or endeavors to disclose, to any other person the contents of any wire, oral, or electronic communication, knowing or having reason to know that the information was obtained through the interception of a wire, oral, or electronic communication in violation of this subsection;

d) intentionally uses, or endeavors to use, the contents of any wire, oral, or electronic communication, knowing or having reason to know that the information was obtained through the interception of a wire, oral, or electronic communication in violation of this subsection; or

e)

(i) intentionally discloses, or endeavors to disclose, to any other person the contents of any wire, oral, or electronic communication, intercepted by means authorized by sections 2511(2)(a)(ii), 2511(2)(b)–(c), 2511(2)(e), 2516, and 2518 of this chapter, (ii) knowing or having reason to know that the information was obtained through the interception of such a communication in connection with a criminal investigation, (iii) having obtained or received the information in connection with a criminal investigation, and (iv) with intent to improperly obstruct, impede, or interfere with a duly authorized criminal investigation,

shall be punished as provided in subsection (4) or shall be subject to suit as provided in subsection (5).

2)

a)

i) It shall not be unlawful under this chapter for an operator of a switchboard, or an officer, employee, or agent of a provider of wire or electronic communication service, whose facilities are used in the transmission of a wire or electronic communication, to intercept, disclose, or use that communication in the normal course of his employment while engaged in any activity which is a necessary incident to the rendition of his service or to the protection of the rights or property of the provider of that service, except that a provider of wire communication service to the public shall not utilize service observing or random monitoring except for mechanical or service quality control checks.

ii) Notwithstanding any other law, providers of wire or electronic communication service, their officers, employees, and agents, landlords, custodians, or other persons, are authorized to provide information, facilities, or technical assistance to persons authorized by law to intercept wire, oral, or electronic communications or to conduct electronic surveillance, as defined in section 101 of the Foreign Intelligence Surveillance Act of 1978, if such provider, its officers, employees, or agents, landlord, custodian, or other specified person, has been provided with –

A) a court order directing such assistance or a court order pursuant to section 704 of the Foreign Intelligence Surveillance Act of 1978 signed by the authorizing judge, or

B) a certification in writing by a person specified in section 2518(7) of this title or the Attorney General of the United States that no warrant or court order is required by law, that all statutory requirements have been met, and that the specified assistance is required,

setting forth the period of time during which the provision of the information, facilities, or technical assistance is authorized and specifying the information, facilities, or technical assistance required. No provider of wire or electronic communication service, officer, employee, or agent thereof, or landlord, custodian, or other specified person shall disclose the existence of any interception or surveillance or the device used to accomplish the interception or surveillance with respect to which the person has been furnished a court order or certification under this chapter, except as may otherwise be required by legal process and then only after prior notification to the Attorney General or to the principal prosecuting attorney of a State or any political subdivision of a State, as may be appropriate. Any such disclosure, shall render such person liable for the civil damages provided for in section 2520. No cause of action shall lie in any court against any provider of wire or electronic communication service, its officers, employees, or agents, landlord, custodian, or other specified person for providing information, facilities, or assistance in accordance with the terms of a court order, statutory authorization, or certification under this chapter.

iii) If a certification under subparagraph (ii)(B) for assistance to obtain foreign intelligence information is based on statutory authority, the certification shall identify the specific statutory provision and shall certify that the statutory requirements have been met.

b) It shall not be unlawful under this chapter for an officer, employee, or agent of the Federal Communications Commission, in the normal course of his employment and in discharge of the monitoring responsibilities exercised by the Commission in the enforcement of chapter 5 of title 47 of the United States Code, to intercept a wire or electronic communication, or oral communication transmitted by radio, or to disclose or use the information thereby obtained.

c) It shall not be unlawful under this chapter for a person acting under color of law to intercept a wire, oral, or electronic communication, where such person is a party to the communication or one of the parties to the communication has given prior consent to such interception.

d) It shall not be unlawful under this chapter for a person not acting under color of law to intercept a wire, oral, or electronic communication where such person is a party to the communication or where one of the parties to the communication has given prior consent to such interception unless such communication is intercepted for the purpose of committing any criminal or tortious act in violation of the Constitution or laws of the United States or of any State.

e) Notwithstanding any other provision of this title or section 705 or 706 of the Communications Act of 1934, it shall not be unlawful for an officer, employee, or agent of the United States in the normal course of his official duty to conduct electronic surveillance, as defined in section 101 of the Foreign Intelligence Surveillance Act of 1978, as authorized by that Act.

f) Nothing contained in this chapter or chapter 121 or 206 of this title, or section 705 of the Communications Act of 1934, shall be deemed to affect the acquisition by the United States Government of foreign intelligence information from international or foreign communications, or foreign intelligence activities conducted in accordance with otherwise applicable Federal law involving a foreign electronic communications system, utilizing a means other than electronic surveillance as defined in section 101 of the Foreign Intelligence Surveillance Act of 1978, and procedures in this chapter or chapter 121 and the Foreign Intelligence Surveillance Act of 1978 shall be the exclusive means by which electronic surveillance, as defined in section 101 of such Act, and the interception of domestic wire, oral, and electronic communications may be conducted.

g) It shall not be unlawful under this chapter or chapter 121 of this title for any person—

   i) to intercept or access an electronic communication made through an electronic communication system that is configured so that such electronic communication is readily accessible to the general public;

   ii) to intercept any radio communication which is transmitted –

      I) by any station for the use of the general public, or that relates to ships, aircraft, vehicles, or persons in distress;

      II) by any governmental, law enforcement, civil defense, private land mobile, or public safety communications system, including police and fire, readily accessible to the general public;

      III) by a station operating on an authorized frequency within the bands allocated to the amateur, citizens band, or general mobile radio services; or

      IV) by any marine or aeronautical communications system;

   iii) to engage in any conduct which –

      I) is prohibited by section 633 of the Communications Act of 1934; or

      II) is excepted from the application of section 705(a) of the Communications Act of 1934 by section 705(b) of that Act;

iv) to intercept any wire or electronic communication the transmission of which is causing harmful interference to any lawfully operating station or consumer electronic equipment, to the extent necessary to identify the source of such interference; or

v) for other users of the same frequency to intercept any radio communication made through a system that utilizes frequencies monitored by individuals engaged in the provision or the use of such system, if such communication is not scrambled or encrypted.

h) It shall not be unlawful under this chapter –

i) to use a pen register or a trap and trace device (as those terms are defined for the purposes of chapter 206 (relating to pen registers and trap and trace devices) of this title); or

ii) for a provider of electronic communication service to record the fact that a wire or electronic communication was initiated or completed in order to protect such provider, another provider furnishing service toward the completion of the wire or electronic communication, or a user of that service, from fraudulent, unlawful or abusive use of such service.

i) It shall not be unlawful under this chapter for a person acting under color of law to intercept the wire or electronic communications of a computer trespasser transmitted to, through, or from the protected computer, if –

I) the owner or operator of the protected computer authorizes the interception of the computer trespasser's communications on the protected computer;

II) the person acting under color of law is lawfully engaged in an investigation;

III) the person acting under color of law has reasonable grounds to believe that the contents of the computer trespasser's communications will be relevant to the investigation; and

IV) such interception does not acquire communications other than those transmitted to or from the computer trespasser.

3)

a) Except as provided in paragraph (b) of this subsection, a person or entity providing an electronic communication service to the public shall not intentionally divulge the contents of any communication (other than one to such person or entity, or an agent thereof) while in transmission on that service to any person or entity other than an addressee or intended recipient of such communication or an agent of such addressee or intended recipient.

b) A person or entity providing electronic communication service to the public may divulge the contents of any such communication –

i) as otherwise authorized in section 2511(2)(a) or 2517 of this title;

ii) with the lawful consent of the originator or any addressee or intended recipient of such communication;

iii) to a person employed or authorized, or whose facilities are used, to forward such communication to its destination; or

iv) which were inadvertently obtained by the service provider and which appear to pertain to the commission of a crime, if such divulgence is made to a law enforcement agency.

4)

a) Except as provided in paragraph (b) of this subsection or in subsection (5), whoever violates subsection (1) of this section shall be fined under this title or imprisoned not more than five years, or both.

b) Conduct otherwise an offense under this subsection that consists of or relates to the interception of a satellite transmission that is not encrypted or scrambled and that is transmitted –

i) to a broadcasting station for purposes of retransmission to the general public; or

ii) as an audio subcarrier intended for redistribution to facilities open to the public, but not including data transmissions or telephone calls,

is not an offense under this subsection unless the conduct is for the purposes of direct or indirect commercial advantage or private financial gain.

5)

a)

i) If the communication is –

A) a private satellite video communication that is not scrambled or encrypted and the conduct in violation of this chapter is the private viewing of that communication and is not for a tortious or illegal purpose or for purposes of direct or indirect commercial advantage or private commercial gain; or

B) a radio communication that is transmitted on frequencies allocated under subpart D of part 74 of the rules of the Federal Communications Commission that is not scrambled or encrypted and the conduct in violation of this chapter is not for a tortious or illegal purpose or for purposes of direct or indirect commercial advantage or private commercial gain,

then the person who engages in such conduct shall be subject to suit by the Federal Government in a court of competent jurisdiction.

ii) In an action under this subsection –

A) if the violation of this chapter is a first offense for the person under paragraph (a) of subsection (4) and such person has not been found liable in a civil action under section 2520 of this title, the Federal Government shall be entitled to appropriate injunctive relief; and

B) if the violation of this chapter is a second or subsequent offense under paragraph (a) of subsection (4) or such person has been found liable in any prior civil action under section 2520, the person shall be subject to a mandatory $500 civil fine.

b) The court may use any means within its authority to enforce an injunction issued under paragraph (ii)(A), and shall impose a civil fine of not less than $500 for each violation of such an injunction.

§2512. Manufacture, distribution, possession, and advertising of wire, oral, or electronic communication intercepting devices prohibited

1) Except as otherwise specifically provided in this chapter, any person who intentionally –

   a) sends through the mail, or sends or carries in interstate or foreign commerce, any electronic, mechanical, or other device, knowing or having reason to know that the design of such device renders it primarily useful for the purpose of the surreptitious interception of wire, oral, or electronic communications;

   b) manufactures, assembles, possesses, or sells any electronic, mechanical, or other device, knowing or having reason to know that the design of such device renders it primarily useful for the purpose of the surreptitious interception of wire, oral, or electronic communications, and that such device or any component thereof has been or will be sent through the mail or transported in interstate or foreign commerce; or

   c) places in any newspaper, magazine, handbill, or other publication or disseminates by electronic means any advertisement of –

      i) any electronic, mechanical, or other device knowing or having reason to know that the design of such device renders it primarily useful for the purpose of the surreptitious interception of wire, oral, or electronic communications; or

      ii) any other electronic, mechanical, or other device, where such advertisement promotes the use of such device for the purpose of the surreptitious interception of wire, oral, or electronic communications,

   knowing the content of the advertisement and knowing or having reason to know that such advertisement will be sent through the mail or transported in interstate or foreign commerce,

   shall be fined under this title or imprisoned not more than five years, or both.

2) It shall not be unlawful under this section for –

   a) a provider of wire or electronic communication service or an officer, agent, or employee of, or a person under contract with, such a provider, in the normal course of the business of providing that wire or electronic communication service, or

b) an officer, agent, or employee of, or a person under contract with, the United States, a State, or a political subdivision thereof, in the normal course of the activities of the United States, a State, or a political subdivision thereof,

to send through the mail, send or carry in interstate or foreign commerce, or manufacture, assemble, possess, or sell any electronic, mechanical, or other device knowing or having reason to know that the design of such device renders it primarily useful for the purpose of the surreptitious interception of wire, oral, or electronic communications.

3) It shall not be unlawful under this section to advertise for sale a device described in subsection (1) of this section if the advertisement is mailed, sent, or carried in interstate or foreign commerce solely to a domestic provider of wire or electronic communication service or to an agency of the United States, a State, or a political subdivision thereof which is duly authorized to use such device.

§2513. Confiscation of wire, oral, or electronic communication intercepting devices

Any electronic, mechanical, or other device used, sent, carried, manufactured, assembled, possessed, sold, or advertised in violation of section 2511 or section 2512 of this chapter may be seized and forfeited to the United States. All provisions of law relating to (1) the seizure, summary and judicial forfeiture, and condemnation of vessels, vehicles, merchandise, and baggage for violations of the customs laws contained in title 19 of the United States Code, (2) the disposition of such vessels, vehicles, merchandise, and baggage or the proceeds from the sale thereof, (3) the remission or mitigation of such forfeiture, (4) the compromise of claims, and (5) the award of compensation to informers in respect of such forfeitures, shall apply to seizures and forfeitures incurred, or alleged to have been incurred, under the provisions of this section, insofar as applicable and not inconsistent with the provisions of this section; except that such duties as are imposed upon the collector of customs or any other person with respect to the seizure and forfeiture of vessels, vehicles, merchandise, and baggage under the provisions of the customs laws contained in title 19 of the United States Code shall be performed with respect to seizure and forfeiture of electronic, mechanical, or other intercepting devices under this section by such officers, agents, or other persons as may be authorized or designated for that purpose by the Attorney General.

§2514. Repealed

§2515. Prohibition of use as evidence of intercepted wire or oral communications

Whenever any wire or oral communication has been intercepted, no part of the contents of such communication and no evidence derived therefrom may be received in evidence in any trial, hearing, or other proceeding in or before any court, grand jury, department, officer, agency, regulatory body, legislative committee, or other authority of the United States, a State, or a political subdivision thereof if the disclosure of that information would be in violation of this chapter.

§2516. Authorization for interception of wire, oral, or electronic communications

1) The Attorney General, Deputy Attorney General, Associate Attorney General, or any Assistant Attorney General, any acting Assistant Attorney General, or any Deputy Assistant Attorney General or acting Deputy Assistant Attorney General in the Criminal Division or National Security Division specially designated by the Attorney General, may authorize an application to a Federal judge of competent jurisdiction for, and such judge may grant in conformity with section 2518 of this chapter an order authorizing or approving the interception of wire or oral communications by the Federal Bureau of Investigation, or a Federal agency having responsibility for the investigation of the offense as to which the application is made, when such interception may provide or has provided evidence of –
   a) any offense punishable by death or by imprisonment for more than one year under sections 2122 and 2274 through 2277 of title 42 of the United States Code (relating to the enforcement of the Atomic Energy Act of 1954), section 2284 of title 42 of the United States Code (relating to sabotage of nuclear facilities or fuel), or under the following chapters of this title: chapter 10 (relating to biological weapons), chapter 37 (relating to espionage), chapter 55 (relating to kidnapping), chapter 90 (relating to protection of trade secrets), chapter 105 (relating to sabotage), chapter 115 (relating to treason), chapter 102 (relating to riots), chapter 65 (relating to malicious mischief), chapter 111 (relating to destruction of vessels), or chapter 81 (relating to piracy);
   b) a violation of section 186 or section 501(c) of title 29, United States Code (dealing with restrictions on payments and loans to labor

organizations), or any offense which involves murder, kidnapping, robbery, or extortion, and which is punishable under this title;

c) any offense which is punishable under the following sections of this title: section 37 (relating to violence at international airports), section 43 (relating to animal enterprise terrorism), section 81 (arson within special maritime and territorial jurisdiction), section 201 (bribery of public officials and witnesses), section 215 (relating to bribery of bank officials), section 224 (bribery in sporting contests), subsection (d), (e), (f), (g), (h), or (i) of section 844 (unlawful use of explosives), section 1032 (relating to concealment of assets), section 1084 (transmission of wagering information), section 751 (relating to escape), section 832 (relating to nuclear and weapons of mass destruction threats), section 842 (relating to explosive materials), section 930 (relating to possession of weapons in Federal facilities), section 1014 (relating to loans and credit applications generally; renewals and discounts), section 1114 (relating to officers and employees of the United States), section 1116 (relating to protection of foreign officials), sections 1503, 1512, and 1513 (influencing or injuring an officer, juror, or witness generally), section 1510 (obstruction of criminal investigations), section 1511 (obstruction of State or local law enforcement), section 1581 (peonage), section 1584 (involuntary servitude), section 1589 (forced labor), section 1590 (trafficking with respect to peonage, slavery, involuntary servitude, or forced labor), section 1591 (sex trafficking of children by force, fraud, or coercion), section 1592 (unlawful conduct with respect to documents in furtherance of trafficking, peonage, slavery, involuntary servitude, or forced labor), section 1751 (Presidential and Presidential staff assassination, kidnapping, and assault), section 1951 (interference with commerce by threats or violence), section 1952 (interstate and foreign travel or transportation in aid of racketeering enterprises), section 1958 (relating to use of interstate commerce facilities in the commission of murder for hire), section 1959 (relating to violent crimes in aid of racketeering activity), section 1954 (offer, acceptance, or solicitation to influence operations of employee benefit plan), section 1955 (prohibition of business enterprises of gambling), section 1956 (laundering of monetary instruments), section 1957 (relating to engaging in monetary transactions in property derived from specified unlawful activity), section 659 (theft from interstate shipment), section 664 (embezzlement from pension and welfare funds), section 1343 (fraud by wire, radio, or television), section 1344 (relating to bank fraud), section 1992 (relating to terrorist attacks against mass transportation), sections 2251 and 2252 (sexual exploitation of children), section 2251A (selling or buying of children), section 2252A (relating to material constituting or containing child pornography), section 1466A (relating to child obscenity), section 2260 (production of sexually explicit depictions of a minor for importation into the United States), sections 2421, 2422, 2423, and 2425 (relating to transportation for illegal sexual activity and related crimes), sections 2312, 2313, 2314, and 2315 (interstate transportation of stolen property), section 2321 (relating to trafficking in certain motor vehicles or motor vehicle parts), section 2340A (relating to torture), section 1203 (relating to hostage taking), section 1029 (relating to fraud and related activity in connection with access devices), section 3146 (relating to penalty for failure to appear), section 3521(b)(3) (relating to witness relocation and assistance), section 32 (relating to destruction of aircraft or aircraft facilities), section 38 (relating to aircraft parts fraud), section 1963 (violations with respect to racketeer influenced and corrupt organizations), section 115 (relating to threatening or retaliating against a Federal official), section 1341 (relating to mail fraud), a felony violation of section 1030 (relating to computer fraud and abuse), section 351 (violations with respect to congressional, Cabinet, or Supreme Court assassinations, kidnapping, and assault), section 831 (relating to prohibited transactions involving nuclear materials), section 33 (relating to destruction of motor vehicles or motor vehicle facilities), section 175 (relating to biological weapons), section 175c (relating to variola virus), section 956 (conspiracy to harm persons or property overseas), a felony violation of section 1028 (relating to production of false identification documentation), section 1425 (relating to the procurement of citizenship or nationalization unlawfully), section 1426 (relating to the reproduction of naturalization or citizenship papers), section 1427 (relating to the sale of naturalization or citizenship papers), section 1541 (relating to passport issuance without authority), section 1542 (relating to false statements in passport applications), section 1543 (relating to forgery or false use of passports), section 1544 (relating to misuse of passports), or section 1546 (relating to fraud and misuse of visas, permits, and other documents);

d) any offense involving counterfeiting punishable under section 471, 472, or 473 of this title;

e) any offense involving fraud connected with a case under title 11 or the manufacture, importation, receiving, concealment, buying, selling, or otherwise dealing in narcotic drugs, marihuana, or other dangerous drugs, punishable under any law of the United States;

f) any offense including extortionate credit transactions under sections 892, 893, or 894 of this title;

g) a violation of section 5322 of title 31, United States Code (dealing with the reporting of currency transactions), or section 5324 of title 31, United States Code (relating to structuring transactions to evade reporting requirement prohibited);

h) any felony violation of sections 2511 and 2512 (relating to interception and disclosure of certain communications and to certain intercepting devices) of this title;

i) any felony violation of chapter 71 (relating to obscenity) of this title;

j) any violation of section 60123(b) (relating to destruction of a natural gas pipeline), section 46502 (relating to aircraft piracy), the second sentence of section 46504 (relating to assault on a flight crew with dangerous weapon), or section 46505(b)(3) or (c) (relating to explosive or incendiary devices, or endangerment of human life, by means of weapons on aircraft) of title 49;

k) any criminal violation of section 2778 of title 22 (relating to the Arms Export Control Act);

l) the location of any fugitive from justice from an offense described in this section;

m) a violation of section 274, 277, or 278 of the Immigration and Nationality Act (8 U.S.C. 1324, 1327, or 1328) (relating to the smuggling of aliens);

n) any felony violation of sections 922 and 924 of title 18, United States Code (relating to firearms);

o) any violation of section 5861 of the Internal Revenue Code of 1986 (relating to firearms);

p) a felony violation of section 1028 (relating to production of false identification documents), section 1542 (relating to false statements in passport applications), section 1546 (relating to fraud and misuse of visas, permits, and other documents), section 1028A (relating to aggravated identity theft) of this title or a violation of section 274, 277, or 278 of the Immigration and Nationality Act (relating to the smuggling of aliens); or

q) any criminal violation of section 229 (relating to chemical weapons) or section 2332, 2332a, 2332b, 2332d, 2332f, 2332g, 2332h 3 2339, 2339A, 2339B, 2339C, or 2339D of this title (relating to terrorism);

r) any criminal violation of section 1 (relating to illegal restraints of trade or commerce), 2 (relating to illegal monopolizing of trade or commerce), or 3 (relating to illegal restraints of trade or commerce in territories or the District of Columbia) of the Sherman Act (15 U.S.C. 1, 2, 3);

s) any violation of section 670 (relating to theft of medical products); or

t) any conspiracy to commit any offense described in any subparagraph of this paragraph.

2) The principal prosecuting attorney of any State, or the principal prosecuting attorney of any political subdivision thereof, if such attorney is authorized by a statute of that State to make application to a State court judge of competent jurisdiction for an order authorizing or approving the interception of wire, oral, or electronic communications, may apply to such judge for, and such judge may grant in conformity with section 2518 of this chapter and with the

applicable State statute an order authorizing, or approving the interception of wire, oral, or electronic communications by investigative or law enforcement officers having responsibility for the investigation of the offense as to which the application is made, when such interception may provide or has provided evidence of the commission of the offense of murder, kidnapping human trafficking, child sexual exploitation, child pornography production, gambling, robbery, bribery, extortion, or dealing in narcotic drugs, marihuana or other dangerous drugs, or other crime dangerous to life, limb, or property, and punishable by imprisonment for more than one year, designated in any applicable State statute authorizing such interception, or any conspiracy to commit any of the foregoing offenses.

3) Any attorney for the Government (as such term is defined for the purposes of the Federal Rules of Criminal Procedure) may authorize an application to a Federal judge of competent jurisdiction for, and such judge may grant, in conformity with section 2518 of this title, an order authorizing or approving the interception of electronic communications by an investigative or law enforcement officer having responsibility for the investigation of the offense as to which the application is made, when such interception may provide or has provided evidence of any Federal felony.

§2517. Authorization for disclosure and use of intercepted wire, oral, or electronic communications

1) Any investigative or law enforcement officer who, by any means authorized by this chapter, has obtained knowledge of the contents of any wire, oral, or electronic communication, or evidence derived therefrom, may disclose such contents to another investigative or law enforcement officer to the extent that such disclosure is appropriate to the proper performance of the official duties of the officer making or receiving the disclosure.

2) Any investigative or law enforcement officer who, by any means authorized by this chapter, has obtained knowledge of the contents of any wire, oral, or electronic communication or evidence derived therefrom may use such contents to the extent such use is appropriate to the proper performance of his official duties.

3) Any person who has received, by any means authorized by this chapter, any information concerning a wire, oral, or electronic communication, or evidence derived therefrom intercepted in accordance with the provisions of this chapter may disclose the contents of that communication or such derivative evidence while giving testimony under oath or affirmation in any proceeding held under the authority of the United States or of any State or political subdivision thereof.

4) No otherwise privileged wire, oral, or electronic communication intercepted in accordance with, or in violation of, the provisions of this chapter shall lose its privileged character.

5) When an investigative or law enforcement officer, while engaged in intercepting wire, oral, or electronic communications in the manner authorized herein, intercepts wire, oral, or electronic communications relating to offenses other than those specified in the order of authorization or approval, the contents thereof, and evidence derived therefrom, may be disclosed or used as provided in subsections (1) and (2) of this section. Such contents and any evidence derived therefrom may be used under subsection (3) of this section when authorized or approved by a judge of competent jurisdiction where such judge finds on subsequent application that the contents were otherwise intercepted in accordance with the provisions of this chapter. Such application shall be made as soon as practicable.

6) Any investigative or law enforcement officer, or attorney for the Government, who by any means authorized by this chapter, has obtained knowledge of the contents of any wire, oral, or electronic communication, or evidence derived therefrom, may disclose such contents to any other Federal law enforcement, intelligence, protective, immigration, national defense, or national security official to the extent that such contents include foreign intelligence or counterintelligence (as defined in section 3 of the National Security Act of 1947 (50 U.S.C. 401a)),1 or foreign intelligence information (as defined in subsection (19) of section 2510 of this title), to assist the official who is to receive that information in the performance of his official duties. Any Federal official who receives information pursuant to this provision may use that information only as necessary in the conduct of that person's official duties subject to any limitations on the unauthorized disclosure of such information.

7) Any investigative or law enforcement officer, or other Federal official in carrying out official duties as such Federal official, who by any means authorized by this chapter, has obtained knowledge of the contents of any wire, oral, or electronic communication, or evidence derived therefrom, may disclose such contents or derivative evidence to a foreign investigative or law enforcement officer to the extent that such disclosure is appropriate to the proper performance of the official duties of the officer making or receiving the disclosure, and foreign investigative or law enforcement officers may use or disclose such contents or derivative evidence to the extent such use or disclosure is appropriate to the proper performance of their official duties.

8) Any investigative or law enforcement officer, or other Federal official in carrying out official duties as such Federal official, who by any means authorized by this chapter, has obtained knowledge of the contents of any wire, oral, or electronic communication, or evidence derived therefrom,

may disclose such contents or derivative evidence to any appropriate Federal, State, local, or foreign government official to the extent that such contents or derivative evidence reveals a threat of actual or potential attack or other grave hostile acts of a foreign power or an agent of a foreign power, domestic or international sabotage, domestic or international terrorism, or clandestine intelligence gathering activities by an intelligence service or network of a foreign power or by an agent of a foreign power, within the United States or elsewhere, for the purpose of preventing or responding to such a threat. Any official who receives information pursuant to this provision may use that information only as necessary in the conduct of that person's official duties subject to any limitations on the unauthorized disclosure of such information, and any State, local, or foreign official who receives information pursuant to this provision may use that information only consistent with such guidelines as the Attorney General and Director of Central Intelligence shall jointly issue.

§2518. Procedure for interception of wire, oral, or electronic communications

1) Each application for an order authorizing or approving the interception of a wire, oral, or electronic communication under this chapter shall be made in writing upon oath or affirmation to a judge of competent jurisdiction and shall state the applicant's authority to make such application. Each application shall include the following information:
   a) the identity of the investigative or law enforcement officer making the application, and the officer authorizing the application;
   b) a full and complete statement of the facts and circumstances relied upon by the applicant, to justify his belief that an order should be issued, including (i) details as to the particular offense that has been, is being, or is about to be committed, (ii) except as provided in subsection (11), a particular description of the nature and location of the facilities from which or the place where the communication is to be intercepted, (iii) a particular description of the type of communications sought to be intercepted, (iv) the identity of the person, if known, committing the offense and whose communications are to be intercepted;
   c) a full and complete statement as to whether or not other investigative procedures have been tried and failed or why they reasonably appear to be unlikely to succeed if tried or to be too dangerous;
   d) a statement of the period of time for which the interception is required to be maintained. If the nature of the investigation is such that the authorization for interception should not automatically terminate when the described type of communication has been first obtained, a particular description of facts establishing probable

cause to believe that additional communications of the same type will occur thereafter;

e) a full and complete statement of the facts concerning all previous applications known to the individual authorizing and making the application, made to any judge for authorization to intercept, or for approval of interceptions of, wire, oral, or electronic communications involving any of the same persons, facilities or places specified in the application, and the action taken by the judge on each such application; and

f) where the application is for the extension of an order, a statement setting forth the results thus far obtained from the interception, or a reasonable explanation of the failure to obtain such results.

2) The judge may require the applicant to furnish additional testimony or documentary evidence in support of the application.

3) Upon such application the judge may enter an ex parte order, as requested or as modified, authorizing or approving interception of wire, oral, or electronic communications within the territorial jurisdiction of the court in which the judge is sitting (and outside that jurisdiction but within the United States in the case of a mobile interception device authorized by a Federal court within such jurisdiction), if the judge determines on the basis of the facts submitted by the applicant that –

a) there is probable cause for belief that an individual is committing, has committed, or is about to commit a particular offense enumerated in section 2516 of this chapter;

b) there is probable cause for belief that particular communications concerning that offense will be obtained through such interception;

c) normal investigative procedures have been tried and have failed or reasonably appear to be unlikely to succeed if tried or to be too dangerous;

d) except as provided in subsection (11), there is probable cause for belief that the facilities from which, or the place where, the wire, oral, or electronic communications are to be intercepted are being used, or are about to be used, in connection with the commission of such offense, or are leased to, listed in the name of, or commonly used by such person.

4) Each order authorizing or approving the interception of any wire, oral, or electronic communication under this chapter shall specify –

a) the identity of the person, if known, whose communications are to be intercepted;

b) the nature and location of the communications facilities as to which, or the place where, authority to intercept is granted;

c) a particular description of the type of communication sought to be intercepted, and a statement of the particular offense to which it relates;

d) the identity of the agency authorized to intercept the communications, and of the person authorizing the application; and

e) the period of time during which such interception is authorized, including a statement as to whether or not the interception shall automatically terminate when the described communication has been first obtained.

An order authorizing the interception of a wire, oral, or electronic communication under this chapter shall, upon request of the applicant, direct that a provider of wire or electronic communication service, landlord, custodian or other person shall furnish the applicant forthwith all information, facilities, and technical assistance necessary to accomplish the interception unobtrusively and with a minimum of interference with the services that such service provider, landlord, custodian, or person is according the person whose communications are to be intercepted. Any provider of wire or electronic communication service, landlord, custodian or other person furnishing such facilities or technical assistance shall be compensated therefor by the applicant for reasonable expenses incurred in providing such facilities or assistance. Pursuant to section 2522 of this chapter, an order may also be issued to enforce the assistance capability and capacity requirements under the Communications Assistance for Law Enforcement Act.

5) No order entered under this section may authorize or approve the interception of any wire, oral, or electronic communication for any period longer than is necessary to achieve the objective of the authorization, nor in any event longer than thirty days. Such thirty-day period begins on the earlier of the day on which the investigative or law enforcement officer first begins to conduct an interception under the order or ten days after the order is entered. Extensions of an order may be granted, but only upon application for an extension made in accordance with subsection (1) of this section and the court making the findings required by subsection (3) of this section. The period of extension shall be no longer than the authorizing judge deems necessary to achieve the purposes for which it was granted and in no event for longer than thirty days. Every order and extension thereof shall contain a provision that the authorization to intercept shall be executed as soon as practicable, shall be conducted in such a way as to minimize the interception of communications not otherwise subject to interception under this chapter, and must terminate upon attainment of the authorized objective, or in any event in thirty days. In the event the intercepted communication is in a code or foreign language, and an expert in that foreign language or code is not reasonably available during the interception period, minimization may be accomplished as soon as practicable after such interception. An interception under this chapter may be conducted in whole or in part by Government personnel, or by an individual operating under a contract with the Government, acting under the supervision of an investigative or law enforcement officer authorized to conduct the interception.

6) Whenever an order authorizing interception is entered pursuant to this chapter, the order may require reports to be made to the judge who issued

the order showing what progress has been made toward achievement of the authorized objective and the need for continued interception. Such reports shall be made at such intervals as the judge may require.

7) Notwithstanding any other provision of this chapter, any investigative or law enforcement officer, specially designated by the Attorney General, the Deputy Attorney General, the Associate Attorney General, or by the principal prosecuting attorney of any State or subdivision thereof acting pursuant to a statute of that State, who reasonably determines that –

  a) an emergency situation exists that involves –

    i) immediate danger of death or serious physical injury to any person,

    ii) conspiratorial activities threatening the national security interest, or

    iii) conspiratorial activities characteristic of organized crime,

that requires a wire, oral, or electronic communication to be intercepted before an order authorizing such interception can, with due diligence, be obtained, and

  b) there are grounds upon which an order could be entered under this chapter to authorize such interception,

may intercept such wire, oral, or electronic communication if an application for an order approving the interception is made in accordance with this section within forty-eight hours after the interception has occurred, or begins to occur. In the absence of an order, such interception shall immediately terminate when the communication sought is obtained or when the application for the order is denied, whichever is earlier. In the event such application for approval is denied, or in any other case where the interception is terminated without an order having been issued, the contents of any wire, oral, or electronic communication intercepted shall be treated as having been obtained in violation of this chapter, and an inventory shall be served as provided for in subsection (d) of this section on the person named in the application.

8)

  a) The contents of any wire, oral, or electronic communication intercepted by any means authorized by this chapter shall, if possible, be recorded on tape or wire or other comparable device. The recording of the contents of any wire, oral, or electronic communication under this subsection shall be done in such a way as will protect the recording from editing or other alterations. Immediately upon the expiration of the period of the order, or extensions thereof, such recordings shall be made available to the judge issuing such order and sealed under his directions. Custody of the recordings shall be wherever the judge orders. They shall not be destroyed except upon an order of the issuing or denying judge and in any event shall be kept for ten years. Duplicate recordings may be made for use or disclosure pursuant to the provisions of subsections (1) and (2) of section 2517 of this chapter for investigations. The presence of the seal provided for by this subsection, or a satisfactory explanation for the absence thereof, shall be a prerequisite for the use or disclosure of the contents of any wire, oral, or electronic communication or evidence derived therefrom under subsection (3) of section 2517.

b) Applications made and orders granted under this chapter shall be sealed by the judge. Custody of the applications and orders shall be wherever the judge directs. Such applications and orders shall be disclosed only upon a showing of good cause before a judge of competent jurisdiction and shall not be destroyed except on order of the issuing or denying judge, and in any event shall be kept for ten years.

c) Any violation of the provisions of this subsection may be punished as contempt of the issuing or denying judge.

d) Within a reasonable time but not later than ninety days after the filing of an application for an order of approval under section 2518(7)(b) which is denied or the termination of the period of an order or extensions thereof, the issuing or denying judge shall cause to be served, on the persons named in the order or the application, and such other parties to intercepted communications as the judge may determine in his discretion that is in the interest of justice, an inventory which shall include notice of –

1) the fact of the entry of the order or the application;

2) the date of the entry and the period of authorized, approved or disapproved interception, or the denial of the application; and

3) the fact that during the period wire, oral, or electronic communications were or were not intercepted.

The judge, upon the filing of a motion, may in his discretion make available to such person or his counsel for inspection such portions of the intercepted communications, applications and orders as the judge determines to be in the interest of justice. On an ex parte showing of good cause to a judge of competent jurisdiction the serving of the inventory required by this subsection may be postponed.

9) The contents of any wire, oral, or electronic communication intercepted pursuant to this chapter or evidence derived therefrom shall not be received in evidence or otherwise disclosed in any trial, hearing, or other proceeding in a Federal or State court unless each party, not less than ten days before the trial, hearing, or proceeding, has been furnished with a copy of the court order, and accompanying application, under which the interception was authorized or approved. This ten-day period may be waived by the judge if he finds that it was not possible to furnish the party with the above information ten days before the trial, hearing, or proceeding and that the party will not be prejudiced by the delay in receiving such information.

10)

    a) Any aggrieved person in any trial, hearing, or proceeding in or before any court, department, officer, agency, regulatory body, or other authority of the United States, a State, or a political subdivision thereof, may move to suppress the contents of any wire or oral communication intercepted pursuant to this chapter, or evidence derived therefrom, on the grounds that –

        i) the communication was unlawfully intercepted;

        ii) the order of authorization or approval under which it was intercepted is insufficient on its face; or

        iii) the interception was not made in conformity with the order of authorization or approval.

Such motion shall be made before the trial, hearing, or proceeding unless there was no opportunity to make such motion or the person was not aware of the grounds of the motion. If the motion is granted, the contents of the intercepted wire or oral communication, or evidence derived therefrom, shall be treated as having been obtained in violation of this chapter. The judge, upon the filing of such motion by the aggrieved person, may in his discretion make available to the aggrieved person or his counsel for inspection such portions of the intercepted communication or evidence derived therefrom as the judge determines to be in the interests of justice.

    b) In addition to any other right to appeal, the United States shall have the right to appeal from an order granting a motion to suppress made under paragraph (a) of this subsection, or the denial of an application for an order of approval, if the United States attorney shall certify to the judge or other official granting such motion or denying such application that the appeal is not taken for purposes of delay. Such appeal shall be taken within thirty days after the date the order was entered and shall be diligently prosecuted.

    c) The remedies and sanctions described in this chapter with respect to the interception of electronic communications are the only judicial remedies and sanctions for nonconstitutional violations of this chapter involving such communications.

11) The requirements of subsections (1)(b)(ii) and (3)(d) of this section relating to the specification of the facilities from which, or the place where, the communication is to be intercepted do not apply if –

    a) in the case of an application with respect to the interception of an oral communication –

        i) the application is by a Federal investigative or law enforcement officer and is approved by the Attorney General, the Deputy Attorney General, the Associate Attorney General, an Assistant Attorney General, or an acting Assistant Attorney General;

    ii) the application contains a full and complete statement as to why such specification is not practical and identifies the person committing the offense and whose communications are to be intercepted; and

    iii) the judge finds that such specification is not practical; and

b) in the case of an application with respect to a wire or electronic communication –

    i) the application is by a Federal investigative or law enforcement officer and is approved by the Attorney General, the Deputy Attorney General, the Associate Attorney General, an Assistant Attorney General, or an acting Assistant Attorney General;

    ii) the application identifies the person believed to be committing the offense and whose communications are to be intercepted and the applicant makes a showing that there is probable cause to believe that the person's actions could have the effect of thwarting interception from a specified facility;

    iii) the judge finds that such showing has been adequately made; and

    iv) the order authorizing or approving the interception is limited to interception only for such time as it is reasonable to presume that the person identified in the application is or was reasonably proximate to the instrument through which such communication will be or was transmitted.

12) An interception of a communication under an order with respect to which the requirements of subsections (1)(b)(ii) and (3)(d) of this section do not apply by reason of subsection (11)(a) shall not begin until the place where the communication is to be intercepted is ascertained by the person implementing the interception order. A provider of wire or electronic communications service that has received an order as provided for in subsection (11)(b) may move the court to modify or quash the order on the ground that its assistance with respect to the interception cannot be performed in a timely or reasonable fashion. The court, upon notice to the government, shall decide such a motion expeditiously.

§2519. Reports concerning intercepted wire, oral, or electronic communications

1) In January of each year, any judge who has issued an order (or an extension thereof) under section 2518 that expired during the preceding year, or who has denied approval of an interception during that year, shall report to the Administrative Office of the United States Courts –

a) the fact that an order or extension was applied for;

b) the kind of order or extension applied for (including whether or not the order was an order with respect to which the requirements of sections

2518(1)(b)(ii) and 2518(3)(d) of this title did not apply by reason of section 2518(11) of this title);

c) the fact that the order or extension was granted as applied for, was modified, or was denied;

d) the period of interceptions authorized by the order, and the number and duration of any extensions of the order;

e) the offense specified in the order or application, or extension of an order;

f) the identity of the applying investigative or law enforcement officer and agency making the application and the person authorizing the application; and

g) the nature of the facilities from which or the place where communications were to be intercepted.

2) In March of each year the Attorney General, an Assistant Attorney General specially designated by the Attorney General, or the principal prosecuting attorney of a State, or the principal prosecuting attorney for any political subdivision of a State, shall report to the Administrative Office of the United States Courts –

a) the information required by paragraphs (a) through (g) of subsection (1) of this section with respect to each application for an order or extension made during the preceding calendar year;

b) a general description of the interceptions made under such order or extension, including (i) the approximate nature and frequency of incriminating communications intercepted, (ii) the approximate nature and frequency of other communications intercepted, (iii) the approximate number of persons whose communications were intercepted, (iv) the number of orders in which encryption was encountered and whether such encryption prevented law enforcement from obtaining the plain text of communications intercepted pursuant to such order, and (v) the approximate nature, amount, and cost of the manpower and other resources used in the interceptions;

c) the number of arrests resulting from interceptions made under such order or extension, and the offenses for which arrests were made;

d) the number of trials resulting from such interceptions;

e) the number of motions to suppress made with respect to such interceptions, and the number granted or denied;

f) the number of convictions resulting from such interceptions and the offenses for which the convictions were obtained and a general assessment of the importance of the interceptions; and

g) the information required by paragraphs (b) through (f) of this subsection with respect to orders or extensions obtained in a preceding calendar year.

3) In June of each year the Director of the Administrative Office of the United States Courts shall transmit to the Congress a full and complete report

concerning the number of applications for orders authorizing or approving the interception of wire, oral, or electronic communications pursuant to this chapter and the number of orders and extensions granted or denied pursuant to this chapter during the preceding calendar year. Such report shall include a summary and analysis of the data required to be filed with the Administrative Office by subsections (1) and (2) of this section. The Director of the Administrative Office of the United States Courts is authorized to issue binding regulations dealing with the content and form of the reports required to be filed by subsections (1) and (2) of this section.

§2520. Recovery of civil damages authorized

a) In General. – Except as provided in section 2511(2)(a)(ii), any person whose wire, oral, or electronic communication is intercepted, disclosed, or intentionally used in violation of this chapter may in a civil action recover from the person or entity, other than the United States, which engaged in that violation such relief as may be appropriate.

b) Relief. – In an action under this section, appropriate relief includes –
   1) such preliminary and other equitable or declaratory relief as may be appropriate;
   2) damages under subsection (c) and punitive damages in appropriate cases; and
   3) a reasonable attorney's fee and other litigation costs reasonably incurred.

c) Computation of Damages. – (1) In an action under this section, if the conduct in violation of this chapter is the private viewing of a private satellite video communication that is not scrambled or encrypted or if the communication is a radio communication that is transmitted on frequencies allocated under subpart D of part 74 of the rules of the Federal Communications Commission that is not scrambled or encrypted and the conduct is not for a tortious or illegal purpose or for purposes of direct or indirect commercial advantage or private commercial gain, then the court shall assess damages as follows:

   A) If the person who engaged in that conduct has not previously been enjoined under section 2511(5) and has not been found liable in a prior civil action under this section, the court shall assess the greater of the sum of actual damages suffered by the plaintiff, or statutory damages of not less than $50 and not more than $500.

   B) If, on one prior occasion, the person who engaged in that conduct has been enjoined under section 2511(5) or has been found liable in a civil action under this section, the court shall assess the greater of the sum of actual damages suffered by the plaintiff, or statutory damages of not less than $100 and not more than $1000.

2) In any other action under this section, the court may assess as damages whichever is the greater of –
   A) the sum of the actual damages suffered by the plaintiff and any profits made by the violator as a result of the violation; or
   B) statutory damages of whichever is the greater of $100 a day for each day of violation or $10,000.
d) Defense. – A good faith reliance on –
   1) a court warrant or order, a grand jury subpoena, a legislative authorization, or a statutory authorization;
   2) a request of an investigative or law enforcement officer under section 2518(7) of this title; or
   3) a good faith determination that section 2511(3) or 2511(2)(i) of this title permitted the conduct complained of;
is a complete defense against any civil or criminal action brought under this chapter or any other law.
e) Limitation. – A civil action under this section may not be commenced later than two years after the date upon which the claimant first has a reasonable opportunity to discover the violation.
f) Administrative Discipline. – If a court or appropriate department or agency determines that the United States or any of its departments or agencies has violated any provision of this chapter, and the court or appropriate department or agency finds that the circumstances surrounding the violation raise serious questions about whether or not an officer or employee of the United States acted willfully or intentionally with respect to the violation, the department or agency shall, upon receipt of a true and correct copy of the decision and findings of the court or appropriate department or agency promptly initiate a proceeding to determine whether disciplinary action against the officer or employee is warranted. If the head of the department or agency involved determines that disciplinary action is not warranted, he or she shall notify the Inspector General with jurisdiction over the department or agency concerned and shall provide the Inspector General with the reasons for such determination.
g) Improper Disclosure Is Violation. – Any willful disclosure or use by an investigative or law enforcement officer or governmental entity of information beyond the extent permitted by section 2517 is a violation of this chapter for purposes of section 2520(a).

§2521. Injunction against illegal interception

Whenever it shall appear that any person is engaged or is about to engage in any act which constitutes or will constitute a felony violation of this chapter, the Attorney General may initiate a civil action in a district court of the United States to enjoin such violation. The court shall proceed as soon as practicable to the hearing and determination of such an action, and may, at any time before final determination, enter such a restraining order or prohibition, or take such other action, as is warranted to prevent a continuing and substantial injury to the United States or to any person or class of persons for whose protection the action is brought. A proceeding under this section is governed by the Federal Rules of Civil Procedure, except that, if an indictment has been returned against the respondent, discovery is governed by the Federal Rules of Criminal Procedure.

§2522. Enforcement of the Communications Assistance for Law Enforcement Act

a) Enfortcement by Court Issuing Surveillance Order. – If a court authorizing an interception under this chapter, a State statute, or the Foreign Intelligence Surveillance Act of 1978 (50 U.S.C. 1801 *et seq.*) or authorizing use of a pen register or a trap and trace device under chapter 206 or a State statute finds that a telecommunications carrier has failed to comply with the requirements of the Communications Assistance for Law Enforcement Act, the court may, in accordance with section 108 of such Act, direct that the carrier comply forthwith and may direct that a provider of support services to the carrier or the manufacturer of the carrier's transmission or switching equipment furnish forthwith modifications necessary for the carrier to comply.

b) Enforcement Upon Application by Attorney General. – The Attorney General may, in a civil action in the appropriate United States district court, obtain an order, in accordance with section 108 of the Communications Assistance for Law Enforcement Act, directing that a telecommunications carrier, a manufacturer of telecommunications transmission or switching equipment, or a provider of telecommunications support services comply with such Act.

c) Civil Penalty. –

1) In general. – A court issuing an order under this section against a telecommunications carrier, a manufacturer of telecommunications transmission or switching equipment, or a provider of telecommunications support services may impose a civil penalty of up to $10,000 per day for each day in violation after the issuance of the order or after such future date as the court may specify.

2) Considerations. – In determining whether to impose a civil penalty and in determining its amount, the court shall take into account –

A) the nature, circumstances, and extent of the violation;

B) the violator's ability to pay, the violator's good faith efforts to comply in a timely manner, any effect on the violator's ability to continue to do business, the degree of culpability, and the length of any delay in undertaking efforts to comply; and

C) such other matters as justice may require.

Title II: Stored Communications Act, 18 U.S.C. 2701–2712

§2701. Unlawful access to stored communications

a) Offense. – Except as provided in subsection (c) of this section whoever–
   1) intentionally accesses without authorization a facility through which an electronic communication service is provided; or
   2) intentionally exceeds an authorization to access that facility;

   and thereby obtains, alters, or prevents authorized access to a wire or electronic communication while it is in electronic storage in such system shall be punished as provided in subsection (b) of this section.

b) Punishment. – The punishment for an offense under subsection (a) of this section is –
   1) if the offense is committed for purposes of commercial advantage, malicious destruction or damage, or private commercial gain, or in furtherance of any criminal or tortious act in violation of the Constitution or laws of the United States or any State –
      A) a fine under this title or imprisonment for not more than 5 years, or both, in the case of a first offense under this subparagraph; and
      B) a fine under this title or imprisonment for not more than 10 years, or both, for any subsequent offense under this subparagraph; and
   2) in any other case –
      A) a fine under this title or imprisonment for not more than 1 year or both, in the case of a first offense under this paragraph; and
      B) a fine under this title or imprisonment for not more than 5 years, or both, in the case of an offense under this subparagraph that occurs after a conviction of another offense under this section.

c) Exceptions. – Subsection (a) of this section does not apply with respect to conduct authorized –
   1) by the person or entity providing a wire or electronic communications service;
   2) by a user of that service with respect to a communication of or intended for that user; or
   3) in section 2703, 2704 or 2518 of this title.

§2702. Voluntary disclosure of customer communications or records

a) Prohibitions. – Except as provided in subsection (b) or (c) –

 1) a person or entity providing an electronic communication service to the public shall not knowingly divulge to any person or entity the contents of a communication while in electronic storage by that service; and

 2) a person or entity providing remote computing service to the public shall not knowingly divulge to any person or entity the contents of any communication which is carried or maintained on that service –

   A) on behalf of, and received by means of electronic transmission from (or created by means of computer processing of communications received by means of electronic transmission from), a subscriber or customer of such service;

   B) solely for the purpose of providing storage or computer processing services to such subscriber or customer, if the provider is not authorized to access the contents of any such communications for purposes of providing any services other than storage or computer processing; and

 3) a provider of remote computing service or electronic communication service to the public shall not knowingly divulge a record or other information pertaining to a subscriber to or customer of such service (not including the contents of communications covered by paragraph (1) or (2)) to any governmental entity.

b) Exceptions for disclosure of communications. – A provider described in subsection (a) may divulge the contents of a communication –

 1) to an addressee or intended recipient of such communication or an agent of such addressee or intended recipient;

 2) as otherwise authorized in section 2517, 2511(2)(a), or 2703 of this title;

 3) with the lawful consent of the originator or an addressee or intended recipient of such communication, or the subscriber in the case of remote computing service;

 4) to a person employed or authorized or whose facilities are used to forward such communication to its destination;

 5) as may be necessarily incident to the rendition of the service or to the protection of the rights or property of the provider of that service;

 6) to the National Center for Missing and Exploited Children, in connection with a report submitted thereto under section 2258A;

 7) to a law enforcement agency –

   A) if the contents –

     i) were inadvertently obtained by the service provider; and

     ii) appear to pertain to the commission of a crime; or

8) to a governmental entity, if the provider, in good faith, believes that an emergency involving danger of death or serious physical injury to any person requires disclosure without delay of communications relating to the emergency.

c) Exceptions for Disclosure of Customer Records. – A provider described in subsection (a) may divulge a record or other information pertaining to a subscriber to or customer of such service (not including the contents of communications covered by subsection (a)(1) or (a)(2)) –

1) as otherwise authorized in section 2703;
2) with the lawful consent of the customer or subscriber;
3) as may be necessarily incident to the rendition of the service or to the protection of the rights or property of the provider of that service;
4) to a governmental entity, if the provider, in good faith, believes that an emergency involving danger of death or serious physical injury to any person requires disclosure without delay of information relating to the emergency;
5) to the National Center for Missing and Exploited Children, in connection with a report submitted thereto under section 2258A; or
6) to any person other than a governmental entity.

d) Reporting of Emergency Disclosures. – On an annual basis, the Attorney General shall submit to the Committee on the Judiciary of the House of Representatives and the Committee on the Judiciary of the Senate a report containing –

1) the number of accounts from which the Department of Justice has received voluntary disclosures under subsection (b)(8);
2) a summary of the basis for disclosure in those instances where –
   A) voluntary disclosures under subsection (b)(8) were made to the Department of Justice; and
   B) the investigation pertaining to those disclosures was closed without the filing of criminal charges; and
3) the number of accounts from which the Department of Justice has received voluntary disclosures under subsection (c)(4).

2703. Required disclosure of customer communications or records

a) Contents of Wire or Electronic Communications in Electronic Storage. – A governmental entity may require the disclosure by a provider of electronic communication service of the contents of a wire or electronic communication, that is in electronic storage in an electronic communications system for one hundred and eighty days or less, only pursuant to a warrant issued using the procedures described in the Federal Rules of Criminal Procedure (or, in the case of a State court, issued using State warrant procedures) by a court of competent jurisdiction. A governmental entity may require the disclosure by a provider of electronic communications services of the contents of a wire or electronic communication that has been in electronic storage in an electronic communications system for more than one hundred and eighty days by the means available under subsection (b) of this section.

b) Contents of Wire or Electronic Communications in a Remote Computing Service. –

   1) A governmental entity may require a provider of remote computing service to disclose the contents of any wire or electronic communication to which this paragraph is made applicable by paragraph (2) of this subsection –

   A) without required notice to the subscriber or customer, if the governmental entity obtains a warrant issued using the procedures described in the Federal Rules of Criminal Procedure (or, in the case of a State court, issued using State warrant procedures) by a court of competent jurisdiction; or

   B) with prior notice from the governmental entity to the subscriber or customer if the governmental entity –

   i) uses an administrative subpoena authorized by a Federal or State statute or a Federal or State grand jury or trial subpoena; or

   ii) obtains a court order for such disclosure under subsection (d) of this section;

   except that delayed notice may be given pursuant to section 2705 of this title.

   2) Paragraph (1) is applicable with respect to any wire or electronic communication that is held or maintained on that service –

   A) on behalf of, and received by means of electronic transmission from (or created by means of computer processing of communications received by means of electronic transmission from), a subscriber or customer of such remote computing service; and

   B) solely for the purpose of providing storage or computer processing services to such subscriber or customer, if the provider is not authorized to access the contents of any such communications for purposes of providing any services other than storage or computer processing.

c) Records Concerning Electronic Communication Service or Remote Computing Service. –

   1) A governmental entity may require a provider of electronic communication service or remote computing service to disclose a record or other information pertaining to a subscriber to or customer of such service (not including the contents of communications) only when the governmental entity –

   A) obtains a warrant issued using the procedures described in the Federal Rules of Criminal Procedure (or, in the case of a State court, issued using State warrant procedures) by a court of competent jurisdiction;

    B) obtains a court order for such disclosure under subsection (d) of this section;

    C) has the consent of the subscriber or customer to such disclosure;

    D) submits a formal written request relevant to a law enforcement investigation concerning telemarketing fraud for the name, address, and place of business of a subscriber or customer of such provider, which subscriber or customer is engaged in telemarketing (as such term is defined in section 2325 of this title); or

    E) seeks information under paragraph (2).

  2) A provider of electronic communication service or remote computing service shall disclose to a governmental entity the –

    A) name;

    B) address;

    C) local and long distance telephone connection records, or records of session times and durations;

    D) length of service (including start date) and types of service utilized;

    E) telephone or instrument number or other subscriber number or identity, including any temporarily assigned network address; and

    F) means and source of payment for such service (including any credit card or bank account number),

of a subscriber to or customer of such service when the governmental entity uses an administrative subpoena authorized by a Federal or State statute or a Federal or State grand jury or trial subpoena or any means available under paragraph (1).

  3) A governmental entity receiving records or information under this subsection is not required to provide notice to a subscriber or customer.

d) Requirements for Court Order. – A court order for disclosure under subsection (b) or (c) may be issued by any court that is a court of competent jurisdiction and shall issue only if the governmental entity offers specific and articulable facts showing that there are reasonable grounds to believe that the contents of a wire or electronic communication, or the records or other information sought, are relevant and material to an ongoing criminal investigation. In the case of a State governmental authority, such a court order shall not issue if prohibited by the law of such State. A court issuing an order pursuant to this section, on a motion made promptly by the service provider, may quash or modify such order, if the information or records requested are unusually voluminous in nature or compliance with such order otherwise would cause an undue burden on such provider.

e) No Cause of Action Against a Provider Disclosing Information Under This Chapter. – No cause of action shall lie in any court against any provider of wire or electronic communication service, its officers, employees, agents, or other specified persons for providing information, facilities, or assistance in accordance with the terms of a court order, warrant, subpoena, statutory authorization, or certification under this chapter.

f) Requirement To Preserve Evidence. –

1) In general. – A provider of wire or electronic communication services or a remote computing service, upon the request of a governmental entity, shall take all necessary steps to preserve records and other evidence in its possession pending the issuance of a court order or other process.

2) Period of retention. – Records referred to in paragraph (1) shall be retained for a period of 90 days, which shall be extended for an additional 90-day period upon a renewed request by the governmental entity.

g) Presence of Officer Not Required. – Notwithstanding section 3105 of this title, the presence of an officer shall not be required for service or execution of a search warrant issued in accordance with this chapter requiring disclosure by a provider of electronic communications service or remote computing service of the contents of communications or records or other information pertaining to a subscriber to or customer of such service.

§2704. Backup preservation

a) Backup Preservation. –

1) A governmental entity acting under section 2703(b)(2) may include in its subpoena or court order a requirement that the service provider to whom the request is directed create a backup copy of the contents of the electronic communications sought in order to preserve those communications. Without notifying the subscriber or customer of such subpoena or court order, such service provider shall create such backup copy as soon as practicable consistent with its regular business practices and shall confirm to the governmental entity that such backup copy has been made. Such backup copy shall be created within two business days after receipt by the service provider of the subpoena or court order.

2) Notice to the subscriber or customer shall be made by the governmental entity within three days after receipt of such confirmation, unless such notice is delayed pursuant to section 2705(a).

3) The service provider shall not destroy such backup copy until the later of –
    A) the delivery of the information; or
    B) the resolution of any proceedings (including appeals of any proceeding) concerning the government's subpoena or court order.

4) The service provider shall release such backup copy to the requesting governmental entity no sooner than fourteen days after the governmental entity's notice to the subscriber or customer if such service provider –
    A) has not received notice from the subscriber or customer that the subscriber or customer has challenged the governmental entity's request; and

B) has not initiated proceedings to challenge the request of the governmental entity.

5) A governmental entity may seek to require the creation of a backup copy under subsection (a)(1) of this section if in its sole discretion such entity determines that there is reason to believe that notification under section 2703 of this title of the existence of the subpoena or court order may result in destruction of or tampering with evidence. This determination is not subject to challenge by the subscriber or customer or service provider.

b) Customer Challenges. –

1) Within fourteen days after notice by the governmental entity to the subscriber or customer under subsection (a)(2) of this section, such subscriber or customer may file a motion to quash such subpoena or vacate such court order, with copies served upon the governmental entity and with written notice of such challenge to the service provider. A motion to vacate a court order shall be filed in the court which issued such order. A motion to quash a subpoena shall be filed in the appropriate United States district court or State court. Such motion or application shall contain an affidavit or sworn statement –

A) stating that the applicant is a customer or subscriber to the service from which the contents of electronic communications maintained for him have been sought; and

B) stating the applicant's reasons for believing that the records sought are not relevant to a legitimate law enforcement inquiry or that there has not been substantial compliance with the provisions of this chapter in some other respect.

2) Service shall be made under this section upon a governmental entity by delivering or mailing by registered or certified mail a copy of the papers to the person, office, or department specified in the notice which the customer has received pursuant to this chapter. For the purposes of this section, the term "delivery" has the meaning given that term in the Federal Rules of Civil Procedure.

3) If the court finds that the customer has complied with paragraphs (1) and (2) of this subsection, the court shall order the governmental entity to file a sworn response, which may be filed in camera if the governmental entity includes in its response the reasons which make in camera review appropriate. If the court is unable to determine the motion or application on the basis of the parties' initial allegations and response, the court may conduct such additional proceedings as it deems appropriate. All such proceedings shall be completed and the motion or application decided as soon as practicable after the filing of the governmental entity's response.

4) If the court finds that the applicant is not the subscriber or customer for whom the communications sought by the governmental entity are

maintained, or that there is a reason to believe that the law enforcement inquiry is legitimate and that the communications sought are relevant to that inquiry, it shall deny the motion or application and order such process enforced. If the court finds that the applicant is the subscriber or customer for whom the communications sought by the governmental entity are maintained, and that there is not a reason to believe that the communications sought are relevant to a legitimate law enforcement inquiry, or that there has not been substantial compliance with the provisions of this chapter, it shall order the process quashed.

5) A court order denying a motion or application under this section shall not be deemed a final order and no interlocutory appeal may be taken therefrom by the customer.

§2705. Delayed notice

a) Delay of Notification. –
   1) A governmental entity acting under section 2703(b) of this title may –
      A) where a court order is sought, include in the application a request, which the court shall grant, for an order delaying the notification required under section 2703(b) of this title for a period not to exceed ninety days, if the court determines that there is reason to believe that notification of the existence of the court order may have an adverse result described in paragraph (2) of this subsection; or
      B) where an administrative subpoena authorized by a Federal or State statute or a Federal or State grand jury subpoena is obtained, delay the notification required under section 2703(b) of this title for a period not to exceed ninety days upon the execution of a written certification of a supervisory official that there is reason to believe that notification of the existence of the subpoena may have an adverse result described in paragraph (2) of this subsection.
   2) An adverse result for the purposes of paragraph (1) of this subsection is –
      A) endangering the life or physical safety of an individual;
      B) flight from prosecution;
      C) destruction of or tampering with evidence;
      D) intimidation of potential witnesses; or
      E) otherwise seriously jeopardizing an investigation or unduly delaying a trial.
   3) The governmental entity shall maintain a true copy of certification under paragraph (1)(B).

4) Extensions of the delay of notification provided in section 2703 of up to ninety days each may be granted by the court upon application, or by certification by a governmental entity, but only in accordance with subsection (b) of this section.

5) Upon expiration of the period of delay of notification under paragraph (1) or (4) of this subsection, the governmental entity shall serve upon, or deliver by registered or first-class mail to, the customer or subscriber a copy of the process or request together with notice that –

   A) states with reasonable specificity the nature of the law enforcement inquiry; and

   B) informs such customer or subscriber –

      i) that information maintained for such customer or subscriber by the service provider named in such process or request was supplied to or requested by that governmental authority and the date on which the supplying or request took place;

      ii) that notification of such customer or subscriber was delayed;

      iii) what governmental entity or court made the certification or determination pursuant to which that delay was made; and

      iv) which provision of this chapter allowed such delay.

6) As used in this subsection, the term "supervisory official" means the investigative agent in charge or assistant investigative agent in charge or an equivalent of an investigating agency's headquarters or regional office, or the chief prosecuting attorney or the first assistant prosecuting attorney or an equivalent of a prosecuting attorney's headquarters or regional office.

b) Preclusion of Notice to Subject of Governmental Access. – A governmental entity acting under section 2703, when it is not required to notify the subscriber or customer under section 2703(b)(1), or to the extent that it may delay such notice pursuant to subsection (a) of this section, may apply to a court for an order commanding a provider of electronic communications service or remote computing service to whom a warrant, subpoena, or court order is directed, for such period as the court deems appropriate, not to notify any other person of the existence of the warrant, subpoena, or court order. The court shall enter such an order if it determines that there is reason to believe that notification of the existence of the warrant, subpoena, or court order will result in –

1) endangering the life or physical safety of an individual;

2) flight from prosecution;

3) destruction of or tampering with evidence;

4) intimidation of potential witnesses; or

5) otherwise seriously jeopardizing an investigation or unduly delaying a trial.

§2706. Cost reimbursement

a) Payment. – Except as otherwise provided in subsection (c), a governmental entity obtaining the contents of communications, records, or other information under section 2702, 2703, or 2704 of this title shall pay to the person or entity assembling or providing such information a fee for reimbursement for such costs as are reasonably necessary and which have been directly incurred in searching for, assembling, reproducing, or otherwise providing such information. Such reimbursable costs shall include any costs due to necessary disruption of normal operations of any electronic communication service or remote computing service in which such information may be stored.

b) Amount. – The amount of the fee provided by subsection (a) shall be as mutually agreed by the governmental entity and the person or entity providing the information, or, in the absence of agreement, shall be as determined by the court which issued the order for production of such information (or the court before which a criminal prosecution relating to such information would be brought, if no court order was issued for production of the information).

c) Exception. – The requirement of subsection (a) of this section does not apply with respect to records or other information maintained by a communications common carrier that relate to telephone toll records and telephone listings obtained under section 2703 of this title. The court may, however, order a payment as described in subsection (a) if the court determines the information required is unusually voluminous in nature or otherwise caused an undue burden on the provider.

§2707. Civil action

a) Cause of Action. – Except as provided in section 2703(e), any provider of electronic communication service, subscriber, or other person aggrieved by any violation of this chapter in which the conduct constituting the violation is engaged in with a knowing or intentional state of mind may, in a civil action, recover from the person or entity, other than the United States, which engaged in that violation such relief as may be appropriate.

b) Relief. – In a civil action under this section, appropriate relief includes –
1) such preliminary and other equitable or declaratory relief as may be appropriate;
2) damages under subsection (c); and
3) a reasonable attorney's fee and other litigation costs reasonably incurred.

c) Damages. – The court may assess as damages in a civil action under this section the sum of the actual damages suffered by the plaintiff and any profits made by the violator as a result of the violation, but in no case shall a person entitled to recover receive less than the sum of $1,000. If the violation is willful or intentional, the court may assess punitive damages. In the case of a successful action to enforce liability under this section, the court may assess the costs of the action, together with reasonable attorney fees determined by the court.

d) Administrative Discipline. – If a court or appropriate department or agency determines that the United States or any of its departments or agencies has violated any provision of this chapter, and the court or appropriate department or agency finds that the circumstances surrounding the violation raise serious questions about whether or not an officer or employee of the United States acted willfully or intentionally with respect to the violation, the department or agency shall, upon receipt of a true and correct copy of the decision and findings of the court or appropriate department or agency promptly initiate a proceeding to determine whether disciplinary action against the officer or employee is warranted. If the head of the department or agency involved determines that disciplinary action is not warranted, he or she shall notify the Inspector General with jurisdiction over the department or agency concerned and shall provide the Inspector General with the reasons for such determination.

e) Defense. – A good faith reliance on –
   1) a court warrant or order, a grand jury subpoena, a legislative authorization, or a statutory authorization (including a request of a governmental entity under section 2703(f) of this title);
   2) a request of an investigative or law enforcement officer under section 2518(7) of this title; or
   3) a good faith determination that section 2511(3) of this title permitted the conduct complained of;
   is a complete defense to any civil or criminal action brought under this chapter or any other law.

f) Limitation. – A civil action under this section may not be commenced later than two years after the date upon which the claimant first discovered or had a reasonable opportunity to discover the violation.

g) Improper Disclosure. – Any willful disclosure of a "record", as that term is defined in section 552a(a) of title 5, United States Code, obtained by an investigative or law enforcement officer, or a governmental entity, pursuant to section 2703 of this title, or from a device installed pursuant to section 3123 or 3125 of this title, that is not a disclosure made in the proper performance of the official functions of the officer or governmental entity making the disclosure, is a violation of this chapter. This provision shall not apply to information previously lawfully disclosed (prior to the commencement of any civil or administrative proceeding under this chapter) to the public by a Federal, State, or local governmental entity or by the plaintiff in a civil action under this chapter.

§2708. Exclusivity of remedies

The remedies and sanctions described in this chapter are the only judicial remedies and sanctions for nonconstitutional violations of this chapter.

§2709. Counterintelligence access to telephone toll and transactional records

a) Duty to Provide. – A wire or electronic communication service provider shall comply with a request for subscriber information and toll billing records information, or electronic communication transactional records in its custody or possession made by the Director of the Federal Bureau of Investigation under subsection (b) of this section.

b) Required Certification. – The Director of the Federal Bureau of Investigation, or his designee in a position not lower than Deputy Assistant Director at Bureau headquarters or a Special Agent in Charge in a Bureau field office designated by the Director, may, using a term that specifically identifies a person, entity, telephone number, or account as the basis for a request –

1) request the name, address, length of service, and local and long distance toll billing records of a person or entity if the Director (or his designee) certifies in writing to the wire or electronic communication service provider to which the request is made that the name, address, length of service, and toll billing records sought are relevant to an authorized investigation to protect against international terrorism or clandestine intelligence activities, provided that such an investigation of a United States person is not conducted solely on the basis of activities protected by the first amendment to the Constitution of the United States; and

2) request the name, address, and length of service of a person or entity if the Director (or his designee) certifies in writing to the wire or electronic communication service provider to which the request is made that the information sought is relevant to an authorized investigation to protect against international terrorism or clandestine intelligence activities, provided that such an investigation of a United States person is not conducted solely upon the basis of activities protected by the first amendment to the Constitution of the United States.

c) Prohibition of Certain Disclosure. –

1) Prohibition. –

A) In general. – If a certification is issued under subparagraph (B) and notice of the right to judicial review under subsection (d) is provided, no wire or electronic communication service provider that receives a request under subsection (b), or officer, employee, or agent thereof, shall disclose to any person that the Federal Bureau of Investigation has sought or obtained access to information or records under this section.

    B) Certification. – The requirements of subparagraph (A) shall apply if the Director of the Federal Bureau of Investigation, or a designee of the Director whose rank shall be no lower than Deputy Assistant Director at Bureau headquarters or a Special Agent in Charge of a Bureau field office, certifies that the absence of a prohibition of disclosure under this subsection may result in –
      i) a danger to the national security of the United States;
      ii) interference with a criminal, counterterrorism, or counterintelligence investigation;
      iii) interference with diplomatic relations; or
      iv) danger to the life or physical safety of any person.

2) Exception. –
    A) In general. – A wire or electronic communication service provider that receives a request under subsection (b), or officer, employee, or agent thereof, may disclose information otherwise subject to any applicable nondisclosure requirement to –
      i) those persons to whom disclosure is necessary in order to comply with the request;
      ii) an attorney in order to obtain legal advice or assistance regarding the request; or
      iii) other persons as permitted by the Director of the Federal Bureau of Investigation or the designee of the Director.
    B) Application. – A person to whom disclosure is made under subparagraph (A) shall be subject to the nondisclosure requirements applicable to a person to whom a request is issued under subsection (b) in the same manner as the person to whom the request is issued.
    C) Notice. – Any recipient that discloses to a person described in subparagraph (A) information otherwise subject to a nondisclosure requirement shall notify the person of the applicable nondisclosure requirement.
    D) Identification of disclosure recipients. – At the request of the Director of the Federal Bureau of Investigation or the designee of the Director, any person making or intending to make a disclosure under clause (i) or (iii) of subparagraph (A) shall identify to the Director or such designee the person to whom such disclosure will be made or to whom such disclosure was made prior to the request.

d) Judicial Review. –
    1) In general. – A request under subsection (b) or a nondisclosure requirement imposed in connection with such request under subsection (c) shall be subject to judicial review under section 3511.
    2) Notice. – A request under subsection (b) shall include notice of the availability of judicial review described in paragraph (1).
e) Dissemination by Bureau. – The Federal Bureau of Investigation may disseminate information and records obtained under this section only as

provided in guidelines approved by the Attorney General for foreign intelligence collection and foreign counterintelligence investigations conducted by the Federal Bureau of Investigation, and, with respect to dissemination to an agency of the United States, only if such information is clearly relevant to the authorized responsibilities of such agency.

f) Requirement That Certain Congressional Bodies Be Informed. – On a semiannual basis the Director of the Federal Bureau of Investigation shall fully inform the Permanent Select Committee on Intelligence of the House of Representatives and the Select Committee on Intelligence of the Senate, and the Committee on the Judiciary of the House of Representatives and the Committee on the Judiciary of the Senate, concerning all requests made under subsection (b) of this section.

g) Libraries. – A library (as that term is defined in section 213(1) of the Library Services and Technology Act (20 U.S.C. 9122(1)), the services of which include access to the Internet, books, journals, magazines, newspapers, or other similar forms of communication in print or digitally by patrons for their use, review, examination, or circulation, is not a wire or electronic communication service provider for purposes of this section, unless the library is providing the services defined in section 2510(15) ("electronic communication service") of this title.

§2711. Definitions for chapter

As used in this chapter –

1) the terms defined in section 2510 of this title have, respectively, the definitions given such terms in that section;

2) the term "remote computing service" means the provision to the public of computer storage or processing services by means of an electronic communications system;

3) the term "court of competent jurisdiction" includes –

   A) any district court of the United States (including a magistrate judge of such a court) or any United States court of appeals that –

      i) has jurisdiction over the offense being investigated;

      ii) is in or for a district in which the provider of a wire or electronic communication service is located or in which the wire or electronic communications, records, or other information are stored; or

      iii) is acting on a request for foreign assistance pursuant to section 3512 of this title; or

   B) a court of general criminal jurisdiction of a State authorized by the law of that State to issue search warrants; and

4) the term "governmental entity" means a department or agency of the United States or any State or political subdivision thereof.

§2712. Civil actions against the United States

a) In General. – Any person who is aggrieved by any willful violation of this chapter or of chapter 119 of this title or of sections 106(a), 305(a), or 405(a) of the Foreign Intelligence Surveillance Act of 1978 (50 U.S.C. 1801 *et seq.*) may commence an action in United States District Court against the United States to recover money damages. In any such action, if a person who is aggrieved successfully establishes such a violation of this chapter or of chapter 119 of this title or of the above specific provisions of title 50, the Court may assess as damages –
   1) actual damages, but not less than $10,000, whichever amount is greater; and
   2) litigation costs, reasonably incurred.

b) Procedures. –
   1) Any action against the United States under this section may be commenced only after a claim is presented to the appropriate department or agency under the procedures of the Federal Tort Claims Act, as set forth in title 28, United States Code.
   2) Any action against the United States under this section shall be forever barred unless it is presented in writing to the appropriate Federal agency within 2 years after such claim accrues or unless action is begun within 6 months after the date of mailing, by certified or registered mail, of notice of final denial of the claim by the agency to which it was presented. The claim shall accrue on the date upon which the claimant first has a reasonable opportunity to discover the violation.
   3) Any action under this section shall be tried to the court without a jury.
   4) Notwithstanding any other provision of law, the procedures set forth in section 106(f), 305(g), or 405(f) of the Foreign Intelligence Surveillance Act of 1978 (50 U.S.C. 1801 *et seq.*) shall be the exclusive means by which materials governed by those sections may be reviewed.
   5) An amount equal to any award against the United States under this section shall be reimbursed by the department or agency concerned to the fund described in section 1304 of title 31, United States Code, out of any appropriation, fund, or other account (excluding any part of such appropriation, fund, or account that is available for the enforcement of any Federal law) that is available for the operating expenses of the department or agency concerned.

c) Administrative Discipline. – If a court or appropriate department or agency determines that the United States or any of its departments or agencies has violated any provision of this chapter, and the court or appropriate department or agency finds that the circumstances surrounding the violation raise serious questions about whether or not an officer or employee of the United States acted willfully or intentionally with respect to the violation, the department or agency shall, upon receipt of a true and correct copy of the decision and findings of the court or appropriate department or agency promptly initiate a proceeding to determine whether disciplinary action against the officer or employee is warranted. If the head of the department or agency involved determines that disciplinary action is not warranted, he or she shall notify the Inspector General with jurisdiction over the department or agency concerned and shall provide the Inspector General with the reasons for such determination.

d) Exclusive Remedy. – Any action against the United States under this subsection shall be the exclusive remedy against the United States for any claims within the purview of this section.

e) Stay of Proceedings. –

1) Upon the motion of the United States, the court shall stay any action commenced under this section if the court determines that civil discovery will adversely affect the ability of the Government to conduct a related investigation or the prosecution of a related criminal case. Such a stay shall toll the limitations periods of paragraph (2) of subsection (b).

2) In this subsection, the terms "related criminal case" and "related investigation" mean an actual prosecution or investigation in progress at the time at which the request for the stay or any subsequent motion to lift the stay is made. In determining whether an investigation or a criminal case is related to an action commenced under this section, the court shall consider the degree of similarity between the parties, witnesses, facts, and circumstances involved in the 2 proceedings, without requiring that any one or more factors be identical.

3) In requesting a stay under paragraph (1), the Government may, in appropriate cases, submit evidence ex parte in order to avoid disclosing any matter that may adversely affect a related investigation or a related criminal case. If the Government makes such an ex parte submission, the plaintiff shall be given an opportunity to make a submission to the court, not ex parte, and the court may, in its discretion, request further information from either party.

Title III: Pen Registers and Trap and Trace Devices, 18 U.S.C. 3121–3127

§3121. General prohibition on pen register and trap and trace device use; exception

a) In General. – Except as provided in this section, no person may install or use a pen register or a trap and trace device without first obtaining a court order under section 3123 of this title or under the Foreign Intelligence Surveillance Act of 1978 (50 U.S.C. 1801 *et seq.*).

b) Exception. – The prohibition of subsection (a) does not apply with respect to the use of a pen register or a trap and trace device by a provider of electronic or wire communication service –

1) relating to the operation, maintenance, and testing of a wire or electronic communication service or to the protection of the rights or property of such provider, or to the protection of users of that service from abuse of service or unlawful use of service; or

2) to record the fact that a wire or electronic communication was initiated or completed in order to protect such provider, another provider furnishing service toward the completion of the wire communication, or a user of that service, from fraudulent, unlawful or abusive use of service; or (3) where the consent of the user of that service has been obtained.

c) Limitation. – A government agency authorized to install and use a pen register or trap and trace device under this chapter or under State law shall use technology reasonably available to it that restricts the recording or decoding of electronic or other impulses to the dialing, routing, addressing, and signaling information utilized in the processing and transmitting of wire or electronic communications so as not to include the contents of any wire or electronic communications.

d) Penalty. – Whoever knowingly violates subsection (a) shall be fined under this title or imprisoned not more than one year, or both.

§3122. Application for an order for a pen register or a trap and trace device

a) Application. –

1) An attorney for the Government may make application for an order or an extension of an order under section 3123 of this title authorizing or approving the installation and use of a pen register or a trap and trace device under this chapter, in writing under oath or equivalent affirmation, to a court of competent jurisdiction.

2) Unless prohibited by State law, a State investigative or law enforcement officer may make application for an order or an extension of an order under section 3123 of this title authorizing or approving the installation and use of a pen register or a trap and trace device under this chapter, in writing under oath or equivalent affirmation, to a court of competent jurisdiction of such State.

b) Contents of Application. – An application under subsection (a) of this section shall include –

1) the identity of the attorney for the Government or the State law enforcement or investigative officer making the application and the identity of the law enforcement agency conducting the investigation; and

2) a certification by the applicant that the information likely to be obtained is relevant to an ongoing criminal investigation being conducted by that agency.

§3123. Issuance of an order for a pen register or a trap and trace device

a) In General. –

1) Attorney for the government. – Upon an application made under section 3122(a)(1), the court shall enter an ex parte order authorizing the installation and use of a pen register or trap and trace device anywhere within the United States, if the court finds that the attorney for the Government has certified to the court that the information likely to be obtained by such installation and use is relevant to an ongoing criminal investigation. The order, upon service of that order, shall apply to any person or entity providing wire or electronic communication service in the United States whose assistance may facilitate the execution of the order. Whenever such an order is served on any person or entity not specifically named in the order, upon request of such person or entity, the attorney for the Government or law enforcement or investigative officer that is serving the order shall provide written or electronic certification that the order applies to the person or entity being served.

2) State investigative or law enforcement officer. – Upon an application made under section 3122(a)(2), the court shall enter an ex parte order authorizing the installation and use of a pen register or trap and trace device within the jurisdiction of the court, if the court finds that the State law enforcement or investigative officer has certified to the court that the information likely to be obtained by such installation and use is relevant to an ongoing criminal investigation.

3)

A) Where the law enforcement agency implementing an ex parte order under this subsection seeks to do so by installing and using its own pen register or trap and trace device on a packet-switched data network of a provider of electronic communication service to the public, the agency shall ensure that a record will be maintained which will identify –

   i) any officer or officers who installed the device and any officer or officers who accessed the device to obtain information from the network;

   ii) the date and time the device was installed, the date and time the device was uninstalled, and the date, time, and duration of each time the device is accessed to obtain information;

iii) the configuration of the device at the time of its installation and any subsequent modification thereof; and

iv) any information which has been collected by the device.

To the extent that the pen register or trap and trace device can be set automatically to record this information electronically, the record shall be maintained electronically throughout the installation and use of such device.

B) The record maintained under subparagraph (A) shall be provided ex parte and under seal to the court which entered the ex parte order authorizing the installation and use of the device within 30 days after termination of the order (including any extensions thereof).

b) Contents of Order. – An order issued under this section –

1) shall specify –

A) the identity, if known, of the person to whom is leased or in whose name is listed the telephone line or other facility to which the pen register or trap and trace device is to be attached or applied;

B) the identity, if known, of the person who is the subject of the criminal investigation;

C) the attributes of the communications to which the order applies, including the number or other identifier and, if known, the location of the telephone line or other facility to which the pen register or trap and trace device is to be attached or applied, and, in the case of an order authorizing installation and use of a trap and trace device under subsection (a)(2), the geographic limits of the order; and

D) a statement of the offense to which the information likely to be obtained by the pen register or trap and trace device relates; and

2) shall direct, upon the request of the applicant, the furnishing of information, facilities, and technical assistance necessary to accomplish the installation of the pen register or trap and trace device under section 3124 of this title.

c) Time Period and Extensions. –

1) An order issued under this section shall authorize the installation and use of a pen register or a trap and trace device for a period not to exceed sixty days.

2) Extensions of such an order may be granted, but only upon an application for an order under section 3122 of this title and upon the judicial finding required by subsection (a) of this section. The period of extension shall be for a period not to exceed sixty days.

d) Nondisclosure of Existence of Pen Register or a Trap and Trace Device. – An order authorizing or approving the installation and use of a pen register or a trap and trace device shall direct that –

1) the order be sealed until otherwise ordered by the court; and

2) the person owning or leasing the line or other facility to which the pen register or a trap and trace device is attached or applied, or who is obligated by the order to provide assistance to the applicant, not disclose the

existence of the pen register or trap and trace device or the existence of the investigation to the listed subscriber, or to any other person, unless or until otherwise ordered by the court.

§3124. Assistance in installation and use of a pen register or a trap and trace device

a) Pen Registers. – Upon the request of an attorney for the Government or an officer of a law enforcement agency authorized to install and use a pen register under this chapter, a provider of wire or electronic communication service, landlord, custodian, or other person shall furnish such investigative or law enforcement officer forthwith all information, facilities, and technical assistance necessary to accomplish the installation of the pen register unobtrusively and with a minimum of interference with the services that the person so ordered by the court accords the party with respect to whom the installation and use is to take place, if such assistance is directed by a court order as provided in section 3123(b)(2) of this title.

b) Trap and Trace Device. – Upon the request of an attorney for the Government or an officer of a law enforcement agency authorized to receive the results of a trap and trace device under this chapter, a provider of a wire or electronic communication service, landlord, custodian, or other person shall install such device forthwith on the appropriate line or other facility and shall furnish such investigative or law enforcement officer all additional information, facilities and technical assistance including installation and operation of the device unobtrusively and with a minimum of interference with the services that the person so ordered by the court accords the party with respect to whom the installation and use is to take place, if such installation and assistance is directed by a court order as provided in section 3123(b)(2) of this title. Unless otherwise ordered by the court, the results of the trap and trace device shall be furnished, pursuant to section 3123(b) or section 3125 of this title, to the officer of a law enforcement agency, designated in the court order, at reasonable intervals during regular business hours for the duration of the order.

c) Compensation. – A provider of a wire or electronic communication service, landlord, custodian, or other person who furnishes facilities or technical assistance pursuant to this section shall be reasonably compensated for such reasonable expenses incurred in providing such facilities and assistance.

d) No Cause of Action Against a Provider Disclosing Information Under This Chapter. – No cause of action shall lie in any court against any provider of a wire or electronic communication service, its officers, employees, agents, or other specified persons for providing information, facilities, or assistance in accordance with a court order under this chapter or request pursuant to section 3125 of this title.

e) Defense. – A good faith reliance on a court order under this chapter, a request pursuant to section 3125 of this title, a legislative authorization, or a statutory authorization is a complete defense against any civil or criminal action brought under this chapter or any other law.

f) Communications Assistance Enforcement Orders. – Pursuant to section 2522, an order may be issued to enforce the assistance capability and capacity requirements under the Communications Assistance for Law Enforcement Act.

§3125. Emergency pen register and trap and trace device installation

a) Notwithstanding any other provision of this chapter, any investigative or law enforcement officer, specially designated by the Attorney General, the Deputy Attorney General, the Associate Attorney General, any Assistant Attorney General, any acting Assistant Attorney General, or any Deputy Assistant Attorney General, or by the principal prosecuting attorney of any State or subdivision thereof acting pursuant to a statute of that State, who reasonably determines that –

1) an emergency situation exists that involves –
   A) immediate danger of death or serious bodily injury to any person;
   B) conspiratorial activities characteristic of organized crime;
   C) an immediate threat to a national security interest; or
   D) an ongoing attack on a protected computer (as defined in section 1030) that constitutes a crime punishable by a term of imprisonment greater than one year;

that requires the installation and use of a pen register or a trap and trace device before an order authorizing such installation and use can, with due diligence, be obtained, and

2) there are grounds upon which an order could be entered under this chapter to authorize such installation and use;

may have installed and use a pen register or trap and trace device if, within forty-eight hours after the installation has occurred, or begins to occur, an order approving the installation or use is issued in accordance with section 3123 of this title.

b) In the absence of an authorizing order, such use shall immediately terminate when the information sought is obtained, when the application for the order is denied or when forty-eight hours have lapsed since the installation of the pen register or trap and trace device, whichever is earlier.

c) The knowing installation or use by any investigative or law enforcement officer of a pen register or trap and trace device pursuant to subsection (a) without application for the authorizing order within forty-eight hours of the installation shall constitute a violation of this chapter.

d) A provider of a wire or electronic service, landlord, custodian, or other person who furnished facilities or technical assistance pursuant to this section shall be reasonably compensated for such reasonable expenses incurred in providing such facilities and assistance.

§3126. Reports concerning pen registers and trap and trace devices

The Attorney General shall annually report to Congress on the number of pen register orders and orders for trap and trace devices applied for by law enforcement agencies of the Department of Justice, which report shall include information concerning –

1) the period of interceptions authorized by the order, and the number and duration of any extensions of the order;
2) the offense specified in the order or application, or extension of an order;
3) the number of investigations involved;
4) the number and nature of the facilities affected; and
5) the identity, including district, of the applying investigative or law enforcement agency making the application and the person authorizing the order.

§3127. Definitions for chapter

As used in this chapter –

1) the terms "wire communication", "electronic communication", "electronic communication service", and "contents" have the meanings set forth for such terms in section 2510 of this title;
2) the term "court of competent jurisdiction" means –
   A) any district court of the United States (including a magistrate judge of such a court) or any United States court of appeals that –
      i) has jurisdiction over the offense being investigated;
      ii) is in or for a district in which the provider of a wire or electronic communication service is located;
      iii) is in or for a district in which a landlord, custodian, or other person subject to subsections (a) or (b) of section 3124 of this title is located; or
      iv) is acting on a request for foreign assistance pursuant to section 3512 of this title; or

B) a court of general criminal jurisdiction of a State authorized by the law of that State to enter orders authorizing the use of a pen register or a trap and trace device;

3) the term "pen register" means a device or process which records or decodes dialing, routing, addressing, or signaling information transmitted by an instrument or facility from which a wire or electronic communication is transmitted, provided, however, that such information shall not include the contents of any communication, but such term does not include any device or process used by a provider or customer of a wire or electronic communication service for billing, or recording as an incident to billing, for communications services provided by such provider or any device or process used by a provider or customer of a wire communication service for cost accounting or other like purposes in the ordinary course of its business;

4) the term "trap and trace device" means a device or process which captures the incoming electronic or other impulses which identify the originating number or other dialing, routing, addressing, and signaling information reasonably likely to identify the source of a wire or electronic communication, provided, however, that such information shall not include the contents of any communication;

5) the term "attorney for the Government" has the meaning given such term for the purposes of the Federal Rules of Criminal Procedure; and

6) the term "State" means a State, the District of Columbia, Puerto Rico, and any other possession or territory of the United States.

Index

Cybersecurity Law, First Edition. Jeff Kosseff.
© 2017 John Wiley & Sons, Inc. Published 2017 by John Wiley & Sons, Inc.
Companion Website: www.wiley.com/go/kosseff/cybersecurity